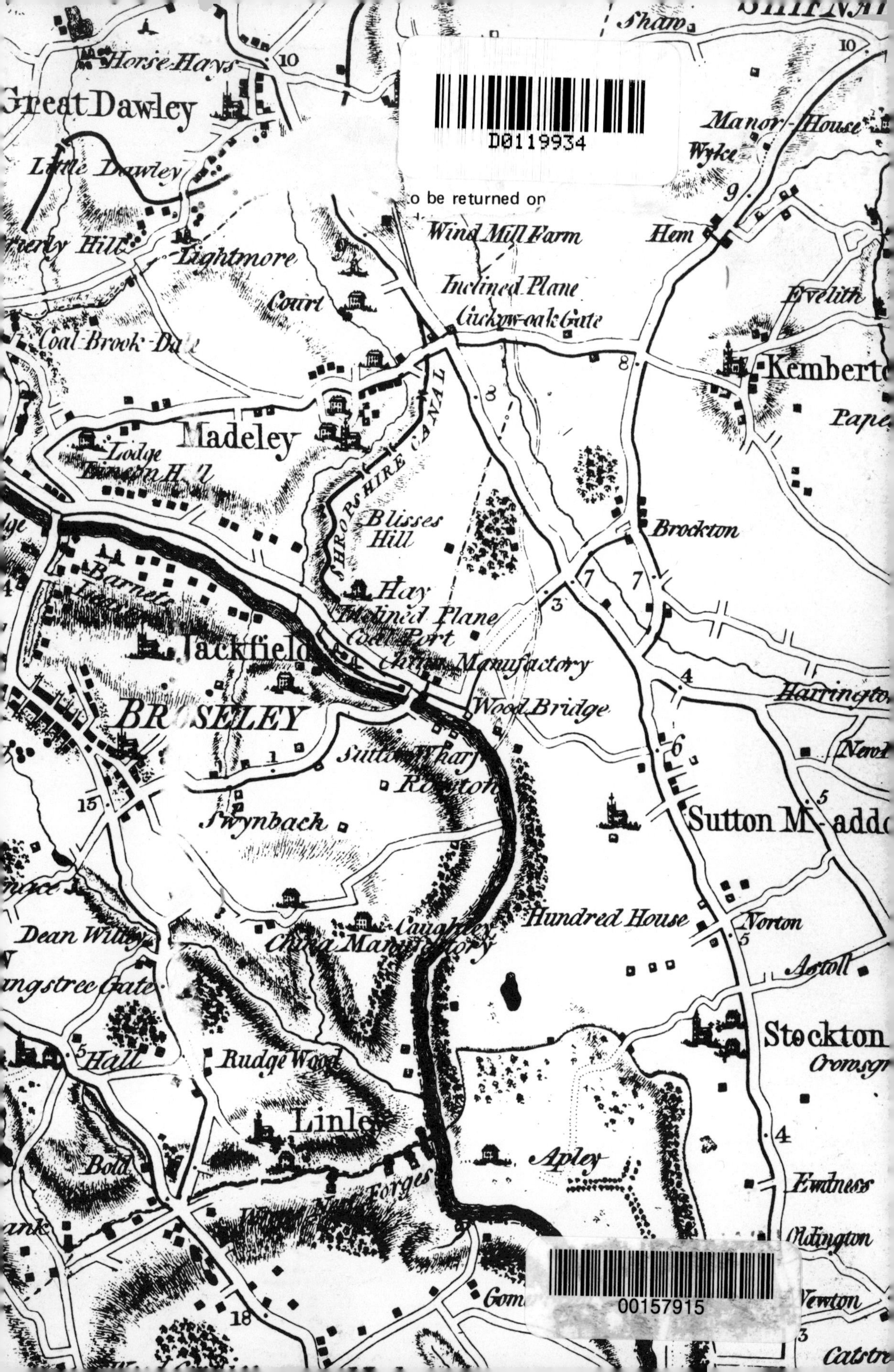

Shaw
Horse Hays
Great Dawley
Little Dawley
Lightmore
Coal Brook Dale
Court
Wind Mill Farm
Inclined Plane
Cuckow-oak Gate
Manor House
Wyke
Hem
Eveleth
Kemberton
Madeley
Lodge
SHROPSHIRE CANAL
Blisses Hill
Brockton
Hay
Inclined Plane
Coal Port
China Manufactory
Jackfield
BROSELEY
Wood Bridge
Harrington
Sutton Wharf
Swynback
Sutton Maddock
Hundred House
Norton
Dean
China Manufactory
Astoll
Stockton
Rudge Wood
Hall
Linley
Apley
Forges
Ewdness
Oldington
Newton

THE
INDUSTRIAL REVOLUTION
IN SHROPSHIRE

Frontispiece: The Iron Bridge by T. F. Burney, 1784. Note the team of bowhaulers bringing a barge upstream (*Ironbridge Gorge Museum Trust*)

The Industrial Revolution in Shropshire

BARRIE TRINDER

PHILLIMORE

1981

Published by
PHILLIMORE & CO. LTD.
London and Chichester

Head Office: Shopwyke Hall,
Chichester, Sussex, England

ISBN 0 85033 428 4

Printed and bound in Great Britain
by Billing and Sons Limited
Guildford, London, Oxford, Worcester

CONTENTS

LIST OF ILLUSTRATIONS

Frontispiece: View of the Iron Bridge, by T. F. Burney

(between pages 20 and 21)

End papers: The Severn Gorge

From Robert Baugh's Map of Shropshire, c. 1808

By courtesy of the Ironbridge Gorge Museum Development Trust

PREFACE TO FIRST EDITION [1973]

This book sets out to examine the economic and social history of the east Shropshire coalfield, principally between 1700 and 1851. No attempt is made to examine industrial developments elsewhere in the county, although the lead mines of the Stiperstones area and the attempts, generally unsuccessful, to establish textile factories in and around Shrewsbury are aspects of the Industrial Revolution which are worthy of investigation. This is not, primarily, a study of industrial monuments, although where relevant, archaeological evidence is used. In the latter part of the book, topics which have their origins in earlier times, the Severn Navigation, the iron industry and revivalism, have been followed through, in some cases beyond 1851, while others, like teetotalism, railways and elementary education, which are relatively new, are not examined in detail.

All of the principal known collections of original sources relating to the area have been used, with the exception of the great mass of Botfield Papers in Manchester University Library.

Any work of this kind which touches on numerous historical sub-disciplines inevitably owes much to many other historians. This does not claim primarily to be a work of technical history, but to write it without some understanding of ironmaking processes would have been impossible. I am indebted to the late Reg. Morton, first Honorary Curator of the Ironbridge Gorge Museum, who patiently explained many ironmaking problems to me, and to W. K. V. Gale, from whose writing, correspondence and lectures I have received much assistance, James Lawson, the historian of the Shropshire iron trade of the 16th and 17th centuries, has provided me with several fruitful ideas, and has recommended numerous sources. At the opposite end of the chronological span of the book, my account of the development of standard gauge railways is drawn largely from the writings of John Horsley Denton, who first introduced me to many aspects of Shropshire industrial history. Robert Machin of the University of Bristol has generously allowed me to quote from his unpublished researches into the Willey ironworks, and first explained to me the remarkable archaeological remains of the works and its transport systems. John Golby of the Open University kindly made available some of his researches into the social history of Madeley, and Christopher Nankivell has allowed me to quote from his studies of Shropshire towns. I have also received information of various kinds from David Adams, Ivor Brown, Neil Clarke, John Corbett, Alec Gaydon, T. C. Hancox, R. E. James, Mrs. M. Kent, Dr. M. J. T. Lewis, Miss D. McCormick, Norman Mutton, John Paget, David Pannett, T. W.

Pollard, Trevor Rowley, Christopher Tongue, Roger Tonkinson, John Vickers and W. H. Williams, to all of whom I wish to record my thanks.

The Rt. Hon. Earl of Dundonald has kindly granted me permission to quote from the Dundonald Papers. Lady Labouchere, Mr. W. Lawrence and Mr. A. H. Simpson have generously made available to me documents in their private collections. My understanding of many points has been considerably enlarged by the privilege of viewing Mr. S. Morley Tonkin's incomparable collection of Shropshire drawings, engravings and paintings. I wish also to thank the various individuals and institutions who have granted me permission to use items in their possession as illustrations. They are acknowledged individually in the captions.

Like all historians I owe a debt to numerous archivists and librarians, and am most grateful to the staff of the Shropshire Record Office, the Shrewsbury Borough Library, the Ironbridge Gorge Museum Trust and the other institutions listed in the Bibliography. I wish particularly to record my thanks to Mrs. Marion Halford, senior assistant archivist at the Shropshire Record Office, who has brought to my attention numerous useful sources, to Mr. Andrew Anderson of the Scottish Record Office who brought the Dundonald papers to my notice, to Mr. F. B. Stitt of the Staffordshire Record Office for his advice on the Sutherland Papers, and to Norman Fenn and Jo. Kennedy, two librarians who have gone to considerable pains to secure copies of rare books.

My employers, the Shropshire Education Committee, have encouraged and assisted much of the research on which this book is based. Many of the ideas in the book have been discussed at length with members of adult classes to whom I am indebted for many corrections, refinements and new insights. For the same reason, I am grateful to Mr. E. P. Thompson for the opportunity of taking part in seminars at the Centre for the Study of Social History at the University of Warwick. Other particular debts are recorded in the footnotes. I am, of course, solely responsible for any errors which remain.

Finally, I am deeply grateful to my wife, who has not only drawn the maps for the book, but has provided encouragement throughout the whole of its preparation.

Shrewsbury.   BARRIE TRINDER.
October 1972.

PREFACE TO SECOND EDITION [1981]

Nearly a decade has passed since the first edition of *The Industrial Revolution in Shropshire* was written. Some of the preoccupations of the early 1970s now seem less urgent, while new questions demand to be considered. The growth of the Ironbridge Gorge Museum has once more brought international attention to the Shropshire coalfield, and has also given a substantial stimulus to research. Understanding of the history of the area has been extended on many fronts. Nevertheless much of the new work has been concentrated on the nineteenth century, or on the century and a half before 1750, and relatively little has been concerned with the events in the second half of the 18th century which form the core of this study. In this new edition chapters X and XVII have been completely re-written, the former because important new sources on the Iron Bridge and Coalport Bridge came to light in the mid-1970s, and because our knowledge of the artists who portrayed the Ironbridge Gorge in the late 18th century has been greatly extended, and the latter because the whole approach to the development of industrial communities in the first edition seemed to require revision. Elsewhere corrections have been made and new material has been incorporated where appropriate, but the underlying arguments of each chapter remain unaltered.

I would like to record my gratitude to those reviewers of the first edition whose helpful and constructive suggestions have been incorporated in this revised version. Many colleagues at the Ironbridge Gorge Museum, including Neil Cossons, Stuart Smith, Tony Herbert, David de Haan, Alistair Penfold, Ian Lawley and Grant Muter, have passed on information or made suggestions which have aided the task of revision. I also owe a considerable debt to members of my research class on the Social History of Telford, particularly to Jeff and Nancy Cox for their work on inventories, and to Ken Jones whose patient labours with the tape recorder are vastly enlarging our understanding of the Shropshire coalfield at the end of the 19th century. I would also like to record my gratitude for information and suggestions from George Baugh, Tony Carr, Robin Chaplin, Colin Dews, Roger Edmundson, Peter Forsaith, Professor J. R. Harris, Barbara Jarvis, John Lenton, Sula Rayska, Michael Rix, Margaret Roake, Gaye and Denis Blake Roberts, Alan Rose, Ian Standing, Dr. Jennifer Tann, Dr. Hugh Torrens, Dr. Malcolm Wanklyn and Dr. Angus Winchester. I am also grateful to Pat Read for allowing me to use some of her splendid drawings as illustrations. I hope that in its new form this study will be of continuing usefulness.

Ironbridge.   BARRIE TRINDER.
January 1981.

ABBREVIATIONS

B.M.	British Museum
B.P.P.	British Parliamentary Papers
B.R.L.	Birmingham Reference Library
B.T.H.R.	British Transport Historical Records [Public Record Office]
B.U.L.	Birmingham University Library
B. & W. Colln.	Boulton and Watt Collection
Cal. Chartism Shropshire	Calendars of Letters and Documents relating to Chartism in Shropshire
CBD MS	Coalbrookdale Manuscripts
Childrens' Emp. Comm. Rep.	Childrens' Employment Commission. Appendix to the first Report of the Commissioners, 1842. British Parliamentary Papers
D.N.B.	Dictionary of National Biography
F.T.C.	Fletcher Tooth Collection
I.A.R.	Industrial Archaeology Review
I.B.G.M.	Ironbridge Gorge Museum
Lill. Co.	Lilleshall Company
L.S.F.	Library of the Society of Friends
M.A.R.C.	Methodist Archives and Research Centre
Mich.	Michaelmas
N.L.W.	National Library of Wales
P.R.O.	Public Record Office
S.B.L.	Shrewsbury Borough Library
Scot. R.O.	Scottish Record Office
S.N.L.	Shropshire Newsletter
S.R.O.	Shropshire Record Office
Staffs. R.O.	Staffordshire Record Office
T.N.S.	Transactions of the Newcomen Society
T.S.A.S.	Transactions of the Shropshire Archaeological Society

INTRODUCTION

The part of Shropshire designated as the new town of Telford was for decades one of Britain's more desolate industrial scars. About a third of the new town's 21,000 acres are affected by the results of shallow mining in past centuries. Until recently much of its landscape has been one of Romantic decay: pit mounts, slag tips, roofless engine houses, ash heaps providing homes for sand martins, the battered wrecks of blast furnaces, crazily tilted pit head stocks collapsing into their own shafts, wharf walls subject to constant erosion by the fast flowing Severn. Eighteenth-century workers' cottages in long, formal, company-built rows, or in twos and threes haphazardly scattered on what was once parish waste, remained in occupation. The predominant communal memories have not been of prosperity but of depression; of the need to migrate in search of employment, of the gradual decline of once flourishing trades, of the withering away of chapel congregations, friendly societies and other institutions. Almost 200 years have passed since the area of the new town, which takes its name from the builder of the Longdon Aqueduct and the Holyhead Road, was the leading iron-producing district in Great Britain and the scene of most of the principal innovations in iron-making in the 18th century. From this part of Shropshire came the materials which made possible economic expansion elsewhere; steam engines, bridges, iron frames for textile mills, giant water wheels, pans for the processing of chemicals, frames for machinery, canal and roadside furniture. As iron-making made possible industrial growth in other parts of Great Britain, in the immediate vicinity it stimulated the development of subsidiary industries based on coal and clay, and of transport systems of great ingenuity. If the term 'industrial revolution' can be meaningfully used to describe what happened in any part of Britain in the late 18th century, it can be applied to the events of that period in the region around Coalbrookdale.

It is the object of this study to examine the economic development of the east Shropshire coalfield in a broad social context, attempting, by the employment of the approaches of the economic, social, ecclesiastical and transport historian, as well as by making use of archaeological evidence, to draw together the many strands of local history which are already well known. Some attempt will also be made to examine some hitherto neglected problems; the ways in which the steam engine was employed in the 18th century as distinct from its mechanical development, the commercial as well as the technical history of the iron trade, the failure of attempts to diversify the local economic structure, the place of riots and threats of riots in local society, and the revivals of the 19th century as well as the Evangelical Revival of the 18th.

Ironmasters feature prominently in the study but the emphasis will be on the multiplicity of their local contacts as well as on their records as innovators. They will be seen not just as entrepreneurs, but as turnpike trustees, patrons of churches and chapels, and as magistrates. Foundrymen, colliers and potters will be regarded not just as work people but as local preachers, bull-baiters and readers of the radical press. Shropshire was important in the late 18th century not just because the technology of its iron industry was particularly advanced, but because it saw the development of a new type of society, one shaped as much by Evangelicalism as by industrialisation. Many problems in the history of the district can only be approached by consideration of local society in a broad context. There is, for example, no ready explanation in terms of engineering or administrative history of why the Severn navigation was not improved in the late 18th century. Some examination of the social structure of the Severn barge trade at least suggests some clues. The use of a variety of historical techniques has produced some fruitful results through cross-fertilisation. The journals of John Wesley, an obvious source for the history of religion in Fletcher's Madeley, also contain significant scraps of information about the building of the Iron Bridge. The accounts of the iron-making partnerships reveal a great deal about the Severn bargemen and about turnpike roads. Accounts of riots have revealed important information about technical as well as social history.

This study is written in full realisation of the inadequacy of current knowledge of some quite major aspects of the history of the district, which may well be remedied by future research or new deposits of records. The study will achieve its aims if it makes a first step towards the integration of the many strands of historical interest which have previously been shown in east Shropshire, if it can establish that the invention of iron rails, the sermons of John Fletcher, John Wilkinson's contacts with Boulton and Watt and the building of workers' cottages were not separate and diffuse activities but different aspects of what was essentially one society.

II

THE RIVERSIDE ECONOMY

The east Shropshire coalfield is a plateau of generally 400 to 600 ft. above sea level which lies to the east and north of the Wrekin. The coalfield extends for a little over 10 miles from north to south, from Lilleshall to Linley and Willey, and at its broadest is no more than three miles from east to west. At its southern end it is riven by the Severn Gorge, a valley 300 ft. deep created when the pent-up waters of a glacial lake which covered north Shropshire gained an escape eastwards. Apart from a variety of coals, the geological resources of the district include iron ore, several clays suitable for potting and brick-making, fireclays, sand which can be used in foundries, pyrites, natural bitumen and brine springs. There are outcrops of carboniferous limestone at Lilleshall and Steeraway, silurian limestone at Lincoln Hill and to the south from the cliffs of Benthall Edge to Gleedon Hill and Wenlock Edge. The distribution of the coal measures is considerably complicated by faults, most of which run from south-west to north-east. There are several major outcrops of the coal strata, most of them on the western side of the coalfield, which were the main centres of mining until well into the 18th century. The deepest coal seams to the east were not worked until the middle of the 19th century.[1]

The ancient parochial structure of the district was complex. In the north the parish of Lilleshall formerly extended south from Lilleshall village to the settlement now known as St. George's on the Roman Watling Street, and included the township of Donnington. West of Lilleshall lay the small parish of Wombridge, which had formerly been the demesne of Wombridge Priory, and Wrockwardine Wood, a detached portion of the parish of Wrockwardine five miles to the west. To the east Wombridge and Lilleshall were bounded by the chapelry of Priorslee, the most westerly portion of the extensive parish of Shifnal. To the south and west lay the large parish of Wellington of which the townships of Ketley, Lawley, Arleston and Hadley were on the coal measures. Between Wellington and Wombridge and the River Severn were Dawley, with its three townships of Great Dawley, Little Dawley and Malins Lee, Stirchley, Little Wenlock and Madeley. The latter included the ancient ironworking settlement of Coalbrookdale, and the 18th-century canal village of Coalport. The riverside portion of the parish was known before 1780 as Madeley Wood. The largest coalfield parish south of the Severn was Broseley, which included the riverside hamlet of Jackfield. Benthall also lay largely on the coal measures, and some coal was also found in the small parishes of Barrow, Willey and Linley, and in the extra-parochial district of Posenhall. A number of parishes on the fringe of the coalfield contained important raw

3

materials or industrial installations. There were limestone mines and quarries at Church Aston, brine pits at Preston on the Weald Moors and a canal basin at Wappenshall in Eyton parish. A small part of the coal measures lay in Sheriffhales, adjacent to Lilleshall. To the west, Buildwas parish was an important source of sand, and Much Wenlock of limestone. On the south-eastern side, Sutton Maddock contained part of Coalport and the railway terminus at Sutton Wharf.

The most unusual feature of the civil government of the district was the Borough of Wenlock, until 1966 the largest non-county borough in England. It included the industrial parishes of Benthall, Broseley, Little Wenlock, Madeley and Willey. The borough, created by charter in 1468, comprised most of the lands owned by the Cluniac priory of St. Milburgh at Much Wenlock, and included parishes as far apart as Little Wenlock in the north and Stoke St. Milburgh in the south, and Eaton-under-Haywood in the west and Beckbury in the east, although its size was successively reduced by the Municipal Corporations Act of 1835 and the Local Government Act of 1889. The borough enjoyed 'an unusually privileged position among the boroughs of England', Its courts held wide powers of civil and criminal jurisdiction, and dealt with many matters which were normally part of the business of Quarter Sessions.[2]

The boundary of the Franchise of Wenlock also determined the ecclesiastical geography of the east Shropshire coalfield. The Severn formed the ancient boundary between the dioceses of Lichfield to the north and Hereford to the south, but those parishes north of the river in the ancient Franchise of Wenlock were in Hereford diocese.

As industrial development gained momentum in east Shropshire so the pattern of settlement came to bear less and less resemblance to the formal political and ecclesiastical boundaries. Markets became established at the meeting points of parish boundaries, while mining settlements, taking their names from fields or charter masters, grew up in situations entirely remote from the churches of the parishes to which they belonged.

The east Shropshire coalfield lies approximately 15 miles from the county town of Shrewsbury to the west, and from the edge of the south Staffordshire coalfield in the Wolverhampton area to the east. The north Staffordshire Potteries lay about 25 miles to the north, Manchester and the Merseyside ports 50 to 60 miles in the same direction. Birmingham lies 30 miles to the south-east. London is about 140 miles away. In the 18th century convenience of communication rather than distances determined economic patterns, and it was the superiority of river over road transport which largely shaped the economic development of east Shropshire. The principal road serving the area and the first to be turnpiked was the Roman Watling Street from London to Wroxeter which passed through Oakengates and Ketley, but the road was of little economic significance to the coalfield in the early 18th century.

The Shropshire coalfield was essentially part of a riverside economy until the age of the railways. The Severn gave easy and direct access to markets as far away as Bristol, more than 80 miles from Coalbrookdale. The river carried Shropshire coal downstream to Tewkesbury and upstream to Shrewsbury and mid-Wales. It was the principal means of communication between the many ironworks of the Borderland. From its barges the tobacco pipes of Broseley were distributed throughout the Midlands and the coarse mugs of Jackfield gave their name to inns along the whole length of the river. From the ports of the upper Severn, Uffington, Shrewsbury, Montford, Llandrinio, Pool Quay and Clawdd Coch road links extended into Wales, Cheshire and Lancashire. To Bridgnorth and Bewdley, the ports of the mid-Severn, came packhorses

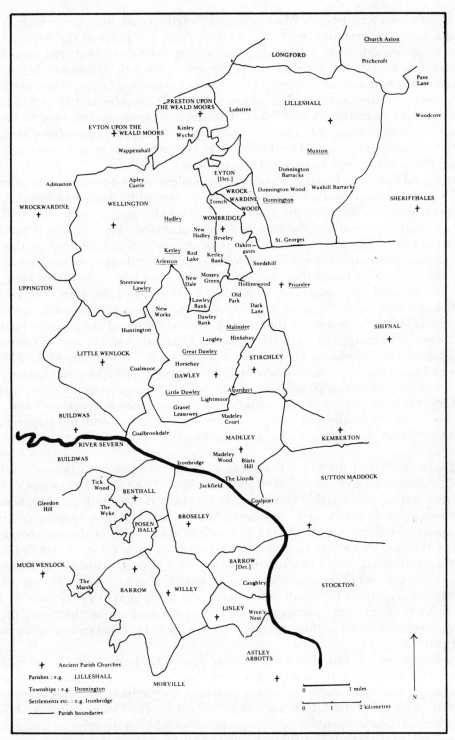

Figure 1.   The East Shropshire Coalfield: Parishes and Settlements.

and waggons with textiles from Manchester and earthenware from north Staffordshire. Difficulty of access probably kept such cargoes from the ports of the Severn Gorge. Indeed so inadequate were the roads approaching the Gorge that iron bound from Coalbrookdale to Stafford sometimes was carried by river to Bridgnorth before being transferred to packhorse or waggon. The upstream carriage of tea, wine, spirits and tobacco created important commercial ties between Shropshire and Bristol. The Severn's tributaries extended its usefulness. The Avon took Shropshire coal to Pershore and iron products to Stratford. The Wye conveyed a variety of cargoes from Shropshire to Brockweir and Monmouth. The Tern and Teme gave access to ironworks near their mouths. The Vyrnwy took barges to Llanymynech.[3]

Commercial links which extended beyond the valleys of the Severn and its tributaries were few and tenuous. Valuable products could be carried by road to or from Cheshire and Lancashire, but the route by river and coastal shipping from Coalbrookdale to Chester by way of Bristol and the Irish Sea was still preferred for pig iron in the 1770s. There were some links with the east-Midlands' economy which centred on the Trent by way of road connections to Burton or Wilden Ferry, but these were more remarkable for the difficulties they posed than for the frequency with which they were used.

The Severn navigation was well established by the end of the 16th century. Commercial traffic was using the river at Bridgnorth in the late 12th century, and by the middle of the 13th the monks of Buildwas Abbey had secured the right to load wool on to barges at Cressage. In 1415 the Abbot of Lilleshall was accused of causing the obstruction of barge traffic to Shrewsbury at Bridgnorth.[4] The orders of the Commissioners of Sewers for Shropshire made in 1575 suggest a flourishing navigation. They called for the regulation of 28 weirs and stakings in the county which were, 'noisome and dangerous to all passengers . . . with floates of wood, cobles, barges or owes'.[5] Coal traffic grew rapidly in the last quarter of the 16th century, and the importance of general carrying at this time is indicated by the building of Mardol Quay in Shrewsbury in 1607.[6]

Coal was the first of the mineral resources of east Shropshire to be exploited on a large scale. Outcrops were mined in the Middle Ages. The Cistercian monks of Buildwas Abbey were granted rights to mine coal by Philip de Benthall in 1250, while the Cluniacs of Much Wenlock in 1322 allowed Walter de Caldbrook to mine coal at the Brockholes in Madeley parish. At the time of the dissolution of the monasteries the monks of Wombridge had an income of £5 a year from their mines. Later in the 16th century Leland noted, 'coles be digged hard by (W)Ombridge where the Priory was' and Camden regarded Oakengates as, 'a small village of some note for the pit cole'. In Donnington township in Lilleshall parish there was a 'Colpytt Way' as early as 1592.[7] In the Severn Gorge, and particularly in the parishes south of the river, the coal industry developed into a highly organised and highly capitalised enterprise in the late 16th century.

A leading figure in this development was James Clifford, lord of the manor of Broseley. His character contrasts sharply with those of the unambitious free miners of the Forest of Dean who might well have provided competition for Shropshire coal in the Severn Valley.[8] In 1575 Clifford was presented by the Commissioners of Sewers because he had, 'made a coaldelf or coal pit in his lordship of Broseley at a place called the Tuckeyes, and cast all the rubbish, stone and earth into the deepest part of the River Severn'. The Commissioners ordered him to remove it at his own cost.[9] In 1605–06 he became involved in a dispute with freeholders in Broseley as he attempted to assert his right to minerals over the whole of the manor. The dispute revealed that there was in use in the parish a wooden railway, employed to convey coal between the pits and the riverside, only the second such railway of which evidence survives in England.[10] Clifford brought immigrant miners to Broseley and provided plots on which they could build cottages, but his freeholders were strongly antagonistic to the new-comers. One described them as, 'lewd persons, the Scums and dreggs of many countries, from whence they have bine driven . . . thieves . . . horible Swearers . . . daillie drunk-erds, some havinge towe or three wyves a peece now liveing, others . . . notorious whore mongers'.[11]

James Clifford exhibited many of the qualities of later capitalist entrepreneurs, characteristics which were shown to an even greater degree in the career of John Weld of Willey. Weld was born in 1585, the son of a London merchant. His two sisters married London merchants who were buying Shropshire estates, and in 1618 Weld purchased the manor of Willey. The following year he bought the adjacent manor of Marsh, and in 1620 a third part of the manor of Broseley. He determinedly bought up freehold land on all of his manors. A memorandum on his estates written for the benefit of his heirs in 1631 when he was seriously ill gives a clear picture of his industrial activities and of the changes which he contemplated. He built or re-built the Old Willey blast furnace, and urged his descendants to make use of the bloomery cinders he had found on old ironworking sites. He anticipated the smelting of iron with coal,

It may fall out iron may hereafter be made with pit-coal, then my coal will stand instead for my furnace, and coals may be brought to my furnace by waggons, either from a place where coal breaks out on the other side of the hill or from a place in the new Park.

He well understood the profitability of the coal trade and the importance to it of river navigation. He estimated the coals in Willey to be worth £5,000, 'if I can procure a constant way to the Severn', and proposed to hinder the development of competitors' mines:

Corbet . . . cannot convey his coals out of his grounds . . . in places where there is no common way without my consent. Corbet cannot carry by wain any coals that can possibly be gotten in any out of his grounds to Bridgnorth, Wenlock, Brosely &c. except he have leave to pass over my grounds, which I will never yield unto, for it would hinder my own delphs.

Weld noted the existence of clay suitable for the making of tobacco pipes in Shirlett, and wondered if it might be possible to operate a glasshouse or soaphouse in Broseley or Willey.

He recovered from his illness in 1631 and lived until 1665. He was probably not the largest coalmaster in Shropshire in the mid-17th century, for the estate of Lawrence Benthall in the 1640s was even larger. Nevertheless in his determination to make the most of the natural resources of his estate, even to the extent of frustrating his neigh-bours' activities, his awareness of the possibilities of new processes, his realisation that his agent, 'may do me much good or hurt', were all characteristics which he shared with the great ironmasters of the 18th century.[12]

The prosperity of the coal trade of the Severn Gorge in the 17th century was reflected until recent years by the fine timber-framed houses which flanked the riverside, most of which have now been demolished. Near to the present road bridge between Iron-bridge to Jackfield there formerly stood two splendid early 17th-century mansions on the north bank of the river, The Lloyds, a timber-framed house of 1621, and Bedlam

Hall, a Jacobean brick structure. On the opposite bank stood a timberframed house of 1654, later converted into a public house and named *The Dog and Duck*.[13]

The mines of Broseley, Benthall and Madeley were important throughout the 17th century. Their productivity was such that in the 1670s Shropshire coal sold at Tewkesbury at 6s. a ton was cheaper than coal bought in Bristol and Nottingham, which were adjacent to coal mines, and about a third of the price of Newcastle coal sold in London.[14] The Shropshire coal trade was highly centralised. A report of 1695 advocating a tax on coal argued that a duty on coal shipped along the Severn could easily be imposed since almost all of the trade was with the three great collieries of Broseley, Benthall and Barr.[15]

The most important innovation in the Shropshire mining industry in the 17th century was the development of the longwall system of working, by which the whole of a seam of coal was removed as working advanced from or retreated towards shaft bottoms, the space previous taken up by the coal, known as the gob or goof, being packed with rock or slack and its roof supported by pit props. The longwall system replaced earlier methods of working in Shropshire in the early or mid-17th century and gradually spread to other districts.[16] Little other detailed evidence survives about the early methods of mining coal in Shropshire. In the Severn Gorge adits were widely used throughout much of the 18th century. The railways running into these horizontal mines in Madeley were described by Francis Brokesly in 1711, 'cole mines into which they descend not as in other places into pits, but go in at the side of the hill into which are long passages both straightforward and from thence on either side, from whence they dig the coles which by small carriages with four wheels of about a foot diameter thrust by men, they convey not only out of the long underground passages but even to the boats which lie in the Severn'.[17] As late as the 1790s the geologist Robert Townson regretted that he was prevented from obtaining an accurate stratification of the southern part of the coalfield 'from the pits not having been lately sunk through the upper strata, but from a level or adit in the side of the hill'.[18]

In the latter decades of the 17th century several new industrial uses for coal were developed in Shropshire. A mug dated 1634 is the earliest evidence for the pottery trades of Jackfield.[19] Broseley parish was well known for its tobacco pipes early in the 17th century. They were at first made with local white clays, then from the early 18th century with Devonshire clays. Archaeological evidence suggests a boom in pipe-making in the 20 years after 1680 when there were more pipe makers active in Broseley than at any time before the mid-19th century.[20]

By the middle of the 1690s several large cauldrons were set up in Jackfield for the extraction of tar, pitch and oil under the patent of Martin Eele. They stood alongside the river, near to the railways leading from the pits to the Severnside wharves.[21] The manufacture of glass in the coalfield was established between 1673 and 1676 when Abraham Bigod, a glass-maker from Amblecote near Stourbridge, built a glasshouse at Snedshill, which was still making window panes and bottles in 1696.[22] Salt-making also was probably established before the end of the 17th century. By 1707 there were two adjacent salt-boiling works near Preston on the Weald Moors.[23]

Shropshire coal was also used for the smelting of lead ore, an industry which was established in the Severn Gorge in the 1730s if not earlier. The Gorge with its ample supplies of cheap coal was well situated to smelt Welsh ores delivered by river, and to despatch the pigs onwards to Bristol, the principal centre of the lead trade. In 1731 Thomas Barker of Gadlis, Flints., built a smelthouse at Benthall in association with

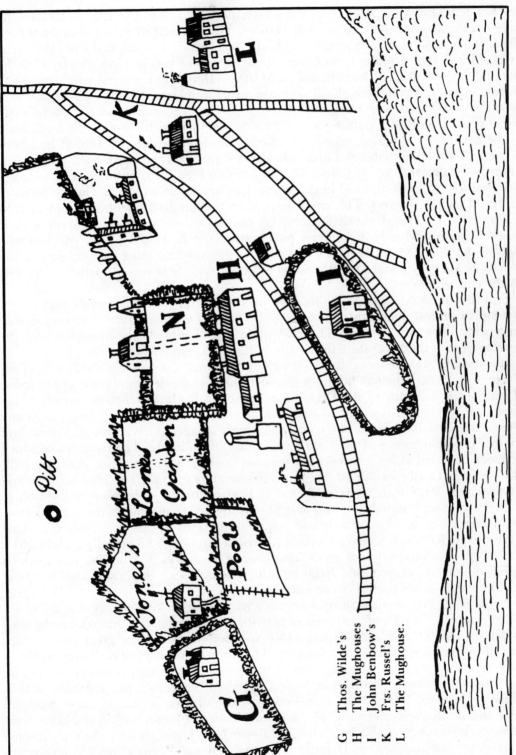

Figure 2. The Calcutts, Jackfield, in the mid-18th century.
Re-drawn from the Broseley Estate Book, Shrewsbury Borough Library Colln.

G Thos. Wilde's
H The Mughouses
I John Benbow's
K Frs. Russel's
L The Mughouse.

the London Lead Company. Two years later he leased from the Earl of Craven the mines in the nearby township of Little Dawley. The Benthall smelthouse used ore from the London Lead Company's mines at Llangynog, which was shipped from the wharf at Llandrinio. The London Lead Company ceased operations in 1736, and by 1739 the Benthall smelthouse had been leased to Matthew Dore and partners, who were using there ores which came from the Bog mines on the Stiperstones. This smelthouse was probably near the Bower Yard, and it is depicted in operation in several of the early prints of the Iron Bridge published in the 1780s. Another smelthouse on the south bank of the Severn was situated near to the site of the Iron Bridge. By 1765 it had been converted into a malthouse.[24] There was also a furnace on the north bank of the river in the mid-eighteenth century. In 1730 and again in 1734 the Coalbrookdale Company sold iron to the 'Smelting Lead Furnace near Coalbrookdale' in which Thomas Stringer of Bristol had an interest. This could have been the Benthall smelthouse, but in 1756 and again in 1774 Coalbrookdale Company deeds mention a smelter adjacent to their property on the riverside in Madeley parish near Dale End. In 1760 the partners who worked the Bog lead mines on the Stiperstones proposed building a smelthouse in the Lloyds in Madeley parish. Whether they did so or not, there was a smelter in the area by the end of the century.[25]

Industry in the Shropshire coalfield in the 17th century was intensively capitalised. It adopted several important innovations. By the end of the century it was using coal for a wide range of new uses. The coal trade was to provide the foundation for the development of the Shropshire iron trade in the 18th century.

Iron-making was well established in east Shropshire by the time of the Reformation. Three of the local religious houses were operating bloomeries for the direct reduction of iron ore at the time of the Dissolution, although in the absence of records of lay estates for this period it would be unwise to assume that iron manufacture was in any sense a monastic monopoly. There was a bloomery adjacent to Wombridge Priory, and another on the demesne of the Cistercian Abbey of Buildwas. The Cluniacs of Much Wenlock operated at least two separate ironworks in the Shirlett area, and they built bloomeries in Coalbrookdale which were still operating in 1545. The blast furnace, and its associated forge with finery and chafery hearths for the conversion of pig iron to wrought iron, were introduced into east Shropshire before the end of the 16th century. Sir Walter Leveson, whose family had acquired the lands of Lilleshall Abbey, granted a lease to Richard and Vincent Corbett to erect a furnace in Lilleshall parish in 1591. In 1599 John Slaney acquired an existing lease of ironworks in Morville parish, which included a finery, chafery and hammer mill. There was an important steel works at Coalbrookdale in the early 17th century.[26]

By the early 18th century Shropshire was a major iron-making county, but the works in the county were part of a pattern of activities which extended throughout the west Midlands and the Borderland, and which was dominated by the great partnerships formed by the Foley and Knight families. The ultimate product of the many works in the region was wrought iron in the form of bars sold either to market town ironmongers or to craftsmen who fabricated it into useful objects. The greatest concentration of such craftsmen, nailers, locksmiths, chain-makers and tool-makers, was in south Staffordshire and north Worcestershire. The greatest density of forges was in the same area, particularly in the Stour Valley, but other forges were found all over the region, some in such remote locations as Dolobran (Monts.) on the Vyrnwy, and Strangeworth (Hereford.) on the Arrow. Pig iron for the forges came from blast furnaces situated on streams within reach of charcoal supplies adjacent to most of the sources of iron ore in the region.

Not all of the iron made at charcoal blast furnaces was converted into wrought-iron bars. There was a thriving trade in cast-iron products in Shropshire well before the end of the 17th century. Of 20 surviving probate inventories for the ironworking parish of Leighton made between 1660 and 1700 which detail household possessions, 16 include domestic ironware, in many cases specifically cast iron. Items recorded in houses in Leighton include firebacks and grates, pots, kettles, pudding plates, frying pans and smoothing irons.[27]

One of the characteristics of the charcoal iron trade was the transport of semi-finished iron over very long distances as it moved from one stage of production to the next. The complicated nature of such movements can be seen in any of the surviving records of the trade. The forge at Wytheford on the River Roden to the north east of Shrewsbury in 1687–88 obtained some of its pig iron from Coalbrookdale and Willey, but used some which came from the Forest of Dean.[28] In the 1720s iron from the Leighton and Kemberton furnaces in east Shropshire was being taken up the Severn to the forge at Dolobran (Monts.) managed to John Kelsall. In his journal Kelsall describes a visit to Shropshire to buy iron in 1725. At a Shrewsbury inn he discussed with James Colley and William Vickers the price of pig iron from Leighton. He visited Leighton the following day, probably saw the iron he was buying, and proceeded to an inn at Buildwas where he met with a barge and arranged with the master for the carriage upstream of his purchases.[29]

The list of ironworks prepared by the Sussex ironmaster, John Fuller, in 1717[30] makes it possible to survey the state of the trade in Shropshire in the early 18th century with some accuracy. The seven blast furnaces in the county comprised two groups, Bringewood, Charlcotte and Bouldon, which drew their supplies of ore from the Clee Hills, and Coalbrookdale, Kemberton, Willey and Leighton, which relied upon the mines of the east Shropshire coalfield for their ore. All four of the latter were situated on streams on edge of the coal measures. Several ironworks known to have operated in the district in the 17th century had apparently closed by 1717. Fuller's list makes no mention of the Earl of Shrewsbury's furnace in Shifnal parish, nor of the Foley family furnaces at Lilleshall and Wombridge.[31]

The greatest concentration of forges in Shropshire in 1717 was in the valley of the River Tern and its tributaries, where seven of the 15 forges listed by Fuller were situated. These were for the most part within easy reach of the furnaces around the coalfield, but they drew their pig iron from all over the Borderland region. Pre-eminent among the Tern Valley forges was that built in 1710 near to the river's confluence with the Severn at Atcham, where by 1717 the output of manufactured iron amounted to 300 tons a year, and where the installations included mills for rolling brass plates and iron hoops, a slitting-mill, a wire-mill and a steel furnace.[32]

Another concentration of ironworks in the eastern part of Shropshire was in the valley of the Worfe and its tributaries between Tong and its confluence with the Severn above Bridgnorth. The Slaney family of Hatton owned the blast furnace at Kemberton, the Lizard forge near Tong, and a slitting-mill at Ryton built shortly before 1692. There was at least some integration of the works, for both slitting-mill and blast furnace were leased to the same tenants in 1714, and at the same time the lessees agreed to slit iron made by the Slaneys at Lizard forge.[33]

The iron-working trades, nailing, locksmithing, needle-making and the like were represented in east Shropshire in the first half of the 18th century. Some evidence survives of nail-making. Migration of workers in these trades between Madeley parish and the Black Country. It is doubtful whether these craftsmen had anything more than a local significance, and certainly they never multiplied in Shropshire as they did in south Staffordshire and north Worcestershire.[34]

The east Shropshire coalfield at the beginning of the 18th century was important in the iron trade only as a source of iron ore for the four blast furnaces on its perimeter. These furnaces, together with the forge at Coalbrookdale, were part of a much wider pattern of activities, which was controlled by partnerships whose interests were not primarily local. This traditional charcoal iron trade was far from decline in the early 18th century. It forms the backcloth against which the development of the coke iron trade must be viewed.

III

THE COALBROOKDALE IRONWORKS 1708–1750

In 1708 the blast furnace at Coalbrookdale was leased by Thomas Dorsett and Richard Corfield to Abraham Darby, a Bristol ironfounder.[1] The furnace was already an old-established one, and there is no valid reason for doubting that the date 1638 on the beam above its hearth is the date of its erection. It had previously been worked by the Wolfe family, who had sheltered the fugitive Prince Charles at Madeley after the battle of Worcester, and in 1695 was being operated by one Shadrach Fox who left when the pool dam burst some time afterwards.[2] July 1706, a time of great floods in north Wales has been suggested as the likeliest time of this disaster,[3] but whenever it happened, the furnace was derelict when Darby leased it.

Abraham Darby I was born on 14 April 1678, the son of John Darby, a Quaker locksmith of the Wren's Nest near Dudley. He was apprenticed to Jonathan Freeth, a maker of malt mills in Birmingham, and after the completion of his apprenticeship and his marriage set up business in 1699 as a maker of malt mills in Bristol. In 1702 he became a partner with other Quakers in the Bristol Brass Wire Company, and began to take an interest in the founding of brass pots.[4] He withdrew from the Brass Wire Company, probably in 1706, set up an iron foundry in Cheese Lane, Bristol, and in 1707 took out a patent for the casting of iron-bellied pots in sand.[5]

Abraham Darby I blew in the Coalbrookdale furnace in January 1709 (N.S.). That from the first he made use of coke instead of charcoal as his fuel, and that this was the first occasion on which iron ore had been successfully smelted with mineral fuel, are now generally accepted. Darby's discovery did not bring about a sudden change in the economy of the district, nor was the invention of coke smelting widely copied, for the iron he produced, while of a quality well suited for founding, could not satisfactorily be converted to wrought iron. The introduction of coke smelting has in the past been the subject of much dispute among scholars, and its chronology and circumstances need to be examined in some detail.

The primary source for the events of the autumn of 1708 and the early months of 1709 at Coalbrookdale is the Sales Book which contains Abraham Darby's accounts for the period.[6] The accounts show that in the period after 20 October the furnace was largely rebuilt.[7] By January 1709 the furnace was in operation; its five regular workmen, supplemented by casual labourers paid by the day or the task, received their first wages on 17 January 1709. Some time before this the making of coke from coal had begun. On 3 January Richard Darrall received 6s. for, 'Charking Coles'. The accounts show that 'coles' were being purchased from Lawrence Wellington, Edward Darrall and

Richard Hartshorne among others.[8] It has been argued that 'charcking coles' at this period could mean either making coke from coal or making charcoal from cordwood,[9] but the word 'coles' was that normally used to denote mineral fuel in Shropshire, and one entry in the accounts, albeit a deleted one, shows beyond reasonable doubt that the 'coles' being purchased for the Coalbrookdale furnace in 1709 were mineral fuel and not charcoal. In the payments for the period up to 30 April 1709 occurs the item 'to coals reserved by Roger Cock from Darrall's *pit* – 9 stack 7 loads. . . .' [10] This item was probably written in the wrong book, since Darby is known to have kept other accounts. On the basis of the evidence in the sales book therefore there is no reason to doubt that from the first Darby employed coke rather than charcoal as the fuel for his furnace.

There remain some doubts about the introduction of coke smelting. While the accounts show that coke was used from January 1709, the recollections of the development of the process by Hannah Rose and Abiah Darby suggest a number of stages, in which first charcoal and then raw coal were employed.[11] Samuel Smiles, who saw a Blast Furnace Memorandum book for 1709 and subsequent years which is now lost, also suggested several stages in which different fuels were mixed together. His conclusion that a mixed charge of 'five baskets of coke, two of brays, one of peat', was used[12] has been discounted by Dr. R. A. Mott on the grounds that brays meant not charcoal but small pieces of coke. Dr. Mott admits however that in the period of the next Coalbrookdale records between July 1718 and February 1721 charcoal was used on three occasions when the furnace was not driving well.[13] While peat was not being used in this period, the presence of turf in the coalyard when an inventory was taken at Coalbrookdale in July 1718 suggests that it could have been used earlier.[14] While there is no room for doubt that in 1709 Abraham Darby used coke and coke alone as his fuel, over the next eight years, a period for which no documents survive, it seems likely that experiments were made with charcoal, peat and possibly raw coal as well as coke, and probably these experiments account for the suggestions that there were successive stages in the introduction of coke smelting which occur in the memoirs of Hannah Rose and Abiah Darby.

How much Abraham Darby I knew of earlier attempts to smelt iron with coal instead of charcoal will probably never be known.[15] That he was born near Dudley makes it tempting to suggest that he may have known of the experiments of Dud Dudley in the 17th century, but such suggestions are based on no historical evidence. The use of coke in the smelting of iron ore was only one of a long succession of innovations in the use of mineral fuel for industrial purposes. It had been foreseen in Shropshire by John Weld as early as 1631. Coal had been used in salt-making, tar-distilling, glass-making, and in the brick and pipe industries, all of which were established in east Shropshire by 1700. Coal was employed by the 1690s for the smelting of lead, copper and tin ores, and was used for such purposes by the Bristol Quakers with whom Darby was acquainted. Even more significant is the use of coke in the malting trade. Darby was apprenticed to a maker of malt mills, and engaged in malting as a subsidiary occupation after his arrival at Coalbrookdale. In her account of his discoveries Abiah Darby noted that 'he had the coal coak'd into Cynder, as is done for drying malt'.[16] Darby had an advantage over Dud Dudley and others who had previously attempted to smelt iron ore with mineral fuel in that Shropshire coal was relatively free of sulphur.

Abraham Darby I's works developed largely as a pot foundry, although some of the pig iron which he made was sent to the works in Bristol in which he retained an interest, probably until 1715.[17] He supplied grates, kettles, pots, smoothing irons and similar items to country ironmongers throughout the Borderland. Cast-iron equipment for various manufacturers was being produced as early as 1709–10 when 40 cast-iron bars were made for a brass-maker, and a 104 gall. 'furnace' (i.e. a bellied pot) for a soap-maker.[18]

Darby's commercial intentions when he moved to Coalbrookdale are difficult to determine. His main interest was in founding – he sent for patterns from Bristol within a month of blowing-in the Coalbrookdale furnace[19] – but it is certainly possible that he hoped to involve himself in the mainstream of the iron trade by supplying pig iron to forges. He was closely involved with the partners who set up the forge at Atcham near the mouth of the River Tern in 1710. Five of the partners were Bristolians, two of whom, James Peters and Griffin Prankard held shares in the Coalbrookdale works, and another was Thomas Harvey, Darby's brother-in-law. Darby also had contacts with the Backbarrow ironworks in the Lake District, and with the furnace at Vale Royal (Cheshire) both of which were involved in the traditional iron trade.[20]

Further light on Darby's intentions may be shed by investigation of the state of charcoal supplies in east Shropshire. The furnace at Coalbrookdale had been out of blast for some years when Darby leased it, and it is possible that the locally-available supplies of charcoal had been bespoken for some years ahead by the operators of other ironworks. That there were some difficulties in supplying the furnace is suggested by the areas from which he drew iron ore and limestone. If, later in the 18th century, 'the geography of the site he chose', became, as Dr. Raistrick has suggested, 'an ideal gravity feed system,'[21] this was not so in the time of Abraham Darby I and his immediate successors. Limestone was obtained not from Lincoln Hill, which adjoins Coalbrookdale, but from Much Wenlock and Gleedon Hill, south of the Severn. After Darby's death in 1717 ironstone was being purchased from Ladywood in Broseley parish[22] and from Benthall, both south of the river, and barge owners were employed to ship it across to Ludcroft on the Madeley side. If the operators of the Coalbrookdale works had to go to the inconvenience of transporting some of their limestone and iron ore across the Severn by barge – for there was no bridge between Buildwas and Bridgnorth until 1780 – then it is certainly conceivable that local supplies of charcoal were unavailable.

Abraham Darby I's intentions and achievements will be better understood as knowledge of the charcoal iron industry increases. In particular the introduction of coke smelting will appear in a clearer light when the degree of control which the charcoal ironmasters exercised over the quality of their products is more fully appreciated. There is some evidence to suggest that by the 17th-century ironmasters were aware that certain types of ore would produce pig iron suitable for conversion into wrought iron, while other types made an iron which could not be so converted although it was suitable for foundry work.[23] It is possible therefore that Darby made iron for castings rather than for forging not through an accidental choice of ores, but as a result of a deliberate decision based on metallurgical knowledge which was familiar to the iron trade at the time.

That there were considerable difficulties in the successful application of coke smelting is suggested by the slowness with which it was adopted at other ironworks. The year after Darby's discovery two master colliers, George Benbow and Richard Hartshorne, the latter Darby's chief supplier, leased mines in Dawley from Robert Slaney and undertook to supply coal and ironstone to Slaney's blast furnace at Kemberton. They received specific authority in the lease to 'convert coals into charcoal', (i.e. coke) at hearths, which were not to be more than 30 yards from the pit mount. In 1714 Slaney leased the furnace to William Cotton, Edward Kendall and William Wright, and assigned to them his contract with Hartshorne and Benbow for the supply of coal and ironstone.[24] Evidence that ironstone was actually smelted with coke at Kemberton is lacking, but Slaney's agreements suggest that at least experiments with coke were tried there, and they show conclusively that the use of coke at Coalbrookdale did not remain a closely guarded secret. It is probable that the lessees of Kemberton furnace after 1714 reverted to the use of charcoal, for in the 1720s the furnace was part of the mainstream of the iron trade, engaged chiefly in the supply of pig to forges.

For 40 years after 1710 the use of coke for smelting iron ore spread slowly. Darby's successors at Coalbrookdale took up the practice at furnaces which they leased at Willey and Bersham. It was introduced at Chester-le-Street (Durham), Little Clifton and Maryport (Cumberland) and at Redbrook in Dean, but these represented only a tiny proportion of the ironworks in Great Britain.[25] One reason for the slow adoption of coke was the limited output of a coke blast furnace. As late as 1753 a Swedish visitor to Coalbrookdale noted that the blast furnaces there made only between 12 and 13 tons of iron a week, compared with the 18 or 19 tons which could be expected from a charcoal furnace.[26] Another reason was the inferior quality of coke-smelted iron. As late as 1761 a Bristol merchant advertised wrought iron, 'inferior to none in goodness or quality and made and drawn out with wood coal only . . . no foreign or pit coal iron will be sold'.[27] Metallurgical research will probably in due course identify more of the technical problems which inhibited the spread of coke smelting. The evidence at present available is sufficient only to show that there were severe technical drawbacks to the process, that it produced an iron inferior for most purposes to charcoal iron, in smaller quantities than were normally obtained from charcoal furnaces. Such difficulties, rather than a Quaker obsession with secrecy, explain why over 40 years elapsed between Darby's discovery in 1709 and the 'take-off' of the coke iron industy.

'In the year 1700', wrote George Perry of Coalbrookdale in the 1750s, 'the whole village consisted of only one furnace, five dwelling houses and a forge or two; about forty years ago the present Iron Foundery was established, and since that time its trade and buildings are so far increased that it contains at least 450 inhabitants and finds employment for more than 500 people'. When Abraham Darby II and his partners renewed the lease of the Coalbrookdale works in 1756, the indenture recorded that since 1734 the works had, 'much increased'.[28] The prosperity of Coalbrookdale depended essentially on the growing trade in cast-iron holloware, but if the works had been no more than a successful pot foundry it would have little historical significance. Coalbrookdale is important in the economic history of Great Britain because, in the 45 years following the settlement of Abraham Darby I in the district, most of the principal restrictions which had inhibited the growth of the English iron trade were overcome by those who operated the works. It had previously been almost unknown for more than one blast furnace to be sited in one place because of limitations on the supply of charcoal, but the discovery of coke smelting removed this constraint. Coal for coking could be obtained in any quantities which an 18th-century ironworks was likely to require. In 1714 Abraham Darby I leased the Great, Upper, Middle and Plate Forges at Coalbrookdale, and it was probably on the site of one of them that he constructed a second blast furnace in 1715.[29]

After the death of Abraham Darby I in 1717 the control of the Coalbrookdale works passed to Thomas Goldney of Bristol to whom half of the works had been mortgaged, and to Mary Darby's son-in-law Richard Ford. Thomas Goldney's interests were taken over by his son, Thomas Goldney II, after his death in 1731. The son of Abraham Darby I, also called Abraham, was aged only six at the time of his father's death. His interest and that of his brothers and sisters in the ironworks was represented by a three sixteenths share held on their behalf by Joshua Sergeant. Abraham Darby II began to participate in the management of the works in 1728, and by 1732 seems to have been acting as deputy to Richard Ford. New terms of partnership which recognised his new role gave him one quarter of the rights privileges and advantages of the tenancy of the works, and a salary of £50, were drawn up in 1732, and in 1738 by a further deed he was recognised as a full partner.[30]

Ford and Goldney spent much of their energy developing the trade in cast-iron holloware. Both partners visited fairs to sell their products – in the autumn of 1718 Ford went to Bishop's Castle and Montgomery, while Goldney visited Shrewsbury and Oswestry. In the spring of 1720 Ford went to Wrexham while Goldney visited Newcastle-under-Lyme and Congleton. Customers were chiefly ironmongers from the Midlands and the Borderland. Goods were supplied to Welsh merchants as far afield as Machynlleth and Dolgelley, and there were many customers in the market towns of Cheshire, Derbyshire, north Staffordshire and south Lancashire. The ironmongers from the small market towns of Shropshire naturally drew supplies of holloware from Coalbrookdale. Large quantities of pots and kettles, often over £200-worth at a time were sent to the Bristol merchant Nehemiah Champion, presumably for export. The most distant inland customer was John Ives of Gainsborough whose goods were carried by road to Wilden Ferry on the Trent, or by river to Bristol and thence by sea and the Trent Navigation.

The most important items supplied to industrial users were the cast-iron parts for Newcomen atmospheric engines. The significance of the foundry's involvement in this trade was twofold: it brought the works to the attention of mine owners all over Britain, and the familiarity thus gained with the atmospheric engine led to its application locally, first to pump water from pits and later to serve the iron industry. The Newcomen engine was to prove an effective means of ensuring a constant supply of water at ironworks through the summer months, hitherto one of the principal impediments to the growth of the iron industry.

The first full-size engine to the design of Thomas Newcomen, the Dartmouth ironmonger, was installed near Dudley Castle only 20 miles from Coalbrookdale by 1712, and by 1717 there were also engines at the Griff collieries in Warwickshire and at Hawarden, Flints., the former being the property of one Stanier Parrot. The first recorded orders for steam engine parts at the Coalbrookdale works were met in 1718–19 when three 6 ft. 6in. cast-iron pipes and a 'cast box' were supplied to 'Stanier Parrot of ye Fire Engine'.[31] It is quite possible that steam engine parts were being cast at Coalbrookdale before the death of Abraham Darby in 1717. About June 1719 an atmospheric pumping engine came into operation in the Madeley glebe coalworks.[32] The surviving records of the Coalbrookdale works do not commence until July 1718, and it is likely that the cylinder for the Madeley engine would have been supplied before that date, since the erection of an engine would obviously have taken a considerable time. The first clear reference to the making of a cast iron-cylinder for a Newcomen engine occurred in 1722, and at least 10 cylinders were cast between that year and 1730.[33]

The patent governing the use of the Newcomen held by the 'Proprietors of the Invention for raising Water by Fire', expired in 1733, which led Richard Ford to anticipate that business relating to 'ye Fire Engine' would increase. In the years immediately before 1733 there was a rise in demand, perhaps anticipating the expiry of the patent. Seven cylinders were cast in 1731 and 10 in 1732, and in the 15 years after 1733 over 50 cylinders and large quantities of pump equipment and pipes were sold. Even so, the account books may give an inadequate picture of the sales of engine parts. A new boring mill for the finishing of cylinders was installed in 1734.[34]

All power-using industries in the early 18th century suffered from the unreliability of water supplies in the summer months. Most water-dependent ironworks ceased operation for a period in the summer. Dr. Raistrick has shown that it was usual at Coalbrookdale in the 1720s to begin an iron-making campaign in September or October, with a steep rise in output to a peak between December and February, checked on some occasions for a time between the running out of the water impounded behind the dams during the summer break and the coming of rains in autumn. After the mid-winter peak output normally fell and reached a low level in April, which was maintained until the furnace was blown out for a period of about 12 weeks in mid-summer.[35]

In 1735 at a time of unusually low rainfall, Richard Ford suggested to Thomas Goldney the use of horses to work pumps to return water from the pools below the furnaces at Coalbrookdale to those above. These pumps were working within four months when Ford forecast that with the engine and new water wheels there would be no need in future to fear water shortages.[36]

In the summer months of 1742 work began on the construction of a Newcomen engine at Coalbrookdale to replace the horse-driven pumps. In June the pits for the 'Fire Engine' were being dug and bricks purchased. In October the regulating beam was purchased for £10 15s. and more timber was floated down the Severn for the engine in December. Most of the construction was done in December 1742 and January 1743 and in the four-week period ending on 13 January 1743 £62 12s. 0½d. was paid out in wages to 24 individual workmen or partnerships. In subsequent months when the finishing touches were being put to the engine fewer workers would have been needed, and this is reflected in lower wage bills. The engine began to work in the four-week period ending 24 September 1743 when small payments were made in addition to the normal wages of two workmen, 'allowed before ye Engine work'd'.[37] The use of the Newcomen engine to return once used water to the pools whence it had flowed was an innovation of major importance which to a great extent relieved ironworks from their dependence on rainfall. It was an innovation which was used in most of the new Shropshire ironworks of the 1750s.

In the time of Richard Ford and Thomas Goldney numerous contacts were maintained between Coalbrookdale and other iron works. In 1733 Ford and the second Thomas Goldney acting on their own accounts and not as partners in the Coalbrookdale works took over the blast furnace at Willey, which they blew in for the first time on 12 September 1733. Coke was used for smelting at Willey, but considerable difficulties were experienced in obtaining a sufficient supply of water for working the bellows. In 1731 Ford and Goldney took over the Bersham blast furnace near Wrexham where coke smelting had been introduced by Charles Lloyd in 1721. One of their objects must have been to supply holloware to Cheshire and Lancashire which lay beyond the easy trading routes of the Severn valley, but some customers at Manchester and Chester were still being supplied from Coalbrookdale as late as 1738.[38] Ford and Goldney operated Old Willey furnace until their lease ran out in 1757, while Bersham was given up to Isaac Wilkinson in 1753.

During the 1720s Ford and Goldney developed the forges in Coalbrookdale. While the pig iron from the adjacent furnaces was unsuitable for forging into wrought iron experiments were made from time to time with small quantities of it. Much of the pig iron for the forge during the 1720s and '30s came from the nearby furnace at Leighton, but other sources included Kemberton, Bouldon in the Corvedale, Vale Royal (Cheshire) and the American colonies. Five tons of 'Baltimore piggs' were noted on an inventory taken at the works in July 1740, and 'Potomack' pigs were received there the following year.[39]

Richard Ford I died in 1745. His three sons retained some connections with Coalbrookdale, Richard Ford II being clerk of the company until 1748, but about 1756 his concerns and those of his brother, which included the blast furnace at Leighton, the forges at Caynton and Sambrook and the slitting-mill at Tibberton, became bankrupt, and Abraham Darby II acquired the Ford family interests in Coalbrookdale. The Goldney connection in the concerns was maintained, and Thomas Goldney II was Darby's principal partner in the great expansion of the 1750s.[40]

For 40 years after the discovery of coke smelting the Coalbrookdale ironworks remained essentially a pot foundry, yet close connections with the traditional charcoal iron trade were maintained, and the advantages which might be gained if a type of iron suitable for forging could be obtained by smelting iron ore with coke must always have been obvious. The works' accounts books suggest that from time to time experiments were made with this object in view. Apart from the small quantities of Coalbrookdale iron used at the adjacent forges, small amounts were sent to the Tern forge at Atcham, and to Leighton furnace, the latter presumably for despatch to a forge with Leighton pigs.[41]

The surviving works' account books cease in 1748, at which time most of the output of the Coalbrookdale furnaces was either cast into pots and kettles or sold as pig to other foundries. Soon after 1748 Abraham Darby II began to make forgeable iron using coke as his fuel. The period of this important innovation is almost entirely undocumented, but from the practices at the new Horsehay ironworks opened in 1755, it would seem that Darby discovered by experiment that he could make iron for forging by smelting particular types of iron ore mined in the northern part of the coalfield, which happened to have a low phosphorous content. The most reliable account of this development is the recollection of Darby's wife Abiah, written about 1779,

> ... about 26 years ago my Husband conceived his happy thought – that it might be possible to make bar from pit coal pigs – upon this he sent some of our pigs to be tryed at the Forges, and that no prejudice might arise against them, he did not discover from whence they came, or of what quality they were. And good account being given of their working, he errected Blast Furnaces for pig Iron for Forges. – Edward Knight Esqr. a capitol Iron Master urged my Husband to get a patent, that he might reap the benefit for years of this happy discovery: but he said he would not deprive the publick of Such an Acquisition which he was Satisfyed it would be; and so it has proved[42]

Something of the tension of this period of experiment is perhaps preserved in the rather garbled account by Hannah Rose of Abraham Darby's six days and nights

without sleep at the furnace top, after which, having produced a satisfactory iron, he
fell asleep and was carried home by his furnace crew.[43]

The initial experiments in which iron for forging was made by using coke as a fuel
must have taken place at Coalbrookdale, but once success was achieved the Dale
furnaces reverted to the production of iron for foundry purposes, and Darby and
Thomas Goldney II began a new works for the manufacture of iron for forging, a works
which was to revolutionise the iron trade.

1. The Iron Bridge at Dawn (*Photo: E. G. Webb*)

2. The Old Furnace, Coalbrookdale (*Ironbridge Gorge Museum Trust*)

3. A Perspective View of Coalbrookdale, by George Perry and T. Vivares, *c.* 1758. On the left is the upper blast furnace, with its surrounding foundry buildings. An engine cylinder is being hauled by the team of horses in the left foreground, while on the edge of the furnace pool coal is being coked in open heaps. In the background can be seen the mixture of ironmasters' houses and workers' cottages which characterised Coalbrookdale, and on the far side of the pool a railway waggon descends into the Dale on the line from Coalmoor (*Ironbridge Gorge Museum Trust*)

4. The Calcutts Ironworks, 1788, by George Robertson (*Ironbridge Gorge Museum Trust*)

5. The Madeley Wood furnaces during restoration (*Photo: Author*)

6. A View of Lincoln Hill with the Iron Bridge in the distance taken from the side of the River Severn, by George Robertson, engraved by James Fittler, 1788 (*Ironbridge Gorge Museum Trust*)

7. Ludcroft Wharf, Coalbrookdale, *c.* 1860 (*Photo: Author's Collection*)

8. Ludcroft Wharf, Coalbrookdale, *c.* 1880 (*Photo: Author's Collection*)

9.   The cast iron grave slab of Eustace Beard in Benthall church yard. The full inscription reads: The Body of Eustace Beard of this parish, Trowman, who departed this life October the 28th 1761, Aged 61 Years.

From rocks and sands the Lord deliver'd me,
And many times from danger set me free,
My body home he brought, among my friends to rest,
My soul sing Hallelujah with the best.

(Photo: Author)

10. The restored Shropshire Canal at the Blists Hill open air museum, with a wrought iron tub boat afloat on it, and a plateway running alongside (*Photo: Author*)

11. Dual gauge plateway siding at Rose Cottage, Coalbrookdale (*Ironbridge Gorge Museum Trust*)

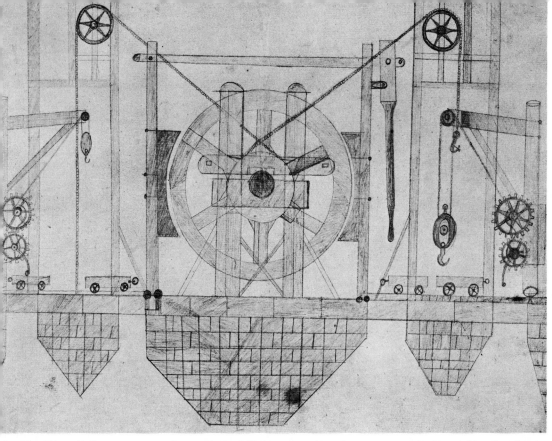

12. The winding apparatus of the Brierly Hill Tunnel and Shafts system on the Shropshire Canal near Coalbrookdale (*From the William Reynolds Sketch Book. Photo: Science Museum, London*)

13. Lost among trees. The tunnel of the 200-year old tunnel-and-shaft system at Hugh's Bridge on the Donnington Wood Canal, which was superseded by an inclined plane in 1796 (*Photo: Author*)

IV

REVOLUTION IN THE IRON TRADE

For most of the second half of the 18th century more iron was produced in Shropshire than in any other county in Great Britain. The foundations of the prosperity of the Shropshire iron trade were the coke blast furnace, the application of the steam engine to iron-making and mining, and the use of coal and coke in the forging of wrought iron. The instrument by which expansion was achieved was the large, vertically-integrated partnership. The 'take-off' into the well sustained growth of the second half of the century came in the mid-1750s. In 1754 there were three coke blast furnaces in the east Shropshire coalfield and its immediate vicinity. By 1759 there were 12.[1] This was the period when coke blast iron for the first time gained a place in the traditional iron trade. What happened in Shropshire during these five years therefore demands detailed scrutiny.

Between 1709 and 1753 most of the major obstacles to the expansion of the iron trade had been overcome by the Darbys and their partners. Coke smelting removed the industry's reliance on limited supplies of charcoal. The application of a Newcomen engine to maintain a water circuit to operate the wheels which drove furnace bellows reduced the industry's dependence on regular rainfall. Railways were shown by 1750 to be as useful to ironmasters for the supply of raw materials to furnaces as they were to coalmasters for taking coal to the Severn. Experiments with different ores about 1750 showed that it was possible to smelt iron for forges using coke instead of charcoal. Many minor but vital modifications to furnace lines, blowing techniques, &c. remain unrecorded.

In the late 1740s and early '50s the Coalbrookdale partners began to integrate their concerns vertically. In earlier decades most of the raw materials used at the works had been mined by independent producers and sold to the partners. They had been delivered to the works by pack horse or wain. By 1750 the partners were using their own railway for this purpose, and they were beginning to take a more active part in the mining of their own raw materials. On 25 March 1754 Abraham Darby II leased from R. A. Slaney the mines in the township of Great Dawley, and on the same day concluded an agreement with Slaney to rent an isolated tenement in the north of Dawley parish known as Horsehay Farm, with an old corn mill adjacent to it, a pool and dam, and some nearby rough ground. The agreement stipulated that Darby would be free to erect furnaces on the land. At about the same time Darby leased the mines in the lordship of Ketley from Earl Gower, and was making preparations to erect an atmospheric pumping engine to drain them in December 1754. While Abraham Darby operated the Dawley and Ketley mines on his own account, Thomas Goldney II was his partner in the projected ironworks.[2]

The conversion of the old mill site at Horsehay into an ironworks required civil engineering works on a prodigious scale. At Coalbrookdale a fast running stream through the valley naturally favoured iron-making. At Horsehay it was necessary to create an entire new landscape. The mill stream and pond were altogether insufficient to provide power for furnace bellows, and a system of pools had to be constructed to store sufficient water to allow operations to continue during the summer months. The main pool lay behind a large and at first somewhat unstable dam. In December 1754 a not entirely benevolent observer reported, 'a great part of the Mighty dam is Tumbled down', and counted about 60 men plugging the leaks in the remainder with coke and charcoal dust.[3] An atmospheric engine for pumping back water to the pool was supplied from the Coalbrookdale works. Vast quantities of building materials were brought to Horsehay; timber from Kemberton, Wrockwardine and Hadley, bricks and firebricks from Broseley, furnace hearth and timp stones from Highley, and alabaster from Bristol.[4]

The survival of so many documents relating to the Darbys and their partners has meant that much of the history of the Shropshire iron trade has been written as a success story with the Darbys as heroes. It is possible to look at events at Horsehay in 1754–55 from a different and less flattering viewpoint. William Ferriday had since the early 1730s been supplying raw materials to the Coalbrookdale partners in his capacity as agent for the lands of William Forester in the parish of Little Wenlock. He employed the Coalbrookdale partners' railway to take coal from Little Wenlock to the Severn. Ferriday was a man of great experience in the coal trade, and regarded the activities of Darby and Goldney at Horsehay as an extravagant folly. He informed his master in March 1755,

> the dale Gentlemen (as their men call 'em) are such for wasting money that I never knew – nor so very little done for it. One can scarce see anything the forwarder but daily hear A Monstrous Braging Noise of what they will do. I think the Engine at Ketley will not work much before Midsummer, and that the Horsehay furnace never will to any purpose, that poole runs out all the water, it was never near full yet this winter – I am pretty sure 20 pounds a week hath not cleared the charge there in odd work, a great part of it carrying the charcoale dust and dirt in a boat and putting in the pool to muddy that little water as is in it, they make good pay and boast loudly of it. However, I am glad you are paid all to last Michs. I cannot perceive where the money comes, But fancy if the Horsehay furnace misses one may hear soon.[5]

The Horsehay blast furnace was prepared for blowing-in during the first four months of 1755. Coking of coal began in January, and early in April the pumping-engine came into operation. Deliveries of iron ore from Lawley commenced on May Day. A fortnight later the furnace was in blast and making iron.[6] It quickly justified Abraham Darby II's confidence and confounded his pessimistic critics. An average production of over 15 tons a week was soon achieved, and in the best weeks it proved possible to make as much as 22 tons. For the first time a coke blast furnace had been proved conclusively superior to a charcoal-fired furnace in the production of iron for forging. In April 1756 Darby and Goldney agreed to erect a second furnace at Horsehay.[7] Something of the partners' elation at their success can be seen in a letter from Darby to Goldney later in the year,

The Horsehay work may surely be said to be got to a top pinnacle of prosperity. Twenty and twenty two tons per week and sold off as fast as made at profit enough will soon find money enough for another furnace and for the pocket too[8]

In May 1757 the second Horsehay furnace was blown in, an event celebrated by a dinner described by Darby's wife,

We . . . dined upwards of 300 people so that our Family that day was large with the poor folks besides. We killed a fat Cow, and the fatted Calf: hams: and 10 large puddings full of fruit: and 2 hogs heads of drink. We carried it up in Railway Wagons and had 4 tables spread under cover.[9]

Goldney and Darby also projected an ironworks at Ketley. About 14 acres of land known as 'the Allmoores', south of Watling Street and east of Ketley Brook were leased from Earl Gower in October 1756. The following year shares in the works were divided into three equal portions, one Darby's, one Goldney's, and the third that of Darby's son-in-law Richard Reynolds, who had recently moved to Shropshire from Bristol. The first of the Ketley blast furnaces began operation in December 1757, and the second during the following year. As at Horsehay civil-engineering works were extensive. At least three pools were constructed, and an atmospheric engine, 'one of the largest in England', was supplied from Coalbrookdale to return used water to the uppermost of them.[10]

The Horsehay and Ketley works depended on railways for the supply of their raw materials and for the despatch of their pig iron to Coalbrookdale and the Severn wharves. Carriage of the large quantities of raw materials needed for the blast furnaces would scarcely have been impossible with any other means of transport available in the 1750s.

The mines which Abraham Darby II leased in Ketley and Dawley were insufficient to supply the needs of the new blast furnaces. Iron ore from Donnington Wood and Wrockwardine Wood was from the outset used at Horsehay, and in December 1756 Darby leased the mines in those areas from Henry Barber, who himself leased the Donnington mines from Earl Gower.[11]

In June 1759 Darby leased from Robert Burton a further mining area on the borders of Dawley and Wellington parishes which gained the name of the New Dale estate. According to a garbled story preserved by John Randall, Darby and Goldney proposed to move their foundries from Coalbrookdale to the new site when John Smitheman, lord of the manor of Madeley threatened not to renew the lease at Coalbrookdale. Randall maintained that the partners built casting houses, moulding shops and ware-houses, and actually commenced operations at New Dale, but that the enterprise was given up after the site of the Coalbrookdale works was purchased from Smitheman. This account cannot be wholly accurate. The lease of the Coalbrookdale works was renewed in 1756, and it was not until 1776 that Abraham Darby III purchased those portions of the lordship of the manor which made him ground landlord of Coalbrook-dale. But there are indications that there is some truth in Randall's story. Firebars and hammer heads were supplied to New Dale from Horsehay in 1759, and in 1761 some pig iron was sent there,[12] suggesting that a foundry may have been in operation. Certainly the village of New Dale was built not long after the land was leased from Burton. A Quaker meeting house was registered in New Dale in 1762, and in 1770 Abiah Darby referred in her journal to 'all those families' who lived there.[13] New Dale became a mining village however and if a foundry ever started there its life was short.

Abraham Darby II died in 1763 at the age of 52. His eldest son was only 13, and his son-in-law Richard Reynolds moved from Ketley to manage the whole of the partnership's enterprises from Coalbrookdale.[14] Darby's death necessitated the re-negotiation of a number of mining leases, including those for the Donnington collieries for which new agreements came into operation in August 1764, and those at Ketley which were concluded in the following September.[15]

Abraham Darby II brought coke smelted iron into the mainstream of the traditional iron trade. The purchasers of Horsehay pig iron were almost all forgemasters, many of them from the Stour valley, the greatest concentration of forges in the West Midlands. They included the Knight and Foley partnerships, Francis Homfray, William Ellwell, the Caynton Company, Francis Dorsett, William Barker and the Bellbroughton Company.[16] Such success would have attracted imitators at any time, but the high prices for iron stimulated by the outbreak of the Seven Years War in 1756 created an additional incentive for the setting up of blast furnaces in Shropshire as it did in South Wales and Scotland.[17] At least three other major partnerships built ironworks in east Shropshire within three years of the blowing in of the first furnace at Horsehay. This was recognised at the time as a period of unprecedented economic expansion. 'My husband delights in laying out money', wrote Abraham Darby's wife in May 1757, 'and when he'll stop I don't know'. 'This is a time yt every body is building Furnaces', wrote a financially-embarrassed local landowner in July of the same year, 'so this is the only time to sell one's Mine [i.e. iron ore] and I shall never again have ye same opportunity '.[18]

The New Willey Company, formed in 1757 took over the old furnace on George Forester's estate from the Ford-Goldney partnership which had held it since 1733 and received authority to build one or more new furnaces. The partners were Brooke Forester, the family's mining agent William Ferriday, John Skrymster of Shrewsbury, Edward Blakeway a Shrewsbury draper, six Bristol merchants, and John Wilkinson of Bersham, Ironmaster.[19]

In 1757 John Wilkinson was aged 30. He was the son of Isaac Wilkinson, a pot-founder of Wilson House, Furness, and since 1753 of the Bersham ironworks near Wrexham. After the death of his first wife in 1756, John Wilkinson married in 1763 Mary Lee of Wroxeter, whose sister was the wife of Edward Blakeway. Apart from his interest in the New Willey Company, Blakeway was associated with several other ironworks in Shropshire and South Wales, and he later became one of the founders of the Shropshire porcelain industry.[20] It was he who in 1774 introduced John Wilkinson as a Burgess of the Borough of Wenlock.[21] In 1762 Wilkinson's sister Mary married Dr. Joseph Priestley, Unitarian minister, schoolmaster, and the discoverer of oxygen. John Wilkinson, his father, and his brother, William, had connections with the iron trade in many parts of Britain. They retained their interests in the Furness and Denbighshire works. Isaac Wilkinson held partnerships in the Dowlais and Plymouth works near Merthyr. In 1766 John Wilkinson obtained the land in Bilston where he founded the Bradley ironworks and laid the foundations of the South Staffordshire iron trade. His connections with Broseley seem to have begun even before the founding of the New Willey Company. In 1752 a John Wilkinson, almost certainly the same man, was buying coal from the Weld estates in the parish. Wilkinson made one of his several homes in Broseley. He leased land from Thomas Stephens in 1778 on which he built a new house which he occupied until 1800.[22] However much he was drawn by business

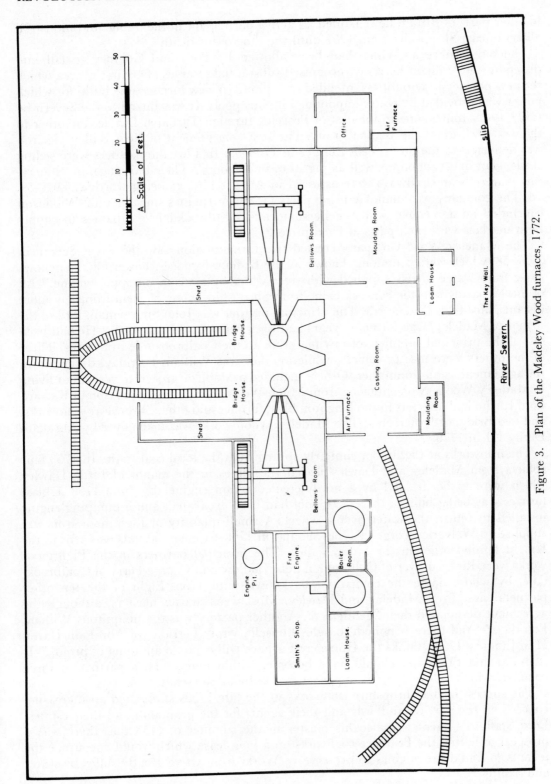

Figure 3.   Plan of the Madeley Wood furnaces, 1772.

to other parts of Britain he remained an active participant in the public and industrial affairs of east Shropshire from 1757 until the time of his death.

The old furnace at Willey had been allowed by Ford and Goldney to fall into disrepair, but William Ferriday recognised substantial reserves of ore in the area which the new partnership doubtless intended to exploit.[23] A new furnace was built, for which power was provided by water impounded in four pools. It was linked to the Severn by two railway routes, one to the east of Broseley through Tarbatch Dingle, the other to the west by way of the Benthall rails. The first consignment of New Willey pig iron was delivered to the Stour Valley forges in 1758–59. In 1761 the partners were selling shells, shot and cannon, as well as pig iron, in London.[24] Their buildings, machinery, raw materials and railways were assessed in August 1761 as being worth £26,910 5s. 1d. The company was manufacturing parts for steam engines since in 1762 Wilkinson concluded an agreement with the Bersham and Coalbrookdale companies to supply most markets with such parts at fixed prices.[25]

The Madeley Wood Company erected two furnaces alongside the River Severn in 1757–58, which were commonly known as the Bedlam furnaces. Power for the bellows came from water wheels supplied with river water by a steam pumping engine.[26] All of the 12 partners in the concern came from Shropshire, none of them from any more distant place than Bridgnorth. The principal partner was John Smitheman, lord of the manor of Madeley, who for many years had been active in the coal trade. He had been one of the principal suppliers of raw materials to the Coalbrookdale ironworks. Three of the others were master colliers, while another was William Ferriday, described in the agreement as an ironmaster. Others included a Madeley grocer, a clergyman living in Madeley Wood, two gentlemen from Much Wenlock, Edmund Ford, son of Richard Ford I, who had interests in the Leighton blast furnace and other Shropshire ironworks, and two Bridgnorth mercers.[27] The Madeley Wood works was taken over by Abraham Darby III in 1776.

The ironworks at Lightmoor similarly sprang from the local coal trade. In 1753 four colliers from Madeley and Dawley leased the mines in the manor of Little Dawley which were to be drained by a newly-erected steam engine. By June 1758 a blast furnace was being built, a three-acre pool had been excavated, and a pumping engine installed to return the water over a wheel. A small quantity of Lightmoor iron was supplied to Wolverley Forge in 1758–59, and in 1760–61 over 150 tons was sent to the Knight family forges in the Stour Valley. The principal partners in the Lightmoor works were Richard Syer of Culmington near Ludlow and George Perry of Coalbrookdale, by whose name the company was known until 1765. Eight of the ten other partners came from Madeley and Dawley. Most were charter masters, although the agreement designated them 'gentlemen'. Another partner was the ubiquitous William Ferriday.[28] 'And there is nobody besides himself', wrote Ferriday of Abraham Darby II in January 1755, 'thinks the Horsehay Furnace will come to anything of profit'.[29] It is ironic that the writer should have become, within four years, a partner in three concerns which followed the example set by Darby at Horsehay.

The success of the Shropshire ironworks in the late 1750s stimulated an increasing concern on the part of landlords and their agents for the profitability of their estates. Lord Stafford's agent wrote to his master in the summer of 1755 that there was a prospect of letting the Priorslee coalworks on a long lease which would encourage the tenants to 'build fire engines to preserve ye Works from wt ye greatly suffer by water and damps'.[30]

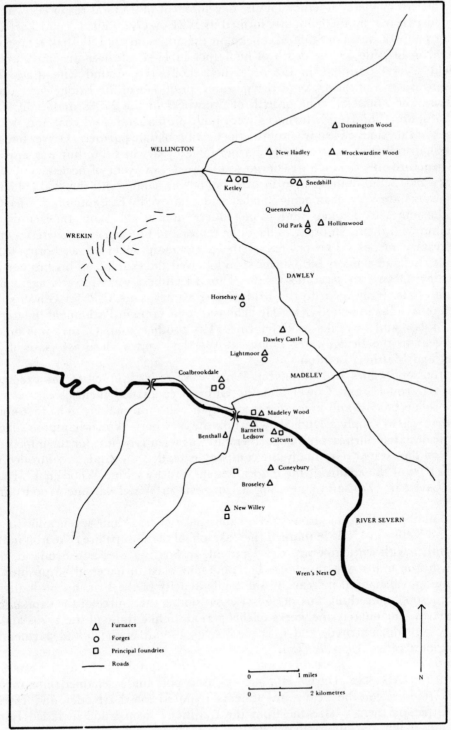

Figure 4. Ironworks in East Shropshire 1755–1810.

The concern of the aristocracy for the development of mineral resources was exemplified most clearly by the company formed in 1764 by Granville, second Earl Gower, and later first Marquess of Stafford, to exploit the mines on his Lilleshall estate. Gower succeeded to his title on the death of his father in 1754. He was an active politician who held several positions in the royal household. His second wife, Lady Louisa Egerton, was sister of the Duke of Bridgewater, promoter of the Bridgewater Canal in Lancashire and Cheshire. The growth of ironworks in the 1750s materially affected Gower's estates. The Ketley furnaces were built on his land, and coal and iron from his mines in Lilleshall parish was sold to the Coalbrookdale partners. Gower had leased his Lilleshall collieries to one Henry Barber for 21 years in 1756, but was apparently dissatisfied with this tenant's discharge of his trust, 'for want of necessary drains for the water and skilful management in carrying on the same, both the said colliery and the limeworks are very near being spoiled and destroyed'. In September 1764 Gower leased the mines to Thomas and John Gilbert, and at the same time entered into partnership with them, 'in order to have the mines and limeworks recovered by proper and necessary means'. The powers of the partnership included authority to build navigable cuts and sluices, and Gower soon followed the example of his brother-in-law by building a canal to serve his estate. Thomas Gilbert was Gower's agent for the Lilleshall estate, legal agent to the Bridgewater estates, and M.P. for Gower's pocket borough of Newcastle-under-Lyne. He achieved some fame in Parliament in later years as a poor law and turnpike road reformer. His brother John Gilbert was land and mines agent to the Bridgewater estates at Worsley, and a close associate of James Brindley and Matthew Boulton.

The ironstone mines in Donnington Wood were re-let in 1764 to the executors of Abraham Darby II, and Gower and the Gilberts concerned themselves much more with the domestic coal and limestone trades than with iron-making. The first object of their canal was to supply a landsale wharf on the Newport–Wolverhampton road, and one of the declared purposes of the partnership was to supply lime for the improvement of farms on the estate.[31] Gradually the company extended the lands it controlled in the northern part of the coalfield, buying estates in Wrockwardine Wood in 1771 and in Mossey Green in 1775, and extending its interests in Wrockwardine Wood mines in 1783.[32]

The building of five new ironworks in the space of less than seven miles between Willey and Ketley in 1755–58 marked the 'take-off' of the Shropshire coke iron industry, and, together with contemporary developments in South Wales and Scotland, that of the British iron industry as a whole. The nine new blast furnaces in Shropshire alone represented a substantial increase in the total capacity of the British iron industry. A crucial question concerning this period of expansion is the source of the capital for the new furnaces. Fortunately the works of this period, unlike those of the 1770s and '80s, are fairly well documented, and it is possible to list all of the initial partners from surviving deeds (See *Appendix One*).

Analysis of the list suggest three major sources of capital. One was the established iron industry. Abraham Darby II's success as a potfounder enabled him to amass sufficient reserves for the heavy investments required for the Ketley and Horsehay works. Other partners who came from the traditional iron trade included Edmund Ford, John Wilkinson and William Hallen. A second source was the city of Bristol. Thomas Goldney II provided a large part of the capital for Horsehay and Ketley, six Bristol merchants helped to finance the New Willey Company, and the arrival of

Richard Reynolds at Coalbrookdale in 1756 and his subsequent marriage to the daughter of Abraham Darby II brought further money from Bristol into Shropshire. The third major source of capital was the local coal industry. Both the Lightmoor and Madeley Wood partnerships were essentially combinations of local master colliers. Some major shareholders match none of these categories; little is known for example of Richard Syer or Joseph Biddle. Edward Blakeway's career is of particular interest. Originally he was a Shrewsbury draper, and his entry into the iron trade at this period seems a significant transfer of resources from an old and largely moribund industry to a new and dynamic one.

The scale of investment involved in the new ironworks of the 1750s is difficult to measure. Detailed accounts survive only for the Horsehay works and since these were so closely related to the Coalbrookdale and Ketley concerns the real significance of the figures is often obscured. The atmospheric pumping-engine at Horsehay cost over £750, and between August and November 1754 £363 9s. 0d. was spent on buildings on the site, exclusive of the blast furnace.[33] All of the works of the period necessitated considerable expenditure on pools, dams and watercourses. Investment was not confined to the ironworks themselves. The needs of the furnaces greatly increased the demands upon the local mines and the new investments in mining of the period are typified by the large atmospheric engine which the Coalbrookdale partners built in 1761 to drain their mines in the Dawley Field which cost £710 11s. $7^3/_4$.[34]

The 1750s were a period of social as well as economic change in east Shropshire. The first recorded food riot in the district took place in 1756. In 1760 the Evangelical John Fletcher accepted the Vicarage of Madeley with the apparent intention of attempting to solve what he saw as the special problems of an industrial and particularly Godless parish. The changes seem least dramatic when seen as part of the activities of the Coalbrookdale partnership, which for several decades had been accustomed to innovations. The pace of expansion can be better judged in the context of an enterprise of a very different kind.

V

THE ECONOMY OF A LANDED ESTATE

A large part of the lands of the Charlton family, of Apley Castle near Wellington, lay in the parishes of Wombridge and Wrockwardine Wood in the Shropshire coalfield. The estate extended in a north-westerly direction to Wytheford in Shawbury parish, 10 miles from Wombridge, and included land in Preston-on-the-Weald Moors, Wappenshall and Muckleton, a considerable number of properties in the town of Wellington, and several holdings in more distant parts of Shropshire. Apart from agricultural, the main resources of the estate were its coal and its timber, but iron ore, clay, limestone and salt were also exploited. For much of the first half of the 18th century the estate was administered by Thomas Dorsett, who was succeeded by his son Francis in the mid-1740s.

Coalmining on the Charlton estate was well established before the end of the 17th century. By the early 1720s the mines in Wombridge were let at £250 a year to Robert Brooks and John Lummas, who, from 1722, were experiencing considerable difficulties. By 1728 they owed the estate nearly £1,000, and had given up the mines to Richard Hartshorne, the leading entrepreneur of the time in the Shropshire coal trade, who paid only £200 a year for them.[1]

Under Hartshorne's tenancy the mines were considerably improved. Early in 1729 work began on the installation of an atmospheric pumping-engine in Wombridge which was erected at the joint cost of landlord and lessee, Hartshorne paying one third and the estate two thirds. The construction of the engine cost over £350. This engine was probably that for which payment by Richard Hartshorne is recorded in the Coalbrookdale works' accounts in 1731. A cylinder, a bottom, two pipes, one piston, six buckets and clacks and 12 iron bars were supplied at a total cost of £70 9s. 8d.[2] The original site of the engine is not known, but a level which it drained ran from Queenswood at the southern extremity of Wombridge parish. In 1738 the engine was removed to Greenfield, an area of increasing mining activity on the site of the present playing fields at Hadley Road, Oakengates.[3] Hartshorne also expanded the mines in Wrockwardine Wood, where 11 new pits were sunk in 1731.

Hartshorne died in January 1733, and after his death the mines came directly under the control of the Charlton estate being administered by Thomas Dorsett. The production of coal at Greenfield, the New Sough and Wrockwardine Wood in the half year from October 1730 amounted to 2,770 stacks, mined by 10 different charter masters. While directly comparable figures for different years are difficult to obtain, there is no indication that output increased substantially during the 1730s. In 1736–37

30

the Wrockwardine Wood mines were leased to Walter Stubbs of Beckbury at an annual rent of £45, and details of operations there cease to appear in the estate accounts. In 1743–44 the half-yearly output at Greenfield and the Sough amounted to 1,431 stacks as against 1,921 in 1730–31.[4]

A further period of expansion began in 1747. Borings were made, 'to see how the coals lay', in the old-established Greenfield work, while in a previously unexploited area, the Horsepasture on the high ground to the north east of the present Oakengates town centre, new pits were sunk and new headings made. A wooden railway was constructed to the Horsepasture pits, probably linking them with a wharf on Watling Street. This was probably the first railway in the northern part of the coalfield. The first waggon of coals passed along its rails on 26 September 1747, when Francis Dorsett gave the workmen 1s. to celebrate. Like the coalmasters of Madeley and Dawley, Dorsett used iron wheels from Coalbrookdale for his railway waggons. In the half year ending on Lady Day 1748, 1,765 stacks of coal were raised from the seams under the Horsepasture. The total production of the Wombridge mines amounted to 2,375 stacks, which realised £526 10s. 11d. as against costs of £436 15s. 9½d, much of which was incurred in expenditure on capital equipment.[5]

Most of the coal raised at this period was sold for domestic purposes, going by road to such places as Shifnal, Edgmond, Sheriffhales, Newport, Sambrook and Weston Park. In 1749–51 special consignments were sent to the Charlton family's home at Apley Castle, 'to burn in the rooms that have pictures in them'. There are no records of coal being taken to the Severn for export at this period, and most of it went to places within a five-mile radius of Wombridge. Large quantities were consumed by various enterprises on the estate, at brick kilns at Wellington, Oakengates and Wytheford, at the salt works at Preston-on-the-Weald Moors, and at a limekiln.[6]

The timber resources of the Charlton estate were as important as its coal mines, and a large part of the estate's woodland was on the high ground of Wombridge and Wrockwardine Wood which had probably never been cultivated. The estate was heavily coppiced, and the coppices in the coalfield area protected by gates and thorn hedges. 11 acres of Cockshutt Piece and 28 acres of Wombridge Farm were newly planted in 1744, and coppicing also took place on the Horsepasture and the Nabb. In 1747 there was a sawpit in the Horsepasture, and William Jervis was paid a guinea a year for taking care of the woods at Oakengates.[7]

During a felling of trees in Oatermoorwood, Wombridge, in August and September 1748, over £37 was paid out for felling and sawing, and for hedging and draining the coppice land. 54 oak saplings, eight tons of ash, and 70 unspecified trees were felled, producing over 200 cords of wood for burning into charcoal, large quantities of 'coalpit wood' (pitprops), in addition to heavy timber. Customers for cordwood are not listed, but it is likely that much of it went as charcoal to the forge at Wytheford. Pitprops were supplied to the Wombridge mines, particularly during the periods of expansion in 1729–31 and in 1747–48. Some timber was sold in 1729 to the trustees of the Watling Street turnpike road, and over 11 tons was sent for the building of Preston Church in 1732. The railway of 1747 was constructed of timber from the estate, as were the bodies of the vehicles which ran on it. From time to time wooden parts were supplied for the mills at Wombridge, including trows and a wheel arm in 1736, and in 1753 a new helve hammer was sent to Wytheford Forge.[8]

One of the enterprises of the Charlton estate was the salt works at Kingsley Wyche in Preston-on-the-Weald Moors, two and a half miles from Wombridge. The works was situated on the same reddish sandstone which produced the spa waters of Ad-maston which were popular in the 18th century. The springs yielded 4,000–5,000 galls. of brine every 24 hours. There were two adjacent salt works at Preston, one that of the Charlton family, the other, known as the Charity Salt Works, belonged to the Hon. Thomas Newport in 1707, when an agreement defining rights of access was negotiated. The Charity Works continued until at least 1736 when its coal was being purchased from the Wombridge mines.[9]

The first recorded tenant of the Charlton family's saltworks was Samuel Stringer who surrendered his lease in 1721, upon which it was let to Richard Brooks and John Lummas, then tenants of the Wombridge coal mines. In 1726, probably on the occasion of the collapse of the partnership of Brooks and Lummas, the works was taken over by Richard Hartshorne along with the Wombridge mines. On Hartshorne's death in 1733 it was administered by the estate, and from 1739 to 1760 it was operated by Francis Dorsett on his own account.[10]

The works stood on over an acre of ground, and salt was made by boiling brine, extracted from a pit by a horse-operated pump. From the pit the brine went to a cistern from which it was fed to iron pans in which it was boiled on iron grates fired by slack coal obtained cheaply from the Wombridge mines. Wrought-iron plates and various tools were obtained from Cornelius Hallen of the Lower Forge, Coalbrookdale. Like the salt makers of 16th-century Germany described by Georgius Agricola, the workers at Kingsley Wyche added blood to the boiling brine to accelerate the rate of evapor-ation. Blood was brought to the works in barrels from butchers in Shrewsbury, Newport and Wellington. The salt was moulded in baskets or 'barrows' and delivered to cus-tomers by road, a regular composition for tolls being paid to the Watling Street turnpike trust. It was sold to merchants as far away as Bishops Castle and Welshpool, and to at least five different customers in Shrewsbury. Richard Hartshorne paid a rent of £50 a year for the saltworks in 1726, when the value of the equipment was £64 13s. 3d. In the Michaelmas quarter of 1730, 121 fires were lit in 13 weeks. In the half year ending Lady Day 1730, 2,588 bushels of salt were sold and 182 remained in stock.[11]

In 1736 Dorsett gave up the works and it was let to John Briscoe, who held the neighbouring Kingsley Farm, and William Ball a collier from Wrockwardine Wood. The works was standing derelict in 1799,[12] and was probably never used afterwards, although it retained the name Kingsley Wyche until the end of the 19th century.

The iron trade was not prominent in the affairs of the Charlton estate in the first half of the 18th century, although an old blast furnace stood derelict by Wombridge mill until the 1730s. The forge at Wytheford was operated by the Dorsetts on their own account as tenants of the estate.[13] Some iron ore was mined in Wombridge: in 1736, 100 dozen were supplied to the Leighton furnace for example,[14] but this trade was of small account compared with that in coal. The estate gained some benefits from its proximity to the innovating Coalbrookdale ironworks. The cylinder for its pumping-engine and the wheels for its railway waggons came from the Coalbrookdale foundry, and salt pans from the Coalbrookdale forge, but mineowners as far from Shropshire as Tyneside bought Coalbrookdale cylinders, and numerous forges could have supplied salt pans.

In the mid-1750s the mines of the Charlton estate were suddenly swept into the orbit of the expanding Shropshire coke iron industry. In the summer months of 1757, as the second Horsehay furnace came into blast, the Wrockwardine Wood mines began to supply the Coalbrookdale partners with Black Stone iron ore. Production began on 19

September 1757 and in the following year 1,994 dozens of ironstone were supplied. A dozen, or douzon, consisted of 11 customary measures of ironstone on a furnace bank, and measured 6 ft. 4 in. long, 3 ft. 4 in. broad, and 2 ft. high. The following year over 5,000 dozens raised by 24 charter masters were supplied to the Dale partners' works at Coalbrookdale, Horsehay and Ketley. In 1759–60 4,334 dozens were raised. St. J. Chiverton Charlton benefited considerably from royalties on iron ore. He received only 1/3 of the money due for mineral rights in Wrockwardine Wood, since the lordship was shared with the Earl of Shrewsbury and the Hill family, but in 1758–59 this amounted to £236 14s. 7d., as compared with a mere £67 12s. 3³/₄d. realised from the operation of the coal mines in Wrockwardine Wood. The following year Charlton received £33 1s. 11d. in profits from the coal mines, but £198 12s. 10d. for his share of a year's ironstone royalties.[15]

On 4 March 1761 the account books record that Richard Reynolds, 'enters upon the road through the wood'. It seems that from this time Reynolds worked the mines on the Charlton estate on his own account. From 1761 supplies of ore to the Horsehay works ceased altogether, and only an occasional small consignment was sent to Coalbrookdale. Most of the ore mined went to Ketley where Reynolds held larger interests than in the other works.[16]

It was not until the late 1770s that iron making became established in the Oakengates area, but the sudden impact of the demand for iron ore on the economy of the Charlton estate in the late 1750s shows how substantial were the changes taking place in Shropshire industry following the blowing in of the first Horsehay furnace. This revolution in the iron trade has several times been described from the point of view of the Quaker entrepreneurs who promoted it. From the viewpoint of the miners in Wombridge and Wrockwardine Wood the changes appear no less startling.

VI

THE GREAT IRON-MAKING PARTNERSHIPS

'The number of blast furnaces for iron between Ketley and Willey exceeds any within the same space in the Kingdom', wrote Thomas Telford in 1800. In the 30 years between 1776 and 1806 the Shropshire iron trade reached the apex of its prosperity.

In 1775 a French observer recorded that there were 14 blast furnaces in Shropshire. If each produced 15 tons of iron a week, a conservative figure, the total made in the county would have been 12,000 to 13,000 tons a year. National production in the early 1770s has been estimated at about 32,000 tons, of which the Shropshire proportion would have been about 40 per cent. In 1788, 21 coke and three charcoal blast furnaces in Shropshire made 24,900 tons of iron per year, about 37 per cent of the total made in Great Britain. In 1791 23 Shropshire works made 31,096 tons. By 1796 there were 23 works in the county using coke blast furnaces which produced 32,969 tons in a year, about 27 per cent of the national total. While this shows a steady increase in capacity in Shropshire the county was being eclipsed by other areas. In South Wales where only 8,400 tons was made in 1788, 34,101 tons were produced in 1796. The same trends can be observed during the remainder of the wars with France. Production in Shropshire continued to increase, but the scope for expansion was less than in South Wales or south Staffordshire, and the proportion of the national output made in the county slowly declined. In 1805–06, 54,967 tons were made in Shropshire, over twice as much as in 1788, and about four times as much as 30 years previously, but this represented only about 22 per cent of the national output of just over a quarter of a million tons.[1]

The changes of this period were not confined to an increase in smelting capacity. The iron trade itself became more sophisticated, and the interests of the iron-making partnerships became more varied and more extensive. The most marked development was the growth of the works in which furnace and forge were fully integrated. When Dr. Joseph Priestley arrived in the United States in 1795 he remarked to John Wilkinson that to his surprise the ironworks were all 'upon the old plan'. 'No one here', he wrote, 'has got into the way of connecting all the processes in one concern. The ore is carried to the furnace, the pigs some miles to the chafery, the bars some miles to the mills and so on'.[2] Priestley was defining in negative terms the type of ironworks which Wilkinson and his contemporaries had pioneered in Shropshire.

The growth of the new type of works depended upon a number of technical factors, among which the application of the steam engine to the blowing of blast furnaces and the operation of forge machinery, and the development of new methods of making wrought iron were the most important. John Wilkinson succeeded for the first time in

34

applying the steam engine to work blowing apparatus at a blast furnace when he set to work the second Boulton and Watt engine at New Willey in 1776. The Watt rotative engine was employed at Shropshire forges almost as soon as it was available.

The capacity of blast furnaces was substantially increased in the closing years of the 18th century. In 1791 the weekly average production of the Shropshire furnaces was only 26 tons. Output at Horsehay after 1799, for which full records survive, was substantially higher. During 1799 the two furnaces then in blast varied between 20 and 30 tons a week, but by December there seems to have been an increase in demand, and throughout that month the No. 2 furnace was maintaining an output over 30 tons a week, reaching 40 tons in the first week of 1800, and remaining above 30 tons for most of the year. The output of the No. 1 furnace was almost as high. In 1801 there was again an increase with an output of over 54 tons in a week achieved at No. 1 furnace in February. On 17 May 1805 the No. 3 furnace was blown in for the first time: 'When of Verry Well' wrote the clerk in the works' memorandum book. Before the end of the year it was making well over 40 tons a week. No. 1 furnace was blown out a week before No. 3 began production, but was blown in again in June 1806. In the early months of 1807, obviously a period of very high demand, the three furnaces were making as much as 150 tons of iron in some weeks.[3]

An interesting technical development recorded by Gilpin in 1804 was the building of small 'Snapper' furnaces with an output of 10 to 15 tons a week which could be used to work surplus ore and coal at times of heavy demand. There were two such furnaces at Ketley, and one each at the Calcutts and Coalbrookdale, the latter presumably the 'new furnace' which is now part of the works' museum.[4]

Changes in forging methods were rather more complex. In 1766 the brothers Thomas and George Cranage of Coalbrookdale took out a patent for making wrought iron in a reverberatory furnace using coke as the fuel instead of charcoal, which was used in the finery and chafery process. Experiments with the method devised by the Cranages were being carried on as late as the autumn of 1767, but it proved wasteful in its consumption of pig iron, the brothers lost money on the trial and they seem to have been discontinued. In 1783 it seemed that the work of Peter Onions would enable wrought iron to be produced with coal as a fuel at Coalbrookdale, but early in the following year Onions could see little hope of success, and left Shropshire for Dowlais.[5] The most commonly-used method of manufacturing wrought iron in Shropshire in the last quarter of the 18th century was that patented by John Wright and Richard Jesson of West Bromwich in 1773 which involved the heating of broken pieces of pig iron in clay pots.[6] This process was used at the forges at Ketley, Horsehay, Coalbrookdale and Old Park, as well as at Wright and Jesson's own Wren's Nest works. In 1784 Henry Cort of Fareham took out his patents for the puddling and rolling of iron, which incorporated a number of previous innovations, including those of the Cranage brothers. In the same year he demonstrated this process at Ketley. Puddling furnaces were built there and an agreement made with Cort to pay him 10s. for each ton of wrought iron produced by the new method. There were 25 puddling furnaces in Shropshire in 1788. The puddling process was subsequently adopted more slowly in Shropshire than in South Wales, where, due to its use by Richard Crawshay, it earned the nickname of the 'Welsh method', while the Wright and Jesson process was often called the 'Shropshire method'. In 1796 Joshua Gilpin referred to stamping and potting as the old mode and to puddling as the new.[7] By 1800 puddling had gained more general acceptance in Shropshire although stamped iron was still being made a decade later.

The economy of east Shropshire in the late 18th century was dominated by nine major iron-making concerns: John Wilkinson, Banks and Onions, Alexander Brodie, Wright and Jesson, William Reynolds and Co., the Coalbrookdale Co., Addenbrooke and Homfray, T., W. and B. Botfield, and John Bishton. These companies had many of the characteristics of colonial governments, exploiting all the resources of their territories, closely controlling the lives of their work people, and often taking their names from the areas they owned or leased. In 1804 the iron-making capacities of the groups varied from Wright and Jesson and John Wilkinson, each with two blast furnaces, to William Reynolds and Co. with nine and Bishton with eight.[8] The four partnerships with the smallest concerns in Shropshire all had substantial iron-making interests elsewhere.

In order to obtain the raw materials for iron-making the great partnerships became involved in a wide variety of activities and in the selling of many different by-products. Typically an iron-maker would lease mining rights from one or more landlords. He would invest capital in sinking pits, and in such substantial items of mining equipment as steam engines, gins, weighing machines and pit props. Mines were normally worked on behalf of the ironmasters by sub-contractors or charter masters, who provided their own labour force, small tools and candles. Once raised to the surface, raw materials were conveyed to blast furnaces, usually by railways owned by the ironmaster. Only iron ore, clod coal, and relatively small quantities of other good coal and slack were required at the ironworks. Other coal would be sold for domestic purposes. Coke might be manufactured from coal in ovens which produced tar and other by-products for sale. Most of the ironmasters raised clay from their pits and manufactured bricks for their own use and for sale, consuming in the process some of their surplus coals. Clay might be sold in a raw or milled state to customers outside the iron trade. Limestone for blast furnaces was often obtained at a greater distance than coal or ore, and sometimes from mines or quarries owned by several iron-making concerns in partnership. Some limestone was unsuitable for use as a flux in furnaces, and would be burnt to make building or agricultural lime, for the ironmasters' own use or for sale. At the blast furnace the ironmasters produced pig iron and made some castings direct from the furnaces. Some pig iron would be sold to other foundries or forges, but much of it would be consumed at the partnership's own works. Wrought iron made at the partnership's forges would be sold as merchant bars or plates, or sometimes as blooms to other forges. The foundries produced a great variety of items, some like bridges, steam engines or cannon requiring a high degree of skill, and necessitating the provision of boring mills and other specialised workshops.

The iron-making combines were also drawn into building, agriculture and the food trades. While Shropshire in the 18th century was in no way as remote as the iron-working areas of Sweden in the same period, there are a number of interesting parallels between the two districts.[9] Cottages for workers had to be built, since the existing housing stock was inadequate to meet the needs of migrants attracted by the growth of the ironworks and their associated undertakings. Places of worship, schools, roads and recreational amenities were also provided in some cases. Ironmasters had, from time to time, to secure food for their employees when their needs were not met by conventional market forces, and they regularly supplied them with alcohol in their places of work. Several of the iron-making partnerships owned or leased substantial tracts of agricultural land. Abraham Darby II and his son purchased the Hay Farm in 1757 and by 1784 controlled Madeley and Sunniside Farms as well. The Lilleshall

Co. leased over 300 acres of farm land from the Marquess of Stafford in the early 19th century. William Reynolds and Co. in 1803 rented a farm at Ketley worth £250 a year. Thomas Botfield had a farm at Stirchley which he showed off to visitors in 1819. Benjamin Rowley kept a celebrated herd of Durham cattle on his farm at Priorslee.[10]

Involvement in agriculture gave to ironmasters some degree of control over the sale of food to customers outside the district in period of high prices, a control so important to Richard and William Reynolds in 1782 that they contemplated the building of a steam corn mill. Farms provided fodder for the horses needed for haulage on railways and canals. They provided a reserve of road haulage teams which could be employed to carry especially large loads or on occasions when droughts prevented the use of the Severn. Control of agriculture may even have helped ironmasters to check the exodus of workers from mines and ironworks to the farms at hay or harvest time, which persisted until well into the 19th century.[11]

The nature and extent of investment in the Shropshire iron industry in the last quarter of the 18th century is less well documented than that of the 1750s. Partnership agreements or sets of accounts have rarely survived, and some doubts must remain about the dates and even the owners of a number of major works. Nevertheless certain features of the investment pattern seem reasonably clear. There was certainly a boom during the American War of Independence, stimulated by the demands of the war, and made possible by the application of the steam engine to iron-making. 'The advancement of the iron trade within these last few years has been prodigious', wrote Richard Reynolds in 1784.[12] There was a similar boom in the late 1790s extending beyond the turn of the century, occasioned by the wars with revolutionary France. Nevertheless industrial growth between 1776 and 1806 seems to have been fairly consistent. Several ironworks, including the very large one at Old Park, were begun in the years of peace between the conclusion of the American War and the beginning of hostilities with France.

The leading figure in the Shropshire iron industry in the 1770s was John Wilkinson, the greatest ironmaster of the age, active in Staffordshire, Denbighshire, Anglesey and Furness as well as in Shropshire. When the New Willey Company was formed in 1757 he was the only partner with direct experience of the iron trade. His capital augmented by his marriage in 1763, he gradually acquired a controlling interest in the company, and by 1774 became sole lessee of the works. The same year, at a time of depression in the iron trade, he ceased operating the Old Willey furnace.[13]

In the early 1770s Wilkinson became interested in the possibilities of applying an atmospheric engine to blow a blast furnace direct, without having to work bellows by a waterwheel. Experiments with a 49 in. Newcomen engine proved unavailing since its work rate was too unsteady for the purpose. Wilkinson's boring machine, patented in 1774 brought him into contact with Matthew Boulton and James Watt who required accurately-bored cylinders for the latter's steam engines. The Watt engine promised a more constant work rate than the atmospheric, and only the second of the engines produced under Watt's patents was applied to the blowing of the blast furnace at New Willey in 1776. Wilkinson probably provided most of the parts himself, only drawings and valves being supplied by Boulton and Watt. The new engine proved all too successful, maintaining at first such a high pressure that the works almost blew up, and a water regulator was applied to keep up a constant pressure.[14]

Wilkinson continued to develop the Willey ironworks after his success with the Watt engine. The pools which had previously provided power for the furnace were employed to operate a boring machine, used, it seems principally for cannon, most of Wilkinson's engine cylinders being produced at his Bersham works. A second Watt engine to return used water to the upper pools was installed by the summer of 1777. In January 1788 a rotative steam engine was applied to power the boring-mill.[15]

In January 1778 Wilkinson set to work a Boulton and Watt engine to pump out mines which he held at Snedshill, Oakengates. In the early months of 1780 another engine began to blow two new blast furnaces at Snedshill, the first in Shropshire on a site wholly independent of water power.[16] At the same time Wilkinson invested large sums in the development of the mining resources of the Oakengates area. By 1793 he had installed steam winding-engines at pits in the vicinity. Associated with the Snedshill ironworks was another furnace at Hollinswood on the Randlay brook, also developed by Wilkinson although its date of blowing in is not known. The earliest documentary references to it do not occur before the late 1780s.[17]

In many of his enterprises John Wilkinson worked in partnership with his brother William who spent a considerable period in France in the 1780s, and on his return in 1787 was greeted with some reserve by his brother. Slowly a quarrel developed between them. The precise issue is uncertain, but it probably arose from John Wilkinson's purchase of the Brymbo estate near Wrexham, adjacent to the Bersham ironworks, which the brothers owned jointly. By 1793 John Wilkinson seems to have realised that the quarrel would necessitate the selling of some of his works, and in November of that year he was contemplating the sale of Snedshill and Hollinswood.[18] By 1794 the dispute was public. In July of the following year news of it reached Joseph Priestley in America, who wrote to John, 'hardly anything that has ever happened to me has given me so much concern'.[19] The dispute was put to the arbitration of William Reynolds, William Robertson and Joshua Walker in the summer of 1795 and the sale of Bersham was recommended. The works was auctioned in December and purchased outright by John Wilkinson against the opposition of a Chester solicitor bidding on behalf of William. It was probably in order to raise money for the purchase of Bersham that John Wilkinson sold some of his Shropshire interests. The Snedshill coal mines were being operated by John Bishton, John Onions and others by the end of 1793, and by February 1794 the Snedshill blast furnaces were also in their hands.[20] The Hollinswood works closed at this period. Little is known of its history, but since it was the first purpose-built coke blast furnace in Shropshire to go out of use, it was probably far from successful. The dispute between the Wilkinson brothers revealed that John had built many steam engines employing the Boulton and Watt patents without paying the appropriate premiums, and a long legal dispute with the Soho partners ensued.

In 1791 John Wilkinson bought an estate in Hadley from Catherine Freeman and Richard Emery. He was buying timber for the mines on the estate in 1793–94, and pumping equipment in 1796. By 1800 he was building an ironworks on the site. One furnace was brought into blast by May 1804 and another not long afterwards. The Hadley works seems to have replaced that at Willey which went out of use in the same year. It was not notably successful. William Wilkinson reported in 1807 that most people in the iron trade thought his brother had been mistaken in not confining his activities at Hadley to the colliery.[21]

John Wilkinson died in 1808, his estate reputedly worth £120,000,[22] about £20,000 more than that of his contemporary William Reynolds who died in 1803. The succession was uncertain, and during the ensuing disputes between his legitimate and illegitimate heirs some works were closed, while others were leased to rival ironmasters. The industrial empire which John Wilkinson had created disappeared, never to re-emerge as a power in the iron trade.

The Calcutts ironworks was one of the most celebrated in Great Britain at the end of the 18th century. The site, in a valley above the confluence of the Severn and a stream which flowed from Broseley, already had a long industrial history by 1750. The valley of the stream was the site of the first recorded wooden railway in Shropshire in the early years of the 17th century, and a line called the Jackfield Rails used the same route in the 18th century. On the downstream side of the confluence were four 'mug houses' making earthenware. In the 1790s two corn mills survived on the stream above the confluence.[23]

The Calcutts estate was leased from Sir Onesiphorus Paul, the Gloucestershire woollen mill owner, by George Matthews of Broseley on 5 May 1767.[24] Two furnaces were built soon afterwards and Calcutts pig iron was being sent to the Stour Valley forges by 1771–72. The furnace bellows were operated by water wheels, water being returned to a reservoir above the ironworks by a steam engine. Matthews was active in the local coal trade, and it was probably he who wrote to Boulton and Watt in November 1776 enquiring whether they could supply a rotative engine for use in mines. By 1778 he was working in partnership with one of the Homfray family, and by 1786 the Calcutts works was being operated by a partnership known as Baille Pocock and Co. In February of that year the works was offered for sale. It included two blast furnaces capable of making 40 tons of iron a week, air furnaces, two forges for making bar iron, three steam engines, a water corn mill, a brick kiln, 12 coke and tar ovens, and 96 acres of land 'abounding with coal, rich iron ore and brick earth'. The works already had a reputation in the armaments trade, for the sale notice claimed that during the American War of Independence it had supplied cannon 'of the best quality which can be justified by the proof book at Woolwich Warren'.[25]

The Calcutts works was purchased in 1786 by Alexander Brodie, a self-made Scotsman, who had worked as a blacksmith in London. He soon ceased to work the forge, and concentrated on the foundry, particularly on the manufacture of cannon and of ships' stoves of a type he patented in 1764. Charles Hatchett went to the Calcutts in 1796 and watched 32-pounder cannon being cast two at a time, and then bored seven or eight at a time in a boring-mill powered by a steam engine. In August of the same year the Prince and Princess of Orange included the Calcutts on their tour of Shropshire. They were saluted by the firing of guns and were taken to see the boring of 10 cannon at a time. A Swedish visitor to the works in 1802–03 found 11 horizontal borers worked by the steam engine in the boring-mill.[26]

A plan of the Calcutts works about the turn of the century shows three blast furnaces, one of them, the 'old furnace' standing inland from the bank of the Severn below a reservoir. Another furnace was being built on the site in 1803. By 1811 when Alexander Brodie I died the works included two large blast engines, a water-pumping engine, three coal winding-engines, a cannon boring-mill powered by steam, a boring-mill for cylinders, and a boring- and turning-mill worked by a water wheel. The coke and tar ovens established at the Calcutts in the time of George Matthews were built by Lord Dundonald, to whom Brodie may have been distantly related, and were the most successful of the ovens of this kind built in Shropshire in the 18th century.[27]

The Benthall ironworks, like that at the Calcutts, was situated in a tributary valley of the Severn, and was originally powered by a water wheel with a pumping-engine to return water from the pools below the wheel to those above. Subsequently a 30 h.p.

atmospheric engine blew the furnaces direct. The furnaces were in blast by the late 1770s, and were supplying pig iron to the Cookley and Wolverley forges by 1778–79. By 1784 the Benthall works was capable of manufacturing steam engines, and had a labour force of about 700 men. The Harries family, lords of the manor of Benthall were closely associated with the works, and from 1778 if not earlier at least until 1801 their partners were William Banks and John Onions.[28]

A range of coke ovens like those at the Calcutts was established at the Benthall ironworks by Lord Dundonald in the autumn of 1787, but they had a short life being demolished before 1799. A water-powered boring machine on John Wilkinson's principles was installed at Benthall in 1781.[29] The Benthall furnaces specialised in pig iron for castings, much of it consumed in the works' own foundry. A list of products of c.1810 shows a range of cast-iron goods of all sizes, very similar to that of the Coalbrookdale ironworks.[30]

A third ironworks on the south side of the Severn was that at Coneybury on the estate of the Davenport family, which was also called the Broseley Bottom Coal furnace. The works probably began to operate in 1786–87 and commenced the supply of pig iron to the Stour Valley forges in 1788–89, when it was owned by Messrs. Banks and Onions. By 1800 it was being worked by William Banks and John Onions in association with a large foundry on the eastern edge of Broseley. The whole mining, furnace and foundry complex was valued at £13,464 6s. $2^3/_4$d. in 1820.[31] The Onions family also gained control of a second Broseley furnace, built in 1806–07 by Thomas Guest, soon after it began to work.[32]

The other major ironworks south of the Severn were owned by Richard Wright and Richard Jesson, forgemasters of Handsworth and West Bromwich, and patentees in 1773 of a process for producing wrought iron with coal by heating pieces of pig iron in clay pots. They were using Shropshire iron in their West Bromwich forge as early as 1775. By February 1777 they had acquired a site for a group of forges at Wren's Nest, near to the confluence of the Severn and the Dean Brook, downstream from Broseley. A Watt steam engine was set to work on 27 April 1779 to pump back water from the Severn to pools above the forges. In 1791 it was converted to rotative motion and applied to work forge hammers. By 1808 the narrow valley at Wren's Nest contained the greatest concentration of forges in Shropshire, five being situated alongside the Dean Brook within 700 yards of its confluence with the Severn.[33]

In 1796 Wright and Jesson acquired land on the banks of the Severn at Barnetts Leasow, Broseley where they built two blast furnaces blown by Watt engines which came into operation in 1797 and 1801, and doubtless supplied pig iron to the Wren's Nest forges. The partnership was dissolved in 1812, following the deaths of Richard Wright and Richard Jesson, and taken over by Thomas Jesson and Samuel Dawes.[34]

The affairs of the Coalbrookdale partnership in the late 18th century were complex. Abraham Darby II died in 1763 and the affairs of the company were subsequently dominated by Richard Reynolds. Born in Bristol of a Quaker family in 1735, Reynolds went to Coalbrookdale in October 1756 as representative of Abraham Darby II's partner Thomas Goldney. In 1757 he married Hannah the daughter of Abraham Darby II and set up house with her at Ketley Bank, where his eldest and most talented son William was born in 1758. Hannah Reynolds died in 1762 and the following year Reynolds married Rebecca Gulson of Coventry. His daughter by his first marriage became the wife of William Rathbone, of the Liverpool Quaker family who came to play a considerable part in the Shropshire iron trade after Abraham Darby III and his

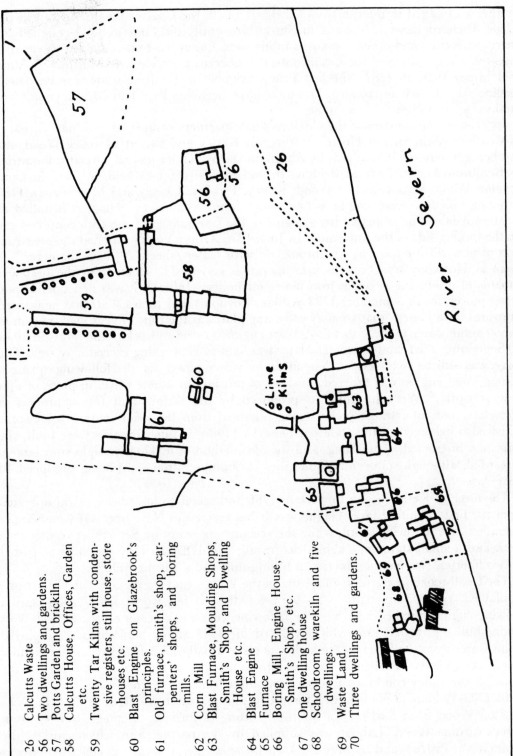

26 Calcutts Waste
56 Two dwellings and gardens.
57 Potts Garden and brickiln
58 Calcutts House, Offices, Garden
    etc.
59 Twenty Tar Kilns with conden-
    sive registers, still house, store
    houses etc.
60 Blast Engine on Glazebrook's
    principles.
61 Old furnace, smith's shop, car-
    penters' shops, and boring
    mills.
62 Corn Mill
63 Blast Furnace, Moulding Shops,
    Smith's Shop, and Dwelling
    House etc.
64 Blast Engine
65 Furnace
66 Boring Mill, Engine House,
    Smith's Shop, etc.
67 One dwelling house
68 Schoolroom, warekiln and five
    dwellings.
69 Waste Land.
70 Three dwellings and gardens.

Figure 5. Plan of the Calcutts Ironworks, c. 1800.
Re-drawn from the Broseley Estate Book, Shrewsbury Borough Library Colln.

brother mortgaged to them many of their shares in the Coalbrookdale concern in the 1780s. Richard Reynolds stayed in Shropshire until 1804, but in 1789 resigned his shares in Ketley and other ironworks to his sons. On at least one occasion Reynolds's reserves of capital saved the Coalbrookdale concerns from closure. Matthew Boulton told James Watt in 1782, 'the last Prime Minister of Coalbrookdale was very near settling fast the whole concern. It would have been the case had Mr. Reynolds not strained every power to raise money'.[35]

In 1776 the enterprises of the Coalbrookdale partners comprised two blast furnaces at Coalbrookdale, two at Horsehay, three at Ketley and two at Madeley Wood, the last being purchased in that year by Abraham Darby III, forges and specialist foundries at Coalbrookdale, a forge at Bridgnorth and extensive mines held on lease in Donnington Wood, Wrockwardine Wood, Ketley, Dawley, Lawley and Madeley. In 1780 a boring-mill for steam engine cylinders on John Wilkinson's plan was installed at Coalbrookdale. The principal investments of the last quarter of the 18th century were on the forging side of the iron trade. In June 1776 Arthur Young watched the construction of new slitting-mills at Coalbrookdale with water wheels 20 ft. in diameter.[36] A forge at Horsehay was brought into operation c.1781–82, which from the first was capable of producing wrought iron plates for boilers. Initially it was dependent upon water power, for in September 1783 William Reynolds told James Watt that he wanted drawings for a boiler, 'that we may order the plates as the time of year gives reason to expect some water to draw them'. A Watt engine was set to work in the forge on 29 or 30 September 1784, and a fortnight later was said to be working exceedingly well. The forge was still to some extent dependent on water power for the following spring a second Watt engine was ordered, 'instead of putting up a new wheel in place of that now at work'.[37] Wrought iron was produced by the Wright and Jesson process at Horsehay, pots of refractory clay being obtained from the neighbouring brickworks which also belonged to the Dale partners. In 1798 puddling furnaces were built, the forgemen instructed in puddling, and the old method of making wrought iron largely discarded, although some small quantities of 'stamped' iron were being produced 10 hears later.[38]

The forge at Ketley began to work in 1785 and seems to have been steam operated from the first. The first forge engine was being erected in November 1784 and began operations the following April, while the second was ready by September of the same year, and a small stamping-engine was installed in 1787. In 1794 the forge consisted of two fineries, two melting fineries, a rolling-mill and a slitting-mill.[39]

The Coalbrookdale partners made use of the Watt steam engine soon after it became available. A pumping-engine was built for the Ketley works in 1778–79 and a blowing-engine supplied in 1780. The following year work began on the largest Watt engine built up to that time which replaced the 1743 atmospheric engine[40] employed to lift water from the lower to the higher pools at Coalbrookdale. Two smaller engines were subsequently installed at the Coalbrookdale forges, but the greater part of the works in the valley continued to derive its power from water wheels.

In 1783 William Reynolds and Joseph Rathbone leased 36 acres of land in Donnington Wood from Earl Gower for the building of furnaces to smelt iron ore from Wrockwardine Wood. Labour was supplied by the partnerships which worked the mines in the district, and by May 1783 when the engine pit was sunk construction was in progress. The furnace came into blast early in December 1785 when William

Reynolds sanctioned the expenditure of 6s. 8d. on ale. Earl Gower contributed £2,000 towards the cost of the furnace.[41]

The Coalbrookdale partnerships were in the vanguard of technological progress in the 1780s, but they were far from profitable at the end of the decade. In 1789 it was reported that no dividends had been paid for several years, and the account of the Dale works itself was heavily indebted to Richard Reynolds. In December 1793 the proprietors were still worried about the company's large debts, and the 'general un-profitable and unproductive state of the concerns'. In May 1794 the preponderance of women in the partnership was given as the reason for trying to sell off such concerns as could easily be detached from the rest.[42]

In July 1796 after a long series of negotiations an agreement was reached to separate the concerns of the Rathbone and Darby families from those of William and Joseph Reynolds. The former retained the foundry complex and forges at Coalbrookdale and the Horsehay ironworks. The Reynolds brothers took the Madeley Wood and Ketley ironworks. The Donnington Wood works was purchased by John Bishton and John Onions in February 1796, and they succeeded to the lease of the premises the following year. Before 1796 there had been a considerable interchange of semi-finished iron between the works at Ketley and Horsehay, but this gradually diminished.[43]

A memorandum drawn up in 1799 calculated that of the Coalbrookdale partners' enterprises, the Horsehay ironworks with the Lawley and Dawley coalfields, and the Coalbrookdale forges, were profitable, but the foundry complex at the Dale was losing money due to the high cost of carrying raw materials and the difficulties of costing the variety of goods made at the foundry. Coal and iron ore cost 10s. a ton more at Coalbrookdale than at Horsehay. It was proposed to transfer the foundry to Horsehay. The alternative, taking Horsehay pig iron to Coalbrookdale and closing the ancient water-powered blast furnaces, was not suggested in 1799.[44]

The Coalbrookdale works did not enjoy an unsullied reputation in the 1790s either for punctuality or for good workmanship. James Watt Jun. wrote in 1795 of 'the inconquerable *vis inertia* of the Dale Company'. In 1800 Boulton and Watt complained that work on a cylinder had not begun four months after it had been ordered, and that the customer for the engine for which it was intended was making urgent demands. The following year Boulton and Watt demanded the immediate delivery of the last of four cylinders ordered from Coalbrookdale, and complained that of three already received not one was sound in boring, the metal was very porous, and there were several large sand flaws on the working surfaces. After 1802 it seems that Boulton and Watt ceased to place orders for pig iron or engine parts with the Coalbrookdale partners.[45]

The Ketley ironworks under the administration of William Reynolds was celebrated throughout Europe for its innovations and its size. In 1806 it was the second largest works in Shropshire and the fifth in Great Britain with an annual output of 7,510 tons of pig iron. In 1804 the works included six blast furnaces, two of them small 'Snapper' furnaces. A large furnace at Queenswood a mile and a half away was built, 'to supply the Ketley works with pig iron'. By 1802 Queenswood was making iron which Boulton and Watt 'found to answer very well'. The forge at Ketley included puddling furnaces, a mill for rolling boiler plate, a slitting mill for making merchant rods and two large pairs of powered shears. Steel was made at Ketley by a process developed by William Reynolds which involved adding 40 lbs. of Exeter manganese to a charge of 270 lbs. of refined iron in a puddling furnace. The Ketley foundry was capable of making the largest castings for civil and mechanical engineering purposes, and included facilities for turning and boring cylinders and for fitting up steam engines. The value of the works at the time of William Reynolds's death in 1803 was over £112,000, the capital being shared equally with his half-brother Joseph.[46]

William Reynolds's Madeley Wood concern, the 'Bedlam' blast furnaces with their associated collieries in Madeley, was on a much smaller scale than Ketley with a capital value of only £15,000 in 1803. One of the two furnaces was taken out of blast in 1794 before the separation of the Reynolds and Darby interests, but was brought back into production before 1800. Some months before the death of William Reynolds the partnership was reconstituted, Reynolds taking three quarters of the shares and the remaining quarter going to his nephew William Anstice. At the same time the small foundry at the works ceased operation.[47]

The Lightmoor ironworks, like Madeley Wood built in the boom of the late 1750s, was taken over in 1787 by members of the Homfray family, long established in the Broseley coal trade and in the forging trade in the Stour valley. In 1783 Francis Homfray and his three sons Thomas, Jeremiah and Samuel moved from Broseley to South Wales and after a brief connection with the Cyfarthfa works, set up the Penydarren ironworks at Merthyr. Lightmoor was controlled by a Francis Homfray, according to one source a brother of the Samuel Homfray of Penydarren, and by John Addenbrooke, who had changed his name from Homfray. Both partners had interests in ironworks in the Stourbridge area, Homfray at Hyde and Addenbrooke at Wollaston.[48]

By 1796 there were three blast furnaces at Lightmoor and the following year half blooms from the forge at the works were being sent to Horsehay for rolling. A visitor in 1802 found three blast furnaces and a few refineries and bloom or balling furnaces. Most of the iron was sent to Worcestershire to be worked into plate, bar and rods at the other works owned by the partners. In 1800–01 Boulton and Watt supplied the works with a blowing engine which was erected by William Murdock, who made drawings of the furnaces while the job was in progress. Murdock was apprehensive of the strength of the beam, which as he feared it might, split a few weeks after the engine began to work.[49]

Most of the supplies for the Lightmoor ironworks doubtless came from the adjacent mines. There was apparently a surplus of top and flint coals which the company was selling to the Coalbrookdale works in 1800–01. Limestone went to Lightmoor from Buildwas, being conveyed by barge to the Meadow Wharf which the company rented from the Coalbrookdale partners.[50]

Earl Gower and Co. or the Marquis of Stafford and Co. as the partnership was known after 1786, did not take an active part in the iron trade but were content to act as ground landlords to iron-makers and producers of coal and limestone. Yet their successors the Lilleshall Co. were one of the foremost ironmaking concerns in Great Britain in the 19th century. This change of emphasis was brought about by John Bishton who became agent on the Marquess of Stafford's Lilleshall estate in 1788. Bishton was a member of a family of minor gentry whose lands were at Kilsall near Albrighton. He had shares in coal workings and in the Whitecliffe Furnace in the Forest of Dean.[51] During the 1790s Bishton acquired holdings in two ironworks in the northern part of the Shropshire coalfield, in each of which his principal partner was John Onions of Broseley. In 1802 Bishton took some of his iron-making interests into the Lilleshall Company which was formed to succeed the earlier partnership of the

Marquess of Stafford and the Gilbert brothers, and in 1807 after Bishton's death, his other ironworks were brought under the same control.

Bishton's first industrial interests in east Shropshire were in mines in Priorslee and Snedshill. In February 1793 in partnership with Benjamin Rowley he leased mines in Priorslee from the Beaufoy family. The next month John Onions and John Asprey Smith made an agreement with Edward Plowden concerning other mines in Priorslee which Plowden leased from the Jernigham family. In December of the same year Bishton, Rowley, Onions and Smith formed a partnership to work the mines in the district. At the same time they were negotiating with John Wilkinson to take over his interests at Snedshill as Wilkinson was becoming embarrassed by his dispute with his brother. Bishton and his partners took over the Snedshill ironworks, probably early in 1794. Subsequently Bishton consolidated his own holding in the partnership. Smith and Rowley resigned their shares to him; Onions allowed Bishton to act on his behalf in Snedshill matters, and Bishton's sons, John and William, were assigned shares in the partnership.[52]

John Bishton's interest in the Donnington Wood ironworks, like that in Snedshill, arose through the troubles of another company, in this case the Coalbrookdale partnership. In January 1796 the Marquess of Stafford gave William Reynolds licence to assign the lease of the ironworks, and in February of the following year it was formally granted to Bishton and his partners, William Phillips, John Onions and James Birch. Two weeks later the Marquess of Stafford renewed the lease on the furnace in Bishton's favour, and at the same time the Marquis of Stafford and Co. leased to Bishton the ironstone mines in Donnington Wood and Wrockwardine Wood. Bishton and his partners built two new blast furnaces at Wrockwardine Wood in 1801, and in the following year added a third to the pair at Donnington Wood.[53]

The Lilleshall Company was formed in 1802 to continue the work of the old partnership of the Marquis of Stafford and Co. which dated from 1764. The Marquess had reached the age of 81, and the Gilbert brothers were both dead. Like the old partnership the Lilleshall Company was a combination of landed interests and entrepreneurial and technical skills. The landed interest was represented by Lord Granville Leveson Gower, son of the Marquess of Stafford by his third wife, and the entrepreneurial interest by John Bishton and his partners. Lord Granville Leverson Gower acquired the Gilberts' holdings in the old company in February and March 1802, and the following month his father assigned him a further half share in the coal, iron and lime works in Lilleshall and adjoining parishes. The articles of partnership of the new company were signed on 24 June 1802, with Gower taking a half share, John Bishton five sixteenths, and James Birch, John Onions and William Phillips one sixteenth each. Only the Donnington and Wrockwardine Wood interests of Bishton, his family and partners were brought into the new company, the Snedshill concerns remaining separate. The partnership soon underwent substantial changes. The shares of James Birch and of the Onions family were made over to the Bishtons in 1805–06. By 1806 John Bishton Sen. was dead, and was succeeded as agent on the Lilleshall estates by his sons, first by John Bishton Jun., then by George Bishton. In 1807 a new partnership was negotiated between John Bishton's sons and executors and Gower under which the Snedshill mines and ironworks were brought under the control of the Lilleshall Co. By 1813 the partnership was joined by William Horton, previously associated with William Reynolds and the Coalbrookdale Co., and he and his son John were prominent in the affairs of the Lilleshall Co. for much of the 19th century.[54]

By 1806 the largest ironworks in Shropshire and the second largest in Great Britain was that at Old Park, Dawley, controlled by the Botfields, a family with deep roots in local industrial history. Beriah Botfield, collier of Great Dawley, was one of four partners who in 1753 leased land for mining at Lightmoor. He died and was buried at Dawley in April of the following year. His son Thomas, baptised in 1738, became one of the partners in the Lightmoor ironworks in June 1758. In 1783 he became involved in mining enterprises on the Clee Hills but in 1790 returned to Dawley to build furnaces on Isaac Hawkins Browne's Old Park estate. Within the next seven years over 50 houses for workmen were built in the vicinity, and there were large investments in mines, including the installation of a pumping-engine, two winding-engines and weighing-machines. By 1801 four blast furnaces had been erected and a 56 h.p engine from Boulton and Watt was applied to a new rolling-mill in a forge which was enlarged and converted from the Wright and Jesson process to puddling under the supervision of Gilbert Gilpin.[55]

Thomas Botfield died in 1801. He was one of the most successful of Shropshire entrepreneurs. He had landed estates in Ystrad-fawr, Breconshire, Hopton Wafers in south Shropshire and Norton in Northamptonshire. He was concerned with mining in Flintshire and at Tipton (Staffs.) as well as at Old Park and in the Clee Hills. He retained an interest in the Lightmoor ironworks, and developed paper mills at Hopton Wafers. After his death his estate passed to his three sons, Thomas, William and Beriah. William Botfield managed the Old Park works, but the three met there each quarter to divide the profits and each carried his money home with him. In 1805–06 the output of pig iron totalled 8,359 tons, and the following year rose to 9,200 tons, half of which was converted to wrought iron in the forges at the works. A profit of £15,000 was realised in 1806. After the break up of the Reynolds-Darby partnership in the 1790s, the death of William Reynolds in 1803 and the contraction of John Wilkinson's activities in Shropshire, the Botfields attained a pre-eminent position in local industry. 'They will' wrote William Wilkinson in 1807, 'govern the iron trade of Shropshire with the Bishtons and others with a lordly sway'.[56]

The traditional charcoal-using, water-powered ironworks of Shropshire and the Borderland were profoundly affected by the rise of the great iron-making partnerships of the coalfield. The smelting of iron ore with charcoal had almost ceased by the end of the 18th century. In 1791 only two charcoal-using furnaces were still in operation in the county, those at Bringewood and Bouldon. Of the other furnaces which had been in blast 70 years earlier, Leighton and Kemberton had become corn mills, Charlcotte was permanently closed. Bouldon, 'noted and always esteemed for making the best tough Pig Iron in the kingdom' was sold in 1795 and it is doubtful whether iron was ever made there afterwards. The water supply was used to power a paper mill. Charlcotte is the best documented of the charcoal furnaces, and its accounts show that the third quarter of the 18th century was a time of discontinuous output and heavy financial losses.[57]

The effects of mineral fuel and steam power on the forging side of the iron industry were less dramatic. The majority of the Shropshire forges listed in 1717 by John Fuller were still working in 1791. While there were no more than seven coke-using forges in the Shropshire coalfield by 1800, there were in 1791 14 water-powered forges still in operation in other parts of the county, as well as a slitting-mill and a rolling-mill. Although there were successful steam-powered forges on the coalfield, water was regarded as the natural source of power for a forge as late as 1800, when Thomas Telford considered that one of the strongest arguments for controlling the Severn was that it would allow the use of river water to power iron forges since, 'at present this great and increasing business is chiefly carried on by means of trifling brooks, often dry in summer, and at all times of very inadequate quantity'.[58] It was not until the second decade of the 19th century that the water-driven forge became the exception rather than the rule, and even afterwards several showed remarkable resilience.

The availability of cheap coke-blast iron alongside the Severn stimulated the building of two important new water-powered forges near to the river between Bridgnorth and Bewdley. In 1777–78 John and William Wheeler built the upper forge on the Mor Brook at Eardington, and added a second forge almost on the banks of the Severn in the mid-1780s. In 1796–97 John Thompsom built forges using both water and steam power at Hampton Loade at the confluence of the Severn and the Paper Mill Brook, two miles from Eardington. Both works later came under the control of James Foster, and survived for a considerable time, Hampton Loade until 1866 and Eardington until 1889.[59]

Eardington and Hampton Loade were built during the Indian Summer of the charcoal iron trade when there were still gaps in demand which the integrated works of the great partnerships could not competently fill. Their success should not obscure the major and far reaching changes which took place in the last quarter of the 18th century. In 1750 the iron industry of the West Midlands and the Borderland was widely dispersed on streams near to coppices supplying cordwood. By 1800 it was increasingly concentrating on the Shropshire coalfield, the South Wales valleys and the south Staffordshire plateau, and was dependent almost entirely on mineral fuel and steam power. While the partnerships controlling the trade in 1750 had been specialists concerned almost entirely with iron, the great companies which dominated the Shropshire iron trade in 1800 were wholesale exploiters of the minerals on the lands they leased, engaged in many commercial activities other than ironmaking, and creating whole new communities to provide labour for their enterprises.

VII

TRADING ACCOUNTS

The Shropshire ironmasters of the late 18th century were involved in a wide variety of trading activities. While their main concern was with iron and goods made from iron, they also traded in raw materials and products like bricks which were surplus to their own requirements. At one end of the commercial scale they sold armaments to governments and steam engines to other entrepreneurs. At the other they provided lime for local farmers and coal for cottagers.

Most of the pig iron smelted at Horsehay between 1767 and 1781[1] was sold to forge masters in south Staffordshire and north Worcestershire who had been regular buyers of Horsehay iron since the furnaces went into blast in 1755. The largest quantities were taken by the Knight family partnership who often purchased as much as 300 tons a quarter for their forges at Mitton, Wolverley and Cookley. Until 1776 the Foley partnership regularly bought quantities only slightly smaller. Mary Croft used Horsehay pig iron at the Powick forge on the Teme in the late 1760s, and at Cradley in the early 1770s. Sampson, Nehemiah and Charles Lloyd with forges at Norton, Calves Heath and Powick, Thomas Hill and Co. of the Titton Forge and the Homfray family at Broadwaters Forge were other important customers in the same area. John Wilkinson bought some Horsehay iron which was delivered to Compton near Wolverhampton and to Bilston, but larger quantities were consigned to his works in North Wales. The forges at Pool Quay and Mathrafal were regular users of Horsehay pig iron throughout the period from 1767 to 1781.

On the lower Severn Thomas Hawkins of Newnham was a customer for melting iron throughout the period as were Sayse Williams and Co. of Chepstow from 1777. Large quantities of Horsehay melting pig were exported through the port of Bristol. Most of the iron purchased by John Wilkinson for his north Wales works was delivered by way of Bristol and Chester, over 190 tons going by that route between March and October 1775. Iron was also carried from Bristol by coastal vessels to London where Crawshay and Moser were the principal customers, taking over 140 tons between March and October 1775, 258 tons between February and June of 1776, and well over 500 tons between September 1776 and July 1777. About 1770 a substantial trade with Ireland began to develop, the iron being forwarded from Bristol to Belfast or Dublin. Between March and August 1778 21 tons were sent to Stewart Hadkiss of Belfast and 80 tons to various customers in Dublin. From 1780 onwards increasing quantities of Horsehay iron went to the enlarged forges in Coalbrookdale.

Throughout the 1780s and 90s large quantities of pig iron from the furnaces of the

48

Coalbrookdale Company were sold to the Knight family partnerships for the Stour Valley forges, the annual amount ranging between 387 tons in 1785–86 and 1,543 tons in 1795–96.[2] The Knight partnerships remained customers for Horsehay iron in 1807, although the quantities they purchased slowly declined. Sir Walter and later Sir Edward Blount, heads of another old-established West Midlands forging partnership, were regular customers between 1795 and 1806. The mid-Wales forges continued to buy iron from Horsehay: sales to Mathrafal are recorded until 1796 and to Pool Quay until 1805. Samuel George purchased pig iron for the three old forges which he operated at Bringewood, Cleobury and Brewood.[3] Until 1800 considerable quantities of iron were delivered to the forge at Powick, and small amounts to customers at Chepstow. From the turn of the century there was a growing concentration on a limited number of very large customers. In 1801 the Horsehay works began to sell iron to Wright and Jessons' forges at the Wren's Nest, and in the trading year ending August 1803 delivered them 451 tons of iron. Smaller quantities were sent to the same partners' forge in West Bromwich. In 1806–07 a substantial trade began with John Bradley and Co. of Stour-bridge who took 143 tons in November 1808 and 190 tons the following month.

From other Shropshire ironworks large quantities of foundry pig iron were sent to Lancashire in the 1790s. Aikin, the Lancashire historian, wrote in 1795 that the foundries in Manchester had recently grown considerably and that most of their pig iron was brought by canal from the Old Park works of the Botfields and Alexander Brodie's furnaces near the Iron Bridge.[4] The Manchester engineering firm of Bateman and Sharratt were customers for wrought iron from Horsehay in the 1790s but do not seem to have bought pig from the Coalbrookdale partners.[5]

Fragmentary accounts for the pig iron trade of the Snedshill ironworks of Bishton and Onions for the quarter ending midsummer 1799 suggest that its trade followed a similar pattern to that of Horsehay. During the quarter 758 tons of iron were sold, 158 tons of melting pig, 533 tons of forge pig and 40 tons of 'hard iron'. The principal customers for melting iron were Messrs. Crawshay who took 125 tons, and Boulton and Watt who had 30 tons. The main buyers of forge iron were John Knight who purchased 100 tons, John Addenbrooke with 60 tons, Wright and Jesson with 150 tons, and Pemberton and Stokes of the Eardington forge who also took 150 tons.[6]

In 1796 Matthew Boulton and James Watt opened their Soho Foundry in Smethwick so that they would be able to undertake the complete manufacture of steam engines after the expiry of their patents in 1800. Previously they had obtained large castings from other firms, principally from John Wilkinson, from whom supplies were inter-rupted by the ironmaster's quarrel with his brother. The Soho Foundry was opened on 30 January 1796 and from the first Shropshire ironmasters were among its principal suppliers of pig iron. Between 1797 and 1801 Bishton and Onions sent as much as 70 tons a quarter, Alexander Brodie up to 30 tons a quarter, and William Reynolds and Co. as much as 80 tons a quarter. Other Shropshire firms from whom pig iron was obtained included the Benthall Company, Wright and Jesson and the Old Park Company. Deliveries of pig iron to Soho were continually hampered by low water on the Severn and this trade must have been precarious indeed as new furnaces in south Staffordshire came into blast.[7]

The Coalbrookdale partnership accounts alone shed light on the trade in Shropshire wrought iron. Much of the iron made at the Horsehay forge was supplied in the form of bars to such merchants as Dearman and Co. and William Ward in Birmingham, John Stokes and Thomas Rushton in Wolverhampton, and various firms in the Potteries. Mining concerns in Shropshire and further afield bought large quantities of wrought-iron bars. A typical order was for 3 tons 15 cwt. for the Lilleshall Co.'s limestone works in 1803. In the first decade of the 19th century there was a considerable increase in trade in bar iron with Bristol merchants. In the quarter ending Lady Day 1802 125 tons of bar iron were sent to Harvey and Co. of Bristol, and in the month ending 14 February 1807 96 tons went to three different merchants in the city. Trade with London iron merchants was also of some importance in this period, the principal customers being Crawshay and Co. and William Payne and Co.[8]

The Horsehay works also sold large quantities of wrought iron in the form of blooms and half blooms for rolling by the customer. Crawshay and Co. bought considerable amounts in this form in the mid-1790s, and in 1807 John Bradley and Co. of Stourbridge began to buy this type of iron as well as pig iron from Horsehay. They were taking over 100 tons of blooms and half blooms a month by the summer of 1807.[9] Boiler plates were rolled at the Horsehay forge and the sale of finished boilers and replacement plates was an important aspect of its trade. Sales of boilers are analysed elsewhere, but several special orders of this kind are of particular interest. In 1803 and 1805 wrought-iron still bottoms were supplied to the British Tar Company's works at the Calcutts, and at least two orders for salt-pan plates were supplied, one for the Winsford salt works in 1806 and one for William and Thomas Cotterell of Birmingham in the following year.[10]

Much of the wrought iron produced at Horsehay was sent to the partnership's Coalbrookdale forge for re-rolling to small sizes: – a typical order was that of December 1795 when 103 bars were sent to be rolled to a thickness of $1/8$ in. and various widths. A substantial amount of Horsehay wrought iron, as much as 170 tons a month, was marketed by the Coalbrookdale works whether or not it received further processing there. Records of shipments from Coalbrookdale show a steady increase in the trade in wrought iron in the early years of the 19th century. In the year ending August 1799 433 tons of bar iron were carried to Stourport, Worcester and Chepstow, and 564 in the following year. The bar iron trade to Chepstow ceased during the next 12 months, but 771 tons went to Stourport and Worcester.[11]

The Horsehay works had numerous links with forges belonging to other partnerships in the district. In the mid-1790s there was a considerable interchange of products with the Ketley works, but this diminished after the separation of the Reynolds and Darby concerns. Nevertheless in 1798 bars from Horsehay were still being sent to the slitting-mills at Ketley. From time to time blooms and slabs from the forges at Lightmoor, Old Park and Snedshill were rolled at Horsehay, presumably to sizes which could not be accommodated on the mills at those forges.

The puddling process as developed by Henry Cort was only really effective when a pig iron low in carbon and silicon was employed, and since iron of this sort could only with difficulty be produced in a blast furnace, it became customary for most forge masters to remove some of the carbon and silicon from their pig in a separate hearth, called a refinery, before it was charged to the puddling furnaces. Some of the refined iron made at Horsehay was sold to other forges in the early 19th century. Pemberton and Stokes of Eardington were taking as much as 100 tons a quarter in 1803–04. By 1806 the Staffordshire firm of Parsons and Firmstone were buying as much as 30 tons a month, and in 1807 John Bradley and Co. began to purchase up to 70 tons a month.[12]

The best-known products of east Shropshire in the late 18th century were those of the local foundries which ranged from steam engines, bridges and threshing-machines to pots, pans and kettles. The principal foundries were those at Ketley, Coalbrookdale, Willey, the Calcutts, Broseley and Benthall, although some cast-iron goods were made direct from the blast furnaces at other works. The Benthall and Coalbrookdale foundries in particular produced an astonishing variety of castings from sophisticated parts for bridges or engines to small domestic utensils. The Benthall works about 1810 offered clock weights, frying pans, cider and cheese presses, soap boilers and threshing-mill castings. Goods made at Coalbrookdale in 1801 included bedsteads, book cases, engine cylinders, enamelling stoves, mortars and pestles, ovens, pudding plates, salt pans, window frames and waggon slips. In the year ending August 1800 864 tons of castings from Coalbrookdale were shipped downstream on the Severn, apart from consignments to Bristol.[13]

The Ketley foundry at this time specialised in heavy industrial castings like engine parts, doors for puddling furnaces, pipes, cylinders, anvils, railway wheels and crane arms. The Calcutts foundry produced principally cannon, stoves and shot furnaces for the Navy. Rails were normally cast straight from blast furnaces. Most were for local use but in 1776 nearly 2,500 were supplied by the Horsehay works to the Staffordshire and Worcestershire Canal Co., and in 1800–01 iron rails were sold by the Coalbrookdale partners to the Irish Coal Co.[14]

One of the most important aspects of the foundry trade was the manufacture of steam engines and steam engine parts. Most of the Shropshire foundries supplied cast-iron parts for engines, and several could undertake the production of complete engines.[15]

Another important source of power for industry was the cast-iron water wheel, many of which were produced in Shropshire in the late 18th and early 19th centuries together with large quantities of other castings for millwrights. Two particularly large wheels adorned the Severn Gorge, one at Benthall Mill and one at Swinney Mill near Coalport. Both the Coalbrookdale and Benthall foundries offered mill wheels and castings among their products and a large water wheel for a corn mill in Shrewsbury was one of the last products of the foundry at Madeley Wood in 1803.[16]

By the second half of the 1790s the manufacture of castings for iron bridges had become an important part of the trade of several local foundries. The celebrated Iron Bridge, which is considered in detail below, was opened in 1781. It was not until the 1790s that it was equalled or surpassed in size or load-bearing capacity, but it seems at least possible that during the ill-documented 1780s the Coalbrookdale Company was producing smaller structures to carry carriage drives in ornamental parks, or the towpaths of waterways. In 1791 the company exported a bridge 'to be thrown over one of the canals in Holland'. In 1793 the company was asked by the agent of the Marquess of Stafford to produce alternative designs for a bridge to cross the Trent at the Marquess's principal country house at Trentham, Staffs. Within less than three weeks six alternatives were submitted all displaying a versatility and confidence which suggest that the company was well accustomed to receive such orders. The design selected had a span of 90 ft. and was erected in the summer and autumn of 1794. The construction of iron bridges after 1795 was stimulated by the great flood of 10–12 February of that year which severely damaged every bridge on the Severn except the Iron Bridge which remained undamaged:

the noble arch . . . exulting as it were in the strength of its connected massy ribs, reared its lofty head triumphantly above the mighty torrent, and would have given an undaunted and generous reception to double the quantity; neither huge logs of timber nor parts of houses which came with such mighty force made any impression on it – It firmly stood and dauntless braved the storm.[17]

Among the casualties of the flood was the ancient stone bridge at Buildwas, which was replaced by Thomas Telford's iron arch on the Schaffhausen principle in 1795–96. The ribs were cast at Coalbrookdale, at a time when the ironworks was also engaged in building two other bridges. One carried the Shrewsbury–Much Wenlock turnpike road over the Cound Brook at Cound. The other crossed the River Parrett at Bridgwater, Somerset. In 1797 the Coalbrookdale works cast the parts for John Nash's second bridge over the River Teme at Stanford, Worcs., and a 36 ft. bridge carrying a minor road over a brook at Cound, which still stands, and bears the inscription 'Cast at Coalbrookdale 1797'. The Wooden Bridge over the Severn at Preens Eddy, opened in 1780, was also damaged in the flood of 1795, and was rebuilt in 1799 with three iron arches, which carried a wooden superstructure. This curious hybrid structure survived until 1818 when one of the half-ribs cracked and was replaced, two additional ribs were added, and the wooden portions of the bridge were replaced with iron deck-plates, bearers, parapets and spandrel frames. In 1800 the Coalbrookdale Company supplied two iron footbridges to cross the Kennet and Avon Canal in Sydney Gardens, Bath, and in 1805–06 they provided two sets of bridge castings to the Bristol Dock Co., part of an order worth more than £3,000 which also included a 10 h.p. steam engine. In 1807 they despatched a 50 ton iron bridge to Jamaica.[18] The flood of 1795 seems firmly to have established the popularity of iron for bridge construction in Shropshire. Between that year and 1835 seven bridges on major roads were constructed for the county quarter sessions. Iron bridges were not universally welcomed. Robert Southey said that to look at them, 'you would actually suppose that the architect had studied at the confectioner's and borrowed his ornaments from the sugar temples of a dessert'.[19]

Aqueducts as well as bridges were realised in iron. The aqueduct carrying the Shrewsbury Canal over the Tern at Longdon built by Thomas Telford in 1795–96 was cast at Ketley, and in 1809–10 the same works supplied the aqueduct carrying the Grand Junction Canal over the Ouse at Wolverton (Bucks.).[20]

One of the most spectacular contributions of the Shropshire foundry trade to the development of British industry, although the work of a foundry in Shrewsbury and not in the coalfield, was the construction of the world's first multi-storied cast-iron framed building. The typical 18th-century textile mill had five or six storeys, and was constructed of brick or stone load-bearing walls, with wooden floors supported on timber beams, themselves supported by timber uprights. As the mechanisation of spinning advanced so the amount of fluff and thread in the atmosphere of such mills increased, greatly enlarging the risk of fire. During the late 1780s and early '90s there was a succession of disastrous fires in textile works which led to the first use of iron in mill construction. Between 1792 and 1795 several buildings connected with the textile trade in Derbyshire were constructed by William Strutt with iron upright pillars although they retained wooden beams. Strutt corresponded with Charles Bage a Shrewsbury wine merchant, who in 1796 undertook to design a mill for the flax spinners John Marshall of Leeds and Thomas and Benjamin Benyon of Shrewsbury. Their new mill in Leeds, opened in 1795 was destroyed by fire in February 1796 and the partners decided in consequence to erect a new mill in Shrewsbury. Bage designed a building with five storeys, 177 ft. 3 in. long and 39 ft. 6 in. wide with both beams and upright pillars in cast iron, the floors being carried on brick arches springing from the beams of the storey below. Bage created a building in which no timber was used at all, which afforded a better protection against fire than any other erected at that time.[21] In making his calculations for the building Bage drew on tests made at Ketley during the design of the Longdon-on-Tern aqueduct, and at the time the mill was being built he was collaborating with Thomas Telford in the building of the octagonal parish church of St. Michael, Madeley.[22] The beams and pillars for Bage's mill were cast at William Hazledine's foundry in Shrewsbury,[23] doubtless from pig iron smelted in the Shropshire coalfield. It is doubtful whether the production of structural members for buildings ever became a particularly important activity in the Shropshire iron trade because there was little demand in the immediate vicinity for mills and other structures for which iron was particularly suitable, although the Coalbrookdale ironworks did offer 'arches for cotton mills' among its products in 1801.

Armaments formed an important part of the trade in iron castings in Shropshire. Cannon and shot had been made at ironworks in the county during the Civil War, but were not manufactured at the Coalbrookdale ironworks for 30 years after the Darby family moved there. In January 1740 however cannon patterns were brought up the Severn from Bristol and in the following April a new boring-mill was under construction at Coalbrookdale. The outbreak of war in 1739 probably stimulated the partners to begin to make guns, in contradiction to the traditional Quaker policy of abstaining from the armaments trade. The Coalbrookdale partners maintained their interests in the manufacture of cannon and shot during the Seven Years War. In 1759 they paid the Willey Company for six swivel guns, and made similar payments for shot in 1763 to both the Willey and Leighton companies. During a press correspondence about the manufacture of armaments at Coalbrookdale in 1859, 'one employed at the works' claimed that ordnance had been made there until about 1790, and then ceased 'on account of a trial which took place in London and caused the Company a great deal of trouble'.[24] The New Willey Company was heavily involved in the armaments trade. In 1761 the partnership's sales included quantities of shells, shot and cannon sold in London. In subsequent years armaments remained one of the staple products of the Willey works, and in both the American War of Independence and the wars with revolutionary France, the Calcutts ironworks made many cannon.[25]

Long before the expansion of the Shropshire iron industry in the 1750s Madeley and Broseley coal had been shipped up and down the Severn for domestic consumption. In the second half of the 18th century the quantity of coal available for Severn or land sale increased as large sums were invested in mines with the object of providing coking coal and iron ore for blast furnaces. The coal trade in this period came to be controlled by the great iron-making partnerships.

Many innovations in mining were introduced in the 1780s and '90s. The steam engine was applied to the winding of pits. Wrought-iron chains replaced the traditional hemp winding-ropes. Many more steam pumping-engines were built. The Curr type iron railway was adopted for underground haulage. Nevertheless a high proportion of Shropshire coal still came from foot rids, as drift mines were called in the district, and from small shallow pits.

Some if not all of the industrial partnerships in the Shropshire coalfield accounted for all the principal overheads of mining, sinking pits, drainage, building railways, &c. as part of the costs of iron-making, so that the marginal costs of producing domestic coal were very low. Sales of domestic coal were generally handled by charter masters in the 1770s,[26] but afterwards they came increasingly under the control of the great partnerships.

Most of the domestic coal mined in east Shropshire was conveyed to its buyers along the Severn. Landsales from the northern part of the coalfield covered a much smaller area. During the last quarter of the 18th century Staffordshire coal began to gain access to the markets of the Severn and Avon valleys, following the opening of the Staffordshire and Worcestershire Canal, but sales of Shropshire coal do not seem to have been adversely affected. The coal trade gained considerable benefits from the local tub boat canal system. The Donnington Wood, Shrewsbury and Shropshire canals all seem to have been constructed primarily to meet the needs of coal-sellers. The latter canal was particularly important in this respect since it gave the owners of collieries in the northern part of the coalfield access to the profitable markets along the Severn.

Coherent statistical information about the Shropshire coal trade in the 18th century is almost impossible to obtain. Perry in 1758 calculated that 100,000 tons of coal a year were shipped from the collieries of Broseley and Madeley by the Severn barges. In 1799 Townson estimated with the help of William Reynolds that the total amount of coal mined annually in the whole of the coalfield was in the region of 260,000 tons.[27]

The available figures for individual groups of mines give only a patchy picture of the amount of coal produced and of the proportions which went to the ironworks and for general trade. In the collieries of the Weld family in Broseley and Willey in the early 1750s there were about 20 pits. In the year beginning at midsummer 1752 they produced 3,676 tons of coal, of which 762 tons were delivered to the Old Willey Furnace. In the following year 4,360 tons were mined, of which 1,002 tons went to the furnace. In the Ketley mines in 1777 the Reynolds's pits produced 20,733 tons of clod coal for coking, but only 2,741 tons of other types, suggesting that production was directed almost entirely towards the supply of the ironworks. Mining for general sale at Ketley was discouraged by the terms of the lease under which a royalty of 6d. per ton was paid for furnace coals, and 8d. a ton for coals for landsale.[28]

The Madeley Field coalworks which supplied the 'Bedlam' blast furnaces on the banks of the Severn were probably more concerned than most collieries with the production of coal for export by river. In 1772 a spur from the railway which supplied the blast furnaces 'for the coals for Severn sale' dived steeply through a tunnel from the high line of the furnaces to emerge on the quay in front of the furnaces' casting houses. In the first six months of 1791 the total sales of minerals from the pits in the Madeley Field realised £5,147 14s. 3d., of which £3,248 came from sales of ore and coking coal to the furnaces. In 1795 the furnaces consumed 9,600 tons of coal in the manufacture of $1,624^1/_2$ tons of iron.[29]

The importance of the coal trade to the partnerships in the northern part of the coalfield is shown by an agreement of 1797 in which Thomas Botfield of the Old Park Company arranged with his landlord, Isaac Hawkins Browne to convey to the Severn 1,200 tons of coal a month from the Malins Lee area by canal or railway. The Coalbrookdale accounts suggest that the importance of the Severn sale of coal was growing in the late 1790s and early 1800s. The partnership's trade in coal was rather irregular in 1797 and 1798. No coal at all was sold in some months, and the total sales for the year beginning August 1797 amounted to only 2,380 tons, and those for the following year 2,381 tons. In 1802–03 sales reached 7,810 tons and the lowest monthly total was 95 tons. There was a steady growth in the period up to 1807–08 when 18,079 tons were sold, and the lowest monthly total was over 1,000 tons.[30]

Investments in mining in order to raise raw materials for iron making seem thus to have stimulated a substantial increase in the trade in domestic coal carried on by the large industrial partnerships in Shropshire. The coal trade was to prove a more enduring source of profits than the iron trade in the depression which followed the peace of 1815.

In most mining districts more economical ways of making coke were developed in the 18th century than the open heaps employed from the time of Abraham Darby I, which simply copied the methods of the charcoal burners. Gabriel Jars saw beehive ovens in use on Tyneside as early as 1765.[31] In Shropshire some of the iron-making partnerships began to make experiments in the 1780s and '90s with ovens which would produce coke and preserve such useful by-products as tar.

In the Severn Gorge such experiments already had a long history. Pitch was extracted from bituminous shales in Broseley under Martin Eele's patent as early as the 1690s, and when Abraham Darby III purchased the Madeley Wood ironworks in 1776 there was a range of 'coal tar buildings' on the premises. These tar ovens were apparently unsuccessful, for Darby ceased to work them in 1779.[32]

The outstanding figure in the Shropshire coke and tar industry was Archibald Cochrane, ninth Earl Dundonald, who took out a patent for the manufacture of tar by the 'stewing' of coal in 1781. Dundonald owned extensive mineral-bearing estates in Scotland,[33] and following the development of his tar process set up five works in the English Midlands, three in Staffordshire and two in Shropshire.

Between 1784 and 1786 Dundonald built 12 kilns or stoves for the manufacture of coke and tar adjacent to the Calcutts ironworks. Following Alexander Brodie's purchase of the works in 1786, eight further kilns were constructed sometime before 1800. Dundonald's second Shropshire works adjoined the Benthall furnaces. The kilns there were in production by 1787 when Dundonald told William Reynolds that they were being fired only with clod coal. In 1790 a composite fee was paid to the proprietors of the Iron Bridge to enable tar to be taken from the Benthall kilns along the bridge company's road to the Severn.[34]

There were two principal stages in Dundonald's method of making coke and tar. First, coal was slowly burned in kilns in such a way that complete combustion was avoided, and coke was produced. The smoke from the smouldering coals was led by horizontal tubes into a funnel supported on brick arches, and covered with a sheet of water. As the smoke was cooled it condensed, and the resulting tar fell to the bottom of the funnel, whence it was led into a cistern. From the cistern it was piped to a boiler, where it was heated to form pitch, and the resulting gasses in turn were condensed into an oil used for varnishing and japanning. The pitch was sold for naval and building purposes, and the oils probably found a market in the Birmingham papier mâché trades.[35]

The kilns at the Calcutts were operated as part of the adjacent ironworks which drew its coke supplies from them. The remainder of the installation, the condensers and 'refridgeratories' were worked by Dundonald's British Tar Company. A similar arrangement seems to have prevailed at Benthall. The Tar Company's interests were managed by Dundonald's brother, John Cochrane, a Captain Dumaresque and one George Glenny. With the opening of the Benthall works Dundonald apparently came to regard his Shropshire interests very highly, and in 1787 took a lease of The Tuckies, a mansion overlooking the Severn about half a mile from the Calcutts.[36] Among local customers for tar produced at the works were the Shropshire Canal Company and the

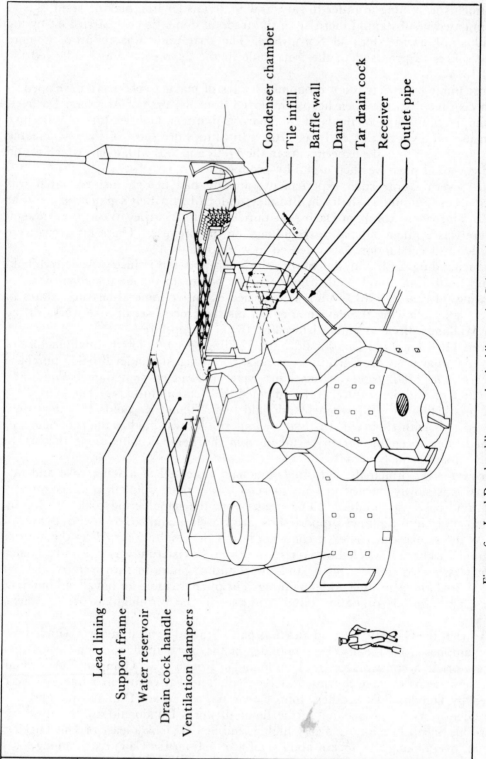

Condenser chamber
Tile infill
Baffle wall
Dam
Tar drain cock
Receiver
Outlet pipe

Lead lining
Support frame
Water reservoir
Drain cock handle
Ventilation dampers

Figure 6.   Lord Dundonald's tar and coke kilns at the Calcutts ironworks.
*A reconstruction of the Calcutts Tar Kilns, taken from a plan in the Dundonald Collection.
Scottish Record Office GD33/109/6/8-9, reproduced by permission of the Rt. Hon. Earl of Dundonald,
and drawn by the late Derek Jobber.*

Horsehay and Coalbrookdale ironworks, and in 1788 a coat of clear varnish prepared by the British Tar Company was applied to the Iron Bridge.[37]

In 1789 and subsequent years the British Tar Company encountered severe financial difficulties, not necessarily because of technical defects in its processes or unsound management of its English works, but because huge sums were lost in unsuccessful mineral prospecting in Scotland. In September 1789 the company owed over £45,000. Lord Dundonald's whole industrial career was marked in no small degree with financial naïveté, and he suffered severely in the collapse of the Tar Company. It seems that' by declaring themselves bankrupt, Dundonald's brothers and George Glenny avoided personal responsibility for the company's debts, and arranged for most of Lady Dundonald's fortune to be laid out in a mortgage on the works. By March 1791 Dundonald was excluded from the management of what he now called the British Tar Company, and could not understand how the company could survive since they were paying only 4 per cent on debts contracted at 5 per cent.[38]

The three Staffordshire works and that at Benthall did not survive, all of them being dismantled by 1799, but that at the Calcutts remained in operation as long as the adjacent furnaces were in blast. In 1799 tar from the Calcutts kilns was being marketed by Anly, Birch and Wright, a firm of Limehouse ships' chandlers, who paid to Lady Dundonald a mere £30 a year for the works, on which Lord Dundonald calculated they made a profit of between £600 and £700 a year. The kilns were operated by Alexander Brodie of the Calcutts ironworks who charged Anly, Birch and Wright a fixed rate per barrel. The kilns consumed between 10,000 and 11,000 tons of coal a year, from which between 1,000 and 1,100 barrels of pitch were produced. Anly, Birch and Wright were interested only in the pitch and allowed the oils and 'coal tar water' to run to waste. Dundonald's interest by this time was minimal. His brothers and George Glenny made considerable fortunes, but he himself had lost all his money in the Tar Company and was involved in its affairs only because he tried to secure an adequate return for his wife.[39]

Dundonald's attempt to utilise the by-products of coke making was copied by a number of Shropshire ironmasters. In 1786 he was a frequent diner at the tables of the Coalbrookdale partners, and the following year William Reynolds discussed with him the building of tar kilns at Madeley Wood but their plans were delayed by Reynolds's partner William Rathbone who was at first unwilling to lease additional land for the erection of the kilns. Dundonald invited Reynolds 'to come and bring Rathbone to eat a bit of mutton with me at the Tuckies', and apparently convinced him of the merits of his process. By February 1789 the kilns at Madeley Wood were complete and producing coke. In the autumn of the same year William Reynolds was building kilns and distilleries at Ketley, for which in March 1790 he purchased lead from the British Tar Company's works at the Calcutts and Benthall. These initial installations seem to have been on a small scale and Reynolds's plans to build many more kilns in the summer of 1790 were frustrated by the collapse of the British Tar Company. In November 1799 Reynolds consulted Dundonald about the erection of further kilns, and there was a prospect that he might have taken over the Calcutts kilns, but these schemes came to nothing. The kilns at Ketley continued in operation for some years. In 1802 the Horsehay ironworks was buying 'coal oil' both from the British Tar Company at the Calcutts and from Ketley.[40]

John Wilkinson also experimented with coke ovens, although he was not, as folk lore claims, the first to make coke in kilns and extract oils. He had kilns, probably at

Willey, where according to Dundonald, coke was made in the same way as in William Reynolds's kilns at Ketley.[41]

The 18th-century experiments with coke and tar ovens in Shropshire were not conspicuously successful, though how much the reasons for their failure were commercial and how much technical is now difficult to determine. Ovens offered the prospects of additional profits to ironmasters through the sale of tar and of oils, but there was considerable prejudice among ship-builders against the use of coal tar, which they claimed rotted ropework, and the introduction of copper plating on ships probably reduced the overall demand for tar. It is clear that there were difficulties in the operation of the kilns. John Randall suggested that the Calcutts works failed because the kilns were constantly blowing up after the ignition of coal gas.[42] This is, at first sight, absurd, for the Calcutts kilns operated with tolerable success for about 40 years, and Dundonald was well aware of the properties of coal gas, but Randall's garbled account probably does draw on a local tradition of accidents at the Calcutts. Dundonald's processes were not generally copied by Shropshire ironmasters, and following the deaths of William Reynolds and John Wilkinson and the closure of the Calcutts works later in the 19th century there seems to have been a total reversion in the district to making of coke in open heaps. This was the only method used in Shropshire in the early 1840s, and while some coke ovens were built later in the 19th century, at most works open heaps were used as long as iron ore was smelted, and the method survived into the 20th century.

The burning of limestone began in Shropshire in medieval times, and quarrying on a considerable scale was taking place in the coalfield in the late 17th century, but the need for fluxing stone for blast furnaces brought about a marked expansion of the industry in the second half of the 18th century. The iron-making partnerships became involved in the production of limestone, and transport facilities constructed for the supply of fluxing stone to blast furnaces were used in addition for carrying building and agricultural lime.

Not all of the local limestone was suitable for use as a flux in blast furnaces, but quarries and mines where white stone for fluxing was extracted, often produced in addition the grey stone which could be used in calcined form as cement, or as fertiliser.[43]

The working of the carboniferous limestone around Lilleshall was well established before the end of the 17th century. The limestone in Lilleshall parish was on the land of the Gower family, but that in neighbouring Church Aston belonged to the Leekes, although it was leased to the Gowers or their partners for most of the 18th and 19th centuries. The exploitation of the Lilleshall limestone was one of the chief purposes of the partnership formed between Earl Gower and the Gilbert brothers in 1764, and one of the partners' objects in building the Donnington Wood Canal was to carry coal to fire the limekilns. Subsequently the white stone from Lilleshall was used extensively in local blast furnaces. Lilleshall lime was being used as an hydraulic cement as early as 1767. The workings at Lilleshall and Church Aston were a complex mixture of mines and quarries, the deepest of the former having a 248 ft. shaft. In December 1805, 3,700 tons of limestone were produced at Lilleshall.[44]

The limestone quarries on the land of the Forester family at Steeraway in the parish of Little Wenlock were also established before 1700. By the late 1730s a railway linked them with wharves on the Watling Street turnpike road where lime could be sold to farmers and builders. Steeraway was among the sources of limestone for the Horsehay furnaces in their first years of operation. By the beginning of the 19th century the

Steeraway workings were being operated by a partnership of Rowley and Emery, and after 1805 by Emery and Clayton. The purchase of a steam winding-engine in 1803–04 shows that deep mines as well as quarries were being worked, and by 1840 shafts 120 ft. deep were being used.[45]

The limestone workings at Lincoln Hill, Coalbrookdale, were similarly a confusing mixture of quarries, adits and shaft mines. The hill has been drastically distorted by the effects of centuries of working. George Perry described it in 1758 as 'a huge Rock of limestone . . . cut hollow to a great depth so that the top of it now appears like a vast pit, 440 yard long and 52 wide, each side being a frightful precipice'. Another writer saw it as 'an immensely large Quarry . . . being the work of many ages. At the bottom there are several prodigous caverns of Limestone, supported by several stupendous pillars of stone left for that purpose . . . a quarry about 150 feet deep and almost perpendicular, at the bottom of which are several large limekilns and immense caverns supported by huge pillars [which] has all the appearance of the horrible'. The Lincoln Hill workings were owned by the Reynolds family in the early 19th century. Fluxing stone was sold to Horsehay, Madeley Wood and other ironworks, but the kilns were operated by independent contractors.[46]

To the south of the Severn the limestone workings on Benthall Edge were linked with the river by a railway inclined plane which ran down to a row of limekilns on the river bank. Benthall Edge was one of the most important sources of limestone in the district but its workings are almost totally undocumented.[47]

To the south of Benthall Edge and further upstream on the Severn were two other important limestone workings. Around Tickwood and the Wyke was the Wenlock Limestone Concern in which William Reynolds had a third share with Thomas Parry and John Morris. It was linked to the Severn by a railway, owned jointly by Reynolds and his partners, and by Wright and Jesson, and Alexander Brodie, who probably operated other quarries in the vicinity. The railway probably ran to a wharf on the river downstream from Buildwas Bridge, known in the 19th century as the Stone Port. Another railway reached the Severn about three quarters of a mile above the same bridge, linking a wharf with limestone quarries in the Gleedon Hill area. These were probably the workings known as the Buildwas Limerocks from which in 1800 the Madeley Wood, Ketley, Horsehay and Lightmoor furnaces were supplied by river.[48]

Mining and iron-making both demand large quantities of bricks and most of the large industrial partnerships in Shropshire became involved in brick-making. Common building bricks had been made in the district long before the 1750s, but it was probably not until about that time that fire bricks were made locally. In the 1790s Robert Townson recorded that three strata in the Wombridge area, the Upper Clunch, Linsed Earth and Bannack clays were used for making firebricks, and that the cheap sulphurous or Stinking Coal was used for burning bricks. All of these strata were found in close proximity to the most commonly-mined coals. In the 1720s firebricks for the Coalbrookdale ironworks were imported from Stourbridge, but most of those used for the erection of the Horsehay furnaces in 1754–55 came from Broseley. At the same time brick-making facilities were developed at Horsehay itself, from where by 1756 bricks and fireclay were being supplied to ironworks in the Wye valley operated by Richard Reynolds's father.[49]

The protests made by ironmasters against the proposed tax on bricks in 1784 show how important a place brick-making occupied in the economies of the iron-making partnerships. John Wilkinson, William Reynolds and the Earl of Dudley complained about the effects the tax would have, declaring that they used a million bricks a year. Richard Reynolds wrote to Earl Gower, 'as to the tax on bricks and tiles, if it is not confined to those used in building dwelling houses, it will be very heavy on those concerned in collieries &c.'.[50]

The importance of brick-making can be seen in the development of one particular part of the coalfield. The right to dig clay and make bricks was among those granted by Earl Gower to Thomas and John Gilbert when the three formed their partnership in 1764, and similar authority was given to William Reynolds and Joseph Rathbone when they leased the land for the Donnington Wood blast furnaces from the Gower family in 1783. The colliers working the ore mines of Donnington Wood were supplied with locally produced bricks throughout the 1760s, and by 1776 some bricks were being sold to outside customers. In 1783–85 vast quantities were made in the area for the new Donnington Wood blast furnace. In November and December 1783 the brick-man, John Jones, made 594,200 bricks 'below the furnace', 70,800 'at the Navigation', 31,000 'at the Crown Pool' and 209,000 'in the Moss, Wrockwardine Wood'. Whether these were permanent brickworks or temporary clamps it is impossible to say, but by 1793 there were certainly established groups of kilns at the Nabb and the Moss which were supplying the Donnington mines.[51]

Most of the major ironworks were linked with brickworks by the 1770s. The Madeley Wood concern had kilns among the coalpits in Madeley Field, at the Lloyds and at Blists Hill. Firebricks for Horsehay in the 1770s were made by Andrew Bradley and Co. at Coalmoor, a works with 40 acres of mining land, 13 cottages for workers and a manager's residence. Bradley offered the works for sale in 1788, and it was probably at that time that Richard Reynolds acquired it. There were brick kilns at Hollinswood and the Calcutts, and probably at most of the other major ironworks.[52]

Roofing tiles were also manufactured in the district. Arthur Young noted in 1776 that large quantities of blue tiles were burned at Benthall, although this was probably not an activity of the iron-making partnerships. In 1772 Thomas Botfield supplied 7,500 roofing tiles to the Horsehay ironworks perhaps for the building of new engine houses. In 1777 Horsehay obtained roofing and ridge tiles from the Coalmoor kilns which supplied the works with firebricks.[53]

A more sophisticated industrial pottery was added to the existing brickworks at Horsehay in the 1790s. Buildings erected there in 1796–97 included a roundware throwing-house, dish moulding and dish tempering houses, a sagger-house and a dish warehouse. Products included clay drainage pipes, pots for the Wright and Jesson forging process and ground clay for glass- and porcelain-making.[54]

VIII

PATTERNS OF TRANSPORT

The iron-making partnerships which dominated the economy of the Shropshire coalfield in the late 18th century made enormous demands on the transport facilities of the district, and innovations in transport in the period were as remarkable as those in iron-making. Some of the new departures, the tub boat canal system, for example, were enterprising solutions to daunting problems, but at the end of the century long distance transport was still unhealthily dependent on the ever less reliable Severn.

In the 17th century the River Severn was, according to Professor Nef, the second busiest in Europe after the Meuse.[1] During the 18th century the river carried away much of the iron from the furnaces, foundries and forges of the Severn Gorge and its vicinity. It was heavily used until the expansion of standard gauge railways in the 1850s and '60s. In the 1750s the river was the most convenient means of access to the coalfield for the less active traveller. Members of the Darby family and their guests often went by boat to and from Worcester. In 1750 a midshipman en route from mid-Wales to the coast left Shrewsbury in a wherry in the early morning, breakfasted at Atcham, dined at Bridgnorth, drank tea at Bewdley and arrived in Worcester at 9 p.m.[2]

Two authors described the Severn Navigation in the mid-18th century. Richard Cornes writing in 1739 said that the river was 'navigable for about 140 miles and has a great number of vessels continually plying upon it'. The most common freight was 'pit coal from Broseley, very famous for its collieries'. George Perry listed the numbers of vessels plying from the ports on the river between Welshpool and Gloucester in 1756. Writing two years later he remarked that since his survey was taken the total had increased from 376 to more than 400. Over the next half century some staple traffics were diverted from the river to other forms of transport, but such was the rate of industrial expansion that the volume of goods carried continued to increase, and by the early 19th century another writer estimated that the number of boats was double that quoted by Perry.[3]

According to Perry there were two types of vessel in use on the Severn in the 1750s, 'the lesser kind . . . barges and frigates, from 40 to 60 ft. in length, a single mast, square sails . . . carry from 20 to 40 tons' and the 'trows or larger vessels, from 40 to 80 tons burthen, a main and top mast about 80 ft. high, with square sails . . . some have mizzen masts . . . generally from 16 to 20 ft. wide and 60 ft. in length'. Perry probably over-simplified the situation, for other sources suggest a wide variety of commercial vessels ranging in size from the 80 ton trows to wherries of only five or six tons.[4] There seems to have been a real distinction however between vessels which were capable of navigating the lower reaches of the Severn and sailing up the Avon to Bristol, which probably only rarely ventured upstream from Coalbrookdale, and those which did not normally sail further downstream than Gloucester, but which could reach any destination on the Upper Severn. Numerous references in the records of the Coalbrookdale ironworks show that goods were frequently conveyed direct from the Severn Gorge to Bristol. Shropshire boats were often fitted out with ropes and tackle in Bristol. Three Broseley trows, *The Success*, *The Industry* and *The William* were regularly trading to Bristol in 1787. There were other Broseley trows in Bristol at the time of the Reform riots in 1831, and in 1836 Owner Barnett of Broseley lost his trow on a journey to Bristol.[5]

A considerable amount of evidence suggests that the larger vessels did not normally sail upstream from Coalbrookdale. A list of Shrewsbury barges in 1837 shows that the largest was only a 50-tonner. Freight carried between Shrewsbury and Bristol was almost invariably transhipped at Gloucester in the 19th century, although in 1787 two Shrewsbury vessels had been sailing direct to Bristol. Numerous advertisements in Shrewsbury newspapers refer to connections made by Shrewsbury barge owners with Bristol trows at Gloucester. In 1817 John Jones, who had just taken over his father's fleet of barges, announced that his vessels would continue to go to and from Gloucester every spring tide to meet the Bristol trows. In 1811 two trow owners operating between Bristol and Gloucester urged Shrewsbury customers to mark their goods for transfer to their particular vessels at Gloucester.[6]

The variety of vessels used on the Severn is shown by a list of boats belonging to the Coalbrookdale Company in 1807, which included a trow the *Friend* valued at £660, another trow the *Trial* valued at only £130, a deal flat, the *Victory* worth £190, and two barges the *William* and the *Mary* and a frigate the *Hermaphrodite* worth together £459. In Shrewsbury in 1837 there were two 50 tonners, one 45, five 40, two 35 and two 30-tonners, as well as a number of lighters or wherries of between five and 12 tons. While Perry reckoned a fully-equipped trow to be worth about £300 in 1756, coal barges were being sold in Broseley at about the same time for as little as £22. As late as the 1830s three barges sold in Broseley realised only amounts between £22 10s. 0d. and £35.[7]

While trows were used principally for the carriage of iron and general cargoes, bulk traffics, particularly coal were usually conveyed in the smaller vessels. In 1791 in a report of an accident near Bridgnorth a distinction was drawn between a 'boat' loaded with coal, and 'a large Trow under a gale of wind' which overwhelmed the former and drowned one of its crew. The many paintings and engravings of the Ironbridge in the late 18th century show that most of the vessels awaiting cargoes of coal in the vicinity were small ones. There were recognised limits on the lower reaches of the Severn beyond which the smaller barges did not normally operate. The borough court of Wenlock records a case in which an owner from Broseley complained that the defendant had hired his barge to take 19 tons of coal to the Forest of Dean, but that he went beyond the Forest 'out of the common roadway into strange waters' and damaged the boat. The smaller barges would also have been used for carrying iron upstream from the Gorge to Pool Quay and Llandrinio, the ports for the forges of mid-Wales.[8]

The range of the barges which operated from the wharves of the Severn Gorge was extended by the use of the Severn's tributaries. On the Tern the survival of a lock near to the present confluence with the Severn suggests that it was possible for small boats to sail to Tern Forge, and possibly beyond to Upton Forge, and even to ironworks

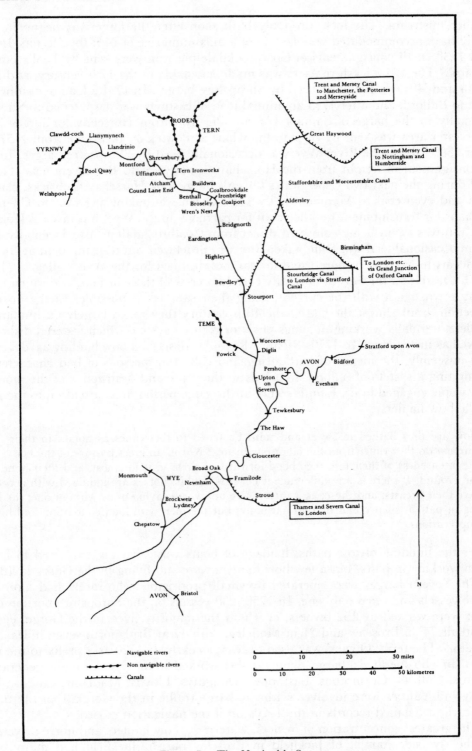

Figure 7. The Navigable Severn.

further upstream. The lock, probably built soon after the forge was begun in 1710, could have accommodated vessels only of a maximum size of 24 ft. by 7ft. 6in. In 1737 and 1738 small consignments of Coalbrookdale pig iron were sent by Pool's barge to 'Tearn'.[9] The Warwickshire Avon was made navigable in the 17th century, and in the 1730s and '40s was regularly used by Shropshire barges. In 1731 a load of castings was sent to Bidford, and after 1735 an annual load of castings was despatched to Stratford, normally in the barge of Samuel Lloyd.[10] Pig iron from Horsehay for forges in the Worcester area was sent by river to the wharf at Powick on the Teme from 1757 until after 1800.[11] Even the River Wye was occasionally used by Shropshire barges. In 1756 a consignment of freight from the Horsehay works went to Brockweir near Tintern, and during the next two years James Owen's barge took Horsehay firebricks, clay, pig iron and even coal to Monmouth. By 1759 Owen was taking pig iron to Chepstow, perhaps for transhipment to other craft for carriage up the Wye, but in 1773 Horsehay pig iron was again being conveyed direct from Coalbrookdale to Brockweir, By 1776–77 an occasional load was being taken direct to Brockweir but transhipment at Glouces-ter seems to have been more usual for cargoes destined for the Wye Valley.[12]

The vessels on the Severn normally carried a crew of three or four 'watermen'. They went downstream with the current, using their sails when possible. In the upstream direction, until almost the end of the 18th century they relied largely on human bow haulers, normally working in gangs of six or eight, a system which fostered dishonesty as well as inefficiency. In 1770s Richard Reynolds described bow hauling as 'degrading and unseemly, the means of harbouring and collecting persons of bad character and facilitating a system of plunder injurious to the trade and destructive of the morals of the people engaged in it'. John Fletcher at the same period drew attention to the plight of the bow haulers,

How are they bathed in sweat and rain. Fastened to their lines as horses to their traces, wherein do they differ from the laborious brutes? Not in an erect posture of the body, for in the intenseness of their toil, they bend forward, their head is foremost, and their hand upon the ground. If there is any difference it consists in this: horses are indulged with a collar to save their breasts; and these; as if theirs were not worth saving draw without one; the beasts tug in patient silence and mutual harmony; but the men with loud contention and horrible imprecations.[13]

After the building of tow paths, haulage of boats was normally entrusted to horses, often working in pairs, but a few bow haulers were still living in the Gorge in 1851.

The Severn barges were operated by small proprietors who rarely had more than three vessels and often only one. In 1756, 250 vessels on the Shropshire portion of the river were worked by 152 owners, of whom the majority lived in the Gorge, eight in Benthall, 55 in Broseley and 21 in Madeley, with 47 at Bridgnorth seven miles down-stream.[14] The term 'Owner' was used at least as early as 1720 as a prefix to the name of a man who operated a barge. Some families worked on the river for many generations. Beards, Cullises, Crumptons, Easthopes, Doughtys, Lloyds, Madelins, Owens, Tran-soms and Yateses were involved with the barge traffic in the Gorge from the time of the earliest detailed records in the 1720s until the navigation ceased.

The greatest concentration of owners, watermen, bow haulers and horse drivers was in the riverside hamlet of Jackfield in Broseley parish. Jackfield had many of the characteristics of a sea port; cheap lodging houses, brothels and numerous public houses including *The Boat*, *The Severn Trow* and *The Tumbling Sailors*. Bow haulers and watermen were notoriously dishonest. Sheep and game from riverside meadows and coverts were considered a normal part of their diet, and ingenious means were employed for removing buckets full of cider, perry, porter, wine or spirits from casks being carried up river, or for the surreptitious removal of portions of the dry groceries among the cargoes. Even the downstream bulk loads of coal were subject to misappropriation through the alteration of tickets of weight. Richard Ford continually complained to Thomas Goldney in the 1730s of the negligence of barge owners who mislaid important consignments.[15]

The way of life of the bargemen is well portrayed in a commonplace book kept by a member of a barge-owning family in Jackfield between 1828 and 1836.[16] One Francis Yates, son of Owner Yates the saltman, had a scuffle with a china-maker in an inn in Coalport and was taken by the magistrates but escaped. The same Francis Yates a few months later was forced to do penance in Madeley church for calling a mason's wife a whore in a show at Ironbridge. The goods of a bankrupt owner, Tom Madelin, were sold for the benefit of his creditors, but the attorney who sold them kept the money. John Transom and his brother James were 'fighting like two tigers' one night at their father's house after he was in bed. Samuel Davis beat his uncle James Lloyd, 'in a most dreadful manner', at the *Black Swan* Jackfield, and nearly killed him. The same month Jack Lowe who lived at the Calcutts beat his sweetheart and gave her two black eyes. George Ball beat his wife and three women that stood by at the same time, and on the same day Thomas Doughty beat his wife and also a man who took her part. In 1833 one Teddy Lloyd, a Jackfield barge owner, had his pocket picked while with a whore at Gloucester. In October 1831 four Broseley trows were stranded at Bristol because their crews had been detained in prison. They had taken the opportunity during the Reform Bill riots in the city to steal valuable property from the burning Custom House and to hide it on their vessel, where it was found by the magistrates.

The same commonplace book describes something of the dangers of the Severn navigation. Several Broseley sailors were lost overboard between 1828 and 1836, usually while their vessels were moored and while they themselves were intoxicated. In 1831 a barge sank at Coalport causing the death of one of its crew. In 1836 a vessel sank at Gitchfield Ford at the downstream end of the Gorge apparently after a collision. Several vessels were lost after going aground at a spot called Eave's Mount, causing the loss of three barges within 18 months in 1831–32. Two vessels, one from Broseley and one from Bristol, were lost on the lower Severn while coming upstream from Bristol with groceries.

The barge owners were active participants in the Severn coal trade. They collected from wharves in the Gorge cargoes of coal which were usually delivered by railway to the riverside. The sidings at one such wharf at the Calcutts are shown on the pictorial map in Figure 5. In 1748, 122 wagons of coal from the Weld estates were awaiting transhipment in these sidings. Coal was taken from the wharves on credit, and the owner would sell his cargo wherever he could find a market. When George Weld of Willey died in 1748, 51 barge owners owed him over £1,600 for coal taken from his wharves. Most of the owners were from the Severn Gorge, but there were several from Bridgnorth, and some from as far away as Worcester and Gloucester.[17] Between July 1790 and April 1793, 74 different owners were engaged in the Severn Sale coal trade of the Madeley Field coalworks, of whom 33 came from Broseley, 15 from Madeley, nine from Bridgnorth, and five from other ports. 11 were identified only by the names of their vessels.[18]

The Coalbrookdale ironworks records suggest that vessels carrying iron operated under charter to particular customers and did not take cargoes on credit. The company employed many fewer barge owners than the two coal concerns mentioned above. Only 14 owners carried iron from Horsehay between 1774 and 1781, and the majority of these only took single cargoes at times of pressure. Normally one or two owners were employed for long periods to carry iron to a particular destination or group of destinations. Between 1756 and 1781 Richard Beard took most of the iron for places between Bewdley and Gloucester, only rarely venturing as far as Bristol or upstream to Shrewsbury. In the same period Samuel Jones took most of the Horsehay iron consigned for Bristol, and Severn ports below Gloucester. The latter were also served by Edward Lloyd and James Owen, both of whom took cargoes to ports on the Wye. Upstream from Coalbrookdale, forge pig iron for Pool Quay was generally taken by William Price, Owner Vaughan, Thomas Rogers or Edward Tipton. In Fogerty's *Lauterdale* set in the 19th century, the contract for the carriage of Coalbrookdale holloware to Bristol was let to a maltster who conveyed the cargo in three barges at a time when the river was falling. Fogerty probably based his character on one of the brothers Francis and John Yates who were both maltsters and barge owners at Coalbrookdale.[19]

The extent to which the Coalbrookdale partners relied on individual barge owners is best exemplified by the career of Eustace Beard of Benthall, born in 1700. He probably took over a barge from his father in 1724, when he was employed to deliver iron to Gloucester. Throughout the 1720s he took similar cargoes of iron to Gloucester, Worcester and Bewdley, sometimes returning with fireclay and Stourbridge bricks. From time to time he went upstream to Shrewsbury with cast-iron pots, often bringing back forge pig iron, probably from blast furnaces in Lancashire or Cheshire, which he loaded at Uffington Quay. In 1734 Beard sailed to Bristol with a new trow. Richard Ford then called him, 'as careful a man as any goes by ye river and deserves encouragement', and urged a friend to allow Beard credit if he should want to buy ropes and sails for the new vessel in Bristol. Beard was regularly employed by the Coalbrookdale partners throughout the rest of the 1730s and '40s. In the normal course of events Beard took goods to Gloucester for transhipment, but quite frequently Ford would warn his partner that Beard was sailing through to Bristol. Between 1754 and the summer of 1756 Beard carried many cargoes for the new Horsehay ironworks, including the hearth and timp stones for the blast furnace, brought up from Highley, and some of the first loads of pig iron from Horsehay which he took to Bewdley and Gloucester. In the summer of 1756 he seems to have handed over his business to his son Richard. He died in 1761 and is commemorated in Benthall churchyard by a cast-iron slab adorned with broken anchors.[20]

The accounts of the Horsehay ironworks show something of the quantities of iron conveyed by river. In the three months beginning 22 November 1755 Eustace Beard delivered 178 tons 7 cwt. of pig iron to Bewdley. In April and May 1757, 19 tons 6 cwt. went to Shrewsbury, 20 tons to Monmouth, 90 tons to Bewdley, 10 tons to Powick and 60 to Bristol. In April and May 1761 20 tons went to Shrewsbury, 10 to Cound Land End, 372 tons to Bewdley, 40 to the Clothhouse Wharf nearby, eight to Bridgnorth and 31 to Bristol.[21]

The pattern of trade with the Worcestershire ports was substantially altered by the opening of the Severn's first canal tributary. The Staffordshire and Worcestershire Canal extends 46 miles from Great Haywood on the Trent and Mersey Canal, past Aldersley near Wolverhampton, where there is a junction with the Birmingham Canal

Navigation, to reach the Severn at a place known in the 1760s as Lower Mitton, but which soon afterwoods gained the name Stourport. The canal was usable from a point near Wolverhampton to the Severn by November 1770, and the basin at Stourport came into use the following year. In May 1772 the whole canal was opened, and the following September the junction with the Birmingham Canal was completed. Navigation from the Staffordshire and Worcestershire through to the Trent was possible from the time of its opening, but it was not until 1777 that it was possible to sail through to the Mersey. In 1779 the opening of the Dudley and Stourbridge Canals created a new route between Stourport and the Black Country.[22]

In 1767 a cargo of Horsehay iron for one of Edward Knight's forges was despatched to 'Stourmouth', the first reference in the Coalbrookdale Company accounts to any such place, and possibly an indication that work had already begun on the basin at what was to become Stourport. By June 1770 consignments were being sent specifically to 'the basin at Stourmouth', and by November of that year to 'the Canal Baison at Stourmouth'. In April 1771 the accounts mention Stour*port* for the first time, and for another two years they refer simultaneously to Stourmouth and Stourport. In November 1772 a load of Horsehay melting pig ordered by John Wilkinson for his Bilston works was sent by way of Stourport, being transhipped there from Richard Beard's trow on to a narrow boat.[23] This route became the principal link between Shropshire and the Black Country and Birmingham.

The Staffordshire and Worcestershire Canal gave access to through canal routes to places even further afield. When the Calcutts ironworks was offered for sale in 1786 prospective purchasers were offered navigation to Liverpool and Hull as well as to Bristol. In 1774 Horsehay iron was being sent to a customer in Nottingham by way of Stourport. Castings from Coalbrookdale were sent to Stourport en route to Liverpool, over £400 being spent in the year ending August 1800 on freights on this route. Steam engines for collieries in the Potteries and bricks for a customer at Gainsborough were among other Shropshire commodities which were delivered by way of the basin at Stourport.[24]

The expansion of the iron industry greatly increased the volume of traffic between Coalbrookdale and the Worcestershire ports in the last quarter of the 18th century. In the year ending August 1800 pig iron, wrought iron and castings sent to Stourport from the Coalbrookdale and Horsehay works totalled 1,440 tons, and by 1807–08 the figure for the same traffics was over 3,000 tons.[25] This was at a time when only six of the 40 or so blast furnaces in east Shropshire were operated by the Coalbrookdale partners, and most of the other ironmasters must have been using the river to a similar extent.

The river trade in Shropshire was considerably affected by the Thames and Severn Canal opened in 1789 from Lechlade on the Thames to Stroud at the head of the Stroudwater Navigation which connected with the Severn at Framilode. One of the objects of the canal was to provide 'an inland communication from the capital with Bristol, Gloucester, Worcester and Shrewsbury'. Iron from Coalbrookdale carried by this route was being handled at Hambros Wharf, London by 1793. By the end of the 1790s the Coalbrookdale Company was despatching castings to customers by way of Brimscombe on the Thames and Severn Canal, where they were transhipped; 120 tons in 1798–99, 30 tons the following year and 78 tons in 1800–01. Traffic by this route fell off during the next few years, but had revived by 1807 when 18 tons of castings and 24 tons of bar iron were despatched. In July 1800 Benjamin Yates, a Coalbrookdale barge owner, made the first through voyage from the Severn Gorge to Hambros Wharf by way of the Thames and Severn Canal. The 400-mile journey took him 14 days. Notices of changes in rates on the Thames and Severn Canal frequently appeared in Shrewsbury newspapers, and writers on Shrewsbury in 1808 and 1825 regarded the canal as the most usual route for freight to London.[26]

High hopes were also entertained of through traffic by waterway between Shropshire and London by way of Stourport and the various canal routes through the Black Country to points south of Birmingham. In 1793 the promoters of the Stratford-upon-Avon Canal anticipated that the traffic they would collect from the Dudley Canal would include castings from Coalbrookdale and earthenware from Broseley, which they would pass on to the Warwick and Birmingham Canal at Kingswood Junction. In the main these hopes were disappointed, although some Shropshire iron did pass along the Stratford Canal by this route.[27]

The reliability of the Severn was actually deteriorating in the late 18th century. According to Thomas Telford this was because the enclosure and drainage of water meadows in north Shropshire prevented their acting as a sponge as they had done in the past. In times of heavy rainfall water ran off the land more quickly, causing dangerous floods down river, and in dry period there was no water to trickle off the meadows to maintain the level of the river. In the 1780s there was usually sufficient water for traffic to operate through the winter, but in the summer there were delays lasting for months at a time when no boats at all could use the river. In 1796 only eight weeks of navigation were possible in the whole year.[28] Such was the need to take full advantage of favourable levels of water that boats often sailed through the night. In 1818 Richard Matthews, a Shrewsbury waterman, was drowned near Upton-on-Severn owing to negligence on the part of the steersman of his boat at two o'clock on a Sunday morning.[29]

As the reliability of the river diminished the demands made upon it by ironmasters increased. In the early 18th century a barge load of pig iron would probably last a charcoal forge for a month or more, and a year's supply could be delivered in a few weeks of favourable water. By the late 1790s several Black Country forges and foundries depended on regular week-by-week supplies of very large quantities of Shropshire iron. The frustrations caused by the inadequacies of the Severn Navigation are vividly illustrated in the correspondence of Boulton and Watt whose pig iron normally went by barge from the Severn Gorge to Stourport and thence by canal narrow boat to Soho. In February 1799 urgent requests were sent to three Shropshire ironmasters to despatch orders to Stourport as soon as the state of navigation should permit. A year later a similar batch of panic-stricken pleas went out. 'Particular inconvenience is caused to us by delays in the supply of our iron' Gregory Watt complained to Bishton and Onions. 'We have been for some time anxiously expecting some melting pig from you', he wrote to the manager at the Barnetts Leasow works. Lack of water in the river caused further delays in the supply of pig iron to Soho in August 1800. In the summer of 1803 when the water level was 'lower than ever remembered by the oldest and most experienced waterman now living', Boulton and Watt engaged a waggoner Thomas Radwell of Ettingshall, to collect Shropshire iron from the *Horns Inn*, Boningale on the county boundary on the Shifnal–Wolverhampton road, to which it was delivered by teams from the ironworks. Radwell took it to Wolverhampton wharf for transfer to a narrow boat which conveyed it to Soho. The following September Boulton and Watt told the Old Park Company, 'if there is any chance of getting down the Severn, send it [i.e. 50 tons of iron] to Stourport, if not by any means you think expeditious'. By

October the Old Park Company had delivered 82 tons to Soho via Boningale. At this period iron from the Lilleshall partnership's furnaces was being delivered by road to the Heath Forge wharf near Kingswinford on the Staffordshire and Worcestershire Canal then by narrow boat, to Soho.[30] While these examples illustrate the unreliability of the Severn, they are also a testimony to the cheapness of river transport. Road carriage was employed only as a very last resort.

In such circumstances it is not surprising that the Staffordshire and Worcestershire Canal Company backed by most of the Shropshire ironmasters was anxious to improve the Severn, which had previously been cleared of obstacles only in the most informal and unorganised fashion. In June 1741 the Coalbrookdale partners contributed 5s. towards, 'clearing the Foards in the Severn'.[31] In 1784 the Staffordshire and Worcestershire Canal Company commissioned William Jessop to draw up plans for the removal of shallows and the building of locks and weirs between Diglis, Worcester, and the Meadow Wharf at Coalbrookdale. Jessop proposed 13 or 14 locks and building reservoirs to hold back floodwaters which would have given an all season passage for vessels drawing 4 ft. of water. His plans, in an engraved version by George Young, were included in a bill presented to Parliament in 1786, which was withdrawn after opposition from the promoters of a canal from Stourbridge to Worcester. The Staffordshire and Worcestershire company undertook some dredging downstream from Stourport, but was inhibited by legal action and by the direct interference of the boatmen. There was determined opposition from Shropshire barge owners to any proposal to impose tolls on the river, and Jessop was reduced to pleading the case for improvements in advertisements in the Shrewsbury newspapers. As late as 1859, Shropshire barge owners recalled how 'when George III was King, they shouted themselves hoarse and tossed their caps in honour of victory over attempts to improve the channel'. When locks were built on the Severn after 1842, they were confined to the section below Stourport.[32]

The Severn barge traffic was the only significant sector of the economy of the Shropshire coalfield which the ironmaking companies failed to control, although the Coalbrookdale Company did, for a short period, operate a fleet of its own. The ironmasters built their own waggonways, they controlled the local canals through their shareholdings and the roads through membership of turnpike trusts, but the barge traffic remained in the hands of the small owners of Jackfield and Madeley Wood, who remained resolutely opposed to the improvement of the river.

The only effective change in the Severn Navigation in Shropshire was the construction of horse towing paths which enabled the replacement of the bow haulers by horses. A plan for a towpath was first discussed in 1761 in Worcestershire, and in 1772 an Act was obtained authorising the building of a path between Bewdley and Coalbrookdale. The idea of a towpath was opposed by those who upheld the concept of a free and open navigation, and for many years the project lay dormant. In 1796 William Reynolds began construction of a towpath through the Ironbridge Gorge at his own expense. Two years later the powers granted under the 1772 Act were renewed and by September 1800 the towpath was completed from Bewdley to Coalbrookdale. A newspaper commented, 'the vessels are now drawn by horses, so that the degrading employment of hauling by men will be done away, and we hope these stout fellows, who have heretofore done the work of brutes, will find a more honourable employment'. Subsequently the path was extended to Diglis in 1804, and to Gloucester soon after 1811. In 1809 an Act authorised a path from the Meadow Wharf, Coalbrookdale to Mardol and Frankwell Quays at Shrewsbury, which was completed by 1 December of that year.[33]

Many cargoes other than coal and iron were carried on the Severn. In the 1730s goods delivered from Bristol to Richard Ford at Coalbrookdale included wine, gunpowder, corks, Hot Wells water and anchovies. The most important of these supplies was timber. In 1742 wood for the Coalbrookdale pumping-engine was floated down the river, and in 1770 five large pieces of oak to make the beam for a new engine at Horsehay were conveyed to Coalbrookdale from Apley by a trow returning from Bristol. In 1767 large quantities of oak and ash rails and sleepers were delivered-by barge to Coalbrookdale, and, in January 1770, 27$^1/_2$ waggon loads of timber arrived off the river for the construction of a railway bridge. In 1792 the Madeley Field coalworks were bringing pit props from Pool Quay along the Severn. As late as 1772 timber was still being despatched in rafts down the river, for a man was drowned at Atcham during that year after falling off one such 'float'.[34] Throughout the 18th century hay and straw were brought down the Severn for the ironworks, and charcoal for slicking moulds and for forges also came from the upper reaches of the river. Bricks and clay from Stourbridge were being carried from Bewdley as early as 1731, and in the mid-1790s Stourbridge clay was being carried up river for the Horsehay Potteries.[35] Hearth stones for blast furnaces came from Highley throughout the 18th century, as did grindstones from Gloucester.[36]

The growth of the iron trade in the mid-1750s stimulated the carrying of a range of new cargoes. In 1756–57 alabaster, limestone, steel, gunpowder and tar were carried from Bristol to Coalbrookdale for the Horsehay works. In 1759–62 nine loads of Cumberland iron ore from John Gale of Whitehaven were carried up the Severn for use at Horsehay. The loads varied between 14 and 26 tons, and were transhipped from sea going vessels at Broad Oak and Chepstow. The Horsehay Potteries were receiving lead by river in 1798. Considerable quantities of food were carried upstream from Bristol which rarely figure in industrial records, but the Coalbrookdale accounts refer to the arrival of rice at a time of shortage in 1800 and to the back freight of fish from Bristol in 1807. Fish delivered by boats returning from the January fair at Bristol, was a traditional Lenten dish in Shropshire and Montgomeryshire.[37]

The Shropshire ironmasters were not always able to make use of the raw materials nearest their works, and those on the north side of the Severn often had to seek supplies south of the river, over which there was no bridge between Buildwas and Bridgnorth until 1780. There was an intense traffic to and fro across the river in the Gorge and from wharf to wharf on the same bank. In 1719 and for some years afterwards hay for the Coalbrookdale ironworks arrived at Ludcroft wharf from Shrewsbury and was ferried about 500 yards upstream to the partnership's own wharf at the Meadow. In the 1720s and '30s ore for the Coalbrookdale furnaces came from Ladywood in Broseley parish and had to be ferried over to Ludcroft wharf on the north bank. In February 1739–40 the need for Broseley iron ore was so great that the Coalbrookdale partners paid 3s. for ice on the river to be broken to enable it to be ferried across. Limestone was also conveyed from the south bank for the Coalbrookdale furnaces, and in the 1750s Horsehay limestone came from the same sources. In 1756 Eustace Beard was ferrying limestone across the Severn from Benthall Edge and also fetched 14,000 firebricks from Broseley for the building of Horsehay No. 2 blast furnace. Such tasks may have provided work for the trows, which normally went to Bristol, when they were awaiting jobs. In 1773–74 John Wilkinson was using Horsehay iron at Willey which was ferried over the Severn from the north bank to the south, either to the wharf at the end of the Benthall rails or to Willey wharf at the end of the Tarbatch Dingle railway three miles downstream. In the first decade of the 19th century boats conveyed lime-stone between wharves at the end of railways near Buildwas Bridge, and wharves and furnaces in the Gorge. In the period June–September 1801 a barge on this work made 21 voyages and a 'boat' 14.[38]

The cost of bringing goods up the Severn was much higher than that for downstream traffic. In 1756 George Perry estimated that the normal freight for goods from Shrews-bury to Bristol was 10s. and the return rate 15s. In 1732 rates for castings from Coalbrookdale were 5s. to Bewdley, Gloucester and Shrewsbury and 7s. 6d. to Bristol. In 1757 pig went to Bewdley and Powick for 3s. to Shrewsbury for 5s., to Chepstow for 7s. 6d., to Bristol for 8s., and to Monmouth for 10s. In 1798 the rate were for pig iron to Wren's Nest 2s. 6d., to Stourport 4s. 6d. for pig iron and 6s. for castings, to Worcester 7s. for pig and 9s. for castings, to Powick 7s. for pig, to Chepstow and Brimscombe 10s. and to Bristol 12s. Return freights from Gloucester at this time were 15s. and by 1805 the rate from Bristol was 22s. Rates were always quoted per ton. Extra charges were imposed by barge owners when water was particularly low. Such charges normally amounted to 12–15 per cent of the usual rate.[39]

The timing of journeys on the Severn naturally varied considerably. A downstream voyage to Gloucester was reckoned to take 11 to 24 hours. A fortnight was considered a good time for a return trip to Bristol by 1850.[40]

The outstanding innovation in the Severn Navigation in the 18th century was the introduction of iron boats on to the river by John Wilkinson. The first iron boat, the *Trial* was constructed by John Jones, a blacksmith at the Willey ironworks, and was launched on 6 July 1787. It was similar to canal narrow boats of the period, 70 ft. long, with a beam of 6 ft. 8$^{1}/_{2}$ in. It was constructed of $^{5}/_{16}$ wrought-iron plates bolted together in the same way as a contemporary copper, or steam-engine boiler. There were wooden stern posts and the gunwhale was lined with elm planks. The total weight was eight tons, and the vessel drew 8 to 9 in. of water when light; and could carry 32 tons in deep water. The *Trial* could operate both on the Severn and on narrow canals and her first voyage was to Birmingham, where she arrived before the end of July 1787 with a cargo of 22 tons 15 cwt. of iron. In September 1787 Wilkinson launched a second vessel designed for use on the Birmingham Canal, and the following month completed a third, a 40-ton barge, for the Severn. A Swedish visitor in 1802 observed several wrought-iron narrow boats at Wilkinson's Bradley works which were superior in many ways to wooden vessels but cost three or four times as much. He learned that Wilkinson's wrought-iron barge on the Severn was unsuccessful but could not find out why. In spite of Wilkinson's pioneering work the typical Severn barge remained a wooden vessel, although several experimental iron boats were made in Shropshire in the 19th century.[41]

A wooden railway between the River Severn at the Calcutts and a pit in Birch Leasows, Broseley, was the subject of a dispute between James Clifford and his tenants in 1605. The existence of a railway at such an early date evidences the advanced technology of the Shropshire coal industry at the time, for this was one of the first railways of which records survive in Great Britain. Several other lines were built in the district in the 17th century, all having, as far as can be ascertained, wooden rails, with wooden-flanged wheels on the vehicles which used them. Dr. M. J. T. Lewis has shown that a type of railway was developed in Shropshire in the 17th century which was quite distinct from that in Northumberland and Durham. Gauges of Shropshire railways were no more than 3 ft. 9 in., which was about the narrowest to be found in the North East. While railways on Tyneside and Wearside employed large chaldron waggons, the vehicles on Shropshire lines were low-sided wagons of much smaller size. The Shropshire type of railway spread to Wales, Scotland and Lancashire. Like the longwall method of mining coal, it was an innovation of major importance which influenced the growth of mining throughout Britain.[42]

By 1700 several railways linked coal mines both north and south of the Severn with wharves on the river bank. In 1692 the lessees of mines north of the Much Wenlock–Shifnal road in Madeley parish agreed to spend £200 on a 1,500 yard wooden railway to the Severn. This was probably the line which in 1741 linked the Lane and Paddock pits in Madeley with the river at Ludcroft Wharf. In 1728 a line known as the Jackfield rails ran down the Calcutts valley from Broseley to the Severn on an alignment which must have been close to James Clifford's line of 1605. In the same year Richard Hartshorne built a line from Little Wenlock to the riverside at Strethill, 'for the advantage of carrying of sand, coles, mines and minerals'. Hartshorne had authority 'to lay rails and make a wharf for the carrying and landing of coals, wood and other things to and from the Severn and also to convert into charcoal such coles'.[43]

By the middle of the 18th century railways were also taking traffic to wharves on the Shrewsbury–London turnpike road. In 1738 lines linked the road near the Old Hall, Wellington, with limestone workings and coal mines on the lands of the Forester family at Steeraway. In the middle of the next decade a railway was built on the Charlton estate in Oakengates from mines in the Horsepasture to a wharf on the turnpike road.[44]

Iron-flanged wheels were cast for the first time at Coalbrookdale in 1729 when 18 were supplied for Richard Hartshorne, perhaps for his new railway from Strethill to Little Wenlock. The same year other iron wheels were supplied to other local colliers. The most regular customer for railway wheels in the 1730s was J. U. Smitheman, Lord of the Manor of Madeley and landlord of the Coalbrookdale works, who was supplied with over 200 between 1732 and 1738. William Ferriday received 36 in the same period. Most of the wheels cast in this period weighed about 30 lbs. but a few were as heavy as 85 lbs. In 1741 iron wheels and axles were employed on the waggons used on the line from the Lane Pits to Ludcroft Wharf.[45]

The first recorded use of rail transport by ironmasters, as distinct from coalmasters, in Shropshire occurred in 1747 when the Coalbrookdale partners paid a workman for the supply of rails, perhaps at Benthall Quay. In 1748 they constructed a small line known as the Lakehead Footrid near the Severn, which probably did no more than bring coal from an adit.[46] In 1749 the partners began the construction of a line about two miles long from the Forester mines at Coalmoor in Little Wenlock parish to the blast furnaces at Coalbrookdale and the wharves on the Severn.[47]

The growth of the Coalbrookdale partners' ironworks in the 1750s was to a great extent dependent on railways. Large sums were spent in the spring of 1755 building lines to the Horsehay blast furnace. The entry in Abiah Darby's Journal for 31 January 1756, 'First Waggon of Pigs came down the Railway' probably refers to the opening of a new direct line from Horsehay to Coalbrookdale. In 1757 the railway network was extended as far as the Ketley furnaces. Three years later iron ore from Donnington Wood destined for Horsehay was being conveyed as far as 'the rails at Ketley' by packhorse or cart and thence by rail, but by 1788 there was a direct line from Ketley all the way to Donnington Wood.[48]

Some at least of the Coalbrookdale Company railways differed in several respects from the typical Shropshire railway. The waggons were larger, resembling more closely the Newcastle chaldrons than the low-sided vehicles favoured in Shropshire. They were 10 ft. long and 4 ft. wide, running on cast-iron wheels with an average weight of 3 cwt. They could carry over two-and-a-half tons, and were normally drawn by three horses.[49]

In 1757–59 the New Willey Company constructed a line from their furnace by way of Swinbatch and Tarbatch Dingle to the Severn. They enjoyed an alternative route to the river by way of the Benthall rails. Other lines linked the Willey furnaces with the mines from which they were supplied with raw materials. Three different lines radiated from the Madeley Wood ironworks to coal and iron ore pits.[50]

The wooden rails used on mid-18th century railways in Shropshire were of various sizes. John Randall, who drew on information from people who remembered wooden railways in operation, said that the railways in Coalbrookdale were laid with, 'rails of plain oblong pieces of wood, 6 ft. × 8 in. × 4 in. in depth'. On other lines Randall knew of rails with a $3^1/_2$ by $4^1/_2$ in. section. A batch of rails from Lawley Coppice for the Horsehay-Coalbrookdale line in 1768 came in two sizes, $3^1/_2$ by $4^1/_2$ in. and 3 by 4 in. Both ash and oak rails were supplied for the lines running to the Horsehay ironworks in the 1760s[51]

By the 1760s, the Coalbrookdale partners were using two section 'double way' rails, the lower sections 9 in. square and those on which the waggons actually ran 4 in. square. In 1767, at the instigation of Richard Reynolds, iron rails were introduced as the top sections of these rails. They measured 6 ft. by $3^1/_4$ in by $1^1/_4$ in. In order to prepare a suitable foundation for them, large parts of the existing wooden railways of the Coalbrookdale partnership were rebuilt with wider wooden rails on which the iron plates could be placed. It is generally accepted that the rails introduced at Coalbrookdale in 1767 were the first iron rails. They were introduced as an act of deliberate policy and not as a means of storing cast iron during a period of glut.[52] By the early 1770s rails were being cast in large numbers at Ketley and at Horsehay where a total of over 17,000 were produced between October 1768 and the end of the first quarter of 1774. Arthur Young in 1776 and Lord Torrington in 1782 both noted the presence of iron rails in the district, and in 1785 Richard Reynolds claimed that he and his partners had more than 20 miles of iron railway.[53] Iron rails on wooden under-rails were also used on lines in the Caughley area where John Randall was able to examine 'flat pieces of iron pegged down with square wooden pegs to long pieces of timber, sawn and squared, and so arranged that the flanged wheels of the ginney carriages could run on the inner side'.[54]

Some of the civil engineering of the Shropshire railways of the mid-18th century was quite ambitious. A bridge on the Park railway, which led to the Horsehay ironworks was built in 1769, using $27^1/_2$ loads of timber, and over a dozen workmen took several months to build it. A fine two-arched masonry bridge, probably built soon after 1759 still survives at New Dale. Several railway embankments which remain suggest that the major lines of the mid-18th century were built with considerable forethought and skill. Inclined planes were a notable feature of the Shropshire railways. The line from Coalmoor to Coalbrookdale approached the latter by an incline on which the waggons were let down 112 yards. In 1776 Arthur Young noted that the waggonways descending to Coalbrookdale from the Lincoln Hill limeworks were 'so contrived that the loaded waggon winds up the empty one on a different road'. A writer in 1801 described the typical inclined plane of the district as, 'a simple piece of machinery at the top, compos'd of a barrel & friction wheel, & the road laid with iron rails; two ropes being fasten'd to the barrel, & connected to the waggons at top & bottom; the superior weight of the load at the top descending, brings up the inferior from the bottom, working up & down 2 sets of Iron rails alternately'.[55]

Figure 8.   Plateway track and truck.   *Ironbridge Gorge Museum.*

In the mid-1790s the angled L-section iron rail was introduced to the Shropshire railways, probably by John Curr its inventor, who gave advice on the Brierly Hill terminus of the Shropshire Canal in 1793, although similar rails had been used on the Ketley canal inclined plane five years earlier. Charles Hatchett in 1796 notes that Curr's rails were used in the Coalbrookdale area.[56] The Curr-type railways in Shropshire seem generally to have been called Ginney, Jinney or Jenny rails. The Coalbrookdale Company records show considerable evidence of a change to the new type of railway in the late 1790s. Jenny carriages were in use around the Horsehay furnaces in January 1797, and a month later Jenny rails were being extended thence to the coke hearths. In June 1797 pennystone ore from pits at New Works was being 'jennyed' to Horsehay. In 1798 Jenny rails were being laid to the Horsehay clay pit. In the following year it was forecast that the introduction of Jinney Carriages on the railways to Coalbrookdale would halve the cost of transporting coal and ore to the furnaces. A new 'Curr railroad' was laid from the Donnington Wood Canal to the Lilleshall limekilns in 1795.[57]

Thomas Telford in 1800 noted the rapid spread since 1797 of 'roads with iron rails laid upon them, upon which the articles are conveyed in waggons containing from 6 to 30 cwt'. 'On a railway well constructed and laid with a declivity of 55 ft. in a mile', he claimed, 'one horse will readily take down waggons containing from 12 to 15 tons and bring back the same waggons with four tons in them'.[58] The introduction of plateways did not alter the character of the waggons used on most of the Shropshire railways which had always been rather small, but it did lead to the disappearance of the larger type of Coalbrookdale waggons. Curr-type rails were laid in most parts of Britain on stone blocks but on almost every line in east Shropshire there were cast-iron sleepers. One line in Donnington Wood, the Yard Rails did have stone blocks similar to those used in other parts of Britain. The plateways of east Shropshire were bewilderingly varied. At least six different gauges were used, and some companies employed more than one gauge on their own lines. Two German engineers who visited Coalbrookdale found that the line leading from the ironworks to the Severn was of mixed gauge, 20 in and 36 in.[59] A portion of this dual-gauge plateway still survives at Rose Cottages, Coalbrookdale. Some lines in the district were as narrow as 18 in. Shropshire plate rails came in many lengths between 4 ft. and 15 ft., both in wrought and cast iron. The space between the rails was normally filled in to provide a path on which a horse might walk. Usually this was done with bricks laid on edge, but sometimes with slag or ashes.

Plateways were apparently much cheaper than railways using edge rails. The rapid construction of lines of this sort doubtless owed much to the boom conditions in the Shropshire iron trade during the wars with France. The building of plateways was entirely unco-ordinated, and the variety of gauges must have led to daunting difficulties when the industry settled to a more sober pace of expansion. By 1800 many of the railways of east Shropshire were being adapted to a new role dictated by the building of canals.

When Earl Gower formed his partnership with John and Thomas Gilbert for the development of the Lilleshall estate in 1764, among the powers he granted was that to make 'railways navigable cuts and sluices'. Gower was brother-in-law to the canal-building Duke of Bridgewater, and John Gilbert was agent on Bridgewater's Worsley estate. Thomas Gilbert first brought his brother and Bridgewater into contact with James Brindley, who built for the Duke the Barton aqueduct to carry his canal over the Irwell, advised on the continuation of the Bridgewater canal from Manchester to Liverpool, and became the most celebrated of the first generation of British canal engineers. With such contacts it is not surprising that Earl Gower and Co. began to build a canal at Lilleshall.[60] By February 1765 30 men were employed on the construction, 'upon the same principles as the duke of Bridgewaters', of a waterway from Donnington Wood to Pave Lane on the Newport-Wolverhampton road, where a land-sale wharf for coal was subsequently set up. To take coal to the limekilns at Lilleshall a change of level was needed which was achieved by a junction at Hugh's Bridge where a tunnel took a low level canal from the limeworkings into the side of the ridge on which ran the main line. Two shafts 42 ft. 8 in. deep were sunk linking the tunnel with the bank of the main line, and goods in containers were hoisted up and down by a winch, a system very similar to that employed at the Duke of Bridgewater's Castlefields terminus in Manchester. The Lilleshall branch descended 35 ft. by means of seven small locks below the mouth of the Hugh's Bridge tunnel, and there were five branches at its extremity serving various quarries and mines. At the opposite end of the canal in Donnington Wood underground navigable levels connecting with the main line were carried right up the coal faces. Again this closely followed the example of the Bridgewater canal which ran into the mines at Worsley. Both the Pave Lane and Lilleshall lines were completed by the autumn of 1767.

The canal was best known as the Donnington Wood Canal, but after Earl Gower was created Marquess of Stafford in 1786 it was sometimes referred to as the Marquess of Stafford's Canal, and when the second Marquess became Duke of Sutherland in 1833 it acquired a third name. The vessels employed on the canal were tub boats about 20 ft. long and 6 ft. 4 in. broad which set a pattern which later canals in the district were to follow. By 1798 109 vessels of three types were working on the canal, 70 eight ton boats worth £22 each, 20 five ton boats worth £14 each, and 19 'large boats' valued at £40 apiece.[61]

Two decades passed between the building of the Donnington Wood Canal and the construction of the next canals in east Shropshire. In 1786–88 William Reynolds was responsible for three short private waterways. In 1786 his miners began to cut an underground canal from a point on the north bank of the Severn in Madeley towards

Figure 9.   A Shropshire tub boat.

Ironbridge Gorge Museum.

the shafts of mines in the Blists Hill area. After driving the tunnel for 300 yards the miners struck a spring of natural bitumen, which was diverted into a stream, processed at the entrance to the tunnel, and sold either as British Oil for medicinal purposes, or as pitch. The tunnel's original transport function was fulfilled by a plateway constructed in 1796 alongside the culvert which drained water from the mines. At the opposite end of the coalfield Reynolds built a canal one and three quarter miles long linking the blast furnaces at Donnington Wood with mine workings near Wombridge church. At the top of a hill at the Wombridge end was a curious tunnel whose purpose is difficult to determine. At the opposite end a junction was made with the existing Donnington Wood Canal.[62]

In 1787 work also began on a canal about one and a half miles long linking the Ketley ironworks with mines in Oakengates. The canal passed through a short tunnel, but its most important engineering feature was the inclined plane by which William Reynolds carried boats 73 ft. down into the valley where the ironworks stood. The workings of the inclined plane doubtless owed much to contemporary railway inclines. There were two parallel sets of rails, and the descending load of superior weight drew up the ascending inferior load, the two being linked by ropes and pulleys to a common winding-drum to which a brake wheel was attached. A pair of parallel locks was built at the top with lock gates at the incline ends and chain operated vertical sluice boards at the other. A cradle would await the downward boat in one of the locks. When the boat was attached to the cradle the water was drained from the lock into a reservoir through culverts. The lock gate would be opened and the cradle with the boat upon it would descend. When the upward-bound cradle and boat had been safely hauled into the other lock by the action of the descending load, the gates would be closed and a small steam engine pumped back the water from the reservoir which had previously been drained from the first lock. The ropes or chains attaching the boats to the cradle would be undone and the boat floated away. The Ketley inclined plane was the first to be successfully employed on a canal in Great Britain. It proved possible by 1802–03 to make 24 hauls in an hour. That it was entirely self-acting limited its capacity for upward haulage. Telford reckoned that the loaded boat going down could bring up 'another boat containing a load nearly equal to one third part of what which passed down'. Loaded boats certainly were carried up the Ketley incline, for the accounts of the Horsehay ironworks in the 1790s show iron from Ketley arriving by canal.[63]

On 18 January 1788 a meeting was held at the *Tontine Hotel*, Ironbridge, to consider a more ambitious project, a canal to carry coal, iron and lime from the vicinity of

Oakengates to the Severn. The new line had been surveyed by William Reynolds during 1787. An Act of Parliament was obtained, and the first formal meeting of shareholders took place on 12 June 1788.[64]

The Shropshire Canal Company, as the new venture was called had a nominal capital of £50,000. Its shareholders included most of the ironmasters and principal landowners in the coalfield, but the Coalbrookdale partners were particularly prominent. The two largest shares, each of £6,000 were taken by Richard Reynolds and Joseph Rathbone, with £4,100 being taken by other members of the partnership. The Lilleshall partners, the Marquess of Stafford and Thomas Gilbert, took £2,000 and £1,000 respectively. John Wilkinson took the third largest individual share, £5,500, while his relative by marriage, Elizabeth Clayton, who owned land on the route of the Canal at Dark Lane, took another £1,000. Other substantial shareholders included the Earl of Shrewsbury and Lord Berwick, two of the joint lords of the manor of Wrockwardine Wood, Sir William Jerningham, Isaac Hawkins Browne, and William Parton of Madeley Court.[65]

The northern end of the Shropshire Canal was at Donnington Wood, where it joined the two existing canals, and almost immediately rose 120 ft. by an inclined plane to a summit level which began on the rough open land of Cockshutt Piece. It then passed through Oakengates where there was a junction with the Ketley Canal, beneath the turnpike roads from Shrewsbury to Ivetsey Bank and Shifnal, and went through two short tunnels. It then approached the Hollinswood ironworks before crossing an area hitherto little affected by industrial growth around Dark Lane, Stirchley and Hinkshay. After passing through a tunnel at Southall Bank on the border of Dawley and Madeley parishes the canal divided into two branches. The western branch was planned to cross the Wellington-New Inns turnpike road on a stone aqueduct, to pass through Little Dawley, to approach the Horsehay ironworks, and after skirting the Lightmoor works to descend to a level near the New Pool at Coalbrookdale, and then to continue along the ridge of Lincoln Hill to the Rotunda from which it was to plunge to a short section parellel with the Severn at Styches Weir where the stream flowing through Coalbrookdale joined the river. The eastern branch was to descend 126 ft. at Windmill Farm almost immediately after the junction, and then to pass through Maddeley, along the side of the valley of the Hay Brook, and to descend 207 ft. down the slope of the Severn Gorge near the Hay Farm, to a low level section parallel with the river, through the Watt and Sheepwash meadows, as far as the border of the parishes of Madeley and Sutton Maddock. The plans for the canal envisaged five inclined planes, at Wrockwardine Wood at its northern extremity, at Windmill Farm and Hay Farm on the eastern branch, and above the New Pool and below the Rotunda on the western line. There were to be three short branches to serve collieries or ironworks, one to Horsehay, and two which ran westwards from the main line between Southall Bank and Dark Lane towards mines in Dawley.[66]

The high, broken land of the coalfield was not the most favourable terrain for a canal. On the summit section water was difficult to obtain and in the vicinity of old mine workings still more difficult to keep. The wastage of water caused by locking was impossible to contemplate, and the proprietors doubtless intended from the first to utilise inclined planes, like that built by William Reynolds at Ketley, although there were many hesitations before the final form of the inclines was settled.

Thomas Telford thought that the Shropshire Canal showed that artificial waterways could be built across any sort of terrain. 'This canal', he wrote, 'carried over high and

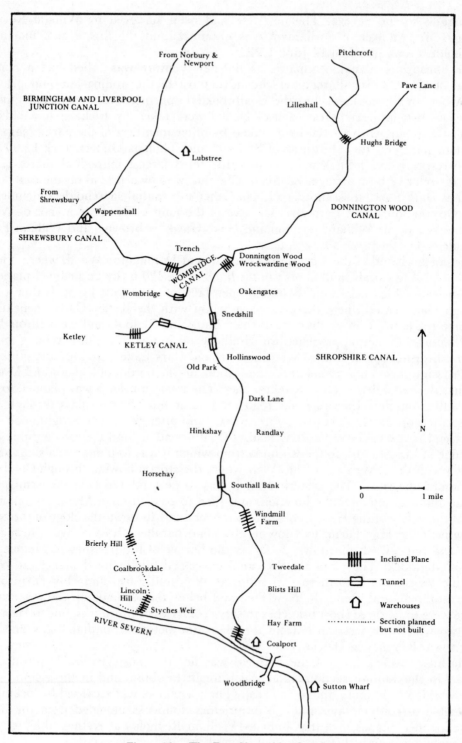

Figure 10.   The East Shropshire Canals.

rugged ground, along banks of slipping loam, over old coal mines and over where coal mines and iron stone are now actually worked under it, is a satisfactory proof that there is scarcely any ground so difficult, but where, with proper exertions and care, a convenient water conveyance may always be obtained'.[67]

It seems doubtful whether the Ketley inclined plane was entirely successful for the proprietors decided at their second meeting in June 1788 to hold a competition for persons who could discover and inform them of 'the best means of raising and lowering heavy weights from one navigation to another'. Even the competition was not regarded with confidence for a month later Matthew Boulton and James Watt were asked for their advice on how to achieve changes of level. The prize in the competition was awarded in October 1788 to a plan devised by Henry Williams and John Lowdon. Lowdon was already surveyor to the company, although he resigned before the end of 1789. Henry Williams was an engine erector for the Coalbrookdale partners. He was soon employed by the canal company, in 1794 became superintendent surveyor, and was to enjoy a distinguished career in local industry. Although the proprietors gave their prize to Williams and Lowdon it was some time before their plan was finally adopted. In May 1789 William Reynolds pressed James Watt for advice 'as we have the Shropshire Canal now navigable nearly to Donnington Wood where there is 120 ft. perpendicular fall, and something must be fixed upon very soon'.[68]

The scheme put forward by Williams and Lowdon was a modification of the inclined plane at Ketley. Instead of building locks on the main slope of the incline they recommended reverse slopes at the top, running into two parallel docks. The water in the main canal remained permanently in the docks, coming up to the sills where the main and reverse slopes met. The rails on which the cradles ran continued down the reverse slopes into the docks, and in order to maintain the cradles in a horizontal position they were fitted with overlapping wheels at the upper ends which ran on ledges on the sides of the docks, lifting the ordinary wheels at those ends off the rails. Boats and cradles were drawn out of the dock by a small winding-drum mounted above the top of the main slope, which was operated by a steam engine. If the ascending load was sufficiently light, the cradle and boat would descend by their own momentum, attached by pulleys and ropes to a main winding-drum set behind the small one, and drawing up the boat and cradle on the parallel track. If the ascending load was too heavy to be drawn by the descending boat, the steam engine could be employed to turn the main winding drum. When the ascending boat reached the top of the main slope the steam engine was employed to raise it over the sill into the docks. The running of cradles and boats up and down the main slope was controlled by a brake wheel on the main winding-drum.

The Lowdon and Williams inclined plane was a basically simple device well within the capacity of the technology of the time. It was employed on the three inclined planes built on the Shropshire Canal, on an incline which in 1796 replaced the tunnels and shafts at Hugh's Bridge on the Donnington Wood Canal, and later at Trench on the Shrewsbury Canal. The Hay incline remained in use for just over a century and that at Trench for over 120 years. In 1800 chains replaced the ropes at Windmill Farm and the Hay. The first rails were plate rails, replaced in the 19th century by conventional main line railway track. An inclined plane could be operated by only four men, and could pass a pair of boats in three and a half minutes.[69]

The summit level of the Shropshire canal was filled from reservoirs in the Stirchley–Randlay area which drew their water from streams and mine workings whence it was

pumped by steam engines. Some water was obtained from the lower canal at Donnington Wood from which it was pumped by steam engines to the higher level. The
section between the Windmill and Hay inclines drew water from the Mad brook via
a culvert near to the *Cuckoo Oak* inn. The lower section below the Hay incline was fed
by a stream in Sheepwash Meadow.[70]

Construction of the canal began in the autumn of 1788 with the section from
Donnington to Hollinswood, which was followed by that from Hollinswood to Southall
Bank. In December 1788 it was decided that the third portion should be from Southall
Bank to 'the top of the Hill above the New Engine at Coalbrookdale', although the
contract for this section was not awarded until November 1789. In February 1790
William Reynolds proposed to open a direct link between the canal and the Coalbrookdale works by sinking shafts from the canal side at the end of the third section to
tunnels driven into the side of the hill 120 ft. below. It seems that soon afterwards the
proprietors decided to make this point the terminus of the western branch, although
the decision is not recorded in the minutes. The line along Lincoln Hill and down to
the Severn at Styches Weir was abandoned. It would have involved the building of
two inclined planes with a total fall of over 330 ft. The final descent to the Severn off
the abrupt limestone cliff of Lincoln Hill would have been spectacular indeed. Powers
to build three collateral cuts were likewise given up. That to Horsehay was replaced
by a railway from the ironworks to 'Horsehay wharf'.[71]

The eastern branch below the Windmill incline was being built by May 1789 and
a year later was complete as far as the Broad Meadow in Madeley. Work on the section
to the Hay incline went on rapidly during the summer of 1790, and in July the short
section below the incline through Watt and Sheepwash Meadows was begun.[72]

In October 1790 traffic was being carried on the canal for short distances although
the Hay and Windmill inclines and the Southall Bank tunnel were not completed. A
year later men and horses were being used to drag boats up the still uncompleted
inclines. The canal probably became fully operational in 1793, for it was not until
December 1792 that the building of the steam engine at the Hay incline was finally
authorised. The tardy completion of the engines was due to disputes with canal users
over the rates to be charged on the inclines.[73]

The canal company's decision not to complete the western branch to the Severn was
taken by October 1792 when the proprietors inclined to purchase from the Coalbrookdale partners the tunnels and shafts at Brierly Hill, but to allow the latter to charge
tolls of 3d. per ton for goods let down the shafts, and 2d. for goods conveyed from the
bottoms to the Severn.[74]

At the Brierly Hill terminus the canal separated into four arms enclosing three small
islands or peninsulas. On the central island stood a large winding-drum, and on the
outer ones began the shafts, 10 ft. in diameter, which descended to the tunnels 120 ft.
below. Above the shafts were headstocks similar to those used in coal mines. Most of
the goods conveyed on the western branch travelled in iron containers about 5 ft.
square. At first, when a boat came alongside one of the pit tops, a container would be
lifted from it by a crane, attached to the rope suspended from the headstock, and when
a signal was given from the bottom of the other shaft that an ascending load was ready,
the container would be released, and as it descended would lift the load in the parallel
pit. Its movement was controlled by a brake wheel on the winding-drum. The process
was entirely self-acting. At the pit bottoms the containers were loaded on to horse-
drawn railway waggons.[75]

The tunnels and shafts were in operation by July 1791. Accounts kept by the Coalbrookdale Company date from 24 Janauary 1793. The company used the terminus for sending cast-iron rails to Ketley, and sent up the shafts such cast-iron goods as anvils and grates. The Ketley Company sent down pig iron for loading on to Severn barges, wrought-iron bars for re-rolling at the Coalbrookdale forges, and supplies for the Lincoln Hill limeworks. The Old Park Company sent coal, pig iron and wrought-iron half blooms to the Severn wharves.[76]

In March 1793 the upward traffic in castings came to a halt and early in May the downward traffic also ceased. It seems likely that the system suffered a serious break-down, for during that month the Coalbrookdale Company asked John Curr of Sheffield to give advice on the improvement of the terminus. Curr suggested the installation of cages in the shafts, in which rails would be laid to carry two trucks side by side. When containers arrived in boats at the terminus, they were to be lifted on to railway trucks which would then be pushed along rails into the cages. When the cages reached the tunnels at the bottom of the shafts the trucks with their containers would be pushed out into a siding where they waited until a train of six waggons was ready to be drawn out of the tunnels by a horse. Meanwhile the men at the shaft bottom were to push into the cage waggons and containers from another siding. Curr's letter suggests that work was already in progress to alter the system for he claimed that his suggestions would not necessitate 'one brick to move in the Tunnel or any other openings made'. It seems likely that Curr's alterations were carried into effect, for, apart from the provision of the cages, they necessitated only the re-siting of the cranes at the shaft tops and some changes in the layout of the railways in the tunnels. A drawing in the William Reynolds Sketch Book shows the system altered according to Curr's suggestions.[77]

The terminus re-commenced operations on 11 July 1793 and was heavily used. There was a substantial traffic in the downward direction of coal and iron from Old Park, Horsehay and Ketley. Upward traffic was surprisingly heavy and varied, including iron rails, two ropes for the Ketley inclined plane, timber from Richard Reynolds's timber yard, and, most surprisingly, some new tub boats. The problems of extricating the boats from beneath the headstocks must have been formidable. The most consider-able upward traffic was limestone from Lincoln Hill and Buildwas Rocks, consigned to Ketley and Wombridge. The downward coal traffic increased substantially from the beginning of September 1793, most of it coming from the Coalbrookdale Company's pits in Dawley and Lawley. In the fortnight ending 26 September nearly 700 tons of the company's coal went down the shafts. It is doubtful whether the terminus was working efficiently. The difficulties of ensuring that downward loads were sufficiently heavy to lift up such weighty commodities as cast iron rails must have been formidable. It seems that about the beginning of October a decision was taken to cease using the terminus for bulk traffic. This was probably not brought about by a sudden breakdown since there was a rush of coal and limestone traffic during the last few days of operation early in October. After 13 October the coal traffic ceased and only occasional and insignificant cargoes of limestone were carried. The shafts remained open for sundries, timber, gunpowder, lime bags, ropes, a little wrought iron from Ketley to Coalbrook-dale, for another year, but the number of consignments steadily dwindled. In December 1793 the Coalbrookdale partners formally decided to replace the tunnels and shafts with a railway incline down the cliff at Brierly Hill, and a railway from its foot along the ridge of Lincoln Hill, to descend to the Severn bank by another incline near the Lower Forge, a route similar to that originally proposed for the canal.[78]

By Mary 1794 57 waggons for the new railway had been completed and 45 were under construction. The railway probably came into use in September 1794 when the last consignment was carried through the shafts. The iron containers which had been used for traffic through the tunnels and shafts remained in use on the new railway. In 1796 the Coalbrookdale Company purchased more land at Brierly Hill, and in October 1800 they were permitted by the canal company to construct a railway along the towpath from Horsehay Wharf to Brierly Hill, linking with the line thence to the Severn, on condition that they paid a toll of 1d. a ton for goods carried along it. The railway was further extended along the towpath to Doseley Wharf, traffic from which paid a toll of $1^1/_4$d. per ton. The new railway was probably open by February 1802 when limestone was being drawn from Brierly Hill to Horsehay Wharf, and was certainly complete by the following May. The new line replaced the Horsehay–Coalbrookdale railway which had been opened in 1756. In November and December 1802 nearly 10 tons of old rails from Gighouse (or Jiggers) Bank, the inclined plane by which the original line ascended out of Coalbrookdale, were taken up and consigned to the Horsehay blast furnaces. The new line was heavily used; nearly 10,000 tons of goods being carried along it in its first three months of operation. In each of the next five years over 30,000 tons were carried, with a peak of 49,143 tons in 1806–07. The building of the railway along the towpath doubtless brought an end to traffic on the canal. When the canal company's land between Horsehay and Brierly Hill was leased in 1832 it was described as 'a slang . . . formerly used as a canal'. The new railway itself was comparatively short-lived, for it was replaced during the 1820s by a plateway running from Horsehay to Coalbrookdale through the Lightmoor valley.[79]

The western branch of the Shropshire Canal was named first of the two lines to the Severn in the Act of Parliament in which there was nothing to suggest any subsidiary status. Most of the wharves in the Severn Gorge in 1788 were at its western end, while the eastern end, as Telford remarked, was little more than a rugged uncultivated bank. Yet it was the eastern branch of the canal which developed into its main line, and the eastern branch which stimulated the growth of a new 'canal village' at Coalport.

Development at the eastern end of the Severn Gorge only began with the building of the Preens Eddy bridge on the site of the present Coalport Bridge in 1780. The proprietors received authority to construct wharves, warehouses, quays and cranes within 60 yards of the bridge, on both sides of the river upstream and downstream, facilities which they duly provided. In 1786 William Reynolds began the underground canal in the area which developed into the Tar Tunnel. In 1787–88 the riverside meadows upstream from the bridge company's wharf on the north bank were bought from Abraham Darby III by Richard Reynolds, who leased them to William Reynolds in 1793, acknowledging that he would be able to build houses, warehouses, wharves, quays, landing places, cranes, weight beams &c. This property included the Watt and Sheepwash Meadows, named in the Shropshire Canal Company Act as the terminus of the canal's eastern branch.[80]

The canal company let the contract for building the canal alongside the Severn below the Hay incline in July 1790. The construction of this section would have presented few difficulties, and by May 1792 the company agreed with William Reynolds to pile the canal banks so as to support wharves. In the same year Reynolds erected a large warehouse straddling the canal and reaching out over the Severn. The original plans for the canal provided for a pair of locks at the terminus of the eastern branch to allow boats to descend 22 ft. 10 in. into the Severn. The locks were constructed for the accounts of Reynolds's Madeley Field coalworks in September 1792 record the payment of £84 3s. 1d. to one Thomas Ford, 'on account of building ye Watt Meadow lock'. It is probable that the lock or locks were removed during subsequent alterations at the terminus, and no trace of them can now be seen.[81]

The new canal-river interchange in the Severnside meadows soon proved successful, and was being called 'Coalport' by the early months of 1794.[82] William Reynolds soon began to encourage new industries to settle around the site. In 1803 complaints were made to the canal proprietors about the 'many inconveniences arising from want of more room at the wharves at Coalport'. In 1810 the wharf was enlarged, several new unloading places provided, and a basin excavated which could accommodate 60 tub boats. Coal and other bulk materials were conveyed over the 20 or so yards of sloping ground between canal and river by seven self-acting, diamond-shaped, inclined railways, on which ran vehicles called 'trams'. Goods were shot into the holds of waiting Severn barges from drawbridge-like constructions extending over the river. On its river side the wharf was supported by a substantial stone wall, part of which was constructed on arches built on piles driven into the river bed, and topped with bricks set in cast-iron frames. Several cranes were installed along the river frontages. By about 1800, 50,000 tons of coal a year were being exported from Coalport, and the wharves were being used to import general cargoes for the traders of Newport, Shifnal and Wellington.[83]

William Reynolds rented, from the proprietors of the Preens Eddy bridge, the wharf on the north bank of the river and took over responsibility for the roads on either side of the bridge, as well as for the 'Coalport Road' which ran from the new settlement to Madeley and Ironbridge.[84]

When Reynolds died in 1803 the value of the wharves at Coalport was no more than £63 1s. 0d., although it must considerably have increased after the improvements carried out by his executors during the next seven years. In the year ending July 1806 receipts at the wharves totalled £764 16s. 3d. of which £233 3s. 4d. was profit. Both receipts and profits fell the following year but trade continued to grow and profits of £319 17s. 7d. were realised in 1808–09 and £378 18s. 2d. in 1809–10. Charles Lumley was employed by Reynolds and his executors as clerk at the wharves. By 1805 Lumley had formed a partnership with William Horton and George Pugh to control the export of coal from the port. Horton had acted closely with William Reynolds in the development of Coalport, and Pugh had previously acted as shipping agent for the Old Park Company, in later years becoming a partner in the Coalport China works.[85]

Most of the boats which sailed on the Shropshire Canal were owned and operated by the iron-making partnerships. A variety of cargoes was carried by water, often for remarkably short distances. Stourbridge clay delivered to Coalport by Severn barge was sent on to Horsehay by canal. Ground refractory clay from Horsehay was sent to Coalport for the china works. Sand from Wombridge, and wrought iron for re-rolling from Lightmoor and Ketley arrived at Horsehay by canal, while goods despatched included ground clay and bricks for the Donnington Wood glassworks, wrought iron for the Snedshill and Old Park ironworks and for the Lilleshall lime-workings, and pig and bar iron to Coalport for export by barge. The value of the canal for short distance traffic is shown by its use for carrying iron from Lightmoor to Horsehay, a journey of a little over a mile of which only half could be undertaken by canal.[86]

A despatch book kept by a charter master working pits at Wrockwardine Wood in 1801–02[87] throws some light on the operation of the Shropshire Canal. Almost all the cargoes he despatched were of Flint Coal, Lump Coal and slack, sent to Coalport for William Horton, probably in his capacity as a forwarding agent. The book begins on 27 August 1801 and in the four months afterwards most of the boats engaged in the traffic made between 14 and 20 return journeys to Coalport, which suggests that turn rounds within two days of reaching the lower canal, regarded as desirable in 1810, were not being achieved. In the period between August and December 1801 less than 60 boats were employed, but the number was gradually increasing during the period. On 16–17 September six new boats numbered 27 to 32 were brought into use, to be followed by nine more numbered 33 to 41 on 3 October. In the early part of January 1802 the canal was apparently frozen over and no boats were despatched. One of the blast furnaces at Horsehay was stopped for want of coals at this time.[88] The day navigation became possible again 21 boats were despatched and larger than usual numbers went out for the next 10 days. 13 boats in this period went to Lightmoor, the only ones recorded in the book to go anywhere other than Coalport. There was another stoppage, probably due to the freezing of the canal between 20 January and 22 February. The dislocation caused by the stoppages is reflected by the employment after the resumption of traffic of many vessels which were not normally used on the route.

Not long after the Shropshire Canal was opened disputes began between the company and the coalowners from the northern part of the coalfield led by John Bishton and Isaac Hawkins Browne, over the right of the company to levy additional tolls for the use of the inclined planes. In October 1794 the company threatened to remove the engines from the planes if the coal did not agree to pay the additional tolls, a threat which was renewed in 1796. In May of the following year the company staff were told to refuse use of the inclines to all canal users who would not consent to pay 2d. per ton for their use.[89]

One consequence of the dispute was the construction of a rival means of transporting coal between the northern part of the coalfield and the Severn. In October 1797 Thomas Botfield agreed with his landlord Isaac Hawkins Browne that he would carry 1,200 tons of coal a month from Malins Lee 'to some convenient wharf or quay adjoining to the River Severn, and to the Railway intended to be made by Messrs. John Bishton and Co. and the said Thomas Botfield, or to some intermediate wharf or bank between the said works and the River Severn upon the line of the intended railway'. Subject to three months' notice, Botfield could also send the coal by canal to Coalport or the Meadow Wharf, Coalbrookdale. The railway was built at about a tenth the cost of the canal, and conveyed goods more cheaply. It was working before the end of 1799, and ran from Sutton Wharf on the Severn below Coalport to Hollinswood, connecting from there with several iron and coalworks to the north. Its total length was about eight miles. Whether or not the Botfields had a share in building it, Bishton and Onions of Snedshill were certainly involved, and by 1812 it was the property of the Lilleshall Company. In June of that year the Shropshire Canal Company instructed Henry Williams to negotiate with the Lilleshall Company about the conveyance of their coal and iron to the Severn, and in April 1815 William Horton, by now acting for the Lilleshall Company, agreed that the railway would be closed on the payment to the company by the canal proprietors of £500.[90]

The tub boat canal system was extended from the coalfield to the county town by the building of the Shrewsbury Canal, authorised in 1793, and promoted by many of

14. The Hay Inclined Plane in the late 19th century (*Ironbridge Gorge Museum Trust*)

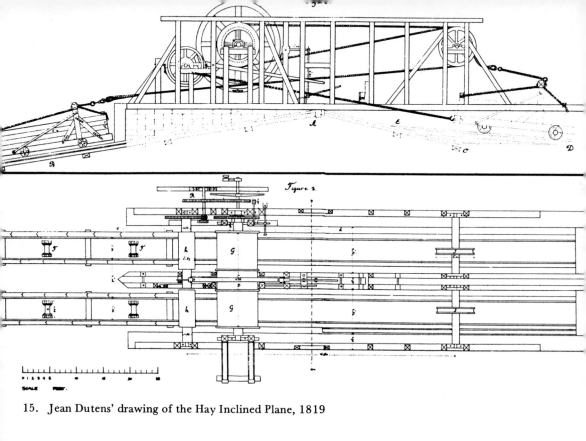

15. Jean Dutens' drawing of the Hay Inclined Plane, 1819

16. The restored Hay Inclined Plane (*Photo: Author*)

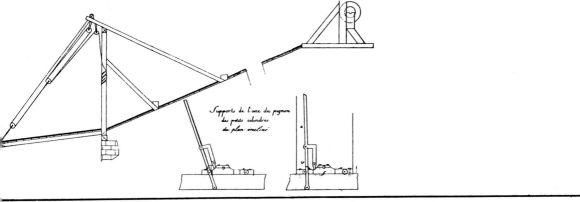

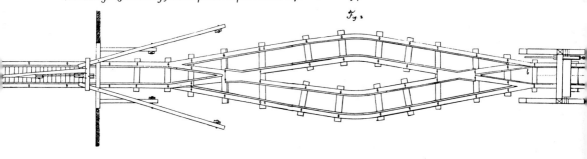

Chemin en fer ("Rail-Way") établi au port de Coalport à la suite du plan incliné de Hay pour la descente des charbons dans les bateaux de la Severn.

Fig. 2

17.   Jean Dutens' drawings of the inclined railways used to carry coal between canal and river at Coalport

18.   Coalport Bridge, showing the stone abutments of the Wood Bridge (*Photo: Brian Bracegirdle*)

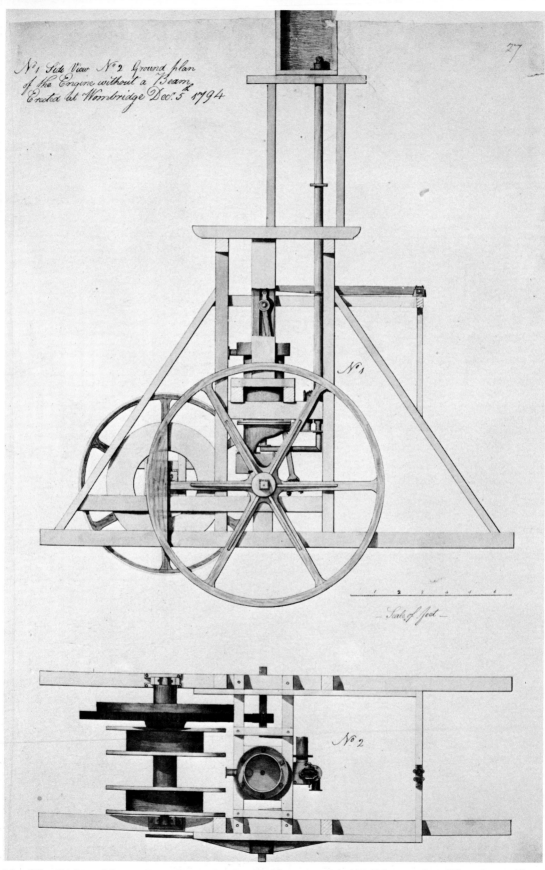

No. 1 Side View No. 2 Ground plan
of the Engine without a Beam
Erected at Wombridge Decr. 5th 1794

No. 1

Scale of feet

No. 2

19. 'The Engine without a Beam Erected at Wombridge Decr. 5th 1794' (*From the William Reynolds Sketch Book. Photo: Science Museum, London*)

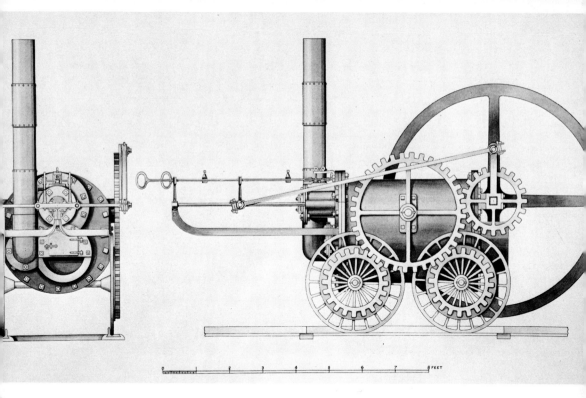

20. Richard Trevithick's Coalbrookdale Locomotive, c. 1803. Museum drawing based on an original contemporary sketch (*Crown Copyright, Science Museum, London*)

21. A Newcomen winding engine belonging to the Coalbrookdale Company, c. 1880 (*Ironbridge Gorge Museum Trust*)

22. The Iron Bridge, by W. Smith, 1810. Note the timber land arch erected *c*. 1800, and replaced with the present iron land arches in 1821 (*Ironbridge Gorge Museum Trust*)

23. Gazebo with ogee and circle ornamentation, in the grounds of No. 27 Broad Street, Ludlow, a house restored by Thomas Farnolls Pritchard, who used similar motifs on the Iron Bridge (*Photo: Author*)

24.   Coalport Masked Jug with the Iron Bridge (*Ironbridge Gorge Museum Trust*)

25. The regal image of John Wilkinson, on a trade token, *c.*1790 (*Ironbridge Gorge Museum Trust*)

the same people who had been responsible for the Shropshire. The new company took over 1 mile 188 yds. at the Donnington Wood end of the Reynolds's Wombridge canal, at the south end of which they built an inclined plane, which descended 75 ft. in the direction of the Wellington-Newport road at Trench. 11 locks, built to accommodate four tub boats at a time, continued the descent to Longdon, whence the canal remained on the same level until it reached Shrewsbury. Josiah Clowes was appointed engineer in 1793 and was responsible for building most of the canal although it was unfinished at the time of his death. In February 1795 he was succeeded by Thomas Telford. Clowes envisaged the construction of three aqueducts crossing the Tern at Longdon, the Roden at Roddington and a stream at Pimley. The latter two were completed, but the unfinished masonry of the structure at Longdon was swept away in a flood in February 1795. After the appointment of Telford to succeed Clowes on 28 February, a meeting of the company on 14 March sanctioned the erection of an iron aqueduct at Longdon, to be cast by William Reynolds and Co. at Ketley. The aqueduct was 62 yd. long, linking masonry abutments probably built by Clowes. It was completed within a year.[91]

The other major engineering work on the Shrewsbury Canal was the 970-yard Berwick tunnel three miles from Shrewsbury, notable for the towpath cantilevered from the side wall, built at the suggestion of William Reynolds.

The first section of the canal to be opened was that from Trench to Long Lane which was operating by December 1794. It was open to Berwick wharf at the eastern end of the tunnel in March 1796, but it was not until November 1796 that cutting at the Shrewsbury end was completed. It was finally opened throughout in February 1797.[92]

Coal and lime wharves were built along the Shrewsbury Canal which offered profitable outlets for the products of the coalfield. From Long Lane wharf it was hoped to supply the Shawbury area by road. A wharf was constructed at Longdon, another at Pimley, and Lord Berwick gave his name to one on the edge of his Attingham Park estate. The canal signally failed to meet the expectations of those citizens of Shrewsbury who confidently predicted that it would bring down the price of coal. By the winter of 1799–1800 complaints were being aired that coal cost 2 or 3s. a ton more than it did before the canal was built, and in 1803 after coal delivered by the canal was increased in price by 10d. a ton a newspaper urged the completion of the Shrewsbury branch of the rival Ellesmere Canal.[93]

The tub boat canals provided the ironmasters of east Shropshire with a cheap and, in many ways, convenient means of transporting materials in bulk. The extent to which the canals were utilised even for journeys of no more than a mile or so shows how economical they were compared with road transport or even tramways. The tub boats carried up to eight tons. One horse usually drew about a dozen loaded boats and it was not unknown for as many as 20, all controlled by one steersman walking on the towpath, to be attached in a train to one horse.[94] The boats were relatively cheap, many costing less than £20 each.

Visiting engineers were for the most part favourably impressed by the ingenuity of the engineering of the Shropshire canals. Thomas Butler in 1815 described how at the Windmill Farm incline, 'vessels are drawn with amazing facility from the lower to the higher level', and he thoroughly enjoyed a ride down the plane on a vessel loaded with coal.[95] The Longdon aqueduct, the Berwick tunnel with its cantilevered towpath and the complex system of reservoirs supplying the summit level of the Shropshire canal, all witness to the skill of the canal builders. Yet the system had distinct disadvantages.

Its only links with the national canal system before 1835 were by way of the unpre-dictable Severn, and involved at least two transhipments. As the canals grew older mining was extended beneath them, and subsidence became a threat to the water supply, particularly on the long summit section of the Shropshire, and a danger to the inclined planes.

Road transport conveyed cargoes of great importance, and ironmasters were as concerned with roads as with other forms of transport. In the early 18th century roads in Shropshire were as bad as in most other parts of England. The mines in the northern part of the coalfield which relied on road transport sent their coal no further than 10 miles away. The collieries in Madeley and Broseley with easy access to the Severn sold theirs throughout the Severn valley. Packhorses were extensively used for carrying ore to charcoal blast furnaces. Adam Luccock, a centenarian interviewed by John Randall in the early 19th century could remember going with strings of packhorses through the woods from the mines above Coalbrookdale to Leighton, with bells tinkling on the horses' necks to warn of their coming.[96]

The first significant attempt to improve the roads serving the coalfield was the turnpiking, in 1725–26, of Watling Street between Crackley Bank in Shifnal parish and Shrewsbury, with connecting roads to Cotwall, Shifnal and Crudgington. As in most turnpike acts of the period, the preamble gives a melancholy picture of the state of the roads, 'by reason of the soil of the said roads and lanes and the heavy Carriages frequently passing through the same . . . [the roads are] very much out of repair . . . many parts thereof even in the Summer Season, after great rains are impassable'. The act specified that horses with coals passing many times in the day could be charged twice at the toll gates, suggesting that coal was already an important traffic. Within four years the trustees obtained another act which doubled most of the tolls since the roads had been in such a ruinous state in 1726 that it had been necessary to borrow large sums which could not be repaid without increases. A special clause enabled the trustees to charge higher rates between October and May for waggons loaded with coal or lime.[97] After the road was turnpiked, compositions for tolls begin to appear in the accounts of industrial concerns in the district.

In the 1750s industrial traffic on Shropshire roads was handicapped by the Broad Wheels Act of 1753 which restricted the number of horses used to four on waggons and three on carts unless the vehicles had broad wheels. William Ferriday who was sending coal to Shrewsbury from the rail-served wharf at Old Hall on Watling Street, found during the winter of 1754–55 that sales of coals were much less than expected, even when coal was fetching 12s. a ton in Shrewsbury, on account of the restrictions imposed by the Act. 'They cannot get along the road with four horses in a waggon and three in a cart to carry any [coal] worth their trouble, not even from the Old Hall, there is not many go now to Salop', he wrote, and added, 'Salop would have been quite starv'd', if he had not sent coal to the county town by barge. Another Salopian critic of the Broad Wheels Act argued that one of its consequences would be to cause unemployment among miners.[98] Watling Street continued to be used for the carriage of coal to Shrews-bury until the opening of the Shrewsbury Canal in 1797.

The Watling Street turnpike served many interests other than those of the coal and ironmasters, but the Madeley turnpike roads, for which an Act of Parliament was obtained in 1764 served local industry more directly. The system consisted of two principal routes; in the shape of a letter 'X' crossing at the *Cuckoo Oak Inn*, Madeley. One led from a junction with Watling Street in the *Buck's Head*, Wellington, through

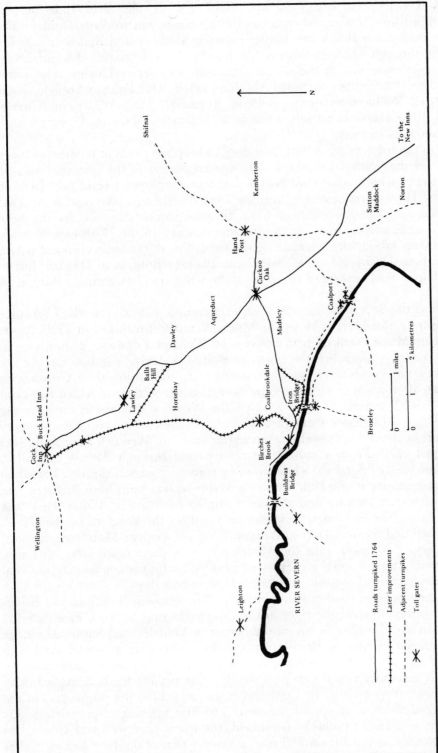

Figure 11. The Madeley Turnpike Roads.

Lawley Bank, Dawley, Cuckoo Oak and Beckbury to the New Inns on the Shropshire-Staffordshire border, whence connecting roads ran towards Dudley. The other led from the Birches Brook, the border between Madeley and Buildwas parishes near the Severn, through Madeley town to 'the hand post in the parish of Kemberton'. The principal toll house was at the *Cuckoo Oak*, with another at Lawley. The active trustees in the late 18th century included Abraham Darby III, Thomas Botfield, Isaac Hawkins Browne, William Ferriday, William Reynolds, John Wilkinson, Charles Guest, Francis Blithe Harries and John Onions, an indication of the road's significance for local iron-making interests.

The records of the trustees show that their duty to keep the roads in repair was taken seriously. In 1774 they ordered markers to be placed on five of the principal hills on their roads between which additional horses could be employed free of toll. In 1776 Abraham Darby III was requested to 'put the Lincoln Hill turnpike road in as good a state as it was in when he began to work his lime works, the road having been damaged by the spoil arising from getting the lime works'. In the 1770s extensive use was made of statute labour in the repair of the roads under the supervision of parish surveyors, Abraham Darby III in Madeley and Thomas Botfield in Dawley, but in 1782 William Dukes was appointed surveyor of the whole road at annual salary of 10 guineas.[99]

To the south of the Severn ironmasters were concerned with a network of turnpike roads radiating from the Market House at Much Wenlock, turnpiked in 1756. Apart from roads linking Much Wenlock with Bourton on Wenlock Edge and Beambridge in the Corvedale, the trust controlled the routes to Buildwas Bridge and Broseley. In the late 18th century the Wenlock trustees promoted their own route from Cressage to Bridgnorth as an alternative to the main Shrewsbury–Bridgnorth road which had been turnpiked in 1751–52. An act of 1778 enabled the Wenlock trustees to turnpike the road from Cressage to Wenlock through Sheinton. The new route avoided 'that very disagreeable part of the old road well known by the name of Wenlock Edge', and was opened in August 1779. From Wenlock the road passed through Barrow to Willey, Nordley Common and Bridgnorth, while Broseley travellers passed through Posenhall to their destination. Early in the 19th century a new road was built from Broseley past Willey furnace towards Barrow and the old turnpike road across Willey Park was closed to the public. The list of new trustees appointed for the Wenlock roads in 1778 included Abraham and Samuel Darby, William Ferriday, George Matthews, Richard Reynolds and John Wilkinson. Like the Madeley system, these roads were obviously important to ironmasters. Special powers were granted so that waggons carrying coal or lime could be charged at the toll gates more than once a day.[100]

Before 1780 there was no road crossing of the Severn between Buildwas and Bridgnorth. The first bridge to span the river in the Gorge was that between Preen's Eddy in Broseley parish and the Sheepwash on the border of Madeley and Sutton Maddock which was completed in time to be used by travellers attending a special market in Broseley on 25 April 1780. After the construction of William Reynolds's 'new town' in the 1790s, it was generally called Coalport Bridge. The project for building a bridge at Preen's Eddy was first mooted in 1775, and in January 1776 the proprietors of the Iron Bridge agreed to offer no opposition to it. The first meeting of proprietors was held at the home of Daniel Onions of Gitchfield, the ironmaster who was credited in 19th-century accounts with a substantial role in the erection of the Iron Bridge. Other shareholders included the ironmasters George Matthews, William Banks, Francis Hom-

Figure 12. The Wooden Bridge at Coalport.

Ironbridge Gorge Museum.

fray and Edward Blakeway, but no member of the Coalbrookdale partnership was involved in the project. The bridge was a two-span structure in wood, designed by William Hayward, designer of the bridges over the Tern at Atcham and the Thames at Henley. It was constructed by Robert Palmer, a Madeley timber merchant. By 1789 the bridge was in serious disrepair, and over £1000 was spent on rebuilding it in 1791–93. Following severe damage in the flood of 1795 it was rebuilt in 1799 as a single-span structure with main ribs of cast-iron. The bridge proprietors constructed the road from Broseley over the bridge to a junction with the Madeley turnpike road near Brockton.[101]

The impact of the Iron Bridge on local roads was much greater. The siting of the Bridge was determined in part by the existing roads. The Madeley turnpike descended off the coalfield plateau to the riverside by the road now called Lincoln Hill, and then ran parallel with the Severn to the Birches Brook. A river crossing along this stretch was ruled out by the sheer limestone cliffs of Benthall Edge which fronted the opposite shore. What principally determined the site of the bridge was the easy approach on the southern side down the valley of the stream on which stood the Benthall ironworks, which gave easy access to the Broseley–Wenlock turnpike road at the valley head.

The Madeley Turnpike Trust began work on a new link between the north end of the Ironbridge and the existing turnpike road during the summer of 1779. This was the road now called Church Hill which climbs from the Market Place at Ironbridge, which it leaves by a steep and acute bend, to a junction with the old turnpike on Lincoln Hill. This route was known in 1779 as the 'new road under Hodge Bower'. The road parallel with the river between the Iron Bridge and the bottom of the hill was in existence by 1748, although it did not formally become part of the Madeley turnpike until 1806, and even then users of the wharves over which it passed were entitled to leave piles of goods where they wished upon it. The Madeley Trust erected a new toll gate near to the Meadow Wharf in 1789 to collect dues from the traffic attracted by the Iron Bridge. In 1806 an Act was obtained for an entirely new road rising from the north end of the Iron Bridge up the side of the Severn Gorge to join the old turnpike near the Lane Pits on the edge of Madeley town. The new road, one of the most impressive examples of civil engineering in the district, was completed by 1810, when the Madeley trustees sought contributions towards its costs from other road authorities who would benefit from it.[102]

Another road directly influenced by the Iron Bridge was the so-called Leighton or Buildwas turnpike. In 1778 an Act of Parliament was obtained for turnpiking a series of lanes between Tern Bridge on Watling Street and the Madeley turnpike road at the Birches Brook, through Wroxeter and the village of Leighton where the solitary toll-gate was situated. Abraham Darby III invested in the road, and Thomas Addenbrooke, secretary to the Iron Bridge proprietors, was also concerned with it. The road was opened to traffic in September 1779, its first users including people anxious to see the Iron Bridge under construction. It formed part of the route of the *Diligence*, the first stage coach to use the Iron Bridge, which ran from Shrewsbury to London via Broseley, Bridgnorth, Alcester and Stratford. Coach proprietors sometimes advertised the crossing of the Bridge as one of the attractions of their services. The operator of the *Marquess Cornwallis* in 1798 drew attention to it as 'that striking specimen of Art and so much admired object of travellers'. Many attempts were made to popularise the route from Bridgnorth to Shrewsbury across the Bridge at the expense of that through Much Wenlock, which are still reflected in the inscriptions on the mileposts between Bridgnorth and the Iron Bridge which give distances to the county town.

On the south side of the Iron Bridge the proprietors built the road up the valley of the Benthall brook to join the Broseley–Wenlock turnpike, voting £50 for work on the road in February 1779. The road was crossed by a railway and John Randall recalled coaches tipping over when the wheels slipped on the rails. In 1781 the road was blocked by piles of limestone cinders and ashes from the Benthall furnaces, and obstructions were caused in the same year by a wall around the boring-mill recently built at the ironworks. The following year there were complaints about stacks of iron ore in the road near the furnaces. In 1783 a potter's oven was demolished in order to widen the road, and in 1791 a further scheme at John Thursfield's pottery near the Pitch Yard involved the demolition of a building and the removal of slip pans from the roadside. A direct link from the Iron Bridge to the Broseley–Bridgnorth road was established in 1828, avoiding the obstructions of the Bridge Road.[103]

The accounts of the Coalbrookdale partners illustrate the changing role of road transport in the 18th century. In the first half of the century many of the customers for domestic holloware must have been supplied by road, since there was no other way of taking pots and pans to such places as Bishop's Castle, Macclesfield or Ellesmere. Road transport was also employed to take pots and kettles for John Ives, a regular customer from Gainsborough, as far as Wilden Ferry or Burton-on-the-Trent. It is a reflection on the state of the roads that in 1722 a pot for John Ives was lost 'when George Benbow's waggon was overthrown'.[104]

The costs of road transport in the first half of the 18th century were formidably high. In 1733 goods were going to Ashbourne, 45 miles from Coalbrookdale at 3s. a hundred-weight, compared with a rate of 7s. 6d. per ton to Bristol, over 80 miles away by river. It was more usual to calculate costs rather less precisely by the 'load'. In 1733 a load to Church Stretton cost 1s. 8d., to Shrewsbury 1s. 6d., to Bishop's Castle and Ludlow 3s., to Much Wenlock and Wellington 8d., and to Leominster 5s. In 1761 Horsehay iron was being waggoned to Upton Forge, a distance of eight miles at 6s. a ton, when the contemporary rate by barge to Bristol was only 8s.[105]

For traffic to Shrewsbury the Coalbrookdale partners always used both road and water transport, and by the late 1760s both were being employed on a number of other routes. Some consignments of iron for Richard Jordan, normally sent by barge to Quatt, were being waggoned in 1768. In the 1770s other loads from Horsehay were being sent by rail to Ketley whence they were forwarded by road to Shrewsbury, Bersham, Calves Heath and Norton Canes. In 1774 curbs were delivered from Coalbrookdale to Chester and Warrington by teams from Abraham Darby's Sunniside Farm.[106]

By the mid-1790s in spite of the growth of railways and canals some quite considerable quantities of iron and raw materials were going between different sites within the coalfield by road, in some cases even over routes where canal connections were convenient. Bricks and clay went by waggon from Horsehay to the Wrockwardine Wood glasshouse, although some loads went by canal. Sand for Horsehay was brought by carts and waggons through the turnpike gate at Lawley, and from time to time road carriers took Horsehay iron for shipment to Coalport and Coalbrookdale.[107]

Iron for the mid-Wales forges in the 1790s was despatched either by road or river, with road transport steadily becoming more usual. In May 1805 10 tons of pigs for Pool Quay forge were sent from Horsehay for despatch by barge, but in the event were sent from Coalbrookdale by waggon to Shrewsbury. The county town was often used as a staging point for goods bound for North Wales, which were sent there by waggons supplied by the ironworks, and forwarded thence by vehicles supplied by the Welsh customers. As early as 1774 iron for John Wilkinson at Bersham was sent by road to await collection at Joseph Crump's in Shrewsbury, but the more usual route for this traffic was then by river and sea via Bristol and Chester. In April 1796 five tons of pigs for Mathrafal forge were forwarded from Horsehay to the *Cross Guns* inn in Frankwell, Shrewsbury in two waggon loads.[108]

Another developing road traffic in the 1780s and '90s was the conveyance of goods for northern and eastern England along Watling Street to the wharf at Gailey, where the Roman road crossed the Staffordshire and Worcestershire canal, 14 miles from Oakengates. Wrought iron for customers in the Potteries was often sent by this route. Iron for customers in Wolverhampton was often delivered direct by waggon and occasionally a canal wharf in that town was used for northbound traffic in preference to Gailey. Some London canal carriers delivered goods for the Wellington area by boat to Wolverhampton and thence by road after the opening of the Grand Junction Canal in 1805. By 1816 castings from Coalbrookdale to Liverpool were being taken by road to the wharf at Edstaston between Wem and Whitchurch, and thence by the Ellesmere Canal.[109]

Several stage waggon services linked the coalfield with London. A Shrewsbury–London service via Bridgnorth which began in February 1782 travelled through Much Wenlock and Broseley where it picked up barrels of bitumen from the Coalport Tar Tunnel. Another waggon began to run in June 1782 serving the north of the coalfield as it made its way from Shrewsbury through Wolverhampton, Birmingham and Coventry to London.[110]

The steady increase in the use of road transport by Shropshire ironmasters in the 1790s, which continued until in the early 1830s wrought iron for Birmingham was being delivered direct by road, probably arose from the frustrations of the Severn Navigation and the lack of direct contact with the national canal system rather than from the intrinsic merits of operating waggons on turnpike roads. The quantities which could be forwarded by one waggon were small – no more than three and three quarter tons. Waggons employed a great deal of labour for long periods. In January 1806 a three-horse team was employed to take an urgent load of castings from Coalbrookdale to the Potteries. The team took four days to make the return journey. Even in the 1830s a return trip to Wolverhampton or Whitchurch took two days, while three days were required to go to Birmingham, Ludlow or the Potteries. 'Deliveries and shipments', wrote the historian of the Horsehay ironworks, 'have always been an expensive and troublesome supplement to the cost of ironmaking at Horsehay'. Certainly the lack of adequate transport facilities, in spite of the skill of local engineers, was one of the most severe impediments to the continued growth of industry in Shropshire after 1800.[111]

IX

STEAM POWER

That the Industrial Revolution in Great Britain was largely made possible by the development of the steam engine is a common-place of the older economic history textbooks. How many steam engines there were in 18th century England, of what types they were, who built them, who used them and for what purposes, are problems which historians have only rècently begun to examine. They are questions which are receiving answers which would have surprised previous generations.[1] The density of steam engines in any district in 1800 is a good measure of the state of its economic development. It is probable that there were more steam engines to the square mile in the Shropshire coalfield than in any other part of Britain, and an examination of how they were used throws a good deal of light on the general problems connected with the application of steam power in Great Britain.

Conveniently, the answers to some of the most important questions about steam engines in Shropshire were computed in the late 18th century. In a footnote in Telford's article on industry in Plymley's account of the agriculture of Shropshire appears an estimate by William Reynolds that in 1802 at the different coal and ironworks in east Shropshire there were 25 engines south of the Severn and 155 north of the river. 30 years previously there were less than 20 in the district. Reynolds's calculation are confirmed by the estimate of another writer who said that in 1801 within a radius of five miles from Lawley Bank in the centre of the coalfield, 'it is suppos'd that there are upwards of 200 steam engines erected for different purposes.'[2] If allowance is made for engines employed in other places than coal and ironworks this estimate accords very well with that of William Reynolds. It seems reasonable to accept that there were about 200 steam engines in the coalfield at the end of the 18th century, the great majority of which had been installed in the last quarter of the century.

Like the answers printed at the back of an old-fashioned arithmetic textbook these figures are insufficient in themselves. If the most important questions about the role of the steam engine in Shropshire are to be answered it is necessary to re-calculate Reynolds's sums. Fortunately there are sufficient documentary sources to begin a serious examination of these problems.

The practical atmospheric engine, which could pump out mines, but which could not be employed rotatively to turn machinery, was developed by Thomas Newcomen, the Dartmouth ironmonger, in the first decade of the 18th century.[3] The first full-size engine was put to work to pump water from a colliery near Dudley Castle in 1712. Because Thomas Savery in 1698 had been granted a patent covering all sorts of machines for raising water by fire, Newcomen engines could only be erected on payment of royalties to Savery, and after his death in 1715, to a syndicate who acquired his rights. To some extent the royalties inhibited the building of engines until the patent rights expired in 1733. James Watt's first major improvements to the Newcomen engine, the steam jacket around the cylinder and the separate condenser were made in 1765 and patented in 1769. In 1774 Watt moved from Scotland to Birmingham where he entered into partnership with Matthew Boulton, and the following year his patents were extended until 1800. The first full-size engines incorporating Watt's improvements were built in 1776. Until 1800 the owners of all engines in which they were legally incorporated were obliged to pay one third of the saving in fuel costs over an atmospheric engine to Boulton and Watt. This was regarded by many as an unduly heavy imposition, and there were many attempts to take advantage of Watt's discoveries without infringing the letter of his patent rights. In 1782 Watt patented his double-acting rotative engine. On engines of this sort a fixed royalty of £5 per h.p. per annum was charged outside London. Again, engineers found that similar, though less efficient, rotative action could be achieved by other means without infringing the letter of the patents. Boulton and Watt did not, until the opening of their Soho Foundry in 1796, supply more than expertise and valves for their engines, but relied on various iron-masters, including several in Shropshire for the supply of iron castings. The critical dates in the history of steam power are those when the first successful applications of new inventions were made, 1712, 1776 and 1782, and those when patent rights expired, 1733 and 1800. Professor Harris has estimated that there may have been 60 engines built in Great Britain between 1712 and 1733, 223 between 1733 and 1781, with perhaps 1,200 in all during the whole of the 18th century.[4]

The manufacture of cast-iron cylinders for the Newcomen atmospheric engine at the Coalbrookdale ironworks after 1722 has already been considered. Several attempts have been made to list all of the engines for which items were manufactured at Coalbrookdale, and of these, the latest painstaking survey by Dr. R. A. Mott[5] is likely to prove definitive unless further documents relating to the works are discovered. Mott has calculated that before the expiry of the patents held by 'the Proprietors of the Invention for Raising Water by Fire', in 1733, parts for at least 23 engines had been cast at Coalbrookdale.

A proposal was made in 1715 to use a steam engine to drain a mine in Broseley, but the first authenticated engine in Shropshire was erected by the partners in the Madeley glebe coalworks, and came into operation about the middle of 1719, pumping water from pits which had previously cost about £300 a year to drain by conventional methods. The site of the engine is not known, but it stood to the north of the Shifnal–Much Wenlock road through Madeley parish. In 1726 an agreement relating to mining in the New Leasow, another portion of the Madeley glebe, refers to 'Smiths Gin pit situate and being in the Lloyds where ye Fire Engine now stands and belonging to ye Hay estate.' The Lloyds is near to the Severn and well south of the Shifnal–Much Wenlock road, which suggests that a second engine had been erected by 1726, although it is possible that the first had been moved.[6] In 1722 the Coalbrookdale ironworks supplied engine parts to the coalmaster Richard Hartshorne who had many mines in the district but none in the Madeley glebe. In 1731 the works sold Hartshorne a cylinder which was probably installed in the engine he was building at that time on the Charlton family estates in Wombridge.[7]

There were probably four atmospheric engines operating in the coalfield by 1733 when the patents on the engine expired. Since a supplier of engine parts was so close at hand this is perhaps a surprisingly low figure for such a productive coalfield. It is probably explained by the ease with which outcrop coal could still be exploited in the 18th century in the Severn Gorge and its tributary valleys. If coal could be won by drift mines and very shallow pits an expensive engine would have offered few advantages.

For the same reasons the expiry of the patents on the Newcomen engine in 1733 did not stimulate Shropshire coal-masters to buy engines. The Coalbrookdale ironworks cast parts for at least 44 different engines between 1733 and 1748, but few of them were for local customers.[8] In May 1745 the company accounts allowed 7s. for the workmen at 'a new Engine in Madeley Wood.' This was presumably for drink to mark the completion of the company's work on an engine supplied to pump out the mines being worked by J. U. Smitheman.[9] It is possible that an engine was built in the Lightmoor area about 1740, although evidence for it is inconclusive, but in 1754 an engine certainly was erected at Evans Yard, Lightmoor, to keep down the water level in the adjacent coalworks.[10]

The first application of the Newcomen engine in the iron trade occurred in 1743 when an engine was applied to pump back water over the wheels which supplied power to the Coalbrookdale ironworks. This same pattern of operation was followed at all the works built during the first great boom in the Shropshire iron trade in the 1750s. Two engines were installed at Horsehay, two at Ketley, one at Lightmoor and one at New Willey, to pump back water over wheels to high level pools, and at Madeley Wood two engines pumped water from the Severn to drive the wheels.[11]

By the time the Watt engine was perfected in the mid-1770s five or perhaps six of the 20 or so engines William Reynolds believed were then working in east Shropshire were mine pumping-engines erected before 1755. 11 engines were at ironworks, pumping water back over wheels which drove blast furnace bellows. Two, and probably several more, were pumping water from mines which had been opened up since the boom in the iron trade in the 1750s. This accounts for at least 18 of Reynolds's engines. Unfortunately the surviving Coalbrookdale Company records for the period after 1748 refer only to engines built for the partners' own works, although they were certainly supplying engine parts to coal mines in all parts of Britain.

It was through John Wilkinson that the Shropshire ironworks became involved in the improvements which were being made to the design of the steam engine by James Watt at the Soho Manufactory. Wilkinson began the production of castings for atmospheric engines at Willey soon after the formation of the New Willey Company. In 1762 he made an agreement with Abraham Darby II acting for the Coalbrookdale Company, and his father Isaac Wilkinson, acting for the Bersham Company, on a common pricing policy for cast-iron engine parts, for all parts of Britain except South Wales, Cornwall, Somerset and the Bristol and London regions. Bored work was to be charged at £30 a ton, unbored pipes at £18 a ton, and pistons, plates and bars at £12 a ton. The parties agreed that they should be free, on consulting the others, to charge less if they encountered competition for particular orders from Walker's foundry at Rotherham.[12]

In 1774 Wilkinson took out a patent for a machine for boring cannon, in which the solid cannon casting was rotated horizontally between bearings, and the stationary boring head was advanced by a toothed rack on the boring bar, which was worked through gearing by a handwheel. Wilkinson's machine worked on the same principles as one introduced at Woolwich Arsenal by a Dutchman Jan Verbruggen in 1770.

Wilkinson's rights were challenged by the Board of Trade, and the patent revoked in 1779. In the same year that Wilkinson obtained his patent James Watt moved from Scotland to Birmingham, where his new partner, Matthew Boulton, urged him to put his steam engine into production. Watt's innovations demanded standards of engineering accuracy well beyond those needed for the Newcomen engine, and Wilkinson whose cannon-boring machine was well known, was asked to supply cylinders. The boring of cylinders posed different problems from those encountered when boring cannon, since to bore a cylinder from the solid was obviously impossible, and Wilkinson modified his machine to bore a casting of far greater diameter than a cannon, which was opened at both ends. On the new machine the cylinder was fixed upon a supporting frame, and the revolving cutter bar passed right through it, being supported at both ends in bearings.[13]

In 1776 Wilkinson set to work the second Boulton and Watt engine at the Willey ironworks where it was applied to blow the blast furnaces, James Watt personally supervising its construction. Within the next four years he built three more Watt engines at his Shropshire works, one an inverted cylinder 'Topsy Turvey' engine, to pump back the water which powered a boring-mill at Willey, one to pump mines at Snedshill and one to blow the Snedshill blast furnaces.[14]

The Coalbrookdale and Ketley partners quickly became aware of the success which Watt and Wilkinson had achieved. 'Mr. Watts [sic]', wrote William Reynolds to William Rathbone in 1777, 'is I believe one of the greatest Philosophers in Europe & has made the greatest improvements in Fire Engines that have ever been since the first discovery of that very useful and most powerful machine.'[15]

On 29 January 1778 Richard Reynolds made an agreement with Boulton and Watt for the erection of an engine at the Ketley furnaces, for which Reynolds himself was to supply the cast-iron parts. The engine was not to blow the blast furnaces direct, but simply to replace the existing atmospheric pumping-engine. On 2 April 1779 a trial took place at Ketley between the new and the old engines to determine standards of fuel consumption by which the premiums paid to Boulton and Watt by all their customers were to be reckoned. At first the Ketley engine was far from successful. The injection valves, piston, boiler and flues were all faulty and the men had received so little instruction that they dreaded having to stop the engine. Gradually its performance improved, and Boulton and Watt supplied a second engine to the Ketley works in 1780.[16]

In 1781–82 the pumping-engine which returned water from the lower pools at Coalbrookdale to the one above the upper furnace was replaced by a very large Watt engine which had a cylinder 66 in. in diameter with a 9 ft. stroke, and a beam allegedly made from eight large oak trees. *Resolution*, as the engine was called, did not work well at first and was modified several times during the 1780s. It seems to have been much improved after a new cylinder was fitted in 1789.[17]

Shropshire ironmasters were among the first to be interested in the rotative engine. Its application in the county was being considered even before Watt's development of his sun and planet motion, for in 1782 William Reynolds told Watt that he and his father had for some time thought of putting up a corn mill, 'to be worked by a common fire engine and crank.' Reynolds explained that his father had been to Birmingham and was 'so pleased with your new rotative motion', that he wished to know the price of an engine to work two pairs of common mill stones. The first Watt rotative engine was employed to operate a hammer at John Wilkinson's Bradley ironworks in Staffordshire where William Reynolds saw it working before the end of May 1783. The following year Watt rotative engines were ordered for the forges at Ketley and Horsehay, soon to be followed by a number of small engines for stamping and hammering at the Ketley forge.[18]

Steam power was applied rapidly in east Shropshire because there were several local firms capable of making parts for engines. The role of the Coalbrookdale ironworks has already been described. The associated works at Ketley had a foundry by the 1790s capable of casting engine parts, and space for the erection of engines. John Wilkinson was a noted builder of steam engines, but concentrated these activities at his Bersham ironworks in Denbighshire. The boring machine at New Willey was probably used only for the manufacture of cannon.[19] In 1784 Banks and Onions of Benthall were making rotative engines, and in 1789 were reported to have order books full for two years ahead. In 1801 John Onions's new foundry at Broseley was making what William Wilkinson described as 'the neatest castings I have seen anywhere', and was erecting several engines. An 80 h.p. engine built by Onions, with a 60 in. cylinder and a cast-iron beam, was offered for sale at a colliery near Bath in 1813. Alexander Brodie was able to make engine parts at the Calcutts ironworks, and certainly made many engines at the works of Brodie, McNiven and Ormrod in Manchester. The Lightmoor Company supplied the first engines for the Old Park Ironworks in 1789–90. Boulton and Watt ordered engine castings from Bishton and Onions at Snedshill and from the Madeley Wood ironworks, where engines and engine parts were made until the closure of the foundry portion of the works in 1803.[20] Wrought-iron plates for boilers were less commonly manufactured, and probably the rolling-mills at Horsehay and Ketley were the only Shropshire works capable of producing them.

As in other parts of Britain, relatively few of the steam engines built in Shropshire in the late 18th century were constructed on Boulton and Watt's principles since the premiums which had to be paid to the Soho partners were prohibitively high. Local engineers displayed considerable ingenuity in the construction of rotative engines which avoided the infringement of Watt's patents. One of the best known was the engine patented in July 1790 by Adam Heslop, than an employee of the Ketley ironworks. Heslop placed two cylinders on a small Newcomen type engine, one a hot cylinder, the other at the opposite end of the beam for condensing. The hot cylinder worked as a single acting steam powered cylinder, while the cold one acted on the same principle as an atmospheric engine. William Reynolds put the Heslop engine into production in 1790 in the belief that it might supersede the Boulton and Watt engine for the winding of pits. Between 1791 and 1795 Heslop built several engines at mines in his native Cumberland, but was still working for William Reynolds in 1797 when he was erecting new engines in the Madeley Field coalworks. Three Heslop engines were still employed at the Madeley Wood Company's pits in 1880.[21]

James Sadler, the balloonist, was also concerned with the development of the steam engine in Shropshire before he took up an appointment with the Board of Naval Works in 1796. In 1792–93 several small tandem single-acting rotative engines which he designed were erected in and around Coalbrookdale. Another Shropshire engineer who took out patents for the improvement of the steam engine at this period was James Glazebrook a carpenter who was closely associated with Alexander Brodie at the Calcutts ironworks, where one of the blast engines was constructed according to his principles. In 1796 Boulton and Watt sought evidence about the Glazebrook engine in the belief that it might have infringed their patents.[22]

The most inventive genius among all of those who applied their talents to the improvement of the steam engine in the 1790s and 1800s was Richard Trevithick, whose contribution to the development of steam power was as great as Watt's. Trevithick first visited Coalbrookdale in 1796, and a number of his most important experiments were carried out at the works or using castings made there. In 1802 parts to the value of £246 were cast at Coalbrookdale for an experimental engine which Trevithick demonstrated in August of that year. Local engineers were most impressed, 'If I had 50 engines,' wrote Trevithick, 'I cud sell them in a Day at any price I wod ask for them'.[23] The Coalbrookdale partners were then building a steam locomotive on Trevithick's principles to run on their plateway. It is now generally accepted that this is the locomotive depicted in a drawing which survives in the Science Museum.[24]

It seems doubtful whether the locomotive was ever put to use. There is no evidence that it ever pulled a train at Coalbrookdale, and a detailed journal kept by a workman at the Dale in this period fails to mention it. Why it was not used is difficult to understand. William Reynolds was to some extent concerned with Trevithick's experiments and his death in 1803 may have brought them to an end. In January 1802 William Wilkinson wrote after a visit to Reynolds, 'he has great faith in his engine but very little was said of it'. Since Reynolds had built any number of stationary engines, this is obviously a reference to some quite exceptional machine. Reynolds commissioned a model of the locomotive, later broken up by his nephew, who was given it as a toy. It is puzzling in view of Reynolds's obvious connections with the experiments that they were carried out at the Coalbrookdale works, in which he had no direct interest, and not at Ketley, where the engineering facilities were comparable with any in Britain. It is possible that a trial of the locomotive was made at which there was an accident, causing the death of a workman, which led to the ending of the experiments. Randall recalls one such accident but dates it to the 1780s when Reynolds himself was contemplating the building of a steam locomotive. Trevithick's Coalbrookdale locomotive was soon broken up, the cylinders surviving at Coalbrookdale ironworks until the 1880s, at which time the boiler was still serving as a water tank at a pit at the Lloyds.[25] Trevithick looked elsewhere for assistance and it is now generally accepted that the first steam locomotive to pull a train was that which successfully hauled 25 tons at Penydarren, South Wales, in 1803.

The Coalbrookdale Company continued to build stationary engines on Trevithick's plans. In 1804–05 a 'horizontal engine on Trevithick's plan as per Engine Book' was supplied to one William Heath, probably the same William Heath of Fenton Park, North Staffordshire, for whom a boiler was made at Horsehay at the same time. In the following year another Trevithick engine with an 18-in. cylinder was sold to John Burlingham of Worcester at a total cost of £688 6s. 8d. Trevithick's high pressure engines were also built at John Hazledine's foundry at Bridgnorth in which Alexander Brodie had interests. One of the products of this foundry, rescued from a scrap-heap at Hereford in the 1880s, survives in the Science Museum.[26]

Experiments were also made in Shropshire about 1800 with the application of the steam engine to propel boats. When William Reynolds died in 1803 he left unfinished an engine designed by James Glazebrook intended to be applied to a pleasure boat. He kept two pleasure boats, one on the Severn, the other on the Shropshire Canal at Coalport. The brass cylinders from one of them were exhibited at Coalbrookdale in 1871. In 1804 Richard Trevithick tried to apply a 10-in. engine bound for a cotton works at Macclesfield to propel a barge on the Severn at Coalbrookdale.[27]

The activities of Heslop, Sadler, Glazebrook and Trevithick do not exhaust the experimental work done on the steam engine in Shropshire between 1790 and 1810. William Reynolds made a series of sketch books containing pen and ink and wash drawings of a host of inventions. These books were used by Randall in the 1880s but all but one are now lost. The surviving volume shows that Reynolds was deeply committed to the development of the steam engine. It includes drawings of Sadler's and Heslop's engines, and some original designs, such as the engine without a beam set up at Wombridge in 1794, which are known by no special names. Typical of these engines was one erected early in the 19th century which survived to be photographed in 1899 at the Rats Pits, Hadley. This was a double-acting beam engine, apparently without a condenser, geared for winding a pit. It belongs to no definable type, and was far removed from the high standards of design and craftsmanship associated with the Boulton and Watt engines of the period.[28]

By 1800 the Shropshire ironworks depended chiefly upon steam as their source of power, although some of them, notably Coalbrookdale, still operated most of their machinery by water power, and used steam engines only to return water to high level reservoirs. The development of the rotative engine in the 1780s meant that steam could be employed to power most ironmaking processes, boring-mills, rolling-mills, hammers, grinding and blacking mills. Appendix Two lists the steam engines known to have been working at Shropshire ironworks about 1800. 42 can be positively identified, and allowance must be made for at least four more which must have existed but about which no details are known.

Of the 42 engines, over 20 were built on Boulton and Watts' principles, several without payment of the requisite premiums. Blowing blast furnaces and operating rolling- and boring-mills were exacting tasks, and it is not surprising that ironmasters should have installed the best available engines for such purposes. How highly they regarded the improved efficiency which could be obtained from a Watt engine is shown by the almost indecent haste in which the blast furnaces at Horsehay were stopped between 21 September and 6 October 1800 'to alter the engine to Watts', immediately the patents expired.[29] The proportion of Watt engines in Shropshire ironworks certainly seems to have been higher than in Lancashire cotton mills in the same period.[30] Nevertheless the appendix shows that any task which could be done by a Boulton and Watt engine could also in 1800 be done less efficiently if perhaps more cheaply by an atmospheric engine. Although John Wilkinson had found great difficulty in applying an atmospheric engine to blow a blast furnace direct, atmospherics were used to blow furnaces at Benthall, Snedshill, Hollinswood and Horsehay. Rotative atmospheric engines worked the rolling-mill at Horsehay, the boring-mill at Ketley, and the forge hammers at Snedshill and Old Park. There were several 'pirate' engines in Shropshire ironworks, built in infringement of the Boulton and Watt patents without the payment of premiums. Between 1795 and 1798 Alexander Brodie erected four such engines at the Calcutts, two of them in the ironworks and two in the adjacent mines. When the offence was pointed out, Brodie protested that the infringements were made by no order of his, and that many engines built by other people employed separate condensers, but nevertheless agreed to pay £602 in compensation. The best known of all pirates of the Boulton and Watt patents was John Wilkinson, but among the many engines he built illegally, the only one in a Shropshire ironworks was the boring-mill engine of 1788 at Willey.[31]

The list of engines in *Appendix Two* shows that there must have been between 40 and

50 engines employed at Shropshire ironworks at the beginning of the 19th century. This leaves about 130 of those counted by William Reynolds still to be identified. Most of them were certainly employed in the local mines.

Some of these were the ancient Newcomen pumping-engines whose installation has been considered above. Several were large pumping-engines built for mines sunk in the late 18th century to meet the ever-growing demand for iron ore and clod coal. In 1782 John Wilkinson agreed with Boulton and Watt to erect a 37.8 h.p. engine with a 42 in. × 8 ft. cylinder which was probably that installed on the Nabb, the high ground to the north of Oakengates. In 1779 the brothers Gilbert obtained from Boulton and Watt an engine with a 30 in. × 8 ft. cylinder for pumping mines at Donnington Wood. Between 1790 and 1797 Thomas Botfield erected a large engine in the Old Park area to drain the clod coal and ironstone levels. At Lightmoor in 1788 there were three pumping-engines, the old, new and upper engines, within a radius of half a mile.[32]

At the Calcutts in 1797 Alexander Brodie built 'a powerful water engine' to drain his mines. Three large 'water engines' drained John Wilkinson's New Hadley mines in the early years of the 19th century. William Reynolds owned a large pumping-engine called 'the Bank Water Engine' at Ketley Bank. The Lilleshall partners in 1793 had a pumping-engine at Lawley Bank from which water ran by a level to 'the pool in Mossey Green meadow' about a mile away. Richard Banks, who was operating pits in Wombridge in 1796, owned the 'Wombridge Water Engine'. Most of these pumping-engines were large ones, and it is clear that the greater part of the coalfield was drained by steam power by 1800. Allowing for the older atmospheric engines which continued in use, there were probably between 15 and 20 large pumping-engines in the district. Some pumping-engines were quite small however, and could have drained no more than one or two pits. The Coalbrookdale Company's 'Water Engine No. 3', for example, moved from New Works to Lawley in 1805–06, was a mere 12 in. engine, valued with its pumps at only £85. In one of the coal pits near the Ketley ironworks an atmospheric pumping-engine was installed 80 yards underground shortly before 1781. It cost one sixth more than an engine built on the surface and the engine house was 'very hot and disagreeable for the engine tender,' but there were considerable operating economies.[33]

The steam winding-engine, or whimsey, was by 1800 one of the dominant features of the landscape of industrial Shropshire. A spectator looking towards Little Dawley from the hills above Coalbrookdale in 1801 saw 'several Steam Engines, erected for the purpose of raising Coals, Ironstone &c. from the Pits, they being now in almost general use instead of horses, performing the business much quicker & at considerably less expence, the apparatus of which being so simple and yet so substantial that the person who has the management of it has so far at his command, as to stop the machine in a moment; so that accidents very seldom happen to the workmen, perhaps not more than work'd by horses'. In 1842, an old miner born 63 years earlier recalled times 'when there was not a single steam engine in the district to draw up the water or the coals'. His memory was at fault as regards pumping-engines, but his impression of his youth as a period when many steam engines were installed in Shropshire pits is a valid one.[34]

The exact date of the introduction of the steam winding-engine in Shropshire is uncertain. George Matthews of the Calcutts ironworks approached Boulton and Watt for a winding-engine as early as 1776, but his suggestion apparently came to nothing. William and Richard Reynolds began work on a steam winding-engine on Watt's principles at Wombridge early in 1787, and at the same time were contemplating installing another engine of 8 h.p. to wind a pit 100 yards deep. The Wombridge engine was not set to work until March 1789. Two months later William Reynolds reported, 'it answers our purpose exceeding well, and now we have made a large trial of it proves more and more useful to us'. This was probably the first pit winding-engine in the district, although one source suggests that the Reynoldses first experimentally applied a Boulton and Watt rotative engine to wind a pit in Madeley. Certainly the Wombridge engine stimulated the ordering of a series of similar machines. In May 1788 two 6 h.p. engines were requested and during the next two years nine slightly larger engines were ordered by the Reynoldses for their own concerns and for the Coalbrookdale Company.[35]

While the Boulton and Watt rotative engine was well suited for the winding of pits, it remained expensive, and the great majority of pit winding-engines in Shropshire in 1800 were mongrel or atmospheric engines. In 1790 William Reynolds was building Heslop engines at Ketley in considerable numbers. He thought them particularly suitable for the winding of pits since they could easily be moved from one site to another, the initial cost was far less than that of a Watt engine, and they were less expensive to operate. The Sadler engine also was applied to the winding of pits and the William Reynolds Sketch Book shows several other ingeniously designed engines intended for winding coals. Not all were built on new principles, for many of the winding-engines of the period were simply small atmospherics, adapted by means of a crank for rotative motion.[36]

To locate the site, maker and owner of every winding-engine at work in Shropshire in 1800 is an impossible task, but the available evidence is sufficient to show that such engines were very numerous and that most of the engines were built in the last decade of the 18th century. The multiplication of winding-engines in the 1790s is well illustrated in the surviving records of the Madeley Field coalworks. In 1790 there were three engines operating in the field, the Union, Wharf and Cape engines, not all of which were necessarily winding-engines. By the end of 1794 a fourth, the Brick Kiln Leasow engine had been built. During the next three years, nine new engines were constructed, three in Rough Park, a second at Brick Kiln Leasow, one each at the Pinneystone pits in the Lloyds, the Crawstone pit, the New Dingle pit and the Lane pits, and one known as the Cumberland Engine No. 4. Of the nine, four were beamless, and most of the parts for them were cast at the Madeley Wood ironworks.[37]

The records of other mining concerns suggest that they operated similarly large numbers of winding-engines by 1800. The Coalbrookdale Company employed at least 12 in the New Works and Lawley mines by 1802. In their Lawley and Dawley collieries in 1827, after two decades when there had been very little change, 16 pumping- and winding-engines were in use at 43 coal and ironstone pits. There were six engines, all of them apparently used for winding, at the Broseley pits connected with the Coneybury furnace in 1820. When the Ketley works was sold in 1817 there were in the adjacent collieries eight Boulton and Watt winding-engines and 'several' beamless, 'common atmospherical engines'. In 1798 the Marquess of Stafford and Co. had six engines in the Donnington colliery, and three in the Lilleshall and Church Aston limeworkings. By 1800 one of their engines was number 18, and in 1805 engines numbered, 2, 5, 9 and 13 were winding ironstone pits in Wrockwardine Wood. At the Calcutts in 1811 were 'three coal winding engines all complete'. There were two winding-engines in the Old Park Company pits at Malins Lee in 1797. A map of the mines on the New Hadley estate developed by John Wilkinson made in 1809 shows winding-engines at three of the 24 pits within a short distance of the New Hadley furnaces, one of which was a 'pirate' engine with a 24-in. cylinder built at Bersham in 1795. At Hollinswood, Wilkinson had a 14-in. engine which he set to work winding a pit in July 1790.[38]

Many more collieries which employed steam engines can be identified from the accounts of boilers manufactured at the Horsehay ironworks. In 1795–96 several boilers were sent to Wombridge for new steam engines then being installed at pits in the area. One boiler was sent to 'Wombridge New Field' in December 1795, another to a coal winding-engine in Wombridge in March 1796, and a third was despatched in the same month to Richard Banks acting for the Wombridge Company. Earl Gower and Co. and their successors, the Lilleshall Company, were regular customers for Horsehay boilers. One was supplied to the Lilleshall limeworks in 1796, one to the Hugh's Bridge inclined plane in April 1802, a second to the limeworks in October of that year, two to pits in Donnington Wood early in 1803, and another to the limeworks in 1805. Between 1795 and 1798 other buyers of Horsehay boilers in the coalfield included the Madeley Wood Company, the Benthall Company, the Snedshill Company and Mr. Barker of Benthall. From 1802 to 1805 boilers were purchased by Thornwill and Addenbrooke, for mines in Langley Field, Dawley, F. R. Rowlands for mines at Hadley, and by Emery and Clayton for the Steeraway limestone mines.[39]

The large number of steam engines in Shropshire in 1802 is thus to a great extent explained by the rapid mechanisation of pit winding between 1789 and the end of the century. If about 50 engines were employed in ironworks, if there were between 20 and 30 mine pumping-engines, and about 20 employed on the canals and for miscellaneous purposes, there must have been well over 100 winding coal, ironstone and limestone from pits in the district. That there were so many in areas where detailed identification is possible and that the Horsehay accounts show boilers being supplied to almost every part of the coalfield, suggest that this is not an exaggerated figure.

The east Shropshire canals employed about 10 steam engines in 1800. A small pumping-engine emptied and refilled the locks on the Ketley inclined plane, and winding-engines, at least two of them Heslop engines, worked on the five other inclines in the district. It is uncertain how many pumping-engines were used on the Shropshire Canal, but there are references in the company minutes to at least four, one at Randlay, one at Hinkshay and two at Wrockwardine Wood.[40]

Some steam engines were used in Shropshire clay works. There is no evidence that any brickworks or pottery used atmospheric engines for pumping back water over millwheels, as did the Turners of Lane End in 1772, nor was any Shropshire potter, like Josiah Wedgwood, among the first customers for Boulton and Watt engines. There was a steam engine at the Reynolds, Horton and Rose porcelain works at Coalport by 1814, which probably dated from the start of the works in 1800. In 1821 Joshua Field came across 'the most miserable engine driving a clay mill', in Madeley. John Randall, writing in the early 20th century, could remember an ancient atmospheric engine turning a mill for grinding refractory clay near the Iron Bridge.[41] It is doubtful whether there were more than five or six engines at work in the Shropshire clay trades by 1802. The local porcelain industry was small, the earthenware trade unprogressive, and the mechanisation of brick-making did not come until well into the 19th century.

A few steam engines were used for other purposes. John Randall believed that one of the first Boulton and Watt rotative engines was employed at a corn mill at Ketley as proposed by William Reynolds in 1782, and it is possible that there were one or two other steam mills in the coalfield. By about 1810 the portable steam engine was well established on the larger farms in the surrounding countryside. In the first six months of 1812 two small engines, one of them by Onions of Broseley, were offered in a farm sale at Stirchley Hall, and a 6 h.p. engine in a sale at Longdon-on-Tern. Some steam engines were used to wind railway inclined planes if only for short periods. Charles Hatchett observed in 1796 that plateway inclines were being wound by steam engines and one of the surviving drawings of a Sadler engine suggests that it was so employed.[42]

The building of so many steam engines in Shropshire in the late 18th century is partly explained by the relatively low cost of the small atmospheric engine. An engine to blow a blast furnace, work a rolling-mill or pump dry a large area of underground workings was a major investment. T., W. and B. Botfield of Old Park bought two engines from Boulton and Watt in 1801, a blowing-engine which cost £828 and a rolling-mill engine, a 36 in., double-acting engine, with an iron beam, which cost £1,675. The 44-in. blowing-engine which Boulton and Watt supplied to Addenbrooke and Homfray to blow two furnaces and four fineries at Lightmoor in 1800 cost £1,283 3s. 4d. The Botfields' mine pumping-engine at Malins Lee was valued at £1,400 in 1797. Such large engines were very expensive to operate. Fuel for the *Resolution* pumping-engine at Coalbrookdale, the largest engine in the coalfield, cost £1,141 10s. 0d. in the year ending august 1799, and £971 10s. 3d. in the year ending August 1804. The Coalbrookdale partners had to pay Boulton and Watt a premium of £200 a year for the engine. By contrast the cost of coal for all of the winding-engines in the Dawley coalfield in 1797–98 was only £74 17s. 9d., and in the New Works district £68 11s. 0d. Such engines could use the very cheapest grades of fuel – the value of the coal used at the New Works engines was only 2d. per ton. The capital costs of the small atmospherics were also very low. The Coalbrookdale winding-engine No. 2 with a 20-in. cylinder was valued at £210 in 1800, while the 22-in. No. 11 was reckoned to be worth £260. The Botfields' two winding-engines at Malins Lee in 1797 were valued at £240 each. Five of the six winding-engines at the mines supplying Coneybury furnace in 1820 were estimated to be worth £120 each and the other £90, but by then they were probably about 20 years old. A new 26-in. cylinder winding-engine from the Coalbrookdale Company in 1802–03 cost £440 7s. 0d. complete, plus installation charges of £36. A 26-in. engine was larger than most of those used for winding. In 1804–05 a Trevithick horizontal engine was sold for as little as £260, although an 18-in. engine of this type in 1805 cost £688 6s. 8d.[43]

What conclusions can be drawn about the place of the steam engine in the economy of the Shropshire coalfield? The Coalbrookdale ironworks for much of the middle part of the 18th century was the principal supplier of cast-iron cylinders for Newcomen engines, but in spite of this, local coalmasters were slow to adopt the engine, probably because they did not need it. The iron-smelting industry on the other hand depended entirely on the atmospheric pumping-engine in the first phase of its expansion in the late 1750s. During the last quarter of the century steam power was extensively used in local ironworks, but the variety of engines employed was considerable, and engines other than those which were built according to James Watt's principles were to be found doing every task for which steam power was employed in ironworks. That there were so many steam engines in Shropshire in 1802 is largely explained by the instal-lation of engines of all sorts, atmospherics, Boulton and Watt's, Heslop's, Sadler's and others to the winding of pits in the 1790s. Except in the ironworks, the proportion of the steam engines working in Shropshire built according to James Watt's principles was not very high. The Boulton and Watt Engine Book records a total of only 30 engines supplied to customers in east Shropshire between 1776 and 1801, when allowance is made for double counting. It makes some obvious omissions which are well documented elsewhere, Wilkinson's second engine at Willey, and the small blowing engine at Coalbrookdale forge, for example, but even allowing for such errors, and for the pirate engines in the district, it is doubtful whether more than between a fifth and a quarter of the steam engines in Shropshire in 1800 conformed to Watt's patents.

The steam engine was vital to the development of the Shropshire iron industry. It enabled blast furnaces to be sited away from streams on sites which could easily be supplied with raw materials. It enabled the mechanisation of many of the forging processes. Pumping and winding-engines made possible the exploitation of the deeper seams in the coalfield, without which the iron industry could not have grown. The east Shropshire canals could not have operated without the engines which wound their inclines and filled their reservoirs. Steam power was also applied in the brick and porcelain industries, on railway inclines and in flour mills. The 200 steam engines between Lilleshall and Willey were probably the most densely concentrated in Great Britain. In the scale of its investment in steam power as much as in its capacity for producing pig iron, the Shropshire coalfield was unequalled by another other region in the second half of the 18th century.

How much the ironmasters realised their indebtedness to steam power is shown by the pride with which they regarded their engines. The practice of naming engines seems to have begun among the Coalbrookdale partners in the 1780s. The great pumping-engine at Coalbrookdale was called *Resolution* and the blowing-engines at Ketley, *Adventure* and *Conviction*. The latter was originally named the *Convincement* by Richard Reynolds in 1782 as a riposte to critics who alleged that the Boulton and Watt engines stopped working every half hour. Perhaps the most ostentatious pride in an engine was that displayed by William Botfield in the huge and powerful rolling-mill engine which he purchased from Boulton and Watt in 1801. 'He is so much pleased with it', wrote William Wilkinson the following year, 'he keeps a woman at 8/- per week to wash the engine house every day more than once and to keep the ironwork well blacked and everything clean, which is a difficult task in a place where there is so much dirt as in a Forge Rolling Mill'.[44]

X

THE PHENOMENON OF THE AGE

'The works & the vicinity are frequently visited by numbers of people, of most ranks & stations in life, who seem much astonished at the extensiveness of the Manufactory & the regularity with which it is conducted', remarked the author of a description of Coalbrookdale in 1801. He went on to explain for the benefit of visitors how permission could be sought to enter the works, and the best times for observing the tapping of the furnaces. People interested in industrial innovations, in social change, or merely in the spectacular, visited the Severn Gorge in the 1780s and 90s as they visited Manchester in the 1830s and 40s.[1]

Visitors to the district included many of the most distinguished engineers and innovators of the period. Thomas Telford was surveyor of Shropshire from 1787 until his death in 1834, and maintained close connections with the iron-making part of the county. Matthew Boulton and James Watt both visited the district, and were customers of, and suppliers of engines to most of the principal iron-making concerns. John Loudon McAdam visited Lord Dundonald at the Tuckies in 1789[2]. William Jessop, the greatest canal engineer of the age, advised on the route of the Shropshire Canal and on projected improvements to the River Severn.[3] Benjamin Outram, Jessop's partner in the Butterley Ironworks, and a distinguished engineer in his own right, visited Shropshire to inspect canal inclined planes in 1795.[4] John Curr, the most talented of 18th-century mining engineers, advised on the tunnels and shafts at Brierly Hill on the Shropshire Canal in 1793. The young Richard Trevithick carried out some of his early experiments with steam locomotion at Coalbrookdale.

Well-known visitors to the district were not drawn only from those actively involved in engineering or manufacturing. Arthur Young wrote a lengthy description of the Severn Gorge when he passed through Shropshire in 1776. John Byng, fifth Viscount Torrington, observed iron railways at Coalbrookdale in 1782. John Wesley was a regular visitor to the district and watched preparations for the erection of the Iron Bridge in 1779. The distinguished geologists Charles Hatchett and Robert Townson wrote accounts of the coalfield during the 1790s. Charles Dibdin the actor explored the Tar Tunnel during a visit about 1790. Many published accounts of tourists' journeys in the early 1800s include descriptions of the Gorge.[5]

Many foreign visitors explored the Severn Gorge in the late 18th century. The Frenchman, Marchant de la Houlière inspected Broseley and Coalbrookdale during his investigation of English methods of making cannon in 1775. Jean Dutens who visited Coalbrookdale not long after the peace of 1815, left the most complete set of drawings of the Hay inclined plane. Two other Frenchmen, P.-C. Lesage and M. de Givry observed iron railways at Madeley Wood in 1784. Two Prussian engineers wrote a valuable account of local railways some years later, and a Bavarian, Joseph Ritter von Baader, made the only surviving measured drawings of the first type of iron rail used in Shropshire. Charles Fulton, the American inventor, investigated the Shropshire inclined planes during the 1790s. A Monsieur Fastre, a member of a mining partnership from Namur, demanded to be shown Coalbrookdale while conducting business with Matthew Boulton in Birmingham in 1782. Three Swedish engineers, Reinhold Angenstein, Johan Ludwig Robsahm and Bengt Quist Andersson visited Coalbrookdale in 1753, 1761 and 1766 respectively, the latter observing the attempts of the brothers Cranage to make wrought iron from pig iron using mineral fuel. Another Swede, Erik T. Svedenstierna thoroughly explored the coalfield in 1802–03 and published his findings in Stockholm. A Venetian aristocrat wrote an account of the Severn Gorge in 1787. Princess Carbristka of Poland and her son embarked on a tour in 1790 'to inspect the curiosities of Coalbrookdale'. The Stadtholder William V of Orange and his wife Princess Wilhelmina concluded a visit to Shropshire in 1796 by visiting the Coalbrookdale and Calcutts ironworks, the Coalport porcelain factory and the Hay inclined plane.[6]

The Coalbrookdale ironworks and such natural curiosities as the burning well as Broseley were already attracting visitors like Dr. Richard Wilkes of Willenhall and Professor Mason of Cambridge, in the 1740s, and the first engravings of the district were published as early as 1758, but it was during the last quarter of the century that the Severn Gorge achieved its greatest fame. Visitors came to see the furnaces, the inclined planes, the Tar Tunnel and the chinaworks, but above all they were attracted by the single-span iron bridge which linked Benthall with Madeley Wood.

The lack of a bridge over the Severn between Buildwas and Bridgnorth considerably impeded the economic development of the Gorge. There was a heavy cross-river traffic in semi-finished iron and raw materials,[7] and there is much evidence to suggest that socially the inhabitants of the parishes on either side of the river formed a single community. For passengers, the crossing by ferry of the swift and treacherous currents must have been both disagreeable and dangerous.

Samuel Smiles and John Randall both deduced from sources no long available that Abraham Darby II planned a bridge over the Severn, but it was not until the 1770s that such a project became a reality. The proposal to construct an iron bridge in the Gorge was made in 1773 by Thomas Farnolls Pritchard in a letter to John Wilkinson. Pritchard was born in 1723 and was apprenticed as a joiner in Shrewsbury. By 1760 he was acting as co-ordinator of a team of talented craftsmen specialising in the refurbishing of the interiors of old houses. His architectural works included Swan Hill Court in Shrewsbury, Hatton Grange near Shifnal and Croft Castle, Herefordshire. He designed fireplaces and ceilings in many other houses, and numerous church memorials. He was closely involved with the construction of the English Bridge at Shrewsbury and the Severn Bridge at Atcham in the late 1760s, and was surveyor for the magnificent bridge over the Teme at Bringewood Forge which was constructed in 1772.[8] In 1773 he was appointed surveyor for the bridge over the Severn at the new canal town of Stourport. He originally proposed a timber structure, but it seems that he later decided to build a brick bridge on an iron centre, lightened in the buttresses with circular perforations.[9]

Pritchard was well-known to the entrepreneurs of the Coalbrookdale coalfield. He designed the memorial for John Wilkinson's first wife in Wrexham parish church, and later worked at Wilkinson's house in Broseley. He designed fireplaces at Broseley Hall and Benthall Hall, and the presence of his plasterer Joseph Bromfield among the craftsmen working for Abraham Darby III at Hay Farm, Madeley in the mid-1770s suggests that he may have provided desgns for the re-furbishing of the building. He commissioned the Coalbrookdale ironworks to cast fireplaces for Shipton Hall in the Corvedale, and probably elsewhere.[10]

It was suggested in 1832 that Pritchard 'made a gradual progress in the application of iron to the erection of bridges', and that after the completion of Stourport, he suggested that a bridge consisting entirely of iron should be constructed, a project in which he was encouraged by 'the spirited ironmasters of Coalbrookdale', including John Wilkinson and Abraham Darby III. Thomas Telford and Thomas Tredgold concluded, after examining family papers in the 1820s, that it was Pritchard who first suggested building a bridge in iron, and his many connections with the ironmasters make this a wholly credible thesis.[11]

Petitions calling for the building of an iron bridge in the Gorge were circulated during the winter of 1773–74,[12] and the first formal meeting of the promoters took place at the house of Abraham Cannadine, a Broseley cooper, and probably an innkeeper, on 15 September 1775. A design by Pritchard was accepted, and Abraham Darby III was appointed to construct the bridge and to act as treasurer. A petition seeking authority to build a bridge was presented to the House of Commons on 5 February 1776 when Lord North, the Prime Minister, asked that plans should be displayed on the table of the House. The subsequent parliamentary bill received the Royal Assent on 25 March 1776.[13]

The project was supported by a wide cross-section of local entrepreneurs and land-owners. The dominant figure was Abraham Darby III, who held more shares than any other individual and was personally responsible for the direction of the project. John Wilkinson, Edward Blakeway and Samuel Darby were among other ironmasters involved in the scheme. The secretary to the proprietors was Thomas Addenbrooke, a lawyer who lived at Buildwas. Other shareholders were the Revd. Edward Harries, lord of the manor of Benthall, Charles Guest a Broseley grocer and proprietor of a soap works, Leonard Jennings who worked the two windmills at Broseley and sold bran to Abraham Darby III, John Thursfield, a surgeon, a partner in a coal mine, and a member of the family of earthenware potters, John Morris, a Broseley maltster very active in the public affairs of the parish, and John Nicholson, licensee of the Swan Inn, Coalbrookdale, where the trustees often met.[14]

For eighteen months after the Act of Parliament was passed the trustees were undecided upon the design of the bridge, and during 1776 a schism seems to have developed between Darby, Wilkinson, Jennings and Pritchard, who still favoured an iron bridge, and a group comprising a majority of the shareholders but possessing a minority of the shares, who preferred a more conventional structure. It was not until October 1777, after counsell's opinion had been sought, that a new assignment of shares was made which enabled work to commence.[15]

The various narrative accounts of the construction of the bridge, the accounts of money expended by Abraham Darby III as treasurer, and occasional references in newspapers and journals provide a reasonably coherent chronology of the construction process, a matter on which the shareholders' minutes are singularly uninformative. Construction began in November 1777, but the small sums expended in wages for the first three months suggest that few men were employed. Work was being carried out on a considerable scale throughout the spring and summer of 1778, with the exception of a slack period in August. An expenditure of over £20 a fortnight suggests that 20 to 30 people were employed, with perhaps twice as many for certain short periods. It is likely that most of 1778 was spent in building the foundations of the bridge, and possibly the stone abutments, although one speculative account of the construction process suggests that the latter were added after the ironwork was completed.[16]

It was during the summer of 1779 that the iron ribs were erected. Expenditure on wages did not fall below £28 per fortnight between April and November of that year. On 26 March John Wesley preached at Broseley and went to see 'the bridge that is shortly to be thrown over the Severn', noticing particularly its great weight; and remarking 'I doubt whether the Colossus at Rhodes weighed much more'.[17] The parts of the bridge were hauled into position with ropes costing over £60, attached to a scaffold built from the considerable quantities of timber purchased by the proprietors during 1779. Dantzic timber worth £82 16s. 0d. was obtained from Harford Ring and Co. and fir timber costing £55 14s. 6d. from William Goodwin. A trow belonging to Owner Thomas Sutton was employed during the construction process. The first pair of main ribs was hauled into place on 1 and 2 July 1779, and the expenditure of nearly £6 on ale in mid-August perhaps celebrated the completion of the main structure. The process in all took three months and was carried out without an accident of consequence and without interrupting the river traffic. The scaffolding was removed in November 1779. Nevertheless much of 1780 was taken up with the building of access roads and it was not until New Year's Day 1781 that the bridge was opened to traffic.[18]

Abraham Darby III was principally responsible for the construction of the bridge. It is clear from the shareholders' minutes that during 1776 and 1777 the project was largely sustained by his personal commitment to it. He probably assumed a large degree of financial responsibility. Lord Torrington in 1784 repeated a tradition that he had been meanly treated, and it is possible that he had to pay for all of the iron, stone and other materials used in the bridge. The accounts show that £2,373 4s. 4d. was expended on construction, mainly on labour and equipment, which in 1775 had been estimated to cost only £550. At that time it was anticipated that the iron castings would cost over £2,100, and the dressed stone for the abutments over £500. The full cost of the bridge was apparently between £5,000 and £6,000.[19]

Thomas Farnolls Pritchard died on 21 December 1777 when work on the bridge had scarcely commenced. The bridge which was finally built differed in many respects from his original plans, but he remained a shareholder up to the time of his death, and was probably responsible for the design of the bridge which was eventually built. In September 1779 his brother received from the proprietors a payment of £39 19s. 0d. for 'Thos. F. Pritchard's bill for making drawings, models &c.' There is also a visual connection between the bridge and another of Pritchard's works. The structure's only decorative features are sets of ogees between the uprights and the abutments, and circles between the smallest sets of ribs and the deck plates. They resemble closely the ogees and circles in the stucco ornamentation of a gazebo at 27 Broad Street, Ludlow, a house which Pritchard re-modelled, and comprise a signature which suggests that whoever inscribed on Pritchard's portrait 'Thomas Farnolls Pritchard, Archt., Inventor of Cast Iron Bridges, 1774', was essentially correct.[20]

John Wilkinson clearly played a crucial part in the initial promotion of the project, but he neither designed nor built the structure. Among those who supervised work on

An Estimate for erecting a Cast & Iron Bridge (with Stone Abutments) over the River Severn between Madeley & Broseley. —

The Quantity of cast & wrought Iron as near as
can be computed amounts to 300 Tons at £7ꝑ Ton £2100 .—

786 Yds Cube of Stone Work in Abutments . . . at 10/— . . . . 393 .—

2520 Feet Superf.t of Wrought Ashler face to d.o at 6ᵈ — 63 .—

448 Feet Cube Stone in Parapet . . . . at 8ᵈ — — 14 . 18 .—

720 Feet Superf.t of Work in d.o . . . . . . — at 6ᵈ . . . . — 18 . —

Vases & Lamp Irons . . . . — 11 . 2 .—

600 Yards of dig.g & clearing . . . . at 1/— . . 30 . —

511 Yards Gravelling . . . . at 1/— . . 20 . 11 .—

Pumping Car.g & Scaffolding to erect the Bridge . — 200 . —

Making Drawings, Surveying & other Incidents . . . . 150 . —

Making Roads . . . . — 200 . —

£ 3200 . 11 . —

The above Estimate made by Abraham Darby & Thomas Farnolls Pritchard
Subscribed, as follows —————

John Wilkinson . . . . 630 . — . —

Abraham Darby . . . . — 787 . 10 . —

Edward Blakeway Esq.r . . . . 105 . — . —

Charles Guest . . . . 105 . — . —

Roger Kynaston Esq.r . . . . 52 . 10 . —

Edward Harries Clerk . . . . . . 525 . — . —

Leonard Jennings . . . . . . 525 . — . —

John Morris . . . . 105 . — . —

John Thursfield . . . . . . 52 . 10 . —

Serjeant Roden . . . . . . 52 . 10 . —

John Harthorne . . . . . . 52 . 10 . —

Thomas Farnolls Pritchard . . . . . . 105 . — . —

John Nicholson . . . . . . 52 . 10 . —

£ 3150 . — . —

Figure 13. Estimate for the Iron Bridge.

Lady Labouchere.

the bridge was one Thomas Gregory. Using sources which are no longer available, Samuel Smiles concluded in 1863 that Gregory was Darby's foreman pattern maker and was responsible for the plan of the bridge as it was erected, but the documents presently available do not sustain this view. Thomas Tredgold, Thomas Telford and John White, who likewise drew on sources which have not survived, all associated Daniel Onions with the bridge. Onions was one of the partners in the Benthall iron-works, and was very active in public affairs, but he was not a shareholder and the surviving minutes and accounts do not mention his name.[21]

It seems likely that the order of construction of the parts of the Iron Bridge was rehearsed with a model, and Pritchard's brother was certainly paid for providing such a model. It was probably sold to Sir Edward Smythe of Acton Burnell, who in 1782 paid a firm of heraldic painters £2 12s. 0d. for painting a model of the bridge. Such a sum would have paid the wages of two skilled men for about two weeks, which suggests that the model was a large one. The mahogany model of the bridge now in the Science Museum was made in 1785 by Thomas Gregory and in 1787 was presented by Abraham Darby III to the Society of Arts, who, 'sensible of the magnitude and importance of the Iron Bridge', awarded him their gold medal the following year.[22]

Many of the proprietors of the Iron Bridge, among them Abraham Darby III, Samual Darby, Edward Harries, John Wilkinson, Edward Blakeway and Thomas Addenbrooke, were also shareholders in the Tontine Hotel at the north end of the bridge which was built in the early 1780s, the first part of which was designed by John Hiram Haycock of Shrewsbury and the second by Samuel Wright of Kidderminster. Many of the proprietors were also involved with the turnpike road through Leighton which linked the Iron Bridge with Shrewsbury, and it seems probable that they also laid out the market square at the north end of the Bridge.[23]

The Iron Bridge became one of the great spectacles of the time, an eye-catching Gothic monument, deliberately promoted by its proprietors, and recorded in the iti-neraries and sketchbooks of countless connoisseurs of the curious. Perhaps no other industrial structure so excited the imagination of artists. The completion of the bridge coincided with a marked change in the attitude of painters and writers towards the scenery of the Severn Gorge.

The two earliest prints of Coalbrookdale, drawn by Thomas Smith of Derby and George Perry engraved by T. Vivares and published in 1758, aimed to show that 'Arts and Manufactures contribute greatly to the Wealth and power of a nation'. They are restrained in style. A team of horses is shown hauling a cylinder past the Upper Furnace Pool, while a waggon descends the hill on the other side. The smoking coke hearths and the flaming furnace top hardly disturb the settled landscape of ironmasters' mansions and workers' cottages with their surrounding gardens on the hillside.[24] The next artist to portray Coalbrookdale was William Williams who made two paintings of the valley, in the morning and in the afternoon, in 1777.[25] The morning view is dominated by an immense vertical stack of smoke arising from the chimney of the pumping-engine house. The Darby residence, Sunniside, stands severely on its emin-ence to the west, facing the rising sun. The top of the old blast furnace is licked with flames, while an amorphous cloud of smoke billows from the coke hearths. Three horses and a man with a rod check the progress of a railway waggon down an inclined plane. The afternoon painting shows the same column of smoke originating in the engine house, but orange flames now burst from the coke hearths. Coalbrookdale appears as a smoke-filled valley, intruding into a serene pastoral landscape, its wooded slopes insulating it from the neatly parcelled fields which extend towards the Wrekin. Williams's painting expresses much the same feelings that Arthur Young experienced at Coalbrookdale the previous year:

> Colebrook Dale . . . is a very romantic spot, it is a winding glen between two immense hills which break into various forms, and all thickly covered with wood, forming the most beautiful sheets of hanging wood. Indeed too beautiful to be much in unison with that variety of horrors art has spread at the bottom: the noise of the forges, mills &c. with all their vast machinery, the flames bursting from the furnaces with the burning of the coal and the smoak of the lime kilns, are altogether sublime.[26]

The most significant feature of William's afternoon view is the attitude of the people he depicts. A red-coated gentleman looks away from the ironworks, directed by a rustic woodman, while his two elegant lady companions are engaged in gossip.

In no respect did the erection of the Iron Bridge more completely change the attitude of artists towards industrial monuments, for in almost every view of the bridge people are shown actively inspecting it. The visual qualities of the bridge were speedily recognised. The tenant of the *Swan Inn* boasted in July 1781 that her hostelry was situated near 'that most incomparable piece of architecture, the Iron Bridge'. Views of the bridge by 'a capital artist' were being advertised as early as June 1780, six months before it was opened to traffic. In October of the same year Abraham Darby III paid William Williams 10 guineas for a view of the bridge.[27] In 1780 also Michael Angelo Rooker, scenery painter at the Haymarket Theatre, travelled to Coalbrookdale to make a drawing of the bridge, his fee and expenses amounting to £29. Engravings by William Ellis of his drawing were on sale the following May.[28]

Rooker shows a barge moored on the south bank of the river, a coracle bobbing below the bridge, watched by a man and a woman on the shore, while a poacher stalks along the north bank followed by his dog. At the foot of the south abutment two gentlemen earnestly examine the structure. Horsemen crossing the bridge are dwarfed by railings of exaggerated size, while beyond the bridge rises a crag, terrifying in its ruggedness, but altogether subsidiary to the man-made bridge which occupies the centre of the picture.

In 1788 George Robertson published a series of six views of industrial scenes in the Severn Gorge. Unlike Rooker, Robertson showed the Iron Bridge as something insubstantial, in most cases altogether dwarfed by the overpowering mountains around it. The bridge remains nevertheless the *raison d'être* of his pictures. In the view engraved by Francis Chesham a horseman pauses beneath the bridge to examine the ribs. In one of the two engraved by James Fittler, two travellers apparently discuss the bridge with a man escorting a packhorse. Robertson turned his attention to other spectacles in the neighbourhood a coal mine at Broseley, the casting house of a blast furnace and the Calcutts ironworks.[29]

The Iron Bridge continued to attract artists to the Coalbrookdale area in the 1790s and early 1800s, but like Robertson many turned from the bridge to other sublime scenes in the neighbourhood. Philip James de Loutherbourg, like Rooker a scenery painter, depicted several views of the Gorge before 1800. The best known, *Coalbrookdale by Night*, which actually portrays the Bedlam furnaces, shows a railway waggon hauled at headlong speed by two horses, their heads bowed down in fright. The whole scene is lit up as if in daylight, perhaps because a furnace is being tapped. The fires illuminate a litter of huge steam engine pipes, while a nearby tree is wracked in a fearsome gale.[30]

In 1789 Joseph Farington passed through the Gorge and drew the pools in Coal-brookdale, a distant view of the Iron Bridge, and the only surviving view of the Preen's Eddy Bridge. In 1802 the young John Sell Cotman toured Shropshire with Paul Sandby Munn. Cotman painted the Bedlam furnaces and sketched horse gins and a riverside salt warehouse. Munn depicted the Iron Bridge with its wooden land arches under construction, the water wheel at Benthall Mill, and the lime kilns on Lincoln Hill, with dwarf-like workmen shrouded in vast clouds of smoke.[31] Thomas Rowlandson painted Ludcroft Wharf, Coalbrookdale towards the end of the 18th century. He shows a cast-iron pot arriving on a horse-drawn railway waggon. The wharf is littered with disorderly piles of cannon and other hardware, while a plump swain and his mistress rest on a pile of timber.[32] Samuel Ireland of Wem drew a variety of scenes on the Severn and wrote a dramatic description of the tapping of one of the Coalbrookdale blast furnaces. J. M. W. Turner visited Coalbrookdale early in the 19th century. His powerful yet serene view of the Lincoln Hill limeworks is in marked contrast to the frenetic activity shown in most paintings of industrial scenes.[33]

The Severn Gorge in the late 18th century, its hills, woods, tributary valleys, the man-made furnace fires, coke hearths and lime kilns, the eccentric motions of steam engines and horse gins, such curiosities as the inclined planes, the giant water wheels and the Tar Tunnel, comprised a landscape which a generation addicted to Romantic follies, Gothic novels and Evangelical religion found particularly moving. Artist, divine and poet found in the landscape an almost apocalyptic significance. 'I thank you for your view of the iron bridge', wrote John Fletcher from Switzerland to a correspondent in Broseley in February 1781, 'I hope the word and the faith that works by love will erect a more solid and durable bridge to unite those who travel together towards Zion'.[34] Thomas Harral was impressed by:

> These regions of volcanic-like eruptions, from flaming apertures, projecting huge columns of smoke, intermingled into a dense atmosphere, and groups of sooty labourers like demons of the lower world.

Another writer was moved by:

> the flaming furnaces and smoking limekilns (which) form a spectacle horribly sublime, while the stupendous iron arch, striding over the chasm presents to the mind an idea of that fatal bridge made by sin and death over chaos, from the boundaries of hell to the wall of this now defenceless world.[35]

An Italian visitor enjoyed much the same experience in 1787:

> The approach to Coalbrookdale appeared to be a veritable descent to the infernal regions. A dense column of smoke arose from the earth; volumes of steam were ejected from the fire engines; a blacker cloud issued from a tower in which was a forge; and smoke arose from a mountain of burning coals which burst out into turbid flame. In the midst of this gloom I descended towards the Severn, which runs slowly between two high mountains, and after leaving which passed under a bridge, constructed entirely of iron. It appeared as a gate of mystery, and night already falling, added to the impressiveness of the scene, which could only be compared to the regions so powerfully described by Virgil'.[36]

In 1798 Henry Skrine reacted in a similar manner:

> We made a precipitate descent to the Romantic scene of Colebrooke Dale, where the river winding between a variety of high, wooded hills, opposite to the forges of Broseley, is crossed by a bridge of one arch, 100 ft. in length, and formed entirely of cast iron, with strong stone

abutments, which present at once a striking effect in landscape and a stupendous specimen of the powers of mechanism.

. . . .By day, the busy scene in this neighbourhood, and the vast quantity of craft with which the river is busy, add not a little to the interest in view; while by night the numerous fires arising from the works on the opposite hills, and along the several channels of the two valleys, aided by the clangour of forges in every direction, affect the mind of one unpractised in such scenes with an indescribable sensation of wonder, and transport in fancy the classic observer to the workshop of Vulcan or an epitome of infernal regions'.[37]

Iron-making was the most awe-inspiring of industries in the 18th century and its products the most spectacular. Visitors of all sorts, artists, poets, engineers, were both horrified and fascinated by what they found in the Severn Gorge. Coalbrookdale and its environs were not just the location of a rapidly-growing new series of industrial processes: they formed a sublime Romantic spectacle in which man appeared puny both in relation to the grandeur of the surrounding natural scenery and to his own creations. The Iron Bridge was no mere milestone in the history of civil engineering. It was the phenomenon of the age.

XI

THE MASTERS

Why did certain entrepreneurs in the mid-18th century set in motion manufacturing processes on an entirely new scale? Did they do so to become rich, to exercise new-found technological skills, in pursuit of fresh knowledge, as a means of providing employment for the poor, or of benefiting humanity with their products? Were they conditioned to undertake risks by their religious beliefs, by their education, or by their social background? Consideration of the Shropshire ironmasters gives no easy and simple answers to these most challenging questions about the entrepreneurs of the Industrial Revolution. While certain tentative conclusions about the ironmasters can be advanced, in general the dissimilarities of background, beliefs and motives are more impressive than the characteristics they shared. Judgments about entrepreneurs are notoriously liable to distortion as a result of the uneven survival of evidence. While some of the principal figures in Shropshire industry, Richard Reynolds, Abraham Darby II, John Wilkinson, Thomas Gilbert, are tolerably well documented, others, of major importance in their own times, are, like Saxon ealdormen, known only as signatories of legal documents.

The difficulties of investigating entrepreneurs are well illustrated by two leading figures in Shropshire in the early 18th century, Abraham Darby I and Richard Hartshorne. The first Abraham Darby is the least known of the succession of Quaker ironmasters who bore that name, but thanks to the records of the Society of Friends and a number of reminiscences by his family and household, and the importance of his discovery of coke-smelting, the outline of his life is tolerably well known, although of sources which might reveal something of his motivations and objectives there are few. Yet far more important to his contemporaries than Abraham Darby I was Richard Hartshorne, who is the 20th century in an even less substantial figure. Hartshorne was, without any doubt, the leading Shropshire coalmaster of the early 18th century. He was one of the first users of a Newcomen engine in Shropshire, the first to employ iron railway wheels, and the principal supplier of raw materials to Darby's furnace at Coalbrookdale. He produced coke for the first ironworks where Darby's coke smelting process was copied. He leased mines in Wombridge from the Charltons, in Ketley from the Gowers, in Great Dawley from the Slaneys, in Little Wenlock and Huntingdon from the Foresters, and probably in Little Dawley from the Cravens. He built a railway from Little Wenlock to the Severn in 1727. He operated the Kingsley Wyche saltworks. He probably built the elegant Ketley Bank House which bears the date 1721 and the initials RJH – Richard and Jane Hartshorne. His death in January 1733 led the

Coalbrookdale partners to fear for the continuance of their iron ore supplies. He was remembered by miners in the 1750s as a coalmaster of outstanding abilities. His wife's probate inventory made in 1737 shows that she had two residences, Ketley Bank Hall and a house in Wellington, which was probably the Old Hall. The total value of the inventory was £546 14s. 0d. which included mining stock and equipment in Dawley, Hollinswood, Snedshill and Ketley, where there was a steam engine worth £200. Both houses displayed the characteristic marks of wealth and luxury of the early 18th century, sets of cane chairs, clocks, china, maps, pictures and looking glasses. The way of life of Richard and Jane Hartshorne was obvious very different from that of Walter Hartshorne, who died in 1696 and was probably the father of Richard, and was a typical yeoman collier, with cows, sheep, horses and pigs worth £49, in contrast with mining tools worth £6 and coal on the pit bank valued at £20. He lived in a six room house in which beer was brewed, yarn was spun and cheese was made. Richard Hartshorne remains a name which appears in leases, rentals and accounts, whose influence can now only dimly be perceived through the impact he made on others.[1] If it were possible to discover as much about Hartshorne, (or in a later period about John Onions, Edward Blakeway, Richard Jesson or Alexander Brodie), as is generally known of the Coalbrookdale partners, the history of the Shropshire coalfield might appear in a very different light.

The Quaker ironmasters of Coalbrookdale are better known than any other group of Shropshire entrepreneurs. They were indeed a 'dynasty of ironfounders'.[2] But it is as misleading to see them as a group with identical outlooks which did not change over 150 years as it is to regard them as typical of other ironmasters. The Coalbrookdale partners have often been portrayed as sharing in most respects the outlook of the Quaker saint Richard Reynolds, the only one of the partners to have been accorded a full-length biography. The Reynoldses and Darbys were individuals whose attitudes to many problems were markedly different.

Richard Reynolds was a supremely successful man of business, with large interests in the West of England and South Wales quite apart from his Shropshire concerns. Of all of the Coalbrookdale partners he was the most positively concerned with philanthropy and the welfare of his employees. A visitor in 1767 found him, 'a Quaker who seemed particularly careful of his speech.' His funeral in Bristol was attended by thousands of the poor, who lined the streets out of respect to his memory.[3]

Reynolds was an active member of the Society of Friends and much of his correspondence is filled with religious concerns. In a letter to his wife in 1773 he seems to disavow all interest in making money

> I am thankful I can say I am at all times enabled to consider the things of this life in that degree of subordination and inferiority to the concerns of the next, that whether an increase or a decrease of outward riches seems most probable is a matter of great indifferency to me, and when I consider further the ill effects riches frequently have upon the mind, especially of young people, together with the remembrance that where there is but little given there is but little required, I am inclined to contemplate a state of inferiority to former expectations, if not with a positive desire for it, at least with a cheerful acquiescence in it. If I attain to purity of heart and meekness of temper, how little of worldly riches will be sufficient, and if either one or the other of the former will be prevented by my having even so much as I have of the latter, may I be deprived of it[4]

Reynolds shared the traditional Quaker horror of indebtedness, and recommended to his son frugality in the early years of life as the foundation of subsequent prosperity.[5]

The second Abraham Darby, builder of the Horsehay and Ketley ironworks, was, like Richard Reynolds, his son-in-law and partner, a strict member of the Society of Friends. In December 1756 when the first Horsehay furnace was proving successful he wrote to his partner Thomas Goldney that it was making as much as 22 tons of iron a week, 'sold off as fast as made at profit enough will soon find money enough for another furnace *and for the pocket too*'. Six months later, after the second Horsehay furnace had been blown in, Darby's wife wrote to her sister, 'My husband delights in laying out money: and when he'll stop I don't know'.[6]

Abraham Darby II's wife saw the innovations made by her husband and son-in-law as achievements of benefactors of mankind, to be contrasted with those of soldiers, the destroyers of mankind. They were *ad hoc* solutions to practical problems which, by improving the iron trade, improved the lot of the nation generally.[7] A rather different attitude is to be observed among Shropshire ironmasters in the last quarter of the 18th century: a delight in innovation for its own sake, a deep interest in science, a concern to make the maximum use of all available resources. The lack of any distinct urban centre in the coalfield prevented the growth of any formal scientific body like the Birmingham Lunar Society in Shropshire, but there is abundant evidence that several leading ironmasters of the late 18th century were concerned with scientific investigation for its own sake, and some attempts were made to provide intellectual activities of the sort customarily found in the larger towns of the period. A subscription library was established in Ironbridge in 1802, and scientific lecturers sometimes visited the district. A Dr. Ketterfeld spoke about magnetism and demonstrated a microscope at Broseley and Coalbrookdale in 1793, and a lecturer on Astronomy demonstrated an orrery at Wellington and Broseley in 1800. Abraham Darby III carried on scientific experiments in his home, and exchanged geological specimens with Erasmus Darwin. His cash book in 1771 reveals the purchase of a camera obscura and an 'electrical machine'.[8]

No other ironmaster could match the intellectual stature or the scientific imagination of William Reynolds, son of Richard Reynolds by his first wife, Hannah Darby. Like Abraham Darby III, Reynolds was interested in electricity, and in 1777 was experimenting with Leyden Jars and reading the works of Joseph Priestley. He was keenly interested in geology. 'His shafts', wrote John Randall, 'to him were mere inlets to the deep storehouse of the globe where Providence had treasured means whereby to enrich future inhabitants of the surface'. In a letter in 1779 Reynolds complimented Lord Dundonald on his knowledge of 'the good things which we have in this neighbourhood', and hoped that a visit would show him 'that we know how to make good use of some of them', and are proceeding to lay the rest under requisition as fast as we can'. In a variety of fields, Reynolds attempted to apply scientific knowledge to industrial processes. In 1799 he took out a patent for the manufacture of manganese steel, and sent samples to John Wilkinson, William Crawshay and to James Watt. He built tar kilns based on those of Lord Dundonald. He was a partner in the Wrockwardine Wood glassworks, and patron of John Biddle's Wombridge alkali works. He planned with Lord Dundonald a vast integrated chemical complex at Coalport. He was involved with Richard Trevithick's experiments with a steam railway locomotive, and he himself attempted to employ steam power to propel pleasure boats. He even pursued lines of research which generations later were to lead to the internal combustion engine. In 1799, in collaboration with James Glazebrook, he was trying to make 'something different from Steam Engines', which was to achieve mechanical effects by using 'oil or tar', one of the hydrocarbons produced at Lord Dundonald's works at the Calcutts.

26. Morning View of Coalbrookdale (William Williams, 1777)
(*Clive House Museum, Shrewsbury*)

27. The Coalport China Works in the early 19th century (T. Jewitt) (*Ironbridge Gorge Museum Trust*)

28. The China Works and the restored bed of the Shropshire Canal at Coalport (*Photo: Author*)

A Wrockwardine Wood glass jug
(Crown Copyright, Victoria and
Albert Museum)

Holy Trinity Church, Wrockwardine Wood, designed by Samuel Smith and consecrated in 1833. In the background are the English glass cones of the Wrockwardine Wood glassworks which closed c.1840 (Shropshire Record Office)

31. The Coalbrookdale turnpike gate at the foot of Jiggers Bank before the building of the railway in 1864 (*Photo: E. G. Webb*)

32. Thomas Telford's Ketley embankment on the Holyhead Road. The main road on the left crosses Telford's embankment, built over the original forge houses of the Ketley ironworks. The old road ascending from the valley floor can be seen on the right (*Photo: Author*)

One of the largest of the Shropshire ironworks of the 19th century: the Lilleshall Company's Lodge ast furnaces, built in the 1820s (*From Samuel Griffiths's* Guide to the Iron Trade, *1873*)

Barrack houses surrounded by pit mounts near Donnington Wood brickworks (*Photo: Author*)

35. John Fletcher (*From an original in the John Fletcher School, Madeley, Telford, copied by courtesy of the headmaster*)

36. The Vicarage Barn, Madeley, and St. Michael's Church. Designed by Thomas Telford, and consecrated in 1797 (*Shropshire Record Office*)

37. The gallery for the poor installed by the Botfield family in St. James's Church, Stirchley (*Photo: Reg Preedy*)

38. Finger Road Primitive Methodist Chapel, Dawley, 1863 (*Photo: H. Griffiths*)

More than any other ironmaster, Reynolds was active in the social and intellectual circle which revolved around Joseph Plymley of Longnor Hall, archdeacon of Ludlow, and author of *A General View of the Agriculture of Shropshire*. Other members of the circle were Thomas Telford, Archibald Alison, the naturalist and philosopher, Thomas Dugard, a surgeon whom Reynolds recommended for a post at the Royal Salopian Infirmary, Robert Townson, the eccentric geologist, and Thomas Clarkson, the anti-slavery advocate. Like Clarkson and most other members of the circle, Reynolds took an active part in the local agitation against slavery. William Reynolds was a less rigid Quaker than his father. He was excluded from the Society of Friends for marrying his cousin, and while he retained his links with the society, conscientiously refusing to pay church rates, always being recognised by his Quaker's broad-brimmed hat, and always being regarded by his workmen as a Quaker, he and his wife 'gradually relaxed in their attachement' to the Friends, and after his death his widow brought up their children in the Established Church. Reynolds seems to have enjoyed an easy and congenial relationship with his workmen and with the local community in general. In 1795 he presided over the warming of the *Tontine Inn* when a new landlord took over. He offered rewards to his miners for bringing him fossils, and was always ready to talk about geology with them. He was not immune from unQuakerly displays of annoyance. By repute he broke the windows of the cottage of the Coalport ferryman who had refused to get out of bed to fetch him over the river, and he repeatedly passed through a turnpike gate at night to disturb the rest of a tollkeeper who had charged him unjustly. He had a zany delight in science and its achievements. Visitors to his home at Ketley Bank were usually shown his laboratory, his library and his collection of fossils. He also displayed a gigantic glass bottle with a capacity of 70 or 80 gallons made at his Wrockwardine Wood works, and explained to one of his guests a scheme for making a flute 150 ft. long and 2 ft. 6 in. in diameter, which was to be blown by a steam engine and played on by barrels.[9] Reynolds died in 1803 at the age of 45. If he had lived as long as his father, who was 81 when he died in 1816, the industrial history of Shropshire might have been very different.

John Wilkinson's temperament and way of life were in most respects very different from those of William Reynolds, but he did share Reynolds's scientific interests, although his concern was much more with the practical applications of discoveries than with the pursuit of pure knowledge. His development of the boring machine, his application of the steam engine to blow blast furnaces and his iron boats are described elsewhere.[10] Among his other innovations was an attempt to introduce a coal-cutting machine, an 'iron man', into his mines, but this is a particularly ill-documented incident.[11] Modesty was not Wilkinson's most obvious characteristic, and it is difficult to distinguish those of his claims to innovations which were justified from those which were merely aggressive attempts to establish a position in a dispute, or those which sprang sincerely from his considerable reserves of conceit. Wilkinson claimed that he made a material contribution to the development of the separate condenser, without which Boulton and Watt would have made no more progress with their engines in the second half of the 1770s than in the first. With what justice this claim was made it is now impossible to judge. James Watt remarked of this period 'As Mr. Wilkinson was perpetually scheming new works he used to tax our brains pretty heavily upon such occasions and used to talk as if he had been doing us a favour by using our inventions'.[12] This may well be a just comment on Wilkinson's lack of gratitude and scruple. It is at the same time a compliment to his thrusting curiosity. He was probably not an original thinker, although he would often claim to have experimented with ideas like coke ovens or manganese steel before other people.[13] Few of his successful innovations were based on his own ideas. His boring machine was probably copied from continental examples built on the plans of Jan Verbruggen. His iron boat was the creation of a skilled blacksmith. His coke ovens were probably copied from those of Dundonald or William Reynolds. Yet his contribution to technological progress in the late 18th century was probably as great as that of any other single ironmaster. The intellectual excitement of his enterprises is well preserved in the young Joseph Priestley's description of the Bradley ironworks in 1790, 'independent of the scope there is for exertion in every branch of the business, there is a pleasure and advantage in being concerned in a works of such large extent and where so many improvements are daily making that no consideration can overbalance'.[14]

Shropshire produces no instant solution to the problems associated with the relationship of religion and industry in the 18th century. While the Darbys and Reynoldses were Quakers, and it is possible to produce an impressive array of evidence that their success sprang from their adherence to Quaker discipline, other equally successful ironmasters had totally different religious backgrounds. John Guest paid half the cost of the Birch Meadow Baptist chapel in Broseley in 1801, and John Onions was buried in the graveyard attached to the chapel. John Wilkinson had a Presbyterian upbringing, and in spite of occasional protests to the contrary, was probably a free-thinker in adult life. Earl Gower and his partners were Anglicans. Granville Leveson-Gower, the second Marquess of Stafford and John Bishton built and endowed the church of St. George, Oakengates in 1806. Isaac Hawkins Browne, landlord of the Old Park Company built the church of St. Leonard, Dawley in 1805, while his partners the Botfields were conventional Anglicans, who provided a gallery for the poor in Stirchley parish church. If Quaker virtues brought success in the 18th-century iron trade, then Anglican virtues, even free-thinking virtues were equally effective.

Conventional virtues were not necessarily more acceptable among entrepreneurs in the 18th century than in the 20th. The quarterly meetings of ironmasters at Stourbridge brought together a number of Quakers and Quaker business was sometimes transacted at the same time. Yet the quarterly meetings themselves were far from being earnest assemblies of the pious. Richard Reynolds dreaded the temptations which they offered, and in 1789 wrote to his son:

> It occurs to me that the quarterly meetings of the iron masters at Birmingham and Stourbridge are in the course of next week. This has occasioned me to reflect on years that are past and the sentiments that so prevailed in my mind before I went to them, as well as the reflections upon them after my return home. I will not say that the consideration of the dangers to which I was about to be exposed, and the desire that sometimes accompanied it for preservation from them, was always attended with that degree of watchfulness and circumspection which would have ensured the plaudits of my own conscience after it was over. For though I may say, with humble thankfulness, I hope my conduct did not bring any reproach on my religious profession . . . yet, when I reflected upon the levity of the conversation (to speak of it in the mildest terms) and how far I had contributed to it, or at least, contenanced it by sitting longer among them than was absolutely necessary, it has brought sorrow and condemnation on my part.

He warned his son against 'those who would triumph if they could lead thee, or any other sober young man into excess or intemperance'. In 1791 he described the quarterly meetings as 'times of peculiar trial', and admitted that he had often gone to them with fear as well as dislike.[15]

The 18th-century Quaker ironmaster enjoyed contacts through the Society of Friends with men of business in all parts of Great Britain and the American colonies who shared the same standards of self-discipline, and who, in an age when trade was uncertain, could be relied upon to pay their debts and meet their obligations. Quaker ethics, with their emphasis on restraint, frugality and the avoidance of debt were obviously conducive to survival in business if not to an outstanding rate of growth. It is likely, nevertheless, that the distinctive culture of the Society of Friends made Quakerism as much an obstacle as a benefit to success in the iron trade. It imposed barriers which must have handicapped relations between Quakers and other ironmasters, their workpeople and the local ruling class. While membership of the Society of Friends was an important link between the ironmasters and some of their principal employees, it may equally well be argued that it might have been a divisive force in the local community. It could certainly have excluded skilled non-Quakers from positions of responsibility. Quakers were distinct from the majority of their employees in dress, in their manner of speech and in their whole way of life. There seems certainly to have been a basic lack of understanding, a feeling of puzzlement rather than bitterness, between the élite who practised restraint and frugality to a most unusual degree, and their workers, among whom lavish spending and reckless abandonment to pleasure, came as of nature.

About no 18th-century entrepreneur were opinions more divided than about John Wilkinson, although none could have regarded his successes as the just rewards of conventional virtue. Wilkinson drove harder bargains than his contemporaries, his prices were higher and his credit terms shorter. He was heartily hated by many. 'I do believe him to be one of the most hard hearted, malevolent Old Scoundrels now existing in Britain', wrote Lord Dundonald in 1800, and went on to speak of 'the Invidiousness, the Malevolence and the Badness of John Wilkinson's heart'. On another occasion Dundonald quoted James Keir, the chemist, as saying, 'his heart is as hard as his pig iron'.[16] Wilkinson's dispute with his brother William gave rise to many similarly abusive statements. Other ironmasters distrusted him and sometimes directly impeded his enterprises. Dr. Joseph Priestley thought that his son failed to gain an appointment as manager of the Coalbrookdale works in 1790 only because of his former employment with Wilkinson. 'It is certainly a singular hardship', Priestley complained to Wilkinson, 'that my son's relationship to you should be of this material disadvantage to him'.[17] In 1797 William Wilkinson noted that his brother had no facilities for making boiler slabs, and could not buy them from others, 'into such a scrawl he is got with the trade'.[18] Hatred of John Wilkinson was not universal however, and much hostility doubtless sprang from worsted rivals. Dr. Joseph Priestley, his brother-in-law, regarded his actions in the dispute with William Wilkinson as fair, unexceptionable and generous, and commented, 'I particularly admire the excellent temper that you have always shown with respect to it'. For one journalist Wilkinson was the embodiment of numerous virtues: 'in the private sphere he adds to the character of the most affectionate of husbands, the habit of benefitting the meritorious part of his fellow creatures, of whatsoever country, in whatsoever situation, and of whatsoever persuasion, religious or political'.[19]

John Wilkinson's ambitions in the iron trade persisted even into old age. In 1800 his brother told James Watt Jun. that he was, 'much taken up in scheming and is now decided to have eight furnaces in blast in the course of this year . . . being decided to have more furnaces than any one man in Britain of his own'. By this time the high reputation for quality which had brought Wilkinson the custom of Boulton and Watt in the 1770s had been sullied. William Wilkinson, not the least biased of witnesses, commented on his plans in 1800, 'I think before he makes new ones [i.e. furnaces] he ought to make the old ones turn out better'.[20] James Watt remarked in 1795 that one of the great objections which he and Boulton had to Wilkinson's erecting engines according to their patents was that, 'his engineers threw them together so inaccurately and kept them in such shocking order that they were the disgrace to the invention, and we believe have more than once prevented our receiving orders from other people'.

Hostility to John Wilkinson arose as much from dislike of his political and religious opinions as from fear of his entrepreneurial aggression or dismay at the quality of his products. He strongly identified himself with his brother-in-law, Joseph Priestley, when the latter's house in Birmingham was sacked by a church-and-king mob in 1791, and James Watt believed that it was the 1791 riots which caused Wilkinson never to visit Birmingham.[21] Wilkinson sympathised with the French Revolution, and in 1791 purchased assignats, describing France as, 'a country which appears to me most likely to become the place of refuge from persecution in religious matters, as it will be of advantage to those engaged in Manufactures and Commerce, which will alway flourish *most* where Church and King interfere least'.[22] There was a curious irony about the epitaph which Wilkinson prepared for himself,

> Delivered from Persecution of Malice and Envy, here rests John Wilkinson, ironmaster, In certain hope of a better estate and Heavenly Mansion, as promulgated by Jesus Christ, in whose gospel he was a firm believer. His life was spent in action for the benefit of man, and he trusts in some degree to the glory of God as his different works that remain in various parts of the kingdom are testimonials of increasing labour[23]

Wilkinson displayed no close regard for conventional morality. In 1795 his brother described one of his affairs, 'his favourite handmaid Betty, is discharged, or report says, and like Hagar of old is left to bemoan the loss of her Virginity without its reward'. In the early years of the 19th century he had three children by another servant girl, Mary Ann Lewis, while his second wife was still alive, the youngest of them fathered when he was 77. Gilbert Gilpin told William Wilkinson of an incident in the friendship in 1804: John Wilkinson had been,

> over at B. Rowley's (at Snedshill) with his girl, She, poor creature, while there had nearly died of indigestion from having gorged herself with eating salmon. Old Shylock and her withdrew from the table: and having laid on the bed together for a few hours, she returned perfectly recovered.[24]

Alone among 18th-century Shropshire entrepreneurs John Wilkinson was regarded among his workpeople as something of a folk hero. On several occasions he took energetic action to overcome local shortages of small coinage by issuing his own notes and tokens, the latter struck with his own image bearing some resemblance to that of the King on the contemporary coins of the realm. He was reputed to grant pensions to aged workmen who had served him well. In 1815 he was confidently expected to return from the dead to aid his former employees when trade was slack. Wilkinson was the only Shropshire ironmaster commemorated in folk song:

Before I proceed with my lingo
You shall all drink my toast in a bumper of stingo
Fill up, and without any further parade,
John Wilkinson, boys, the supporter of trade.

May all his endeavours be crowned with success
And his works ever growing prosperity bless
May his comforts increase with the length of his days
And his fame shine as bright as his furnace's blaze.

That the wood of old England would fail, did appear,
And tho' iron was scarce because charcoal was dear,
By puddling and stamping he cured that evil,
So the Swedes and the Russians may go to the devil.

Our thundering cannon, too frequently burst,
As mischief so great he prevented the first,
And now it is well known they never miscarry
But drive on our foes with a blast of Old Harry.

Then let each jolly fellow take hold of his glass
And drink to the health of his friend and his lass.
May we always have plenty of stingo and pence,
And Wilkinson's flame blaze a thousand years hence.[25]

Wilkinson was not, of course, the inventor of coke smelting, nor of the puddling furnace nor of the stamping and potting process, but errors in the detail of the song should not detract from the truth of its main theme, that without Wilkinson's energy many important innovations in iron-making would have been applied less rapidly. Without displaying the Evangelical concern for the souls of his workmen shown by other Shropshire ironmasters, he secured a reputation as a good employer and as a folk hero.

The three sons of Thomas Botfield who succeeded to the Old Park ironworks in 1801 were rather different from most Shropshire entrepreneurs of the late 18th century. They were less closely involved with the day-to-day operation of the ironworks, and with the processes carried on therein. Rather than plough back all of their profits into iron-making, they invested large sums in landed property. Gilbert Gilpin who re-organised the Old Park forges from 1799 onwards found there was so much distance between himself and his employers that he contemplated leaving. William Wilkinson noted in 1802 that William Botfield lived 'in Style' and was, 'not much attached to Business'. In 1807 Gilpin told William Wilkinson that Beriah Botfield's income in the previous year from land and trade was more than £13,000 and that he 'would take no part in any business and is the least pleasant of any of the three brothers'.[26] Nevertheless the Botfield concerns flourished and grew more rapidly in the first half of the 19th century than any other Shropshire iron-making partnership.

If there is a career pattern typical of Shropshire ironmasters in the 18th century it is not that of a Quaker born into an iron-making family and inheriting his father's concerns, but of an Anglican agent proving himself capable in his master's service and eventually receiving a share of the capital in his master's industrial enterprises. Many agents were themselves men of considerable social standing, landowners in their own rights, and not penniless men of ability.

The complexity of the agent's position can be observed in the careers of Thomas and Francis Dorsett, agents to the Charlton family of Apley Castle. Thomas Dorsett with Richard Corfield held the freehold of the Coalbrookdale works when Abraham Darby I leased the site in 1708. His association with the Charltons began in the mid-1720s when he began to act as their estate steward and took over the operation of the forge at Wytheford in his own right. He lived at this time at Madeley Court which suggests considerable wealth. By 1733 he was in control of the blast furnace at Leighton. His son Francis became agent to the Charltons in the mid-1740s, and began at the same time to operate the Kingsley Wyche saltworks and the neighbouring farm in his own right. Francis Dorsett did not inherit Wytheford Forge on his father's death in about 1747, but in 1750 leased the forge at Upton-on-Tern. As research on the charcoal iron industry progresses so more will be learned about the Dorsetts. They were not leading figures in the Industrial Revolution in Shropshire but their careers do illustrate a number of factors common in the careers of Shropshire entrepreneurs. They were themselves landowners. While acting as agents to other, larger, landowners, they themselves leased some of the enterprises on their masters' estates and worked them in their own right. Ultimately they acquired sufficient capital to extend their operations elsewhere.[27]

Numerous Shropshire entrepreneurs began their careers as agents or as experts in iron-making or pottery for landowners or capitalists who knew little of industrial processes. The more traditional estate agent, ignorant of technological developments, laboured under some disadvantages in the mid-18th century. In 1755 Francis Paddy, agent on the Shropshire estates of Lord Stafford, recommended his master to lease his mines in Priorslee to someone who would build 'fire engines' to drain them, and lamented, 'for your Lordship's sake only I wish I was a Master of such works'.[28] John Wilkinson was no more than a hired authority on iron-making when he was granted a one twelfth share in the New Willey Company in 1757. He ultimately took control of the company and the Forester family, on whose land it operated, withdrew from direct involvement in its affairs. Another Forester agent, William Ferriday, became a considerable entrepreneur in his own right, after observing with some pessimism the building of the Horsehay ironworks, becoming within four years a partner in three similar concerns. Thomas Botfield was a figure of some local standing when he acted as agent to Isaac Hawkins Browne in the exploitation of the Old Park Estate in Dawley after 1790. He sprang from an old Dawley mining family, had been one of the partners in the original Lightmoor ironworks and had experience of the industries of the Clee Hill area. The details of the first Old Park partnerships are at present unknown, but it seems likely that Botfield was agent to Browne with a share in the partnership in 1790, and that within a few years he gained complete control of the company. The role of agents is even more notable in the history of the Lilleshall partnerships. In 1764 Earl Gower's partners in the company he formed for the exploitation of his estates were John Gilbert, the Duke of Bridgewater's agent at Worsley, and Thomas Gilbert, his own land agent. When the new Lilleshall partnership was formed in 1802 a leading member was John Bishton, a member of a family of minor gentry from Kilsall near Tong, who became agent to the Gowers' Lilleshall estates in 1788, and was succeeded by his son in 1805. Another dynasty of agents came to prominence in the Lilleshall Company later in the 19th century. William Horton, one-time clerk to the Coalbrookdale Company and partner with William Reynolds in the development of Coalport was working for the Lilleshall Company by 1815 when he acted for the partnership in a dispute with the Shropshire Canal Company. In that year his son John, 'a very pleasant young man and very civil', was managing the Snedshill ironworks for the Lilleshall Company. By 1851 John Horton was living at the company's headquarters at Priorslee Hall and was a leading partner in the concern.[29]

The number of progressions from agent or 'expert' to entrepreneur in Shropshire industry could be multiplied many times. Henry Williams first appears in a prominent role about 1779 when he was erecting Boulton and Watt engines at Wren's Nest, Coalbrookdale and Ketley. In 1782 he entered the service of Richard Reynolds to keep his engines in proper order. In 1788 he perfected the canal inclined plane. He became the Shropshire Canal Company's principal engineer and manager. He was responsible for the building of part of the Holyhead Road through the coalfield. In 1818 he was one of the partners who took over the Ketley ironworks after it was relinquished by the Reynolds family. Another partner at Ketley in 1818 was William Hombersley, then a miller but previously the Marquess of Stafford's underground bailiff in the Ketley mines. Another agent who became a capitalist in his own right was Gilbert Gilpin, one time employee of John Wilkinson, later agent to the Botfields, who became a chain-maker at the Aqueduct and Coalport. The brothers John and Thomas Rose followed similar careers in the porcelain industry, John Rose under the patronage of Edward Blakeway and Thomas Rose under that of William Reynolds and William Horton.[30]

The sources of capital for the expansion of the Shropshire iron trade in the 1750s have been discussed above. The ploughing-back of profits from the established coal and iron trades, important in the 1750s, doubtless remained so for the rest of the century. There are few signs of profits being expended on conspicuous consumption in Shropshire before 1800. Fortunate marriages were also a significant source of capital. John Wilkinson seems to have owed much of his success to two alliances with wealthy heiresses. Alexander Brodie, almost penniless when he left Scotland for London, began to accumulate the capital which he invested in the Calcutts ironworks when he married his master's widow. Extravagance was not among his more obvious vices. He was remembered as, 'an old man who never saw a rusty nail but he carried it to the scrap heap, or a stray cottle of coal but he saved it from being wasted, who was not against darning his own stocking and who had a partiality for sheeps' heads on the grounds of economy, but was a good master nevertheless'.[31]

Most Shropshire landowners from the mid-18th century onwards seem to have been content to profit from the rents and royalties paid by their lessees rather than hazard their own capital in the risky world of iron-making. The experience of Brooke Forester in the New Willey Company may have deterred other landowners from similar enter-prises. Isaac Hawkins Browne's direct involvement in the Old Park Company seems to have been short-lived, and that of the Harries family in the Benthall ironworks spasmodic. The direct concern of the Leveson Gower family in the exploitation of their Lilleshall estate was exceptional. Landowners were more active in public utilities than in manufacturing or extractive industries. A considerable amount of landed capital was subscribed for the building of the Shropshire Canal, and local landowners were prom-inent among turnpike and bridge trustees in the coalfield.

Several Shropshire entrepreneurial families expanded into other areas, sometimes leaving their local interests as insignificant portions of their extended estates. John Guest, a member of an old-established family of Broseley colliers became manager of the Dowlais ironworks and a partner there in 1782. The Guests retained some land and other interests in Broseley, but their fortunes were made at Dowlais. In 1783 Francis Homfray moved from Broseley to South Wales to lease part of the Cyfarthfa ironworks. This lease was given up but the family later acquired the Penydarren works near Merthyr, although they retained an interest in Shropshire through the Lightmoor ironworks. The Onions family also had extensive interests outside the coalfield. When John Onions, 'father of the Shropshire iron trade', died in 1819 less than half of his estate worth about £15,000 was in Broseley and Madeley, the rest, worth over £20,000 was in Brierley Hill, Staffordshire.[32] Similarly John Wilkinson had interests in Bilston, Denbighshire and Anglesey, the Botfields in Tipton, Flintshire and the Clee Hills.

There are exceptions to every generalisation about entrepreneurs in 18th-century Shropshire. Nevertheless there were certain common characteristics among the Shropshire ironmasters which clearly distinguish them from the typical ironmasters of other districts. Shropshire iron-making partnerships were large, vertically-integrated concerns, something which may have been dictated by the way in which mines were leased by landowners. Capital came largely from the ploughing-back of profits rather than from borrowing. Thomas Butler visited the Horsehay works in 1815 and found very little work in progress because the rich proprietors could afford to do little at a time of low prices. 'Not so', he said, 'with some, nay most of the Staffordshire works, they must go on or stop for ever, because in general not only their own capitals but the proprietors have other people's capitals employed, and if they stop, there is nothing but ruin'. In 1816 a correspondent of the *Wolverhampton Chronicle* observed that 'the great Coal and Iron Formation in Staffordshire' was 'generally divided into small parcels among numerous individuals'. Gilbert Gilpin in 1819 contrasted Staffordshire and Shropshire:

> In Staffordshire landed property is very much divided; and, naturally all the proprietors desirous of turning their coal and iron mines to immediate account. Hence there is a colliery in almost every field. As there is not sale for such an immense quantity of coal and ironstone, several of these little proprietors unite as partners to direct the concerns, the tradesmen of the towns in the vicinity who can raise a hundred or two hundred pounds, form part of the firm; and it is in this way that the iron works have been multiplied in that county. The proprietors embark all their property, and all that they can borrow, in these establishments. This slippery foundation is rendered still more so by an inferiority in the quality of their iron when compared with that of South Wales and Shropshire ... The works in Staffordshire, will therefore continue to multiply in direct ratio with the advance in the price of iron. In short, that county is 'a millstone hung around the neck of the iron trade' and from which it cannot extricate itself.[33]

In a local context it is difficult to find common characteristics in such diverse entrepreneurs as Richard Reynolds, John Wilkinson, Beriah Botfield and Thomas Gilbert. Observed from afar, they have much in common in their scale of their operations and their sources of capital. Collectively they were very different from the majority of their contemporaries in south Staffordshire.

XII

INDUSTRIAL DIVERSIFICATION

The great iron-making partnerships did not control all the economic activities in the coalfield in the late 18th century. This was a period of innovation and expansion in the old-established pottery trades of the district, the glass industry was revived, and at the terminus of the eastern branch of the Shropshire Canal the most talented of the ironmasters tried to develop an economically-balanced community with many of the characteristics of a 20th-century new town. The long term failure of these attempts to diversify the local economy did as much to shape local society as the contemporary successes of the ironmasters.

The pottery trade in Jackfield, the riverside hamlet in Broseley parish, was well established before 1700. The principal masters in the trade in the 18th century were the Thursfield family. Richard Thursfield of Stock-on-Trent took over a pottery in Jackfield from a Mr. Glover in 1713, and was succeeded in due course by his son, John Thursfield I, (1707–1760), his grandsons John Thursfield II, (1733–1789), and William Morris Thursfield, (1748–1783), and his great-grandson John Thursfield III, who died in 1816. In 1742–43 John Thursfield I establised a new pottery at Haybrook in Posenhall, and John Thursfield II subsequently built another works on the opposite side of the Broseley-Much Wenlock road in Benthall parish. The works of the Thursfields and of other potters in the district in the early 18th century made coarse earthenware mugs, the usual drinking vessels in the Severnside inns, a number of which were called 'mughouses'. The same name was given to the potteries – Haybrook works was the 'Mugus' in local dialect. Other products included milk pans, washing pans, dishes and horn-shaped drinking vessels called 'tots'. Some of the potteries made slipware dishes similar to Welsh ware, and there is some evidence of the manufacture of 'Dutch tiles'. From about 1750 the Thursfields began to make 'Jackfield ware' a highly vitrified black earthenware. Products included mugs and teapots, but the most celebrated were the large jugs called 'black decanters', often decorated in gilt with flowers or figures. Morris Thursfield is most generally credited with the making of these wares, probably in conjunction with Aaron Simpson who took over the Jackfield works from John Thursfield II in 1772. Jackfield ware was exported to the American colonies and Morris Thursfield died in Philadelphia in 1783 when selling a cargo of earthenware which he had escorted across the Atlantic. Jackfield ware was not manufactured at the Benthall and Haybrook potteries, which continued to make the staple, coarser products.[1]

The works at Jackfield consisted of several kilns built on to the ends of cottages in a cluster of buildings on the eastern side of the confluence of the Severn and the stream which powered the Calcutts ironworks. Like the contemporary pottery trade in north Staffordshire that in Shropshire about the middle of the 18th century was little more than a haphazard collection of family businesses. The introduction of Jackfield ware, a product of particularly high quality, shows that well before the introduction of porcelain manufacture into the district the Shropshire potters were already beginning to specialise in luxury products. After the death of Morris Thursfield in 1783 the Jackfield pottery passed to Edward Blakeway, subsequently to be joined by John Rose, who was to become the founder of the Coalport porcelain works.[2]

The manufacture of porcelain began in Shropshire in the mid-1770s, about 30 years after the setting up of the first English porcelain works in London. About 1772 Thomas Turner, a potter who had served his apprenticeship at the Worcester porcelain works, set up a porcelain manufactory at Caughley, on the south side of the Severn, half a mile from the river bank and about a mile and a half south east of Broseley. Coal and refractory clay were to be found there near to the surface. Turner was making porcelain at Caughley by November 1775, and there were about 100 people employed at the works 18 years later. By the turn of the century the Caughley premises comprised two acres in all, with warehouses, counting houses, kilns and store houses, with an adjacent colliery, and outlying grinding-mills at the Smithies and the Calcutts. This was no mere extension of a local craft but a major investment in a relatively new industrial process, as significant in the history of the Shropshire clay trades as Horsehay No. 1 furnace in the development of iron-making. The clock which was such a prominent feature of the factory indicates that here was a sophisticated and disciplined economic unit, far removed in spirit from the cottage-based earthenware potteries of Jackfield.[3]

Thomas Turner used local coal and probably local fire clays for saggers in his porcelain factory. Soapstone came from a quarry near the Lizard, and doubtless china clay also came from Cornwall or Devon. Feldspar could have been obtained from North Wales or Derbyshire. Turner manufactured at Caughley large quantities of fine white porcelain which went to Chamberlain's works at Worcester for decoration. Products completed at Caughley included blue and white porcelain decorated in Chinese styles, enamel services, 'of various much approved patterns' and tea and coffee services, 'richly executed in burnished gold'. The Salopian Porcelain Manufactory, as Turner called his works, enjoyed much fashionable patronage and by 1797 included the Prince of Wales, the Dukes of York, Albany and Clarence, and the Grand Duke of Tuscany among its customers. Turner was obviously concerned about the loss of trade secrets which might come about when apprentices absconded. In February 1788 he warned others against employing an apprentice painter who had left the works before his time was up, admitting that he had 'great reason to fear the said apprentice with others hath been advised by some evil designed person . . . to betray their engagement to the great injury of the Manufactory'. Three apprentices who absconded in 1787 were vividly described in newspaper advertisements. John Adams a 16-year-old painter, was wearing a blue top and undercoat, a striped waistcoat and nankeen breeches. Another Painter, Edward Lloyd, was 'a poor decrepid youth, an object of great charity'. Samuel Whitehouse, an apprentice to the pressing branch, wore a blue coat with large metal buttons, a broad-striped linen waistcoat, a pair of broad striped corduroy breeches, a pair of spotted stockings, and a remarkable large pair of plated buckles on his shoes.[4]

Subsequent developments of the Shropshire porcelain industry for the most part took place at William Reynolds's 'new town' of Coalport, and the history of this development must be considered before they can be further examined.

The eastern part of the Severn Gorge was, until the last quarter of the 18th century, less developed than the western end, where wharves and warehouses had been established for two centuries. The land alongside the river at the eastern end consisted of meadows belonging to Hay Farm. In 1780 the Preens Eddy bridge was completed across the river in the area, and the proprietors were given powers to lay out wharves, quays and warehouses.[5]

Abraham Darby III acquired Hay Farm by 1772. In 1787–88 as the building of the Shropshire Canal was being discussed, he sold some of the riverside meadows belonging to the farm to Richard Reynolds. For a time Reynolds leased them back to the Coalbrookdale Company, but the lease was surrendered in 1792, and in the following year they were let to William Reynolds to be developed as a canal/river interchange. By May 1794 the land near the interchange had acquired the name 'Coalport'. Its advantages as an industrial site were obvious. The bulky resources of the coalfield, coal, clay and iron could easily be delivered by canal. Less heavy, more valuable, raw materials like china clay could be brought from a distance by river. At a time when the Severn was the basic means of carrying goods away from the district, there was no better site in east Shropshire for the distribution of finished products.[6]

The best known of the enterprises which grew up at Coalport was John Rose's porcelain factory. John Rose was born at Barrow near Broseley in 1772, and apprenticed to Thomas Turner at Caughley. About 1793 he moved to the former Thursfield pottery at Jackfield in partnership with Edward Blakeway. Shortly afterwards, in association with Blakeway and his brother Richard Rose, he set up a new porcelain works in Coalport. It seems likely that a large part of the capital for the works was provided by William Reynolds. Before the end of 1795 fireclay from the Coalbrookdale Company's clay mill at Horsehay and firebricks from the adjacent brickworks were being delivered to Rose's new site. The lease of the works was concluded in 1796, and production had certainly begun by the summer of that year when the factory was visited by Charles Hatchett and by the Prince and Princess of Orange. Rose's works was situated on the north bank of the canal about 100 yards from the entrance to the Tar Tunnel. Rose obtained china clay from Cornish sources controlled by Wedgwoods of Etruria. In December 1798 he purchased $44^{1}/_{2}$ tons of doubles coal from the Coalbrookdale partners, but they were not his usual suppliers.[7]

On 12 October 1799 Rose and Blakeway leased the Caughley factory from Thomas Turner who declined trade due to his indifferent state of health. The conjunction of the two enterprises created what was probably 'the largest and most expensive porcelain producing estate in Great Britain during the early years of the 19th century', with a yearly rental of over £7,000. The growth of the industry caused a shortage of skilled labour since Rose, Blakeway and a new partner, Robert Winter, had to appeal in the Press during 1799 for 36 workmen for gilding, enamelling and blue painting. Rose's rising status in the local community is illustrated by his leasing of John Wilkinson's former house in Broseley in 1800. Expansion may have been unhealthily rapid, for by 1803 Rose and Blakeway were bankrupt. The works were purchased by Cuthbert Johnson and William Clarke, but the buyers seem not to have been engaged in the porcelain trade themselves and were content to leave the business under the management of John Rose, who for a time after 1803 lived in one of William Reynolds's cottages at Coalport. His name was to be linked with the factory throughout the 19th century, even long after his death.[8]

About the time that Rose established his Coalport porcelain works the 'Coalport Delfwork' of Walter Bradley came into operation. The owner was probably the same Walter Bradley who in January 1796 was working as a clerk at William Reynolds's Madeley Wood ironworks. Bradley was taking delivery of ground fireclay from Horsehay by April 1796, and earthenware from his manufactory was being sold in Shrewsbury the following year. His products included creamware tankards, black basalt teapots and candlesticks. The works was probably that mentioned by Telford in 1800 as a manufactory of Queensware. It may well have been situated near to John Rose's factory at Coalport, between the canal and the Severn, but until wares attributable to Bradley are found on the site its location must remain a matter for conjecture. It is possible that it was adjacent to the great wheel at Swinney Mill, downstream from Coalport Bridge. Walter Bradley probably died in 1809, for a press notice in January 1810 called the creditors of 'Walter Bradley of Broseley, accountant' to meet his executors.[9]

A third pottery was established at Coalport in 1800 when a partnership was formed between William Reynolds, William Horton and John Rose's brother Thomas. The original shares were each worth £2,695 18s. 10d., but £2,621 12s. 3d. of Rose's contribution was met by a loan from William Reynolds. Thomas Rose lived in one of William Reynolds's cottages in Hortons Row, Coalport. The partnership traded as Reynolds, Horton and Rose, and was obviously a large and important concern. The half yearly rental of the partners' premises in 1803 was £142 3s. 1d. compared with only £55 1s. 6d. paid by Blakeway and Rose. When William Reynolds died in 1803 his share was purchased by his cousin Robert Anstice, and the company was normally known as Anstice, Horton and Rose thereafter. The works was situated between the Shropshire Canal and the Severn, and included a steam engine, a flint mill and a clay mill. Its importance is illustrated by the number of patterns issued by the partners, over 1,419 between 1800 and 1814, a period in which only two other works in England issued more than 1,000. John Rose's works produced a mere 350 before 1814.

In 1814 the Anstice, Horton and Rose works was offered for sale, and purchased by John Rose. The Caughley factory was closed and all porcelain manufacture concentrated at the combined works at Coalport where over 400 people were employed by the early 1820s. The factory remained a large one by the standards of the industry, employing 500 people in 1851, but it was an isolated centre of the trade. In the manufacture of porcelain east Shropshire shared most of the natural advantages and historical traditions of north Staffordshire, yet after 1814 there was never any prospect that Shropshire would develop to the same extent as the Potteries. Apart from Coalport, the only other porcelain factory was that set up in Madeley by Thomas Martin Randall about 1826. Randall produced wares of the most exquisite quality and he employed painters of the highest skill, but economically the significance of his works was slight, and about 1840 he closed and removed to Stoke-on-Trent. The earthenware trades of Broseley survived into the 19th century but showed few signs of substantial growth. The Broseley clay pipe industry positively flourished in the mid-19th century but the units of production were for the most part very small, although one producer in 1871 claimed to be a 'tobacco pipe manufacturer by steam'. Coalport apart, the Shropshire potteries remained little more than cottage industries until the growth of decorative tile-making late in the 19th century.[10]

The clay in the Coalport meadows was suitable for making common bricks, and when William Reynolds leased the site from his father in 1793 he agreed to pay a royalty of 6d. per 1,000 bricks made there. A brickworks worth £84 5s. 8d. was erected by 1803. It afterwards provided materials for the building of Madeley Wood Hall, for the repair of cottages at Coalport, and for the reconstruction of the wharves. It was still active in 1810 but probably went out of production not long afterwards.[11]

William Reynolds was always anxious to exploit to the full the resources of his estates, and his development of the Coalport Tar Tunnel well demonstrates both his scientific understanding and his commercial acumen. In October 1786 Reynolds's miners were driving a tunnel into the side of the Severn Gorge with the object of making a canal to bring out coal from pits about a mile away. After the tunnel had been driven for about 300 yards a spring of natural bitumen was struck, yielding as much as 450 gallons a day. Reynolds quickly had trials made of the substance by Samuel More, secretary of the Society of Arts. The tunnel was completed and for the most part lined with bricks. A number of side passages were mined to expedite the flow of the tar, and a stream flowed along the side of the tunnel. The bitumen fell from the walls on to the surface of the stream which conveyed it to pits at the entrance where it was deposited as a sediment. In a cast-iron cistern at the entrance some was rectified to be sold as Betton's British Oil for medicinal purposes, and some boiled into pitch. British Oil had been made from bituminous rocks quarried from an outcrop alongside the Coalbrookdale–Horsehay railway as early as 1767. In September 1787 the output of tar was 55 gallons a week, which, at the current price of 16s. per barrel, would have brought Reynolds an income of £2,288 a year. The tunnel was extended well beyond the distance necessary for the collection of tar in order to bring out coal from mines beneath Blists Hill, and to serve as a ventilation outlet and drainage level. Charles Hatchett who explored the tunnel in June 1796 recorded that it was 1,040 yards long, and he himself went 760 yards inside. In the following November Joshua Gilpin went 1,100 yards into the tunnel and saw preparations being made for linking it with the mines. In the same year a plateway was laid through the tunnel to bring out coal, large quantities of which were travelling along it in 1801. The springs of bitumen began to diminish as early as 1791, and passages were driven off to the sides of the tunnel in order to gain new supplies. The 'Native Tar Concern', as it was known, was taken over from William Reynolds's Executors by the Madeley Wood Co. in 1805. By 1824 the annual production was no more than 20 barrels a year, a quantity which steadily fell until sales ceased altogether in 1843.[12]

William Reynolds's principal partner in the development of Coalport was William Horton, once clerk to the Coalbrookdale Company. Horton had a third share in the Reynolds Horton and Rose porcelain works, and developed a number of small concerns on his own account. A ropeworks at Coalport on land leased from William Reynolds was supplying winding ropes to the Coalbrookdale partners' mines as early as 1794, and was considerably enlarged in 1806. Horton also had a timber yard big enough for the building of the 20-ft. tub boats used on the Shropshire canals, of which 29 were sold to the Coalbrookdale Company in January 1803. Both the ropeworks and timber yard were flourishing in the early 1820s.[13]

William Horton also began one of two chainworks established at Coalport. The second was developed by Benjamin Edge, a Quaker who moved to Coalport from Tivetshall, in Norfolk, in 1799. By 1802 both works were supplying winding chains to the Coalbrookdale partners, and buying from the partners best, tough, charcoal-iron

Figure 14.   Wheel and Pot Works at Coalport, c. 1810. Artist unknown.
The mill was built about 1805. The kiln might have been part of Walter Bradley's short-lived Coalport
Delfware works, or it may have been used for calcining flints to be ground at the mill.
By about 1820 its site was occupied by the Rock House.

Ironbridge Gorge Museum.

bars, and some scrap wrought iron for the manufacture of chains. Another Shropshire pioneer of the manufacture of wrought-iron chains was Gilbert Gilpin, one-time agent for John Wilkinson, and later for the Botfields at Old Park. About 1803–04 Gilpin developed the idea of working chains on barrels with grooved pulleys. These were not entirely satisfactory and subsequently the three link chain was developed. About 1810 Benjamin Edge began to use wooden keys for holding the links together. Gilpin developed a chainworks at the Aqueduct and subsequently operated the Horton works in Coalport for a while, although it reverted to the control of the Horton family after his death.[14]

Figure 15.   Drawing of 3-link chain.

Ironbridge Gorge Museum.

Another enterprise at Coalport with which William Horton was concerned was a water mill at Swinney about 600 yards downstream from Coalport Bridge on the north bank of the river. The mill was apparently that for which one Thomas Thomas was paid three guineas in 1805 for making a drawing. By 1810 the mill was erected. It had a 76-ft. diameter wheel fed by a long, elevated trough built out from the hill side. Although designed as a corn mill, it was being used by the Hortons in 1824 for crushing linseed and was subsequently employed for the grinding of materials for the Coalport china works.[15]

William Reynolds may have been concerned at Coalport with the smelting of lead ore, for the accounts of his executors make several references to a 'smelthouse'. One of the rows of cottages erected by Reynolds in Coalport was called Smelthouse Row in 1803–04, and in 1810 a smelthouse on the estate was pulled down and re-erected. The smelting of lead ore was never well established in the district however, and in the late 18th century, with the development of the Hanwood collieries, it probably became cheaper to smelt south Shropshire ores nearer to the mines whence they were extracted.[16]

Coalport was a 'new town' of the late 18th century, a centre of new industries like porcelain manufacture and chain-making, where roads, wharves and the ferry traffic were controlled by the developer of the estate. The interest with which Coalport was regarded in the 1790s shows how unusual an enterprise it was. Thomas Telford in 1802 was optimistic about Coalport's future:

> The works at Coalport which were established by Mr. William Reynolds on the banks of the Severn at the termination of the Shropshire Canal . . . have succeeded to a very considerable degree, and they are striking proof of the good effects of an improved inland navigation. Formerly the place consisted of a very rugged uncultivated bank, which scarcely produced even grass, but owing to the judicious regulations and encouraged by Mr. Reynolds, joined to the benefit arising from the canal and river, houses to the number of 30 have been built there, and more are still wanted, to accommodate the people employed at a large china manufactory, a considerable earthenware manufactory, another for making ropes, one for bag making and one for chains which are now taking the place of ropes for the use of mines and for other purposes.[17]

Telford's account is not without minor inaccuracies, but it is a striking testimony to the sort of development which Reynolds was trying to achieve. Another writer was even more emphatic in his praise of Reynolds's work.

> The whole of this lively and beautiful place [i.e. Coalport] with its erections, belongs to Willm. Reynolds, who . . . since the commencement of its erections, has still continued planning & erecting for himself and others, sparing neither labour nor expence to render it as complete as possible; in which improvements proceeds with that noble ardour, so truly characteristic of himself, as a liberal promoter of the different Arts and sciences, in whose bosom merit in every station always finds a place, and to whom the nation at large stands greatly indebted.[18]

Apart from the capital invested in various industries in Coalport, Reynolds spent large sums on the port installations and on the repair of roads in the area. He owned a half share with Thomas Bryan of the Tuckies estate in the passage boat which linked Coalport with Jackfield on the opposite shore of the Severn which brought each day large numbers of workers to the china and other factories. Reynolds had the course of the Severn diverted near to the passage boat at a cost of over £350. As Telford remarked, Reynolds built cottages for workers at Coalport and at one time numbered John and Thomas Rose and Benjamin Edge among his tenants. In 1805 one group of cottages adjacent to the canal inclined plane were leased to William Horton and his partners in the coal agency, and in 1807 another terrace was leased to John Rose of the china works.[19]

In 1800 William Reynolds moved from Ketley Bank to the Tuckies, the mansion in Jackfield which overlooks Coalport. His health was already failing and he died in 1803. His executors continued to invest substantial sums at Coalport but they did no more than build up projects which had already started. The extensive plans for new works being entertained by Reynolds in the last years of his life were never realised. Before these ambitious projects can be considered in detail it is necessary to examine the general development of the heavy chemical industry in Shropshire.[20]

The tar trade and its associated by-products have been considered above. The manufacture of tar in ovens which also produced coke was essentially a corollary of iron-making, and in the 18th century was carried on entirely by the iron-making partnerships.

There was a large soapworks adjacent to Ludcroft Wharf, Coalbrookdale, where, in 1805, Charles Guest had an alkali furnace, two cast iron boilers, four cast iron vats, and evaporating pans for making 'British Barilla'. Coal and limestone were obtained from nearby mines and trade was reckoned to be very good. The works was probably set up in 1792, for in 1809 there remained 82 unexpired years of a 99 year lease.[21]

Glass-making in the coalfield began in the late 17th century but there is no evidence that it survived in the early years of the 18th, and when the glass industry was revived in the district it was on a new and impressively large scale. In October 1791 William Reynolds proposed to his partners in the Coalbrookdale Company that they should be associated with one William Phillips in a glass house at Donnington Wood. The scheme was rejected but William Reynolds and his brother Joseph went ahead on their own account with Phillips and signed articles of agreement in July 1792. Phillips was a man of some consequence in the district and later became a partner with John Bishton in the ironworks of the Lilleshall partnership.[22]

The new glassworks was erected in the township of Wrockwardine Wood, but only about 200 yards from the boundary of Donnington Wood in Lilleshall parish, and on different occasions it took its name from both places. Surviving plans and a picture of the works show two, high, conical structures, about 80 yards south east of Wrockwardine Wood parish church, (which was not built until 1833). The manager's house, the present rectory, contained a pane of glass engraved, 'Donnington Wood Glass House, 6 August 1792', which may well be the date when production started.[23]

In 1794 the glasshouse was being supplied with Stourbridge clay for its crucibles, which was ground in the clay mill at Horsehay. Refractory bricks some of them measuring 28 × 15 × 9 in. were also obtained from Horsehay. Slag from the Donnington Wood blast furnaces was being used to make glass at Wrockwardine Wood. In 1799 Reynolds contemplated making use of locally-pumped brine but was frustrated by the complications of excise regulations. In 1805 the glasshouse was using Black Rock stone extracted from Lord Craven's land in Little Dawley.[24]

By 1796 the Wrockwardine Wood glasshouse was being managed by Richard Mountford, and between 1800 and 1803 ownership passed to a partnership formed by Mountford with William and Henry Cope and John Biddle. The principal products of the glasshouse were bottles for the French wine trade, but some items of table ware in green glass with splashes of white, red and yellow opaque glass were manufactured there, and other products included walking sticks with barley sugar centres, striped glass rolling pins, ornamental buttons and massive door stoppers of dark green glass full of air bubbles. William Reynolds displayed in his house a 70 gallon bottle blown at the works.[25]

William Cope left the partnership in 1816, and the glassworks was operated under the name of Biddle and Mountford until it closed after Richard Mountford died in 1841. Only eight glassworkers were living in Wrockwardine Wood at the time of the 1841 census, and there is evidence from the 1851 census that some of them moved to St. Helens. The Copes, Biddle and Mountford were associated in several other enterprises including a bank in Shifnal.[26]

William Reynolds was also interested in a chemical works at Wombridge. This was originally a sulphuric acid works, using iron pyrites from local coal mines as its raw material, but about 1799 John Biddle began to make alkali there. He used the process developed in France by Malherbes and Athenais, in which ferrous sulphate and salt were calcined with coke, producing sodium sulphide, dyes and soap. Biddle's mode of working was strenuously criticised by Lord Dundonald who himself took out patents for the manufacture of alkali during the 1790s. Dundonald's criticisms may well have been justified for the alkali works had a short life, and probably did not continue after Biddle became a partner in the Wrockwardine Wood glasshouse about 1803.[27]

The most ambitious chemical undertaking in Shropshire was never completed, but its planning merits examination since it shows something of the close relationship of science and industrial development in the late 18th century, and also how much the local economy suffered by the early death of William Reynolds. Lord Dundonald met William Reynolds shortly after he arrived in Shropshire in the mid-1780s, and their collaboration over the construction of tar kilns has been discussed above. Dundonald regarded Reynolds highly, 'I never knew a man in life whom I could put such reliance in, or invited my conscience so much as yourself', he wrote in 1791. Reynolds acknowledged Dundonald's scientific talents and sympathised with his misfortunes, 'My blood almost boils when I consider how you have been treated by those in power and the public in general', but he had a shrewder sense of business than Dundonald, and took care to procure second opinions on Dundonald's schemes.[28]

In December 1799 Dundonald put to Reynolds a plan for the construction of an integrated chemical works which would manufacture alkali, soap, glass, alum, white lead, dyes, iron and fertilisers, all of which could be 'united like the links of a chain'. He was anxious to associate his proposed factory with an established ironworks and held the highest hopes of Reynolds. Reynolds encouraged his expectations and Dundonald sent him a list of the necessary raw materials, salt or brine, pyrites (ferrous sulphite), green vitriol (ferrous sulphate), clay, coal, sawdust or other vegetable matter, muriate (chloride) of Potash, litharge (lead oxide), furnace slag, sand, tallow, iron and limestone, pointing out that all but litharge and tallow were available on Reynolds's estate. Reynolds welcomed the scheme, finding it congenial to his ambitions to develop the mineral resources of his lands to the full. In January 1800 Dundonald visited the Tuckies, but missed seeing Reynolds, and left with William Horton a draft indenture making over to Reynolds his patents for making coal tar and for preparing Glauber Salts, Alum, Alkaline Salts and White Lead.[29]

William Reynolds then suggested to Dundonald that a chemical works should be built at Coalport, the capital to be confined to the Reynolds and Cochrane families, and the site to be the slopes of the Severn Gorge between the Hay inclined plane and the Preens Eddy bridge. Dundonald wrote in reply, 'I highly approve of the situation of the sloping ground above Coalport for an Alkali work. The Minerals, solutions or salts may be made to go upon their own legs from one process to another until at last the finished goods are turned out at a little above the level of your store house'. To ensure security he suggested walls 20 ft. high. Reynolds may well have had a scheme of this sort in mind some years earlier in 1795 when he obtained from the Shropshire Canal Company permission to use the engine on the Hay inclined plane when it was not raising boats, a permission which was renewed in 1800.[30]

Subsequently Dundonald regretted the choice of Coalport as a site for the works, thinking it too near the place of his failure with the British Tar Company at the Calcutts. He tried to persuade Reynolds to allow him to direct the Wombridge alkali works in place of John Biddle whose failure he prophesied. Reynolds still regarded Dundonald's proposals for a large integrated works with favour, and in May 1800 was making plans for his proposals to be examined by experts in London.[31]

Dundonald revealed himself more and more as a potentially disastrous partner. He led the life of a perpetual fugitive, often staying incognito at lowly inns, frequently pursued by creditors of long standing, seeking small loans from wealthy friends in industry, and suffering from a profound, if largely justified, persecution complex. In March 1800 Reynolds's health was failing, and Dundonald urged him to take care. In November he decided to retire for a while from all manner of business. Dundonald's processes were not given the chance 'to make a dozen of the largest fortunes ever made in Britain'. In January 1802 William Wilkinson found Reynolds still 'very busy in exploring the bowells of Madeley', and was shown over the whole of his speculative concerns. Reynolds was then intending to take advantage of the Peace of Amiens to take his family to France for a year, but the following year he died and the stills, kilns and pipes of a chemical works did not appear opposite the Tuckies on the slopes above the Severn.[32]

There was at least one cotton mill in the Coalbrookdale coalfield. In 1792 Messrs. Jennings, Latham and Jennings announced that they would supply shopkeepers with woollen drapery and cotton goods from their warehouse adjacent to the 'Cotton Manufactory' in Broseley. One of the partners was probably Leonard Jennings, a prominent shareholder in the Iron Bridge, but the history of the concern is otherwise totally obscure.[33]

Apart from Coalport, the alkali works at Wombridge and the Wrockwardine Wood glasshouse there were no serious attempts to diversify the economic structure of the Shropshire coalfield in the late 18th century. A few old-established crafts like pipe-making and earthenware potteries survived as cottage industries. Some trades subsidiary to mining and iron-making such as boat-building and rope-making continued to prosper. The successes of glass-making at Wrockwardine Wood and of porcelain manufacture at Coalport were in terms of the whole economy of the district very limited. Coalport did not become another Stoke-on-Trent nor did Wrockwardine Wood and Wombridge develop into a second St. Helens. The industrial structure of the district at the beginning of the 19th century depended almost entirely upon the prosperity of the iron trade, a dependence which in later years was cruelly to expose the people of the area to the cold winds of the trade cycle.

XIII

THE NINETEENTH CENTURY

The attempts made by William Reynolds, William Horton and Lord Dundonald to diversify the economy of the Shropshire Coalfield in the 1790s and early 1800s were largely unsuccessful. Local industry in the 19th century was dominated by the great iron-making partnerships, whose range of activities tended to contract after the peace of 1815. Foreigners coming to England in the 1830s and '40s to experience something of industrial society went to Manchester, Liverpool or Birmingham, or to the model textile villages of Lancashire rather than to Coalbrookdale and Ketley. If industrial society could be epitomised in a single picture in 1840 it was a view of a multi-occupied house in 'Little Ireland' or a steam locomotive crossing a viaduct rather than of the iron arch linking Madeley Wood with Benthall. Leon Faucher, Alexis de Tocqueville and Friedrich Engels do not mention Shropshire in their accounts of England in the 1830s and '40s. Shropshire industry was not distinguished for its innovations in this period. Improvements in iron-making were applied tardily and hesitantly. Yet the coalfield remained a major centre of industrial activity. In 1830 Shropshire still produced over 10 per cent of the pig iron manufactured in Great Britain, and the volume of production doubled by 1860, although the proportion of the British output fell to about 4 per cent.[1] If the area ceased to attract distinguished foreigners, the scale of industrial activity could still impress visitors. Charles Hulbert, the Shrewsbury topographer, wrote in 1836 of:

> this world of mines, canals, railroads, iron foundries and smoke . . . Only let us imagine, a surface of more than 30 square miles, on which, within this last half century, have arisen many new towns, villages and hamlets; chapels of ease, Methodist and Dissenting chapels; hundreds of flourishing establishments; comprising works of lime, bricks, earthenware, china, glass; and probably the most complete and extensive IRON WORKS in the world. This district may be said to commence within two miles of Newport, taking a south eastern direction with some variation, to the iron foundry half a mile south of Broseley, a length of 10 or 12 miles. The whole, densely populated, is in some places, as from Pain's Lane to Ketley or from Priors Lee to Steeraway Lime Works, four miles from east to west. Among the places which have risen to eminence are the Dawleys, Ironbridge, Pain's Lane, where there are markets, as at Oakengates, Ketley and Ketley Bank, the Trench and Donnington Wood, Lawley Bank Horsehay, Malins Lee, Madeley Wood, Coalport &c. In all these places new establishments, streets of houses, &c. are continually arising . . . In this respect the Shropshire mining district resembles the neighbourhoods of Birmingham, Manchester, Stockport, &c. where populous towns rush into existence as if by the power of magic.

Hulbert described the Severn Gorge, the two miles of riverside settlements between Coalbrookdale and Coalport as:

> the most extraordinary district in the world: the two banks on each side are elevated to the height of from 3 to 400 feet, studded with Iron Works, Brick Works, Boat Building Establishments, Retail Stores, Inns and Houses, perhaps 150 vessels on the river, actively employed or waiting for cargoes, while hundreds and hundreds of busy mortals are assiduously engaged, melting with the heat of the roaring furnace; and though enveloped in thickest smoke and incessant dust are cheerful and happy.[2]

The wartime boom in the Shropshire iron trade began to ebb in 1812 when the Coalbrookdale partners decided to blow out one of their blast furnaces at Horsehay because of the low price of iron. The group's profits fell from over £30,000 in 1807 to no more than £3,571 in 1813. The most sensitive indicator of the state of the iron trade was the price of forge pig iron which had reached £6 15s. 0d. per ton in 1806, probably the most prosperous of the wartime years. It did not fall below £6 until 1812 when it reached £5 10s. 0d. although the following year it again reached £6. In 1816 it fell to £3 15s. 0d., and apart from a slight recovery in 1818–19 remained at a very low level until 1825.[3] The post-war years were in consequence a time of acute depression in the coalfield.

1816 was the worst year of the depression. In July men from Ketley pulled cartloads of coal to Shrewsbury bearing the text 'We would rather work than beg and rather beg than steal'. In August only 10 of the 34 blast furnaces in the Coalbrookdale region were working and several companies had vast stocks of unsold iron. By the end of the year many coalmines and the Wrockwardine Wood Glassworks had suspended operations, and the early onset of winter and a bad potato harvest intensified local distress. Colliers who had been accustomed to earn 4s. a day were working for as little as 1s. 6d. Expenditure on poor relief in the district reached a peak between October 1816 and April 1817. 3,300 of the 8,213 inhabitants of Wellington, 703 of the 1,938 who lived in Wrockwardine Wood and 1,250 of the 5,000 residents in Broseley were receiving relief during that winter. In October 1817 Gilbert Gilpin estimated that 20 Shropshire furnaces were in blast and 12 not working. Only two rolling-mills were operating in the coalfield in 1817, and the local production of manufactured iron steadily declined between 1816 and 1820, from 7,702 tons to 6,765 a year. There were signs of an improvement in trade towards the end of 1817 but prices fell again in 1819. Gilpin claimed that the fall was attributable to the low prices of inferior Staffordshire iron.[4]

Many of the Shropshire ironworks were ill-fitted to face competition from the newer works of South Wales and the Black Country. The majority relied on furnaces which dated from before 1800, and many were sited to take advantage of water supplies, which were no longer necessary after the application of the steam engine to ironmaking, and of coal and ironstone mines which had been worked out. Two engineers who visited Shropshire during the depression were impressed by the obsolescence of much of what they saw.[5] Thomas Butler the Yorkshire ironmaster in September 1815 found the once great Calcutts ironworks and the Coneybury furnace almost in ruins. At Madeley Wood he noted that the company found little profit in the iron trade, an impression which is confirmed by their accounts. At Coalbrookdale he observed, 'these furnaces are blown by a water wheel, all the machinery old and clumsy and all the works seem to be conducted upon the old plans of forty years ago'. Horsehay ironworks was doing very little, and gave Butler 'a melancholy picture of the iron trade'. Joshua

Field visited Shropshire in August 1821. At Coalbrookdale he found the works 'in a great measure deserted', the furnaces were not in blast and only some small castings and a badly designed, and little understood, sugar mill were being made in the foundry. The forges were still producing a little wrought iron, and were still powered by water wheels. The great *Resolution* steam engine was being demolished. The Horsehay rolling-mill Field found 'tolerable good but old and dirty'.

Butler considered that the vast profits made during the wars with France enabled the proprietors of Coalbrookdale and Horsehay safely to do little business when prices were low. Both he and Gilpin contrasted the situation in Shropshire with that in Staffordshire where proprietors were so heavily indebted that they could never afford to blow out furnaces. Several Shropshire ironmasters reduced their commitments in the county in order to deploy their capital more profitably in other districts.

The Ketley ironworks, according to Gilbert Gilpin was the oldest and most celebrated in Shropshire. By the standards of the time it was very large and highly mechanised. In the time of William Reynolds the puddling furnace and manganese steel had been the subjects of experiments there. It lay at the centre of dense network of railways on which ran 350 waggons. It was the terminus of a branch canal on which the owners operated over 200 tubs boats. The offices were much admired by Thomas Butler: 'The counting houses are very spacious, divided into different offices for the various departments, occupied by several clerks, and a noble office for the principals . . . the whole may be compared to the Commons, Lords and King'. After the death of William Reynolds in 1803 control of Ketley passed to his half-brother Joseph, who in 1805 became a partner in the bank of Eyton, Reynolds and Wilkinson at Wellington; Ketley thereafter being left in the charge of managers. In 1816 Joseph Reynolds decided to concentrate on his banking activities and give up the ironworks. In April 1817 the works was offered for sale, but failed to attract a purchaser. In July Reynolds was offended when the Coalbrookdale Company refused to buy the rolling-mill and engine.[6]

The social consequences of the closure of the Ketley works were disastrous. In October 1817 Gilpin wrote 'Ketley . . . is becoming an appendage to the Wellington workhouse'. Expenditure on poor relief in Wellington parish soared to £9,495 in 1817 and £6,109 in 1818. It sank to £4,262 in the following year and never again exceeded £4,000 before 1836. 196 men were thrown wholly on the parish and employed on the roads, and 133 obtained part-time work and had their wages supplemented from parish funds. Many workers left the district altogether.[7]

The Ketley works was eventually re-opened by a new company. Early in 1818 it was leased by Richard Mountford of the Wrockwardine Wood glassworks, Henry Williams the civil engineer who perfected the Shropshire Canal inclined planes, William Shakeshaft, a banker and tenant of Leegomery farm, John Ogle of Preston on the Weald Moors, and William Hombersley, a miller who had formerly been underground bailiff in the Ketley mines. Three blast furnaces were brought back into use, and by 1823, 4,984 tons of iron per annum were being produced, and 5,763 tons were made in 1830. The Ketley partners built a new furnace at Lawley which was reported to be nearly ready for blast in September 1822. Over 3,000 tons of pig iron were made there in 1830. The Ketley forge was also brought back into production, and contained 20 puddling furnaces by the early 1870s. The Ketley inclined plane ceased to be used after Reynolds gave up the ironworks, although the drowning of a boy playing with chains attached to a boat at Ketley Canal Wharf in 1844, and the presence of a boatbuilder in Ketley in 1821 suggest that the upper level of the Ketley Canal remained in use.[8]

The other major portion of William Reynolds's estate, the Madeley Wood ironworks, passed to the control of William Anstice, son of his cousin, Robert Anstice, who had been admitted to a quarter holding in the concern only a few months before his uncle's death. The ironworks and mines were on a smaller scale than those at Ketley and were valued at just over £11,000 in 1803. Nothing is known of the affairs of the company during the worst years of the depression, although after 1826 its activities are well documented. Thomas Butler remarked in 1815 that the company found the coal trade more profitable than the iron trade, and this is fully confirmed by the surviving statistics, although since the accounts for the iron trade bore the full burden of general charges for pumping from mines, tramways, &c. the figures are a little misleading.

The Madeley Wood Company made profits on its coal trade every year between 1826 and 1850, but these varied from £679 1s. 6d. in 1835 to over £7,000 in 1848. In 1826 the profit was just over £3,000 but this level was not reached again until 1845, and in 1829 and 1835 profits fell below £1,000. After 1845 there was a distinct upturn in the trade. Production as well as profits rose in the 1840s. From 1826 to 1844 the yearly totals varied between 11,160 tons and 18,557 tons, but in 1845 there was a sharp increase to over 25,000 tons and over 32,000 tons were sold in 1849.

If the company's coal trade was steadily profitable, the fortunes of its iron trade were wildly erratic. A profit of £1,710 1s. 0d. was achieved in 1826, but losses were made in each of the next seven years, that of 1827 being over £2,000. The company probably suffered from the siting of its blast furnaces alongside the Severn at a distance from the most productive mines of the period. In 1832 the partners began to remove their ironworks to Blists Hill in the valley of the Hay Brook between Madeley and Coalport, alongside the Shropshire Canal, and within easy reach of several recently-developed deep mines. The advantages of the move were reflected in a profit of a little over £700 in 1834. A loss was made the following year, but the next quinquennium was very profitable indeed, over £5,000 being realised in 1836 and over £6,000 in 1837. In 1841 profits slumped to £21 13s. 11d. which heralded three years of heavy losses. Two more furnaces came into blast at Blists Hill in 1840 and 1844, and the years 1845–48 were very successful with profits of over £10,000 in 1847. Production of iron rose steadily between 1826 and 1850, although it is impossible to relate it precisely to the blowing in of new furnaces since the dates of the blowing out of the furnaces at the old works are not known. In 1826 2,867 tons were produced, and there was a steady increase to 3,853 tons in 1831. In 1832 the figure slumped to 3,303 tons, but rose to 5,267 in 1834, and 6,683 in 1835, doubtless owing to the blowing in of the first Blists Hill furnace. In 1839 production passed 7,000 tons, and over 8,000 tons were made in 1843, more than 9,000 in 1846, and over 10,000 in 1849 and 1850.

The Madeley Wood Company made a slow, but successful, recovery from the post war depression. Its ironworks were re-established on a favourable site, and after the sinking of deeper pits the coal trade became very profitable. A new brickworks came into production in 1841 and 10 years later an extensive brick and tiles works was established at Blists Hill. Some less profitable activities were given up. Tar ceased to be collected from the Coalport Tar Tunnel in 1843–44, and the company's limestone workings in the Buildwas-Much Wenlock area were sold to James Foster in 1849. In spite of its success the company remained conservative in its methods of operation. The tops of its blast furnaces were ultimately closed in but hot blast was never introduced, and until iron-making ceased at Blists Hill in 1912 coke was manufactured in open heaps.[9]

The second two decades of the 19th century were a period of low activity in the history of the Coalbrookdale Company. Its principal iron-making assets were the foundry complex at Coalbrookdale, of which the two ancient blast furnaces formed part, the Coalbrookdale forges, the furnaces, forges and rolling-mill at Horsehay, and the Dawley Castle blast furnaces. The Coalbrookdale works were still water powered in 1815, but the Dawley Castle furnaces were at that time the most recent in the district, having been blown in only in 1810, and the Horsehay rolling-mill of 1809 was reckoned to be far in advance of any other in the area.

An approximate indication of the company's fortunes is given by the sums paid out to the partners between 1805 and 1852. Profits in the wartime years were very high, but between 1810 and 1837 exceeded £10,000 in only two years, 1810 and 1825. The 1840s were by comparison a period of prosperity. Profits never fell below £10,000, and in 1846 and 1847 exceeded £75,000.[10]

This period saw substantial changes in the company's activities. At Coalbrookdale one of the two ancient blast furnaces was still making iron in 1817 but was blown out soon afterwards. The Coalbrookdale forges ceased operation in 1842–43. The foundries were re-organised and became profitable following the renewal of the company's lease after some hesitation in 1827. The trade in domestic holloware was expanded. The company still manufactured steam engines, and from about 1840 began to make art castings. The foundry had produced such items as cast-iron railings and bookcases for over a century, but now lamp posts, fire grates, plaques, garden seats and statues were made in bewildering variety. At the Great Exhibition of 1851 the company provided the ornamental gates which stood at the entrance to the transept of the Crystal Palace, and which now divide Hyde Park from Kensington Gardens, as well as a cast-iron statue of Andromeda, a canopied statue of an Eagle Slayer and a fountain, the Boy and the Swan.[11]

The company's Horsehay ironworks is well documented thanks to a detailed history written by W. G. Norris in 1876.[12] Norris suggested that slack management had reduced the efficiency of the works during the post-war depression, but that after 1830 the active participation of Alfred and Abraham Darby IV, nephews of Abraham Darby III, brought a revolution in management. Slack was substituted for high quality coal for the firing of boilers, saving 600–700 tons of coal a month. The forge was re-organised and new puddling furnaces erected. Forge cinder which contained large quantities of iron was used in the blast furnaces, raising the production of each to about 65 tons a week. New steam engines were built for forges and furnaces. Neilson's hot blast, invented in 1828, was introduced at Horsehay and Dawley Castle 10 years later, enabling the use of raw coal instead of coke in the furnaces, and increasing the output, although reducing the quality of iron. The company took over from sub-contractors the operation of its tramways, and after the opening of Wappenshall wharf began to operate its own fleet of canal narrow boats.

For all this energy, it would be difficult to claim that Horsehay was one of the leading ironworks in Britain in the 1830s and '40s. The changes provoked labour troubles, particularly when the payment of a production bonus at the furnaces led to the disappearance of loose castings from all over the works, and when in 1837 new regulations committed puddlers to given yields and qualities. In contrast with the 18th century, no innovations of importance were pioneered at the works of the Coalbrookdale Company. Joseph Hall's method of producing wrought iron by 'pig boiling' an important improvement of Cort's puddling process, was discovered in the early 1820s. It was not until 1832 that, 'two men came to Horsehay from Joseph Hall's ironworks, south Staffordshire, in order to instruct the Horsehay puddlers in the new mode of puddling iron by boiling it on cinder bottoms'. Similarly the guide rolling-mill introduced in the Black Country before 1820 was not adopted at Horsehay until 1833, when, again, it was introduced by wire rollers from Staffordshire. The closing in of the furnace tops at Horsehay began relatively early, in 1851, and achieved great economies in fuel consumption, but two disastrous explosions led to the ending of the experiment. In the 1830s and 40s the Darby family were closely associated with the construction of iron ships. In 1844 the wife of Abraham Darby IV launched the *Richard Cobden* an iron sailing ship constructed to carry cottons to China. In 1871 the managing owner of the vessel revealed that the iron plates from which it was constructed were made by the Coalbrookdale Company, which, he said, also provided the iron from which Brunel's SS *Great Britain* was built. In 1839 one of the Company's travellers told Barclay Fox of the Neath Abbey ironworks that his employers were producing 800 tons of plates for the *Great Britain*. Apprehension among the Darbys when the *Great Britain* ran aground in Dundrum Bay in 1847 suggests strongly that they had substantial investments in the company which operated her.[13]

In 1839–40 the Coalbrookdale partners acquired the Lightmoor ironworks, then consisting of three blast furnaces and a small foundry, with adjacent coal and ironstone mines, clay pits and cottages. The company were also active in the ceramics trades, particularly when a bed of exceptionally good clay was discovered after the purchase of the Pool Hill estate near Horsehay in 1838. Soon after 1860 the company began to make decorative terra cotta ware.[14]

By 1851 the Coalbrookdale partners employed 3,500 people, and in Dawley alone raised 102,000 tons of coal and 42,000 tons of ironstone a year, and at Horsehay smelted 17,880 tons of iron a year. The company acquired a number of works in South Wales, buying furnaces at Ebbw Vale in 1844, and later at Abersychan, Pontypool and Abercarn. Nevertheless the eager application of the latest knowledge which had characterised the partnership in the 18th century was almost wholly lacking in the 19th.[15]

The Lilleshall Company were, according to Gilbert Gilpin in 1819, 'the greatest pig sellers in the world'. By 1815 the company controlled most industrial activities in the northern part of the Shropshire coalfield. Its iron-making interests included three blast furnaces and a forge at Snedshill, three furnaces at Donnington Wood and two at Wrockwardine Wood. The company had six furnaces in blast in 1823 making nearly 16,000 tons of iron. Before the end of 1825 two new furnaces at the Old Lodge in Lilleshall parish had been built to replace those at Wrockwardine Wood, although they were not then in blast. Production at the two Lodge furnaces and the three at Donnington Wood totalled 15,110 tons in 1830. Snedshill in that year made only 317 tons, and the furnaces ceased production soon afterwards. A new blast furnace was constructed at the Lodge in 1846 to replace one of the three at Donnington Wood, and about 1859 when two more furnaces came into blast at the Lodge, the remaining two at Donnington Wood went out of production. In 1851 a new works at Priorslee with four blast furnaces began to smelt iron ore.[16]

In the mid-19th century the engineering activities of the Lilleshall Company were concentrated in a large works called the New Yard at St. George's. At the 1862 International Exhibition the company exhibited a pair of blast furnace blowing-engines and a contractor's locomotive, and claimed to be 'manufacturers of all kinds of high

pressure expansive and condensing steam engines and colliery and contractor's locom-
otives', as well as of 'pumping engines of all descriptions, condensing winding engines,
horizontal, vertical, direct or beam, coupled or single . . . strong and massive steam
engines for rolling mills, sugar mills and saw mills'.[17]

Lilleshall pig iron enjoyed a high reputation; large quantities of it being used at
the Snedshill forge and by the forge of W. Barrows and Sons of Bloomfield, Tipton.
The company controlled most of the resources of the coalfield north of the Holyhead
Road in the mid-19th century, operating mines in Hadley, Wrockwardine Wood and
Priorslee, as well as those on the Sutherland estate in Lilleshall and Ketley. In 1844–
45 the company was raising over 100,000 tons of coal per annum from the Sutherland
estate alone, using about two thirds of it at their blast furnaces and selling the rest as
domestic fuel. Over 50,000 tons of ironstone was raised from the Sutherland estates in
1845. The company operated the Donnington Wood Canal, the Lilleshall and Church
Aston limeworkings, limestone quarries on Wenlock Edge, and several brickworks. By
any 19th-century standards the Lilleshall partnership was a major industrial concern.
In 1870 it was raising about 400,000 tons of coal a year from its various estates, 105,000
tons of ironstone and 5,000 tons of brick clay; it manufactured over 70,000 tons of iron
a year and employed over 3,000 people.[18]

The Old Park Company, the iron-making concern controlled by the Botfield family
grew to be one of the principal partnerships in Shropshire during and after the wars
with France. In 1815 the company operated only the Old Park works itself which
consisted of four blast furnaces, a forge, and associated collieries. Between 1814 and
1830 the partners acquired lands in Dawley and Stirchley parishes along the banks of
the Shropshire Canal for about two and a half miles between Old Park and the Dawley/
Madeley parish boundary. In 1814 they leased 72 acres at Dark Lane which they
purchased in 1825–26. They bought Hinkshay Farm in 1824, and in the same year
acquired an interest in the adjacent Langley Field estate. Two years later a further
estate on either side of the Shropshire Canal at Stirchley and Hinkshay was bought
from Lord Darlington. In 1825–27 two pairs of blast furnaces at Hinkshay and Stirchley
were brought into operation, and by 1830 the company was making 15,300 tons of pig
iron a year, only 127 tons less than the output of the Lilleshall Company who were
then the largest producers in Shropshire. In 1830 the forge at Stirchley came into
operation, and within the next few years two furnaces at Dark Lane were brought into
blast. Thomas Botfield died in 1843, and his brother William in 1850, and control of
the company passed thereafter to their nephew Beriah, whose father, also Beriah, had
died in 1813. In 1856 Beriah Botfield purchased the Langley Company, with two blast
furnaces at Langley Field, which had been built by George Bishton and Adam Wright
in 1824–26. Like other iron-making companies the Botfields mined coal for general sale
and made bricks and tiles, but they did not venture into engineering, except for the
manufacture of equipment for their own works.[19]

The Ketley, Madeley Wood, Lilleshall, Coalbrookdale and Old Park companies all
had their main centres of operation in Shropshire, and all had substantial reserves of
minerals which they were able to exploit in the post-war period. Other partnerships
were less well endowed, and in the area south of the Severn there was a substantial
contraction of activity after 1815. The first of the major works in the Broseley area to
close was John Wilkinson's Willey furnace which ceased operations in 1804, probably
because the mines from which it was supplied were exhausted. After 1815 other works

suffered the same fate and by the mid-1830s iron ore was no longer smelted south of the Severn in Shropshire.

The partnership of Banks and Onions owned the Broseley Bottom Coal or Coneybury furnace, the Broseley foundry, and had controlling interests in the Benthall ironworks. In the first decade of the 19th century they produced pig iron for sale and operated an extensive trade in castings and engineering products. In 1805 John Onions gave up his holdings in the ironworks of the Lilleshall partnership, and by 1810 had a substantial interest in an ironworks at Brierley Hill, Staffs. In that year tensions developed between Onions and his partner in Broseley because Banks was using a faulty machine to weigh ironstone being sent from Broseley for smelting at Brierley Hill. This is the earliest evidence of the export of ore from Broseley to the Black Country, a practice which was to grow considerably within the next two decades. In 1817 the partners' Broseley furnaces were standing out of blast, but in March of that year Onions purchased mining rights in 19 acres of land at Broseley from John Guest.[20]

John Onions was known as 'the father of the Shropshire iron trade', when he died in November 1819. His Broseley works were worth £13,646, but his Staffordshire estate was valued at over £20,000. By 1820 calcined iron ore was being exported from Broseley to Brierley Hill on a considerable scale. In April of that year 11 boatloads of approximately 20 tons each were despatched, in May, 8, and in June 14. In 1822 John Onions Jun. sold the Brierley ironworks, one of the chief selling points being that Shropshire ironstone could be delivered there 'much cheaper than at any other place around'. The Coneybury and Benthall furnaces saw little activity after the Battle of Waterloo. Both were out of blast in 1823. In 1830 the output at Coneybury was a mere 270 tons a year. John Onions Jun. continued in trade as an ironfounder and brick-maker in Broseley until his death in 1859, and was succeeded by his daughter Penelope Thorn, who kept the works in operation until 1877. The Onions' mines were leased to others and most of the iron ore doubtless exported. The Benthall blast furnace made its last iron in 1821 but a foundry was maintained on the site for some years afterwards by one Stephen Hill.[21]

The other ironworks south of the Severn also ceased to make iron during the post-war period. The Calcutts works was taken over by William Hazledine, friend of Thomas Telford and contractor for the ironwork of the Pontcysyllte aqueduct, about 1817 when two furnaces were in blast. In 1823 1,822 tons of iron were made there. Production apparently continued until 1828 and in 1831 the works was acquired by James Foster. In Hazledine's time it had been unprofitable, and Foster was content to use its railway system to bring iron ore to the banks of the Severn for despatch to his Black Country furnaces. The foundry at the Calcutts was demolished in 1836.[22]

James Foster was also concerned with the Barnetts Leasow furnaces. Between 1812 and 1815 these furnaces, less than 20 years old, were taken over from Wright and Jesson by one Charles Phillips. In 1820 Phillips and his partner William Parsons went bankrupt. The premises were offered for sale in January of the following year when Foster acquired them. He appointed one Benjamin Ball as manager, and continued to produce iron there, making 2,755 tons in 1823, and 1,316 tons in 1830, but the furnaces went out of blast not long afterwards. Like the Calcutts, this was a riverside site, and Foster doubtless used its railways to convey calcined ore to the Severn wharves for transhipment.[23]

James Foster, born in 1786, was one of the most eminent Midlands ironmasters of the early 19th century. Scrivenor thought that he possessed 'possibly a more perfect knowledge of his trade than any other ironmaster'. His main concern was with the Stourbridge ironworks of his half-brother John Bradley, but he had interests in more than 30 other enterprises.[24]

Foster's Shropshire activities were not confined to Broseley. His first ironworks in the county were the forges at Eardington near to the Severn, downstream from Bridgnorth, which he acquired in partnership with John Bradley in 1809. He bought the similarly sited forge at Hampton Loade in 1819. In 1813 Foster and Bradley made an agreement with the executors of John Wilkinson's estate to buy the iron made at the two furnaces at New Hadley for seven years. When this agreement expired the stock at Hadley was valued by Foster's partner, J. U. Rastrick, and the works was apparently taken over by Foster in partnership with Thomas Jukes Collier, a Wellington wine merchant, who had been one of the original partners in John Bradley and Co. of Stourbridge. In 1825 it was thought unlikely that the Hadley furnaces would ever work again. No iron was being made there in 1830 and in 1835 the end of the works was marked by the sale of the blast-engine.[25]

In 1818 Foster leased mines at Wombridge with an obligation to build two blast furnaces within 18 months, on a site only about half a mile from New Hadley. The two furnaces were producing over 5,000 tons of iron a year in 1825 and a third was added in 1824. In 1830 the production of the three totalled over 7,000. In 1827 Foster purchased the Madeley Court estate, where there were large, unexploited reserves of minerals, but he did not start mining there until about 1841, when he was reputed to be making preparation for building furnaces. In October 1841 he complained to the Shropshire Canal Company that he wished to convey Madeley coal to his works at Wombridge and to Shrewsbury, but that the engine on the Windmill Farm inclined plane was incapable of raising fully-loaded boats. In April 1843 he renewed his complaint in stronger terms, but the company found they could do nothing, and he removed his ironworks from Wombridge to Madeley Court, where he constructed three blast furnaces during 1843. The Wombridge furnaces were sold and ultimately operated by others.[26]

By 1830 the number of major iron-making partnerships in the Shropshire coalfield had been reduced from nine to six, the Lilleshall, Ketley, Coalbrookdale, Madeley Wood and Old Park companies, and the various concerns of James Foster. The companies still dominated the local economy, and still bore many similarities to colonial governments, five of them bearing the names of the districts where they operated. Their range of activities had in general contracted since the time of the French wars. Foster sent away much of the ironstone he mined as calcined ore and the rest as pig iron. He had no forge in the coalfield itself. The Madeley Wood Company similarly made no wrought iron, and sent away all of its output as pig. The Old Park Company and the Ketley Company had forges and rolling-mills, and sold some of their iron as pig, some as blooms and some in the form of bars. The Coalbrookdale and Lilleshall partnerships alone had both forges and engineering works. There were several small independent forges and foundries, but they did not consume a significant quantity of the pig iron made in the district.

The benefits of mixing Shropshire and Black Country pig iron in the manufacture of wrought iron were well known, and a high proportion of the pig made in Shropshire was shipped eastwards into Staffordshire. 'The state of the mining district of our own country is in a great measure regulated by the proceedings of the Staffordshire men', commented a Shrewsbury newspaper when riots threatened in 1831.[27] This was true

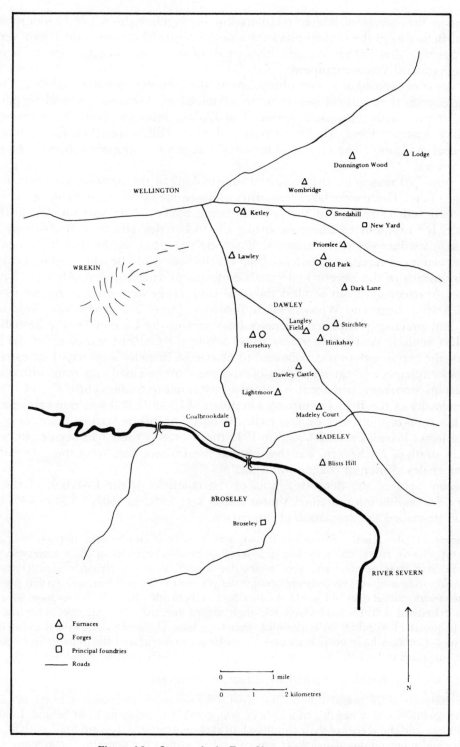

Figure 16.   Ironworks in East Shropshire 1840–1870.

not just in the sphere of labour relations but throughout the whole economy of the district. Before 1790 the coalfield had been at the centre of an economic region centred on the Severn. After 1815 it was an outlying part of an economic region centred between Birmingham and Wolverhampton.

The areas of expansion in east Shropshire in the 19th century were chiefly along the eastern edge of the coalfield, where more advanced mining methods made it possible to exploit previously unworked seams. The Lodge, Priorslee, Dark Lane, Stirchley, Hinkshay, Langley Field, Madeley Court and Blists Hill, were all on the eastern side of the coal measures. The retreat of industry was most pronounced in the area south of the Severn.

The principal reason for the decline of iron-making in the Broseley area was not the shortage of ore. There were large quantities of ironstone in the district still being mined in the mid-19th century, but the ore was being conveyed for smelting to the Black Country. John Onions had been exporting ore to Brierley Hill from Broseley in 1810, and the following year when mines at Easthope's Coppice in the parish were offered for sale, vendors explained to potential buyers that ore could be conveyed in a calcined state by means of the Severn and canals to furnaces at a distance. After 1815 at the Broseley furnaces went out of blast the local iron mines were used more and more to supply Staffordshire and Worcestershire furnaces. James Foster sent ores from mines which had previously supplied Barnetts Leasow and the Calcutts to the Stourbridge area. His nephew W. O. Foster was still working the Calcutts mines as late as 1879. In 1870 the export of ore was reckoned to be one of Broseley's principal industries. A directory explained, 'great quantities of ironstone are calcined and transmitted down the river to Stourport, whence it is conveyed by canal to Staffordshire'.[28]

The closure of the Broseley furnaces between 1815 and 1830 was due principally to the exhaustion of the seams of clod coal, the only Shropshire coal suitable for coking. The geologist Joseph Prestwich said in 1842 that formerly there had been eight or nine furnaces south of the Severn, but they had all been blown out, 'from the exhaustion of the proper description of coals in that part'.[29]

Broseley became the depressed area of the coalfield in the first half of the 19th century. Its population remained almost stationary; 4,832 in 1801, 4,738 in 1851. John Randall described the desolation of the parish,

Broseley, ere the mines became exhausted, was a place of much more importance than at present. Grimy ruins, chimney stacks looking gloomily conscious of their uselessness, and disjointed masses of masonry, give a singular aspect to scenes formerly characterised by manufacturing activity. Grasslands occupy the place of forge and furnace, garden plots and game covers extend over old works, upon a surface beneath which the mines have long since been exhausted. Old pit banks have had their angles lowered, and vegetation year after year has bequeathed so much of its remains, that they look like some Celtick or ancient British barrows. Cottages have been built over shafts long forgotten, and the inmates have ere now been surprised to find the floor give way, as if by the effects of some engulfing earthquake.

Some years later Randall recalled the effects of emigration,

The character of the population (of Broseley) has changed in consequence of the exhaustion of the coalfield, which has driven numbers, who cast many lingering looks behind, from their birthplace and the scenes of their childhood, to seek employment in south Staffordshire, South Wales and other mining districts. It was painful to witness the departure of so many men of bone and muscle, with their families and their household goods, but their bettered circumstances soon reconciled them to the change.[30]

Even after the exhaustion of the clod coal in Broseley the problems of making iron in the parish would not have been insuperable. In the 18th century ore from south of the Severn had regularly been conveyed to the Coalbrookdale furnaces, and ironworks throughout the coalfield drew limestone from Benthall Edge and Much Wenlock. To take coke to Broseley in the 19th century would not have been difficult. Ironmasters doubtless preferred to take Broseley ore to Staffordshire for smelting not because iron-making was impossible in Broseley but because it was more profitable in Staffordshire, due to better transport facilities and nearness to markets.

In other parts of the coalfield shortages of coal and ore were not a serious handicap to iron-making in the mid-19th century. Some ores were imported from north Staffordshire, Cleveland, Cumberland and from abroad in the 1840s and '50s, but the quantities were not large, and they were probably used to achieve certain qualities in pig iron rather than because of a shortage of local ironstone. As early as 1817 forge slag at Old Park was being used in the blast furnaces, and at Ketley in 1851 it was regarded as a valuable source of iron.[31]

While clod coal and iron ore were reasonably plentiful, there was a shortage of limestone. The opening of the canal wharf at Wappenshall in 1835 enabled the import of large quantities from Trevor Rocks and Llanymynech. By the end of July 1835 John Bradley and Co. were delivering as much as 258 tons a week. By 1837 Ketley and Old Park companies were also using limestone from North Wales delivered by this route, and by 1845 the Coalbrookdale and Lilleshall partners were also engaged in the same traffic. In the year ending 31 March 1849 the Botfields received over 10,000 tons of limestone and the Ketley Company over 5,000 tons by this route.[32]

The import of such large quantities of limestone reflected a shortage of local supplies. In 1846 there was no longer any of the white limestone most suitable for fluxing left to be extracted from the Duke of Sutherland's Lilleshall estates, although grey limestone for building and agriculture was still being mined, and the Lilleshall Company were taking white limestone from the adjacent lands of the Leeke family. Limestone was still being mined by the Lilleshall Company at Steeraway in the 1840s, but the company ceased operation there about 1850. By the same date large scale operations to extract fluxing stone seem to have ended on Benthall Edge and Lincoln Hill, and the railways which took stone from the quarries north of Much Wenlock to the wharves at Buildwas no longer worked. By 1842 the Lilleshall Company was obtaining some of its fluxing stone from quarries on Wenlock Edge to the south of Much Wenlock.[33]

Inadequate transport facilities probably imposed the severest handicap on the growth of industry in east Shropshire in the 19th century. Until 1835 there was no direct canal link with the national system. The tub boat canals served the coalfield itself but extended no further than Pave Lane and Shrewsbury. The River Severn was unimproved, and when locks finally were built in the 1840s they extended no further upstream than Stourport. The river continued nevertheless to be an important commercial artery. Coalport in particular remained an impressive place in the 1830s, one to which the ageing Thomas Telford delighted in taking his friends and pupils. In May 1836 Charles Hulbert counted 72 boats as he stood on Coalport Bridge, and estimated that 150 were employed in the whole of the Severn Gorge.[34] Traffic was being attracted from the river to other forms of transport however, even before the building of standard gauge railways.

The road system of east Shropshire was substantially improved during the two decades after the peace of 1815 which led to the transfer of some industrial traffic to the roads, in spite of the small maximum loads and the high costs. This was a period of road improvement in the whole of Great Britain, but in Shropshire the setting up of the Holyhead Road Commission and the need to relieve unemployment in the post-war depression brought about more far-reaching changes than elsewhere.

A committee for the Relief of the Labouring and Manufacturing Poor was set up in Shropshire by 1816, and tried to encourage the employment of the poor by grants to turnpike trusts which covered half the costs of improvement schemes. The Madeley trust financed the widening of the road between the Meadow Farm and the Birches Brook near Coalbrookdale by this method in 1816. The following year an Act was obtained for a direct road from Coalbrookdale to Wellington by way of Jiggers Bank, which was opened in 1818. At the same time a network of good roads was built on the estates of the Marquess of Stafford in Lilleshall and on the Weald Moors giving employment to many of the local poor. Another scheme promoted with the aim of relieving unemployment was the direct link between the south end of the Ironbridge and the Broseley–Bridgnorth road, avoiding the centre of Broseley, which was completed in 1828. The relief committee also made several grants for schemes carried out by local turnpike trustees on the Holyhead Road.[35]

The benefits which accrued to the Shropshire coalfield from the improvement of the Holyhead Road did not come about as the result of local pressures, but arose from the choice of the main road bisecting the coalfield as the principal route between London and Dublin. The union of the English and Irish parliaments in 1800 increased the number of journeys made by politicians between London and Dublin, journeys which 'produced constant irritation and complaints respecting the road through North Wales and gave rise to warm discussions in Parliament'. In 1815 the Holyhead Road Commission was appointed to improve the route on the English and Welsh side of the Irish Sea, and Thomas Telford was instructed to survey the road. The most dramatic changes were made to the west of Shrewsbury, and included the Menai suspension bridge, the Waterloo bridge at Bettws-y-Coed, and the route through the pass of Nant Ffrancon, but a vast programme of widening and realignment was carried out between Shrewsbury and London. The Holyhead Road followed the route of the present A5 and A464 between Shrewsbury and Wolverhampton, bisecting the coalfield between Ketley and Priorslee. Between 1815 and 1835 the entire line of the road over this section was substantially improved. Telford built a massive slag embankment across the valley of the Ketley Brook over the ruins of the original forge houses of the Ketley ironworks. Between Potters Bank and the crossing of the Shropshire Canal at the *Greyhound Inn* an entirely new road, parallel to the Ketley Canal, was laid out before 1819 by Henry Williams on behalf of the local turnpike trust. East of the *Greyhound* Telford re-aligned the ascent of Mumporn Hill and then constructed a new road for a distance of about a mile avoiding Priorslee village. At Shifnal, Telford constructed a by-pass avoiding the congested central market place. Finally in 1836, two years after Telford's death, his scheme for a two and a half mile by-pass avoiding Overley Hill to the west of Wellington was completed.[36] While the Holyhead Road owed little to local initiatives it considerably influenced the local economy, making the carriage of iron to Birmingham and Wolverhampton immeasurably easier.

The Birmingham and Liverpool Junction Canal like the Holyhead Road was not a project which originated in the Shropshire coalfield. The new route from the Staffordshire and Worcestershire Canal at Autherley near Wolverhampton to the Ellesmere and Chester at Nantwich was promoted by canal interests headed by the Marquess of

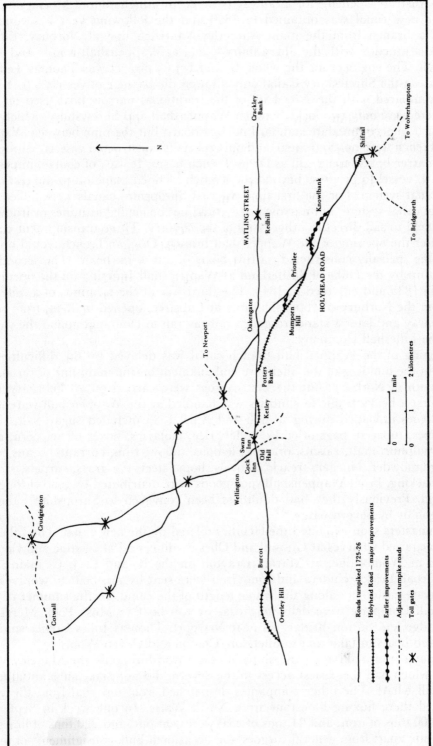

Figure 17. Watling Street and the Holyhead Road.

Stafford to frustrate a scheme for a railway between Birmingham and Merseyside. The Act for the new canal was obtained in 1826 and the following year a second Act authorised a branch from the main Autherley-Nantwich line at Norbury, through Newport to a junction with the Shrewsbury Canal at Wappenshall a mile and a half from Trench. The engineer for the whole B. and L.J.C. project was Thomas Telford.

The locks on the Shrewsbury Canal only allowed the passage of vessels 6 ft. 4 in. in beam, as compared with the 7 ft. 4 in. of the traditional narrow boat used on most canals. There were only two locks between Wappenshall and Shrewsbury, which were both widened to accommodate standard narrow boats, but the nine between Wappenshall and Trench were not so treated, and only specially constructed vessels, 'Shroppies' or 'narrer-narrer boats' could sail as far as Trench basin. It was, of course, impossible for any 70 ft. vessel to progress beyond the Trench inclined plane on to the rest of the tub boat canal system. For the first time the east Shropshire canals were linked with the national canal system, but narrow boats could not be loaded at mines or ironworks in the coalfield to sail direct to other parts of the country. Three transhipment centres grew up after the opening of the Wappenshall branch. One, at Trench, could only be served by the specially constructed narrow boats of 6 ft. 4 in. beam. The second was a wharf set up by the Duke of Sutherland at Wappenshall Junction on the opening of the canal in 1835 and enlarged in 1843. The third was at the terminus of a mile long branch from the Norbury–Wappenshall line at Lubstree, opened in 1844, from which first a tramway and later a standard gauge railway ran to Donnington and the various works of the Lilleshall Company.[37]

The opening of the Wappenshall branch canal was delayed by the difficulties encountered in the building of the Shelmore embankment on the main line of the B. and L. J. C. south of Norbury, but the first cargoes were carried on 28 February 1835. From the first a heavy traffic in sundries was handled at the Wappenshall warehouse. Inward cargoes unloaded during March and April 1835 included sugar, salt, slates, baskets, pipes, tobacco, bags of corks, coffee, rice, molasses, boxes of tin, corn, glass, soap, flax, sulphur, malt, raisins, oranges, lemons, tallow, rum, currants, beans, wine, herrings, gunpowder, vinegar, treacle, shovels, hops, steel, rye grass, carpets, spades, seeds and sacking, From Wappenshall such goods were distributed by road throughout the coalfield. Previously they had doubtless been conveyed to Shropshire either by stage waggon or by Severn barge.[38]

The ironmasters soon exploited the facilities offered by the new canal. The Lilleshall Company acquired wharves at Gnosall and Cheswardine, and Hazledine and Co. who mined coal at Wombridge, at Market Drayton on the B. and L. J. C. main line.[39] Cargoes of coal, bricks, cinders and some iron were sent by tub boat to wharves and even to private customers along the whole length of the canal. In the summer of 1835 the Lilleshall Company were delivering coal by tub boat to Moss Pool, Meretown, Buttery Bridge and Sutton Bridge, all near Newport. Thomas Jukes Collier similarly employed tub boats to take coal to Shebdon, Coaton and Coven Wharf.

Of the major iron-making partnerships in east Shropshire, only the Madeley Wood Company, which had the easiest access to the Severn, did not make substantial use of Wappenshall wharf. The other companies despatched iron and coal from the wharf and received there fluxing limestone from North Wales. In one week in September 1837 over 400 tons of iron, and 24 tons of coal were sent out, and 220 tons of limestone received, quite apart from general cargoes and occasional bulk consignments of timber and grain.

At first most of the ironmasters sent goods to Wappenshall by tub boat for tranship-ment. The Coalbrookdale Company soon found this inconvenient and began to employ road transport between Horsehay and Wappenshall.[40] By 1848 the Ketley Company was similarly using road teams to take iron to Wappenshall and carry limestone back. Waggons also carried wrought iron from Snedshill to the wharf. T., W. and B. Botfield at this period still employed tub boats for the carriage of iron and limestone between their works and Wappenshall. Most of the ironmasters purchased their own fleets of narrow boats. Boat No. 1 of Abraham Darby and Co. (the Coalbrookdale Company) left Wappenshall for the first time on 14 March 1837, with a cargo of iron, in the Nantwich direction, probably bound for Merseyside. By May 1837 an unnumbered butty boat was working with it, and within a year at least nine Coalbrookdale Company narrow boats were sailing from Wappenshall. The company's boats operated all over the linked waterways of southern Britain to Ellesmere Port, Brentford, City Road Basin and Manchester. In December 1841 Orlando Forester, newly-instituted rector of Broseley, waylaid one of the company's boats at Melton Mowbray and arranged for it to take some of his furniture to Wappenshall, whence waggons conveyed it to Broseley.[41] By September 1837 William Hazledine, the Ketley Company and the Lilleshall Com-pany were operating their own narrow boats from Wappenshall, and the Botfields were doing the same by May of the following year. As fleets of narrow boats grew the use of tub boats on the B. and L. J. C. beyond Wappenshall diminished. By September 1837 the Lilleshall Company were using narrow boats even to take coal to Newport.

The Lubstree (or Humber) Arm of the B. and L. J. C. was authorised in the Act of Parliament of 1827 as a branch to Lilleshall. It left the Norbury–Wappenshall line about two miles from Wappenshall near to the ornate Duke's Drive aqueduct, and extended about a mile to a wharf on the road from Preston-on-the-Weald Moors to Donnington. Like Wappenshall, Lubstree wharf was owned by the Duke of Sutherland. The first cargoes were handled on 9 May 1844 and before the end of that month 320 tons of coal were despatched, all from the Lilleshall Company. Most of the iron was pig, consigned for forges in the Black Country. The coal trade was with wharves along the B. and L. J. C. at such places as Newport, Gnosall and Goldstone. Fluxing limestone was handled at Lubstree from the time of its opening, 160 tons arriving during May 1844. Lubstree was complementary to Wappenshall. No sundries traffic was handled there, consignments of anything other than coal, iron or limestone being most unusual.[42]

The Coalbrookdale and Lilleshall Companies transferred to Lubstree most of the traffic which they had previously sent to Wappenshall. When James Foster blew in his Madeley Court furnaces and closed those at Wombridge he ceased to use the canal for the despatch of iron. Nevertheless Wappenshall continued to prosper. In the year beginning April 1848 the Ketley Company despatched 4,902 tons of merchant iron and 200 tons of pig, the Snedshill works 6,406 tons of merchant iron, and the Old Park Company 10,262 tons of merchant iron.

Main line railways came late to the Shropshire coalfield. In 1837 only two years after the opening of the Wappenshall branch canal, the Grand Junction Railway linking Birmingham with Manchester and Merseyside was opened, but there is no evidence that traffic from the coalfield was sent in any quantity along the 14 miles of Watling Street to the G.J.R. at Gailey, in spite of the earlier road links with the adjacent canal wharf. Competition between railways and canals did much to shape the pattern of early railway developments in Shropshire. In May 1845 the B. and L. J. C. was taken over by the Ellesmere and Chester Canal Company, and in the following July the Shropshire Union Railway and Canal Company was formed, bringing together the Montgomeryshire, Shrewsbury and Shropshire Canals with the enlarged Ellesmere and Chester under the tutelage of James Loch, agent to the Duke of Sutherland.[43] A number of railway schemes were proposed by the new company including one for a line from Stafford to Shrewsbury through Wellington. The following year the newly-formed London and North Western Railway offered a perpetual lease to the S.U.R.C.C., which was accepted by the Directors and authorised by an Act in June 1847. Meanwhile in 1846 an Act authorising a railway running from west to east through the coalfield from Shrewsbury to Wolverhampton and Birmingham had been passed, with the section from Shrewsbury to Wellington envisaged as a joint line with the S.U.R.C.C. Shrewsbury–Stafford route. In June 1849 the joint line between Wellington and Shrewsbury and the S.U.R.C.C. Wellington–Stafford lines were opened, and after the completion of the tunnel at Oakengates the Shewsbury and Birmingham line on to Wolverhampton opened the following November.[44]

The effects of the railways on existing transport systems in the district were dramatic. Rails, sleepers and other materials for both railways were unloaded at the canal wharves at Wappenshall and Lubstree, but traffic at the wharves fell immediately after the railways were opened. Between January 1848 and August 1849 the lowest amount collected in tolls at Wappenshall was £41 in a month, with the totals for some months exceeding £90. By September 1849, three months after the opening of the railways income fell to £27, and the highest monthly total in 1850 was also £27, the lowest being no more than £8. Traffic from the Horsehay ironworks was immediately transferred from the canal to the railway, being forwarded by road to the station at Wellington. The effects of the railways on long distance road transport were equally sudden. According to the keeper of the Burcote gate on the Holyhead Road, the opening of the railway from Wolverhampton to Chester 'was the cause of removing nearly all the traffic from the Turnpike roads as if by magic . . . the road that was considered the best in England, namely London to Holyhead, in a few months time was deserted'.[45]

One reason for the suddenness of the transfer of passenger traffic from road to rail was the intensity of competition between the L.N.W.R. which controlled the S.U.R.C.C. and the Shrewsbury and Birmingham, which found expression in a drastic slashing of fares. At Wolverhampton the L.N.W.R. hampered the rival company's approach to Birmingham and packed shareholders' meetings to try to force amalgamation. Such activities only served to push the smaller company towards one of the L.N.W.R.'s most formidable rivals. In 1851 the S. and B. R. made an agreement with the Great Western Railway over the interchange of goods traffic, and in 1854 with the opening of the G.W.R. route from Birmingham to Wolverhampton a junction was made there with the S. and B. R.; in the same year the Great Western absorbed the Shrewsbury and Birmingham and its associated company, the Shrewsbury and Chester, which gave it a main line running from Paddington to Merseyside, and which meant that two rival major companies, the G.W.R. and the L.N.W.R. now controlled the railways of the Shropshire coalfield.[46]

The 10 years after the takeover of the Shrewsbury and Birmingham by the G.W.R. saw the gradual extension of branch lines across the coalfield. First was the Shrewsbury and Birmingham branch from Madeley Junction, between Oakengates and Shifnal, to Lightmoor opened in 1854–55. It had been intended to go to Coalbrookdale but for reasons not now obvious remained uncompleted beyond Lightmoor, which seemed to one traveller 'the ultima Thule of railway progress, the most forlorn and dismal looking railway station which the ingenuity of an unskillful engineer sadly deficient in taste and equally at a loss for funds could possibly have contrived'.[47] In 1858 another line reached Lightmoor, the Wellington and Severn Junction which began at Ketley on the G.W.R. main line, and which had been opened as far as the Horsehay ironworks the previous year. On 31 January 1862 the Severn Valley Railway, authorised 9 years earlier, was opened from Hartlebury to Shrewsbury passing along the south bank of the Severn through the Ironbridge Gorge.[48] The Severn Valley was part of the West Midland Railway and in 1863 along with its parent company it was absorbed by the G.W.R. The same day the Severn Valley line opened, the Wenlock Railway, also part of the West Midland, was opened from Buildwas to Much Wenlock. In 1864 the Great Western completed the short section from Lightmoor to Coalbrookdale to connect with a subsidiary company, the Wenlock No. 2 Railway's line from Buildwas which crossed the Severn by the spectacular Albert Edward Bridge, built at Horsehay. This enabled the through running of passenger trains between Wellington or Shifnal and Much Wenlock, which from 1867 were able to proceed through to Craven Arms on the Shrewsbury–Hereford line. More importantly from an industrial point of view, it gave direct access to the reserves of limestone in the quarries south of Much Wenlock. The Lightmoor–Buildwas line was the last built in the coalfield by the G.W.R. or its subsidiaries, apart from a mineral line from Hollinswood to Stirchley of which the origins remain obscure.

The takeover of the Shrewsbury and Birmingham by the G.W.R. and the opening of the Lightmoor branch in 1854 threatened to rob the L.N.W.R. not only of long distance traffic but also of short hauls on the Shropshire Canal, which it controlled as part of the S.U.R.C.C. By 1855 the canal could be operated only with difficulty. Subsidences and water shortages caused long delays and forced reductions in the loading of the tub boats. Subsidence on the Wrockwardine Wood inclined plane was so serious that a boat on its carriage could hardly pass beneath the winding-drum. In January 1855 the canal manager recommended the conversion of the canal to a railway, a recommendation adopted in an Act of Parliament obtained in 1857. The new branch railway began at Hadley Junction on the Wellington-Stafford line, ran half a mile to the canal bed near Oakengates, and then followed the bed for most of the way to the top of the Windmill Farm inclined plane, whence an entirely new line was laid to Coalport. The canal from the Wrockwardine Wood incline to Tweedale basin in Madeley was completely closed, but the section from Tweedale to Coalport remained in operation. The L.N.W.R. agreed with the Madeley Wood Company in 1857 to buy the great warehouse and canal/river interchange at Coalport, but to keep open the wharf for the transfer of goods between canal and river and to retain the Hay inclined plane in working order. The Madeley Wood Company agreed in return not to build a river wharf. The railway between Hadley Junction and Coalport was opened to freight in 1860 and to passenger traffic in 1861.[49] It provided a useful link between the main lines and the many coal, iron and brick works along the eastern edge of the coalfield. Its passenger trains gave access for the many employees of these works to the shops and markets of Wellington, and more particularly of Oakengates, which probably owed much of its prosperity in the late 19th century to the railway.

All the major Shropshire iron-making companies had direct access to standard gauge railways by the mid-1860s and if the Horsehay works was typical found their transport problems largely solved. After the opening of the Wellington and Severn Junction

Railway according to William Norris 'the conveying and accommodation was such that iron could be rolled, loaded and into Birkenhead before it was cold'.[50] Norris's earlier account of the frustrations of river and canal transport excuses his exaggeration.

Although the links between the ironworks and the canal wharves at Wappenshall and Lubstree and the railway station at Wellington were by road, most of the local industrial transport, particularly of raw materials, was by plateway. Archaeological evidence shows a bewildering variety of gauges, rail lengths and sleeper types, which must largely have prevented through running between different systems. Plateways were extended in the mid-19th century to connect works and mines with standard gauge sidings. They were cheap to lay and inexpensive to operate, but were nevertheless a cul-de-sac in railway development.[51] A unified system in the coalfield could have provided a tolerably efficient form of transport; the diverse network which actually materialised must have ossified the systems for supplying the ironworks with raw materials.

The only new form of railway introduced in the district before the opening of main line railways was the Birkenshaw rail, a wrought-iron edge rail patented in Northumberland in 1820s. James Foster used track of this type on lines between the Madeley Court ironworks and the adjacent mines.[52] Later in the 19th century several standard gauge mineral lines were built in the coalfield giving some of the major works direct access to L.N.W.R. and G.W.R. tracks.

The opening of standard gauge railways brought a rapid demise of the Severn barge traffic, particularly upstream from Coalbrookdale. Traffic between Coalbrookdale and Shrewsbury fell from an average of 42 barge-pulling horses a year in 1845–47 to 24 in 1854–56, and ceased altogether in 1862, the year the Severn Valley Railway opened. The tonnage handled at the canal/river interchange at Coalport steadily diminished, falling from 79,323 tons in 1827, to 66,589 tons in 1837, 67,747 tons in 1847 and 48,680 tons in 1857.[53] Downstream from Coalbrookdale and Coalport traffic remained buoyant in the 1850s, but many of the houses inhabited by barge owners and watermen in Jackfield were swept away during the construction of the Severn Valley Railway. By 1871 there were only five barge owners left in the Gorge, their chief traffics being calcined ore carried from Broseley to the Black Country, bricks and tiles, and a few fine castings which the Coalbrookdale Company feared to entrust to railway waggons. In 1862 John Randall thought there were probably not half a dozen barges left upstream from Stourport. In 1875 the trustees of the Bewdley–Coalbrookdale towpath sought to relinquish their obligations, and actually did so 10 years later blaming the Severn Valley Railway for their loss of trade. By tradition the last barge on the Shropshire section of the river sank in 1895 when it collided with one of the piers of Bridgnorth bridge, and by 1904 the head of navigation was reckoned to be Arley quarries upstream from Bewdley.[54]

Canals too lost ground in the face of railway competition. The surviving records for Wappenshall wharf do not extend beyond 1850, although Lubstree wharf continued to handle a limited range of cargoes into the 20th century. The Coalport inclined plane was probably used for the last time about 1894. In 1905 the L.N.W.R. officially proposed to close it, and formally did so in 1907. Most of the Donnington Wood Canal was closed on Christmas Day 1882, but the short section of the Shrewsbury from Trench basin, up the Trench inclined plane to the Donnington flour mills remained operational until 1921.[55]

Many natives of the Shropshire coalfield became successful entrepreneurs in the 19th century. In 1862 John Randall compiled a long list of examples of the triumph of the principles of self-help: Richard Padmore, M.P., the Worcester ironfounder, formerly a workman in Shropshire, John Russell, the South Wales coal owner, born at Coalbrookdale, G. B. Thorneycroft, the Wolverhampton ironmaster once an employee of John Wilkinson at Willey, George Jones, another south Staffordshire ironmaster and a native of Broseley. Significantly all of the individuals Randall quoted made their fortunes outside the Shropshire coalfield. There seems to have been a considerable outflow of entrepreneurial talent from the district after 1815. To some extent this was no more than a continuation of the process which had taken the Guests and the Homfrays to South Wales in the mid-18th century, but it is certainly possible that the lack of zeal for innovation in the great companies, and the limited opportunities for the founding of new concerns allowed by the major concerns, made the district particularly unattractive to the young man of enterprise. At the same time the proprietors of some of the major companies showed less and less interest in industrial affairs. In 1849 Alfred and Abraham Darby virtually retired. In 1850 Francis Darby died, and the direct connection of the Darby family with the management of the Coalbrookdale Company came to an end. Entrepreneurs from outside Shropshire showed little interest in the coalfield. James Foster was the only outsider to invest substantial sums in the district in the 19th century, and his chief interest was merely to provide his Staffordshire works with pig iron and iron ore. Nor was Foster well pleased with his Shropshire ventures. He told a group of striking miners in 1831 that 'he had brought a great deal of money into the county, tho' he had taken none out and did not expect to take any money out of it'.[56]

Many of the Shropshire ironworks worked well below capacity, relying on high profits in the boom years to compensate for losses in the slack periods. The district achieved its highest annual production of pig iron in the boom year 1869, when nearly 200,000 tons were made, but this was a mere two per cent of national output.[57]

Why did the Shropshire iron trade cease to flourish in the 19th century? To some extent its demise was brought about by a lack of mineral resources. There were local shortages of clod coal and a general shortage of limestone. Iron ore, if plentiful was difficult and expensive to mine. But these shortages were not crucial. The overall production of iron remained remarkably buoyant. The general decline of the area was brought about rather by the diminishing sophistication of the activities of the big companies. Shropshire became more and more a supplier of semi-finished iron and even of raw materials to the Black Country ironworks. Probably the lack of adequate transport facilities and the remoteness of the coalfield from the principal ports and customers for iron contributed to this decline. The Black Country forgemaster had at his doorstep the traditional metal craftsmen of the district, as well as the many iron-using trades of Birmingham. He had direct rail and canal links with London, Lancashire, Yorkshire and South Wales, whereas Shropshire's connections with anywhere but Merseyside and Manchester were much less favourable. There was no local tradition of metal-using crafts and with the exception of the Lilleshall Company engineering declined rather than grew. The low wages paid to Shropshire ironworkers in the 19th century doubtless helped to stimulate the emigration of skilled workers, whom the absence of technical education facilities in most parts of the coalfield made it difficult to replace. That an intelligent entrepreneur like James Foster should prefer to smelt iron ore from Shropshire in Stourbridge indicates that the coalfield offered few positive advantages to the ironmaster after 1815. The local industrial structure, the large and

all-dominant extractive companies, probably allowed few opportunities for the
would-be entrepreneur, who doubtless found much greater openings in the more com-
petitive atmosphere of south Staffordshire or South Wales.

The beginning of the end of the Shropshire iron trade was marked by a visit of the
Iron and Steel Institute in 1871. From Hollinswood Junction they were conveyed in a
special train to the large and prosperous works of the Lilleshall Company, were given
impressive statistics about the company's output, and inspected a wide range of engines
under construction in the New Yard shops. After lunch they went to Coalbrookdale
and Ironbridge where they spent most of their time inspecting old documents and
looking at a display of local tiles and porcelain. Henry Bessemer led a hunt for relics
of Abraham Darby I. Finally the visitors were addressed by William Reynolds Anstice
of the Madeley Wood Company. He described how he himself when a boy had
destroyed a model of a steam locomotive (presumably Trevithick's) which had been
made for his uncle, William Reynolds. 'Shropshire', he said, 'was somewhat in the
position of a man who, while conscious that his own best days were past, regarded
with pride the race of giant sons which had grown up around him'.[58]

XIV

THE MECCA OF METHODISM

The church of St. Michael, Madeley attracted Evangelicals in the late 18th century in much the same way that the Coalbrookdale and Ketley ironworks attracted engineers. John and Charles Wesley, George Whitefield, the Countess of Huntingdon, Captain Jonathan Scott and many less well-known religious leaders were drawn to visit the parish church of John Fletcher, one of the principal theologians of the Evangelical Revival. Fletcher's influence on Madeley and the surrounding coalfield parishes began which he acted as temporary curate at the parish church in the late 1750s. In 1760 he was inducted as vicar, and after his death in 1785 his ministry was extended through the work of his wife and adopted daughters until the early 1840. Madeley remained a place of pilgrimage for the pious long after the organisations he had set up had disappeared. Through Fletcher's career it is possible to observe the impact of Evangelicism on an emerging industrial society in an unusual degree of detail.

Stirrings of religious revival began in east Shropshire two decades before Fletcher went to Madeley. Preaching began in Broseley in February 1741–42 when a chapel was opened which for two years 'had no constant supply but what by the providence of God ministers of other congregations were sometimes sent to assist us'. The meetings developed into a Baptist society which had close links with the Baptists of Leominster, a town where the ferment of Evangelicalism ran particularly strongly. There is no obvious explanation for this sudden establishment of a Nonconformist congregation in the coalfield, but it may well be linked with the exceptionally high mortality in the district in the years 1739–41.[1]

John Fletcher, born at Nyon on Lake Geneva in 1729, migrated to England in 1752 after rejecting a career in the Portuguese army. He became tutor to the two sons of Thomas Hill of Tern Hall, Atcham, near Shrewsbury, and after experiencing an Evangelical conversion, made contacts with John and Charles Wesley and with various religious societies. On 6 March 1757 he was ordained, and the following day was licensed as curate of Madeley. By 1760 Thomas Hill's sons no longer needed a tutor, and Hill offered Fletcher the lucrative living of Dunham in Cheshire, but this Fletcher refused, on the grounds that it posed too many temptations to a luxurious way of life. When Hill met Edward Kynaston, patron of Madeley, at Shrewsbury racecourse, the two arranged for the incumbent of Madeley to move to Dunham and for Fletcher to take his place.[2]

Nowhere is Fletcher explicit about his reasons for choosing Madeley rather than any other parish, but several guarded pronouncements suggest that he particulary wished to confront the social problems of an industrial parish. Certainly he did not, as some biographers have suggested, see Madeley as a quiet rural retreat where he could write theological tracts. He was as aware as anyone of the profound social and economic changes taking place in the district. In 1758 he described his future parishioners as '2,000 souls, which are as sheep scattered without a shepherd, and mostly those who enter first in the kingdom, poor labourers and colliers'. In a letter to John Wesley in 1760 he spoke of 'a chain of providences I could not break', which took him to Madeley. In November of the same year he wrote to Charles Wesley, 'the god of a busy world is doubly the god of this part of the world . . . should the Lord vouchsafe to plant the gospel in this country, my parish seems to be the best spot for the centre of a work, as it lies just among the most populous, profane and ignorant'. Melville Horne, Fletcher's successor, wrote at a time of personal disillusionment in 1796 that 'for a settlement for life I could wish another such wild parish as Madeley with no more religion in it than Madeley when Mr. Fletcher came there'.[3] Fletcher saw as his mission the combating of the busy-ness and sin which he regarded as particular features of industrial society; bad language, drunkenness, misuse of time, self-indulgent recreation, lack of respect for humanity and the flouting of lawful authority.

In the early years of his ministry at Madeley, Fletcher, like John Wesley, did not regard with meticulous respect the conventional ecclesiastical discipline of the Church of England. His congregations, small at first grew during the winter of 1760–61 so that by April 1761 the church could no longer contain them. Evangelicalism was not accepted quietly by many of the parishioners. Churchwardens hindered those from neighbouring parishes who wished to attend the church, and a clergyman called Prothero delivered a bitter attack on Fletcher at the Archdeacon's Visitation in August 1761. By May 1762 Fletcher was holding meetings in the Rock Chapel, Madeley Wood, a tall cottage on the edge of the Severn Gorge, occupied by one Mary Matthews. A mob led by a Roman Catholic demonstrated outside, interrupting the services by beating a drum. Fletcher was threatened with imprisonment by a magistrate, and another clergyman tried to enforce the Conventicle Act against him.[4] The meeting in the Rock Chapel was one of two religious societies which Fletcher formed, the other being at Coalbrookdale.[5]

In 1764 John Wesley preached to large congregations at Madeley, and by the following year there were several Wesleyan societies in Shropshire. A short-lived circuit in Wesley's connexion, based on Shrewsbury, was formed, with Alexander Mather as its itinerant minister. Fletcher agreed with Mather on a division of their labours, and asked for help in visiting some of the societies which he had set up. The following year he addressed a pastoral letter to 'those who love and fear the Lord Jesus Christ about Madeley, Madeley Wood, the Dale, Broseley, Coalpit Bank and the Trench', indicating that he was drawing adherents from settlements throughout the coalfield, both north and south of the Severn. Regular societies were formed at Broseley and Coalpit Bank, but Fletcher was less successful at Little Wenlock where one man 'set about ringing the pan at him and another man threw eggs at him and a man the name of Rogers drove four horses through the congregation'. In 1765 Fletcher began to preach in the town of Wellington.[6]

The mid-1760s marked the zenith of Fletcher's activities in the coalfield at large. Afterwards he was afflicted by failing health, and was increasingly involved in Evangelical affairs at a national level. In 1768 he became Superintendent of the Countess of Huntingdon's seminary at Trevecca, but resigned the post three years later. In 1770 he spent five months in Italy and France with Joseph Benson, later his biographer and then classics master at Wesley's school at Kingswood. In the early 1770s Fletcher's work in the coalfield was largely confined to his own parish. He resisted John Wesley's attempts to persuade him to relinquish his vicarage so that he could prepare to lead the Wesleyan Connexion on its founder's death.[7]

In the summer of 1776 Fletcher's physical condition deteriorated. He spent long periods at the Bristol hot wells and went on a tour of East Anglia in the hope of speeding his recovery. In 1776–77 he arranged the building of a meeting house in Madeley Wood, 'where the children might be taught to read and write in the day, and the grown up people might hear the Word of God in the evenings, when they can get an evangelist to preach it to them'. In November 1777 he left for his native Switzerland, whence he did not return until May 1781. During his absence the parish was served with but little success by a curate, Alexander Greaves. 'A cloud is over my poor parish,' wrote Fletcher on his return, 'the place is not fit for him nor he for it'.[8]

In November 1781 Fletcher married Mary Bosanquet, a pious Evangelical whom he had known for many years, but to whom he had previously been inhibited from proposing marriage by her fortune, which had, by 1781, been dissipated. He introduced his wife to his congregation in January 1782 with the words, 'I have not married this wife for myself only, but for your sakes also'. John Wesley visited Madeley in May 1782 and Fletcher hoped that he and Mary Fletcher would between them revive class meetings in the parish. In 1784–85 a second meeting house in the parish, at Coalbrookdale was begun. Fletcher died in August 1785 having expressed the hope several times during his last years that his congregations would maintain their links with John Wesley's Connexion.[9]

Methodism remained closely identified with the parish church in Madeley for half a century after Fletcher's death. Archdeacon Plymley commented in 1793 that sectaries in the parish were but few 'for though many would be denominated Methodists they frequent the church'. This harmonious relationship sprang from the tolerance which the patrons of the living, and Henry Burton non-resident vicar from 1793 until 1831, allowed to Mary Fletcher. She continued to live in the vicarage, and set up the adjacent barn as a centre for religious meetings. She was allowed to choose Evangelical curates to perform the duties in the parish church.[10]

Fletcher's immediate successor was Melville Horne, one of John Wesley's itinerant preachers, whose successful ministry in Madeley ended in 1792, when he left England for Sierra Leone. He returned from Africa the following year, sadly disillusioned,[11] and tried unavailingly to re-establish himself at Madeley. He was followed as curate by Samuel Walter, who arrived in the parish in May 1792, and subsequently superintended the replacement of the medieval parish church by an octagonal meeting house designed by Thomas Telford.[12] Before Walter agreed to settle at Madeley, Mary Fletcher offered the post to Robert Morris of Shifnal, warning him that 'by coming among Methodists he should not expect to make the world love him'.[13]

Relations between Samuel Walter and Mary Fletcher were always cordial and during his time a three-fold ministry operated from the vicarage, comprising Walter himself as curate of the parish church, the visiting preachers of the Wesleyan Shrewsbury circuit, and Mary Fletcher with her adopted daughters, Sally Lawrence and Mary Tooth, who lived at the vicarage. Charles Hulbert recalled sitting in Madeley Wood chapel with Samuel Walter and the curate of Wellington drawing up Wesleyan preaching plans. The Methodist society at Madeley, together with those which assembled at the meeting houses built by Fletcher at Coalbrookdale and Madeley Wood, and at the Coalport chapel founded by Sally Lawrence, comprised an unofficial sub-circuit. Mary Fletcher and her adopted daughters regularly preached in the meeting house on Sundays and led class meetings during the week. They maintained less formal links with congregations and individual Methodists throughout the coalfield. They were in effect the leaders of a kind of religious order drawn together by the charisma of John Fletcher, for which parallels have to be sought in the primitive or medieval churches rather than in the sober history of English dissent. Madeley became a place of pilgrimage for Evangelicals, both in the time of Mary Fletcher and for many years afterwards. 'A kind of Mecca to methodists', 'a sort of Christian Jerusalem' are phrases which were applied to the parish time and time again in the Evangelical press. I barely avoid the absurdities of some of the Roman Catholics', confessed one Victorian Methodist when describing his affection for Fletcher's memory. The publication of engravings of Fletcher, his church, his vicarage, his bedroom, and of the vicarage barn, became something of a cottage industry. Mary Fletcher and Mary Tooth received a continuous stream of demands for relics, for locks of Fletcher's hair or specimens of his handwriting. His pulpit, communion table, brass lamps and prayer books were carefully preserved, while marks on the wall of his study said to have been made by his heavy breathing while in prayer were readily displayed. Mary Fletcher and Mary Tooth were frequently asked about John Fletcher's appearances on earth after his death, and such visitations were devoutly chronicled in the Evangelical press.[14] How, each Sunday, the adherents of the cult of John Fletcher renewed their devotion to his memory was described by William Tranter, a convert of Mary Fletcher, who entered the Wesleyan ministry:

> On the Sabbath, the pious people, living at the distance of from one to three or four miles from Madeley, usually arrived in time for Mrs. Fletcher's morning meeting. In fine weather the room used generally to be full. The religious services for the day were as follows: after prayer, with which the service always commenced, a beautiful, prepared piece, called 'The Watchword', occupying from ten minutes to a quarter of an hour, was read . . . At the close of this exercise, Mrs. Fletcher spoke to a few, chiefly aged persons, coming from a distance, on their religious experience, giving to each advice, encouragement, or admonition. If any strangers were present, as was often the case, she now gave them an invitation to express, for the edification of others, their own views and feelings. And here she appeared to great advantage . . . If time permitted, after these strangers, any persons present might speak on their own religious experience; and thus the happy moments flow away only too rapidly, but leaving solid and lasting benefits behind. The chiming of the church going bell was then heard, and the assembly separated to meet again in the parish church close at hand, to which the people very generally repaired, Mrs. Fletcher always, if in health; and for its services the preceding exercises were found to be a happy and profitable preparation. Here, too, the Gospel, in those days gave no uncertain sound . . .
>
> The noon hour of the Sabbath was generally spent in the following manner: respectable strangers visiting Madeley for religious purposes, when discovered as such, were usually invited to dine with Mrs. Fletcher at the vicarage-house, where they were sure to find a cheerful welcome to things necessary for their refreshment, and at the same time, by edifying conversation, a feast for the soul. The poor living too far off to allow them to return from their own houses for the afternoon services of the day, partook, if so disposed, of her hospitalities in the vicarage-kitchen. Some, having brought their provision with them, were seen in fine weather in little companies in the fields, holding heavenly conversation and prayer. Others of the respectable portion of these pious persons, wishing to enjoy the remainder of the Sabbath services, had, in an apartment to themselves, a cheap family dinner

provided at the village inn, where great decorum was maintained. Here they too spent the time in edifying conversation and prayer, till the welcome little bell reminded them of Mrs. Fletcher's one o'clock meeting. At this meeting, for the most part numerously attended, she read the life of some eminently holy person ... accompanied with such remarks of her own on the excellency or defects of the character under consideration, as showed her great spiritual discernment ... On the ringing of the bell for the afternoon service, this exercise was suspended. At church there was always a sermon in the afternoon; and those who could remained to hear it and join in the other devotion of the Church. Those who could not, by reason of distance or other circumstances, remain, now repaired to their own homes, to be in readiness for the evening services in their own vicinity, there being several large chapels in the populous parts of the parish, at each of which the Minister officiated every Sabbath evening alternately ... This plan was adopted by Mr. Fletcher and was followed by his evangelical and pious successors for upwards of forty years'[15]

The fundamental loyalty of those who met in Madeley every Sunday and of the 100 or so people who comprised the Wesleyan class there was to a particular way of life and to the memory of John Fletcher. This was a loyalty which overlay formal denominational affiliations. A 'Methodist' in Madeley meant one who took religion seriously, and not the adherent of a particular sect, denomination or connexion. Such an informal, spontaneous religious movement was threatened by growing denominational awareness, both nationally and locally, and by the increasing intolerance of the Wesleyan bureaucracy.

In 1815 Samuel Walter left Madeley and was succeeded by George Mortimer. In June Mary Fletcher was looking forward with pleasure to the arrival of the new curate, but by August she was writing of a division between the Methodists and church people by the desire of the minister. A Wesleyan living in Madeley at the time later recalled 'many acts of unkindness and even bigotry on the part of the then resident clergyman', which forced the Methodists to detach themselves from the parish church. This process of separation was a gradual one, not completed for nearly two decades after 1815.[16]

Mary Fletcher died on 9 December 1815. Her successor, Mary Tooth, was politely requested to vacate the vicarage, and moved to another house near the church. George Mortimer did not identify himself with the Methodists as Samuel Walter had done and the threefold ministry came to an end. In 1816 the Methodists contemplated the building of a separate Wesleyan chapel in Madeley, but this did not materialise, probably because Mortimer allowed Mary Tooth to hold meetings in the Vicarage Barn as Mary Fletcher had done. The Methodists who attended these meetings still went to Anglican services in the parish church in the intervals between their own Sabbath devotions. Relations with the church authorities remained strained. One Methodist suggested to Mary Tooth in 1822 that a small group should be formed to pray that either the present ministry should be converted, or that another should be sent more congenial to the spirit of a pure Gospel.[17]

Wesleyan as well as Anglican antipathy threatened the existence of the Methodist society led by Mary Tooth. In 1823 there were over 1,000 Wesleyans in the Madeley circuit. Many came from parishes like Broseley, where there was traditional hostility between Anglicans and dissenters, or from settlements like Ketley Bank, distant from parish churches, where the Church of England was unrepresented. In 1827 it was proposed to hold preaching services in Fletcher's chapel at Madeley Wood at the same time as morning prayer at the parish church. A Wesleyan minister, appalled at the decision, wrote to Mary Tooth, who likewise opposed it 'Surely this would ill accord with the original design of that blessed servant of Christ who executed the building', pointing out that the decision might prejudice the use of the Vicarage Barn which had been allowed by the incumbents of the parish for over 40 years. In 1828 Mary Tooth and her congregation were again contemplating the erection of a chapel of their own in Madeley town. The same year the Wesleyan ministers of the Madeley circuit insisted to their Local Preachers' Meeting that only preachers whose names were on the circuit plan would be able to take appointments in local chapels, thereby excluding Mary Tooth from Wesleyan pulpits, since women were not normally allowed to become local preachers in the Wesleyan Connexion at this time. By 1829 there was talk of strong party feeling in the Madeley Wesleyan circuit. In 1831 the Wesleyan Superintendent pointed out to Mary Tooth that before accepting a collection from her congregation at Coalport, he 'should be satisfied the chapel from which a collection is to be made, is, in good faith, a Wesleyan Methodist chapel', and promised that he would when he saw her explain the propriety of the regulation.[18]

In 1831 the Vicarage Barn was demolished. Mary Tooth's society continued to meet in the upper room of her house but the Wesleyan circuit decided to build a new Wesleyan chapel in Madeley town within sight of the parish church, which was opened in August 1833. Dissension between Mary Tooth and the circuit authorities continued and she contemplated leaving Madeley. Services at the chapel were timed to coincide with those of her society, but the latter were changed to enable people to attend both. In 1841 the Wesleyans replaced their first small chapel with a larger one at a greater distance from the church, but Mary Tooth's three classes, totalling over 70 members, continued to meet in the upper room of her house until her death in 1843.[19]

Madeley remained a place of pilgrimage for Evangelicals seeking inspiration from Fletcher's memory. Both Anglicans and Methodists claimed to be the true guardians of his spirit, but since the atmosphere of the parish church remained strongly Evangelical, open conflicts did not develop. Visiting Anglicans were favourably impressed with the large Methodist chapels and congregations they found in Madeley, and visiting Methodists liked the atmosphere of the parish church. John Petty the Primitive Methodist minister and historian wrote in 1845,

> The leading doctrines taught by Fletcher are still clearly and forcibly preached. The present excellent vicar has no sympathy with Popery whether within the Church of Rome or the Church of England. He preaches ex tempore, holds class meetings, the same as the Methodists, employs local preachers and exhorters, and conducts prayer meetings in the new school room after preaching in the church on Sunday evenings. A great congregation attends his ministry.[20]

The ministries of John Fletcher, his wife and her adopted daughter lasted for over 80 years. Few parishes in Britain and certainly none in east Shropshire were subjected to such a prolonged exposure to Evangelical influences. How did Madeley differ from neighbouring parishes where Evangelicalism made little or fitful progress? Many Victorian visitors had no doubts about the long term success of Fletcher's work. They were able to point to large Anglican and Wesleyan congregations, and to a great diminution in public disorder, to see Fletcher's name as 'an ointment poured forth among the people'. A minister in the 1880s noted that the people of Madeley were 'as different as possible from the blasphemous, drunken, immortal, brutal crew who at times threatened the life of the saintly Fletcher'.[21] To some extent visitors' impression are confirmed by statistics and other evidence. The places of worship in Madeley in the mid-19th century *were* better attended than those in some neighbouring parishes. Yet to isolate the influence of Evangelicalism from other factors affecting social change remains difficult. The consequences of Fletcher's activities on recreational changes, working conditions and popular disturbances are discussed below.[22] His influence on individuals and that of his wife and of Mary Tooth can also be examined through the voluminous correspondence which survives in the Methodist archives.

The instrument by which Evangelical ideas were spread was the religious society or class meeting. Fletcher formed several societies in Madeley in the early years of his ministry listing as sins for their members to avoid:

> taking the Lord's name in vain, either by profane cursing or trivial exclamations, Sabbath breaking, uncleanness, drunkenness or tippling, or going into a public house or staying without necessity; fighting; quarrelling; brawling; railing, uncharitable conversation; filthy talking, jesting; evil speaking; attendance at balls, plays races, cockfightings and bull baitings; gaming; song singing; reading unprofitable books; softness; needless indulgence; putting on gaudy and costly apparel; smuggling; taking advantage of a neighbour[23]

When Fletcher returned from Switzerland in 1781 the structure of local classes had collapsed and one of the reasons for his marriage was the need for someone who could rebuild it. A Yorkshire Methodist told Mary Fletcher after her marriage that she was in her proper place since there had been no classes or bands at Madeley; and he 'never knew any success to attend our ministry where these were omitted', and they could only be re-established by a wife to John Fletcher. Mary Fletcher wrote shortly after her husband's death, 'besides the great reformation that has taken place in this parish as to outward behaviour, he has left behind him a goodly company of upright, earnest, people, whom he had gathered into little societies'.[24]

One function of the society or class meeting was to provide a breeding place for evangelists like those who, during revivals, went out to mission in the remotest settlements in the coalfield, and for such reprovers of vice, as those who went with Fletcher to public houses to denounce the sins they saw there. The culture of the class meeting is well preserved in letters written to Mary Tooth and Mary Fletcher. One of the former's correspondents described a love feast at Madeley in 1826. 'It was very encouraging to hear a young youth speak, he was on trial, I think, the quarter before, he said how he longed for the time when he should have a ticket and be a member. He like myself, seems to esteem it a privilege to be member of the Wesleyan Methodist Connexion'. The high claims made by Methodists for their own morality led to an almost neurotic defensiveness. A minister told Mary Tooth in 1823 of a Mr. Smith whom he had informed of the necessity to avoid everything likely to arouse suspicion while he held Wesleyan office. Smith agreed that if he brought a stain upon the cause of Methodism he would allow himself to be read publicly out of the society.[25]

The strict discipline of the class meeting often conflicted with the need rapidly to absorb new members. In 1812 John Griffiths, a Wesleyan cooper was executed for the murder of William Bailey a charter master, at Ketley. Charles Cameron, vicar of St. George's, complained that this was a blow against all religion, and criticised the standards of Methodist discipline,

> I urge Methodists to take heed who they admit as members of their society, and still more who they suffer to teach, or speak, or in any way take the lead among them. But while persons, not only whose past character but whose present profession of religion is evidently doubtful, are admitted into their society, while inexperienced men, women and almost children, who can have but little knowledge of themselves, of human nature, or of the Word of

God, and who have not even made a profession of religion long enough to prove what they really are; are suffered to pray or to exhort, or in any way to stand forth as teachers, such woeful departures from their profession, as must disgrace the society to which they belong, tend to its confusion and destruction, and cause the truth of God to be blasphemed in the world.

Cameron's wife wrote a pair of tracts which pursued the same theme. A young dissenter is led by flattery to exhort at cottage meetings, and to assume ministerial airs and postures, while his humble brother is content to remain an obscure but effective Sunday School teacher. The would-be minister marries the daughter of his chief flatterer, works hard to provide his family with luxuries, fine furniture, tea, loaf sugar, white bread and fresh butter, but is eventually led into debt and is struck by illness. He is persuaded by his brother to return to his own family where he dies in Christian humility. 'It is impossible', concludes the narrator of the tale, 'to describe the ridicule which these blind teachers bring upon themselves and those they pretend to teach'.[26]

Class meetings were regarded with deep sentimentality. One of Mary Tooth's correspondents recalled the meetings held in her house, 'your upper room and its furniture – the pulpit, the cushion, the old table and the cloth'. The atmosphere of such meetings bred an uneasy sense of sexual introspection. An anonymous farmer asked Mary Fletcher in a letter whether he should marry a converted woman or an unregenerate one so as to convert her. If she advised the former, he sought her recommendations. In 1785 Betsey Pigott of Astley Abbots was to be married to Thomas Milner of Madeley, and such was the awe in which Fletcher was held that 'the young bride trembled at the thought of coming into his presence on the occasion of her nuptials lest the drapery she wore should call forth some admonition'.[27]

Mary Tooth received a succession of embarrassed proposals of marriage. One Benjamin Longmore, a commercial traveller for the Coalbrookdale Company pleaded for her hand in 1805, declaring himself 'a man of weak constitution, illiberal education and rough manners'.[28]

Members of the societies who left Madeley were often disenchanted with the world outside. In 1812 Samual Walter's son joined the Marines at Plymouth and wrote to Mary Fletcher, 'no one can conceive the sin that goes on here'. A servant girl wrote from Birmingham to Mary Tooth in 1823 that she wished she could hear the ministers whom she had heard in Madeley. The people for whom she worked often went out, then she would go upstairs to pray with the prayer book always reading the burial service because it was so solemn. She asked Mary Tooth to pray that her master and mistress might see the danger of plays and balls.[29]

Attitudes to politics among Methodists in Madeley underwent fundamental changes between Fletcher's arrival in the parish and the death of Mary Tooth. Fletcher himself was an unrepentant controversialist, an outspoken upholder of established authority, in particular a defender of the King's government during the American War of Independence. He gave enthusiastic support to the efforts of Sir Richard Hill, M.P. for Shropshire, to legislate against bull baiting and in favour of various other Evangelical causes. As early as 1778 he wrote to John and Charles Wesley attacking the philosophy of Voltaire, Rousseau, Bayle and Mirabeau. Ironically, in 1799 his widow's income from his Swiss estates was cut off by the 'plunderous atheists' who by then ruled Switzerland.[30]

Both Fletcher and his successors saw politics in Old Testament terms, upholding the concept of national guilt as expressed in Fletcher's sermon on a national fast day in 1762,

> From the gilded palace to the thatched cottage, our guilt calls for vengeance. Wickedness is become so fashionable that he who refuses to run with others into vanity, intemperance or profaneness is in danger of losing his character, on the one hand, while on the other the son of Belial prides himself in excesses, glories in diabolical practices, and scoffs with impunity at religion and virtue. O England! England! happy, yet ungrateful island. Dost thou repay fruitfulness by profaneness, plenty by vanity, liberty by impiety, and the light of Christianity by excesses of immorality[31]

Mary Fletcher was told in 1797 that naval victories over the French showed 'God is for us'. Another correspondent during the French Wars asked her 'what God is doing with England as a nation . . . what is he doing amongst our great men and amongst our lower order of men in London, or where will the present disturbances end?'

While Fletcher actively participated in political controversies, rarely failing to make public his views, by the turn of the century Methodists in Madeley seem to have regarded themselves more as victims of politics, a small group of the virtuous caught in the crossfire of the conflicts of a world hostile on all sides. Some consolation was obtained from accounts of the discomfiture of the wicked, like a description of the death of Tom Paine carefully preserved among the papers of Mary Tooth. Times of political stress brought to the surface particularly vivid fears among the Methodists. In May 1832 as the Reform Bill reached its last stages in Parliament, one of Mary Tooth's friends wrote to her, 'the times are truly awful', and claimed to have found in John Wesley's 'Notes upon the New Testament' prophecies that the year 1832 was fixed upon as the time the Beast would ascend out of the bottomless pit and that the year 36 would be the time of the final overthrow.[32]

The Madeley Methodists are perhaps the best documented of any congregation in Britain in the early decades of the 19th century. The picture of them which emerges from their letters to Mary Tooth and Mary Fletcher is of an inward-looking, rather timorous people, oppressed by ecclesiastical politics, perplexed by secular events which they did not understand, hoping to be saved by divine intervention in the form of a revival, clinging tenaciously to the memory of John Fletcher, which earned them status and respect among Evangelicals throughout Britain. But the Madeley Methodists were not typical of local congregations. If Christianity had been represented in the coalfield in the 19th century only by Fletcher's direct successors it might have been a movement of much greater purity, but it would have been of considerably smaller size.

XV

THE RELIGIOUS EXPERIENCE

By the time that Mary Tooth's congregation in Madeley ceased to meet in 1843 denominational allegiances were firmly established in the Shropshire coalfield. Appendix Three indicates something of the relative strength of the various denominations in the district as revealed by the 1851 Ecclesiastical Census. The level of church attendance in the coalfield was rather below the average for England and Wales as a whole, although higher than in the large towns. If morning, afternoon and evening services are taken together there were 25,486 attendances in the 11 parishes in the coalfield. Using the method employed by K. S. Inglis,[1] this gives an index of 54.7, as compared with the average for England and Wales of 61, for rural areas, 71.4, and for towns of over 10,000 inhabitants, 49.7. The actual number of people attending services would, of course, have been substantially less than 25,486, since many, especially Nonconformists, went to two or three services each Sunday.

No attendance figures were returned for several important congregations in east Shropshire, and forms were not provided for a number of cottage meetings. When comparing attendances in the coalfield with the national average this is of little consequence since there must have been similar omissions throughout the country, but such faults to some extent distort local comparisons between denominations. There are no figures for the parish churches of St. Michael, Madeley and St. Leonard, Malins Lee, for the Wesleyan chapels at Coalbrookdale and Coalport, for the Primitive Methodist chapel at the Aqueduct, nor for at least 52 cottage meetings, although some of those who attended the latter may have been recorded at services at chapels at different times of the day. Of the figures quoted in Appendix Three, those for the Anglicans and Methodists should be somewhat increased, those for the Roman Catholics are approximations only, while those for other dissenting denominations are probably quite accurate.

The three Methodist denominations taken together were the best supported of the churches in the district, having rather more than half of the total attendances, although the largest of them, the Wesleyan Connexion, taken alone had rather fewer attendances than the Church of England. The older Nonconformist denominations were not strongly supported, while the Roman Catholics formed an even smaller proportion of local church goers.

Methodism was in many ways the established church of the Shropshire coalfield. In 1851 the three Methodist denominations recorded over half of all of the church attendances, and between them claimed 3,516 members.[2] In 1793 when the Shrewsbury

Wesleyan circuit was formed there were only 395 members in Shropshire. The Connexion grew rapidly during the French wars, claiming 1,400 members in the whole of
the county by 1810. The association of Methodists and Anglicans which survived at
Madeley was not typical of the county as a whole. Several petitions were sent from
Shropshire congregations to the Wesleyan conference, in the early 1800s, including one
from Broseley, asking for the right to hold Holy Communion services, a sign of complete
separation from the Church of England. In 1815 a circuit centred on Broseley covering
most of the southern half of the coalfield was separated from the Shrewsbury circuit,
taking 683 members and leaving 693 in the parent circuit. In 1817–18 a circuit in the
north of the coalfield, of which Wellington was the centre, was created from the
Shrewsbury circuit, with 350 members. Wesleyanism continued to grow during the
1820s and '30s, and by 1835 each of the two coalfield circuits claimed over a thousand
members, a level which was maintained throughout the 1830s and '40s.

Methodism in east Shropshire was characterised by its revivals, phenomena which
seemed to owe more to their origins in vernacular culture and the environment of the
coalfield than to strictly denominational sources. It was probably because the Methodist
churches allowed, tolerated and sometimes encouraged revivalism that they fulfilled so
perfectly the deep-seated emotional needs of those accustomed to a dangerous and
violent working environment, and enjoyed in consequence more support than the other
more sober churches.

John Fletcher was a leading figure in the Evangelical Revival, but he was not a
revivalist in the 19th-century sense. He was no more a hellfire preacher than John
Wesley himself, and did not encourage religious meetings of excessive size, length or
sentimentality. The first preacher who deliberately used emotional techniques to produce conversions in public meetings who was active in the coalfield appears to have
been Samuel Taylor, a Wesleyan minister appointed to the Shrewsbury circuit in 1798.
Taylor was certainly able to use with some effect the tear-raising techniques of later,
more sophisticated, practitioners. A colleague wrote at the time of his death that he
admired Taylor, although he could not admire panegyric. According to one witness,
'in 1799 and to the Conference of 1800, the Lord greatly blessed the preaching of
Messrs. Taylor and Gill, not only in Coalbrookdale but in every part of the Shrewsbury
circuit, when many precious souls were converted from sin to holiness and from Satan
unto God'. The revival continued during 1801, and raised the membership of the
circuit from 587 in 1799 to 920 in 1803. As new societies were established in villages
hitherto unmissioned, groups of newly converted young men set out to plant Wesleyanism in other settlements. From Lawley Bank, where the Methodist society was one
of the first successes of Taylor's revival, young men went to preach at Little Wenlock
and New Works. The revival at Coalbrookdale led a group to found a society at Little
Dawley.[3]

During the next two decades there were several revivals in the coalfield, but their
effects seem for the most part to have been localised. At Coalbrookdale in 1814, a
Wesleyan noted, 'we experienced a very genuine revival of Religion, many Sunday
School teachers were truly converted to God . . . as were many others of our neighbours'. The effects of this revival seem largely to have been confined to Coalbrookdale
and there were no sudden large increases in church membership over the district as a
whole.[4]

The next revival in the coalfield followed closely upon the Cinderhill riots of 2
February 1821, when the Yeomanry shot two colliers who were among a large group

demonstrating against reductions in wages. After the shooting the 6th Dragoon Guards paraded the district as the striking miners returned to work. In March 1821 a Wesleyan minister congratulated Mary Tooth on the prosperity of Methodism in Madeley and in the same letter asked for news of the riots. In April two Primitive Methodist missionaries from Tunstall began to reap 'an abundant harvest among the men employed in the mines and iron works', to the south of Newport. In May news reached a Liverpool correspondent of Mary Tooth that Methodists in Madeley were 'experiencing times of refreshing from the Lord'. A group of missionaries of the Winfieldite or Revivalist Methodist sect, a small group who had seceded from the Primitives, arrived in Dawley in 1821 and were assisted by Benjamin Tranter, a Wesleyan and mines agent for the Coalbrookdale Company. After being reprimanded by the Wesleyan authorities, Tranter left the Connexion and identified himself with the Revivalists. Both of the new groups opened chapels in the following year, the Primitives at Wrockwardine Wood and the Revivalists at Brand Lee, Dawley.[5]

The impetus of the revival was maintained in 1822 and it was not confined to the two new denominations. In April 1822 the Wesleyan minister in Wellington wrote,

> The Lord is making bare his holy arm and exhibiting the richest of his grace among us . . . our chapels and preaching houses are crowded to excess and everywhere there is a thirst for the Word of Life . . . no noise or disorder is connected with this good work, but the power and the presence of God in a peculiar manner rests upon the people in the prayer meetings, the class meetings and under the public ministry, and many that have been very vile and ignorant as the wild ass's colt have been strangely drawn to hear words whereby they may be saved[6]

A Primitive Methodist conducted an emotional meeting at Coalpit Bank on 29 April 1822,

> It was a shaking time. The people were crying for mercy on every hand and a great many were enabled to rejoice in a sin pardoning God. O Lord still ride on and be glorified in the salvation of sinners.[7]

On 19 May 1822 Hugh Bourne the founder of Primitive Methodism conducted a camp meeting at Coalpit Bank,

> The Lord made bare His arm: souls were in distress in several of the companies and several were brought into liberty. In the afternoon thousands were present and two preaching stands were occupied. The last time the praying companies were out was a very powerful one; and at the first stand there still remained about a thousand persons who had not room to go out. A praying service was held for these and after some time a general cry for mercy was heard among them, but how many got liberty could not be fully ascertained.[8]

Membership statistics reflect the scale of the revival. The newly formed Primitive Methodist circuit in the coalfield claimed 775 members by 1823. The membership of the Wellington Wesleyan circuit rose from 396 in March 1821 to 705 three years later. In Madeley there was an increase from 803 to 1,000 within a year of March 1821.[9] While it is not possible to identify individuals converted in the revival with people who took part in the Cinderhill riots, the connection between the revival and the traumatic political and social defeat of the colliers in February 1821 seems a close one. In an area where a return to work at reduced wages was overlooked by Dragoons, it was not surprising that Methodist missionaries should find a trembling and fearful population. Colliers and ironworkers who had experienced five or six years of unparalleled economic depression, and whose attempts to prevent wages being reduced were met with gunfire from a Yeomanry force comprised of the local ruling class, might well have asked what they might do to be saved. It would be absurd to pretend that every revival in 19th-century Shropshire represented an expression of working class despair at the failures of political agitation, but equally absurd to maintain that in 1821–22 political disappointment and the great tide of popular emotion represented by the revival were not closely linked. Like the great Nottinghamshire revival of 1817–18 which followed the abortive Pentridge Rising, the Shropshire revival of 1821–22 was kindled by a political defeat for the working class.[10]

As prosperity returned to the iron industry in the 1820s so the heat of the revival diminished. Methodist conversion was for many a transitory experience. The year of greatest growth among the Wesleyans was 1821–22, and while membership increased each year until 1825, the rate of increase declined, and numbers began to decrease in 1826, although membership did not shrink to the pre-1822 level. The Primitive Methodist circuit disappeared from the Connexion's official records between 1825 and 1828, when its membership was 304, less than half that of 1824. It fell away still further in the next few years. The Revivalists in Dawley established a circuit with chapels at Brand Lee and Madeley Wood and 10 societies assembling at cottage meetings in the industrial hamlets. Nationally the Revivalist or Winfieldite Connexion was collapsing and in 1829 the Dawley circuit successfully applied for admission to the Methodist New Connexion.[11]

There were signs of a revival in Shropshire in 1829, particularly at Coalbrookdale and among the Wrockwardine Wood Primitive Methodists, but the effects were limited.[12] It was not until 1832–33 that there was a marked increase in the membership of the local Methodist societies. This was no more than the beginning of a slow build-up to a revival which took fire throughout the coalfield in 1835. There were clear signs of revival in Coalbrookdale, 'a glorious effusion of the Holy Spirit's influence in the Wellington circuit', and 'a stir and such a good work amongst the people in Madeley', where, 'blessing was copiously poured upon the church'.[13]

The Primitive Methodists experienced a remarkable series of revivalistic meetings during the summer of 1839. On 4 August a huge camp meeting was held on the cinder hills of the Donnington Wood blast furnaces:

> While engaged in prayer at the opening of the meeting, the people rose unitedly into the exercise of mighty faith; the feeling was heavenly, and at times almost overpowering. Nor did that blessed and powerful influence leave the meeting the whole of the day. The hearts of both the preachers and people were fixed upon God; and divine and eternal things seemed fully to captivate every soul. All the preachings, exhortations, singing and prayer, were attended with such a great degree of Divine Unction that it was clearly discovered (and felt) that the arm of the Lord was revealed . . . in the afternoon this populous country appeared all on a move. The people came crowding in from every quarter, till the congregation soon consisted of about four thousand persons . . . We broke up about five o'clock p.m. and at six o'clock commenced the love feast in our Wrockwardine Wood chapel. It was soon crowded to excess both in the gallery and in the bottom. And the Lord in answer to united prayer, so filled the chapel with His glorious presence that the congregation was shaken throughout. The speaking was powerful, and it went on well until sinners were brought into such deep distress of soul on account of their lost state, that we were obliged to turn it into a prayer meeting. The most distressing cries for mercy were very soon heard from every part of the chapel, in the gallery and below; so that there was full employment for all who knew the Lord. As speedily as possible, four penitent forms were placed, and the mourners and

broken-hearted were invited to come forward to be prayed for. Many came forward volun-
tarily, and fell down before the Lord; others were in such deep distress as to become almost
helpless, and these were brought forward . . . At my two penitent forms eighteen or twenty
precious souls obtained a solid sense of sins forgiven, and were delivered from sin and Satan's
power; and near that number found the like blessing at the other forms and others went away
in distress. This has been a great day: language fails to express what I felt on this occasion.[14]

All three of the local Methodist denominations shared the prosperity of the late
1830s. Even the smallest, the New Connexion, recorded its highest ever total of members in 1837–38. The Primitive Methodists had previously confined their activities to
the part of the coalfield north of the Holyhead Road, apparently by tacit agreement
leaving the Dawley and Madeley area to the New Connexion who had no congregations
north of Hollinswood. In 1839 the Primitives began to expand in Dawley while the
New Connexion, less successfully, started cottage meetings at Trench and Hadley. The
fervour of the revival was sustained in 1841, when at Lawley Bank, after the building
of a large Wesleyan chapel, there was 'a time of breaking down of sinners' hearts'. In
1842 there was a revival among the Primitive Methodists in Wellington where, 'for six
weeks the chapel was open almost night and day and crowded out every night'.[15] The
greatest increases in Methodist membership in the district were recorded between 1840
and 1841, and between 1841 and 1842. There was a further increase the following year,
but the rate of growth had declined, and the mid-1840s saw a falling away of support.
Even so during the decade after 1832 there was an enormous increase in Methodist
membership throughout the coalfield. At the trough of a depression in 1832 there were
a little over 2,000 Methodists in the area. At the peak after the revival, in 1843, there
were 3,669.

The sustained period of revival between 1835 and 1842 cannot easily be explained
by economic or political factors. The late 1830s were a period of prosperity in the iron
trade, the early '40s a time of acute depression. There are no indications that the
revival was in any way affected by disappointment with the failure of Chartist agitation.
The Chartist-inspired miners' strike of 1842 did not end with the same degree of
bitterness and sense of failure that followed the Cinderhill Riots 21 years earlier. The
revival of 1835–42 seem different in kind from that of 1821–22. While the whole coalfield
was swept with religious hysteria from the spring of 1821 until the summer of 1822,
between 1835 and 1842 there seem rather to have been a continuing series of revivalistic
outbursts at particular churches. Like barrels of gunpowder on a burning ship congregations exploded into revivals as they were affected by sparks from their neighbours.

Revivalism in Shropshire in the first half of the 19th century was not so much a
conscious technique of evangelism as a religious aspect of vernacular culture. Although
Wesleyans and Primitive Methodists looked to their itinerant ministers to take a lead
in revivals, numerous accounts emphasise the role of local preachers within their own
communities. At Lawley Bank a succession of revivals in the 1840s was considered the
work of seven or eight local preachers in the Wesleyan society. When a minister went
to live in the village in 1848 lethargy resulted. The success of the Primitive Methodist
revivals in the Wrockwardine Wood area in 1839 was attributed to the good discipline
of the congregations, to the holding of open air meetings and to 'the zealous, pious and
united labours of our travelling and local preachers'.[16]

Local Evangelicalism derived much from the sense of nearness to death engendered
by work in the pits. John Fletcher was celebrated for his readiness to minister to anyone
injured in a mine. Among the Wesleyans at the Nabb the 1835 revival began when:

it pleased Him with whom are the issues of life and death, to call away, suddenly, by one of those awful catastrophes which are so common in mining districts, a very amiable and exemplary man, a member of the Wesleyan society in that place. A massive piece of coal slipped from its dark fastness, and by a part of it, he was so very much bruised that he survived but a short time; this time was however sufficient to exemplify the power of godliness. Death was seen deprived of his sting and the grave of her victory; and all who visited him beheld, amidst the agonies of dissolution brought about by so violent a cause, the soul full of joy and settled piece.[17]

Revivalists consciously and deliberately confronted those who took part in animal cruelty sports. In Oakengates in 1821 the Primitive Methodist missionaries chose to preach at the centre of the village, 'at the sport called the bull ring, where thousands of guilty and depraved human beings rioted in the brutal sport of bull baiting'. A Wesleyan open-air meeting on Easter Monday 1822 was held in a place 'generally resorted to for bull baiting and cockfighting, but on this occasion it was highly gratifying to see these workers of iniquity retiring and leaving us in full and quiet possession of their formerly unhallowed spot'. The Wesleyans of Oakengates in 1835 rejoiced at their success in an area 'the most notorious for vice of every kind, and especially for the grossest violation of the Sabbath and the cruel practice of bull baiting'.[18] Yet animal cruelty sports and revivals were in a sense not mutually exclusive but complementary. They were both aspects of an essentially violent popular culture, in which men and children were accustomed to seeing sudden and painful deaths in the pits, in which riots were often the only means of industrial bargaining. When children no longer went into the pits before the age of 10, when the double shifts at blast furnaces were discontinued, when mining accidents became less frequent, so violent recreation and violent religion declined together.

The Methodist churches recruited most of their members during revivals. One of their functions was clearly to secure the conversion of the children of parents who were already members of Methodist societies, but the revivals which affected the whole coalfield certainly succeeded in attracting outsiders. A revivalistic conversion could mean a complete change of life. William Smith, a Wellington shoe-maker, schooled during his apprenticeship in animal cruelty sports, returned from the tramp to Wellington in 1842 following the death of a friend while bathing. He was converted in the six-week revival then in progress at the Primitive Methodist chapel. Soon afterwards he became an Oddfellow, a Teetotaller, and a local preacher, he began to associate with the sort of people approved by the middle class, he was introduced at the chapel to the woman he later married, and secured a more responsible job as a turnpike toll collector.

Richard Groom of Wellington, a Wesleyan, was converted in 1841, 'during a remarkable religious awakening'. He began to walk 12 miles each Sunday to take a Sunday School, began a timber business and married a fellow Wesleyan. He became a member of the town Improvements Commission, chairman of the Board of Guardians and a county alderman. He was a teetotaller, always paying his workmen on Thursdays so that a good part of their wages would be spent on food before the temptations of the weekend. He was an early riser, so punctual in going to work that clocks were set by him, and was responsible for a programme of civic improvement that destroyed the worst rookery in Wellington.

Thomas Handley who died in Coalbrookdale in 1801 had in his youth 'followed the multitude to do evil, particularly in revelling and what are called pastimes, where he was accustomed to divert himself and his thoughtless companions by playing on the fiddle'. He was converted following the prayers of his mother, and afterwards refused to visit 'those places of vain amusement which he had frequently attended', although he would often go to neighbouring villages to warn the thoughtless to avoid such temptations.[19]

Such conversions show how dramatically a revival could affect the life of an individual. Conversion often marked the rejection of one society, that of the public house, for another, that of the chapel, even before the rise of the Teetotal movement. It meant a conscious standing aside from many traditional pursuits, even those like playing the fiddle which in the 20th century seem relatively innocent. Conversion often brought a change in secular occupation, or an entry into business, frequently with successful results. Conversion meant a more careful use of time and selection of company. In Shropshire as elsewhere blackslidings were common among those converted at revivals, but the influence of the social values imparted during revivals must have been profound. Local society was shaped as much by Evangelicalism as by industrialisation, and the revival was the most potent instrument of the Evangelicals.

The character of revivals in east Shropshire slowly changed during the 1850s. For the Wesleyans this was a period of disruption and schism, but it was not a time of prosperity for the Primitives and the New Connexion who were not so troubled. A new factor was introduced in 1853 when the Yorkshire Evangelist Isaac Marsden was invited to Lawley Bank. There was 'a great deal of wild excitement', and the whole neighbourhood was moved, and over 50 new members converted in a week, but the excitement was soon replaced by 'a dreadfully monotonous spirit of lukewarmness'. The Methodist New Connexion in Dawley in 1856 tried to instigate a revival by the rather improbable means of holding a tea meeting. In the late 1850s the Primitive Methodists experimented with protracted meetings, lasting for many hours if not days, but they seldom recorded more than one or two converts.[20]

The last great revival in the coalfield occurred in 1862. The previous year there were no more than 3,590 Methodist members in the district. By 1863 the total was 4,545, the highest ever recorded. All of the denominations shared in the prosperity of the period. The Wesleyans recorded 2,145 members, almost as many as in 1842, the Primitives 1,645, the New Connexion 245, and the United Methodist Free Church 510. The revival was described in the official organs of all four denominations, but of particular interest is an account written not by a Methodist but by a correspondent of an ultra-Tory and Anglican Shrewsbury newspaper:

Dawley: The Revival. Few people living outside this gloomy and murky district imagine the extent to which this movement has changed the habits of the semi-barbarous population for the better. Without binding ourselves by a sanction of the means in every instance employed by the chief movers in the affair, it is only just to say that a great reformation has been the result. Instead of that filthy language and those disgusting pursuits which pained and sickened those brought into contact with the colliers and forgemen in the district, you hear and see the fruits of a high moral change. Instead of an oath, a refusal and a frown if one man asks a favour of another, there is a readiness to oblige and favours are given and little assistances rendered before they are asked for . . . On Saturday 22nd the men at Mr. Botfield's works at Stirchley, after finishing up the week, held a prayer meeting in the forge. It is a pleasing sight to see these grimy sons of toil, with the dust of the works and the perspiration caused by their fires upon them, bending in perfect recognition of a higher power, and subdued by the gentler influences of religion. In their homes the same change is manifest, and here the revolution is even more complete for wives and children receive the benefit. 'I spent 15s. last fortnight in drink' said one of these in giving his experience at one of these meetings, 'this fortnight I have spent only 7d. with which my wife brought home some small beer, and she and the children have had the difference'. In the streets you see rough looking customers with their short pipes, and hear them asking others where they are going tonight, not as formerly, to riot and get drunk, but to join with their fellow workmen in prayer; some appear to divide their attention between their prayer meeting and the night school, and down to the young ragged urchin on his knees at marbles in the mud. snatches of revival songs are sung.[21]

This was to be the last such revival in the coalfield, for after 1870 the rate of migration from the district was such that it was impossible to achieve permanent increases in church membership.

The controversies which beset the Wesleyan Connexion in the first half of the 19th century had only minor repercussions in the Shropshire coalfield. The Primitive Methodists came to the district as a new denomination nearly a decade after their separation from the Wesleyans. The Revivalists who in 1829 joined the New Connexion became established in Dawley as a result of the support of a wealthy Wesleyan, and gained some strength through defections from Wesleyan societies, but essentially they too came to the district as a new denomination and did not owe their existence to a schism.

The major controversy in the Wesleyan Connexion which followed the publication of the Flysheets in the late 1840s, and led to the formation of the United Methodist Free Church in 1857 did provoke a substantial schism in the Wellington Wesleyan circuit. No Shropshire delegates attended the first meetings of Wesleyan Reformers in 1850 but during that year a pamphlet controversy developed, involving George Hughes, a Wesleyan minister in the Madeley circuit. In June 1850 the local Primitive Methodists declared their neutrality 'in the Wesleyan affair'. The principal schism came in the Wellington circuit and was centred on the chapel at Snedshill which opened in 1850. From the beginning some members, led by John Howells, a charter master, resisted ministerial attempts to assert control over the chapel, and in October 1851, in defiance of Wesleyan discipline, the expelled minister William Griffith was invited to preach at special services. After Howells had refused to allow a Connexional collection at Snedshill in January 1852, the church was omitted from the Wesleyan circuit plan. The leaders at Snedshill began to publish their own plans, and were supported by 21 local preachers, whose Wesleyan membership was subsequently severed. Later in 1852 the Wesleyan Reformers opened a new chapel at Ketley, and two country chapels and five other small societies left the Wellington circuit. In 1853 donations were sent to the national Wesleyan Reform funds. In 1854 and 1855 representatives from the Wellington circuit went to the national meetings of the Reformers, and in the latter year a new chapel at St. George's was opened. The United Methodist Free Church was formally constituted in 1857, and the following year its Wellington circuit claimed 29 local preachers, six chapels, 17 cottage meetings and 300 members. After the revival of 1862 membership rose to 510. The schism only affected the northern part of the coalfield, and apart from the involvement of George Hughes in the early stages of the controversy, the Madeley circuit seems to have been undisturbed, perhaps because the New Connexion offered a democratic alternative to Wesleyanism in that area. Most of the United Methodist chapels in the Wellington circuit were in the coalfield, but several rural societies also joined the new denomination. The Wellington circuit lost 447 members between 1851 and 1854, almost half its membership.[22]

The Church of England recorded less than 40 per cent of church attendances in the

Shropshire coalfield in 1851, but the very large congregations at some parish churches show that the Established Church was a major religious influence among all classes in the district. All Saints, Broseley had a morning congregation of 606 on 30 March 1851, St. Luke's, Ironbridge an evening attendance of 700, All Saints, Wellington a morning attendance of 530, and there were 538 at the evening service at Christ Church, Wellington.

The pattern of settlement in the coalfield created substantial difficulties for a church based on the territorial parish. Mining and iron-making villages grew up with no regard for established ecclesiastical boundaries and remote from parish churches. The difficulties which beset the Church of England in this situation are illuminated by the case of a Sunday School at Lawley Bank, a mining village on the boundary of Dawley and Wellington parishes, over a mile from Dawley parish church and three miles from that of Wellington. In 1802, a joint Anglican-Wesleyan Sunday School was begun in the village, but the Anglicans would not admit children from the Wellington side of the border. The Wesleyans, inhibited by no such sense of legalism, thereupon set up a school of their own, which prospered while that of the Anglicans dwindled away.[23]

Non-residence, pluralism, inadequate buildings and gross variations in clerical incomes were as prevalent in Shropshire as elsewhere in the 18th century. In the part of the coalfield in Lichfield diocese, the incumbents of Lilleshall and Dawley were not residing in their parishes in 1772, and the rector of Stirchley was too ill to do duty. In 1799 the incumbents of Lilleshall, Dawley, Stirchley and Wellington were all non-resident. At Priorslee the congregation was reported to be very small because the only service of the week was held at 1 p.m. on a Sunday, coinciding with the colliers' traditional Sunday lunch. While the churches in the part of the coalfield in Hereford diocese were for the most part rather better served at this period, that at Benthall had only 24 Sunday services per year in the early 1790s.[24]

The obstacles to the creation of the parishes or even to the construction of new chapels-of-ease within existing parishes were formidable in the 18th century. The church of Wombridge was rebuilt in 1756, and those at Wellington and Madeley replaced by new buildings in the 1790s, but otherwise the only new Anglican building constructed in the coalfield in the 18th century was a chapel-of-ease at Jackfield in Broseley parish opened in 1759. One object of the new church was to provide accommodation for the poor, since only 168 of the 786 sittings in Broseley parish church were free, but in practice this aim was hardly achieved for only 70 of the 272 places in the new church were free. St. Mary's Jackfield was built on unstable ground, and was so badly damaged by subsidence that services could no longer be held there in 1793.[25]

The next two Anglican churches to be built in the coalfield were both paid for by ironmasters, and both were the subjects of considerable legal confusion. In Dawley parish in 1799 there were only 29 communicants among a population of 3,869, and the incumbent was a non-resident, who also served three other parishes. Isaac Hawkins Browne, ground landlord of the Old Park Company, was planning the construction of a new church as early as 1800, a project realised in 1805 when the church of St. Leonard, Malins Lee, was opened. The new building designed by Thomas Telford was intended to replace the old parish church about a mile away, which was to have become a chapel serving the surrounding burial ground, but this intention was frustrated by legal difficulties, and both churches remained open, the new building becoming a district chapel in 1843.[26]

Similar ambiguity surrounded the building of St. George's, Oakengates, in the parish of Lilleshall in 1805. The church was endowed by the partners in the Lilleshall Company and constructed with the aid of a large grant from Isaac Hawkins Browne on a plot of land donated by the Marquess of Stafford. The patrons' object was to provide a church for the miners who lived at great distances from their parish churches, 'from a pious and due regard to the worship of Almighty God and with the hope and intent of promoting religion and morality among the said several persons'. The status of the church was undefined, and in 1832 the Vicar of Lilleshall denied all connection with it. In 1851 the curate in charge of St. George's claimed that there was no means of ascertaining by whom the chapel was built, the cost, or how it was defrayed. The settlement served by the church, previously known as Pains Lane, took the name St. George's.[27]

An outstanding figure in the Church of England in the early years of the 19th century was John Eyton, Vicar of Wellington from 1804 to 1823, whose standing in the northern part of the coalfield was almost as great as that of John Fletcher had been in Madeley 20 years earlier. Eyton had known Fletcher, and corresponded frequently with his widow. In 1807 he was consulted on the appointment of Wesleyan ministers for the Shropshire circuit, and he preached the sermon at Mary Fletcher's funeral.[28]

Like Fletcher, Eyton was credited with great successes as a moral reformer. Before his arrival in Wellington:

> The Sacred day was passed in sports profane,
> Unheeded was the church bell's pleasant chime
> By noisy crowds and pleasure seekers vain
> Who owned no law or human or divine.
> The All seeing Eye, it may be, rested on
> The faithful few, who might in secret mourn
> O'er the sad scene, and low before the throne
> Might daily ask a great and glorious town.

> The prayer was heard: the youthful pastor came,
> In all the graces of his early prime,
> Addressed the rebels in the Saviour's name
> And told of pleasures holy and sublime.
> As in his own soul the clear true light
> Shone more and more unto the perfect day
> It shed on all around its radiance bright
> And showed to erring souls the living away.[29]

Eyton worked closely in Wellington with the Wesleyan societies, accompanying them to their own chapels, preaching in their meeting houses, and holding services in private houses in Ketley, Hadley and other outlying townships of the parish. One of his curates who moved from Wellington to Yorkshire regarded 'perfect peace between the Methodists and us', as a normal state of affairs and was surprised when the Bradford Wesleyans opened their chapels during church hours and 'became wholly dissenters', in 1814.[30]

The Acts of Parliament of 1818, 1835 and 1843 which successively granted money to the Church Commissioners for the building of churches in populous areas and the division of parishes, set up the Ecclesiastical Commission, and made possible the creation of new parishes before the building of churches, accelerated the provision of new Anglican churches in the Shropshire coalfield as elsewhere. St. George's was extended with the aid of a grant from the Commissioners in 1823. In the 1830s three churches in the typical architectural style of the Commissioners were built in the district by Samuel Smith of Madeley. In 1833 Holy Trinity Wrockwardine Wood was consecrated, and the following year Wrockwardine Wood became a separate parish. Anglican meetings had been held in a schoolroom in the district by the vicar of Wrockwardine for some years previously.[31] In 1833 the erection of a church at Ironbridge in Madeley parish was proposed, and the building consecrated in 1837. Much of the cost was met from national sources, but the endowment was largely provided by the Madeley Wood Company. Ironbridge became a separate parish in 1845. The third of the churches designed and built by Samuel Smith, Christ Church, Wellington, also received substantial support from the Commissioners and was consecrated in 1839.[32]

Two other new churches were erected in the coalfield during the 1830s. In 1837 the ancient thatched chapel at Priorslee was replaced by a new building in Gothic style with 256 sittings, and free seats for 159 of the poor in two galleries. In the manor of Ketley which included parts of both Wellington and Wombridge parishes, the second Duke of Sutherland spent £1,300 on the provision of the church of St. Mary, at Red Lake on his own estate. The church was consecrated in July 1839. The Duke regarded the church with affection, and in November 1839 attended a service incognito, sitting in a free seat. He found the church decently filled, and the sermon fair with no exaggeration. He was greatly affected by the singing which reminded him of the Kirk.[33]

The pace of church building did not slacken in the 1840s and '50s. In 1845 the crumbling parish churches of Dawley and Broseley were both replaced with large modern buildings, and a third church in Dawley parish was erected at Doseley. The fourth Abraham Darby turned from Quakerism to the Church of England. Services under his patronage began in a schoolroom at Coalbrookdale in 1850, and a church to accommodate them was consecrated in 1854. At the Aqueduct, a settlement which had grown up in the 1840s with the arrival of workers for the Madeley Court ironworks, James Foster built a church in 1851. At Coalport, the clergy of Madeley parish began to hold services in licensed buildings in 1842.[34] In the northern part of the coalfield new churches were erected at Donnington Wood in 1850, Oakengates in 1855, Hadley in 1856 and Lawley in 1865, while the existing buildings at St. George's and Wombridge were replaced by new churches in 1863 and 1869 respectively. South of the Severn a new church by Arthur Blomfield was built at Jackfield in 1863, embodying many of the products of the local tile industry.[35]

During the middle decades of the 19th century the Church of England fought back with vigour against the encroachments of Methodism and Dissent in the Shropshire coalfield. An ecclesiastical census for 1861 or 1871 would probably show considerably higher Anglican attendances than that of 1851.

The non-Methodist dissenting denominations were only weakly represented in east Shropshire with only a little over 10 per cent of church attendances on Census Sunday in 1851. The oldest local congregation was that of the Baptists in Broseley whose formation in 1740–41 was one of the first signs of the Evangelical Revival in the district. In 1801 there was a schism in the congregation, and a new society was formed which built a second Baptist chapel in the town at Birchmeadow in 1802. Neither of the Broseley Baptist congregations was particularly prosperous in the 19th century. The Old Baptists claimed average attendance of 150 and the Birchmeadow congregation of 200 in 1851, but by 1872 they had respectively only 20 and 33 members.[36]

The third Baptist congregation in the coalfield was in Wellington, where a church was opened in 1807 and enlarged in 1828. There was a congregation of 100 in 1851.

Figure 18. Holy Trinity Church, Dawley, prior to demolition in 1845, and showing the effects of mining subsidence. The buttresses had all been erected within the previous half century.
Shrewsbury Borough Library Colln.

A church at Donnington Wood, opened in 1820, also claimed 100 attendances in 1851. A small Baptist chapel was built at Hadley in 1831. At Dawley Bank a Baptist congregation was formed in 1817 by an evangelist who regularly travelled from Birmingham. The society built a chapel in 1846, inspired chiefly by two men called James Jones. One, a farmer, had links with Baptists in Shrewsbury, the other, a charter master, was connected with one of the Broseley congregations. Baptisms at Dawley Bank were performed in the open air in a stretch of water called Morgans Pool among the pit mounts. Two further Baptist churches were built in the coalfield, at Madeley in 1858 and at Oakengates in 1862. If the Dawley Bank congregation was typical, Baptists were vividly conscious of their Nonconformity, conscientiously refusing to pay church rates, and insistent on the right to Christian burial of unbaptised children. The Dawley Bank church numbered several farmers among its members. Most of the Baptist congregations in the coalfield were small, and few were able to afford settled ministers.[37]

Congregationalism was not represented in the coalfield in the 18th century, and that several societies were established in the 19th was due largely to the energetic Salop Association, composed of flourishing churches in other parts of the county, which made numerous attempts to found churches in the mining area. In 1823–24 ministers from Ludlow, Shrewsbury, Hadnall and Newport were sent to Wellington to seek support for a Congregational society, and to find land for the erection of a chapel. A building was opened in 1825 as a result of a donation from Houlstons, the publishers of religious tracts. The church was rarely well supported, and had a succession of ministers who stayed only for short periods. The history of the Congregational church at Broseley was similar. A group of ministers appointed in 1837 by the county association obtained the use of the derelict Friends' meeting house in the town, and in 1840–41 a chapel was built. Support for the new venture, promising at first, rapidly dwindled and ministers changed frequently. At Oakengates the Congregational church was a plantation from the Wellington society, which began to hold meetings in the clubroom of an inn in 1843. The chapel was opened in 1848 and proved more successful than its parent society, sharing with the Methodists the benefits of the revival of 1862. Later in the 19th century two further Congregational churches were established at Dawley and Madeley, the former having a life of a few years only.[38]

The coalfield was not fruitful ground for the old dissenting denominations. Few of the social classes which provided support in other areas for the Baptists and Congregationalists were well represented in the district. The commercial centres of the coalfield were not highly developed. There were no long traditions of independent artisan labour, no weavers and few yeomen-farmers. In the case of the Congregationalists especially, churches owed their existence almost entirely to the wealth and enthusiasm of fellow denominationalists in other parts of Shropshire.

Roman Catholicism survived in the coalfield in the 18th century only in Madeley where it owed its existence to the recusant Brooke family, the lords of the manor. There were 12 Catholic families in the parish in 1716, and in 1767 a total of 72 individual Catholics, including children and a priest. Most of them were working-class including blacksmiths, colliers, a carpenter, a butcher and a shoemaker.[39] John Fletcher argued bitterly with the Madeley Catholics, and when the priest proposed to open a church in the parish, 'declared war on that account . . . and propose to strip the whore of Babylon and expose her nakedness'. Mary Fletcher, by contrast, remained on friendly terms with the parish priest and frequently exchanged books with him.[40] In 1835 a

Catholic congregation was established in Wellington and served by the priest from Madeley.[41]

There was a Meeting of the Society of Friends in Broseley as early as the 1670s, and in 1691–92 a meeting house was built. In 1716 the Meeting was attended by very few inhabitants of the parish itself. A second meeting house was erected in the town in 1742, and a third in 1770, but it seems likely that the Friends had ceased to meet in Broseley by 1778.[42]

When Abraham Darby I arrived in Coalbrookdale in 1708 there were no members of the Society in the coalfield north of the Severn, and Darby, his descendants and successors were closely involved with the affairs of the Broseley meeting. A number of skilled Quaker workmen from Bristol followed Darby to Coalbrookdale, and by 1716 there were eight Quaker families in Madeley parish. Meetings were held in the house which Darby began to build at Coalbrookdale even before it was completed, and a number of other buildings in the Dale including a laundry and a malthouse were licensed for worship in the middle decades of the 18th century. The first purpose-built meeting house was erected in 1741 and was enlarged sometime before 1770. It was replaced by a new building in 1808. In 1798 29 men and 37 women attended, and the largest congregation recorded there in the census of 1851 numbered 25. The meeting house continued in use throughout the 19th century, although the fourth Abraham Darby left the Society for the Church of England in the late 1840s.[43]

A third Quaker meeting house in the coalfield was at New Dale, in the village built by the Coalbrookdale partners on land leased in 1759, which was licensed in 1762. New Dale stood near the boundary of Dawley and Wellington parishes and in 1772 there were four Quaker families in each. In 1798 the meeting was attended by 11 men and 13 women, and supported chiefly by members of the Reynolds family. The meeting house was still in use in 1840 but was no longer regularly used for Quaker meetings by 1851.[44]

Apart from the regular meetings held at Broseley, Coalbrookdale and New Dale, Quaker meetings with an evangelical purpose were occasionally held elsewhere. In the late 1750s and early 60s, Thomas Waring, a Quaker evangelist from Leominster spoke in the open air at Ketley and Horsehay in August 1759, addressed a meeting at Wellington town hall in 1760 against the clamour of the bells of the parish church set in motion by the vicar, held a meeting at New Dale in 1762, and conducted similar missions in 1763 and 1765. In 1826 the celebrated Quaker preacher J. J. Gurney held meetings at New Dale and in the Vicarage Barn at Madeley, and in 1835 he spoke to over 2,000 people in the rolling mill at Horsehay. William and Rebecca Byrd of Dudley addressed meetings in the Coalport warehouse and at New Dale in 1822.[45]

It is doubtful whether the Society of Friends ever had many members among the manual workers at Coalbrookdale or New Dale. The numbers attending meetings in 1798 are small when due allowance is made for the large households of the Darby and Reynolds families. Most available evidence suggests that the meetings were always confined largely to the families of the ironmasters and some of their senior clerical workers and their domestic servants. Richard Reynolds was accustomed to go each year on a picnic to the Wrekin with:

> his family, his relations from Coalbrookdale and the principal clerks in their employment, with their families; and, in short, almost the whole of the members of their small congregation.

A revealing comment on the size of the Coalbrookdale meeting occurs in a description of the explosion at the upper furnace in 1802 which took place 'while the Darby family were in meeting'. Plymley wrote in 1793 that in Madeley 'the Quakers are more considerable in point of property than in numbers'. Fogerty's impression of the meeting was also that it was a small one:

> The proprietors of the works and most of their principal clerks and officials were members of the Society of Friends, who made no converts on principle, but twice a week threw the doors of their large meeting house wide open to all comers, and received those who entered in with courteous, grave civility, but it does not appear that many persons availed themselves of the opportunities thus afforded.[46]

The nature of the religious communities in east Shropshire was shaped much more by local social conditions than by denominational affiliations. The Church of England throughout the coalfield was Evangelical in outlook, and the few churches that served predominantly working-class communities more so than the average. The services at St. Mary, Jackfield about 1880 for example, were 'bright and cheery such as draws a good congregation'. The typical Wesleyan churches were those of the commercial centres, large imposing buildings in which tradespeople were prominent in the congregations, but where Wesleyan chapels were built in the more isolated working class settlements they assumed many of the characteristics of Primitive Methodist societies. At the Little Dawley chapel 13 of the 18 trustees in 1837 were colliers, and the Stirchley and Lawley Bank chapels were framed for their revivalism. The typical Primitive chapels were those in remote mining settlements like Dark Lane, but the large churches in Wrockwardine Wood and Oakengates both architecturally and socially displayed many of the characteristics normally associated with the Wesleyans. Relations between denominations were generally cordial by the middle of the 19th century. The Duke of Sutherland gave plots of land for at least three Primitive Methodist chapels as well as for parish churches. When a new Methodist New Connexion chapel was opened in Madeley in 1859 the minister declared, 'the object of the Connexion in coming to Madeley was to assist and not to rob other churches', and a Baptist minister speaking on the same occasion said, 'the moral condition of Madeley requires new churches – if all of the places of worship were full there would still be many who could not attend'. Methodist local preachers from all four denominations in the district were accustomed to preach in each other's chapels.[47]

Chapels and churches, and particularly the former, remain a memorable feature of the landscape of the Shropshire coalfield, although many are now converted to secular uses. The influence of Evangelical ideas on the development of local society was profound, and the religious societies were the most vital of the formalised social institutions in the district.

39. An artist's view of an ironworks: The Inside of a Smelting House at Broseley, Shropshire by George Robertson, engraved by Wilson Lowry, 1788 (*Ironbridge Gorge Museum Trust*)

41. Carpenters' Row, Coalbrookdale (*Ironbridge Gorge Museum Trust*)

42. The Old Row, Horsehay (*Photo: Author*)

43. The squatter cottage of *c.*1830 from Burrough's Bank, Little Dawley, re-erected at the Blists Hill open air museum (*Photo: Author*)

44. Squatter-type cottages, on the Wharfage, Ironbridge (*Photo: Author*)

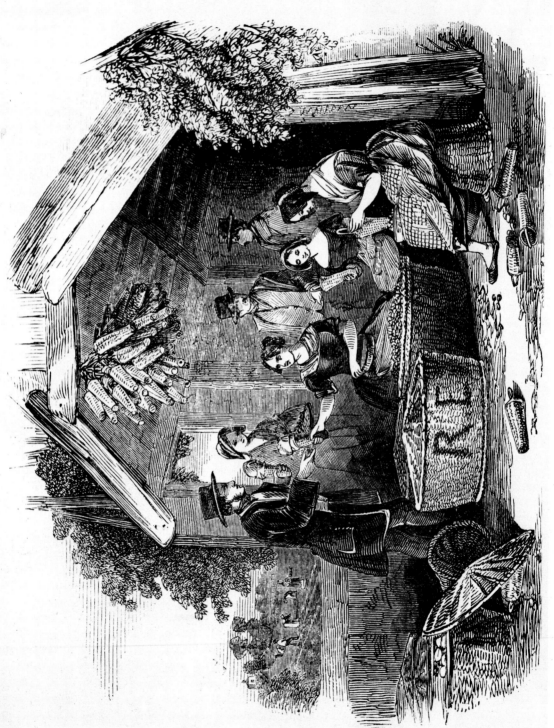

45. Shropshire pit-girls handling strawberries in a market garden, 1846 (Illustrated London News, 27 June 1846)

46. Preparing dogs for bull-baiting at Oakengates Wake. Woodcut from *The Oakengates Wake* by Mrs. Cameron reproduced by courtesy of Mrs. M. Kent, Shrewsbury)

47.   Warehouse re-adapted (i). The Severn Warehouse, Ludcroft Wharf, Ironbridge, built for the Severn trade the Coalbrookdale Company about 1840 (see Plates 7 and 8), then a bicycle workshop, a mineral water factor and a garage, and opened in 1977 as the Ironbridge Gorge Museum's visitor centre (*Photo: Author*)

48.   Warehouse re-adapted (ii). The Great Warehouse, Coalbrookdale, built in the 1830s, and the setting for t Coalbrookdale Museum of Iron, completed by the Ironbridge Gorge Museum Trust in 1979 (*Photo: Author*)

XVI

MIGRANT WORKERS

'They are mustering up all that can be met, of any sort or size, old or young, none escapes them',[1] reported William Ferriday as he observed the preparations for the blowing of the Horsehay No. 1 blast furnace in February 1755. The shortage of labour to which he drew attention persisted in the coalfield for the next half century. The writings of entrepreneurs suggest that they assumed that workers would naturally be in short supply, and that anything which might increase the local population was to be welcomed. There was not, as in most textile areas, a class of poor hand workers made redundant by technical progress, and the need to attract and to keep labour was one of the dominant forces which shaped local society between 1750 and 1810.

George Perry, the Coalbrookdale engineer, writing in the 1750s welcomed the increase of population which the iron trade had brought to the Dale in the previous 40 years, and the opportunities for employment which it offered to the children of the lower class of people. Lord Dundonald in 1791 sent William Reynolds a copy of his pamphlet on the making of bread with potato flour, and commented, 'I am sure that you will join with me in anticipating with peculiar pleasure as stated in my pamphlet, the increased population of Great Britain in consequence of the lower classes of the people being better fed and enabled to do all things at a cheaper rate'. In 1800 a Shropshire ironmaster told the Committee on the Coal Trade, 'there are new furnaces for the smelting of iron constantly erecting and it is now difficult to get pitmen to work the coals'. Unemployment and the consequent burden on the poor rates became severe social problems in east Shropshire after 1815, but before 1810 the need to attract more labourers to the coalfield was one on which most observers were agreed.[2]

The only sophisticated study of the population of east Shropshire in the 18th century covers only the period between 1711 and 1760, and does not therefore reflect the demographic consequences of the great expansion in the iron trade which began in 1755. It shows an increase in the population of the 17 parishes of the coalfield and its periphery in the first half of the 18th century, with an estimated total population of 11,500 in the middle of 1711 rising to over 20,000 by the end of 1760. Growth was not consistent, but was concentrated in the periods 1716–25, 1731–40 and 1746–53. As in other parts of the West Midlands there were several periods of exceptionally high mortality in the first half of the 18th century. 1726–30 was a period of actual decrease in population and there were exceptionally large numbers of deaths in 1741–42. The records of Little Wenlock parish suggest a high incidence of smallpox throughout the first half of the century.[3] From an estimated total of just over 20,000 in 1760 the population of the 17 parishes of the survey rose to over 34,000 by the time of the 1801 census. After 1800 there were marked migrations of skilled workers away from the coalfield, but the total population continued to grow and over 50,000 people lived in the 17 parishes by 1851.

While the large families of the Shropshire colliers and ironworkers and the general healthiness of their children were remarked by several visitors to the district,[4] immigration was certainly a principal factor in the growth of the local population in the 18th century. As early as 1734 Richard Ford and Abraham Darby II agreed with their landlords when renewing their lease of the Coalbrookdale works that they would themselves be responsible for the upkeep in poverty of outsiders brought in to work at the foundries.[5] In Madeley in 1793 over 1,000 of the 3,677 inhabitants had settlements in other parishes.[6]

Evidence of patterns of migration into the coalfield is sparse. Poor law records give only occasional glimpses of the places of origins of migrants. The prosperity of the iron trade was such that it was most unusual for able-bodied workers to need to seek relief. Nevertheless such poor law records as do survive, together with a few crumbs of literary evidence, and the 1851 census do suggest some fairly consistent patterns of migration. Among skilled ironworkers there was a steady movement in both directions between Shropshire and other iron-making areas, particularly the Black Country, and skilled potters likewise often moved between Shropshire and north Staffordshire, Worcester or London. Unskilled workers moved into the coalfield principally from other parts of Shropshire and from Montgomeryshire, Radnorshire and Denbighshire. This pattern of migration over relatively short distances is similar to that which peopled the Lancashire cotton towns.[7]

Population movements in Shropshire as a whole were complex. Many people from the county went to Lancashire as early as the 1780s, and in 1851 there were 1,800 migrants from Shropshire in Liverpool, Manchester and Bolton alone.[8] Most of them probably came from the parts of the county contiguous to Cheshire and Flintshire. Birmingham and the Black Country, the north Staffordshire Potteries, and the lead-mining area around the Stiperstones also competed with the Coalbrookdale region for unskilled migrants from the countryside. The abilities of workers in the Shropshire coalfield attracted entrepreneurs from other industrial regions. In 1796–97 skilled workers from the Coalbrookdale area were sought by coal masters from Dudley, Tipton and Sedgeley, by the owners of the White Grit mine on the Stiperstones, and by Boulton and Watt, who needed moulders and turners for their new Soho Foundry. By the 1840s parties of colliers recruited by agents working for mineowners were embarking on canal boats for Lancashire.[9]

The results of several decades of migration were revealed by a survey made for the Poor Law Commissioners in 1836, which showed that in the principal parishes of the coalfield less was spent per head on poor relief than in almost any others in Shropshire, partly because 'the extensive iron mines and coalfields, and the increasing demands for manufacturing labouring have rapidly absorbed every appearance of a redundancy of population', and partly because many families still had their settlements in distant parishes. The commissioner explained,

> from the nature of the work in the mines settlements are hardly ever given, and consequently whole families have continued in these districts from generation to generation, who trace only a derivative settlement to a distant and agricultural parish. Strangers to each other and

differing in their habits, the one party is as averse to return as the other to receive them[10]

In the Examination Books of the Borough of Wenlock, which included the coalfield parishes of Broseley, Madeley and Little Wenlock and cover the years 1729–43, 1745–53, and 1774–77, pauper ironworkers are conspicuously absent, but a considerable migration of potters from north Staffordshire to the Broseley area is revealed.[11]

50 settlement certificates for the parish of Madeley survive for the period 1698–1730, and 46 for the year 1734–69. Apart from adjacent parishes, two or more certificates were recorded from Shifnal, Much Wenlock, Beckbury, Bridgnorth, Tong and Stottesdon in Shropshire, from Halesowen in the detached portion of the county, and from Harborne, Smethwick, Sedgley, Dudley and Stourbridge. The number of immigrants from the Black Country confirms indications in the Wenlock records that there was a considerable movement between Shropshire and south Staffordshire and north Worcestershire. Later Madeley poor law records show paupers being returned to the parishes of Worfield, Kington (Herefordshire) and Chirk (Denbighshire) between 1781 and 1790.[12]

The destinations of paupers removed from Dawley to their parishes of settlement during the depression of 1816–17 also show something of the pattern of migration into the coalfield. Apart from a few migrants returned to parishes contiguous to the coalfield, most of those re-settled came from Shropshire, the Black Country and Wales. Migrants from Shropshire included people from Clun, Munslow, Condover, Bishop's Castle and Chirbury in the south of the county, and from Upton Magna, Wem, High Ercall and Wroxeter north of the Severn. Migrants from further afield included people from West Bromwich, Bilston and Wolverhampton in the Black Country, Berriew in Montgomeryshire, Chirk and Ruabon in Denbighshire, Oldham (Lancs.), Ledbury (Herefordshire) and Nantwich (Cheshire). Later records of the same parish record the parishes of settlements of paupers receiving relief between 1831 and 1835. They included people from Westbury, Bridgnorth, Chirbury, Kinlet, Pontesbury, Easthope, Coreley, and Much Wenlock in south Shropshire; Shawbury, Weston Lullingfields, Upton Magna and Shrewsbury in north Shropshire; Wolverhampton, West Bromwich, Stourbridge, Dudley and Bilston in the Black Country; Llanfechan, Berriew, and Llanfyllin in Montgomeryshire, Llanelwed and Kinnerton in Radnorshire; Denbigh and Ruabon in Denbighshire, Forton and Stone in north Staffordshire; Bold in Lancashire, and London.[13]

Thomas Cadman, an archetypal Oakengates collier of the early 19th century described in a religious tract, had 'been born in Wales in a little hut on the side of Cader Idris; and had been brought into Staffordshire when he was three years old'. He moved from Staffordshire to Oakengates shortly before his marriage. In 1857 short biographies were composed of six leading Methodists from Lawley Bank, all of them by that time elderly. Two were immigrants, one from Berriew, Montgomeryshire, and one from Kinnerley near Oswestry.[14]

The 1851 census confirms this pattern of migration. Of 149 adults living in Coalport in 1851, 70 were born in the coalfield, 36 elsewhere in Shropshire, 10 in the north Staffordshire Potteries, six in Worcestershire and 27 elsewhere. There was a considerable interchange of skilled workers between the Coalport china works and those in Worcester and Stoke-on-Trent. Migrants to Coalport from other parts of Shropshire included people from Rodington, High Ercall, Morville, Edgmond, Roden and Claverley.

At Dark Lane, a mining village erected about 1830, 156 adults were recorded in the 1851 census. Of these 70 per cent were natives of the coalfield, 20 per cent had been born in other parts of Shropshire, and 10 per cent elsewhere, including five from Wales. The migrants from other parts of Shropshire were primarily from parishes to the north of the coalfield, Market Drayton, High Ercall, Upton Magna, Shrewsbury, Kinnerley, Llanymynech, Bolas, Edgmond and Hadnall.

The nearby village of Hinkshay also dated from about 1830, but unlike Dark Lane which consisted chiefly of miners, it was primarily an iron-making settlement. The census recorded 173 adults at Hinkshay, of whom 104, about 60 per cent, were born in the coalfield, 29, or 17 per cent elsewhere in Shropshire while 35, or 20 per cent were migrants from further afield. Five did not know their places of birth. Of the 35 migrants from outside Shropshire, 27 came from Staffordshire and Worcestershire, chiefly from the industrial parts of those counties. Most were skilled ironworkers who had probably migrated when the Botfields opened their Stirchley forge in 1830. They included William Longmore, a 29-year-old sheet-iron roller born at Kingswinford, James Garrett, a 26-year-old forgeman, born at Darlaston, John Plimmer a 20-year-old puddler born at Bilston, Isaiah Tittley, a 43-year-old hoop-roller from Darlaston, and John Phaysey, a 44-year-old iron-roller from Tipton. Most migrants from other parts of Shropshire were unskilled, and they came from such villages as Cound, Westbury, Wroxeter, Hodnet, Oswestry, Caynham, Tong and High Ercall.

At New Dale, the Coalbrookdale Company's mining village which was over 80 years old by 1851, there were 90 adults recorded in the census. 66, or 73 per cent had been born in the coalfield, 18, or 20 per cent in other parts of Shropshire and 6, or 7 per cent, further afield. The immigrants included a collier born at Bishop's Castle, a miner's wife from Stanton Lacy, a labourer from Baschurch, a miner from Hanmer (Flints.) and a furnaceman from High Ercall.

At Waxhill Barracks, a block of 27 single-storey miners' cottages alongside the Donnington Wood Canal, the proportions of immigrants and locally born inhabitants were similar to those at New Dale. Of 65 adults, 47, or 72 per cent, were born in the coalfield, 13, or 20 per cent, in other parts of Shropshire and 5, or 8 per cent, further afield. Migrants included coal miners from Brymbo (Denbighshire) and Wem, and two brothers, a labourer and an ironstone miner, from Pontesbury.

The riverside hamlet of Jackfield accommodated a variety of immigrants in 1851, farm labourers from north Shropshire and Cheshire, china workers from north Staffordshire, a group of earthenware potters from Church Gresley (Derbyshire) and people from the Severnside ports of Worcestershire and Gloucestershire. The census shows several instances of how migrants were absorbed into industrial society. First generation migrants often worked on the farms in the coalfield, or took jobs which involved the care of animals. Two migrants from the Corvedale and another from Bala, Merionethshire, who lived in the Severn Group in 1851 were employed as horse drivers on the Severn. The sons and grandsons of such migrants usually found employment in mines, ironworks or potteries. Francis Taylor, a farm labourer aged 55 in 1851, had migrated to Jackfield from Much Wenlock, but his two sons aged 15 and 17 were both employed in a brickworks. Another farm labourer, Thomas Taylor, aged 38 in 1851, had been born at Sutton Maddock and had lived for some years at Beckbury before moving to Jackfield. His son was a collier and his step-daughter a labourer in the chinaworks. Ann Flaveard, born in Clungunford, lived in the Lloyds in 1851 and worked as a servant, but her 13-year-old daughter and 11-year-old son worked in nearby ironstone pits. Roger Trundle, born in 1770, was the son of a migrant employed as a servant at the *Seven Stars* inn on the Holyhead Road. He himself became a collier, and in the 1820s two of his sons were employed as puddlers.[15]

There were many Welsh migrants in the coalfield. The 1851 census shows that in the poor law unions of Madeley, Shifnal and Wellington, there were 380 migrants from Montgomeryshire and 130 from Radnorshire.[16] The census also reveals a sizeable Irish settlement in the district, 944 in the three unions. The largest concentration was in Nailors' Row and New Street in Wellington. Many were railway labourers, but there were also farm workers, hawkers, pedlars, dealers in trifles, and an occasional shoe-maker or tailor. There were also migrants from Co. Clare and Co. Mayo in Broseley, some of whom, it seems, had settled there before the famine of the mid-1840s. The 1851 census reveals that some refugees from the famine had settled in mining and iron-making villages and taken up industrial occupations. James Cain from Kilmore, Co. Wexford, aged 26 in 1851, had become a pit banksman, and lodged with his wife and a child born in England in one of the cottages near the Madeley Wood Company's Blists Hill ironworks. Henry Cain, aged 18, and probably his brother, was a labourer, and lodged at the next cottage but one. Another Irishman from Co. Mayo had become a coalminer and also lived at Blists Hill in 1851. Irishmen who had settled in Ironbridge included a silk dyer, a hatter from Co. Roscommon and a cabinet maker. A migrant from Co. Mayo lived in Coalport and worked as a farm labourer.

There was no substantial foreign community in the coalfield. The 1851 census reveals a few individuals, Dominic Rimarosi, an Italian 'traveller', and Dominic Dotti, a jeweller, living in Wellington, a Prussian jeweller in Holywell Lane, and two families of Polish clothiers who lived in Ironbridge, but foreign immigrants as such made no distinctive contribution to local society.

XVII

COTTAGES AND COMMUNITIES

'Industry and commerce', wrote George Perry in his description of Coalbrookdale in the 1750s, 'will soon improve and people the most uncultivated situation'.[1] The migrants attracted to east Shropshire by the prospect of work in the ironworks and coalmines in the late 18th century came to situations which were indeed uncultivated. Furnaces were erected and pits were sunk in places remote from established villages, and still more so from recognisable towns. Nevertheless the Severn Gorge was already a busy industrial area in 1700, with a distinctive pattern of settlement, and elsewhere in the coalfield, along the wide verges of lanes, on the edges of woodland, or on open commons, scattered groups of cottages housed miners and a variety of craftsmen. Such settlements provided a fund of skills, which was one of the bases of local industrial growth, and they proved to be centres around which other housing could readily be provided by the inhabitants themselves or by small-scale speculators, which accommodated incoming migrants without the expenditure of capital by the ironmasters. In many ways the district's lack of cultivation was one of the reasons for the growth of its industries.

In Broseley, Madeley and Benthall, the three parishes which bordered the Severn Gorge, settlement was relatively easy in the late 17th and 18th centuries. While there were estates of considerable size in each parish, manorial control was weak. Landlords were willing to sell freeholds, or to let plots on long leases, and it is evident that it was possible for squatters to settle on common land without impediment. A variety of sources combine to show that the slopes of the Gorge and the banks of the Severn were dotted with small cottages, surrounded by small, irregular enclosures. Whatever the precise legal status of each holding, in appearance the majority resembled the squatter holdings to be found in profusion in rural parts of the West Midlands, and in other upland districts. Frequently such cottages were enlarged into terraces, to accommodate successive generations of a family, or additional houses were built at the extremities of gardens, folds or orchards. The plots themselves were often sub-divided when one generation succeeded another. The number of dwellings in the Gorge could thus be multiplied without control. Few people living in such circumstances could have aspired to great riches, but the very slenderness of their resources was an incentive to industriousness. Those who lived in the Gorge were either miners, boatmen, whose main trade was carrying coal, or tradesmen who provided the infrastructure without which the expansion of mining, and later of ironmaking, would not have been possible.

Architectural research has shown that in the riverside parts of Madeley parish,

186

within a landscape shaped by roads built in the late 18th century and villas erected in the 19th, there survive many cottages which date from before 1750. Houses of this similar type can also be seen in Jackfield, the riverside portion of Broseley parish, and in Benthall. Most follow a single unit plan, with a ground floor kitchen, a small lean-to buttery or brewhouse, and one or two sleeping chambers above. Often they are built of coal measure sandstones, which may have come from mines. It is clear that some of the two- or three-unit houses in the Gorge were originally single dwellings which had extra rooms added.[2]

Numerous wills provide evidence of the sub-division of cottages standing within small enclosures on the slopes of the Gorge. Edward Boden, a collier who lived in the Lloyds, died in 1691, and left his house to his eldest son. His second son was to inherit with the consent of the landlord, a house which Boden had repaired 'in the place called the ground in Madeley wood', together with a new building added to it. A third son had, subject to the landlord's agreement, a house in Madeley Wood built by one John Spencer and his mother, the tenancy of which Boden had purchased for £30. John Bayley, a collier who died in 1712, owned a house in Madeley Wood which he had bought from the lord of the manor. He had divided it into three and he and his wife occupied two sparsely furnished rooms and a brewhouse at the east end. The middle two rooms with an outbuilding and a portion of the garden were the home of a son, and a daughter resided in three rooms at the west end. Another son occupied just a loft and a portion of the garden. Adam Crumpton, a miner who died in 1723, left the east end of his house with a brewhouse and an additional parlour to one son, and two rooms below and two above stairs at the west end to another. The garden was to be divided between them by a line which took in a cockpit, codling trees and a box tree. Robert Holland, a miner who died in 1726 lived in a house in Madeley Wood, of which one end was let to a certain John Lloyd. It had several outbuildings attached, and was surrounded by gardens and orchards. He also had a tenement called the New Building, which likewise stood in a sizeable plot. Edward Owen, a Madeley Wood trowman, who died in 1728, left to his wife his house place, kitchen, buttery and the rooms above, with a garden, orchard and a little house which stood in the orchard, while a son inherited another part of the house, a stable and part of the orchard. Owen Davies, a Broseley tailor who died in 1729, had added two 'little pieces of new building' to his house. The property of William Teece, a Broseley waterman who died in 1727, consisted of a main dwelling house, a little house adjacent, and a little dwelling house at the upper end. William Botteley, a collier who died in 1762, divided his house on the edge of some waste ground in Madeley Wood between two sons, one of whom inherited the kitchen, cellar and parlour, while the other had a 'little room', the room above it and the brewhouse. The plot was to be divided by a line from the 'little room' door to a filbert tree at the bottom of the garden on the bank of a brook. John Bedware, a Madeley Wood carpenter who died in 1761, held three cottages by lease from the lord of the manor. His own, the middle tenement was left to a step-daughter, the upper tenement to another step-daughter, and the lower one to a grand-daughter. William Lloyd, a Broseley collier who died in 1766, made provision for his wife to live in 'that little house lately erected at ye top of ye garden'. Timothy Roper, another Broseley collier, died in 1767, leaving to one son the larger part of his house, while another had the west end with authority to extend it. The first son had leave to build on a portion of the garden, which was divided by a line drawn between the apple and pear trees.[3]

This picture of scattered building within the bounds of small freehold, leasehold or squatter plots is confirmed by map evidence. The Broseley Estate Book of about 1730 shows several properties near the confluence of the Calcutts Brook and the Severn.[4] Several houses had been extended into pairs or short terraces, and stand within their own small enclosures. A small house stands in the corner of one plot, which accords exactly with some of those described in probate records.

Houses of this sort were occupied by families who followed a variety of occupations. While the plots might provide some useful crops, or give pasture to a few cows or pigs, they were wholly insufficient to sustain the needs of a family. Many of those who lived in the Gorge were miners, and because new cottages could easily be built, it was possible to provide accommodation quite readily for newcomers to the district attracted by high wages at times of heavy demand. Many of the cottagers were bargemen, who like the miners could look to their plots when the river was too shallow for navigation, or when there were no cargoes on offer. Both mining and the river trades relied on a complex infrastructure of craft trades. Shipwrights, ropemakers, carpenters, coopers, basket makers, tallow chandlers, blacksmiths, nailers, brass founders and wheel turners were all to be found living in the Gorge in the first half of the 18th century. The dispersed pattern of settlement also encouraged the growth of the small-scale clay trades. The Broseley Estate Book[5] shows several mughouses, cottages with small kilns built on the sides. Both potters and the makers of tobacco pipes occupied such premises. A few manufacturers of metal goods, locksmiths and gunsmiths, also lived in the Gorge, but their numbers were small compared with those following such trades in the Black Country. Such an industrious community provided opportunities for the manufacture of consumer goods, and shoemakers, weavers, tailors and pedlars lived among the craftsmen of the Gorge. The availability of easy settlement also encouraged the growth of new, large-scale industry. Ironworkers at Coalbrookdale like the Hallen, Thomas and Bangham families, owned their own small houses which had been extended into multi-occupation.[6]

There were also squatter-like communities in the parts of the coalfield north of the Severn. Around the outcrop of the coal seams in the manor of Ketley were numerous small cottages standing in irregular enclosures, one of which, occupied by William Davies, a weaver who died in 1742, consisted of a house place, a shop containing three looms, and sleeping space upstairs. He kept a cow and a calf on his plot. Wrockwardine Wood was scattered with similar holdings. One Richard Vickers, who died in 1705, made part of his living by carrying coal on two packhorses. His home consisted of a house place, parlour, two chambers above and a buttery. He had eight cows and two calves, and grew corn, barley and hay. There were similar squatter settlements in slangs alongside the Wellington-Newport road at Trench Lane, and on the open commons at Snedshill and Lawley.[7]

Ketley was probably the largest area of squatter-like settlement outside the Gorge. The settlements of Beveley, Coalpit Bank, Red Lake and Cow Wood were made up of scattered cottages by the 1790s and many more were built during the boom years of the French Wars. In 1812 the administration if the Leveson Gower estate which owned the manor passed into the hands of the redoubtable Scottish agent James Loch, who expended much energy in regulating the area. 'This township', he wrote of Ketley in 1820, 'is occupied by a numerous mining population whose wretched huts have been erected from time to time on the waste'. They were, he thought, little better than the huts on the land of his master in the county of Sutherland. Loch forced out the middlemen, whom he alleged had been exploiting the poor, and made the cottagers the immediate tenants of the estate. The cottages and their inhabitants were regularly surveyed, and buildings which fell into disrepair, often caused by mining subsidence, were demolished. The industrious were encouraged by grants of land for keeping cows and of building materials for extensions, while the idle, the poachers and the sexually promiscuous were forced to leave. Loch's declared intention was 'to breed up a steady, industrious and moral set of persons, resistant to the virus of radicalism'. The area remained one of haphazard, disjointed settlement, but many cottages acquired during repairs or extensions the typical features of Sutherland estate houses, dormer windows, herringbone lintels, and yellow, square-sectioned chimney pots. In appearance and origin Ketley had many of the characteristics of a rural open village, but in the 19th century it was administered with a severe paternalistic concern, typical of that displayed by the landlords of closed villages. The number of cottages in Ketley was reduced during the 19th century. Of the 456 which remained in 1873, 129 had only one bedroom, 266 had two, 51 had three, nine had four and one had five. When the condition of 452 of them was examined, two were assessed as 'wretched', two as 'delapidated', 24 as 'very bad', 16 as 'bad', 90 as 'middling', 27 as 'very middling', 211 as 'tolerable', 64 as 'good' and 16 as 'very good'. Typical of the bad cottages was that of Benjamin Brown a collier living in Red Lake with his wife and seven children. There were two bedrooms in the house, which the surveyor found 'a very dirty place, the roof in bad condition'. At Lawley Bank, in 'a poor old place, all on the ground floor', lived an infirm man, with his wife, his nephew and wife, and four children. By contrast the surveyors found much self-help to commend. The one five-bedroomed house in Ketley had been enlarged by the late tenant, and in 1873 was occupied by his widow, his son, daughter-in-law and their three children, another grandchild and a servant. A collier at Ketley Bank lived in a cottage to which he himself had added a second bedroom and a wash house. The surveyors found some resentment among tenants at the criticisms of their houses implied by their enquiries. One widow living in a single-bedroomed cottage, with her daughter, son-in-law and their seven children, proclaimed that she had reared 10 children in the house without any sickness, and that her daughter had also born 10 healthy offspring.[8]

Holywell Lane, a rambling route which led westwards from Little Dawley towards Little Wenlock, was a much smaller squatter settlement than the manor of Ketley, but it grew with equal rapidity during the last years of the 18th century and the first of the 19th. In 1772 it consisted of six cottages, probably all of squatter origin, built in slangs alongside the lane, apparently in land taken from the verges. By 1825 there were 26 cottages in the lane and six more had been added by 1882. They were closely and untidily crammed together on which had formerly been garden plots. Many of them interlocked, with the bedrooms of some houses extending over the ground floor rooms of others. Some parts had walls consisting of only a single thickness of bricks, and many roof timbers were unsawn. One of the cottages which was standing in 1772 consisted of a ground floor house place about 12 ft. × 11 ft. and a cramped sleeping chamber above. Few of the cottages had as many as four rooms. The staircases were sometimes so narrow that furniture could only be taken to the bedrooms through trapdoors. Holywell Lane grew up on common land on the slackly administered manor of the absentee Earl of Craven. The virtual freeholds which many of the cottagers acquired led to a remarkable degree of stability in the population, which contrasts markedly with the quickly changing occupants of most of the company rows who rarely remained in the same house from the time of one census to that of the next. Several families mentioned in the 1841 census, and even some mentioned in 18th century records, only moved away from Holywell Lane in the mid-1970s when the cottages were cleared.[9]

Holywell Lane was the largest of several clusters of squatter-like cottages in the western part of Little Dawley, where in the mid-18th century a pattern of small enclosed fields merged with the woodlands on the hills above Coalbrookdale. By the 1860s almost the entire township was covered with pit mounts, canals, railways, slag tips, brickworks and the great ironworking complex at Lightmoor. Settlements like Gravel Leasows, Burroughs Bank, Stoney Hill and the Finney grew up to provide accommodation for those who worked within the township and at the adjacent ironworks at Coalbrookdale and Horsehay. One small cottage from the area, from Burroughs Bank, has been preserved in the Blists Hill Open Air Museum. It is a single storey building, erected on pit waste about 1830, and measures approximately 20 ft. × 12 ft., and had two main rooms, originally with earth floors. The walls consist of coal measure sandstones, and the roof was formed of ash and birch timber wallplates, tie-beam and rafters, with the bark still adhering in many places. A collier his wife and five children were living in the cottage in 1851, and ten years later the same couple were still in residence, with seven children aged between five and twenty four. Members of the family remained in the cottage until the 1930s.[10]

However important was the role of the squatter-type communities in the development of industry in east Shropshire, the principal entrepreneurs found it advantageous to provide some accommodation for their workpeople. Such provision doubtless gave them a greater degree of social control over their employees, and, in times of labour shortage, company housing, of a standard which was often above the norms of the district, could be used as an inducement to lure skilled workers from other employments. How effective an inducement a cottage could be was illustrated by William Ferriday in 1755 when he congratulated his master, William Forester, on a scheme to provide housing for miners working in Little Wenlock. Since the proposal had been made public, he reported, 'not one man hath left us . . . but some that were gone are come again'.[11]

The best-known and most spectacular of the communities created by the ironmasters was Coalbrookdale, although the contribution of company housing to the settlement was less than has sometimes been suggested. In 1700 Coalbrookdale consisted of no more than a furnace, one or two small forges, and about five dwelling houses. It was remote from the centre of Madeley parish and had no tradesmen or shopkeepers.[12] The first terraced housing with which the Coalbrookdale Company was concerned appears to have been Nailers' Row, Dale End, which it acquired by lease in 1733. It consisted of a mixture of two and two-and-a-half storey cottages. Tea Kettle Row, a complex terrace of six one-and-a-half storey dwellings, constructed in three stages, was built, according to an inscription in one of the cottages, in the 1740s, but there is no evidence to show that the company was responsible for it. Each house had two rooms and a pantry on the ground floor, although the layout varies. The accommodation is generally more spacious than in later Coalbrookdale Company housing.

The company rows in Coalbrookdale were built in the closing years of the 18th century, and consisted of houses with two rooms on the ground floors, designed to an L-plan. The larger was a living room, usually about 12 ft. square, and the smaller a buttery, set to one side and interlocking with that of the adjacent house, so that each row was a mixture of alternately single- and double-fronted houses. On the first floor were sleeping chambers of similar size, although some dwellings had an extra bedroom above a communal brewhouse. The rows were of brick and tile, with quarry tile floors, and substantial fireplaces. Carpenters' Row and Engine Row, which still survive were typical of this form. The former was built about 1783. School House Row was similar, but has been demolished. Smokey Row was demolished before being recorded. Charity Row, which by tradition was built by the company for the widows of workpeople, is rather different, in that the brewhouses are separate from the main block, and each

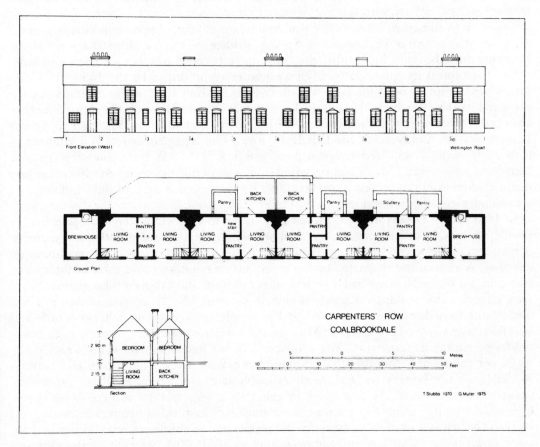

Figure 19.   Carpenters' Row, Coalbrookdale. From: *Grant Muter. The Buildings of an Industrial Community.*

house has a back door, but in spite of alterations, the characteristic L-plan can still be discerned. The five rows built by the company contained only 34 houses, and can have accommodated only a small proportion of those employed in the ironworks. Land in Coalbrookdale was quite minutely sub-divided, and most of the short terraces and pairs of cottages appear to have been built by residents or small-scale speculators. While the Coalbrookdale partners provided most of the communal buildings in the Dale, and while the company came to acquire many of the houses in the settlement in the 19th century, it was responsible for building very few dwellings, relative to the size of the community.[13]

At Horsehay there can have been few dwellings of any kind before the ironworks was erected. The Coalbrookdale Company built a long row of 27 cottages in three stages, alongside the furnace, pool, probably at about the time the furnaces came into blast in the mid-1750s. Originally these cottages, which became known as the Old Row, consisted of four rooms, the two on the ground floor being about 12 ft. square and 12 ft. × 9 ft., with bedrooms of similar size above. In style this group are similar to Tea Kettle Row in Coalbrookdale. Other houses at Horsehay were probably built by the workers who occupied them, while a third group were converted from pottery buildings which became redundant soon after 1800. The ironworks was situated in Dawley parish, which was largely enclosed, but it stood on the border of Lawley township in Wellington, where there was a substantial tract of open common, on which grew up the irregular settlement of Spring Village, within a short distance of the Horsehay furnace pool. Most of its dwellings have been rebuilt, but its plots and lanes reflect the typical irregular patterns of a squatter community. In the 1830s the Coalbrookdale Company built the New or Upper Row at Horsehay, twelve cottages 'for the principal workmen' which also overlook the furnace pool. At much the same time they also built 32 cottages for brickworkers in the vicinity, six at Pool Hill, eight at Frame Lane and 18 at Sandy Bank (or Dill Doll) Row. The latter consisted of a kitchen, 14 ft. × 12 ft., with a coal-fired range, a pantry, 6 ft. 8 in. × 8 ft. 6 in., with a settle, two bedrooms above, and a detached brewhouse. The superior houses in the New Row are distinguished from the brickworkers' cottages by drip moulds around the windows, and ceramic devices above the doors.

In 1851 the 39 houses in the Old and New Rows at Horsehay were occupied by 221 people, an average of 5.66 per house. Most of the householders were skilled ironworkers. 91 per cent of those who lived in the rows had been born in Dawley or the neighbouring parishes. A substantial disparity between the numbers of boys and girls in their teens living in the row, 34 boys and 11 girls, suggests that the families who resided there may have sent their daughters into domestic service. The 26 houses in Sandy Bank and Frame Lane Rows were occupied by 155 people, an average of 5.96 per house, and one had as many as 12 residents. Most of the householders were unskilled, 25 being described simply as labourers. The proportion of the residents who were born locally, 81.94 per cent, was rather less than in the ironworkers' rows. There were 45 dwellings in the Horsehay Pottery in 1851, with 246 occupants, an average of 5.47 per house. Most of the men and boys worked in the iron trade, but 19 miners lived in the area. Eleven girls from the Pottery were engaged in picking ironstone on the pit banks. There was a marked contrast in the proportion of children under 15 in the three parts of Horsehay who were attending school in 1851: 40.5 per cent in the Old and New Rows: 39.22 per cent in the Pottery; and 25 per cent in Sandy Bank and Frame Lane Rows.[14]

In 1759 the Coalbrookdale partners leased land belonging to Robert Burton in the township of Lawley on which they erected a settlement which became the mining village of New Dale. A Quaker meeting house was registered there in 1762, and at about the same time seven cottages were built. A row of 28 back-to-back houses was constructed, probably before 1770, and certainly before 1794. Unfortunately no detailed survey of the row survives, but it is clear that none of the urban traditions or topographical constraints which led to the development of the back-to-back terrace in cities like Leeds and Liverpool could have applied in an open setting like New Dale, and the form may have been adopted simply as the easiest means of providing a large number of dwellings at a low cost.[15]

The Coalbrookdale partners have long been famed for the housing which they provided for their workpeople and some of their records display considerable concern for the lack of housing in the district. In 1792 William Reynolds was appointed to determine the sites for no less than 40 new dwellings, though whether such houses were actually built is uncertain. The company charged a rental of $7^1/_2$ per cent on its cottages in Coalbrookdale in the 1790s, which, while by no means extortionate, was somewhat higher than the 5 per cent which became fashionable among philanthropic providers of housing in the 19th century.[16] The company was in no way unique as a provider of cottages and it is likely that housing was built as much out of economic necessity as from purely philanthropic motives. In conditions of labour shortage the provision of housing was essential if workers were to be attracted and retained. Other companies not owned by Quaker philanthropists were just as active in housebuilding, and some of the dwellings they constructed were of a rather higher standard than those erected by the Darbys and Reynoldses.

Over 50 cottages were built by Thomas Botfield at Hollinswood for workers at the Old Park ironworks in the 1790s. The first were of stone, possibly from the shafts and headings of mines being sunk at the time, and later examples of brick, some of which, like Nos. 21-24 Forge Row, were among the best workers' houses in the district. They had four bedrooms, two downstairs rooms, a wash-house, a cellar and a bread-oven. It is clear from the way the Old Park Company bargained with the workers it took on as its furnaces came into blast that housing was an important bargaining counter in attracting skilled men from other companies. The Madeley Wood Company constructed terraces of cottages for workers at its rather isolated Blists Hill ironworks in the 1830s. There were two terraces adjacent to the Lightmoor Ironworks in 1839, known as Cokers' Row and Pool Row, with five and six houses respectively. Housing was a major part of William Reynolds's development at Coalport in the 1790s. Glasshouse Row and Glasshouse Square stood adjacent to the glassworks in Wrockwardine Wood, and Smelthouse Row by the leadworks in the Lloyds. When James Foster transferred his Shropshire ironmaking concern from Wombridge to Madeley Court in the 1840s, he built six rows of four cottages each to accommodate his skilled men, many of whom moved with him from Wombridge. Later a seventh row was added, together with a house for his furnace manager and an Anglican Chapel of Ease, and the settlement assumed the name of an adjacent group of older houses called the Aqueduct. The best houses in what was called Foster's Row, had a kitchen 10 ft. × 9 ft. 6 in., and a parlour 12 ft. 6 in. × 12 ft. on the ground floor, two bedrooms above, a cellar and a detached brewhouse and privy.[17] As in other works, only a small proportion of the 500 strong labour force at Madeley Court could have been accommodated in company housing. Nevertheless every major industrial concern in the coalfield provided cottages for some of its workpeople.

The least eligible cottages built in any numbers in east Shropshire were probably the single storey 'barrack houses' characteristic of the northern part of the coalfield, and built in the second half of the 18th century. It was probably these houses which were held on lease by the 'middlemen' who were displaced by James Loch when he became agent for the Leveson Gower estate in 1812. Long rows of these houses were to be found in Donnington and Lilleshall, while they comprised the whole of the village of Waxhill Barracks. Shorter groups were built in Wrockwardine Wood, Pains Lane and as far south as Lawley Bank. The barrack houses built at Lilleshall for limestone miners were surveyed before being demolished. The terrace was originally 500 ft. long, but only 12 houses, 350 ft. in total length remained at the time of the survey. The cottages were of one storey, measuring approximately 25 ft. × 12 ft., and contained a living room, a bedroom and sometimes a store. There were wash houses at each end of the row and one in the middle.[18]

The most typical east Shropshire workers' cottages consisted of a large and a small room downstairs, with a narrow open staircase, leading to bedrooms of similar size. The houses at Carpenters' Row at Coalbrookdale, and at Sandy Bank Row were of this pattern. A more complicated group was to be found at the village of Hinkshay Rows built about 1830 by the Botfields. The longest terrace in the village, Double Row, consisted of 38 houses and 10 wash houses in a row 375 ft. long with changes in level as it descended a hillside. Sixteen of the houses were 22 ft. 6 in. long with two rooms downstairs and upstairs. Some were much smaller, with only a 13 × 12 ft. room downstairs and a bedroom of the same dimensions above. An intermediate type had the same two 13 × 12 ft. rooms, with a second bedroom extending over a communal ground floor wash house. The shorter Single Row provided slightly better accommodation, each house having its own larder. A third terrace, New Row, consisted of houses with four rooms, the larger ones, downstairs and up, measuring 10 ft. 6 in. × 13 ft. 9 in. In 1851 428 people lived in the 80 houses in the village, an average of 5.35 per house. There were distinct social differences between the three rows. No labourers lived in New Row, where seven of the householders were skilled ironworkers and the rest tradesmen. In Single Row there were 11 skilled ironworkers and only eight labourers, but of the 41 working heads of households in Double Row, 23 were labourers, and only two skilled ironworkers.[19]

In the nearby mining village of Dark Lane, also built by the Botfields about 1830, the standard of the majority of the dwellings was well below that of many 18th century workers' cottages. The nine houses in the Top or Short Row consisted of one room upstairs and one downstairs, the latter measure 12 × 7 ft. The Long or Top Row was about 550 ft. long and contained some 20 two-storied houses, each with a small and a large room on each floor, the small room interlocking alternately at front and rear. The main downstairs rooms measured approximately 12 × 13 ft. and the small rooms 8 ft. × 6 ft. The third row, the Bottom Row, was originally a little over 500 ft. long and contained about 25 houses. The cottages were slightly larger than those in the Long Row, the bigger rooms on the ground floor being about 13 ft. 6 in. × 13 ft. 8 in. and the smaller rooms 4 × 13 ft. Sixty-eight houses occupied at the time of the 1851 census housed 354 people an average of 5.21 per house.[20]

Not all industrial workers in the coalfield lived in conventional houses. It is some measure of the housing shortage in the district that redundant engine houses, brick kilns and even blast furnaces were adapted as dwellings. In 1793 two inhabited brick ovens were among properties at Hollinswood offered for sale by John Wilkinson. In 1812 four families lived on the first, second, third and fifth floors of the building which once housed the original atmospheric pumping engine of the Ketley ironworks. The fourth floor was apparently untenanted at the time. Two other families lived in disused smith's shops at Ketley. In 1791 a redundant pattern makers' shop at the Old Park Ironworks was converted into a pair of houses. When the Wrockwardine Wood blast furnaces went out of use in the 1820s, they were converted into 11 tenement dwellings which were still inhabited in 1912, when a local government inspector found 'the character of the accommodation furnished by these dwellings is in point of lightness and dryness of rooms superior to many of the ordinary dwelling houses'. A disused conical kiln at the Horsehay Potteries accommodated a family well into the 20th century, and accounts of their efforts to install a corner cupboard retain a place in local folk lore. In 1859 the Duke of Sutherland granted a licence for the conversion of the blast furnaces, engine houses and other buildings at the Donnington Wood iron-works into artificers' dwellings.[21]

Shortages of accommodation led to severe overcrowding in many of the coalfield settlements. In Madeley in 1782 2,690 inhabitants lived in 440 houses, an average of 6.1 per house. Eleven years later 3,677 lived in 750 houses, an average of 4.9, and in 1800, 4,785 in 943 houses, an average of 5.1. According to Plymley this improvement was due largely to Richard Reynolds.[22] It is doubtful whether similar improvements would have been recorded in the same period elsewhere in the district.

The 1851 census reveals many houses where the accommodation must have been severely strained. Forty-seven of the houses at Dark Lane were occupied by five or more people and 21 by seven or more. Most of these houses consisted of no more than a large and a small room downstairs and upstairs. At New Dale 27 of the 39 houses had five or more occupants, and 14 seven or more, and 28 of the houses were the long row of back-to-backs. At Waxhill Barracks, 20 of the 27 single-storey houses had five or more inhabitants and 9 seven or more.

In spite of such overcrowding the ironworks and miners of east Shropshire enjoyed advantages in housing over their fellows elsewhere. Their cottages may have been cramped internally, and crowded together, but they were grouped in dozens and not in hundreds as they were in contemporary Manchester or Leeds. Overcrowding may have been severe, sanitation unreliable, and internal comforts meagre, but the condi-tions of the cottages in the rural north and west of Shropshire in 1870 were without doubt many times worse.[23] The young man from Wem or the Clun Valley who moved to Donnington Wood or Dawley, married, took a company cottage of one and a half rooms downstairs and up, and fathered a family of six, would still in all probability be living in better conditions than those in which he had grown up.

A study of the township of Wrockwardine Wood illustrates many general points about housing in the coalfield in the 19th century. In 1841 the 332 dwellings in the township were occupied by 1,698 people, an average of 5.11 per house. 289 men in the township were engaged in mining, and 83 in ironworking and allied trades, including several filemakers who lived at Pains Lane. Forty-two girls worked as mine pickers on pit banks. The census reveals the decline of the glassworks. Only eight blowers or other glassmakers were living in the township, and only one of them resided in Glasshouse Row. By 1851 408 dwellings in Wrockwardine Wood housed 2099 people, an average of 5.14 per house. There were 309 miners, 84 ironworkers and 63 pit bank girls. During the 1850s the crossroads settlement at Pains Lane gained the name St. George's, and several streets of terraced houses were constructed, mostly within the boundaries of Wrockwardine Wood, to accommodate employees of the Lilleshall Company's New Yard engineering works, and the nearby Priorslee blast furnaces. The population of the township rose by 58 per cent in the decade, to 3,317, and the number of occupied dwellings rose to 596, giving an average of 5.57 per house. The number of workers engaged in ironmaking and engineering rose to 486, an increase of over 575 per cent, while the number of miners grew to 476, and that of pit bank girls to 128. By 1871 the population had risen only to 3,794, a rise of 14 per cent in the decade. The increase was more than matched by the rate of house building. There were 714 houses in the township, occupied by an average of 5.12 people, showing that while the acceleration of industrial growth in the 1850s increased overcrowding, during the 1860s the occupancy rate returned to almost exactly what it had been in 1841 and 1851, and since many houses of a quality superior to that of earlier years had been constructed, overall living conditions must have improved. The growth of the new works brought many migrants to Wrockwardine Wood. In 1851 no less than 90 per cent of the population had been born in the coalfield, but this proportion had fallen to 64 per cent 20 years later. While a significant number of skilled workers had moved in from other industrial districts, most of the migrants were people from the rural parts of Shropshire, who comprised only 1.96 per cent of the population in 1851, but 25.5 per cent in 1871.[24]

The housing in Wrockwardine Wood was in many ways typical of that in the coalfield as a whole. It was remarkably varied. Some houses were of the squatter type, scattered in ones and twos on the open ground of the Nabb and Cockshut Piece, some groups in such clusters as Fenns Fold, and some ranged in slangs along Trench Lane. There were several single storey terraces like the Moss Barracks, some old terraces dating from around 1800, like Glasshouse Row and Glasshouse Square, which were probably built by industrial concerns, and some, like Bonser's Row and Bunter's Row, which may have been erected by speculators. Some people lived in dwellings adapted from redundant industrial buildings like the Wrockwardine Wood furnaces. Many of the workers from the New Yard lived in reasonably spacious urban-style terraces, like those in Albion Street or Granville Street, or in houses groups in twos and threes in the style of a freehold land society estate, like those in New Street, but others, largely the unskilled, lived in the rather cramped terraces known as St. George's or Granville Buildings, constructed at right angles to the Priorslee-Donnington road, almost opposite the New Yard.

There were several particularly unhealthy areas in the coalfield, such as a group of cottages on Lincoln Hill, Madeley, where the cholera epidemic of 1832 was largely concentrated, but most observers found that living conditions in the area as a whole were favourable compared with those of large towns. Members of the Children's Employment Commission in 1842 paid an official visit to the Wesleyan Sunday School at Ketley Bank. They saw about 700 children and commented 'a more healthy set of children could nowhere be seen. The boys were all substantially and decently clothed . . . the girls, more particularly the elder ones and the teachers, understand how to show themselves off to best advantage'.

Matthew Webb a surgeon who had lived at Ketley Bank since 1806 gave evidence to the same commission of the changes which he had observed in the neighbourhood. He thought that living conditions had substantially improved. When he began his practice, 'there was much deformity from bad clothing, bad food, bad nursing in infancy and premature work', but this was no longer so in 1842. Scofula, typhus and scarletina had much diminished due, he thought, to 'moderation in the price of soap and therefore greater cleanliness, the cheapness of cotton, linen and woollen apparel, the improvement in building colliers' houses and the superior ventilation'. He considered that cheap salt and Epsom salts, and vaccination against smallpox had contributed substantially to better health in the district. In 1806 the workers' houses in the Ketley area were 'a sort of barracks in long rows with no upstairs appartments but entirely on the ground floor, and very damp and dirty; their privies and piggeries too near the dwellings, and there was not proper drainage'. By 1842 new houses had been built which had 'well ventilated upstairs chambers and several roods of garden ground and the privies and piggeries . . . at the extremities of the premises. Every man now has from one sixth to a quarter of an acre to grow cabbages and potatoes, and the cultivation of these greatly benefits the health and morals. There are many amateur cultivators of flowers and most of them feed a fat pig'. Certainly many of the worst cottages in Ketley were demolished when they became empty during the depression of 1816–17.[25]

Industrial growth transformed much of the landscape of east Shropshire. In 1772 the vicar of Dawley described his parishioners as mostly farmers. In 1799 his successor said that the parish was 'now full of cottages from one end to the other occasioned by the extension of the coal and iron works'. As early as 1772 the vicar of Wrockwardine described Wrockwardine Wood as an area containing '90 houses scattered about in different places, almost the whole of it being in a working state as a colliery and ironstone work'. Arthur Young passing from Shifnal to Wellington in 1776 noticed 'many collieries and ironworks all the way'.[26] By 1840 pit mounts were the characteristic landscape of much of the district. In 1847 254 acres of Wombridge consisted of waste and pit mounts, and only 380 acres of arable, meadow and pasture. In Wrockwardine Wood, 286 of the 518 acres were given over to mines, works, water, roads and waste. In the parish of Lilleshall, much of which was right outside the coalfield, there were over 400 acres of coal pits and waste.[27]

The coalfield had no recognisable commercial centre, but was rather a grouping of scattered settlements, many of them with no ancient origins. The most influential market town in the district was Wellington, whose centre, a medieval planned town, lay outside the coal measures, although several mining hamlets were within the bounds of the parish. In 1759 the parish contained 780 houses and 4,000 inhabitants. Wellington was never one of Shropshire's most eminent market towns, The range of its trades in the late 17th and early 18th centuries was narrow compared with that of Shrewsbury, Bridgnorth or Ludlow, but its inhabitants included several mercers, dyers and tanners, who operated on a considerable scale, and a host of leather workers, butchers and bakers.[28] Wellington had a range of commercial facilities in the 19th century comparable with those of such rural market towns as Ludlow. It received considerable impetus from the opening of the main line railways. Shifnal, another market town which lay outside the coalfield, but whose parish boundaries included mining hamlets, was the postal town for much of the industrial area until well after the coming of the railways. Wellington was rivalled in the northern part of the district by the twin centres of Oakengates and St. George's. In 1826 a market was established at St. George's on the high ground to the east of Oakengates, which after the opening of two railways through the valley below, migrated down the hill to the present centre of Oakengates, which in 1851 was described as 'one long street which contains many good shops and several respectable inns'.[29]

The same pattern of dispersal can be observed in the south of the coalfield. The ancient medieval market of Madeley had lapsed by the beginning of the 18th century but was revived in 1763. After the opening of the Iron Bridge the market was moved to the new commercial settlement which grew up at its northern end. The centre of Madeley itself had few of the characteristics of a town. In 1851 it was described as, 'irregularly built and consists chiefly of detached ranges of cottages rather than streets'. In contrast Ironbridge had prospered. Charles Hulbert wrote in 1837,

Here we may say is the merchantile part of the town of Madeley, and here is the focus of professional and commercial pursuits, the weekly market, the post office, the printing office, principal inns, draper, grocer and ironmongery, watch-making, cabinet making, timber and boat building establishments, the Subscription Library, Subscription Dispensary, branch bank, Subscription Baths, gentlemen of the legal and medical professions, ladies' boarding school &c.

Nevertheless like St. George's and Oakengates, Madeley and Ironbridge divided facilities which together might have made a more active and lively town.[30]

South of the Severn, Broseley provided another focus of commercial activity. In the late 17th and 18th centuries it had many of the characteristics of a small market town, its inhabitants including surgeons, mercers, dyers, butchers, maltsters and a clock-maker. It possessed an ancient market, and in the period of its prosperity in the 1770s its inhabitants erected a new market hall and town hall. With the decay of the iron trade in the district in the 19th century Broseley's commerce languished, and in 1851 its market was, 'not very numerously attended'.[31]

The only other settlement with more than 5 per cent of the coalfield's commercial facilities in the mid-19th century was Dawley, where the centre had migrated from the old village around the parish church to the junction of the old and new turnpike roads from Wellington to Madeley at the *Lord Hill* inn. There was no market at Dawley until 1867.[32]

For the majority of industrial workers in the coalfield the commercial centres were no more than places to which they might repair to drink on special occasions. The public houses of Oakengates were said in 1846 frequently to be thronged on Reckoning Mondays.[33] The main focus of social life was the village or hamlet. Few of these were in any sense commercial centres. Only Coalbrookdale, Trench, Hadley, Ketley, Ketley Bank and Lawley Bank had any real concentrations of shops and public houses, and each possessed well under 5 per cent of the total facilities in the district. Villages like Dark Lane, Hinkshay, Waxhill Barracks, Sandy Bank Row and Blists Hill had even less. The quality of life in these more remote communities varied greatly.

At one extremity was Coalbrookdale, often quoted as an archetypal creation of Quaker philanthropy, but a settlement quite unique in east Shropshire. The Darbys provided an unusually wide range of communal facilities for their work people, a mill, a laundry, schools, company shops, and cottages for widows. There was a long tradition of skilled work in the village. The 1851 census suggests that the inhabitants of most settlements in the coalfield did no more than mine coal or ironstone and smelt or forge iron. At Coalbrookdale there was a host of sophisticated occupations, fitters, mechanics, 'draftsmen', grate fitters, bronzers, file cutters, pattern-makers, grate and fender polishers, kitchen range fitters, stove grate grinders. With this tradition of skilled work went a tradition of intellectual self-help. William Cooke the first Methodist New Connexion minister to reside in the district noted in 1829:

I have been occupied in giving lectures on Tuesday evenings at Mr. Heaford's at Coalbrookdale. The subjects of these lectures are the doctrines which we teach as contained in our rules. They are well attended by people of respectability from the different communities, and it is thought that good will be done. I have always some sceptics or deists to hear me.

It is doubtful whether deists or sceptics willing to give a peaceful hearing to a Christian minister would have been found in many other east Shropshire communities at this time.

The Methodist shoemaker William Smith kept the turnpike gate at Coalbrookdale for a time in the 1840s and found the village, noted at that time for turning out smart intelligent men and hard thinkers and workers. It was my delight to be amongst these men and be invited to join their discussion classes where good preachers were appointed to train them. These classes proved a great blessing to me and sharpened me up for discussion and preaching and public speaking.[34]

Fogerty, who knew Coalbrookdale in the 1850s said, 'the skilled workmen engaged in the Dale works were a superior class, and as a rule were members of some dissenting body whose ministers looked pretty well after them'. Something of the range of intellectual interests among the labour aristocracy of the Dale can be seen from the possessions of Samuel Cookson, an engineer who died in 1853, which included 300 volumes of historical, scientific and other literature, choice music, musical instruments, a camera obscura, electrical apparatus, glass retorts, a vice and lathe, a quadrant and pit level and three guns. The intellectual aspirations of the Coalbrookdale workers culminated in the founding of an Institute and School of Art, projected in 1853 and completed in 1859.[35]

These were not the only respects in which Coalbrookdale was an unusual settlement. Late in the 19th century a variety of ancient community customs prevailed. A wife beater was sanctioned by a ceremonial mawkin burning. His neighbours would make a mawkin or effigy of old clothes and straw, and process with music made by tin whistles, clappers and tin cans to burn it at his door. Similar rough music would be employed to serenade men persistently late for work at the foundry, who would be brought from their homes and taken to work in a wheelbarrow. In the 1870s one inhabitant of the Dale was living with his fourth wife whom he had bought at an auction at Wenlock Fair and led home with a halter around her neck.[36]

The high intellectual standards of the Coalbrookdale workmen led them into such movements as Chartism and Teetotallism, and the Dale was one of the few settlements in the district to show an acute awareness of conventional politics.

Coalport, although a new settlement of the 1790s, had much in common with Coalbrookdale. It had a tradition of highly skilled work in the china factories, and was like Coalbrookdale the creation of Quaker entrepreneurs. While it lacked the strong community traditions and institutions of Coalbrookdale, its workers, particularly the china painters whose working conditions allowed day-long political conversations, were similarly renowned for their intellectual prowess and their independent spirit. According to John Randall, himself a painter of Coalport china,

Coalport men were usually great politicians; Hunt, Hetherington, Richard Carlile, Sir Francis Burdett and Cobbett had their disciples and admirers; and such was the eagerness to get the Register with its familiar grid iron on the cover, that a man has been despatched to Birmingham for it from one of the rooms, his shopmates undertaking to do his work for him whilst he was away.

Randall describes one china painter, John Crowther, a good-natured recluse, who studied algebra and mechanics to an advanced stage, and claimed that many painters became linguists, engineers and schoolmasters because their intelligence was cultivated through discussion in the workshops.[37]

Coalbrookdale and Coalport were unusual settlements. More typical of the district were the isolated villages, blocks of company houses in some cases with neither shop, public house nor chapel. Inhospitable to strangers, and particularly to the inhabitants of the traditionally hostile neighbouring market towns, such villages were regarded with amazement by newcomers to the area. Lawley Bank about 1800 appeared in retrospect to a Wesleyan minister as,

> notorious for wickedness, and the brutal sports; such as gambling, drunkenness, cockfighting and bull baiting, and that even on the Sabbath-day. Society was then sunk into the lowest depths of degradation; sin abounded to a fearful extent ... there was no counteracting influence brought to bear upon the mind or conduct of men, to restrain the impetuous torrent of evil. Amidst a large and rapidly increasing population there was no church, no chapel, no preaching house, no Sunday or even a day school.[38]

Such villages had all of the characteristics of frontier societies and retained many of them throughout the 19th century. There were distinct differences in culture between villages which superficially were quite similar. Dark Lane, in appearance one of the rawest frontier settlements, was unusual in having no public houses, but its Primitive Methodist society received exceptionally strong support. A congregation of over 100 was meeting in a cottage in 1851. In 1863 a temporary wooden 'tabernacle' was erected, later to be enclosed in bricks. In the 1890s activities of some sort took place at the chapel every night of the week, and throughout Sundays. A highlight of the year at Dark Lane was a performance of a drama, *Joseph and his Brethren*, somewhat inappropriately on Good Fridays.[39]

The alternative focus for community activities to the chapel was the public house. Hinkshay, which unlike nearby Dark Lane had its own public house, significantly showed much less enthusiasm for Methodism. A cottage was for many years used for Wesleyan meetings, but the numbers in the society were small, and no chapel was ever built.

Public houses were closely involved with industry in the district. The *Brewery Inn* at Coalport, first licensed in 1826, was owned by the china works. The *Commercial Hotel*, Coalbrookdale, licensed in 1839, was the property of the Coalbrookdale Company. The *Three Furnaces* near Madeley Court was licensed in 1841 at exactly the time that James Foster was beginning to exploit the minerals in the vicinity. Police records[40] show that in the 1880s only two of the 30 inns in Madeley and only one of the 20 beer houses did not regard 'works' or 'mining' as at least part of their trade. Local newspapers make spasmodic references to friendly societies and benefit clubs which met at public houses. Much remains to be learnt about their role in the community.

The division between the frequenters of public houses and those who belonged to the chapel societies was not absolute. In Dawley, the Tranter family, prominent in the affairs of the Methodist New Connexion kept the *Lord Hill Inn*. They refused to open on Sundays and would never allow bad language or the service of drink to anyone whom they considered to have had sufficient. At Dark Lane one of the leading participants in the annual drama at the chapel not only went to public houses, but was known for his bad language, and the choirmaster at the chapel on one occasion tried to obtain a licence to open a beerhouse in the village.[41]

A study of the communities of the Shropshire coalfield is as essential to an understanding of the reasons for the area's economic growth in the 18th century as an examination of the careers of the local entrepreneurs. The area was one of scattered, non-urban settlement, with no single commercial centre. The communities which existed in the early 18th century provided an environment rich in skills in which the seedlings of large-scale industry could grow. They also proved capable of expanding to accommodate the fast-growing numbers who found work in the mines and ironworks after 1750. The surviving company rows are impressive. Many were well-built and reasonably spacious but they were not typical of the housing in the coalfield. Some company terraces consisted of cramped, badly-built cottages, and the sum total of company housing accommodated only a small proportion of the local population. Most housing was originally provided by its occupants or by small-scale speculators. Dr. David Hey has observed:

> The origins of the Industrial Revolution are to be sought not in those areas where the peasant structure of society was destroyed, but precisely in those regions which long retained the characteristic features of the peasant way of life.[42]

This was as true in Shropshire as in the Pennine region to which Dr. Hey was referring. Industrial growth in the Coalbrookdale coalfield owed as much to initiatives born of the poverty of its inhabitants, of the needs of those who lived in squatter-type dwellings on the slopes of the Severn Gorge, along the verges of lanes, or on the open commons of Ketley or Lawley, to find new sources of income, to develop new skills and new markets for their coal, as it did to the enterprise of ironmasters or to the ambitions of landowners. Edward Darrall, a collier who died in 1726, occupied one of the first squatter cottages to be built in Holywell Lane, with a kitchen, a little room and a buttery on the ground floor and two bedrooms above. His possessions were worth only £4. 13s. 0d. He kept a cow, and his family made butter, brewed beer and spun flax. He appears to have slept on a feather bed while his children slept on chaff. It was probably this Edward Darrall who sold coal to Abraham Darby I in 1709, and burned that coal into coke for iron-making.[43] The community, which probably began with the construction of Darrall's humble cottage, housed more than 30 families by the mid-19th century. The role of Darrall and his descendants in the industrial revolution in Shropshire was as significant as that of Darby and his.

XVIII

THE WORKING CONTEXT

High wages were the most potent of the inducements which drew migrant workers to the Shropshire coalfield. They were a necessary compensation for the way of life which awaited the newcomer. 'In the absence of an inducement of this kind', wrote one observer in 1836, 'few would undergo the slavery of a coal pit who could obtain nearly equal wages in more secure and more congenial employment'.[1] The meagre luxuries bought by the high wages of the coalfield were balanced by the appalling dangers to life and to health in the local pits and by the interminable hours of labour demanded by the ironmasters.

Wages at the ironworks of the Coalbrookdale partners seem to have been considerably above average throughout the 18th century. In 1709 the rates for furnacemen varied between 5s. and 7s. 6d. a week. Two labourers received 2s. and 3s., probably not for a full week's work, and one Daniel Floweree regularly received 16s. 8d. In 1718 rates varied between 6s. and 11s. with additional payments to certain workers for tasks performed outside their normal range of duties. Furnacemens' wages in 1730 and 1732 ranged from 8s. to 10s. with varying additional payments for extra tasks, while wages at the forge were as low as 6s. a week. By 1767 the rates paid at Horsehay were 9s. or 9s. 6d. for filling the furnace, 10s. or 11s. for keeping, 9s. 6d. for stocking the bridge, 12s. for burning iron ore, and 9s. for breaking limestone.[2]

The first wide-ranging survey of the wages in the coalfield was that of Arthur Young in 1776.[3] He found that the normal wage for a farmworker in Benthall or Broseley who received board from his employer was 6s. a week in harvest time and 4s. for the rest of the year. The man who received no board had 1s. 4d. a day or 8s. a week, a rate which had risen from 1s. a day in the previous 10 years. In the old established potteries of Broseley a man's wage was between 8s. and 10s. a week, and in the tobacco pipe works 10s. 6d. North of the Severn a collier's wage was 1s. 8d. a day, which meant 18s. 4d. for the traditional 11-day fortnight. Foundry workers at Coalbrookdale received between 8s. and 10s. 6d. a week according to Young, although the company's accounts show that the wage structure was very complex and that some men received much more than this. The labour of women and children augmented the average family income. Young found the rate for women in agriculture to be 6d. a day with beer and for lads £2 a year. In the potteries boys could earn from 3d. to 9d. a day and girls 3d. and 4d. a day. In the pipe works women could earn 3s. a week, and children 2s. or 3s. In the pits boys drawing coal baskets could earn 1s. a day, a yearly income of £14–£15 as compared with £2 on the farms.

Nearly two decades later Archdeacon Plymley found that the agricultural labourer's wage in the Madeley area was 9s. a week with 10s. in summer. He did not quote a rate for colliers, but found that at the ironworks labourers received 11s. a week with 12s. in summer, and that some workers had as much as £2 a week. In Broseley 'the least able labourer' could earn 10s. a week at common work in husbandry, and ironworkers could get between £1 10s. and £2. Plymley gives no instances of potters' wages, but noted that in Barrow parish where the Caughley works was situated, men at the china factory had higher wages than the average. The wages paid in ironworks and mines influenced the rates paid throughout the adjacent countryside. The condition of the labourers of Beckbury, five miles from Madeley and 10 from Wolverhampton, was not happy in 1793. Most farm work in the parish was done by contract between farmers and labourers, and otherwise men received only a shilling a day and beer. Family incomes were supplemented by a bounty of 1s. 6d. to 2s. 6d. a week paid by Isaac Hawkins Browne, the lord of the manor, but payments were only made to those who attended morning service at the parish church. Nevertheless Plymley noted 'a rise in wages is anticipated since the parish is within the influence of Manufactories, Collieries and Iron Furnaces on almost every side of it'.[4]

Young and Plymley show conclusively that industrial wages, even those of the unskilled, were much higher than those paid to farm workers, although they were somewhat lower than labourers' rate in London or industrial Lancashire in the same period. Their figures suggest a steady rise in money wages between the early 1770s and the end of the century. During the first two decades of the 19th century the situation changed. By 1815 Shropshire wages were lower than those in other iron-working areas. Thomas Butler found rates at Madeley Wood to be 3s. 6d. a day for colliers, 2s. 6d. a day for labourers, and £1 a week with a production bonus for fillers and keepers of furnaces. Butler thought these rates about 15 per cent below those obtaining at the time in the Black Country, and by 1845 Shropshire wages were 20 per cent below those in south Staffordshire which themselves were lower than those in ironworks in northern England. The tradition of low wages in the 19th century was confirmed by Fogerty who claimed that this was compensated, at least for employees of the Coalbrookdale Company, by the management's reluctance to lay off men in slack times.[5]

Estimates of what happened to real wages can be no more than tentative, but a statement by Gilbert Gilpin about wages and prices in Shropshire in 1817 makes an interesting comparison with the figures quoted by Arthur Young for 1776. Colliers, Gilpin estimated, earned 15s. a week, as against about 10s. in 1776. The less skilled workers at the furnaces also received about 15s. as compared with 8s.–10s. 6d. in 1776. Money wages had therefore risen by approximately 50 per cent over 40 years. Gilpin's figures suggest that food prices had risen by about the same amount, butter from 6d. to $11\frac{1}{4}$d. per pound, beef from $3\frac{1}{4}$d. to $4\frac{1}{2}$d., mutton from 4d. to $5\frac{1}{2}$d., bacon from 6d. or 7d. to 10d. These, unfortunately, are the only commodities quoted by both Gilpin and Young. Gilpin estimated that the workman's house and garden rent and his fuel cost about 1s. 6d. a week, or £3 18s. a year. Young noted that labourers' house rents were between £1 and £1 5s. a year, and domestic coals cost 3d. per cwt. If the consumption of coal averaged 1 cwt. a week through the year, the total cost of fuel and housing in 1776 would have been about £1 15s. to £1 18s. a year, so these costs perhaps doubled between 1776 and 1817. The latter year was one of acute depression, and the wages being paid were certainly lower than in earlier and later boom years. It seems nevertheless that while real wages may have risen between 1776 and 1790, a comparison of Young's figures with Plymley's suggests, over the long term between 1776 and 1817 the growth of money wages only just kept pace with the rise in food prices, and may actually have fallen behind the rise in the cost of housing and fuel. The latter may to some extent have been compensated by the falling prices of cotton textiles and soap which were noted by Dr. Matthew Webb.[6]

The accounts of the iron-making partnerships show that the calculation of the sum due to any particular workmen at the end of a week, fortnight or month was a complex and devious process, made the more confusing by piece work and sub-contracting. Miners' incomes are extremely difficult to assess since it is often uncertain whether payments to individually named colliers were for those named alone, or for a group, or whether payments to child assistants had to be met from them. Nor was the situation in ironworks any more straightforward. Throughout the 18th century labour was in short supply, and a man was frequently employed to do more than one job.

Just how complex was the wage system in the ironworks can be seen from the accounts for the Horsehay works in a month during the summer of 1796.[7] At the furnaces, most employees received a fixed sum per week plus a bounty on the production of iron. The two furnace keepers, Richard Jones and William Whitehead received £2 16s. 6d. for the month, made up of four weekly payments of 12s. 6d. plus a bonus of 6s. 6d. The two fillers received £2 13s. 3d. each, the coke fillers £2 12s. 3d. Thomas Skelton and Son, presumably sub-contractors, received £3 3s. 6d. for breaking lime-stone. Thomas Skelton Sen. also received £2 for 24 days moulding castings, while Thomas Skelton Jun. was one of the two furnace fillers, and also had 5s. 3d. for 3½ days' work with 10 other men, 'wheighing plates in the Bridge House'. Humphrey Yates received £2 16s. 0d. for stacking the bridge, apparently his regular job, plus 5s. 4d. for 'assisting the keeper to throw', on 16 occasions. John Wilcox received £2 19s. 7d. for performing three different labouring tasks, while Joseph Baugh, the regular furnacemen's labourer, had only his basic wage of four weeks at 10s. 6d. Apart from the Skeltons, two other sub-contracting teams were employed: Ester Purcell and Co. unloading and burning over 1,200 tons of ironstone, and William Ball and Co. who performed a variety of loading, unloading and carrying tasks.

Payments in the forges were equally complicated. Two men, Samuel Purcell and James Skelton received over £12 during the month for making stamped iron from pigs, an astonishingly high rate for the period if it did not include allowances for payments to assistants or labourers. As at the furnaces, some of the forge work was sub-contracted. Jno. Lambett Sen. and Co. received over £22 for heating, shingling, slabbing &c., and Benjamin Norton and Co. over £10 for planishing oven bars and round iron. William Ball and Co., who were also employed at the furnaces, were paid for some loading and unloading at the forges.

Even the engine keepers' wages at Horsehay were far from straightforward. The keepers of the Blast Engines received £2 per month each, but had in addition about 4s. each for getting out ashes and unloading coals and 1s. 6d. or 1s. 8d. for making an inventory. The rolling mill engine was kept by James Tranter Sen. and John Tranter Jun. who were paid £2 4s. 0d. and £2 respectively, and both had additional sums for unloading fuel.

A busy period at the ironworks increased wages considerably. In March and April 1797 the standard rate for a furnace keeper was still 12s. 6d. as it had been the previous year, but Richard Jones's wages for the month amounted to £3 2s. 2d. since his bonus had nearly doubled with increased production.

The figures quoted by observers like Young and Plymley must therefore have been approximations only, and it is likely that particularly in times of good trade they underestimated the real level of wages rather than the contrary. Their figures probably took no account of the various labouring tasks undertaken by skilled men for which special payments were made. Comparison of wages in Shropshire with those in other areas is complicated by the high incidence of company trading. Much of the advantage of relatively high wages could have been negated by having to buy food at highly priced company shops.

Whatever the uncertainties about wages rates, literary evidence unanimously suggests that high wages determined patterns of spending and recreation in the coalfield. One indication of the prosperity of the district was the high rate of consumption of tea. It was noted in 1795 that in Madeley,

> since the use of Tea is becoming so prevalent, on a moderate calculation, each family consumes $3^1/_2$ lbs. of flour each week more than formerly, by instituting a fourth meal every day. In the days of yore, Breakfast, Dinner and Supper were esteemed sufficient, but now it must be Breakfast, Dinner, Tea, and Supper, which wastes both meal and time, and makes a difference each week in the parish of Madeley of 3,234 lbs. of flour.[8]

High wages were perhaps the greatest cause of class friction in the coalfield. Clergy, magistrates and other members of the middle class frequently expressed their indignation at the ways in which the miners and ironworkers spent their high wages.

Lucy Cameron's archetypal Oakengates miner, Thomas Cadman and his wife earned between them a guinea a week in the early 19th century. 'A guinea a week', remarked the clergyman's wife, 'is fifty two guineas a year, and the clergyman of the parish where Cadman was born had not so much yet he brought up a large family creditably, besides giving much to the poor'. Mrs. Cameron's husband, the first Vicar of St. George's, in a sermon in 1812 deplored the motives of immigrant workers and their modes of spending.

> A large proportion of the people here are perhaps those who, discontented with their original situations and flattering themselves with I know not what golden dreams, were tempted by the hope of large wages to leave their homes and settle among us. These, as might be expected, in general spend what they get in luxury and self indulgence. The rest too, receiving at regular seasons large sums of money which they know not how to use rightly, waste it in the same luxurious living, and the money which is got at the hazard of their lives is spent to the ruin of their souls[9]

Archdeacon Plymley expressed similar fears about the workers of Madeley in 1793,

> it does not appear that these high wages produce more comfort or advantage than at other places – there are 24 ale houses and this additional pay is most spent at these places. These labourers are prone to the indulgences of dainty living, having a pride in buying dear and rare articles at Market for a Sunday's dinner or so, tho' they fare harder during the remainder of the week, and there is little attention paid by any of these people to have comforts, neatness of house or garden, or cleanliness of apparel; nothing indeed seems so difficult as telling whether high or low wages are best for the poor themselves.

At Broseley Plymley noted,

> The small children in this parish can earn something in addition to the parents' gains, so

that here is ample maintenance for the labourers, but it is generally spent in an improper manner, much of their wages is spent at the alehouse and good living at home is preferred to cleanliness and neatness, either in the person of the people, their cloathing, houses or gardens. There are scarcely any instances of a Collier or Mechanic saving money, otherwise than by contributing to Clubs or Benefit Societies.[10]

An ironmaster in 1835 remarked,

The great evil with colliers is, they over-stimulate themselves by their irregular habits of living: after having received their wages, which is once a fortnight, they live on the fat of the land for the first three or four days, and during the remainder they are obliged to starve themselves. With many it is either a feast or a fast.[11]

Lucy Cameron's account of Thomas and Mary Cadman fills out the picture of working-class spending patterns as they were observed from the vicarage window. On their marriage, Mary Cadman's six guineas savings were sufficient to buy a bed, a table, a few chairs and cooking vessels, to which was added on occasions when Thomas Cadman went to town with money in his pocket, 'a bit of showy furniture that caught his eye but seldom anything useful'. Large sums were spent by the Cadmans on their bull dog which was kept for the annual ball-baitings at Oakengates Wake. Like most of their neighbours, the Cadmans ate well after the fortnightly reckoning, but lived poorly in the days immediately before it. A roasted joint of fine fat mutton, with potatoes, followed by a pudding, with a jug of beer from a public house, was the usual meal on Reckoning Sundays. On special occasions a goose would be cooked with other meats. Because Mary Cadman 'knew nothing of management, and very little of any kind of women's work except knitting', she had to pay others to make her husband's shirts. Lucy Cameron thought that she should have made them herself. She also deplored Thomas Cadman's lack of thrift. His only saving was a payment towards a bull for the Wake, although he was a member of a club.[12] A doctor in Madeley in 1830s thought that men generally allowed their wives a fixed sum for house-keeping and spent the remainder of their wages, a large or a small amount according to the state of trade, on their own pleasures.

The propertied classes were much angered by the miners' lack of thrift, and seem to have resented the miners' own benefit societies, over which they had no control. The Assistant Poor Law Commissioner in 1836 demanded the rigorous reform of the field clubs or friendly societies in the district. He claimed that,

the character of the miner is like that of the sailor, greedy of present enjoyment and careless of the future. The very scenes they live in contribute to this feeling, and the maxim they act upon is too unhappily 'let us eat and drink today for tomorrow we die'.

He quoted a speech made to miners by a magistrate during the depression of 1816 in which resentment at the high level of miners' wages approached vindictiveness,

When work and money were to be had, and you were in comparison in a state of prosperity, did you use and enjoy these blessings with moderation, sobriety and thankfulness? When I mention drunkenness do I not name a sin most common, not only among men but among almost children? What scenes of revelling and debauchery, of gambling and even fighting might be witnessed after every reckoning, and even on the Lord's Day itself. But this is not all. Remember the pride and insolence of many: they would work when they pleased and play when they pleased, and often refused to work when wanted to do it, to the great injury of their masters and trade in general. Recollect the extravagance, the luxury, the self-indulgence of numbers. While the men beset themselves with ale, the women more privately indulge in the gin bottle. By how many were almost the whole earnings of a fortnight eaten and drunk in two or three days? Some who are now going to the parish for relief would give any price in the market for poultry, or what they had a fancy to; and even professed not to care for a pound or two, to have one single dress a little finer, or more tasty, as they say, then ordinary.[13]

The high wages and high level of employment in the coalfield meant that the able-bodied rarely sought help from the poor law authorities, who were concerned for the most part with the sick and injured, the orphans and the old. The relief of the unemployed did not become a serious problem until the depression of 1816–17. Industrial development seems to have reduced the average burdens on ratepayers in the 18th century. In Broseley between 1770 and 1793 the rate was reduced by half. In the latter year between 30 and 40 paupers relied on the parish most of them orphans and old people who were accommodated in a workhouse. They have previously been farmed out to contractors but this system proved oppressive and was discontinued. Contractors also tended the poor of Madeley in the late 18th century. In the early 1770s the poor were farmed out to a variety of individuals for between £120 and £130 a year. In 1781 two dwellings were acquired for a workhouse, but the following year one Thomas Roberts contracted to take care of the inhabitants for 2s. 6d. a week, and later to take responsibility for all of the parish poor for £220 a year. A workhouse was again in use in 1784. By 1795 the cost of looking after each pauper in Madeley was reckoned to be 2s. 8d. per week.[14]

The majority of Shropshire miners and many of the unskilled ironworkers were not employed by the great industrial partnerships but by sub-contractors, known variously as charter masters, butties or gaffers. The charter master would contract with the mine owner to get and raise a given quantity of minerals at an agreed price, a proportion of the proceeds if coal was to be mined for sale, or a fixed sum if the minerals were destined for the owner's ironworks. The owner bore the charges for sinking shafts, of providing drainage and winding facilities, and of conveying the minerals from the pit top. The charter master hired all of the workmen, apart from the owner's clerks and agents, and provided horses, tubs, tools and timber for use underground. Most charter masters operated on monthly contracts, so that their incomes and those of the colliers they employed were subject to sudden fluctuations.[15]

A charter master often rose from the ranks of the colliers by becoming first a doggy, a deputy to the charter master responsible for the direct supervision of work underground. By tradition a charter master was rich, fat and illiterate. In Staffordshire the term 'butty' often meant simply a great belly. The system had many advantages for the coal owners, since the charter masters brought new capital into the works. As much as £500 was often needed for cutting out headings below ground before coal could be raised. In an area where formal educational institutions provided no more than the meanest rudiments of literacy, professional managers were few, and in such a situation the substitution of the profit motive for loyalty to the partnership in the supervision of large areas of the company's activities was obviously advantageous. Furthermore, the gulf which existed between entrepreneurs in manners, recreation, religion and speech, and the dangers of work underground, made it essential that direct supervision should be undertaken by men able to communicate with the colliers.

The charter master system probably grew up in Shropshire with the development of the longwall system of mining in the 17th century. One of the most skilled tasks in mining, the sinking of shafts was generally undertaken by specialists paid by the mineowners, but charter masters would take charge of a pit immediately it was ready for production. Coal along a face would be undermined by holers, who would build up cogs or stone supports to keep up the mass of coal. Pikemen would then cut down the undermined coal with 'pikes'. In the early 18th century the occupations of holer and pikemen were separate, but their functions seem to have merged by 1800. Once the coal was cut down, turnsmen or bandsmen would despatch it to the bottom of the shaft. The bandsmen included turners or getters-out, who broke up the largest lumps of coal, and pitchers, teenage boys who loaded the coal on to skips and fastened it down with wrought iron hoops. Other bandsmen propped the roof of the gob, the space left when coal had been extracted, and filled it with rock and slack. The bandsmen were paid by the day, which for most meant a 12-hour shift, although the getters, the most skilful of this grade were accustomed to no more than 10 hours. The pikemen or holers were the aristocrats among the Shropshire colliers. To be a pikeman was considered 'the object of the ambition of every young miner'. Pikemen were also paid by the day, but their 'day' was a stint, the amount of coal which could be cut in six to eight hours, usually about five ft. square of a face. When trade was good an able-bodied pikeman might do one and a half or even two 'days' in a shift, and a fortnight's work of 11 shifts might be as much as 15 or 16 'days'. The rates of wages paid per 'day' to pikemen were generally lower than those paid to bandsmen, but the incomes of the former could easily be substantially higher, since a bandsman could only work as many days as the pit was open, while the pikeman could work as many as his energy and the state of trade permitted.[16] The charter-master system was in origin a natural and logical way of organising an industrial operation where tasks were essentially specialised. It was a system particularly well adapted to the needs of an expanding industry which depended on immigrant labour, since there were numerous tasks suited to the capabilities of an unskilled man new to the pit, and a range of others increasing in skill to which he could turn as he gained acquaintance with mining.

Charter masters very commonly kept public houses. They organised bull baitings on behalf of their men in Broseley.[17] Some were the stewards of Methodist societies. Much remains to be learned about the charter master system, but there are certainly many indications that it was not just a way of organising industrial labour, but a form of social organisation which extended to many activities outside the mines.

Industrial disputes were inherent in the charter master system. The pikemen or holers were highly skilled, and demarcation disputes constantly arose when they were required to clean out roads or do other tasks than cutting out their stints. The allocation of small stints, 'half days' or 'quarter days', was the subject of much argument. It was widely believed that charter masters punished independently-minded colliers by allocating them such stints. For the bandsmen, the hourly paid workers, a projected half or quarter day might be extended to eight or 10 hours by the slowness of the doggy's watch. Sometimes colliers would descend the pit and find the whole day's work suspended because of slackness of trade or a breakdown in the overground transport system. On such occasions, known as 'Buildasses', they received no wages at all. Meal breaks were another cause of dispute. The Botfields' insistence in 1842 that men working a 12-hour shift should be allowed 40 minutes for dinner and 20 for lunch was a move towards reform. The employees of the Coalbrookdale Company's charter masters were allowed to leave work half an hour early if they took meals when they could and missed formal meal breaks.[18]

As potent as the underground abuses of the charter master system were those which arose through the ways in which wages were paid. Miners were paid by the fortnight. Alternate Saturdays were called 'Reckonings'. After work was concluded the colliers would assemble at the charter master's house while the sums due to them were calculated. Often the house was a beershop, and the colliers were expected to buy drinks on credit while they waited. The Sunday following the reckoning was tradition- ally the day for expensive family dinners, and the colliers generally took a holiday on the 'Reckoning Monday', a day when the public houses were generally well frequented. A 12-year-old in 1843 described what happened,

> They reckon on the Saturday. Sometimes we work the Monday after the reckoning, and sometimes the men go to the alehouse and drink, smoke, sing songs sometimes, and make knocks on the table when the song is done. I can drink a pint and a half of strong beer.

A 15-year-old said,

> I get 20d. a day and work 9, 10 or 11 days a fortnight. We generally play on the Monday after we get the money. After the money is received at the butty's house, most of the men go and drink some drink. On the Sunday very few drink but a good many more on the Monday. On the Tuesday morning we all come to work.[19]

Many charter masters kept 'truck' or 'tommy' shops where the colliers they employed were expected to buy their provisions, often at inflated prices.

The charter master system in Shropshire was being attacked by the 1840s, although it survived into the 20th century. During the Chartist inspired strike of 1842 the county magistrates were shocked to discover some of the abuses of the system, and the acting Lord Lieutenant, the Earl of Powis, tried to persuade both the government and the local ironmasters to correct them. He explained to the Duke of Sutherland that the charter masters kept beer and tommy shops, made men wait for their pay on Saturdays, on the excuse that change was short, gave the men credit notes for the tommy shops rather than cash, and allocated quarter and half days to those who did not buy at their beer and provision shops. He told Sir James Graham, the Home Secretary, of the 'tyranny, fraud and injustice constantly practised upon the men by middle men who are denominated butties, charter masters &c'. The system embarrassed the ironmaking partnerships. The ground bailiff to the Madeley Wood Company, himself a former charter master, insisted in 1842 that 'all the great companies in Shropshire are totally above having anything to do with tommy shops'. William Botfield claimed to be surprised at the complaints made by the colliers about the system. The Duke of Sutherland found that on his estate charter masters working for the Ketley Company were allowed to keep beer houses, and declared his intention of trying to halt the practice. In September 1842 the ironmasters agreed to investigate claims about the charter masters and disavowed all connections with the truck system. Ironmasters and magistrates frequently claimed that the abuses of the charter master system were much less in Shropshire than elsewhere, but the evidence which came to light in the strike of 1842 suggests that little more than the pride of Salopians supported this opinion.[20]

'Few or none escape accidents', wrote one Shropshire coalmaster of his workers in 1835, 'and a large proportion meet with accidents which disable them for a longer or short time'. Another owner estimated that in the course of 30 years every miner was likely to meet with an accident, of which 75 per cent would be slight, 15 per cent totally disabling, and 10 per cent fatal. High wages were necessary to persuade men to endure

the conditions underground, and the more dangerous the conditions the greater were
the wages paid.[21]

The scale of mining operations increased in the late 18th century with the adoption
of steam winding engines, and in the 1820s as the deeper seams to the north and east
of the coalfield were exploited the collieries became even larger undertakings. Nevertheless shallow pits operating on a small scale continued to produce a significant
proportion of the coal mined in east Shropshire, and the last of them ceased operation
only in 1970. In the mid-19th century many of the worst practices of earlier years were
retained in such pits long after they had disappeared in the larger collieries.

The conditions which obtained in many pits in the 1840s were described by the
geologist Joseph Prestwich who knew the coalfield well,

> When the seam is very thin, they will have to work almost lying on their sides. Sometimes
> the space they have to work in is not more than two feet high. When the seams are still less,
> and the coal is sufficiently good to make it desirable to work it, the men cut away a little
> below the coal, but chiefly above it, so as to make room; but they are content with the
> smallest room possible so as to conduct their work with as much economy of labour as
> possible. In all the seams the men first cut away a few inches of the indurated clay under the
> coal, and so undermine it, then get it down in as large blocks as possible . . . Boys put the
> coal into wooden sledges, and draw them along to the levels, where it is put into carts and
> drawn by horses to below the mouth of the pit, where it is hoisted up. The boys are dressed
> like the grown men in trousers, shoes and stockings, but with no other clothing, the heat not
> rendering more necessary. There is a rope put round the waist when the height of the work
> will not admit their standing upright, the boys run on all fours drawing the sledge after
> them[22]

The most graphic account of the working conditions of the Shropshire miner is that
of John Fletcher,

> With what hardships and dangers do our indigent neighbours earn their bread! See those
> who ransack the bowels of the earth to get the black mineral we burn; how little is their lot
> preferable to the Spanish felons who work the golden mines. They take their leave of the light
> of the sun, and, suspended by a rope, are let down many fathoms perpendicularly towards
> the centre of the globe; they traverse the rocks through which they have dug their horizontal
> ways. The murderer's cell is a palace in comparison of the black spot to which they repair;
> the vagrant's posture in the stocks is preferable to that in which they labour.
> Form, if you can, an idea of the misery of men kneeling, stooping, or lying on one side, to toil
> all day in a confined place, where a child could hardly stand; whilst a younger company,
> with their hands and feet on the black dusty ground, and a chain about their body, creep and
> drag along like four-footed beasts, heavy loads of the dirty mineral, through ways almost
> impassable to the curious observer. In these low and dreary vaults, all the elements seem
> combined against them. Destructive damps, and clouds of noxious dust, infect the air they
> breathe. Sometimes water incessantly distils on their naked bodies; or bursting upon them in
> streams, drowns them and deluges their work. At other times, pieces of detached rocks crush
> them to death; or the earth, breaking in upon them, buries them alive. And frequently
> sulphureous vapours, kindled in an instant by the light of their candles, form subterraneous
> thunder and lightning. What a dreadful phenomenon! How impetuous is the blast! How
> fierce the rolling flames! How intolerable the noisome smell! How dreadful the continued
> roar! How violent and fatal the explosion!
> Wonderful providence! Some of the unhappy men have time to prostrate themselves: the fiery
> scourge grazes their backs; the ground shields their breasts; they escape. See them wound up
> out of the blazing dungeon, and say if these are not brands plucked out of the fire. A

pestiferous steam and clouds of suffocating smoke pursue them. Half dead themselves, they hold their dead or dying companions in their trembling arms. Merciful God of Shadrach! Kind Protector of Meshach! Mighty deliver of Abednego! Patient preserver of rebellious Jonah! Will not these utter a song – a song of praise to Thee! Praise ardent as the flames they escape – lasting as the life Thou prolongest? Alas they refuse![23]

It is impossible to measure the torments of working in a primitive coal pit, the dangers of dust, of damp and the agony of hours of work in narrow seams. About the dangers of fatal accidents it is possible to be more precise. The records of coroners' inquisitions received at the Shropshire Quarter Sessions show that between 1756 and 1800 the court received notices of 170 deaths brought about by pit accidents in the east Shropshire coalfield. This is not a complete figure since deaths from Madeley, Broseley and Little Wenlock were notified to the Wenlock borough courts. Nearly half of the 170 deaths, 37 per cent, were caused by falls of coal or rock, 28 per cent by accidental falls into the pit shafts, 25 per cent through accidents while ascending or descending the shaft, 7 per cent through suffocation by pockets of carbon dioxide, 2 per cent through fire damp explosions, and one per cent through other causes. Between 1801 and 1819 the Quarter Sessions records list 355 deaths from mining accidents in east Shropshire, and average of 18.7 per year, which represents a considerable increase in the accident rate over early periods, even allowing for inconsistent recording before 1800. The proportions attributable to various causes were not significantly different, except that the percentage of deaths due to fire damp explosions rose from two to six, doubtless due to the opening up of deeper pits. Falls of coal or rock caused 42 per cent of the deaths, falls into shafts 28 per cent, accidents while ascending or descending pits 15 per cent, suffocation by black damp or carbon dioxide 5 per cent, and other causes 4 per cent. Between 1820 and 1830 there were 236 deaths, an average of 21.5 a year. 38.5 per cent were caused by falls of coal or spoil, 22.9 per cent by falls into shafts, 21.7 per cent by accidents during the ascent or descent of shafts, and 14 per cent by fire damp explosions. Other causes included accidents with steam engines and premature explosions of gunpowder.[24]

Roof falls were a common danger wherever the longwall method of working was employed. Accidents in ascending and descending shafts were caused largely by the primitive methods employed. Men either went down in the basket used to haul up coal, which, in the absence of guides, was liable to swing and tip out its occupants, or they descended on the rope, sometimes sitting on a stick or a stool attached to it. The advent of steam winding posed new hazards, since men were sometimes killed by being drawn over the pulley at the shaft top when the engines failed to stop in time. The absence of guides brought danger to those working at the bottoms of shafts for baskets and their contents were liable to break away and fall to the bottom. The number of deaths caused by accidental falls into shafts suggest that the tops were inadequately guarded. They were particularly a hazard to the intoxicated in the hours of darkness. Many of those killed by falls into shafts worked on the banks of ironstone pits separating nodules of ore from clay. Mary Fletcher recorded one such death in 1805,

I was greatly struck by hearing of a young woman who was to have been married next Monday. One of her ungodly companions on the pit bank asked where she intended to keep her wedding. She profanely answered 'In Hell'. Soon after, being at her work near the mouth of the pit, her foot slipped, she fell in and was dashed to pieces.[25]

The Madeley parish records distinguish deaths from mining accidents in the late

18th and early 19th centuries, and show that the lack of references to the parish in the Quarter Sessions records was not because the mines there were unusually safe. In the 24 years between 1789 and 1812, 35 deaths from pit accidents are recorded in the registers. These include several fatal accidents caused by fire damp explosions. This was a hazard not encountered in some parts of the coalfield where pits were still lit by candles at the end of the 19th century.[26]

Even when the safety lamp became available in the second decade of the 19th century it was not always used. In 1843 an explosion which caused a man's death in the Hall Pits, Old Park, led the proprietor to warn his charter masters that they must insist on the use of the safety lamp.[27] Accidents caused by explosions caused more concern in the district than any others, and the funerals of the victims of such disasters were the occasions for vast demonstrations of public grief. The funeral of three young men who died in the Blists Hill pits in 1804 was attended by over 1,000 people according to Mary Fletcher, and by over 2,000 according to the curate of Madeley.[28]

The nearness of death in the pits influenced many aspects of local society. It was difficult for the propertied classes to teach thrift to men who were accustomed to seeing their colleagues crushed or burned to death. The nearness of death may well explain the particular form of emotional revivalism found in the churches in the district. It may explain the brutality of local recreations. Putting a bull to death by allowing dogs to torment it could hardly seem cruel to anyone who had seen miners die in a fire damp explosion.

The evidence collected by the Children's Employment Commission suggests that accidents deeply impressed the consciousness of young miners. A 17-year-old from Ketley described to the commission how he had left the Steeraway pits once after an accident which killed two men, went back, and left again when another man was killed. A 14-year-old from Lawley who was still drawing with the girdle and chain in 1842, described to the commission the death of a man caused by a tree falling down a shaft, which he had personally witnessed.[29]

Children could appreciably increase family incomes by working in the pits, and the Children's Employment Commission found terrifying evidence of what the Tory county newspaper called 'White Slavery in Shropshire'.[30] The commission was seeking evidence to justify legislation, and may have directed its attention to the worst practices. Its own evidence demonstrates that many of the worst methods had been abandoned in many pits by 1842. Yet its report establishes beyond any doubt that many of the most dangerous and unhealthy practices were still employed at a significant proportion of the pits in the district, and it can only hint at the horrors of the mining situation earlier in the 19th century when they were prevalent throughout the coalfield.

The commissioners visited the Hills Lane mine of the Madeley Wood Company where they found working a boy of no more than four years old. They would not have noticed him if his father, a working collier, had not interrupted the ground bailiff who was telling them there were no children under 10 in the pit. William Tranter, mining agent to the Coalbrookdale Company, told the commission that boys entered the pits at the age of six, when they could earn 6d. a day, which rose to as much as 1s. by the age of nine. The eight-year-old son of one Wellington pauper in 1822 was receiving a wage of 4d. per day. A ten-year-old earned 6d., an 11-year-old 8d., and a 14-year-old one shilling. Since the children carried out menial tasks they were employed in the same way as the bandsmen, paid by the day of 12 hours from 6 a.m. to 6 p.m. Boys ususally began to work with the pick, like men, between the ages of 14 and 16. Emanuel

Lovekin, later to be a charter master and a leading Primitive Methodist, entered a coalpit at Donnington Wood at the age of seven and a half in 1827–28, and began work opening and closing ventilation doors, from which he was later promoted to drive a donkey.

The commission was repeatedly told, and there is no reason to doubt it, that the great iron-making companies had substituted dans running on plate rails for the sledges hauled by boys with a girdle and chain for coal transport underground. William Tranter told them that while this was so, many small operators still used the girdle and chain, just as they used horse gins where the big companies used winding engines. Haulage with the girdle and chain was described to the commission by a 12-year-old from Ketley,

> I had not time to eat a bit of meat from morning till night. I have often had blisters on my side; but when I was more used to it it would not blister, but it smarted very badly. The chains was made of the same stuff as the rope [i.e. chain] that goes down the pit. I crawled on hands and feet. I often knocked my back against the top of the pit and it hurt very sore. There was not room to stand to that height. The legs ached very badly. When I came home at night I often sat down to rest me by the way I was so tired. The work made me look much older than I was.

Children in mines were particularly prone to accidents. According to Matthew Webb there were in 1838, 29 deaths of children under 13 in pit accidents in the coalfield.[31]

The 1842 Mines Act prohibited the employment underground of boys under 10, and if the 1851 census can be believed, there were by that time no younger children working in the east Shropshire mines, although a number of nine-year-olds were employed in such unregulated trades as brick-making.

By long tradition, women were not employed underground in Shropshire coal mines, although hundreds of pits girls worked on the banks of ironstone pits, separating nodules of ore from the clays and shales in which they were brought up from underground. The 1851 census shows that some girls were doing this work at the age of ten. A 14-year-old daughter of an Old Park collier was receiving 8d. a day for this work in 1822. Women generally continued to work on pit banks after marriage, but not after they began to bear children. One of the last of the pit girls, who began work about 1898, has recalled that when she joined her sister picking stone at Kemberton pit, her mother brought her a bag apron, new shoes, a basket for food, a print bonnet to wear en route to and from work, and a brown bonnet incorporating a roll made from old stockings, on which the iron boxes of ore were carried. In earlier years women had done other jobs at the pit top, particularly attaching baskets to the ropes going down shafts, and operating hand-worked winding apparatus. There are faint traces of evidence that women sometimes worked underground. In 1804 a women in an ironstone pit in Ketley was killed by a roof fall, and the following year in Wombridge a woman was killed while 'getting stone in a stone pit'. In 1813 a woman died while 'felling soil in a stone pit', in Dawley, and in 1816 a roof fall killed a woman working in a clay pit in Lilleshall.[32] None of these incidents occurred in coal mines, and it seems certain that women were not employed underground in pits of any sort by the 1840s. Much earlier, in about 1688, a group of poor inhabitants of Coalpit Bank petitioned for relief from hearth tax on the grounds that they were so poor that they were forced to send their wives and children into the pits.[33]

Picking out ore on the pit bank was in many parts of the coalfield the only employ-

Figure 20.   A. J. Munby's drawing of a Shropshire pit girl.
The Master and Fellows of Trinity College, Cambridge.

ment open to young women. In the Severn Gorge, the clay trades, particularly the porcelain factories, offered opportunities to women, who could, if sufficiently talented, perform skilled tasks. The 1851 census shows that women travelled to work at Coalport from as far away as Coalbrookdale and the centre of Madeley, and from all over the parish of Broseley.

No such opportunities were available in the Donnington and Oakengates areas where colliers' daughters and even some of their wives walked in droves every May to work in the market gardens around London. Many used the ability to carry heavy weights on their heads, acquired through work on the banks of ironstone pits, to take baskets of fruit from gardens west of London to Covent Garden. A survey of cottages in Ketley in 1836 revealed that the wife and daughter of one collier were 'gone to work in the London gardens', and three daughters of Wellington paupers, aged between 18 and 20, were recorded as being in London in the early 1820s. The historian of Hammersmith described in 1839 how women from Shropshire would make two daily journeys from as far away as Isleworth to Covent Garden, carrying 50 or 60 pounds of strawberries on their heads. After the strawberry season was over, they would gather vegetables and take them to the London markets. They could earn as much as 9s. a day during the forty-day strawberry and raspberry season, but rather less when harvesting vegetables. Their income was traditionally used to build up a dowry. They slept on straw in hovels and barns, ate a 'coarse and simple' diet, and drank tea and small beer. As late as 1870 A. J. Munby, that obsessive chronicler of the ways of working women, spent a June afternoon observing the girls in the orchards and gooseberry fields between Twickenham and Isleworth. He asked in one garden where the girls came from, and was told that 30 of the 48 employed there came from Shropshire and Staffordshire. An Oakengates girl with a cotton hoodbonnet, red neckerchief, smock sleeves and a skirt made of an old sack with the maker's name and the word 'flour' legible upon it, told him 'I've worked on a pit bonk most o'my days'. The girls returned to Shropshire in the autumn in time for the wake at Oakengates, bringing with them, 'many fine clothes, as well as money, which they have gained, some by honest industry alone, but many, it is feared, in a different way'. In 1822 a Wellington girl gave birth at the poor house to an illegitimate son whose father was a maltman from Fulham, and in 1824 another spinster from the parish was delivered of the child of a bricklayer from Bishop's Court, High Holborn. Work in the London gardens may have been a means to finding situations in domestic service in the capital, since many Shropshire girls were so employed in the 1820s.[34]

The miner who escaped death or disablement through accidents could expect that the cumulative effects of damp and foul air would seriously impair his health by the time that he was 50 if not earlier. One observer in 1835 thought that a miner at the age of 40 to 45 was reduced to the state of an agricultural labourer of 60. An anonymous surgeon told the Childrens' Employment Commission that few miners lived to their 51st year, and that most were asthmatic by the time they reached 30. The clerk to the Madeley Poor Law Union found that miners began to apply for relief on the grounds of permanent debility at about the age of 45. After that time he thought few could work underground, but most were able to find employment on the surface.[35]

The limestone mines of Steeraway, Lilleshall and Lincoln Hill were quite unlike the coal and iron ore pits elsewhere in the coalfield. At Steeraway in 1842, 100 men and 20 boys were employed. A seam of 45 ft. was extracted by pillar and stall methods. Because the roof was so high and because explosives were extensively used, limestone mining was extremely dangerous, and the miners in consequence received a higher wage than those who cut coal. The height of the workings made limestone workings much healthier, since there was an abundance of air, although in winter huge fires were lit for warmth. The limestone mines appeared terrifying even to those who worked in them. One Scottish immigrant working an extra shift on a Sunday evening in order to secure money to spend on drink on the Reckoning Monday,

> looked up and saw the stones in the roof, as he supposed ready to fall on him, and thought what must become of him if he should be killed when so employed, and also thought of the pious instructions of his father and mother and minister in his youth . . . felt himself totally unable to work, and got up the shaft as soon as he could, and never since has ventured into such a scene of danger on the Sabbath.[36]

The ironworker did not face the extreme dangers which threatened the miner. Only one fatal accident in an ironworks is recorded in the Madeley parish register between 1789 and 1812, when there were 35 deaths in mines in the parish. The ironworker's high wages were earned by excessive hours or a high degree of skill rather than by exposure to danger. Two sets of men were usually employed at furnaces and forges, working shifts of 12 hours from six o'clock to six o'clock, changing from night to day shift or vice versa each weekend. Wages were normally reckoned every four weeks. Such long hours were normal until well past the middle of the 19th century.

The smelting of iron ore in a blast furnace is a continuous process, and until the second decade of the 19th century all of the Shropshire iron-making partnerships compelled their furnaces crews to work a 24-hour 'double turn' on alternate Sundays when the shifts changed duties. In 1817 the Madeley Wood Company first modified this practice by taking off blast for a six-hour period on Sundays during which the crews were allowed to rest. The Coalbrookdale Company were the next to adopt this practice, in 1830, followed by the Old Park Company and the Lawley Company who abandoned double turns by 1842. The Lilleshall Company, the Wombridge Company and the Ketley Company still imposed the 24-hour shift in 1842, insisting that it was necessary to maintain the quality of their iron.[37]

Forging processes were not continuous so that there was no necessity for double turns. A puddler would normally be expected to work six heats of $3^3/_4$ cwt. of iron in a shift of 12 hours, each heat taking about two hours. Puddlers were always in demand, and more than most skilled workers they tended to migrate in search of higher wages. It was a particularly strenuous occupation, and the puddler's working life was normally over by the time he reached 40.[38]

Children were employed for several unskilled tasks in the Shropshire ironworks. Boys of eight and nine filled boxes with raw materials for the blast furnaces, and the superintendent of the Horsehay forges and rolling mills said in 1842 that he employed boys of seven and upwards for light duties.[39]

Conditions in the iron and coal industries of east Shropshire are well documented from the 1840s, but much less is known of other local occupations. Brickmaking had the reputation in the early 20th century of being 'slavery'. Fogerty wrote in the mid-19th century that while the majority of the colliers in Madeley and Dawley were ignorant and brutal, 'the work people of both sexes in the potteries and brick yards were almost degraded to the level of beasts, and their children were worse savages than those of the Sandwich Island'. In the 1860s many children between ten and fourteen were employed in the summer months in the brickyards of Jackfield, where the brickmakers, their immediate employers, allowed them between 4d. and 1s. 4d. a day.[40] John Randall, who worked at the Coalport china factory, recorded that the painters and the most highly-skilled potters worked in groups in rooms where a sophisticated level of conversation was possible, but in general the works were 'ill designed and badly constructed', portions had been added, 'with no regard to ventilation or other requirements of health'. There were 'the most curious ins and outs, dropsical looking roofs, bulging walls and drooping floors'. The biscuit room and other parts of the factory were noted for having 'a very stifling atmosphere charged with clay or flint'.[41]

XIX

DISCIPLINE: INDUSTRIAL AND SOCIAL

The community of interest between ironmaster and worker in 18th-century Shropshire was slight. The entrepreneur was accustomed to restrain his personal expenditure, a constant ploughing-back of profits being essential to the growth of his business. The collier, whose life might at any time be crushed from him by a roof fall, and who could look forward only to an asthmatic retirement in his 40s, lavishly spent his wages within a few days of the reckoning and fasted afterwards. For Richard Reynolds, a day's party on the Wrekin with his family and other Quaker employees was the principal annual festival.[1] For the collier the annual May Day wakes on the Wrekin or the Oakengates wakes in the autumn were occasions for exceptionally heavy drinking, often with the added excitement of seeing a bull baited. Reynolds was an extreme example of an entreprenurial type, and not every miner was accustomed to drink heavily or to fight, but the contrast between the Quaker ironmaster and the archetypal collier does illustrate a basic difference in life styles, which goes far to explain the pattern of class relationships in east Shropshire.

An ironworks was a heavily capitalised undertaking, many of its processes depending on continuous attention from skilled workmen. The enforcement of regular and punctual attendance and the setting of a high value on the use of time were therefore major concerns of the entrepreneurs. Such objectives were likely to be inhibited by heavy drinking and other excesses on Sundays and holidays, which led ironmasters to take a lead in the suppression of violent recreations. Upon ironworks and mines fell the heaviest burden of poor rates in the coalfield, so that it was in the interest of local entrepreneurs that their employees should save as an insurance against slack trade, sudden death or injury, rather than spend their money within a few days of receiving it.

New forms of work discipline were imposed between 1750 and 1850 by a combination of capitalist self-interest, Evangelical fervour and magisterial authoritarianism, aided by the spread of self-help and evangelical doctrines among the workers themselves. It was generally acknowledged that the colliers and ironworkers of east Shropshire were different from the labouring classes elsewhere in the county. While investigating poverty on his estates in 1833 the Duke of Sutherland noted the exemplary behaviour of those who lived in Lilleshall village, Muxton, and the country part of Donnington, conspicuously omitting the miners and ironworkers of the remainder of the latter township. In 1788 Richard Reynolds regretted the lack of progress of his Sunday School in Ketley, and on hearing that one was to be founded in Wellington remarked with some sadness, 'that being in a market town, I expect will succeed better'. In 1799 the vicar of Wellington described the inhabitants of the outer, industrial, townships of his parish as 'colliers and low educated people not easily brought to the sacrament'.[2]

The difference between industrial workers and others found many ways of expression. Annually at the May Day wakes on the Wrekin colliers fought farm workers for the possession of the summit, the men of the market town of Wellington venturing to join in only when the fight was evenly balanced. Fights between colliers and Severn barge-men took place regularly on market days in Ironbridge. During the miners' strike of 1842 the magistrates of Shrewsbury, 12 miles from the coalfield, feared that the colliers' traditional hostility to the county town would lead them to attack it.[3] Local oral history abounds in stories of clever men from the market town of Wellington who tried to take advantage of the apparently slow wits of Dawley colliers, but were worsted in the attempt. The problems of disciplining a population so different from that of a market town or an agricultural village were formidable. The coalfield, unlike a market town, had virtually no middle class. Unlike most agricultural villages it had no widely respected resident landowners. It was, furthermore, an area where the authority of the established church was particularly weak.

Within an ironworks discipline was relatively straightforward. To a large extent it was imposed by the obvious dangers posed by red hot billets and ladles of molten iron. At Ketley, William Reynolds and Co. enforced a code of approved behaviour upon their employees by a tariff of heavy fines. The basis of most punishments was the fine of absence, 1s., plus loss of the wages due for the time lost. Workmen in responsible positions were said to 'undertake a place', and were consequently known as Place or Plackmen. They, and other employees receiving more than 12s. a week were subject to absence fines of 1s. 6d. plus loss of wages. The absence fine was imposed for lateness, absence from work during the 12-hour shift, drunkenness, or failure to inform the management of absence through illness or accident. Employees lost a quarter of a day's wages if they lingered too long at mealbreaks, 2s. 6d. if they brought alcohol into the works without authority and 1s. more if they drank it. They forfeited 2s. 6d. for striking a fellow workman, and 1s. if they retaliated when struck. These fines were high compared with those imposed in other industries.[4]

Rules alone were insufficient to secure adequate discipline, and where constant supervision was lacking, as at Horsehay in the years immediately before Alfred and Abraham Darby IV took over management in 1830, chaos resulted. The brothers found that beer was supplied to the workers in excessive quantities, and that their constant presence was necessary to ensure that 'sleepy fillers and half-drunken keepers', continued to work. Their new management techniques were to some extent counter-productive. The payment of bounties for high output at the furnaces induced the crews to throw in loose castings from all over the works, rails, wheels and tools, in order to increase the yield. Reforms in the forges in 1837 binding the puddlers to given yields and qualities provoked a month's strike.[5] Industrial relations in the ironworks were relatively good, and it was generally agreed that ironworkers were less unruly than colliers. At Coolbrookdale punctuality was even enforced by community sanctions.

Wages in the mines rose steeply when demand in the iron industry was high. In such periods, particularly the boom years of the Napoleonic wars, going into the pit became almost a voluntary activity. In slack times the charter master could discipline his colliers by the allocation of half and quarter days. When the blast furnaces were ready to consume all of the raw materials which could be raised, such sanctions were self-defeating. In the 1830s and '40s colliers looked back with nostalgia to the war years when they were able to earn more than adequate wages by working only three or four days a week, the efforts of employers to persuade them to go in more often proving largely unsuccessful.[6]

At the workplace discipline was imposed as much by the dangers of the tasks and the motive of self-preservation as by any action of the employers. But the employer's need to discipline his workmen was not confined to the mine or the ironworks. To secure regular attendance it was necessary to control the workers' leisure time activities. Entrepreneurs became more and more concerned with the control of festivals, recreation and education in the late 18th and early 19th centuries.

The public house was, of all institutions, the most frequently blamed for the colliers' irregularities. 'The continued increase of the poor rates', wrote John Fletcher in 1783, 'is occasioned by the corrupted morals of the lower classes of the people who are seduced into idleness and neglect of their families in the public houses to be met with at every turn'. The Madeley Vestry meeting, on which both Evangelical and ironmaking interests were well represented, petitioned local magistrates in 1781 to enforce the acts of parliament regulating liquor sellers, especially those which applied to tippling, which had risen 'to an alarming and shameful height in this and the neighbouring parishes, to the disgrace of Society, the ruin of the morals of the rising generation, the total destruction of piety and virtue and the complete annoyance of every peaceable housekeeper'. The meeting demanded that there should be no more alehouses licensed in the parish and that the existing disorderly ones should be suppressed. The following year magistrates and ironmasters even hoped to put off riots by a closer imposition of controls on licensed houses.[7]

'Our parochial and national depravity', wrote John Fletcher in 1784, 'turns upon two hinges, – the profanation of the Lord's day and the immorality which flows from neglecting the education of children'. About Sunday observance there prevailed a great paradox in an iron-making district. The traditionally expensive Sunday lunch, together with heavy drinking, reduced the worker's fitness for his task on Monday or Tuesday. Yet a rigid imposition of Sabbath rest was frustrated by the necessity to keep furnaces in blast and to carry out maintenance at forges and in pits. 'No one', wrote the vicar of Madeley in 1716, 'blasphemes God's holy name in the parish. No one works on the Lord's day, except the furnacemen'.[8] For an employer whose furnacemen worked 24 hour shifts on alternate Sundays to suggest that his other workmen should exercise restraints in their Sabbath recreation was an obvious hypocrisy. Yet conscious attempts were made to enforce social discipline on Sundays. Joshua Gilpin described the efforts made by John Fletcher,

It was a common thing in his parish for young persons of both sexes to meet at stated times for the purpose of what is called recreation; and this recreation usually continued from evening till morning, consisting chiefly in dancing, revelling, drunkenness and obscenity. These licentious assemblies he considered as a disgrace to the Christian name, and determined to exert his ministerial authority for their total suppression. He has frequently burst in upon these disorderly companies with a holy indignation, making war upon Satan in places peculiarly appropriated to his service. Nor was his labour altogether in vain among the children of dissipation and folly. After standing the first shock of their rudeness and brutality, his exhortations have been generally received with silent submission and have sometimes produced a partial if not an entire reformation in many who were accustomed to frequent these assemblies.[9]

Richard Reynolds provided on the slopes of Lincoln Hill above Coalbrookdale, 'shrubs and fir trees with gravel walks through them and adorned them with temples and other ornamental buildings with iron pillars, rustic seats and other accommodation'. The area was called the Workmen's Walks, and on a Sunday, 'men, accompanied by their wives and children were induced to spend the afternoon or evening there, instead of at the public house'. Whether or not as a result of Evangelical pressures, there was some reluctance among Shropshire miners to drink on a Sunday, however much they might consume at other times.[10]

The diary of Thomas Boycott, a junior clerk at the Coalbrookdale ironworks in 1801– 06 reveals the recreational occasions which he considered important: Samuel Darby's marriage ale, the fair at Much Wenlock in May, the reviews and departures for camp of the Volunteers, the race meeting at Bridgnorth in June, the Club feasts of the local public houses, the *Rodney* and the *Swan*, early in July, and Wenlock wake in August.[11] Boycott did not mention the Wrekin Wake on the Sunday nearest to May Day which was an occasion of great local importance. Ale booths, gingerbread standings, gaming tables, swing-boats, merry-go-rounds and three-sticks-a-penny stalls were set up. Other wakes in the district, Oakengates early in October, Dawley and Madeley in September, and Broseley in November, were marked by bull-baitings. At Oakengates, colliers would save money for months beforehand to subscribe for the bull, against which the courage of their dogs would be matched. The public houses along the main street formed the 'heart' of the wake, but its 'legs and tail' extended far into the surrounding mining districts. Men and women gathered in the public houses and fiddlers provided music for those who wished to *ost* at a dance. Rings were formed when men began to fight. Swings and roundabouts were erected on the Green. There was much gambling, tossing of coins, thimble-rigging, dice-shaking and throwing at sticks. Drunkenness was obtrusive, with men helplessly staggering about the streets in daytime, and lying prone and helpless on the ground by nightfall.[12]

Animal cruelty sports were regarded by many observers as typifying the violence of the coalfield. 'This district', wrote a Wesleyan minister of Oakengates in 1835, 'is the most notorious for vice of every kind, and especially for the grossest violation of the Sabbath and the cruel practice of bull baiting'.[13]

Cockfighting in late 18th-century Shropshire was at one level an aristocratic sport. Matches between the gentlemen of Shropshire and those of neighbouring counties were regularly fought at the most exclusive public houses in the 1770s and '80s. They were aped at a lower social level by matches between the colliers of Broseley and those of south Staffordshire. By 1800 aristocratic participation in the sport was less open, and advertisements for matches became less frequent in the respectable county press. Cock fighting continued among the miners and other workers of the coalfield. About 1830 William Smith was apprenticed to a shoemaker in Wellington who kept a public house, and maintained fighting cocks and bull dogs,

> The game fighting cocks was kept at different places called Mains, usually in the country. It was part of my duties to see to them and fetch and take these birds to different parts of the county. We used to feed these birds before the fight with old beer and eggs, we fought them at what was called Mains. Ten or twelve birds would be laid down by each party or side, and the one that had most killed usually lost a great deal of money in betting &c. I remember one of these cockfights ... [where] ... my employer won so much money ... that he went to London by coach to spend it, and it was no little journey to take, in those days, to go to London by Coach.

The high value attached to fighting cocks is indicated by a reward of five guineas offered in 1778 for the return of 'a pole cat cock with only one eye and a very remarkable speckled hen,' stolen from the gate keeper at Redhill on the turnpike road from Oakengates to Ivetsey Bank.[14]

Bull baiting was less common than cock fighting, perhaps because it was more expensive. At Madeley Wake a bull was baited three times in different places on each of the three days of the wake. At Broseley, according to Randall, bull baiting was patronised by 'the lower class of the people', and was not confined to the wakes.[15]

Such sports linked the colliers with farmworkers outside the coalfield. Miners from Oakengates and Ketley would spend a week each summer at the *Bull's Head* Inn, Rodington, fighting their cocks against those of the local inhabitants. William Smith took his master's dogs to Somerwood, near Rodington, for badger baiting.[16]

Enthusiasm for animal cruelty sports epitomised the difference of the Shropshire coal and ironworker from what middle class opinion considered normal humanity. The curbing of such sports was seen not just as an end in itself but as a means of securing a wider measure of discipline among an unruly population. Evangelicals formed the spearhead of the attack on the sports. Cock fightings and bull baitings were among the events which the members of John Fletcher's Methodist society in 1762 were prohibited from attending. In 1772 Fletcher linked theatrical performances, annual wakes, horse, racing, cock fighting, man fighting and dog fighting as alike to be condemned. Fletcher's opposition to bull baiting was so well known that on one occasion the Madeley Wood colliers determined to set their dogs upon him instead of the bull.[17] Between the 1770s and the 1830s the form of attack gradually changed from moral condemnation, to social sanctions, to direct repression, and finally, after much frustration to legislative control.

Prize fighting had a considerable following. In 1863 about a thousand colliers assembled at Sutton Maddock to watch Thomas Bird fight Charles Harper in a ring defined by a line of men with sticks. 'A greater gathering than has been witnessed for many a day' watched Tom Sayers at Howe and Cushing's circus in Madeley in 1863. His jewels, rings and gold chains astonished the colliers who regarded him as a hero.

In 1788 the Madeley vestry resolved, 'no one shall be relieved that keeps a dog or a fighting cock'. Richard Reynolds in 1796 urged Sir Richard Hill, the Evangelical M.P. for the county, to try to make the proposed tax on dogs as severe as possible with regard to bull dogs so as to aid 'the suppression of the infamous practice of bull-baiting, the ill effects whereof upon the tempers and manners . . . I need not describe . . . a practice which is a disgrace to the nation, inconsistent with religion and degrading to human nature'. In 1822 cockfighters near Wellington were confronted by a revival meeting. In 1811 George Mortimer the curate of Madeley, and one of the Anstice family of the Madeley Wood Company, put down bull-baiting in the parish with a posse of constables, searching widely for the stakes used for tying up the bulls, ripping up the floors of colliers' cottages while they did so. The authorities felt 'satisfaction at the quiet and orderly behaviour . . . of the inferior classes of society who becomingly submitted to the restrictions laid down . . . for the prevention of those cruel excesses which have been generally witnessed at their annual wake'. The Broseley bull-baitings ceased in the 1820s, and by tradition the last in Shropshire took place at Oakengates Wake in 1833. In that year the Duke of Sutherland's agents executed 500 ferocious bulldogs belonging to the cottages of nearby Ketley.[18] Both cock-fighting and bull-baiting became illegal in 1835, and while the latter was difficult to conceal and probably did cease in Shropshire, the former continued for many years.

Similar means were used to attack the annual wakes. By 1826 the Wrekin May Wakes was decaying. It was 'deservedly discouraged by the magistracy' and one of the Cludde family of Orleton Hall on the outskirts of Wellington, led a force of gamekeepers to put it down. Direct action had been preceded by a confrontation with Evangelicals. In April 1808 Hugh Bourne, later one of the founders of Primitive Methodism, heard of the wakes while passing through Shropshire, and brought to the Wrekin a group of his followers from the Potteries, who organised a camp meeting in opposition to the normal festivities. In Dawley in 1851 a group of traders tried to mitigate the effects of the wakes by organising such innocent pursuits as pedestrian displays and obstacle races instead of the usual horse racing. Four local clergy nevertheless thought it necessary to innoculate their flocks from corruption by holding services throughout the wakes.[19]

Colliers and ironworkers from east Shropshire were always well represented at public executions in Shrewsbury. The execution of three Catholic Irish highwaymen in August 1836 drew to the county town crowds totalling well over 10,000, many of whom came from 'the collieries about Wellington, Ironbridge and Shifnal'. In April 1841 when Josiah Mister was hanged for the attempted murder of William Makepeace Mackreth, a *cause cèlèbre* which had aroused nationwide interest, 'the works at Ketley and Wellington sent out their hundreds of spectators'. Employers had been asked by their workers to let them 'have a holiday on Saturday to see the hanging at noon and go to the circus at two'. The opportunities for watching this form of blood sport ceased in the 1840s, soon after the demise of bull baiting.[20]

The attack on animal cruelty sports had far reaching social and political objectives. In one Evangelical tract on bull baiting which circulated in the coalfield, a working man objects that the poor are denied their traditional sports, while the rich are still allowed to shoot, hunt and race. He is told that those who go hunting,

> return home to pass the rest of the day in the society of their own families, sharing, probably, in their own tranquil occupations and making their pleasures their own. In their general habits and character they may also be found all their life long, as kind and compassionate, as gentle and amiable, as it is possible for men to be.

Why such men hunt, was explained as 'a sort of riddle'. By contrast bull baiting was carried on with 'uproar, savage ferocity and tumult', and promoted 'a love of riot and disorder, and cherishes the worst passion of the human heart'. After a baiting, men did not go home to their families but to the alehouse where drinking, gambling and swearing were the order of the day. Bull baiting engendered 'a savage thirst of blood and ferocity, like that of some of the ignobler beasts of prey, a spirit like that which animated the Conspirators of Cato Street'.[21]

Evangelicals were concerned not just to divert colliers from sports which openly inflicted cruelty on animals, but to attack a traditional way of life which encompassed many forms of behaviour, like playing the violin, which were in no way vicious. In 1764 Abiah Darby advised young people to abstain from 'joining in with the world in vain sports, games and from the observation of the times, and what is called wakes – which had their rise in the dark times of popery'.[22] Once bull baiting and cock fighting were put down by law, pressure was applied to the rustic sports, the traditional holiday and festival recreations of the district. When it was proposed to celebrate the end of the Crimean War in Wellington with wheelbarrow and sack races, climbing the greasy pole and diving for live eels, such innocent if unsophisticated pastimes were denounced by a Methodist minister as 'a revival of barbarism'.[23] Formalised athletics were promoted in the place of the traditional sports, and by the time of the Jubilee celebrations of 1887 and 1897 the latter had been entirely eliminated in Shropshire.

By the 1840s most observers agreed that the recreational pattern of the coalfield had been transformed. John Petty, the Primitive Methodist, wrote in 1846 that Oakengates was *'formerly* proverbial for brutal sports and excessive wickedness',[24] and most other contemporary accounts spoke of the animal cruelty sports in the past tense. Evangelicals claimed much credit for their suppression, but in the event direct repression by the magistrates may have been more effective than denunciation, although the creation of a climate of opinion among magistrates favourable to action against the sports probably owed much to Evangelical pressures.

An evangelical conversion which caused a collier or ironworker to abstain from bull baiting or heavy drinking made him a steadier workman, and such results led even Anglican ironmasters to abandon their hostility to Methodism. In 1801 the Botfields gave notice to members of the Wesleyan congregation at Lawley Bank who were employed at the Old Park Ironworks that they would be turned out of their cottages and lose their jobs if the preaching was not given up, but one of their agents, probably Gilbert Gilpin, prevailed upon them to keep the Methodists because they were the best men, without whom the works could not operate.[25]

'The special temptation in a colliery district', wrote a Baptist minister from Dawley at the end of the 19th century, 'is the drink traffic'. Those Evangelicals whose concern to change the recreational pattern of the coalfield extended to a determination to reduce drinking challenged an aspect of local culture that was particularly well entrenched. Quite apart from the influence of the public houses, home-brewing was widespread, many workers' cottages having their own brewhouses, and drinking was positively encouraged in the working context. Beer was provided at most ironworks, and was traditionally dispensed to miners and construction workers when specific tasks, the driving of a level, the building of a waggonway or the erection of an engine, were completed. The miners of Donnington Wood regularly received gin as well as beer in the 1770s and '80s. In 1726 Thomas Goldney even provided a gallon of brandy for his workmen when one of the Coalbrookdale furnaces was blown out.[26]

In the 18th century Evangelicals in Shropshire as elsewhere attacked public houses without attacking the principle of drinking. Neither John nor Mary Fletcher abstained from alcohol, although Victorian teetotallers claimed that they did. Their correspondence shows that they frequently received liquor from friends in London and Bristol which was often distributed to the poor. In 1809 Mary Fletcher's brother sent her 12 bottles of sherry, which he thought she would prefer to Madeira, and two gallons of brandy.

Heavy drinking was often a feature of recreations organised by paternalist employers and landowners for their workpeople. In 1809 John Rose and Co. of Coalport celebrated the 50th anniversary of the king's accession by providing for their potters six fat sheep and two hogsheads of good Shropshire ale. The Lilleshall and Ketley companies distributed roast ox, bread and beer to their employees to mark the marriage of Earl Gower in 1823. Two thousand colliers and ironworkers gathered at Malins Lee in 1828 to eat four fat oxen and drink strong ale to mark the marriage of Beriah Botfield III. The Old Park Company clerks, the workmens' wives and children, and 'the respectable inhabitants of the neighbourhood' celebrated separately. The birth of Alfred Darby's heir in 1850 was commemorated by a procession of between 3,000 and 4,000 Coalbrookdale Company employees, who subsequently ate 15,140 lbs. of beef and mutton and drank a thousand gallons of free ale.[27]

The growth of the Temperance Movement in Shropshire has yet to be investigated in detail but it was clearly well-established in the coalfield by the early 1840s. Teetotalism was being discussed among members of the Wesleyan Society at Coalport in 1837. It gave rise to great enthusiasms in Shropshire as elsewhere. In 1843 a party of colliers and cobblers from Broseley went to hold a temperance meeting in Much Wenlock. They were opposed by 'the respectable inhabitants of the town', who disturbed their meeting with conventional and rough music. While the respectable were drinking in a public house, one of the teetotallers split their drum with a razor, on the discovery of which the teetotallers were drummed out of town, and the windows of the chapel where they had met duly smashed. The Conservative county newspaper heartily approved of the breaking up of the meeting.[28]

The attack on drinking was less successful than that on animal cruelty sports. In 1857 a Wesleyan complained that drink was responsible for most of the backslidings in Methodist societies. To the end of the 19th century the coalfield retained a reputation as an area of heavy drinking, where public drunkenness was usual at weekends and festivals. The temperance movement, perhaps in consequence, continued to prosper. Teetotalism benefited during the great revival of 1862. After a successful meeting at Donnington it was reported that teetotalism 'was engrossing the attention of the working classes for miles around. Numbers are continually signing the pledge, and there is abundant testimony of much good following'. In the Dawley area the Baptists were particularly prominent in temperance movement, and members of the denomination were responsible for the erection of a large temperance hall and the formation of temperance friendly societies.

Numerous societies were formed to encourage thrift and self-improvement in the coalfield in the 1850s and 60s. The Coalbrookdale Literary and Scientific Institution, founded in 1853, was provided by the Coalbrookdale Company in 1859 with a blue and yellow brick building in the Tudor Gothic style, containing lecture and concert rooms, an art studio and a library. There were mechanics' institutes at Wellington and Donnington, a Mental Improvement Society at Little Dawley, a Church Instruction Society at Madeley, and a lodge of the United Brothers at Wellington, who organised a demonstration on the Wrekin in 1860 to draw people away from the temptations of Wellington Fair.[29]

Education was frequently canvassed as a means of controlling the unruly population of the coalfield, but until the mid-19th century its effectiveness was limited by the employment of children in mines and ironworks. There were very few schools in the district in the 18th century. In 1772 in the part of the coalfield in Lichfield diocese only Dawley and Lilleshall parishes had free schools of any kind under the patronage of Isaac Hawkins Browne and Earl Gower respectively, and catering for only about 40 children between them. John Fletcher for a time operated a small school in Madeley.[30] By the 1830s there were day schools in most parts of the coalfield, some like those at Coalbrookdale and Pool Hill, Dawley, built by the ironmasters, others, like those at St. George's and Wrockwardine Wood, provided by the church. Nevertheless the 1851 census shows that many children below 10 years of age were not attending school, and the majority of those more than 10 were working. The Sunday Schools, as the only source of education of a large proportion of the children in the district were institutions of particular importance.

The founding of Sunday Schools in east Shropshire was first suggested by Abiah Darby, widow of Abraham Darby II. In 1784 she wrote to John Fletcher about the schools established in Gloucester and Yorkshire,

> for the benefit of poor children, who have, and are suffered to play and riot about on that day, which is and ought to be dedicated to Divine worship

She asked Fletcher,

> to labour to promote there being set up in this parish as they may be productive of great good to inculcate into the minds of poor children the holy fear of Almighty God and their duty to parents and one another.[31]

Abiah Darby's request was probably the cause of Fletcher's proposals to start six Sunday Schools in the parish, one for boys and one for girls at Coalbrookdale, Madeley Wood and Madeley town, to be financed by subscriptions of £20 a year. Reading and writing as well as the principles of morality and piety were to be taught, and the schools were intended particularly for children who were employed all the week.[32]

In 1786 Richard Reynolds began a Sunday School at Ketley because of 'the very great want of such means of improvement and civilisation among the numerous poor children of the Marquis of Stafford's cottages, whose parents are employed in the works'. He estimated that there were 300 potential scholars and that a building 80 ft. long, 14 ft. wide and 7 or 8 ft. high without a ceiling would accommodate them. Two years later he reported that the school 'doth not much decline; but, from its being situated where the few who can be procured to act as teachers are almost wholly without the aid of visitors, it doth not flourish as I am glad to hear the schools do in many other places'. By 1799 there was a Sunday School in Dawley parish supported by Isaac Hawkins Browne and the Old Park Company, and in the 1830s they were to be found at most of the churches and chapels in the district.[33]

'The principles of morality and piety', were broadly interpreted in the Sunday Schools. Fletcher hoped that the schools by preventing the desecration of the Lord's day and by educating children would remedy some of the worse faults in society,

> our workhouses full of aged parents forsaken by their prodigal children, wives deserted by their faithless husbands; the wretched offspring of lewd women and idle and drunken men.

He quoted with approval a 'pious clergyman', who also advocated Sunday Schools as a means of social reformation, regretting the sight of children,

> who live in gross ignorance and habitual profanation of the Lord's day. What crowds fill the streets and fields, tempting each other to idleness, lewdness and every other species of wickedness. Is it any wonder that we should have so many undutiful children, unfaithful apprentices, disobedient servants, untrusty workmen, disloyal subjects and bad members of society? Whence so much rapine, fornication and blasphemy? Do not all these evils centre in ignorance and contempt of the Lord's day?[34]

The aims of Evangelicals seeking moral reform and of entrepreneurs trying to discipline their labour force closely coincided. They both placed particular stress on the proper spending of time. A dying 10-year-old in Madeley in 1807 told his Wesleyan father how his soul was grieved to see workmen playing and trifling, 'Sure they forget that God sees their every moment'. A child wrote to Mary Tooth about 1802, 'Sarah says I am very idle or I should have more time to read . . . I must pray that God will help me and that I may not waste a moment of my time'.[35]

Robert Southey considered, 'Mr. Wesley's notions concerning education must have done great evil. No man was every more thoroughly ignorant of the nature of children'. John Fletcher's views of education did not differ materially from those of the founder of Methodism. 'How excessively foolish are the plays of children', he wrote in 1772, 'how full of mischief and cruelty the sports of boys! How vain, foppish and frothy the joys of young people!'[36] Many of the Sunday Schools in the coalfield were conducted with much the same attitude to the young.

The tracts written by the wife of the vicar of St. George's in the early 19th century suggest that the teaching of deference was a major objective in Sunday Schools. The non-deferential poor are usually portrayed as vicious and unthinking. 'There is not much to be greedy about in poor folks' houses', retorts the mother of a naughty child to his schoolmaster. 'We may be as greedy over a dish of potatoes and bacon as over the grandest dinner; and a little child may be as greedy and self-indulgent over an apple or a bit of toffee as a grown up man over his ale', retorts the master. The same fictitious school master in another tract discovers a theft, ritually beats the culprit, and takes him from his parents to settle him as a waggoner's boy, justifying his action by saying that a boy who steals a knife unpunished will steal a sheep or a horse when he is a man.[37]

Another tract concerns Edward Davies and Richard Walker, two 10-year-olds who live in a manufacturing country but cannot find employment because trade is bad. Edward Davis earns 1d. by minding a gentleman's horse, after which another gentleman gives him 9d. and he buys a Testament. Richard Walker is given a shilling which he spends on apples and gunpowder. While Edward Davis is at Church, Richard Walker is blinded while playing with gunpowder in an old brick kiln. Edward Davies goes to see his friend, and as he stands by his bed thinks of 'the fearful end of the wicked, the importance of observing the Sabbath, the peace and security which is to be had in the ways of God'. A clergyman tells Richard Walker's parents, 'Had your son been brought up to attend church regularly, had he been taken there by yourselves, and had he been restrained by your commands and your example from buying on the Sabbath, this sad affair could never have happened'. Eventually the boy recovers the sight of one eye. The tract is remarkable for its utter insensitivity to the situation of the child in an industrial society, and for its profound joylessness. There is a complete acceptance of the normality of child labour, it is simply unfortunate that bad trade prevents the boys finding jobs. There is a complete rejection of childlike pleasures; the oranges, mint cakes and tarts in the shop where Richard Walker buys apples are just so many temptations to vice.[38]

Such attitudes bred a deep resentment among the children of the coalfield. 'I do not go to Sunday School now', said a 14-year-old miner in 1842, 'it is too much confinement to us who have been at work all the week'. 'I never sleep in Sunday school', said another miner of the same age, 'for fear of being beat for it'. 'The boys at Madeley Wood Sunday School', said another, 'are obliged to mind what they say for fear of the cane'.[39] Doubtless many people in the coalfield benefited from literacy acquired in Sunday Schools in the early 19th century, but for many scholars they were institutions which served only to prolong the agonies of the working week.

XX

TIMES OF CRISIS

Riots and the threats of riots were as common in east Shropshire as in other industrial parts of England in the 18th century. As elsewhere, rises in the cost of provisions were the most frequent cause of popular discontent, and the measures taken to secure redress of grievances were not blind acts of violence but customary forms of behaviour amounting almost to ritual.[1] Disturbances in Shropshire in the 18th century were marked by an anxious concern on the part of the ironmasters for the safety of their installations, and appeasement was in consequence the normal entreprenurial reaction of the threat of riots. After 1800 the characteristics of crises changed. Disturbances were provoked not by high food prices but by threats of reductions in wages. The reaction of the ironmasters was not to provide cheap food but to call for troops. The anger of the rioters was directed not against farmers, millers and bakers but against their employers and their employers' installations.

At the height of the first great boom in the coke iron industry early in November 1756, the coalfield was disturbed by a whole week of riots.[2] They broke out at a time when 'there was not a bit of bread nor corn nor flower to be had for money for some miles about – so that the country was in the greatest distress'. The first to riot were colliers of Broseley, Madeley Wood and Benthall, who were later joined by other miners from Oakengates and Dawley, by those of the Coalbrookdale partnership, a few Coalbrookdale ironworkers and some Severn bargemen. The rioters assembled each morning to the blowing of horns, and gave themselves the title of 'levellers'.

On Monday 1 November they visited the market at Much Wenlock, on Tuesday they went to Shifnal, on Wednesday to Broseley, on Thursday to Wellington, and on Saturday a visit to Bridgnorth was planned. At Much Wenlock the colliers insisted on buying grain at customary prices, 5s. a bushel for wheat, 2s. 6d. for barley, and 2s. 2d. for oats. Some grain at least was available at the market, and the rioters 'did not comit any great outrage that day'. On subsequent days, farmers declined to expose their produce for sale, and the level of violence steadily increased. On the way to Shifnal the rioters sought contributions from farmers, who gave them food and ale, and they persuaded an elderly magistrate to ride on horseback in the midst of them. At Shifnal many houses were searched for food, and some was taken without payment. At Broseley the Riot Act was read with no effect other than the uttering of a loud 'Huzza'. The colliers told the magistrates that they valued neither the proclamation nor those who uttered it. Bakers' shops were attacked and their bread freely distributed. At Wellington there was again considerable plunder, and the day concluded with a fight between townsmen and colliers after one of the latter snatched a piece of beef from a butcher's stall.

One of the most significant incidents of the week took place at Coalbrookdale on the Thursday morning when the colliers were heading for Wellington. Some of the Dale workmen had been active among the rioters at Shifnal on the Tuesday, and there had been a threat that if the ironworkers were not allowed to march to Wellington the Dale works would be destroyed. When the colliers called at Coalbrookdale on the Thursday morning Hannah Darby said, 'they behaved pretty civil only asking for meat and drink which we were glad to give them to keep them quiet'. Abraham Darby II gave one of his clerks £20 to present to the colliers' leaders if the destruction of the works should be threatened but this was not necessary. The Darbys employed several men to carry buckets of ale down the drive to their gate, and three days' bread was baked for distribution. Quakers were the victims of riots in 1756 throughout Britain, and in spite of this generous treatment it was believed that the plundering of the Darby's house was planned on the Friday.

The riots were put down by possees of farmers and their labourers led by local magistrates. In the north of the coalfield a force led by Edward Cludde and Edward Pemberton, estimated to be nearly 1,500 strong, accompanied by a gang of Wellington tradesmen, encountered the colliers near Ketley, marching towards them along the Coalbrookdale Company's railway line. 10 were taken prisoner and two of them subsequently executed. In the south of the coalfield a force of about 1,000 led by Brooke Forester seized those believed to be ringleaders in the Forester manors of Broseley and Little Wenlock. Many miners had taken provisions underground and some were fetched up with their booty.

On the Saturday positive measures were taken by magistrates to prevent rioting at Bridgnorth market. Sir Thomas Whitmore and Sir Richard Acton instructed their tenants to sell wheat at the customary price of 5s. per bushel, and promised to reduce their rents in consequence. The following year Abraham Darby II petitioned for mercy on behalf of four of the captured rioters who had been reprieved from hanging but sentenced to 14 years' transportation. He insisted that they were honest, industrious and laborious workmen until they were drawn into the riots by the threatenings of others, and with a view to procure sustenance for their starving families.[3]

Many features of the food riots of 1756 indicate the adherence of the rioters to a traditional moral economy, and their belief that they were in some way acting within the law to set right injustices perpetrated by profiteers. The rioters were called together by the sounding of horns, they insisted that a magistrate should accompany them to Shifnal, they collected money as of right, they observed a measure of discipline and restraint. To a large extent the rioters achieved their objectives. The local magistrates took effective measures to hold down grain prices and to ensure that supplies continued to flow to local markets. In the long term, the behaviour of the Darbys set a precedent which was to be followed by paternalist ironmasters for half a century.

In 1782 there were again threats of riots when food prices rose steeply. As in 1756 they occurred in the autumn following a bad harvest. In October while there was rioting in the Wednesbury and Stourbridge areas, colliers threatened to 'go to regulate the market', at Wellington.[4] A meeting was called at the *Talbot Hotel* in Wellington early in November to consider how 'riots among colliers occasioned by the high price of provisions', should be prevented and suppressed. The meeting included a wide cross-section of the ruling classes of the coalfield, landowners and magistrates like

George Forester, Edward Cludde, Richard and Noel Hill, Isaac Hawkins Browne, John Smitheman and Edward Pemberton, entrepreneurs like Richard and William Reynolds, Thomas Botfield and William Ferriday, and Evangelical clergyman like John Fletcher of Madeley and John Rocke, vicar of Wellington. The social isolation of the Quakers is nicely illustrated by the remark of Richard Reynolds's biographer that Reynolds was induced to 'unite with the gentlemen of the neighbourhood' at this meeting.[5]

The meeting at the *Talbot* took actions which reflected the inclinations of all of its varied members. A troop of horse was sent for. A subscription, 'for the relief of such industrious poor as behaved themselves in an orderly and peaceable manner', was begun. The magistrates present agreed to reduce the number of alehouses, particularly suppressing those whose keepers 'should harbour Labourers, Colliers, &c. to drink and tipple on the Lord's Day, or at any unseasonable hours, or shall draw them any more liquor that was necessary for moderate refreshment'. For the first time flour and rice were purchased in Liverpool with the money raised by the subscription, and brought to Shropshire under armed guard by canal, probably by way of Gailey wharf. The meeting's actions seem to have been effective for disturbances on the scale of those of 1756 did not occur, John Fletcher was particularly proud of his part in suppressing the threatened riots. He wrote to Charles Wesley in December,

> The colliers began to rise in this neighbourhood: happily the cockatrice's egg was crushed before the serpent came out. However, I got many a hearty curse from the colliers for the plain words I spoke on that occasion.[6]

The distress of 1782 may well have stimulated the erection of the first rotative steam engine in Shropshire. On 23 November William Reynolds wrote to James Watt asking the price of one of his new rotative engines sufficient to work two pairs of common millstones, explaining that, 'from the high price of provisions and the present distress of the poor that consideration [i.e. the building of a mill] is a material object to us'. John Randall, quoting from sources no longer available, believed that one of the first Watt rotative engines was duly supplied and set to work a corn mill at Ketley. The crisis of 1782 saw the first application of a programme for buying off violence which was employed with some effect during the Revolutionary and Napoleonic Wars. The profound social gulf between masters and men is nowhere more apparent than in the deliberations of the ironmasters, yet there did exist in the 1790s a sense of at least some community of purpose. While colliers and ironworkers demanded the right to purchase provisions at customary prices, ironmasters felt a responsibility to feed their work people. If the final years of the 18th century 'saw a last desperate effort by the people to reimpose the older moral economy as against the economy of the market place', it was an effort on the part of the ironmasters as well as their employees.[7]

The introduction by the Coalbrookdale partners of a new system of regulating wages and hours of work led to the threat of riots in 1791. On Monday 8 August feeling against the new regulations became so intense that about a thousand workers assembled and threatened to destroy Richard Reynolds's house. Reynolds made some concessions which eased the atmosphere, but not before a troop of the Royal Oxford Blues had been summoned from Wolverhampton. The soldiers stayed in the Coalbrookdale region until Friday 12 August, and Reynolds paid them 50 guineas for their services. Three men and a woman were subsequently fined and imprisoned for taking part in riots at Coalpit Bank and Wrockwardine Wood.[8]

Bread prices reached a very high level in January 1795 when subscriptions were raised for the relief of the colliers, and eleven unemployed Ketley men dragged a waggon loaded with coal to Shrewsbury. In July of that year the wants of the poor, according to Richard Reynolds, were 'far beyond what has been at any former time experienced'. Reynolds believed that the total quantity of grain available in the whole country was far short of what would be required before the harvest was brought in. Many families in east Shropshire were entirely without bread.

At a meeting of gentlemen, farmers, millers, tradesmen and ironmasters held in Ironbridge on 9 July 1795 it was resolved to raise a subscription from which food prices would be subsidised. Grain would be purchased at 12s. a bushell to be sold to the poor at 9s. The subscription would be used to cover the loss of 3s. a bushel and the costs of milling. In addition large quantities of Indian Corn were ordered from Liverpool. Subscriptions from local landowners, iron companies and ironmasters were of the order of 100 guineas each, and subscribers included George and Cecil Forester, Isaac Hawkins Browne, the Coalbrookdale Company, Richard Reynolds and John Wilkinson. Reynolds and Wilkinson took advantage of their own involvement in agriculture to bring grain from their farms on to the market below the prevailing prices. Early in August a cargo of corn from Liverpool for the poor of the Wellington area was stopped by a demonstrating crowd as it passed along the Staffordshire and Worcestershire Canal at Radford Bridge near Stafford, but it was allowed to go on after the intercession of a local landowner. Fixing prices and importing grain were not wholly sufficient to maintain public order. On 27 July one of the clerks of the Coalbrookdale Company apologised to Boulton and Watt that the manager was unable to write to them himself because he had been 'very much engaged among the colliers in this neighbourhood who have shown a disposition to riot', and on 30 July the Wrekin Company of the Shropshire Yeomanry Cavalry, raised only three months previously, was employed to disperse rioters at Madeley Wood, which they were able to do with no more than a show of their pistols.[9]

The impact of the French Revolution can be seen in a letter which Richard Reynolds wrote to John Smitheman after the Ironbridge meeting, calling on him to instruct his tenants to make grain available at 12s. a bushel. Reynolds warned that the poor were likely to make demands at houses from which they felt they ought to be relieved, or where they expected to find provisions. If farmers could not show that they had contributed to the relief of local distress mischief might commence, 'the end of which, if once begun, it is impossible to ascertain . . . such is the urgency of the temper of the people, that there is not a day to lose if we are desirous to preserve the poor from outrage, and most likely the country from plunder if not from blood'.[10]

The local situation did not improve after the harvest of 1795, and the following year another subscription was raised to purchase rice for the poor. How grave were the fears of the ironmasters can be seen from the scale of their contributions: £1,500 from John Bishton and Co., £1,500 from the Old Park Co., £2,000 from the Ketley Co., £1,500 from the Coalbrookdale Co., £1,000 from the Madeley Wood Co. and £500 from Richard Reynolds personally.[11]

There were further severe shortages in the autumn of 1799 and the early months of 1800. In September 1799 colliers faced with families who were starving were agitated by the high price of corn and the reluctance of farmers to take it to local markets. A 'rice committee' was formed at a meeting of ironmasters and gentry held on 28 February 1800, and casks of rice were delivered by barge to Coalbrookdale. The scale of contributions was again impressive. The Ketley Co. donated £2,000, the Old Park Co. and

John Bishton and Co. £1,500 each, and the Coalbrookdale and Madeley Wood Companies £1,000 each. The majority of the ironmasters who attended the meeting gave personal contributions of £100, but William Reynolds gave £500. Troops were sent to keep peace in the coalfield, and their general urged landowners to gain control of the price of grain. In the autumn of 1800 millers in the vicinity proclaimed that they would not buy new wheat at a price higher than 12s. a bushel and they were supported by many local farmers and landowners. There was some resistance to the eating of rice. Lucy Cameron's typical pitman's wife 'had no notion of using rice or anything else in the place of bread, and indeed would not do so if it were recommended to her'.[12]

The seven-year period of depression in the iron trade between 1815 and 1822 was one of profound social crisis in Shropshire, a crisis in which an awareness of national political issues was more apparent than in those of the 18th century, and one in which the ancient sense of contract between ironmasters and men, by which the men refrained from damaging works in return for the masters' assuming responsibility for their relief, was no longer evident.

John Randall described the 1820s in the coalfield as a time when,

> it was not so much Whig and Tory, as Tory and Revolutionist. Society was divided into two completely hostile camps. Abuses which no one now will deny existed, but to call for their removal then was to subject oneself to bitter hostility and to be denounced as innovators and rebels against king and country . . . justices of the peace were tools in the hands of others to torture, imprison or banish those who made themselves obnoxious by the least disposition to exhibit an independent spirit.

Randall makes it clear that there was a ready market in east Shropshire for radical publications, and preserved several traditions regarding the methods by which they were surreptitiously distributed.[13]

Initially the issues in the crisis were economic ones. The depression in the iron trade was at its worst in 1816–17, and wage reductions were imposed by the ironmasters in an attempt to keep down costs. In 1817 such reductions led to a strike of Shropshire puddlers, acting in support of their fellow puddlers in the Black Country. Not surprisingly in such a severe recession, the strike proved ineffective. In 1820 a strike of colliers and ironworkers also caused by threatened reductions in wages, led to the calling out of several troops of Yeomanry, who were attacked as they patrolled through Wombridge and Wrockwardine Wood by colliers wielding bludgeons and throwing stones. Colonel Cludde of the Yeomanry persuaded the strikers to accept arbitration by a board of four landowners and a clergyman, none of whom was directly connected with the iron trade. The arbitrators agreed that the men were entitled to their old level of wages and the strike was accordingly called off.[14]

Meanwhile throughout Shropshire the political aspects of the crisis were becoming steadily more apparent. In March 1820 the possession of a copy of the *Black Dwarf* was used as evidence of the bad character of a Shrewsbury man accused of burglary. The news of the result of Queen Caroline's trial in November 1820 was greeted in Madeley by the ringing of bells, bonfires, the public roasting of an ox and several sheep, and a dinner attended by a hundred people at the *Golden Ball* Inn, presided over by a shoemaker disciple of Cobbett. There were also rejoicings in Shrewsbury, Shifnal and Bridgnorth. The county newspapers gave considerable space to reports of the trials of Henry 'Orator' Hunt after Peterloo, and of the Cato Street Conspirators.[15]

The atmosphere of crisis is vividly conveyed in the speeches made at a series of loyalty meetings held by the gentlemen of the county during January 1821. An address adopted at a meeting at Much Wenlock declared,

> We cannot at a moment like the present, when the Standard of Sedition has been unfurled, and every attempt made to delude the Unthinking from their Allegiance, omit this Declaration of our unshaken Devotion to your Majesty's sacred person and to that Establishment so long the Admiration and Envy of surrounding nations.

At a meeting in Shrewsbury on 10 January attempts to amend a resolution of loyalty so that it supported the King instead of the ministry were hastily rejected. One speaker declared that the country would not,

> be misled by the delusions of the philanthropists and the misrepresentations of the disaffected . . . but support that tried and good old Constitution under which we enjoy so many valuable privileges.

Another asked the meeting,

> if they ever heard of a period in which the Altar, the Throne, and the Legislature have been so grossly insulted as within the last few months . . . if publications more disgustingly blasphemous, more seditious could have been composed than those which have appeared in various forms of parodies and libels on all that a good and loyal man holds dear . . . It will no longer be a struggle for power between Whig and Tory . . . it will be a struggle between You who have everything to lose and Wretches who have everything to win.[16]

A few weeks afterwards, on 29 January 1821, wage reductions were announced by most of the Shropshire ironmaking partnerships. Two days later many colliers did not go to work but loitered around the pit tops.[17] Some went to pits which were still operating and demanded that the miners should be brought to the surface. The next day, 1 February, parties of colliers went to the ironworks to encourage men to strike. They visited Ketley, the Ragfield works at New Hadley where boilers were plugged, and the Wombridge ironworks where they brought production to a halt. Between 300 and 500 went to the Lilleshall Co.'s Donnington Wood furnaces where the company's bailiff warned them, 'Lads, I hope you come to do no mischief here, it will be worse for yourselves if you do'. One of the men then replied, 'Damn your eyes, what do you drop the men's wages for?' Others shouted, 'We want a big loaf and our old wages'. Stones were thrown at constables, then the foundry was stopped, the employees in the casting house forced out, and the boilers of the blast engine plugged.

The next day it was intended similarly to bring to a halt the ironworks in the southern part of the coalfield. A large force of colliers, initially between 300 and 400 strong, went first to the Old Park ironworks where the boilers were plugged, all four blast furnaces stopped, and the casting bell rung until it broke. The colliers then went to the pits at Stirchley where men were called up from underground to join them. The marchers proceded to Dawley Castle ironworks where boilers were plugged and the furnaces stopped, to Lightmoor where six boilers were plugged, and to Horsehay where all production came to a halt. They were heading for Coalbrookdale when news came that a body of constables and yeomanry cavalry had been called out. The marchers retreated towards Old Park, where about 3,000 gathered on the cinderhills, the waste-products of 30 years of iron making.

There they were confronted by magistrates, police and military. The reading of the Riot Act was greeted with shouts of, 'We will have our wages', and, 'Yonder they are, let us get together, if we are to fight for it, let's all get together'. The crowd remained very noisy and did not disperse. After an hour a squad of constables and cavalrymen seized two suspected ringleaders, Samuel Hayward and a man called Hassell. The colliers and ironworkers massed on the tips on either side of the road leading towards Wellington, and when the cavalry tried to take the two prisoners to the lock-up in that town, began to pelt them with heavy lumps of slag. The cavalry then opened fire, killing one collier, William Bird, and fatally wounding another, Thomas Gittins. Hayward and Hassell were released, the latter soon to be recaptured, but the former succeeded in escaping altogether. One cavalryman was dangerously wounded when his pistol went off in his pocket. William Turner, the clerk to the magistrates, received a wound in his arm which prevented him from using it for a week, and several cavalrymen were severely wounded by stones.

Several prisoners were taken during the next few days. One of the colliers' leaders, Thomas Palin was discovered because he had a shot wound in his arm, was sentenced to death at the Assize in March and executed on 7 April. Samuel Hayward also received a death sentence but was reprieved. Seven others were gaoled for nine months for rioting.

The day after the riots several other troops of Yeomanry cavalry entered the mining district, to be joined later by a troop of the 6th Dragoons. On Monday, 5 February the horsemen paraded through the coalfield to 'deter the turbulent part of the population', and protect those miners who wished to return to work.

The next day the iron companies in the north of the coalfield, including the Botfields and the Lilleshall Co. compromised with their employees, agreeing to reduce wages by 4d. a day instead of 6d., after which the men went back to work, but in the southern part of the district, the Coalbrookdale, Lightmoor and Madeley Wood companies insisted on the full reduction, in consequence of which the local magistrates feared further disorders.

The Shropshire iron trade recovered during 1822, and until 1830 there was a period of full work in which several new groups of blast furnaces were commissioned. This time of prosperity was succeeded by five years of bad trade, although distress at this time was never so acute as in the years between 1815 and 1822. Early in 1830 William Botfield wrote to the Coalbrookdale Company, 'We have but little demand for any kind of iron', and proposed reductions of colliers' and ironworkers' wages. Conditions did not improve, and at the end of 1831 came a further social crisis.[18]

On 5 December 1831 the miners in the Shropshire coalfield struck in protest against the lack of work at satisfactory wages, and in support of demands made by south Staffordshire colliers who had stopped work some days earlier.[19] The same day orders were sent to the Shropshire Yeomanry Cavalry to assemble at Wellington, and during the remainder of the week the troops were employed to protect ironworks and collieries. On 8 December they frustrated an attempt by the strikers to close the Steeraway limestone mines but on 10 December they were unable to prevent 1,000 people from going to Blists Hill and cutting pit winding-ropes. On Wednesday 14 December a meeting of magistrates and ironmasters was called at which evidence was given by a delegation of strikers. The ironmasters agreed to listen to what the strikers had to say, but refused to enter into any discussion with them. No agreement was reached at the meeting, and widespread violence expected on the following Friday was countered by the parading of the yeomanry through the district. William Botfield entertained the troops to lunch on the lawn of his house at Malins Lee. The commander of the Yeomanry took every opportunity to argue with such strikers as they met, pointing out to them 'the impropriety of their conduct'. At Snedshill the Earl of Powis addressed a group of workmen, and distributed sovereigns to several poor women. The expected disorders did not ensue, and the following day some miners returned to work, to be followed by the remainder on Monday 19 December.

There was a marked division in 1831 between the magistrates, who as in 1820, were anxious for a compromise which would diminish the threat to public order, and the ironmasters who were 'determined not to raise wages in the present state of trade'. The latter issued a handbill deploring the traditional practice among the wealthier classes in the district of giving money to groups of striking colliers, although they raised no public objections when the Earl of Powis dispensed sovereigns at Snedshill. As in other social crises in Shropshire, there was a strong belief among the magistrates in 1831 that disturbances were the result of mischief-making by outside organisers, and that the riotous assemblies were made up of young men and boys. Just as John Fletcher had been prominent in the suppression of the riots of 1782, so Charles Cameron, the Evangelical vicar of St. George's, and like Fletcher an opponent of traditional recreations, was active on the side of the magistrates and yeomanry in 1831.

The miners' strike of 1831 was only one manifestation of the social tensions which persisted in Shropshire during the period of the Reform Bill crisis. Another was the strike of potters at the Coalport china factory in November 1833, 'a memorable event in the history of the works, so much so that in speaking of occurrences it is usual . . . to ask in case of doubt if it happened before or subsequent to the strike'.[20] Throughout 1830 and 1831 incendiarism was rife throughout the county, some of it certainly politically motivated. The County Fire Office announced in February 1831 that its losses in the previous year amounted to nearly £30,000, 'chiefly arising from the destruction of farming and other property by incendiarism'.[21]

The issue of Parliamentary Reform, like that of dealing with strikes and riots, frequently divided ironmasters from the majority of the county gentry. Some iron-making families, like the Botfields, were Conservatives and opponents of reform, but others actively supported it. William Hazledine, owner of the Calcutts ironworks during its last unprofitable years, and of ironworks at Shrewsbury and Plas Kynaston was a speaker at Reform meetings in Shrewsbury. James Foster, owner of the Wombridge ironworks, of mines in Broseley and of the Madeley Court estate, secured election as M.P. for Bridgnorth in 1831 as 'an avowed advocate of Reform'. Two of the partners in the Ketley Company were among those who sat down to a Reform dinner in Shrewsbury in June 1831.[22]

The influence of the ironmasters could have little effect on elections in the overwhelmingly Conservative county constituency – Shropshire was the only English county to return two opponents of Reform to Parliament in 1831 – but their sympathies had greater potential in the borough constituency of Wenlock, which included Madeley, Little Wenlock and Broseley. The politics of Wenlock in the 18th and early 19th centuries were traditionally dynastic. For many years the power of the Forester family of Willey Hall to nominate both members for the borough remained unchallenged, but after a hotly-contested election in 1820, an agreement was made in 1822 that the right to nominate should be shared with the Wynn family of Wynnstay, who, like the Foresters, were considerable landowners in the borough. In 1820 the ironmasters did not involve themselves in the contested election, but lent passive support to the Foresters. In 1832 an independent radical candidate Mathew Bridges, a Bristol lawyer, was brought forward to oppose the nominees of the Foresters and Wynns by 'the

Quaker iron masters of Coalbrook Dale on the radical pledges of vote by ballot, triennial parliaments and the total repeal of the Corn Laws'.[23] Reform was a popular cause in Broseley and Madeley where the passing of the Reform Act had been 'celebrated by a procession of 12,000 people', and Bridges attracted considerable support in the industrial parts of Wenlock. This was wholly insufficient to outweigh the strength of the gentry in the agricultural districts of the borough, and he was heavily defeated. When the victorious George Forester processed through Coalbrookdale on 26 December 1832 he was pelted with mud, and a baker from Much Wenlock who broke his promise to vote for Bridges had his cart upset at Madeley market.[24]

Political divisions between industrialists, both masters and men, on the one hand, and conservative gentry on the other, were common in the West Midlands and the Borderland during the Reform Bill crisis. At Shrewsbury in 1831 the candidature of the Radical Robert Slaney was supported by Henry Benyon the flax master, and contingents of white-aproned flax dressers were prominent in Slaney's victory processions. In Montgomeryshire in 1831 the Liberal Joseph Hayes Lyon received substantial support from spinners and weavers from Newtown.[25] The strike and threatened riots in the Shropshire coalfield in 1831 indicate in this context the complexity of class relationships at this period. The 'genuine divisions' which arose between ironmasters and gentry in Wenlock borough between 1820 and 1832[26] included disagreements on how the threat of riots should be faced, in which the cause of moderation was argued by the gentry. Yet on the issue of Parliamentary Reform there was an enthusiastic solidarity between ironworkers and their employers, directed against the Conservative gentry.

The late 1830s were a time of prosperity in the iron trade, 1839 being a year of particularly good profits, but 1840 was a poor year, and 1842 a very bad one. As was customary in such years, the iron masters tried to reduce wages. The pikeman's daily rate, which had been as high as 3s. 1d. in 1836, and 2s. 10d. in 1830, had sunk to 2s. by January 1842. The bandsman's wage 2s. 6d. compared with 3s. 6d. in 1836 and 3s. 3d. in 1839.[27] In midsummer attempts were made to reduce wages still further. The Ketley Company cut the basic daily rates by 3d. in May, and in July the Lilleshall Company followed suit.[28]

The Chartists were widely blamed for the strike which resulted from the wage reductions. Chartism never had the same appeal in the coalfield that it enjoyed in textile districts or in market towns. The movement received some impetus from the wage reductions in May 1842. An attempt was made to form an association in Oakengates, but public meetings received only limited support. At the end of May meetings were held at Watling Street, Wellington, at Coalbrookdale and at Broseley. The *Northern Star* claimed that over 260 members had been enrolled in the Coalbrookdale Association. On Monday, 16 May a great meeting was planned on the summit of the Wrekin, and since the day was fine large numbers of families were attracted to it, but the police stopped women and children from ascending the hill, which destroyed the holiday atmosphere, and the meeting disappointed its organisers.[29]

A poem, *The book of Demonstration*, in Biblical style verse mildy satirises the Chartists and the failure of the Wrekin meeting.[30] It is dedicated 'to be sung in all the workshops and casting houses in Coalbrookdale and Coalport', and partially indentifies a number of Chartists who had previously been active Free Traders 'Thomas, surnamed Cobbett, who dwelt in Queen Street [Broseley] anunst a doctor's shop', 'John, (who had the appearance of a little child) who dwelt in the valley which runneth towards the Jigger

Bank', (Coalbrookdale), 'William, a maker of woollen garments who dwelt to the eastward of the parish pound as thous goest to Madeley', 'John, professedly a water bibber and lecturer on Theoloy-a-li-ty, who dwelt at Coalport'. Another John, the chairman, had charge of the company warehouse at Coalbrookdale and was also a 'water bibber', or teetotaller, and other Chartists included John, a mechanic, Thomas, a weaver, and William, a baker. In the present state of knowledge of local working class politics it is not possible to identify the Chartists more fully, but the poem does show that the Chartist movement in the district drew its strength from the labour aristocracy of the Coalbrookdale ironworks and Coalport potteries and from among small traders. How much such men influenced the miners' strike is an open question.

The one professed Chartist to be arrested in the district in 1842 was Thomas Halford, a shoemaker, once an Anti-Corn Law League lecturer, formerly a Wesleyan, and later a Methodist New Connexion preacher, who lived at Coalbrookdale and spoke at a number of local Chartist meetings. He was assisted by another lecturer, a Mr. Mogg.[31] There is very little evidence that the miners' strike of July and August 1842 was politically inspired, the six points of the Charter were not stressed at strike meetings, but the Chartists were satisfied to accept the credit for the strike lavished upon them by many local magistrates, and ironmasters were sufficiently concerned by the threat of Chartism to distribute anti-revolutionary propaganda among their workers.

Disturbances began on Wednesday 20 July when the Lilleshall Company announced that wages would be reduced. Machinery was broken and ropes cut as pits in Donnington Wood, Priorslee, and Old Park. It was widely believed that Staffordshire men had inspired the riots, but the supposed ringleaders who were arrested were all local men. Five were taken by the police at Donnington Barracks on the Wednesday night after the crowd had dispersed.

The South Shropshire Yeomanry were summoned and arrived at Priorslee Hall early on the Thursday morning, to be joined by the Bridgnorth troop later in the day. A small body of colliers assembled at Old Park where they forced a number of pits to cease work before proceeding to Ketley Bank. Here they were confronted by a force of cutlass-bearing police who chased them up and down the pit mounts, successfully dispersing them. No prisoners were taken, most of the colliers escaping by mingling with the crowds at Wellington market, although three more were captured at Donnington Wood on the following day.

The activities of the demonstrating colliers were much more like those of their 18th-century forebears than of sophisticated exponents of the Charter. As in 1756, 1795 and 1831, parties went to wealthy households to ask for food or money. Class antagonisms were strongly expressed however. William Bulger, a bailiff in charge of a pit at Priorslee, refused to draw up the men who were underground. Six of the colliers lifted him above the scalding water of the engine boiler and threatened to immerse him, one of them remarking, 'He's just like the masters, he wants to clem us to death'. As in 1821 the demonstrations began in the north of the coalfield, and again as in 1821, the intention of the collieries was to march to Coalbrookdale. Estimates of the number involved on 20 July varied from 300 to 2,000.

A partial return to work followed the arrival of the Yeomanry, but the atmosphere of the coalfield remained tense, and in August many more men struck, so that by the middle of the month almost all of the mines north of the Severn were standing. The strike was confined to the mines. The ironworks continued to operate, although after a fortnight without supplies some blast furnaces were threatened with blowing out. A series of Chartist meetings took place during the strike at which men were advised to stand out for their rights. Some damage was done at the pits, boilers plugged and ropes cut, but all of it during the hours of darkness. More serious disturbances were daily expected, and the citizens of Shrewsbury lived in fear of an armed attack by the colliers.[32]

The crisis was handled by the authorities with a sympathy and understanding[33] quite unlike the attitudes displayed in 1821, although there was available in 1842 an instrument for the containing of disturbances, the police force, which had been lacking 21 years earlier. The Lord Lieutenant, the Duke of Sutherland, remained on his Dunrobin (Co. Sutherland) estates throughout the crisis, and the responsibility for handling the strike was that of his deputy, Edward Herbert, second Earl of Powis. As Lord Clive, Herbert had been Lord Lieutenant of Montgomeryshire in 1839, and in the Chartist riots at Llanidloes had seen what havoc could be created in a tense situation by the irresponsible panicking of local magistrates.[34] Throughout the Shropshire crisis of 1842 his policy was one of restraint. His sympathies with the miners were real, and deepened as his knowledge of the coalfield increased. On 21 August he gave instructions that the uniformed Yeomanry should not be brought into collision with the people, 'particularly when suffering as they are now from want of employment'. The soldiers were carefully concealed at Priorslee Hall during the crisis for use only as a last resort, and the confrontation of the strikers was left to the police. All the Shropshire Constabulary were on duty in the Wellington area by 20 August, and they were aided by special constables, although one magistrate lamented 'the fact is that in the collieries few, if any, can be depended upon in that capacity'.[35]

A month before the disturbances began the Conservative county newspaper had registered profound shock at the findings of the Children's Employment Commission. 'We were by no means prepared', wrote the editor, 'for the facts which the report brings forward relative to the extent of White Slavery in Shropshire'.[36] As in 1820, 1821 and 1831 clear differences of opinion developed between ironmasters and the local gentry, who as magistrates were responsible for law and order in the coalfield. Such differences deepened as the authorities discovered more about conditions in the mining area. On 24 August, over a week after the strike had become general, Powis came to realise that the basis of the miners' complaints was the maladministration of the charter masters. He conveyed this information to Sir James Graham, and to William Botfield, who promised that he would correct such malpractices where they could be identified in his own concerns. On 26 August a meeting of ironmasters admitted that some of the grievances over the charter master system were real ones. They promised reforms, and immediately the miners began to return to work. Powis put pressure upon the ironmasters to check the abuses practised by charter masters, although in public he maintained that the strike was simply the result of mischief wrought by itinerant Chartist agitators. By the end of August most of the men had returned to work, but Powis continued to urge the government and the ironmasters that real grievances ought to be redressed. A meeting of ironmasters on 3 September agreed that the truck system should be disavowed, and that other complaints about charter masters should be examined.[37]

To Powis the government owed the relative peace of Shropshire during the Plug Plot riots which swept the Midlands and the North during the summer of 1842, and which led to considerable violence in some districts. One of Sir James Graham's letters of thanks to Powis as the miners returned to work conveniently epitomises the basic dilemma which faced industrial society in Shropshire and elsewhere in the 1840s,

> No legislative remedy can be applied to the undoubted evils, which prevail to an extent most dangerous to the public peace. They are inherent in the state of society at which we have arrived and which is highly dangerous. It will be seen that a manufacturing people is not so happy as a rural population, and this is the foretaste of becoming the 'Workshop of the World'.[38]

XXI

COLLAPSE AND RENAISSANCE

The middle years of the 19th century were a period of uneasy stability in the Shropshire iron trade. The last three decades of the century were a time of precipitate decline. Iron production by 1885 was less than a quarter of what it had been in the boom year of 1869, and at 45,000 tons p.a. was back to the level of the opening years of the century.[1] The failure to adopt modern methods which had characterised the industry in the 1820s and '30s was still evident. Only one ironworks, the Priorslee works of the Lilleshall Company, went over to the making of Bessemer steel. The difficulties of the iron trade first showed themselves in the mid-1850s when the vast integrated concerns of the Botfields were divided up after Beriah Botfield III failed to agree with his landlords on the terms for renewing his company's lease of a large part of its territory. In the early 1860s the historic Horsehay blast furnaces of the Coalbrookdale Company ceased to make iron, although the forges and rolling-mills on the same site continued.[2]

These difficulties were insignificant in comparison with the spectacular collapses of the 1870s and '80s. The first major ironworks to close altogether was the one-time Botfield works at Old Park, once the second largest in Great Britain, which ceased operations in 1877. The consequent social distress was aggravated by an outbreak of typhoid. The other ex-Botfield ironworks were closed by various successor companies during the 1870s and '80s. The Coalbrookdale Company blew out their Lightmoor and Dawley Castle furnaces in 1883, thus ceasing altogether to smelt iron ore. In 1886 the company closed down the forges at Horsehay, causing unemployment and threats of starvation on a scale to which the district was entirely unaccustomed. The soup kitchen became as much the symbol of the coalfield in the late 19th century as the glowing blast furnace had been at the end of the 18th. W. G. Norris, clerk to the Coalbrookdale Company, wrote in 1887 that he 'did not expect the closing of Horsehay, causing there so great a depreciation of property . . . the condition of the residents at Horsehay is very trying'. He advised one of the remaining Darby shareholders in the company to try and avoid a total liquidation which would bring about a like calamity in Ironbridge and Coalbrookdale. The Horsehay works was taken over by the Simpson family who developed its bridge-making activities.[3]

Other major ironworks followed in the wake of Old Park and Horsehay. The Lilleshall Company's Lodge furnaces ceased work in 1888, the Madeley Court furnaces in 1902, the Blists Hill ironworks in 1912. Iron-making, the staple trade of the district since the 1750s, and the activity to which everything else had been subservient, was effectively destroyed.

239

The Shropshire iron industry, did not, as has often been suggested, migrate to the Black Country. The south Staffordshire iron trade began to decline at exactly the same time and for much the same reasons as that of Shropshire, although because it was a larger industry more of its furnaces remained in operation in the 20th century. The output of pig iron in the Black Country fell from 726,000 tons in 1871 to 293,000 in 1887, while the number of puddling furnaces and mills was halved in the same period. The shortages and high costs of local ores, and the expense of bringing in ores from Northamptonshire or the coast, affected both Shropshire and Staffordshire. While the decline of iron-making in the Black Country was to some extent reversed by the end of the century, with the modernisation of a few major plants, and was mitigated by the growth of other industries, in particular of engineering and of the fabrication of steel manufactured at coastal works,[4] few such developments took place in Shropshire. The Lilleshall Company was a major national engineering concern at the end of the 19th century, but there had been a general contraction of engineering in Shropshire between 1815 and 1870.

The collapse of metal working was not total. Several foundries remained in production, and in 1910 the manufacture of pressed steel car wheels began at a works at Hadley which has since proved one of the principal growth points in the district. But the few survivals and the few new activities introduced should not obscure the magnitude of the economic and social changes which came over the Shropshire coalfield between 1870 and 1914. The large, integrated, 'colonial' iron-making partnership, the characteristic economic unit of the district since the 1750s, had disappeared for ever.

In the Severn Gorge the collapse of the iron companies was offset by the prosperity of the clay industries. The most attractive products of the period, decorative tiles, were produced by two major firms, Maws and Craven Dunhills, whose works were both alongside the Severn in Jackfield. Roofing tiles were manufactured in increasing numbers, and several new works were set up at Jackfield and elsewhere. This was also a time of progress in brick-making, and even the Coalport china manufactory enjoyed a burst of new activity in the 1880s and '90s.

The decline of the iron industry in the 1870s coincided with the growth of trades unions in the district, which provided a convenient excuse for managers trying to explain the collapse of their companies. Until the 1870s there were few unionists in the coalfield. The men of Coalbrookdale wrote Fogerty, were 'free from the deadly influence of designing delegates and committee men'. W. G. Norris of Horsehay wrote in 1873 that he found a union forming in the forge,

> It originated with the shinglers whose work being much easier, I wanted to reduce their wages . . . In these days the Union fever seems to prevail everywhere: but I did not expect much of it here . . . I do not think we can do much except by watching it quietly and getting rid when opportunity offers of any active promoter of it.[5]

The ebbing tide of prosperity in the iron trade was as much a threat to unions as to manufacturers. The two outstanding trade union leaders who sprang from the coalfield, came to prominence not in Shropshire but in the areas to which they had migrated. Albert Stanley, born at Dark Lane in 1863, learnt to read and write at the Primitive Methodist Sunday School there, and by the age of 14 was a local preacher. In the 1870s his family moved to Staffordshire; by 1884 he was secretary of the Cannock Chase Miners' Association and subsequently entered Parliament. Alfred Onions, a Wesleyan born at St. George's in 1858, began work at the age of 10, then in early manhood migrated first to the Potteries and then to South Wales, where in 1888 he became secretary of the Monmouthshire district of the South Wales Miners Federation, and later M.P. for Caerphilly.[6]

The decline of the iron trade caused a substantial exodus from east Shropshire. The population of the 11 parishes in the coalfield (including the whole of Shifnal) fell from 57,572 in 1881, to 49,897 10 years later. The population of every individual parish declined, but the fall was most marked in Dawley, where there were 9,200 people in 1881 and only 6,996 in 1891. The population of the parish in 1861 had been over 11,000. Ironworkers migrated to the new centres of the iron and steel industry, particularly to South Wales, Cleveland and Scotland. Miners were attracted to the new deep mines opened up in the late 19th century on the edges of the south Staffordshire coalfield, particularly in the Cannock area.

A pattern of decline can be observed in every aspect of the life of the coalfield in the late 19th century. The weaker religious denominations were threatened with extinction. The Primitive Methodists found it necessary in 1890 to send a minister to the Dawley and Madeley circuit with instructions, 'either to set the Circuit on its feet or sell out and wind up our connection with the district'.[7]

Construction of new houses in the coalfield almost ceased. In 1965 only 8.5 per cent of the houses in the Telford area had been built between 1881 and 1925, as compared with 23.2 per cent built before 1881. In the area formerly designated as Dawley New Town, the ancient parishes of Dawley and Madeley with the southern townships of Wellington, only 3.2 per cent of the houses were erected between 1881 and 1925, compared with 39.2 per cent before 1881.[8]

The decline of the coalfield in the late 19th century was a social and economic process as complex as its 'take-off' in the second half of the 18th century, and cannot be examined in detail here. It demands a study in its own right.

The predominant communal memories of the coalfield are not of the prosperous years of the late 18th century, but of the depression of the last 100 years, particularly of the 1930s. Some attempts were then made to relieve unemployment by removing some of the more hideous industrial scars, particularly some large pit mounts near to the centre of Oakengates. Nevertheless until the late 1960s the landscape of the coalfield remained much as it had been when the ironworks closed and the pits stopped producing coal. The young L. T. C. Rolt, who discovered the Ironbridge Gorge during World War II, was amazed to find plateways still in use at Horsehay, delivering materials to craftsmen building barges for the Normandy invasions, to see horses still working gin pits, and to talk with a man who still built coracles. 'Everywhere', he wrote, 'I was reminded of the fierce activity of former days, and every stick and stone of the place seemed to have absorbed something of its white hot violence'.[9]

In the last 20 years great changes have occurred in the district, in the landscape, in the treatment of the surviving industrial monuments, and in our understanding of its past. Telford Development Corporation has transformed much of the landscape. The village of Dark Lane and some of the pit mounts of the Botfield empire between Old Park and Stirchley have been flattened to make way for a new town centre, while other mounds survive as a range of miniature hills within a town park, whose lakes are canal reservoirs and clay quarries. Whole villages like Forge Row and Holywell Lane have been cleared, and the balance of the local economy has substantially changed as the older industries have died to be replaced by new ones introduced by the Development

Corporation. The year 1979 marked the end of many centuries of deep coal mining in Shropshire.[10]

At the same time the rich industrial heritage of the coalfield, particularly of the Ironbridge Gorge, has been increasingly recognised. In 1959 Allied Ironfounders Ltd. uncovered the Old Blast Furnace at Coalbrookdale to mark the 250th anniversay of Abraham Darby I's introduction of coke smelting, and established alongside it a small museum of the Coalbrookdale Company's products over the centuries, which became a focus for visitors to the area. In 1968 the Ironbridge Gorge Museum Trust was established to conserve for posterity all of the monuments of the Gorge, and absorbed the older Coalbrookdale Museum in 1970. Since that time it has enjoyed remarkable success. Ironbridge has become once more, as it was about 1800, a place to be visited, a magnet which draws people from all over the world to the scene of events which have shaped the common heritage of mankind. It has also become an object of pride to those who live in Telford, who have discovered at Ironbridge thrills and excitement in their local history, and a sense of dignity which derives from the achievements of their ancestors.

While it is absurd to assert that industrial civilisation began in the Ironbridge Gorge, or, indeed, in any other particular place, it is acknowledged throughout the world that for about 40 years at the end of the 18th century the innovations made in and around Coalbrookdale, made possible by the abilities of the local entrepreneurs, and by the varied skills of the communities which had grown up in the area, made it possible to produce much larger quantities of iron than previously, and to use some of that iron in bridges, buildings, steam engines and ships, which greatly accelerated the general pace of economic growth. Much remains to be discovered about that period. Very little is known of the activities of the Lightmoor Company, of Alexander Brodie, of Wright and Jesson, or of the lead-smelting concerns. The massive 19th century enterprises of the Botfield family still await an historian. Much remains to be discovered about the growth of communities within the coalfield. The mere scale of the Hay inclined plane, the sheer daring of the Iron Bridge, are impressive memorials to the activity of the Shropshire ironmasters of the late 18th century. But monuments alone do not explain all we may wish to know about the society which gave them birth. If we are to understand the great economic leap forward which occurred in Shropshire in the eighteenth century we need to discover more about the commercial operations of the major partnerships, about the ways in which they recruited labour, about the religious habits and recreations of masters and men. That the materials for such investigations will continue to accumulate and that the history of the coalfield will continue to exercise a widespread fascination seems certain. If this study continues to provide a useful framework for investigation it will have achieved its purpose.

SOURCES AND CROSS-REFERENCES

Notes to Chapter II

1. T. H. Whitehead and others, *Memoirs of the Geological Survey of England and Wales: the country between Wolverhampton and Oakengates* (1928), pp. 29–30, 51–52.

2. L. C. Lloyd, ed., *Wenlock 1468–1968* (1968), pp. 6–7, 12–15.

3. For a fuller discussion of the Severn navigation and other aspects of transport, see below pp. 61–71.

4. H. C. Maxwell Lyte, 'The Manuscripts of E. Lloyd Gateacre Esq.' Staffs. R.O. D593/B/2/12/6/16.

5. *Transactions of the Shropshire Archaeological Society* (abbreviated hereafter to *T.S.A.S.*), vol. 11, pp. 425–26. For a discussion of these sites see D. Pannett, 'Fish weirs of the River Severn', *Shropshire Newsletter* (abbreviated hereafter to *S.N.L.*) (No. 41, 1971).

6. Charles Hulbert, *Manual of Shropshire Biography, Chronology and Antiquities*, (1839), *Annals of the River Severn* (unpaginated section) (sub. 1607).

7. William Camden, (ed. and trans. by Richard Gough), *Britannia*, (1789), vol. 2, pp. 397, 419.

8. Shropshire Record Office (abbreviated hereafter to S.R.O.) 38/134. J. U. Nef, *The rise of the British Coal Industry* (1932), vol. 1, p. 97.

9. *T.S.A.S.*, vol. 11, pp. 425–26.

19. J. U. Nef, *op. cit.*, vol. 1, pp. 121, 308–9, 384. M. J. T. Lewis, *Early Wooden Railways* (1970), pp. 95–100.

11. J. U. Nef, *op. cit.*, vol. 2, pp. 150–51.

12. Memorandum of John Weld, S.R.O. 1224/163. M. D. G. Wanklyn, 'John Weld of Willey', in *West Midlands Studies*, vol. 3, (1969), pp. 88–99.

13. H. E. Forrest, *The Old Houses of Wenlock* (1914), pp. 87–89, 100.

14. J. U. Nef, *op. cit.*, vol. 1, pp. 96–98.

15. *Ibid.*, pp. 360–61.

16. T. S. Ashton and J. Sykes, *The Coal Industry in the 18th Century*, 2nd edn. (1964), p. 153.

17. Thomas Hearne, ed., *The Itinerary of John Leland* (1744), vol. 6, p. 93.

18. Robert Townson, 'A Sketch of the Mineralogy of Shropshire', in *Tracts and Observations in Natural History and Physiology* (1799), p. 174.

19. J. Randall, *The Clay Industries . . . on the Banks of the Severn* (1877), p. 27.

20. David Atkinson, The *Tobacco Pipes of Broseley* (1975), p. 41.

21. C. Singer and others, eds., *A History of Technology* (1957), vol. 3, p. 688.

22. John Houghton, 'Periodic Letters on Husbandry and Trade', No. 198, 15 May 1696, Staffs. R.O. D641/2/D/2/4.

23. See below pp. 31–32.

24. F. Brook and M. Allbutt, *The Shropshire Lead Mines* (1973), p. 44.
John Rhodes, 'Lead smelting in the Severn Gorge', *S.N.L.* No. 41, 1971).
Barrie Trinder, 'Lead Smelters of the Ironbridge Gorge', *Journal of the Shropshire Caving and Mining Club* (1979), pp. 31–33.
W. J. Lewis, *Lead mining in Wales* (1967), pp. 157–58. S.R.O. 210/3.
Deed of 26 Mar. 1765, Robert Jones-George Goodwin, summary in Shrewsbury Borough Library (abbreviated hereafter to S.B.L.).

25. S.R.O. 1224/3/16/97, 1224/3/70, 1681/PA; S.B.L. 3190.
William Rees, *Industry before the Industrial Revolution* (1968), p. 280.
Library of the Society of Friends, Friends' House, London (abbreviated hereafter to L.S.F.) Norris MSS., vol. 8.

26. B. L. C. Johnson, 'The Foley Partnerships' in, *Economic History Review* vol. 4, (1952).
B. L. C. Johnson, 'The Charcoal Iron Industry in

the early 18th century' in, *Geographical Journal*, vol. 117, (1951), p. 167 seq.

William Rees, *op. cit.*, pp. 317–334.

Malcolm Wanklyn 'Iron and Steelworks in Coalbrookdale in 1645', *S.N.L.* No. 44, 1973.

27. Inventories deposited in Lichfield Diocesan Record Office, transcribed by members of History of Leighton Adult Education class, 1970–71.

28. Mr. Woodhouse's Forge Acct. 1687–88. S.R.O. 625/15.

29. A. S. Davies, *The Charcoal Iron Industry of Powysland* (1939), p. 24.

30. E. Wyndham Hulme, 'The Statistical History of the Iron Trade 1717–50' in, *Transactions of the Newcomen Society*, (abbreviated hereafter to *T.N.S.*) vol. 9, (1928–29), p. 22.

31. H. R. Schubert, *The History of the British Iron Industry to 1775* (1957), pp. 368, 379.

32. Robin Chaplin, 'A Forgotten Industrial Valley' in *S.N.L.* (No. 36, 1969), pp. 1–6.

33. S.R.O. 796/191–93.

34. J. H. Pavitt, 'Wenlock Poor in the 18th century' in L. C. Lloyd, ed., *Wenlock 1468–1968* (1968), p. 39.

Notes to Chapter III

1. R. A. Mott, 'The Shropshire Iron Industry' in *T.S.A.S.* vol. 56, (1957–60), p. 71. A. Raistrick, *Dynasty of Ironfounders* (1953), p. 34.

2. Hannah Rose, 'Some Account of the Family of the Darbys, being what Hannah Rose has heard her Parents, John and Grace Thomas say concerning them', MS. in Lady Labouchere's collection, Dudmaston.

3. R. A. Mott, 'Coalbrookdale – The Early Years' in *T.S.A.S.* vol. 56, (1957–60), p. 82.

4. Hannah Rose, *op. cit.*

5. Hannah Rose, *op. cit.*

R. A. Mott, 'The Coalbrookdale Story – Facts and Fantasies' in *T.S.A.S.* vol. 58, (1965–68), p. 161. Patent No. 380, 18 April 1707, quoted in A. Raistrick, *op. cit.*, p. 22.

6. S.B.L. MS.328.

7. *Ibid.*, ff. 1,2,7.

8. *Ibid.*, ff. 5,7.

9. M. W. Flinn, 'Abraham Darby and the Coke Smelting Process' in *Economica*, New Series, vol. 26, (1959), p. 54.

10. S.B.L. MS.328 f.13.

11. Hannah Rose, *op. cit.*
Letter of Abiah Darby, c. 1779, MS. in Lady Labouchere's collection, Dudmaston.

12. S. Smiles, *Industrial Biography: Iron Workers and Tool Makers* (1863 ed.) pp. 82–3.

13. R. A. Mott, 'The Coalbrookdale Story – Facts and Fantasies' in *T.S.A.S.* vol. 58, (1965–68), p. 155.

14. S.B.L. MS. 330, f. 1.

15. For a list of patents relating to the use of coal and peat in iron-making in the 17th century see W. Rees, *Industry before the Industrial Revolution* (1968), p. 294–95.

16. Letter of Abiah Darby, c. 1779, MS. in Lady Labouchere's collection, Dudmaston.

17. S.B.L. MS. 32 f. 26.
R. A. Mott, 'Coalbrookdale – The Early Years' in *T.S.A.S.* vol. 56, (1957–60), p. 88.

18. S.B.L. MS. 328 ff. 16,30, 31, 33.

19. *Ibid.*, ff. 7,16,35.

20. R. Chaplin, 'A Forgotten Industrial Valley' in *S.N.L.* (No. 36, 1969), p. 2.
A. Raistrick, *op. cit.* pp. 41–2.
See also above pp. 10–11.

21. A. Raistrick, *op. cit.*, p. 29.

22. S.B.L. MS. 328 f. 30.
S.B.L. MS. 329 *passim*.

23. I am grateful to Mr. James Lawson, the historian of the charcoal iron trade in Shropshire, for suggestions included in this section.

24. S.R.O. 796/192 and 193.

25. R. A. Mott, 'Abraham Darby (I & II) and the Coke Iron Industry in *T.N.S.* vol. 31, (1957–58), pp. 84–88.

26. M. W. Flinn 'The Travel Diaries of Swedish Engineers as sources of Technological History' in *T.N.S.* vol. 31, (1957–58), p. 104.

27. Quoted by Dr. W. H. Challoner in discussion reported in *T.N.S.* vol. 34, (1961–62), p. 68.

28. *A description of Coalbrookdale* (prospectus for engravings), copies in Ironbridge Gorge Museum and S.B.L. f. M66.
Copy of lease of 27 April 1756 in L.S.F. Norris MSS. vol. 8.

29. A. Raistrick, *op. cit.*, p. 103. S.R.O. 1681/139.

30. *Ibid.*, pp. 50–51, 57–58, 63.

31. S.B.L. MS. 330 f. 51.
For Parrott, see A. W. A. White, *Men and Mining in Warwickshire* (1970), pp. 37–45.

32. S.R.O. 2280/3/6.

33. A. Raistrick, *op. cit.*, pp. 130–35.
R. A. Mott, 'The Newcomen Engine in the 18th century' in *T.N.S.* vol. 35, (1962–63), pp. 74–81.

34. Richard Ford–Thomas Goldney, 26 Mar. 1733, 30 Apr. 1734, 1 July 1734, S.B.L., MS. 3190, Nos. 9, 52, 56.
R. A. Mott, 'The Newcomen Engine in the 18th Century' in *T.N.S.*, vol. 35, (1962–63), pp. 74–81.

35. A. Raistrick, *op. cit.*, pp. 108–111.

36. Richard Ford–Thomas Goldney, 2 Feb. 1734, 1 June 1734, 15 June 1734, S.B.L. MS. 3190, Nos.

40, 54, 55.

37. S.B.L. MS. 331, ff. 52, 55, 56, 58, 60, 65, 69.

38. A. Raistrick, *op. cit.*, pp. 58–61.

S.B.L. MS. 3190, *passim*.

39. Coalbrookdale Manuscripts (abbreviated hereafter to CBD MS.) 1, ff. 136, 249, 534.

S.B.L. MS. 330, ff. 145, 291, 431.

Inventory at Coalbrookdale made up 28 7 mo. 1740.

S.R.O. 1987/18.

L.S.F. Norris MSS. vol. 8.

40. A. Raistrick, *op. cit.*, pp. 67–68, 143.

41. CBD MS. 1, ff. 253, 317.

S.B.L. MS. 331, ff. 63, 88.

42. Letter of Abiah Darby, c. 1779, MS. in Lady Labouchere's collection, Dudmaston.

43. Hannah Rose, *op. cit.*

Notes to Chapter IV

1. In 1754: Coalbrookdale (2), Old Willey. In 1759: Coalbrookdale (2), Old Willey, New Willey, Horsehay (2), Ketley (2), Madeley Wood (2), Lightmoor (2). According to one source the Coneybury furnace in Broseley dates from 1756, but this is doubtful.

2. Copy of deed of 28 May 1756 in A. H. Simpson Collection.

S.R.O. 1681/118.

William Ferriday-William Forrester, 6 December 1754. S.R.O. 1224/259.

3. William Ferriday-William Forrester, 28 December 1754. S.R.O. 1224/259.

4. S.B.L. MS. 332, ff. 1–30.

5. William Ferriday-William Forrester, 7 March 1755, S.R.O. 1224/259.

6. S.B.L. MS. 332, ff. 7–13.

7. S.R.O. 1987/20.

8. Quoted in T. S. Ashton, *Iron and Steel in the Industrial Revolution* (1951), p. 131.

9. Abiah Darby-Rachel Thompson, 5 mo. 1757. Copy in A. S. Simpson Colln.

10. Staffs. R.O. D593/B/2/5/11/2.

H. R. Rathbone, *Letters of Richard Reynolds, with a Memoir of his life* (1852), p. 17.

'A short Account of Wellington, 1759' in *Salopian Shreds and Patches*, vol. 1, (1874–75) pp. 132–3.

11. A. Raistrick, *Dynasty of Ironfounders* (1953), p. 82.

12. J. Randall, *The Old Court House, Madeley* (1883), p. 64.

S.B.L. MS. 332, ff. 141/202.

13. R. F. Skinner, *Nonconformity in Shropshire 1662–1816* (1964), pp. 31, 33–34.

14. H. R. Rathbone, *op. cit.* pp. 19–20.

15. Ironbridge Gorge Museum, Lilleshall Company Collection (hereafter abbreviated to I.B.G.M., Lill. Co. Colln.) Catalogue of Deeds, Sundry Deeds Nos. 3, 8.

Staffs. R.O. D593/B/2/5/11/2.

16. S.B.L. MS. 332, *passim*.

17. T. S. Ashton, *Iron and Steel in the Industrial Revolution*, 2nd. edn. (1951), p. 132.

18. Abiah Darby-Rachel Thompson, 5 mo. 1757. E. Purcell to the Earl of Stafford, 1 July 1757, Staffs. R.O. D641/K/1/1.

19. S.R.O. 1224/Box 143.

20. For the Wilkinsons see:

W. H. Challoner, 'John Wilkinson: Ironmaster' in *History Today*, (1951).

W. H. Challoner, 'Isaac Wilkinson: Potfounder' in L. S. Pressnell, ed., *Studies in the Industrial Revolution* (1960).

J. Randall, *The Wilkinsons* (n.d.).

H. W. Dickinson, *John Wilkinson: Ironmaster* (1914).

A. N. Palmer, *John Wilkinson and the Old Bersham Ironworks* (1899).

21. Ex. inf. John Corbett.

22. S.R.O. 1224/173.

S.R.O. 1224/3/436–42.

23. William Ferriday to William Forester, 4 January 1755 and 19 January 1755. S.R.O. 1224/259.

24. S.R.O. 1224/3/537 & 602.

S.R.O. 1224/Box 173. Kidderminster Public Library, Stour Works Accounts, vol. 148.

25. Copy in A. H. Simpson Colln.

26. J. Randall, *History of Madeley* (1880), pp. 178–79.

27. S.R.O. 1681/14.

28. S.R.O. 1681/7–10. Kidderminster Public Library, Stour Works Accounts, vols. 148–155.

29. William Ferriday to William Forester, 4 January 1755, S.R.O. 1224/259.

30. F. Paddy to the Earl of Stafford, 25 June 1755, Staffs. R.O. D641/2/K/1/1.

F. Paddy to W. Stubbs, 5 April 1757, Staffs. R.O. D641/2/G/1/6.

31. For Gower and the Gilberts see *D.N.B.* and H. Malet, *The Canal Duke* (1961), pp. 51–54, 61–62, 100–101.

There are copies of the various agreements of August and September 1764 in I.B.G.M., Lill. Co. Colln., Catalogue of Deeds, Sundry Deeds Nos. 3,4,7,8,9, and in Staffs. R.O. D593/B/2/7/22/1–2.

32. Staffs. R.O. D593/B/2/9/7, D593/B/2/5/11/3, D593/B/2/11/4.

S. R. Broadbridge, 'Joseph Banks and West Midlands Industry, 1767' in *Staffordshire Industrial Archaeology Journal*, vol. 2, (1971), p. 6.

33. S.B.L. MS. 332, ff. 1–5.

34. *Ibid.*, f. 202. *et seq.*

Full details listed in A. Raistrick, *op. cit.*, p. 289.

Notes to Chapter V

1. Rent Rolls Mich. 1722, Lady Day 1725, Mich. 1728. S.R.O. 625/1. For Richard Hartshorne, see below pp. 114–15.
2. Rent Rolls Lady Day 1729, Lady Day 1730, Coal Accts. Lady Day 1731, S.R.O. 676.
CBD MS. 1, f. 187.
3. Coal Accts. Lady Day 1739, S.R.O. 676.
4. Coal Accts. Lady Day 1730, Rent Rolls Mich. 1737, Mich. 1738, Lady Day 1744, S.R.O. 676.
5. Rent Rolls Lady Day 1747, Lady Day 1748, S.R.O. 676.
6. Coal Accts. Mich. 1731, Estate Accts. Lady Day 1752, S.R.O. 676.
7. Rent Rolls Lady Day 1744, Lady Day 1747, S.R.O. 676.
8. Rent Rolls, Lady Day 1720, Lady Day 1732, Mich. 1736, Lady Day 1748, Mich. 1753, S.R.O. 676.
9. Robert Townson, 'A Sketch of the Mineralogy of Shropshire', in *Tracts and Observations in Natural History and Physiology* (1799), p. 179. Articles of Agreement, Charlton-Newport, 10 April 1707, S.R.O. 625/10. Coal Accts. Mich. 1736, S.R.O. 625/1.
10. Lease, Charlton-Hartshorne, Mich. 1726, S.R.O. 625/10.
Sundry Rent Rolls &c. S.R.O. 625 and 676.
11. Rent Rolls, Mich. 1737, Lady Day 1739, Salt Works Accts. Sep.–Dec. 1730 and Dec.–Mar. 1730–31, S.R.O. 676.
Lease, Charlton to Hartshorne, Mich. 1726, S.R.O. 625/10.
Georgius Agricola (ed. by H. C. and L. H. Hoover), *De Re Metallica* (1950), pp. 546–52.
12. Lease, Charlton-Briscoe and Ball, 2 May 1763, S.R.O. 625/10.
Robert Townson, *op. cit.*, p. 179.
13. R. Chaplin, 'A Forgotten Industrial Valley' in *S.N.L.* No. 36 (1969), pp. 4–5.
14. Rent Roll, Mich. 1738, S.R.O. 676.
15. Leeke's Accts., Lady Day 1759, S.R.O. 625/1.
Wrockwardine Wood Coal & Ironstone Accts., 1757–58, 1758–59, S.R.O. 676.
16. Wrockwardine Wood Coal & Ironstone Accts., 1761–62, 1762–63, S.R.O. 676.

Notes to Chapter VI

1. J. Plymley, *A General View of the Agriculture of Shropshire*, (1803) p. 340.
Marchant de la Houlière, 'Report to the French Government on British Methods of smelting iron ore with coke and casting naval cannon' (1775) Trans. and ed. by W. H. Chaloner in *Edgar Allen News* (Dec. 1948/Jan. 1949).
A. Birch, *An Economic History of the British Iron and Steel Industry 1784–1879* (1967), pp. 18, 44–45.
H. Scrivenor, *The History of the Iron Trade* (1967 ed.), pp. 87, 95–99.
2. Joseph Priestley-John Wilkinson, 28 May 1795, Priestley Correspondence, Warrington Public Library.
3. 'An account of the coke furnaces now in work in Great Britain . . . 25 December 1791'. Birmingham Reference Library, (hereafter abbreviated to B.R.L.) Boulton and Watt Collection, (hereafter abbreviated to B. & W. Colln.) M II.
S.B.L. MS. 335, *passim*.
4. S.R.O. 1781/6/28.
5. A. Raistrick, *Dynasty of Ironfounders* (1953), pp. 85–87.
S. R. Broadbridge, 'Joseph Banks and West Midlands industry, 1767', in *Staffordshire Industrial Archaeology Society Journal*, vol. 2, (1971), p. 9. Weale MSS. quoted in A. Birch, *op. cit.*, pp. 32–33.
Patent No. 815, June 1766.
6. Patent No. 1054, Oct. 1773.
G. R. Morton and N. Mutton, 'The Transition to Cort's Puddling Process', in *Journal of the Iron and Steel Institute*, vol. 205 (1967), pp. 722–28.
7. Weale MSS. quoted in A. Birch, *op. cit.*, pp. 36–37, 45.
Memorandum Book of William Reynolds (now lost) quoted in S. Smiles, *Industrial Biography: Ironworkers and Toolmakers* (ed. 1863), pp. 121–22.
Joshua Gilpin's Journals and Notebooks, Vol. 27, Microfilm in B.U.L.
8. S.R.O. 1781/6/28.
9. E. F. Soderlund, 'The Impact of the British Industrial Revolution on the Swedish Iron Industry' in L. S. Pressnell, ed., *Studies in the Industrial Revolution* (1960), pp. 53–64.
10. S.R.O. 749/12.
Abraham Darby's Ledger Accts., S.R.O. 2448/1, ff. 6, 31, 34, 35, 39.
Staffs. R.O. D593/G/4/14/3, D593/F/7.
Northamptonshire Record Office, Journal of John Thornton, Aug.–Sep. 1819. *Shrewsbury Chronicle* (11 Mar. 1814).
11. W. Day, 'Report on Shropshire' in *Second Annual Report of the Poor Law Commissioners for England and Wales* (1836), p. 385.
W. Anstice to Earl of Powis, 31 Aug, 1842, National Library of Wales, *Calendar of Letters and Documents relating to Chartism in Shropshire* (1949) vol. 2, No. 18.
12. Richard Reynolds-Earl Gower, 7 mo. 1784,

H. R. Rathbone, *Letters of Richard Reynolds with a Memoir of his Life* (1852), p. 280.

13. S.R.O. 1224/183 and 184. Ex. inf. Robert Machin.

14. H. W. Dickinson, *John Wilkinson: Ironmaster* (1914), p. 23.
B.M. Egerton MSS. 1941. ff. 29–30.
Ex. inf. Robert Machin.
For Wilkinson's boring machine see below pp. 162–63.

15. List of Engines, n.d., B.R.L., B & W. Colln., Box 20, Bundle 16.

16. Memorandum, n.d., B.R.L., B. & W. Colln., Box 20, Bundle 17.
M. Boulton-J. Wilkinson, 17 July 1777 (copy), B.R.L., B & W. Colln., Box 20, Bundle 16.
Engine Book, B.R.L., B. & W. Colln.

17. I.B.G.M., Lill. Co. Colln., Mr. Wilkinson's Proposals to Messrs. Bishton and Onions, 30 Nov. 1793.
Science Museum, William Reynolds's Sketchbook, f. 36.

18. T. S. Ashton, *Iron and Steel in the Industrial Revolution* (1951), pp. 76–79.
I.B.G.M., Lill. Co. Colln., Mr. Wilkinson's Proposals to Messrs. Bishton and Onions, 30 Nov. 1793.

19. Joseph Priestley-John Wilkinson, 24 July 1795, Priestley Correspondence, Warrington Public Library.

20. I.B.G.M., Lill. Co. Colln., Schedule of Deeds, Snedshill Nos. 1–9.

21. I.B.G.M., Lill. Co. Colln., Portion of the Hadley Estate Map, 1809.
S.R.O. 245/145, Tunnel Accts.
S.B.L. MS. 334, f. 28.
William Wilkinson-James Watt Jun., 28 Mar. 1807, B.R.L., B. & W. Colln., Box 20, Bundle 2.
Ex. inf. Robert Machin.

22. J. Randall, *Broseley and its Surroundings* (1879), p. 115.

23. S.B.L., MS. 2365.

24. Pritchard & Son-James Foster, 17 May 1831. Ex. inf. Norman Mutton.

25. J. Lord, *Capital and Steam Power* (1966), p. 237.
Shrewsbury Chronicle (18 Feb. 1786). Kidderminster Public Library, Stour Works Accounts, vols. 161, 168, 176.

26. J. Randall, *Broseley and its Surroundings* (1879), pp. 119–123.
A. E. Musson and E. Robinson, *Science and Technology in the Industrial Revolution* (1969), p. 452.
A. Raistrick, ed., *The Hatchett Diary* (1967), p. 58.
Salopian Journal 24 Aug. 1796.
W. A. Smith, 'A Swedish view of the West Midlands in 1802–03' in *West Midlands Studies* vol. 3 (1969), pp. 47–48.

For further discussion of Dundonald's activities at the Calcutts, see below pp. 55–58.

27. S.B.L. MS. 2365.
Salopian Journal (19 June 1811).
S.R.O. 2524/13.

28. J. L. McAdam-Lord Dundonald, 11 April 1788, Scot. R.O. GD 233/109/G/1. Kidderminster Public Library, Stour Works Accounts, vol. 168.
C. B. Andrews, ed., *The Torrington Diaries*, (1934), p. 184.
S.R.O. 1190/112.
H. W. Dickinson and Rhys Jenkins, *James Watt and the Steam Engine*, 1927, p. 322.
J. Randall, *Broseley and its Surroundings* (1879), p. 124.
J. Randall, *The Wilkinsons* (n.d.), p. 32.

29. Lord Dundonald-William Reynolds, 24 Dec. 1787, Scot. R.O. GD 233/109/H/2.
J. Dumaresque-William Reynolds, 22 Feb. 1791, Scot. R.O. GD 233/109/H/3.
B.M. Add. MSS. 21018.
L.T.C. Rolt, *Tools for the Job* (1968), p. 56.

30. S.R.O. 245/71.

31. J. Randall, *Broseley and its Surroundings* (1879), p. 124.
J. Randall, *The Wilkinsons* (n.d.), p. 38.
List of the Different Ironworks . . . to the year 1794, B.R.L., B. & W. Colln., M II.
William Wilkinson-James Watt Jun., 17 Jan. 1802, B.R.L., B. & W. Colln., Box 20, Bundle 22.
Boulton and Watt-J. Onions, 20 Dec. 1800, B.R.L., B & W. Colln., Letter Book (Office), Nov. 1800–July 1801, f. 33.
S.R.O. 1190/112. Kidderminster Public Library, Stour Works Accounts, vols. 178, 197.

32. J. Randall, *Broseley and its Surroundings* (1879), p. 125.
Iron Furnaces in Great Britain and Ireland, 31 Dec. 1825, B.R.L., B. & W. Colln., M II.

33. Marchant de la Houlière, *op. cit.,* p. 3.
'Wright and Jessons Proposals for payments on the Wren's Nest Engine, Aug. 1779', B.R.L., B. & W. Colln., Box 2, 'W'.
S.R.O. 245/144, f. 170.
Engine Book, B.R.L., B. & W. Colln.
Robert Baugh, *Map of Shropshire* (n.d. c. 1808).
Ex. inf. Robert Machin.

34. Engine Book, B.R.L., B. & W. Colln.
H. Scrivenor, *op. cit.,* pp. 97–98. *Shrewsbury Chronicle* (13 Aug. 1813).

35. Matthew Boulton-James Watt, 13 April 1782, B.R.L., B. & W. Colln., Parcel D.
A. Raistrick, *op. cit.,* pp. 83–85, 89, 208.

36. A. Young, *Tours in England and Wales* (1932), p. 151.
S. R. Broadbridge, *op. cit.,* pp. 8–9.

37. S.R.O. 245/144, which covers the period up to 1781 at Horsehay, makes no reference to a forge.

William Reynolds-James Watt, 2 Sep. 1783, 29 Nov. 1784, 11 Dec. 1784, B.R.L., B. & W. Colln., Box 2 'R'.

Richard Reynolds & Co.-Boulton and Watt, 4 2mo. 1785, 3 4mo. 1785, B.R.L., B. & W. Colln., Box 4 'R'.

38. S.R.O. 245/145, passim.

For a table showing the decline in the manufacture of pots on the introduction of puddling, see R. A. Mott, 'The Coalbrookdale Company Horsehay Works Pt. II' in, T.N.S. vol. 32, (1959–60), p. 53.

39. William Reynolds-James Watt, 29 Nov. 1784, 14 April 1785, B.R.L., B. & W. Colln., Box 2 'R'.

Richard Reynolds & Co.-Boulton and Watt, 3 9mo. 1785, 14 Feb. 1787, B.R.L., B. & W. Colln., Box 4 'R'.

List of the Different Ironworks . . . to the year 1794, B.R.L., B. & W. Colln., Box 20, Bundle 2.

40. Engine Book, B.R.L., B. & W. Colln.

William Reynolds-James Watt, 19 May 1780, B.R.L., B. & W. Colln., Box 2 'R'.

B. Trinder, ed., A Description of Coalbrookdale in 1801 (1970), pp. 3, 11.

41. Staffs. R.O. D593/B/2/5/11/5, D593/G/4/3/55.

I.B.G.M., Lill. Co. Colln., Charter masters' Book.

42. Coalbrookdale Co.-Boulton and Watt, 5 5mo. 1794, B.R.L., B. & W. Colln., Box 4 'C'.

CBD MS. 3, f. 25.

43. CBD MS. 3, 14 April 1796.

I.B.G.M., Lill. Co. Colln., Schedule of Deeds, Donnington & Lilleshall, No. 14.

44. Memo. on the Dale Works. S.R.O. 1987/20.

45. J. Watt Jun.-William Wilkinson, 30 Dec. 1795, quoted in T. S. Ashton, op. cit., p. 78.

Boulton and Watt-Coalbrookdale Co., 10 Mar. 1800, 26 Aug. 1801, B.R.L. Letter Books (Office) Mar.–Nov. 1800 f. 4, July 1801–April 1802, f. 61.

46. S.R.O. 1781/6/28.

H. Scrivenor, op. cit., p. 99.

A. Birch, 'The Midlands Iron Industry during the Napoleonic Wars' in Edgar Allen News (Aug./Sep. 1952).

Boulton and Watt-William Reynolds & Co., 27 Aug. 1802, B.R.L., B. & W. Colln., Letter Book (Office), April–Dec. 1802, f. 130.

Thomas P. Smith, Conseil des Mines (1803), quoted in A. Birch, Economic History of the British Iron and Steel Industry 1784–1879 (1967), p. 307. Salopian Journal (9 April 1817).

A month's work at Ketley Foundry, S.R.O. 1987/20.

Staffs. R.O. D876/155, ff. 1, 45.

47. Staffs. R.O. D876/155, ff. 1, 43, 66.

CBD MS. 3, 3 May 1794.

H. Scrivenor, op. cit., pp. 97–98.

48. Universal British Directory (1797), p. 868.

N. Mutton, ed., 'An Engineer at Work in the West Midlands' in, West Midlands Studies Special Publication No. 1 (1969), p. 29.

J. P. Addis, The Crawshay Dynasty (1957), pp. xii, 5.

49. H. Scrivenor, op. cit., pp. 95–97.

S.B.L. MS. 334, ff. 162, 211.

W. A. Smith, op. cit., pp. 53–54.

Boulton and Watt-J. Addenbrooke, 13 June 1800, 10 June 1800, B.R.L., B. & W. Colln., Letter Book (Office), Nov. 1800–July 1801, ff. 98, 100.

Boulton and Watt-F. Homfray, 13 May 1801, 9 June 1801, Ibid., ff. 278, 304.

50. CBD MS, 2, ff. 44, 84, 101, 123, 206, 384.

S.R.O. 271/1, f. 184.

51. Memo. by John Bishton, 17 Oct. 1789, John Bishton-Marquess of Stafford, 26 Mar. 1790, Staffs. R.O. D593/L/4/3. Ex. inf. Ian Standing.

52. I.B.G.M., Lill.Co. Colln., Schedule of Deeds, Sundry deeds Nos. 25/26, Snedshill deeds Nos. 1/2/5/9/4/16/17/18/22.

53. I.B.G.M., Lill. Co. Colln., Schedule of Deeds, Donnington & Lilleshall deeds Nos. 10/14/15/16/17/18, Wrockwardine Wood deeds Nos. 8/9/10. CBD MS. 3, 14 April 1796.

H. Scrivenor, op. cit., pp. 97–98.

54. I.B.G.M., Lill. Co. Colln., Schedule of Deeds, Donnington & Lilleshall deeds Nos. 22/23/24/25/26/28/29/31/32/37, Snedshill deed No. 42. Staffs. R.O. D593/B/2/7/22.

55. H. Scrivenor, op. cit., p. 99.

Shropshire Parish Register Society, Register of Dawley Magna (1923).

Engine Book, B.R.L., B. & W. Colln.

William Wilkinson-James Watt Jun., 12 June 1799, B.R.L., B. & W. Colln., Box 20 Bundle 21.

W. H. Williams, 'Thomas Botfield kept his ear to the wall' in Shropshire Magazine December 1965.

56. William Wilkinson-James Watt Jun., 28 Mar. 1807, B.R.L., B. & W. Colln., Box 20 Bundle 22.

57. R. T. Rowley, 'Bouldon Mill' in, Shropshire Magazine, (Feb. 1966). 'List of the Different Ironworks . . . to the year 1794', B.R.L., B. & W. Colln., M II.

N. Mutton, 'Charlcotte Furnace' in, T.S.A.S. vol. 58, (1965–68) pp. 84–88.

58. 'List of the Different Ironworks . . . to the year 1794', B.R.L., B. & W. Colln., M II.

J. Plymley, op. cit., pp. 287–88.

59. N. Mutton, 'The Forges at Eardington and Hampton Loade' in, T.S.A.S. vol. 58, (1967) pp. 235–43.

Notes to Chapter VII

1. S.B.L. MS. 333.
S.R.O. 245/144.

2. S.B.L. MSS. 334, 336, 337. Kidderminster Public Library, Stour Works Accounts, vols. 170–185.

3. S.B.L. MS. 336, ff. 1148, 1430, MS. 337, f. 1688.

4. Quoted in A. E. Musson and E. Robinson, *Science and Technology in the Industrial Revolution* (1969), p. 448.

5. S.B.L. MS. 334, f. 22.
For Bateman and Sharratt see A. E. Musson and E. Robinson, *op. cit.*, pp. 405–06.

6. I.B.G.M., Lill. Co. Colln., The Quarter's orders for Pig at Snedshill, Midsummer 1799.

7. Letter Books (Office), July 1797–July 1805 (9 vols.) *passim.* B.R.L., B. & W. Colln.

8. CBD MS. 2.
S.B.L. MSS. 334, 336, 337.

9. S.B.L. MS. 336, f. 1666.

10. S.B.L. MS. 336, f. 1068, MS. 337, ff. 1378, 1490, 1648.

11. S.B.L. MS. 334, f. 10.
CBD MS. 2, ff. 43, 103, 126.

12. S.B.L. MSS. 336, 337.

13. S.R.O. 245/71.
B. Trinder, ed. *A description of Coalbrookdale in 1801* (1970), pp. 13–15. CBD MS. 2, f. 103.

14. A month's work at Ketley Foundry. S.R.O. 1987/20.
S.R.O. 245/144, ff. 145, 146, 150, 151.
CBD MS. 2, f. 125. *Shrewsbury Chronicle* (4 April 1794).

15. See below p. 97.

16. See A. E. Musson and E. Robinson, *op. cit.*, pp. 68–71.
Staffs. R.O. D876/155. f. 41.

17. *Salopian Journal* (21 May 1794, 18 Feb. 1795), *Shrewsbury Chronicle* (23 May 1794) St.R.O. D593/H/13/39, D593/N/2/1/1/6.

18. Inscription on bridge 'Cast at Coalbrookdale 1797', Nat. Grid. Ref. SJ 555052.
CBD MS. 2, ff. 89, 343, 459.
Salopian Journal, (26 Feb. 1806).
Neil Cossons and Barrie Trinder, *The Iron Bridge* (1979), pp. 82–89, 96.
Barrie Trinder, 'Coalport Bridge: a Study in Historical Interpretation', I.A.R. III, 2 (1979) pp. 153–57.

19. M. C. Hill, 'Iron and Steel Bridges in Shropshire 1788–1901' in *T.S.A.S.* vol. 56, (1957–60), p. 105.
Robert Southey (ed. by J. Simmons), *Letters from England* (1951), p. 44.

20. C. Hadfield, *The Canals of the West Midlands* (1966), pp. 161–62.

A. H. Faulkner, 'The Wolverton Aqueduct' in *Transport History*, vol. 2, (1969), pp. 163–64.

21. The flax mill is now known as Jones's Maltings. For a full account of its building see A. W. Skempton and H. R. Johnson, 'The First Iron Frames' in *Architectural Review*, vol. 131, No. 751 (Mar. 1962).

22. 'S.R.O. 2280/6/95. John Banks, *On the Power of Machines* (1803), pp. 89–91.

23. T. Minshill, *The Shrewsbury Visitor's Pocket Companion or Salopian Guide and Directory* (1803), pp. 47–48.

24. S.B.L. MS. 331, ff. 18, 22, 27.
A. Raistrick, *Dynasty of Ironfounders* (1953), pp. 66–67.
Willey Co.-Thomas Goldney, Leighton Co.-Thomas Goldney, S.R.O. 1987/20. S.B.L. *Watton Colln.*, Vol. X, p. 304.

25. S.R.O. 1224/Box 173.

26. *Shrewsbury Chronicle* (22 Jan. 1778).

27. *Gentlemen's Magazine* vol. 28, (1758), p. 277.
Robert Townson, 'A Sketch of the Mineralogy of Shropshire' in *Tracts and Observations in Natural History and Physiology* (1799), p. 178.

28. S.R.O. 1224/Boxers 171 and 173.
Staffs. R.O. D593/F/3/6/20.

29. B.M. Map Kxxxvi. 16.1.
S.R.O. 271/1.

30. S.R.O. 1150/898.
C.B.D. MS. 2.

31. F. Atkinson, *The Great Northern Coalfield* (1968), pp. 62–63.

32. C. Singer and others, eds., *A History of Technology* (1957), vol. 3, p. 688.
Elwell and others to Darby, 1776. S.R.O. 1987/20.
Abraham Darby's Ledger Accounts, f. 43, S.R.O. 2448/1.

33. Patent No. 1291, April 1781.
See also J. Butt, *The Industrial Archaeology of Scotland* (1967), pp. 147–48.

34. *Shrewsbury Chronicle* (18 Feb. 1786).
S.B.L. MS. 2365.
Lord Dundonald-William Reynolds, 24 Dec. 1787, Scot. R.O. GD 233/109/H/2.
Minutes of the Proprietors of the Ironbridge. S.B.L. MS. 3689, 4 June 1790.

35. For descriptions of the Tar works at the Culcutts see:
The Hatchett Diary, ed. by A. Raistrick, (1967), p. 59.
B.M. Add. MS. 21018. sub Benthall.
W. A. Smith, *A Swedish view of the West Midlands in 1802–03'* in *West Midlands Studies* vol. 3, (1969), p. 48.
J. Randall, *Broseley and its Surroundings* (1879), pp. 118–119.

Letters from Simon Goodrich to General Bentham, giving an account of a tour of engineering works in 1799. Goodrich Collection. Science Museum. There is a detailed plan and elevation of the kilns in Scot. R.O. GD 233/109/G/8, and a less satisfactory sketch in B.R.L., B. & W. Colln. Box 26.

36. Lord Dundonald-George Glenny, 20 June 1789, Scot. R.O. GD 233/111-3/N.
Lord Dundonald-William Reynolds, 11 Sep. 1789, Scot. R.O. GD 233/107/L/5.
Copy of Indenture, 1 June 1787, S.B.L. MS. 2366.

37. British Transport Historical Records (abbreviated hereafter to B.T.H.R.) Shropshire Canal Minutes, 10 Aug. 1789.
S.B.L. MS. 336, f. 1251.
CBD MS. 2, f. 342.
Minutes of the Proprietors of the Iron Bridge, S.B.L. MS. 3689, 6 June 1788.

38. Lord Dundonald-[Richard] Crawshay, 11 Sep. 1789, Scot. R.O. GD 233/109/G4.
Lord Dundonald-William Reynolds, 11 Sep. 1789, n.d. (c.1790), 15 Mar. 1791, Scot. R.O. GD 233/107/L/6, GD 233/109/H/15 and 16.

39. Lord Dundonald-Dr. Campbell, 14 Dec. 1799, Scot. R.O. GD 233/109/G/47.
Lord Dundonald-William Reynolds, 13 Nov. 1799, 6 Dec. 1799, Scot. R.O. GD 233/109/H/22 and 24.

40. Eustace Greg, ed., Reynolds Rathbone Letters and Diaries (1905) p. 44.
Lord Dundonald-William Reynolds, 6 Nov. 1787, 26 Feb. 1789, 10 Nov. 1799, Scot. R.O. GD 233/109/H/1, 4 and 21.
S.B.L. MS. 336, f. 963.

41. J. Randall, The Wilkinsons (n.d.) p. 28–29.
Lord Dundonald-William Reynolds, 14 Feb. 1800, Scot. R.O. GD 233/109/H/3.

42. J. Randall, Brozeley and its Surroundings (1879), pp. 118–19.
J. Randall, The Wilkinsons (n.d.) p. 28.

43. D. R. Adams and J. Hazeley, Survey of the Church Aston-Lilleshall Mining Area (1970), p. 22.

44. Staffs. R.O. D593/I/1/32, D593/M/17/1.
I.B.G.M., Lill. Co. Colln., Schedule of Deeds, Donnington and Lilleshall Deeds, No. 8.
D. R. Adams and J. Hazeley, op. cit., passim.

S. R. Broadbridge, 'Joseph Banks and West Midlands Industry, 1767' in Staffordshire Industrial Archaeology Society Journal vol. 2, (1971), p. 5.

45. CBD MS. 2, f. 276.
S.B.L. MS. 336, f. 1367.
British Parliamentary Papers, Children's Employment Commission, Appendix to first Report of Commissioners, (abbreviated hereafter to Children's Emp. Comm. Rep.) (1842), p. 42.

46. G. Perry, Prospectus for a Description of Coalbrookdale (n.d., c. 1758).
S.B.L. f. M. 66.
B. Trinder, op. cit., p. 12.
I. M. Brown and D. R. Adams, A History of Limestone Mining in Shropshire (1967), pp. 17–18.
Staffs. R.O. D876/155, ff. 121, 123.

47. B. Trinder, op. cit., p. 7.

48. Staffs. R.O. D876/155, ff. 1, 3, 31, 34.
CBD MS. 2, ff. 45, 101, 180, 439.
For the route of the Gleedon Hill railway see Reprint of the first edition of the one-inch Ordnance Survey of England and Wales Sheet No. 41.

49. R. Townson, op. cit., p. 166.
S.B.L. MS. 332, ff. 30, 44, 47, 120.

50. W. H. B. Court, The Rise of the Midland Industries 1600–1838 (1953), p. 187.
H. M. Rathbone, Letters of Richard Reynolds with a Memoir of his Life (1852), p. 282.

51. Staffs. R.O. D593/B/2/7/22/1, D593/B/2/11/5.
I.B.G.M., Lill. Co. Colln., Charter masters' Book Jan. 1776, Dec. 1783.

52. S.R.O. 271/1, ff. 9, 189, 192.
Shrewsbury Chronicle (18 Feb. 1786, 2 Mar. 1788).
I.B.G.M., Lill. Co. Colln., Mr. Wilkinson's Proposals to Messrs. Bishton and Rowley, 30 Nov. 1793.
S.R.O. 245/144, ff. 56, 74, 214, 390.

53. A. Young, Tours in England and Wales (1932), p. 150.
S.B.L. MS. 333 f. 406.
S.R.O. 245/144, f. 165.

54. S.R.O. 245/145, Horsehay Wages Book., passim.
S.B.L. MS. 334, passim.

Notes to Chapter VIII

1. J. U. Nef, The Rise of the British Coal Industry, (1932), vol. 1, p. 97.

2. L.S.F., Journal of Abiah Darby, ff. 47, 49, 68.
Anon., 'Narrative Travels &c., of Capt. William Owen, R.N. in Montgomeryshire Collections, vol. 16, (1883), p. 240.

3. 'A short topographical Account of Bridgnorth, 1739, by Richard Cornes' in T.S.A.S., vol. 9,
(1886), p. 197.
Gentlemen's Magazine, vol. 28, (1758), p. 277.
Thomas Howell, The Stranger in Shrewsbury, 2nd edn. (1825), p. 106.

4. Thomas Phillips, The History and Antiquities of Shrewsbury, ed. by Charles Hulbert, (1837), pp. 5–6.

5. William Bailey, The Bristol and Bath Directory, (1787).
S.R.O. 1649/1.

6. Thomas Phillips, *op. cit.*, pp. 5–6.
Salopian Journal, (27 Feb. 1811).
Ibid., (3 July 1811).
Ibid., (15 Jan. 1817).
7. CBD MS. 2, f. 447.
S.R.O. 1649/1.
S.R.O. 1224/Box 171.
8. L. J. Lee, ed., *A Full List and Partial Abstract
. . . of the Quarter Sessions Rolls* [for Shropshire],
1696–1800, (n.d.). p. 104.
L. C. Lloyd, 'The Records of a Borough Court in
the 18th century' in *Archives*, vol. 7, (1965), p. 14.
9. Ex. inf. Dr. M. J. T. Lewis.
S.B.L., MS. 331, ff. 53, 61, 67, 73, 74, 80.
J. H. Denton and M. J. T. Lewis, 'The River Tern
Navigation', *Journal of the Railway and Canal Historical
Society*, vol. 23 (1977), pp. 56–64.
10. S.B.L. MS. 331, ff. 36, 43, 56, 64, 66, 77, 78,
111, 122, 142.
S.B.L. MS. 329, f. 209.
S.B.L. MS. 333, f. 3 *et passim.*
CBD MS. 2, f. 103.
12. S.B.L. MS. 332, ff. 32, 36, 44, 52, 87, 120.
S.B.L. MS. 333, f. 412.
S.R.O. 245/144, ff. 122, 160, 171.
13. H. R. Rathbone, *Letters of Richard Reynolds
with a Memoir of his Life* (1852), p. 45.
J. W. Fletcher, *An Appeal to Matter of Fact and Common Sense* (1772), pp. 35–39.
14. *Gentlemen's Magazine*, vol. 28, (1758), p. 277.
15. J. Randall, *Broseley and its Surroundings* (1879),
p. 165.
Richard Ford-Thomas Goldney, 1 July 1734, 22
Nov. 1735, S.B.L. MS. 3190, Nos. 56, 94.
16. S.R.O. 1649/1.
17. S.R.O. 1224/Box 171.
18. S.R.O. 271/1.
19. S.B.L. MSS. 332 and 333 *passim.*
S.R.O. 245/144 *passim.*
[J. Fogerty], *Lauterdale* (1873), pp. 212–14.
20. CBD MS. 1.
S.B.L. MSS. 329, 330, 331, and 332.
Richard Ford-Thomas Goldney, 1 July 1734, 23
Jan. 1736, 9 June 1736, S.B.L. MS. 3190 Nos. 56,
99, 110.
21. S.B.L. MS. 332, ff. 21, 52, 216.
22. Charles Hadfield, *The Canals of the West Midlands* (1966), pp. 29–32, 49–51.
23. S.B.L. MS. 333, ff. 5, 237, 273, 299, 315.
24. CBD MS. 2, ff. 81, 99, 100, 212.
Shrewsbury Chronicle (18 Feb. 1786).
S.R.O. 245/144, ff. 131, 150.
25. CBD MS. 2, ff. 103, 413.
26. H. Household, *The Thames and Severn Canal*
(1969), pp. 38, 95.
CBD MS. 2, ff. 37, 43, 103, 126, 493.
John Phillips, *Phillips's Inland Navigation* (1805), p.
592.

Salopian Journal (27 July 1796).
Ibid., (5 Oct. 1808).
Hugh Owen, *Some Account of the Ancient and Present
State of Shrewsbury* (1808), p. 57.
Thomas Howell, *The Stranger in Shrewsbury*, 2nd ed.
(1825), p. 106.
27. Charles Hadfield and J. Norris, *Waterways to
Stratford* (1962), pp. 77, 93.
28. J. Plymley, *A General View of the Agriculture of
Shropshire* (1803), pp. 286–88.
29. *Salopian Journal* (21 Jan. 1818).
30. B.R.L., B. & W. Colln. Letter Books (Office),
July 1798–May 1799 f. 170, May 1799–Mar. 1800,
ff. 241–42, Mar.–Nov. 1800, f. 183, Jan.–Sep. 1803,
ff. 241–42, Sep. 1803–Aug. 1804, ff. 2, 12, 21.
Salopian Journal (27 Aug. 1800).
31. S.B.L. MS. 331, f. 36.
32. Charles Hadfield, *op. cit.*, pp. 54–55.
G. Young, *Plan of the River Severn from the Meadow
Wharf near Coalbrookdale to the City of Gloucester*,
(1786), British Waterways Museum, Stoke Bruerne.
Charles Hadfield and A. W. Skempton, *William Jes-
sop: Engineer* (1979), pp. 27–28.
S.B.L. *Watton Collection*, vol. X, p. 280.
Shrewsbury Chronicle (4 Mar. 1786).
33. S.R.O. 27/1, f. 268.
Salopian Journal (3 Sep. 1800).
Charles Hadfield, *op. cit.*, pp. 55, 124–25.
34. Richard Ford-Gabriel Goldney, 2 Feb. 1733,
Richard Ford-Thomas Goldney, 13 Jan. 1736,
S.B.L. MS. 3190 Nos. 3*, 69, 98.
S.B.L. MS 331, f. 58.
S.B.L. MS. 333, ff. 73, 208, 269.
S.R.O. 271/1, f. 70.
L. J. Lee, ed., *A Full List and Partial Abstract of the
Quarter Sessions Rolls* [for Shropshire] 1696–1800,
(n.d.), p. 38.
35. S.B.L. MS. 329, f. 228.
S.B.L. MS. 334, *passim.*
36. S.B.L. MS. 330, ff. 235, 255.
S.B.L. MS. 331, f. 48.
S.B.L. MS. 332, f.9.
CBD MS. 2, f. 103.
S.B.L. MS. 329, f. 218.
37. S.B.L. MS 332, ff. 30, 42, 74, 170, 178, 180,
199, 243.
S.B.L. MS. 334, ff. 398, 417.
CBD MS. 2, ff. 81, 495.
A. S. Davies, '*The River Trade of Montgomeryshire and
its Borders*' in *Montgomeryshire Collections* vol. 43
(1934), p. 41.
38. S.B.L. MS. 329, ff. 16, 26, 43.
S.B.L. MS. 331, f. 18.
S.B.L. MS 332, ff. 39, 42.
CBD MS. 2, f. 435.
S.B.L. MS. 333, ff. 479.
S.R.O. 245/144, ff. 5, 8.
39. *Gentlemen's Magazine*, vol. 28, (1758), p. 277.

CBD MS. 1, f. 246.
S.B.L. MS. 332, f. 52.
CBD MS. 2, ff. 43, 103, 392.
40. J. Randall, *History of Madeley* (1880), p. 254.
C. Hadfield, *op. cit.*, p. 282.
[J. Fogerty] *Lauterdale* (1873), pp. 213–14.
41. H. W. Dickinson, *John Wilkinson: Ironmaster* (1914), pp. 26, 29.
Gentlemen's Magazine, vol. 57, (1787), p. 732.
J. Randall, *The Wilkinsons* (n.d.), pp. 19–20.
W. A. Smith, 'A Swedish view of the West Midlands in 1802–03' in *West Midlands Studies*, vol. 3 (1969), pp. 66–67.
Salopian Journal (29 Nov. 1843).
42. M. J. T. Lewis, *Early Wooden Railways* (1970), pp. 232–36.
43. S.B.L. MS. 2365.
S.R.O. 1224/256.
S.R.O. 2280/3/7/11–12.
44. S.R.O. 1224/299.
William Ferriday-William Forester, 11 Jan. 1755, S.R.O. 1224/259.
Rent Rolls, Lady Day 1747, Lady Day 1748, S.R.O. 676.
45. CBD MS. 1, ff. 95, 239, 343–4, 356–8, 405–6, 429, 434–6, 452, 484, 492, 516.
S.R.O. 2280/3/11–12.
46. S.B.L. MS. 331, ff. 120, 125.
47. *A Plan of a Waggon Way Design'd to Convey Mr. Forrester's Clod Coals from his Coalworks to Coalbrookdale*, S.R.O. 1224/259.
Agreement, Dukesell-Goldney, 23 Jan. 1749, S.R.O. 1224/259.
William Ferriday-William Forester, 4 Jan. 1755, S.R.O. 1224/259.
48. S.B.L. MS. 332, ff. 1–10, 14.
L.S.F. Journal of Abiah Darby, f. 54.
G. Young, *Plan of a Navigable Canal . . . from the Marquess of Stafford's Canal . . . to the River Severn.*
B.R.L., B. & W. Colln., Steamship Box.
49. R. A. Mott, 'English Waggonways of the 18th century' in *T.N.S.* vol. 37 (1964–65), pp. 8–9.
S.B.L. MS. 332, *passim*.
M. J. T. Lewis, *op. cit.*, pp. 269–70.
S. R. Broadbridge, 'Joseph Banks and West Midlands Industry, 1767' in *Staffordshire Industrial Archaeology Society Journal*, vol. 2, (1971), p. 9.
50. S.R.O. 1224/36.
S.B.L. MS. 333, f. 479.
B.M. Map Kxxxvi. 16.1.
51. J. Randall, *History of Madeley* (1880), p. 291.
V.C.H., Salop, vol. 1 (1908) p. 461.
S.B.L. MS. 333, ff. 73, 123.
52. H. M. Rathbone, *op. cit*, p. 25.
S. Smiles, *Industrial Biography: Ironworkers and Toolmakers* (1863), p. 89.
R. A. Mott, *op. cit.*, pp. 22–23.
M. J. T. Lewis, *op. cit.*, pp. 260–65.

S. R. Broadbridge, *op. cit.*, p. 9.
53. Figs. based on S.B.L. MS. 333 quoted in A. Raistrick, *Dynasty of Ironfounders* (1953), p. 180.
A. Young, *Tours in England and Wales* (1932), p. 150.
C. B. Andrews, ed., *Diary of John Byng* (1934), vol. 1, pp. 184–85.
H. M. Rathbone, *op. cit.*, p. 283.
54. J. Randall, *Broseley and its Surroundings* (1879), p. 77.
55. S.B.L. MS. 333, ff. 185, 186, 193, 208.
R. A. Mott, *op. cit.*, pp. 8–9, quoting letter of Samuel Maude, 16 Sep. 1751.
A. Young, *op. cit.*, pp. 150–51.
B. Trinder, ed., *A Description of Coalbrookdale in 1801* (1970), p. 7.
56. *The Hatchett Diary*, ed. A. Raistrick (1967), p. 60.
M. J. T. Lewis, *op. cit.*, pp. 293–96.
For Curr See F. Bland, 'John Curr: Originator of Iron Tram Roads' in, *T.N.S.* vol. 11, (1930–31), pp. 127–29, and R. Galloway, *A history of Coalmining in Great Britain* (1882), pp. 116–17.
57. S.R.O. 245/145.
Memo. on the Dale Works, S.R.O. 1987/20.
St. R.O. D593/F/3/5/54.
58. J. Plymley, *op. cit.*, p. 312.
59. Specimens of many patterns of rails and sleepers, including stone blocks, in Ironbridge Gorge Museum.
C. von. Oeynhausen and H. von Dechen, *Ueber Scheinenweg in England 1826–27* (1829).
60. Staffs. R.O. D593/B/2/7/22/1 and 2.
H. Malet, *The Canal Duke* (1961), *passim*.
S. R. Broadbridge, *op. cit.*, p. 5.
61. *Salopian Shreds and Patches vol. 7.* (1880/85).
S. R. Broadbridge, *op. cit.*, p. 5.
For a full survey of the canal see D. R. Adams and J. Hazeley, *Survey of the Church Aston-Lilleshall Mining Area* (1970).
For the underground levels see *Plan of the Donnington Wood Colliery* (1788 with later additions). Whereabouts of original unknown. I am grateful to Mr. J. Pagett for the loan of his copy.
For details of boat sizes, see St. R.O. D593/F/3/5/56.
62. For a full account of this project see I. J. Brown and B. S. Trinder, *The Coalport Tar Tunnel* (1971).
Ironbridge Gorge Museum, Guide 4.04 *The Tar Tunnel* (1979).
Shropshire Newsletter Nos. 33 (1967) and 35 (1968).
63. J. Plymley, *op. cit.*, p. 290.
W. A. Smith, *op. cit.*, pp. 55–56, 61.
R. Ll. Tonkinson, *Inclined Planes on the Shropshire Canals* (Birmingham School of Architecture thesis, 1964).
S.B.L. MS. 334, ff. 2, 3, 160.
64. Staffs. R.O. B/2/11/7.

Shrewsbury Chronicle (5 Jan. 1788).
William Reynolds-William Rathbone, 16 Jan. 1788, quoted in A. Raistrick, *op. cit.*, p. 189.
B.T.H.R. Shropshire Canal Minutes 12 June 1788.
  65. Geo. III c. lxxiii.
B.T.H.R. Shropshire Canal Minutes.
  66. 28 Geo. III c. lxxiii.
G. Young, *Plan of a Navigable Canal . . . from the Marquis of Stafford's Canal to . . . the River Severn* (1788), B.R.L., B. & W. Colln., Steamship Box.
  67. J. Plymley, *op. cit.*, p. 296.
  68. B.T.H.R. Shropshire Canal Minutes, 13 June 1788, 18 July 1788, 24 Oct. 1788, D. Davies-Boulton and Watt, 18 July 1788, 20 Aug. 1788, 10 Sep. 1788, B.R.L., B. & W. Colln., Box 4 'D'.
For Henry Williams, see below, p. 209.
  69. B.T.H.R. Shropshire Canal Minutes, 26 Sep. 1800, 1 May 1801, 10 Dec. 1790.
R. Ll. Tonkinson, *op. cit.*
St. R.O. D593/F/3/5/55.
70. B.T.H.R. Shropshire Canal Minutes, 10 Mar. 1790, 17 Oct. 1791, 27 Feb. 1793, 6 Nov. 1795, 10 May 1790, 18 May 1789, 10 July 1790.
  71. B.T.H.R. Shropshire Canal Minutes, 13 June 1788, 12 June 1788, 3 Dec. 1788, 9 Nov. 1780, 24 Feb. 1790, 27 Nov. 1789.
  72. B.T.H.R. Shropshire Canal Minutes, 18 May 1789, 18 May 1790, 19 July 1790, 7 Oct. 1790.
  73. B.T.H.R. Shropshire Canal Minutes, 6 Oct. 1791, 19 Dec. 1792.
  74. B.T.H.R. Shropshire Canal Minutes, 4 Oct. 1792.
  75. J. Plymley, *op. cit.*, pp. 294–95.
  76. The accounts of traffic carried in the tunnels and shafts are taken from S.R.O. 245/145, Tunnel Accts.
M. W. Doughty 'Samborne Palmer's Diary' I.A.R., (III.1.1978), p. 19.
  77. John Curr-Richard Dearman, 25 May 1793. Original in Coalbrookdale Museum. Reprinted in F. Bland, *op. cit.*, pp. 127–29.
Science Museum, William Reynolds's Sketch Book, f. 53.
  78. CBD MS. 3, f. 25, 49–50.
For a further description of the route see B. Trinder, *op. cit.*, p. 7.
  79. B.T.H.R. Shropshire Canal Minutes, 18 April 1796, 4 Oct. 1798, 2 Nov. 1800, 5 Oct. 1832. CBD MS. 2, ff. 149, 175, 208, 275, 334, 384, 437, 494.
S.R.O. 245/145 Horsehay Accts.
S.B.L. MS. 336, f. 992.
  80. J. Plymley, *op. cit.*, p. 315.
S.R.O. 168/153.
For Preens Eddy Bridge see below pp. 87–89.
For the Tar Tunnel see I. J. Brown and B. S. Trinder, *op. cit.*
  81. B.T.H.R. Shropshire Canal Minutes 16 July 1790, 7 May 1792.
Date stone in Ironbridge Gorge Museum.
G. Young, *op. cit.*
S.R.I. 270/1, f. 65.
  82. Earliest references to Coalport are in S.R.O. 245/145, Tunnel Accts., and S.B.L. 334, unpaginated section.
  83. For industries at Coalport see below pp. 127–32, 134–35.
B.T.H.R. Shropshire Canal Minutes, 6 Oct. 1803, 15 June 1810, 13 July 1810.
Staffs. R.O. D876/155, f. 169.
J. Dutens, *Memoirs sur les Travaux Publiques d'Angleterre*, (1819).
J. Plymley, *op. cit.*, p. 84.
Barrie Trinder, *The Most Extraordinary District in the World* (1977), p. 107.
  84. Staffs. R.O. D876/155, f. 53.
  85. *Ibid.*, ff. 1, 52, 111, 158–59.
S.R.O. 1681/181.
  86. S.B.L. MS. 334, ff. 1, 2, 10, 119, 139, 143, 193.
S.B.L. MS. 336, f. 1040.
  87. The Despatch Book of Thomas Dykes, 1801–02.
I am grateful to Mr. W. Lawrence of Wellington for allowing me to examine this document.
  88. S.B.L. MS. 335, 2 Jan. 1802.
  89. B.T.H.R. Shropshire Canal Minutes, 2 Oct. 1794, 3 Nov. 1794, 12 Jan. 1795, 1 Oct. 1795, 6 Oct. 1796, 14 Nov. 1796, 6 Jan. 1797, 21 April 1797, 8 May 1797.
  90. S.R.O. 1150/898.
Robert Baugh, *Map of Shropshire* (n.d., c. 1808) for route of railway from Sutton Wharf as far as Hollinswood.
Letters from Simon Goodrich to General Bentham, giving an account of a tour of engineering works in 1799. Goodrich Collection, Science Museum.
B.T.H.R. Shropshire Canal Minutes 5 June 1812, 18 April 1814, 28 April 1815.
  91. 33 Geo. III, c. cxiii.
C. Hadfield, *op. cit.*, pp. 160–63.
  92. C. Hadfield, *op. cit.*, p. 160.
Salopian Journal (3 Dec. 1794).
Ibid., (23 Mar. 1796).
Ibid., (16 Nov. 1796).
  93. *Salopian Journal* (3 Dec. 1794).
Ibid., (15 Jan. 1800).
Ibid., (18 May 1803).
  94. Stephen Ballard, report in Hereford and Gloucester Canal Minute Book 3 Aug. 1829, quoted in Charles Hadfield, *op. cit.*, p. 159.
  95. A. Birch, 'The Midlands Iron Industry during the Napoleonic Wars' in *Edgar Allen News* (Aug./Sep. 1952).
  96. J. Randall, *History of Madeley* (1880), p. 290.
  97. 12 Geo. I. c. 9.

3 Geo. II. c. 6.

98. William Ferriday-William Forester, 6 Jan. 1755. S.R.O. 1224/259.

R. More-W. Forester, n.d. 1755, S.R.O. 1224/259.

99. 4 Geo. III. c. lccci.

S.R.O. 1681/196.

100. For routes see Robert Baugh, *Map of Shropshire* (n.d. c. 1808), J. Rocque, *Carte Topographique de la Comté de Salop ou Shropshire*, (1752).

29 Geo. II c. lx.

25 Geo. II c.lx.

B.M. Add. MS. 21018.

18 Geo. III c.ixc.

Shrewsbury Chronicle (9 May 1778).

Ibid., (28 Aug. 1778).

101. Barrie Trinder, 'Coalport Bridge: a study in Historical Interpretation', *J.A.R.* (III. 2. 1979), pp. 153–57.

102. S.R.O. 1681/196.

46 Geo. III c. viii.

103. Minute Book of the Proprietors of the Ironbridge, S.B.L. MS. 3689, *passim*.

Abraham Darby III Ledger Accounts, f, 22–23,

S.R.O. 2448/1.

J. Randall, *Broseley and its Surroundings* (1879), p. 238.

104. S.B.L. MS. 330, ff. 143, 205, 213.

105. S.B.L. MS 330, ff. 263, 275, 277, 293, 297. S.B.L. MS. 332, f. 220.

106. S.B.L. MS. 333, ff. 3, 64, 354, 391, 396, 425, 433.

S.R.O. 245/144, ff. 28, 74, 106, 126, 151, 166, 219. Abraham Darby III Cash Book, ff. 17, 18. S.R.O. 1987/19.

107. S.B.L. MS. 334, *passim*.

108. S.B.L. MS. 336, f. 1313.

S.R.O. 245/144, ff. 41, 74.

S.B.L. MS. 334, f. 51.

109. S.B.L. MS. 337, f. 1490.

Salopian Journal (26 Feb. 1806).

110. *Shrewsbury Chronicle* (23 Feb. 1782).

Ibid., (1 June 1782).

S.R.O. 27/1, ff. 157, 160.

111. S.B.L. MS. 337, f. 1393.

W. G. Norris, *The Horsehay Ironworks* (MS), S.R.O. 245/140.

Notes to Chapter IX

1. A. E. Musson and E. Robinson, 'The Early Growth of Steam Power' in *Science and Technology in the Industrial Revolution* (1969), pp. 405–420. J. R. Harris, 'The Employment of Steam Power in the 18th century' in *History* vol. 52, (1967), pp. 133–148.

2. J. Plymley, *A General View of the Agriculture of Shropshire* (1803), p. 340.

3. L. T. C. Rolt, *Thomas Newcomen' The Prehistory of the Steam Engine* (1963), *passim*.

4. J. R. Harris, *op. cit.*, p. 147.

5. R. A. Mott, 'The Newcomen Engine in the 18th century' in, *T.N.S.* vol. 35, (1962–63), pp. 74–86.

6. S.R.O. 2280/3/6 and 9.

L. T. C. Rolt and J. S. Allen, *The Steam Engine of Thomas Newcomen* (1977), pp. 57, 146.

7. R. A. Mott, *op. cit.*, p. 74. See above pp. 48–49.

8. R. A. Mott, *op. cit.*, pp. 75, 81.

9. S.B.L. MS. 331, f. 89.

10. *V.C.H., Salop* vol. 1 (1908), p. 464. S.R.O. 1681/7.

11. J. Randall, *History of Madeley* (1880), pp. 178–79.

See above pp. 22–25.

12. Proposals made and agreed to by the Coalbrookdale Company, the Bersham Company and the New Willey Company, 19 Oct. 1762.

13. L. T. C. Rolt, *Tools for the Job* (1968), pp. 53–56.

W. K. V. Gale, *Boulton, Watt and the Soho Undertakings*

(1952), pp. 10–14.

14. B. M. Egerton MSS. 1941 ff. 29–30. List of John Wilkinson's engines, n.d. B.R.L. B. & W. Colln., Box 20 Bundle 16.

H. W. Dickinson and Rhys Jenkins, *James Watt and the Steam Engine* (1927) pp. 44, 111–12, 115–16.

15. William Reynolds-William Rathbone, 30 12mo. 1777, quoted in A. Raistrick, *Dynasty of Iron-founders* (1953), p. 94.

16. Agreement, 29 Jan. 1778, Henry Williams-James Watt, 24 April 1780. Certificate of Trial of Engine, 2 April 1779, William Reynolds-James Watt, 19 May 1780, Richard Reynolds & Co.-Boulton and Watt, 31 8mo. 1780, B.R.L., B. & W. Colln., Box 40 and Box 2 'R'.

17. James Watt-William Reynolds, 3 Jan. 1781. (Original in custody of Institution of Mechanical Engineers).

Richard Reynolds & Co.-Boulton and Watt, 31 10 mo. 1781, Rathbone & Co.-Boulton & Watt, 16 April 1782, B.R.L., B. & W. Colln., Box 2 'R'.

B. Trinder, ed., *A Description of Coalbrookdale in 1801* (1970), p. 11.

Rathbone & Co.-Boulton and Watt, 13 June 1786, B.R.L., B. & W. Colln., Box XIII.

Coalbrookdale Co.-Boulton and Watt, 17 Nov. 1788, M. Gilpin-James Watt, 2 3mo. 1789, B.R.L., B. & W. Colln., Box 4 'C'.

18. William Reynolds-James Watt, 23 11mo. 1782, 30 5mo. 1783, B.R.L., B. & W. Colln., Box 2 'R'.

Catalogue of Old Engines, B.R.L., B. & W. Colln.

A. Raistrick, *op. cit.*, pp. 152–53.

19. The various lists of engines built by John Wilkinson compiled by Boulton and Watt in their disputes with Wilkinson over 'pirate' engines c. 1795 are all of engines made at Bersham.

20. William Wilkinson-James Watt Jun., 22 Nov. 1801, B.R.L., B. & W. Colln., Box 20, Bundle 22. Letter Box (Office), Nov. 1800–July 1801, f. 176, B.R.L., B. & W. Colln.
H. W. Dickinson and Rhys Jenkins, *op. cit.*, p. 322.
A. E. Musson & E. Robinson, *op. cit.*, p. 425.
S.R.O. 271/1, *passim*.
Hugh Torrens, *The Evolution of a family firm* (1978), p. 24.

21. William Reynolds-William Rathbone, 1 April 1790, quoted in A. Raistrick, *op. cit.*, pp. 154–55.
S.R.O. 270/1 f. 344.

22. A Raistrick, *op. cit.*, pp. 157–59.
S.B.L. MS. 2365.
S. M. Tonkin, 'Trevithick, Rastrick and the Hazledine foundry at Bridgnorth' in, *T.N.S.* vol. 26, (1947–49), pp. 1743–74.
Henry Williams-Boulton and Watt, 21 Sep. 1796, B.R.L., B. & W. Colln., Box 5 'W'.

23. CBD MS. 2, f. 331.
R. Trevithick-David Giddy, 22 Aug. 1802, quoted in A. Raistrick, *op. cit.*, pp. 163–64.

24. E. A. Forward, 'Links in the History of the Locomotive: Trevithick's first Railway Locomotive, Coalbrookdale 1802–03' in *The Engineer* (22 Feb. 1952), pp. 266–68.
G. F. Westcott, *The British Railway Locomotive 1803–53* (1958) p. 3 and Plate I.

25. Thomas Boycott: His Book, S.R.O. 245/14.
William Wilkinson-James Watt Jun., 17 Jan. 1802, B.R.L., B. & W. Colln., Box 20, Bundle 22.
Confession by W. Anstice in speech to Iron and Steel Institute reported in *Salopian Journal* (6 Sep. 1871).
J. Randall, *History of Madeley* (1880), p. 179.

26. CBD MS. 2, ff. 341, 394.
S.B.L. MS. 336, f. 1342.
R. J. Law, *The Steam Engine* (1965), p. 19.
S. M. Tonkin, *op. cit.*, pp. 171–76.

27. Staffs. R.O. D876/155, f. 41.
Salopian Journal (6 Sep. 1871).
J. Randall, *History of Madeley* (1880), p. 179.
A. Raistrick, *op. cit.*, pp. 165–67.

28. William Reynolds's Sketch Book, f. 27. Science Museum.
L. C. Lloyd, 'A beam engine at the Rats Pits' in *T.S.A.S.*, vol. 53, (1949–50), p. 24.
Sula Rayska, *Victorian and Edwardian Shropshire from Old Photographs* (1977), 28.
Ivor J. Brown, *The Mines of Shropshire* (1976), p. 16.

29. S.B.L. MS. 335, 26 Sep. 1800.

30. A. E. Musson & E. Robinson, *op. cit.*, pp. 405–06.

31. Alexander Brodie-Boulton and Watt 4 May 1798 and 10 May 1798, B.R.L., B. & W. Colln., Parcel F 'B'.
Boulton and Watt-Alexander Brodie 28 April 1798, B.R.L., B. & W. Colln., Letter Book (Office), July 1797-July 1798, f. 184.

32. Catalogue of Old Engines, B.R.L., B. & W. Colln.
I.B.G.M., Lill. Co. Colln., Mr. Wilkinson's proposals to Messrs. Bishton and Rowley, 30 Nov. 1793.
S.R.O. 1150/898.
G. Young, *Plan of a Navigable Canal from the Marquis of Stafford's Canal . . . to the River Severn*, (1788), B.R.L., B. & W. Colln., Steamship Box.

33. *Salopian Journal* (19 June 1811).
I.B.G.M., Lill. Co. Colln., Portion of the Hadley Estate Map, 1809.
Staffs. R.O. D876/155, ff. 41, 67.
S.B.L. MS. 334, f. 108.
I.B.G.M., Lill. Co. Colln., Charter masters' Book, 6 July 1793.
CBD MS. 2, f.393.
Henry Williams-Matthew Boulton, 23 Aug. 1781, B.R.L., B. & W. Colln., Box 40.

34. B. Trinder, *op. cit.*, p. 11.
Children's Emp. Comm. Rep. p. 33.

35. William Reynolds-James Watt, 10 Feb. 1787, 16 May 1789, B.R.L., B. & W. Colln., Box 4 'R'.
M. Gilpin-James Watt, 2 3mo. 1789, B.R.L., B. & W. Colln., Box 4 'C'.

36. William Reynolds-William Rathbone, 1 April 1790, quoted in A. Raistrick, *op. cit.*, pp. 154–55.
William Reynolds's Sketchbook, *passim*. Science Museum.
H. Davey, 'The Newcomen Engine' in *Procs. of the Institution of Mechanical Engineers* (1903) includes a photograph of a Coalbrookdale atmospheric winding-engine in Plate 17.

37. S.R.O. 271/1, ff. 9, 140, 149, 152, 166, 176, 198, 215, 281, 312.

38. CBD MS. 2, f. 174.
W. G. Norris, *The Horsehay Ironworks* (MS.), S.R.O. 245/10.
S.R.O. 1190/112.
Salopian Journal (19 June 1811).
Ibid., 9 April 1817.
I.B.G.M., Lill. Co. Colln., Charter masters' Book, 13 Sep. 1800, Wrockwardine Wood Ironstone Reckoning, 1805.
S.R.O. 1150/898.
I.B.G.M., Lill. Co. Colln., Portion of the Hadley Estate Map. 1809.
Lists of Engines built by John Wilkinson, B.R.L., B. & W. Colln., Box 20, Bundles 2 and 16.
St. R.O.; D593/F/3/5/56.

39. S.B.L. MS. 334, ff. 7, 17, 36, 86, 90, 113, 166, 419, 444.
S.B.L. MS. 336, ff. 911, 937, 970, 1001, 1009, 1045,

1134, 1342, 1367.

40. B.T.H.R., Shropshire Canal Minutes, 18 May 1789, 10 Mar. 1790, 10 May 1790.

H. W. Dickinson and Rhys Jenkins, *op. cit.*, p. 316.

41. Bevis Hillier, *Master Potters of the Industrial Revolution* (1965), p. 84.

G. P. Godden, *Coalport and Coalbrookdale Porcelain* (1970), p. 53.

J. W. Hall, 'Joshua Field's Diary of a Tour in 1821 through the Midlands' in, *T.N.S.*, vol. 6, (1925–26), pp. 30–32.

V.C.H., Salop vol. 1, (1908), p. 443.

42. J. Randall, *History of Madeley* (1880), p. 364.

William Reynolds-James Watt, 23 11mo. 1782, 22 July 1783, B.R.L., B. & W. Colln., Box 2 'R'.

The Hatchett Diary, ed. by A. Raistrick (1967), p. 60.

William Reynolds's Sketchbook, f. 6. Science Museum.

43. Letters Books (Office), July 1801–April 1802, f. 208, Nov. 1800–July 1801, f. 278, B.R.L., B. & W. Colln.

S.R.O. 1150/898.

CBD MS. 2, ff. 6, 38, 52, 125, 281, 341, 394.

S.R.O. 1190/112.

44. William Reynolds & Co.-Boulton and Watt, 26 Aug. 1796, B.R.L., B. & W. Colln., Box 2 'R'.

Henry Williams-J. Buchanan, 21 Jan. 1782, B.R.L., B. & W. Colln., Box 40.

William Wilkinson-James Watt Jun., 17 Jan. 1802, B.R.L., B. & W. Colln., Box 20, Bundle 22.

Notes to Chapter X

1. Barrie Trinder, ed., *A Description of Coalbrookdale in 1801* (1970), pp. 6, 15.

Asa Briggs, *Victorian Cities* (1968), p. 93.

2. J. Hamilton-Lord Dundonald, n.d. (1789), Scot. R.O. GD 233/109/H/53.

3. Charles Hadfield and A. W. Skempton, *William Jessop: Engineer* (1979), pp. 27–28.

B.T.H.R. Shropshire Canal Minutes, 15 July 1788.

Shrewsbury Chronicle (4 March 1786).

4. Charles Hadfield, 'Telford, Jessop and Pontcysyllte', in *Journal of the Railway and Canal Historical Society*, vol. 15, (1969), p. 71.

5. A. Young, *Tours in England and Wales* (1932), pp. 145–53.

The Diary of John Byng, ed. by C. B. Andrews (1934), vol. 1, pp. 184–85.

The Journals of the Rev. John Wesley, ed. by N. Curnock (1938), vol. 5, pp. 87, 278, 424, 516–17; vol. 6, pp. 33, 226, 478; vol. 7, pp. 150, 225, 345, 367–68, 480; vol. 8, p. 54.

Robert Townson, 'A Sketch of the Mineralogy of Shropshire' in *Tracts and Observations in Natural History and Physiology* (1799), pp. 164–202.

The Hatchett Diary, ed. by Arthur Raistrick (1967), pp. 56–60.

Charles Dibdin, *Observations on a Tour through almost the whole of England and a considerable part of Scotland in a series of Letters* (1801–02), vol. 2, pp. 309–12.

Selections from these and other accounts of the area are anthologised in Barrie Trinder. *The Most Extraordinary District in the World* (1977).

6. Marchant de le Houlière, 'Report to the French Government on British Methods of smelting iron ore with coke and casting naval cannon' (1775), trans. and ed. by W. H. Chaloner in *Edgar Allen News* (Dec. 1948/Jan. 1949).

Jean Dutens, *Memoirs sur les Travaux Publiques d'Angleterre* (1819).

P. J. Wexler, *La Formation du vocabulaire des Chemins de Fer en France (1788–1842)*, (1955), p. 19.

C. von Oeynhausen and H. von Dechen, *Railways in England 1826 and 1827*, translated by E. A. Forward, ed. Charles E. Lee (1971).

Joseph von Baader, *Neues System der Fortschaffenden Mechanik* (1822).

Charles Hadfield, *op. cit.*, p. 71.

Matthew Boulton-James Watt, 13 April 1782, B.R.L., B. & W. Colln., Parcel D.

M. Flinn, 'The Travel Diaries of Swedish Engineers of the 18th century as Sources of Technological History', in *T.N.S.*, vol. 31, (1957–58), pp. 104–05.

Svedenstierna's Tour in Great Britain, 1802–03; The Travel Diary of an Industrial Spy, ed. M. W. Flinn (1973).

'Viaggio in Einhilterra di Carlo Castone del Torre di Renzionico Comasco', in *Salopian Shreds and Patches* (1890), p. 337.

Wolverhampton Chronicle (7 July 1790).

Salopian Journal (24 Aug. 1796).

7. See above pp. 70–71.

8. John Harris, 'Pritchard Re-devivus', *Country Life*, (29 Feb. 1968).

Robin Chaplin, 'New Light on Thomas Farnolls Pritchard', *Shropshire Newsletter* (no. 34, June 1968).

I am grateful to James Lawson, of Shrewsbury Schools, for access to his extensive researches on Pritchard.

9. John White, 'On Cementitious Architecture, as application to the construction of bridges, with a prefatory note on the first introduction of iron as the constituent material, for bridges of a large span by Thomas Farnolls Pritchard in 1773', *Philosophical Magazine and Annals of Philosophy*, vol. XI (1832), p. 183.

Berrow's Worcester Journal (16 Dec. 1773, 30 June 1774).

10. *Ex inf.* James Lawson.

11. John White, *op. cit.*, p. 183.

Thomas Tredgold, *A Practical essay on the strength of Cast Iron* (1824), pp. 9–10.

Thomas Telford, *Autobiography*, ed. John Rickman (1838), p. 29.

Chambers's Edinburgh Journal, (vol. 13, 1832), p. 21.

12. *Shrewsbury Chronicle* (26 Feb. 1774, 4 Feb., 26 Aug., 9 Sep. 1773).

Berrow's Worcester Journal (24 Feb. 1774).

13. Minute Book of the Proprietors of the Iron Bridge, 1775–1799, Shrewsbury Borough Library MS 3689 (henceforth SBL 3689), 15 Sep., 17 Oct., 21 Oct. 1775.

Estimate for the erection of a Cast Iron Bridge, Copy in Ironbridge Gorge Museum.

Journal of the House of Commons 1774–76, pp. 514, 558, 580, 598, 635, 640, 667, 679.

Journal of the House of Lords 1774–76, pp. 583, 587, 589, 593, 16 Geo. III c. 17, 1776.

Shrewsbury Chronicle (17 Feb. 1776).

14. For details of shareholders see S.B.L. 3689 and the Proprietors' Assignment Book, SBL 3690. Biographical details are drawn chiefly from the *Shrewsbury Chronicle* 1772–1810, and from probate records in the Hereford Record Office.

15. S.B.L. 3689.

16. Abraham Darby III's Ledger Accounts, S.R.O. 2448/1.

Abraham Darby III's Cash Book, 1768–1781, S.R.O. 1987/19.

Shrewsbury Chronicle (10 July 1779, 20 Jan. 1781). Text with woodcut of the Iron Bridge by J. Edmunds in Ironbridge Gorge Museum. This text forms the basis of the well-known account of the building of the bridge in W. Camden, *Britannia*, ed. Richard Gough (1789), vol. 2, pp. 357–58.

17. *The Journal of the Revd. John Wesley*, ed. N. Curnock, (1938), vol. 6, pp. 225–26.

18. S.R.O. 2448/1.

Shrewsbury Chronicle (10 July 1779, 20 Jan. 1781).

19. *The Torrington Diaries*, ed. C. B. Andrews (1934), vol. 1, p. 184.

Estimate for the erection of a Cast Iron Bridge, Copy in Ironbridge Gorge Museum.

S.R.O. 2448/1.

Anonymous diary of a Warwickshire landowner, S.R.O. 2495.

20. *Shrewsbury Chronicle* (27 Dec. 1777).

S.B.L. 3689, 3690.

S.R.O. 1987/19.

I am grateful to Robin Chaplin for bringing the gazebo to my notice, and to Michael Wise for making arrangements for me to see it.

21. Samuel Smiles, *Industrial Biography: Ironworkers and Toolmakers* (1863), p. 91.

Thomas Tredgold, *op. cit.*, pp. 9–10.

Thomas Telford, *op. cit.*, p. 29.

22. S.R.O. 1514/2/820.

S.R.O. 1987/19.

Transactions of the Society of Arts, vol. 6 (1788), pp. 229, 279.

23. Minutes of the Proprietors of the Tontine Hotel, S.R.O. 245/6.

Neil Cossons and Barrie Trinder, *The Iron Bridge* (1979), pp. 41–43.

24. Stuart Smith, *A View from the Iron Bridge* (1979), pp. 14–16.

25. *Ibid.*, pp. 16–17.

The original paintings are in Clive House Museum, Shrewsbury.

26. Arthur Young, *op. cit.*, p. 152.

27. Stuart Smith, *op. cit.*, pp. 18–19.

The original is in the collection of Sir Alexander Gibb and Partners, Reading.

28. Stuart Smith, *op. cit.*, pp. 20–23.

29. *Ibid.*, pp. 26–31.

30. *Ibid.*, pp. 46–47.

31. *Ibid.*, pp. 33–35.

32. *Ibid.*, p. 35.

Arthur Raistrick, *Dynasty of Ironfounders* (1953), facing p. 96.

33. Thomas Harral, *Picturesque Views of the Severn* (1824), vol. 1, p. 229 and plates *passim*.

S. B. Smith, *op. cit.*, pp. 40–42.

34. John Fletcher-William Wase, 14 Feb. 1781, Melville Horne, *Posthumous Pieces of the late Revd. J. W. de la Flechère* (1791), p. 66.

35. Quoted in Charles Hulbert, *A History and Description of the Country of Salop* (1837), vol. 2, p. 350.

36. *Viaggo . . . di Carlo Castrone, op. cit.*

37. Henry Skrine, *Two Successive Tours through the whole of Wales with Several of the English Counties* (1808), p. 618.

Notes to Chapter XI

1. Barrie Trinder and Jeff Cox, Yeomen and Colliers in Telford, (1980), pp. 71, 173–74, 380–84. Richard Ford-Thomas Goldney, 29 Jan. 1733 and 30 Mar. 1733, S.B.L. MS. 3190, Nos. 2 and 11, see also above, pp. 30–32.

2. A Raistrick, *Dynasty of Ironfounders* (1953).

3. H. R. Rathbone, *Letters of Richard Reynolds with a Memoir of his Life* (1852), pp. 1–81.

4. S. R. Broadbridge, 'Joseph Banks and West Midlands Industry, 1767' in *Staffordshire Industrial Archaeology Society Journal*, vol. 2, (1971), p. 7.

5. H. R. Rathbone, *op. cit.*, pp. 32, 126.

6. Abraham Darby-Thomas Goldney, 30 12mo. 1756, S.R.O. 1987.

Abiah Darby-Rachel Thompson, 5 mo. 1757, copy in A. H. Simpson Colln., Garmston.

7. Letter of Abiah Darby, c. 1779, MS. in Lady Labouchere's collection, Dudmaston.

8. Erasmus Darwin, *The Botanic Garden* (1791), vol. I, p. 39.

Abraham Darby III's Cash Book, 1769–81, f. 10, S.R.O. 1987, Box 19.

Shrewsbury Chronicle (6 Sep. 1793, 28 Dec. 1810).

Salopian Journal (11, 18 June 1800).

9. A. Raistrick, Dynasty of Ironfounders (1953), pp. 93–95.

J. Randall, *History of Madeley* (1800), pp. 81–102.

Letters from Simon Goodrich to General Bentham, giving an account of a tour of engineering works in 1799. Goodrich Collection. Science Museum. William Reynolds-Lord Dundonald, 18 Dec. 1799, Scots. R.O. GD 233/109/H/27.

Joshua Gilpin's Journals and notebooks, vol. 26, microfilm in B.U.L.

Shrewsbury Chronicle (11 Sep. 1795).

George Peacock *Memoir of Dr. Thomas Young* (1855), pp. 74–75.

See also pp. 134–5.

10. See above pp. 37–38, 71, 95–96.

11. J. Randall, *The Wilkinsons* (n.d.), p. 31.

12. John Wilkinson-Boulton and Watt, 16 Jan. 1797, Observations by James Watt on the case of Boulton and Watt v John Wilkinson, Nov. 1795, B.R.L., B. & W. Colln., Box 20, Bundles 16 and 17.

13. Lord Dundonald-William Reynolds, 14 Feb. 1800, Scots. R.O. GD 233/109/H/3.

14. J. Priestley Jun.-John Wilkinson, 3 Oct. 1790, Warrington Public Library, Priestley Correspondence, f. 3.

15. H. R. Rathbone, *op. cit.*, pp. 134, 179–80, 186.

16. Lord Dundonald-William Reynolds, 15 Dec. 1799, 14 Feb. 1800, Scots. R.O. GD 233/233/106/C/60, GD 233/109/H/3.

17. Joseph Priestley-John Wilkinson 20 Jan. 1791, Warrington Public Library, Priestley Correspondence.

18. William Wilkinson-James Watt, 7 Mar. 1797, B.R.L., B. & W. Colln., Box 20, Bundle 21.

19. Joseph Priestley-John Wilkinson, 15 Nov. 1796 and 20 Oct. 1796, Warrington Public Library Priestley Correspondence, ff. 46, 50.

Commercial and Agricultural Magazine (November 1799).

20. William Wilkinson-James Watt, 22 Jan. 1800, B.R.L., B. & W. Colln., Box 20, Bundle 21.

21. Observations by James Watt on the case of Boulton and Watt v John Wilkinson, Nov. 1795, B.R.L., B. & W. Colln., Box 20 Bundle 16.

22. J. Wilkinson-J. Priestley, 10 Oct. 1791, Warrington Public Library, Priestley Correspondence, f. 16.

23. A. N. Palmer, *John Wilkinson and the Old Bersham Ironworks* (1899), p. 36.

24. William Wilkinson-James Watt, 24 Oct. 1795, B.R.L., B. & W. Colln., Box 20, Bundle 21.

A. N. Palmer, *op. cit.*, p. 36.

G. Gilpin-William Wilkinson, May 1804, S.R.O. 1781/6/28.

25. P. Mathias, *English Trade Tokens* (1962), pp. 54–55.

John Wilkinson-Boulton and Watt, 6 Mar. 1797, B.R.L., B. & W. Colln., Box 20, Bundle 17.

A. N. Palmer, *op. cit.*, p. 33.

J. Randall, *Broseley and its Surroundings* (1879), p. 115.

26. William Wilkinson-James Watt Jun., 17 Jan. 1802 and 28 Mar. 1807, B.R.L., B. & W. Colln., Box 20, Bundle 22.

27. Richard Ford-Thomas Goldney, 30 Mar. 1734, S.B.L. MS. 3190, No. 11.

For the Dorsetts' roles on the Charlton estates see above Chapter Five.

R. A. Mott, 'The Shropshire Iron Industry' in *T.S.A.S..*, vol. 56, (1957–60), p. 71.

Robin Chaplin, 'A Forgotten Industrial Valley' in, *S.N.L.* No. 36, 1969, pp. 3–5.

28. F. Paddy-Lord Stafford, 25 June 1755, Staffs. R.O., D641/2/K/1/1.

29. For the Hortons see:

B.T.H.R.., Shropshire Canal Company Minutes, 28 April 1815.

A. Birch, 'The Midlands Iron Industry during the Napoleonic Wars' in, *Edgar Allen News* (Aug./Sep. 1952).

30. Henry Williams-James Watt, 28 Aug. 1779, Henry Williams-J. Buchanan, 21 Jan. 1782, B.R.L., B. & W. Colln., Box 40.

Staffs. R.O. D593/I/1/34, D593/M/17/1.

31. S.R.O. 2524/13.

32. J. P. Addis, *The Crawshay Dynasty* (1957), pp. xi, xii, 5.

Broseley Survey 1820, S.R.O. 1190/112 (Box).

33. A. Birch, *op. cit.*

G. Gilpin-J. Wise, 3 Oct. 1819, in M. Elsas, *Iron in the Making* (1960), p. 7.

Shrewsbury Chronicle (26 July 1816).

Notes to Chapter XII

1. Clifton Roberts, 'Salopian China' in *The Connoisseur*, vol. 58, (1919–20), p. 149.

Sir Edward Benthall, 'Some 18th century Shropshire Potteries' in *T.S.A.S.* vol. 55 (1955), p. 160.

J. Randall, *The Severn Valley* (1882), p. 309.

2. Sir Edward Benthall, *op. cit.*, p. 162.

S.B.L. MS. 2365.

3. G. A. Godden, *Caughley and Worcester Porcelains* (1969), p. 1.

Aris's Birmingham Gazette, (3 July 1775).

Roger Edmondson, 'Coalport China Works, Shropshire' in *I.A.R.* vol. 3 (1979), p. 124.
B.M. Add. MSs. 21018.
Salopian Journal, (21 Sep. 1803).
 4. *Salopian Journal* (30 Oct. 1799).
Shrewsbury Chronicle (13, 20 Sep. 1797, 12 Jan., 16 Feb. 1988).
 5. See above pp. 88–89.
 6. Abraham Darby's Ledger Accounts, f. 32, S.R.O. 2448/1.
CBD MS. 3, p. 76.
S.R.O. 1681/131, 137, 153.
S.B.L. MS. 334 (Unpaginated section).
 7. S.B.L. MS. 334, ff. 1, 5, 17.
Salopian Journal (24 Aug. 1796).
CBD MS. 2, f. 17.
The Hatchett Diary, ed. by A. Raistrick (1967), p. 60.
G. A. Godden, *Coalport and Coalbrookdale Porcelains* (1970), pp. 7–8.
Joshua Gilpin's Journals and Notebooks, vol. 26, Microfilm in B.U.L.
Shrewsbury Chronicle (2 Sep. 1803).
Roger Edmundson, *op. cit.*, pp. 126–27.
 8. G. A. Godden, *Coalport and Coalbrookdale Porcelains* (1970), pp. 1, 10, 13–14.
Salopian Journal (2, 9 and 30 Oct. 1799, 24 and 31 Aug. and 21 Sep. 1803).
Staffs. R.O. D876/155, f. 13.
S.R.O. 1224/3/438.
 9. S.B.L. MS. 334, ff. 50, 105, 115.
G. A. Godden, *Coalport and Coalbrookdale Porcelains* (1970), pp. 2–3.
J. Plymley, *A General View of the Agriculture of Shropshire* (1803), pp. 340–51.
Drawing of Wheel and Pot Works at Coalport, Anon. 1810. Ironbridge Gorge Museum.
Madeley Wood Co.-Boulton and Watt 3 Jan. 1796, B.R.L., B. & W. Colln., Box 3 'M'.
S.R.O. 1224/225.
Roger Edmundson, *op. cit.*, pp. 127–28.
Shrewsbury Chronicle (28 April 1797, 12 Jan. 1810).
 10. Staffs. R.O. D876/155, ff. 30, 36, 51, 58, 60.
G. A. Godden, *Coalport and Coalbrookdale Porcelains* (1970), pp. 52–57.
Staffordshire Mercury (5 Mar. 1814).
Salopian Journal (16 Feb. 1814).
T. Gregory, *The Shropshire Directory* (1824), p. 285.
For T. M. Randall see J. Randall, *The Clay Industries . . . on the Banks of the Severn* (1877), p. 52.
 11. S.R.O. 1681/153.
Staffs. R.O. D876/155, ff. 1, 54, 61, 112, 149.
 12. For a fully-documented account of the Tar Tunnel see I. J. Brown and Barrie Trinder, *The Coalport Tar Tunnel* (1971).
For an account with up-to-date survey information and a selection of visitors' impressions, see Ironbridge Gorge Museum, *The Tar Tunnel* (1979).

For earlier extraction of bitumen see S. R. Broadbridge, 'Joseph Banks and West Midlands Industry, 1767', in *Staffordshire Industrial Archaeology Society Journal*, vol. 2 (1971), p. 15.
 13. S.R.O. 245/145, Tunnel Accounts, sub. Coalbrookdale Co. 26 Feb. 1794.
Staffs. R.O. D876/155, ff. 51, 58.
CBD MS. 2, f. 185.
T. Gregory, *op. cit.*, p. 285.
 14. S.B.L. MS. 336, ff. 971, 1030.
S.B.L. MS. 337, ff. 1414, 1464, 1488, 1557.
CBD MS. 2, f. 181.
J. Randall, *The Wilkinsons* (n.d.), Appendix, pp. 6–13.
L.S.F. Norris MSS. vol. 5.
T., W. & B. Botfield-Boulton and Watt, 26 Aug. 1831, B.R.L., B. & W. Colln., Box. 5 VIII.
N. J. Clarke, 'The Aqueduct: An East Shropshire Industrial Settlement Pt. II' in *S.N.L.* No. 40, (1971), pp. 17–18.
 15. Staffs. R.O. D876/155, f. 13.
T. Gregory, *op. cit.*, p. 285.
 16. Staffs. R.O. D876/155, ff. 49, 50, 58.
 17. J. Plymley, *op. cit.*, p. 315.
 18. B. S. Trinder, ed., *A Description of Coalbrookdale in 1801* (1970), p. 13.
 19. Staffs. R.O. D876/155, ff. 9, 41, 111.
 20. *Ibid*, f. 3.
Lord Dundonald-William Reynolds 24 Nov. 1800, Scot. R.O. GD 233/106/C/6.
 21. *Shrewsbury Chronicle* (26 Feb. 1805, 1 Sep. 1809).
 22. See above, p. 45.
CBD MS. 3, f. 18.
I.B.G.M. Lill. Co. Colln., Schedule of Deeds, Sundry Deeds No. 23.
 23. Lichfield Diocesan Record Office, Wrockwardine Wood Tithe Map, 1847.
Print of works c. 1835 in S.R.O. 1254/1.
W. H. Williams, 'The Wrockwardine Wood Glass House' in *The Around and About* (2 Dec. 1961).
 24. S.B.L. MS. 334, unpaginated section sub. 21 May 1794, and ff. 4, 36, 89.
S.B.L. MS. 336, f. 1335.
Joshua Gilpin's Journals and Notebooks, vol. 27, Microfilm in B.U.L.
Lord Dundonald-William Reynolds 15 Dec. 1799 and 16 Dec. 1799, William Reynolds-Lord Dundonald, 1 Dec. 1799, Scots, R.O. GD 233/106/C/60, 106/C/1/1, and 190/H/22.
 25. Specimens of Wrockwardine Wood bottles, walking sticks and door stoppers kindly shown to me by Miss D. McCormick of Wellington. There is a fine Wrockwardine Wood jug in Victoria and Albert Museum, gallery 131, a smaller jug and buttons in the Pilkington Glass Museum, St. Helens, and a variety of items in the Ironbridge Gorge Museum.

Joshua Gilpin's Journals and Notebooks, vol. 27, Microfilm in B.U.L.

S.B.L. MS. 336, f. 1355.

W. H. Williams, *op. cit.*

26. R. S. Sayers, *Lloyds Bank in the History of English Banking* (1957), p. 319.

Ironbridge Gorge Museum, Lilleshall Co. Colln., Box 3.

Shrewsbury Chronicle (23 Aug. 1816).

27. Lord Dundonald-William Reynolds 19 Jan. 1800, Scott. R.O. GD 233/109/H/33.

J. Plymley, *op. cit.*, pp. 72, 340–41.

Memo by Lord Dundonald '. . . on the French Process for preparing Glauber Salt and Soda', Scot. R.O. GD 233/106/C/76.

28. Lord Dundonald-William Reynolds 15 Mar. 1791, William Reynolds-Lord Dundonald 1 Dec. 1799, Lord Dundonald-Anon. 23 Feb. 1799. Scot. R.O. GD 233/109/H/16 and 23, and 106/C/11.

29. Lord Dundonald-William Reynolds, 15 Dec. 1799, 16 Dec. 1799, 23 Jan. 1800, William

Reynolds-Lord Dundonald, 18 Dec. 1799, Draft indenture 22 Jan. 1800, Scot. R.O. GD 233/106/C/ 60, 106/C/7/1, 109/H/22, 24, 36.

For a table listing 18th-century names for chemicals and their modern equivalents see A. and N. Clow, *The Chemical Revolution* (1952), p. 620 *et seq.*

30. Lord Dundonald-William Reynolds, 22 Jan. 1800, 16 Mar. 1800, Scot. R.O. GD 233/107/F, and 109/H/44.

B.T.H.R. Shropshire Canal Minutes, 12 Jan. 1795, 9 Dec. 1800.

31. Lord Dundonald-William Reynolds, 14 Feb. 1800, 17 Mar. 1800, 24 Mar. 1800, Scot. R.O. GD 233/109/H/3, 44, 46.

32. W. King-William Reynolds, 5 Mar. 1800, Lord Dundonald-John Wilkinson and John Wilkinson-William Reynolds, 15 Dec. 1799, Lord Dundonald-William Reynolds, 17 Mar. 1800 and 24 Nov. 1800, Scot. R.O. GD 233/111/M/25 and 26, 109/H/44, 106/C/6.

33. *Shrewsbury Chronicle* (6 July 1792).

Notes to Chapter XIII

1. Alan Birch, *An Economic History of the British Iron and Steel Industry 1784–1879* (1967), pp. 128, 140–1.

2. Charles Hulbert, *The History and Description of the County of Salop* (1837), vol. 2, pp. 172–3, 347–8.

3. A. Raistrick, *Dynasty of Ironfounders* (1953), pp. 238, 297.

T. S. Ashton, *Iron and Steel in the Industrial Revolution* (1951), p. 156.

4. *Annual Register* (Aug. 1816), p. 131.

Salopian Journal (16 Aug. 1816).

Shrewsbury Chronicle (10 July, 9 Oct. 1816).

G. Gilpin-J. J. Guest, 12 Oct. 1817, 23 May 1819 and 19 June 1819, in M. Elsas, ed., *Iron in the Making* (1960), pp. 3–4, 5–6.

S.R.O. 245/101.

S.R.O. 665/6019.

S.B.L. c 37–8.

5. Alan Birch, 'The Midlands Iron Industry during the Napoleonic Wars' in *Edgar Allen News* (Aug./Sep. 1952).

J. W. Hall, 'Joshua Field's Diary of a Tour in 1831 through the Midlands' in *T.N.S.* vol. 6, (1925–26), pp. 30–32.

6. G. Gilpin-J. J. Guest, 12 Oct. 1817 quoted in Alan Birch, *The Economic History of the British Iron and Steel Industry 1784–1879* (1967), p. 147.

S.R.O. 1781/6/28.

Salopian Journal (9 Apr. 1817).

Alan Birch, 'The Midlands Iron Industry during the Napoleonic Wars' in, *Edgar and Allen News* (Aug./Sep. 1952). G. Gilpin-J. J. Guest, 12 Oct. 1817 in M. Elsas, *op. cit.*, p. 4. J. Reynolds-B. Dick-

inson, 5 & 8 July 1817, S.R.O. 245/86, 88.

7. G. Gilpin-J. J. Guest, 12 Oct. 1817 quoted in Alan Birch, *An Economic History of the British Iron and Steel Industry 1784–1879* (1967), p. 147.

W. Day, *Report on Shropshire in Second Annual Report of the Poor Law Commissioners for England and Wales* (1836), p. 380.

Memo on the Marquess of Stafford's English estates, Staffs. R.O. D593/L/2/1.

8. Staffs. R.O. D593/I/1/34.

H. Scrivenor, *The History of the Iron Trade* (1967), p. 96.

Salopian Journal (11 Sep. 1822, 15 May 1844).

9. Staffs. R.O. D876/155, ff. 1, 43.

Madeley Wood Company Annual Statements 1826–50, Staffs. R.O. D876.

J. Randall, *History of Madeley* (1880), p. 174.

10. Valuation, or Profit and Loss Accounts, CBD MS. 4, reproduced in A. Raistrick, *op. cit.*, p. 297.

11. G. Gilpin-J. J. Guest, 12 Oct. 1817, in M. Elsas, *op. cit.*, p. 3.

A. Raistrick, *op. cit.*, pp. 261–2.

CBD MS. 4.

Ian Lawley, 'Art and Ornament in Iron: Design and the Coalbrookdale Company', The Design Council, *Design and Industry* (1980), pp. 18–21.

12. MS. in S.R.O. 245/140.

See also J. Randall. *The Severn Valley* (1862), pp. 284–85.

13. For details of pig boiling, guide mills and the closing of furnace tops see W. K. V. Gale, *Iron and Steel* (1969), pp. 47–49, 53, 54.

For the SS *Great Britain*, see Ewan Corlett, *The Iron*

Ship (1975), p. 24; Ironbridge Gorge Museum Trust, *The Coalbrookdale Company and the SS Great Britain* (Information Sheet No. 4 1979); R. L. Brett, ed., *Barclay Fox's Journal* (1979), p. 148; *Shrewsbury Chronicle* (26 July 1844); Hannah Tothill – Hannah Darby, 29 Aug. 1847, Lady Labouchere's Collection, Dudmaston; John Grantham, 'On the *Richard Cobden* Sailing Ship', *Transactions of the Institution of Naval Architects*, April 1871.

14. S.R.O. 1224/Box 228.
Art Journal Illustrated Catalogue of the International Exhibition of 1862, p. 73.

15. S. Bagshaw, *History, Gazetteer and Directory of Shropshire* (1851), p. 374.
S. D. Chapman, ed. *The History of Working Class Housing* (1971), p. 294.

16. G. Gilpin-J. J. Guest, 12 Oct. 1817 and 18 June 1819, in M. Elsas, *op. cit.*, pp. 3, 5.
I.B.G.M. Lill. Co. Colln., Schedule of Deeds, Donnington and Lilleshall deeds no. 31, Snedshill deeds no. 42.
A. Birch, 'The Midlands Iron Industry during the Napoleonic Wars' in *Edgar Allen News*, (Aug./Sep. 1952).
S.R.O. 245/101.
H. Scrivenor, *op. cit.*, p. 96.
Staffs. R.O. D593/M/17/5, D593/B/2/7/23.

17. *Official Catalogue of the 1862 International Exhibition*, pp. 14, 38–99.

18. For the activities of the Lilleshall Company in the 19th century see *Griffith's Guide to the Iron Trade of Great Britain*, ed. by W. K. V. Gale. (1967), pp. 102–09, 185–59; *Salopian Journal* (6 Sep. 1871).
Staffs. R.O. D593/M/17/5.

19. S.R.O. 1265/75, 76, 119, 128, 216, 217, 218, 220.
H. Scrivenor, *op. cit.*, p. 96.
Iron Furnaces in Great Britain and Ireland, 31 Dec. 1825, B.R.L., B. & W. Colln., MII.
S.R.O. 245/140.
See also W. H. Williams, 'The Botfields' in *Shropshire Magazine* (Dec. 1965 and Jan. 1966).

20. I.B.G.M. Lill. Co. Colln., Schedule of Deeds, Donnington and Lilleshall Deeds nos. 26, 32.
S.R.O. 1190/111 (Box), 1190/112 (Box).
G. Gilpin-J. J. Guest, 12 Oct. 1817, in M. Elsas, *op. cit.*, p. 3.

21. S.R.O. 1190/111 (Box), 1190/112 (Box), 1190/113.
J. Jackson-J. J. Guest, 4 June 1822, in M. Elsas *op. cit.*, pp. 88–89.
H. Scrivenor, *op. cit.*, p. 96.
J. Randall, *Broseley and its Surroundings* (1879), p. 124.

22. H. Scrivenor, *op. cit.*, p. 96.
Charles Hulbert, *op. cit.*, p. 343.
J. Randall, *op. cit.*, p. 123.

23. *Salopian Journal* (31 Jan. 1821).

H. Scrivenor, *op. cit.*, p. 96.
J. Randall, *op. cit.*, p. 123.

24. N. Mutton, ed., 'An Engineer at work in the West Midlands' in *Journal of West Midlands Studies*, Special Publication No. 1, (1969), p. 3.
H. Scrivenor, *op. cit.*, p. 279.

25. J. Randall, *The Wilkinsons* (n.d.) pp. 50–51.
H. Scrivenor, *op. cit.*, p. 96.
Salopian Journal (2 Sep. 1835).

26. N. Mutton, *op. cit.*, pp. 16, 31.
H. Scrivenor, *op. cit.*, p. 96.
N. Clarke, 'The Aqueduct' Pts. I and II, in *S.N.L.* 39 and 40 (1970/71).
I. J. Brown, 'The Mines of the Madeley Court Company' in *S.N.L.* 38, (1970).
Salopian Journal, (23 Nov. 1842).
B.T.H.R. Shropshire Canal Company Minutes, 15 Oct. 1841, 28 April 1843.

27. *Salopian Journal* (14 Dec. 1831).

28. *Salopian Journal* (20 Nov. 1811).
J. Randall, *Broseley and its Surroundings* (1879), p. 78.
E. Cassey, *Directory of Shropshire* (1870), p. 93.

29. *Children's Emp. Comm. Rep.*, p. 78.
J. Prestwich, 'The Geology of the Coalfield of Coalbrookdale' in *Transactions of the Geological Society*, vol. 5 (1840), pp. 440.

30. J. Randall, *The Severn Valley* (1862), pp. 160–61.
J. Randall, *Broseley and its Surroundings* (1879), pp. 95–96.

31. S.R.O. 245/140.
S.B.L. Watton Colln., vol. 10, p. 303.
Staffs. R.O. D593/N/3/12/12, D593/M/17/3.
G. Gilpin-J. J. Guest, 19 June 1819 in M. Elsas, *op. cit.*, pp. 199–200.

32. S.R.O. 972/170, 175.
Staffs. R.O. D593/N/3/8/12.

33. Staffs. R.O. D593/M/17/5.
Children's Emp. Comm. Rep. p. 43.
I. J. Brown, *The History of Limestone Mining in Shropshire* (1967), p. 13.

34. Charles Hulbert, *op. cit.*, pp. 347–50.
Sir Alexander Gibb, *The Story of Telford*, (1935), pp. 280–81.

35. S.R.O. 1681/196, 1649/1.
Salopian Journal (23 Aug. 1816, 1 Jan. 1817, 1 April 1818).
57 Geo. III c. xii.
J. Randall, *Broseley and its Surroundings* (1879), p. 238.
J. Loch, *An Account of the Improvements on the estates of the Marquis of Stafford* (1820), pp. 217–18.

36. *The Life of Thomas Telford*, ed. by John Rickman, (1838), pp. 204–17.
Barrie Trinder 'The Holyhead Road: an engineering project in its social context', in Alistair Penfold, ed., *Thomas Telford: Engineer* (1980), pp. 41–61.
L.T.C. Rolt, *Thomas Telford* (1958), pp. 111–116.

Parliamentary Papers, *Mr. Telford's Reports on the English Parts of the Holyhead Road* (1819 et. seq.).

37. C. Hadfield, *The Canals of the West Midlands* (1967), pp. 161, 183–87.
L.T.C. Rolt, *op. cit.*, pp. 173–86.

38. Details of traffic at Wappenshall come from the following account books unless otherwise stated.
S.R.O. 972/170.
Staffs. R.O. D593/N/3/1 and 12.

39. I.B.G.M., Lill. Co. Colln., Schedule of Deeds, Freehold Property, John Smith to Lilleshall Co. 3 May 1834, Donnington and Lilleshall deeds No. 50.
S. Bagshaw, *op. cit.*, p. 274.

40. S.R.O. 245/140.

41. S.R.O. 245/131–32.

42. C. Hadfield, *op. cit.*, p. 185.
Accounts of Lubstree Wharf in S.R.O. 972.

43. C. Hadfield, *op. cit.*, pp. 231–36.

44. Material on railways comes from the following:
J. H. Denton, *A Tour of the Railways and Canals between Oakengates and Coalbrookdale* (1961).
Shrewsbury Borough Library, *The Age of Steam* (1967).
Salop County Council, *Canals and Railways, A list of Plans &C.* (1969).
E. T. MacDermott, *A History of the Great Western Railway*, ed. by C. R. Clinker. (1964), vol. 1, pp. 177–204.
Rex Christiansen, *A Regional History of the Railways of Great Britain, vol. 7, The West Midlands* (1973), pp. 80–92, 154–61.

45. S.R.O. 972/175.
S.R.O. 245/140.
'The Memoir of William Smith', ed. by B. S. Trinder, in *T.S.A.S.* vol. 58, p. 184.

46. E. T. MacDermott, *op. cit.*, pp. 186–88.

47. [J. Fogerty], *Lauterdale*, pp. 1–2.

48. D. J. Smith, *The Severn Valley Railway* (1968), pp. 7–17, 23.

49. C. Hadfield, *op. cit.*, pp. 237–38.
S.R.O. 1681/185.
Salopian Journal (18 July 1860).

50. S.R.O. 245/140.

51. M. J. T. Lewis, *Early Wooden Railways* (1970), p. 294.

52. B. S. Trinder, 'Early Railways in east Shropshire' in *S.N.L.* No. 39 (1970).

53. C. Hadfield, *op. cit.*, pp. 287–88.
S. Bagshaw, *op. cit.*, p. 19.
Salopian Journal (12 June 1861).

54. S.R.O. Deposited Plan 349.
For the declining years of the Severn Navigation see:
E. Cassey, *op. cit.*, p. 93.
C. Hadfield, *op. cit.*, p. 288.
J. Randall, *The Severn Valley* (1862), pp. 180, 315.
J. Randall, *The History of Madeley* (1880), pp. 254–62.
S.R.O. 890/2 and 3.
Graham Farr, 'The Severn Navigation and the Severn Trow' in *Mariners Mirror*, vol. 32 (1946) p. 77.
Henry de Salis, *Bradshaw's Canals and Navigable Rivers of England and Wales* (1904), pp. 322, 326.

55. C. Hadfield, *op. cit.*, pp. 238, 251.
S.R.O. 1681/185.
Staffs. R.O. D593/B/2/9/17.

56. J. Randall, *The Severn Valley* (1862), pp. 150–51.
A. Raistrick, *op. cit.*, p. 270.
Salopian Journal (21 Dec. 1831).

57. Alan Birch, *The Economic History of the British Iron and Steel Industry 1784–1879* (1967), pp. 128, 140–41.

58. *Salopian Journal* (6 Sep. 1871).

Notes to Chapter XIV

1. Original church minute book (now lost) quoted in J. Randall, *Broseley and its Surroundings* (1879), pp. 222 seq.
For Leominster see L. T. Nyberg, 'A short Sketch of the Awakening in Leominster down to May 12 1769', MS. in John Rylands Library, MS. 1069 (2). For mortality see parish registers of Dawley, Madeley and Broseley.

2. For the exact chronology of Fletcher's ordination &c. see F. W. MacDonald, *Fletcher of Madeley* (1885), p. 58 n.
The institution to the vicarage is recorded in the Register of the Bishop of Hereford, 1755–1771, f. 63.
Peter Forsaith, *The Eagle and the Dove* (1979), p. 9.

3. J. Fletcher-John Wesley, nd. d. 1760, John Fletcher-Charles Wesley, 19 Nov. 1760, in F. W. MacDonald, *op. cit.*, pp. 58, 61.
John Fletcher-Charles Wesley, 26 Dec. 1758, quoted in P. Forsaith, *op. cit.*, p. 10.
Melville Horne-Mary Fletcher 3 Feb. 1796, Methodist Archives and Research Centre (referred to hereafter as M.A.R.C.) Fletcher-Tooth Correspondence (referred to hereafter as F.T.C.).

4. L. Tyerman, *Wesley's Designated Successor* (1882), pp. 26–3, 65, 76–77.

5. John Fletcher-Charles Wesley, 27 April 1761, in Melville Horne, *Posthumous Pieces of the late Rev. J. W. de la Flechère* (1791), p. 108.

6. *The Journals of the Rev. John Wesley*, ed. by N. Curnock, (1938), vol. 5, p. 87.
L. Tyerman, *op. cit.*, p. 100.
R. F. Skinner, *Nonconformity in Shropshire 1662–1816* (1964), pp. 71–73.

7. L. Tyerman, *op. cit.*, pp. 148, 159, 176–77, 263.

8. John Fletcher-William Wase, 18 Feb. 1777, in Horne, *op. cit.*, p. 24. John Fletcher-Charles Greenwood, 12 June 1781; John Fletcher-John Wesley, 6 June 1781, in L. Tyerman, *op. cit.*, pp. 460–61.

9. *Methodist Magazine*, (1800), pp. 219–223. *The Journals of the Rev. John Wesley*, ed. By N. Curnock (1938), vol. 6, p. 345. L. Tyerman, *op. cit.*, pp. 547–48.

10. B.M. Add. MS. 21018. H. Moore, *The Life of Mary Fletcher* (1817), pp. 164, 378–80.

11. Melville Horne-Mary Fletcher, various dates, M.A.R.C., F.T.

12. H. Moore, *op. cit.*, p. 269. S.R.O. 2280/6/95. Bishop of Hereford's Register 1772–1802, f. 201. B.M. Add. MS. 21018. Madeley Parish Register.

13. Mary Fletcher-R. Morris, 1 Mar. 1792, M.A.R.C., F.T.C.

14. J. Randall, *The Severn Valley* (1862), p. 160. Joseph Peake-Mary Tooth, 2 Dec. 1823; M. Robinson-Mary Fletcher, 14 Sep. 1809, M.A.R.C., F.T.C. Charles Hulbert, *Memoirs of Seventy Years* (1852), pp. 220–21. L. Tyerman, *op. cit.*, p. 505. *Methodist Magazine* (1800), pp. 266–67.

15. *Methodist Magazine* (1837), pp. 901–02.

16. Ann Trip-Mary Fletcher, 14 June, 1815, M.A.R.C., F.T.C. H. Moore, *op. cit.*, pp. 378–80. *Methodist Magazine*, (1837), p. 902.

17. Henry Burton-Mary Tooth, 20 Feb. 1816; E. W. Legge-Mary Tooth, 27 April 1816; Sarah Hill-Mary Tooth, 14 Mar. 1816; Joseph Peake-Mary Tooth, 21 Nov. 1822, M.A.R.C., F.T.C. H. Moore, *op. cit.*, p. 382n.

18. J. Cooper-Mary Tooth, 5 July 1827; F. Riggall-Mary Tooth, 12 April 1828; J. Evans-Mary Tooth, 31 July 1828; R. Longmore-Mary Tooth, 13 Aug. 1829; W. Stones-Mary Tooth, 27 Aug. 1831, M.A.R.C., F.T.C.

19. *Methodist Magazine* (1833), p. 876. *Ibid.*, (1843), p. 1036. M. Grigson-Mary Tooth, 15 Jan. 1833; F. Griffiths-Mary Tooth, 5 Feb. 1833; J. Radford-Mary Tooth, 5 Nov. 1833, M.A.R.C., F.T.C. Release of land, 13 Nov. 1832, Madeley Vicarage. J. Randall, *History of Madeley*, (1880), pp. 159–60.

20. *Primitive Methodist Magazine*, (1846), p. 51.

21. Revd. John M'Owan, *A Man of God: a memoir of the Revd. Peter M'Owan*, (ed. G. Osborn, 1873), p. 209. Robert Plummer, *The Successful Class-Leader: A Memorial of Mr. Benjamin Pollard* (1861), p. 73. *Annals of Church Pastoral Aid Work No. 5* (n.d., c. 1855), p. 17.

22. See below chapters 18, 19 and 20.

23. L. Tyerman, *op. cit.*, p. 86.

24. J. Valton-Mary Fletcher 30 Mar. 1784, M.A.R.C., F.T.C. L. Tyerman, *op. cit.*, p. 560.

25. S. Jenkins-Mary Tooth, 10 Sep. 1826; R. Heys-Mary Tooth n.d. (1823), M.A.R.C., F.T.C.

26. C. R. Cameron, *Considerations suggested by the Murder of William Bailey* (1812), pp. 19–20. Mrs. [Lucy] Cameron, *The Novice* Pts. I & II, (n.d.) Houlston Tracts Nos. 43–44. For the Bailey case, see *Shrewsbury Chronicle* (Feb. & Mar. 1812).

27. J. Collins-Mary Tooth, 8 Aug. 1842; 'YX'-Mary Fletcher, n.d., M.A.R.C., F.T.C. *Methodist Magazine*, (1863), pp. 193–201.

28. Benjamin Longmore-Mary Tooth, 18 April 1805. Other proposals from T. Bridgeman, S. Hickling, W. J. Thornbury, M.A.R.C., F.T.C.

29. S. Walter-Mary Fletcher, n.d. (1812); S. Delves-Mary Tooth, 11 June 1822, M.A.R.C., F.T.C.

30. John Fletcher, *American Patriotism: Further confronted with Reason, Scripture and the Constitution; Being Observations on the Dangerous Politics taught by the Rev. Mr. Evans, M.A. and the Rev. Dr. Price*(1776). Richard Hill-John Fletcher, 16 Dec. 1784, M.A.R.C., F.T.C. John Fletcher-John and Charles Wesley, 17 May 1788, in F. W. MacDonald, *op. cit.*, p. 136. J. Randall, *op. cit.*, pp. 138–39.

31. *Methodist Magazine* (1822), p. 153.

32. Mrs. T. C. Marsh-Mary Fletcher 7 Nov. 1797; Benjamin Longmore-Mary Tooth n.d. (c. 1805); M. Grigson-Mary Tooth, 30 May 1832, M.A.R.C., F.T.C.

Notes to Chapter XV

1. K. S. Inglis, 'Patterns of Religious Worship in 1851' in *Journal of Ecclesiastical History*, vol. 11, (1960), pp. 74–86.

2. Figures in this section are taken from annual volumes of the *Minutes of the Wesleyan Conference*.

3. *Methodist Magazine* (1822), p. 691.

'B.B.' *Wesleyan Methodism in Coalbrookdale* MS. in S.R.O. 2280/16/185, W. H. Barclay, *The History of Wesleyan Methodism at Lawley Bank* (1858), p. 33.

4. S.R.O. 2280/16/185.

5. For the Cinderhill Riots see below pp. 232–33.

W. Edwards-Mary Tooth, 6 March 1821; S. Hill-Mary Tooth, 4 May 1821, M.A.R.C., F.T.C.
J. Petty, *History of the Primitive Methodist Connexion* (1860), p. 111.
Methodist New Connexion Magazine (1838), pp. 42–44. See also B. S. Trinder, *The Methodist New Connexion in Dawley and Madeley* (1967), pp. 4–7.
6. *Methodist Magazine* (1822), p. 732.
7. *Primitive Methodist Magazine*, (1823), p. 70.
8. Bourne's Journal, quoted in J. Petty, *op. cit.*, pp. 112–13.
9. Figures from annual volumes of the minutes of the Wesleyan and Primitive Methodist conferences.
10. E. P. Thompson, *The Making of the English Working Class* (1963), pp. 388–391.
11. Statistics from annual volumes of the minutes of the Wesleyan and Primitive Methodist Conferences.
B. S. Trinder, *op. cit.*, pp. 6–7.
12. *Primitive Methodist Magazine* (1830), p. 24.
B. Baugh-Mary Tooth, 20 Aug. 1829, M.A.R.C., F.T.C.
13. S.R.O. 2280/16/185.
M. Grigson-Mary Tooth, Aug. 1836, M.A.R.C., F.T.C.
Methodist Magazine (1835), p. 378.
14. *Primitive Methodist Magazine*, (1841), p. 154.
15. B. S. Trinder, *op. cit.*, p. 8.
W. H. Barclay, *op. cit.*, pp. 13–14.
'The Memoir of William Smith', ed. by B. S. Trinder in *T.S.A.S.* vol. 58, (1965–68), p. 182.
16. W. H. Barclay, *op. cit.*, pp. 14–15.
Primitive Methodist Magazine (1841), p. 329.
John Wesley, *Works* (ed. 1856), col. 11, p. 280.
17. *Methodist Magazine* (1835), p. 378.
18. J. Petty, *op. cit.*, pp. 112–13.
Methodist Magazine (1822), p. 732, 1835, p. 387.
18. 'The Memoir of William Smith' ed. by B. S. Trinder in *T.S.A.S.* vol. 58, (1965–68), pp. 182–83.
Methodist Magazine (1893), pp. 568–72.
Ibid., (1805), p. 505.
20. W. H. Barclay, *op. cit.*, pp. 13–14.
Methodist New Connexion Magazine, (1856), p. 156.
Primitive Methodist Magazine (1858), pp. 43–44.
21. *Salopian Journal* (2 April 1862).
22. *Flysheets Winged*, by George Hughes, (1850), *Letter to the Rev. George Hughes* by William Reynolds, (1850), in Wesleyan Reform Collection, M.A.R.C. I am grateful to Mr. John Vickers for bringing these pamphlets to my attention.
Minutes of the Wrockwardine Wood Primitive Methodist Circuit, sub 8 June 1850. S.R.O. 1861/163.
Wesleyan Methodist Penny Magazine (1853), p. 155.
Ibid., (1854), p. 131.
Ibid., (1855), p. 131.
J. H. Lenton, 'The Snedshill Affair 1851–52' *Bulletin*

of the Wesley Historical Society: Shropshire Branch, vol. 1 (1977).
Annual volumes of minutes of conference of the United Methodist Free Church.
Wellington Circuit of the Methodist Free Church, Preachers' Plan, (1859–60).
S.R.O. 3767.
23. W. H. Barclay, *op. cit.*, p. 10.
24. Parish Returns for the Archdeaconry of Salop, 1772–73, Lichfield Diocesan Record Office, B/V/5.
Visitation of the Archdeaconry of Salop, 1799, copy in S.R.O.
B.M. Add. MS. 21018.
25. Bishop of Hereford's Register, 1755–1771, ff. 127–31. Hereford Diocesan Record Office.
B.M. Add. MS. 21018.
J. Randall, *Broseley and its Surroundings* (1879), pp. 212–13.
26. Visitation of the Archdeaconry of Salop, 1799, copy in S.R.O.
C. Hulbert, *The History and Description of the County of Salop*, vol. 2, p. 146.
Roger Hill, *A Telford Church: St. Leonard's Malinslee* (1980), pp. 3–5.
Bishop of Lichfield's Register, 1792–1811, Lichfield Diocesan Record Office.
Parish Returns for the Archdeaconry of Salop 1832, Lichfield Diocesan Record Office B/V/5.
27. Bishop of Lichfield's Register, 1792–1811, f. 267 *et seq.*
Staffs. R.O. D593/M/17/1.
Parish Returns for the Archdeaconry of Salop, 1832, Lichfield Diocesan Record Office B/V/5.
28. G. Lowe-Mary Fletcher, 28 July 1807, M.A.R.C., F.T.C.
Methodist Magazine (1816), p. 159.
29. Anon. *On the Rev. J. Eyton*. Broadsheet in S.B.L.
30. *Methodist Magazine*, p. 425.
Ibid., (1866), p. 288.
C. Hulbert, *op. cit.*, vol. 2, p. 154.
William Morgan-Mary Fletcher, 5 Feb. 1814, M.A.R.C., F.T.C.
31. G. L. Yate, *Holy Trinity Church, Wrockwardine Wood*, (n.d.).
Bishop of Lichfield's Register vol. I, ff. 687–89, 695–701, 704–06, 710–11.
Lichfield Diocesan Record Office.
32. J. Randall, *History of Madeley* (1880), pp. 168, 350–51.
C. Hulbert, *op. cit.*, vol. 2, p. 348.
B.M. Add. MS. 21018.
Bishop of Hereford's Register 1822–42, ff. 345–357; 1842–47, ff. 272–3, 289. Hereford Diocesan Record Office.
Bishop of Lichfield's Register, vol. L, ff. 456, 459, 464. Lichfield Diocesan Record Office.

33. Bishop of Lichfield's Register, vol. K, ff. 587–597; vol. L, ff. 494–516. Lichfield Diocesan Record Office.
Staffs. R.O. D593/L/2/2a.
34. Bishop of Lichfield's Register, vol. N, ff. 314, 325. Lichfield Diocesan Record Office.
Bishop of Hereford's Register, 1822–42, f. 650; 1842–47, ff. 23, 38, 1847–57, ff. 362, 471, 488, 503–07 Hereford Diocesan Record Office.
S.R.O. 2280/7/1.
35. Bishop of Lichfield's Register, vol. O and vol. P. Lichfield Diocesan Record Office.
Bishop of Hereford's Register, 1857 seq., Hereford Diocesan Record Office.
36. See above p. 157.
J. Randall, Broseley and its Surroundings (1879), p. 222.
Baptist Handbook, (1872), p. 143.
37. Baptist Magazine, (1829).
Shropshire Circular Letter, June 1821, B.R.L. Pamphlet No. 407116.
A. Lester, Fifty Years (1896), pp. 2–4.
38. Ernest Evans, A History of Congregationalism in Shropshire (1898), pp. 213, 251, 275.
Evangelical Magazine (1826), p. 251; (1840), p. 495.
39. Visitation Returns, Box 69, Hereford Diocesan Record Office.
Return of Papists 1767, Hereford Diocesan Record Office.
40. J. Randall. A short . . . sketch of the Lives and Usefulness of the Rev. John and Mary Fletcher, (n.d.), pp. 8–9.
John Reeve-Mary Fletcher, sundry dates 1809–11, M.A.R.C., F.T.C.
41. Samuel Bagshaw, History, Gazetteer and Directory of Shropshire (1851), p. 423.
42. L. S. F. Norris MSS. vol. 10, pp. 4–6.
Bishop of Hereford's Register, 1682–1709, f. 1692, Hereford Diocesan Record Office.

Visitation Returns, Box 69, Hereford Diocesan Record Office.
R. F. Skinner, Nonconformity in Shropshire 1662–1816 (1964), pp. 31, 34.
S.R.O. 1224/3/635.
43. Journal of Abiah Darby, 29/30 7mo. 1750, L.S.F.
Ironbridge Gorge Museum, The Quaker Burial Grounds (1979).
Visitation Returns, Box 69, Hereford Diocesan Record Office.
Hannah Rose, Some Account of the Family of the Darbys, being what Hannah Rose has heard her Parents, John and Grace Thomas say concerning them, MS. in Lady Labouchere's Collection, Dudmaston.
R. F. Skinner, op. cit., pp. 31, 34, 37.
44. Parish Returns for the Archdeaconry of Salop 1772, Lichfield Diocesan Record Office, B/V/5.
R. F. Skinner, op. cit., pp. 31, 37.
Diary of Thomas Graham, in L. S. F. Norris MSS., vols. 6 and 7.
45. Journal of Abiah Darby ff. 61, 68, 89, 120, 148, L.S.F.
Diary of Thomas Graham, in L. S. F., Norris MSS., vol. 6.
46. H. M. Rathbone, Letters of Richard Reynolds with a Memoir of his Life (1852), p. 40.
J. Randall, History of Madeley (1880), p. 292.
B.M. Add. MS. 21018.
[J. Fogerty], Lauterdale (1873), p. 37.
47. J. Randall, Broseley and its Surroundings (1879), pp. 217–18.
Deed of 7 June 1837 in Madeley Methodist Circuit safe. I am grateful to Rev. R. Hewitt for allowing me to examine this and other documents in the safe.
W. H. Barclay, op. cit., pp. 13–16.
Methodist Recorder (28 Feb. 1907).
Methodist New Connexion Magazine (1859), p. 692.

Notes to Chapter XVI

1. William Ferriday to William Forester, 11 Feb. 1755, S.R.O. 1224.
2. A Description of Coalbrookdale . . . with two perspective views thereof, copies in S.B.L. f.M.66 and I.B.G.M.
Lord Dundonald-William Reynolds 15 Mar. 1791, Scot. R.O. DG 233/109/H/16.
T. S. Aston, Iron and Steel in the industrial Revolution (1951), p. 144.
3. Silvi Sogner, 'Aspects of the Demographic Situation in 17 parishes in Shropshire 1711–60' in Population Studies, (Feb. 1964).
4. A Description of Coalbrookdale . . . with two perspective views thereof, op. cit.
A. Young, Tours in England and Wales (1932), p. 145.
5. Copy of lease of 7 Jan. 1734 in L.S.F., Norris MSS., vol. 8.
6. B.M. Add. MS. 21018.
7. Arthur Redford, Labour Migration in England 1800–1850 (1964), pp. 62–64.
8. Ibid., p. 64 and Map E.
9. Shrewsbury Chronicle (18 Dec. 1795, 22, 29 Jan. 1796, 6 Jan. 1797).
Salopian Journal (15 May 1844).
10. William Day, 'Report on Shropshire' in Second Annual Report of the Poor Law Commissioners for England and Wales (1836), pp. 377–78.
11. J. H. Pavitt, 'Wenlock Poor in the 18th Century' in Wenlock 1468–1968 ed. by L. C. Lloyd (1968), p. 39.
12. Analysis of settlement returns by local history research group 1963. I am grateful to the group's

tutor Mr. John Golby for permission to quote from
its findings.
S.R.O. 2280/6/95.
   13. S.R.O. 615/1–2.
   14. Mrs. [Lucy] Cameron, *The Oakengates Wake*
(n.d.), pp. 7–9.

W. H. Barclay, *The History of Wesleyan Methodism at
Lawley Bank* (1858), pp. 19–41.
   15. 1851 Census Enumerators' Book. Wellington
Poor Law Examinations Book, S.R.O. 3129/5/4.
   16. *Census of Great Britain 1851: Population Tables.*
(1854).

Notes to Chapter XVII

   1. *A Description of Coalbrookdale . . . with two perspective views thereof,* copy in I.B.G.M.
   2. W. Grant Muter, *The Buildings of an Industrial
Community: Coalbrookdale and Ironbridge* (1979), pp.
29–31.
   3. Evidence from probate records in Hereford
Record Office. See also Barrie Trinder, 'The Open
Village in Industrial Britain' in Marie Nisser, ed.,
*The Industrial Heritage: Transactions of the Third Inter-
national Congress on the Conservation of Industrial Monuments,* vol. 3, (forthcoming).
   4. See Figure 2.
   5. See Figure 2.
   6. Probate records in Hereford Record Office.
   7. Barrie Trinder and Jeff Cox, *Yeomen and Colliers in Telford* (1980), pp. 15–16, 395–96, 428–29.
   8. James Loch, *An Account of the Improvements on
the Estates of the Marquess of Stafford,* (1820), pp. 181–
83 and Appendix, p. 100.
Eric Richards, 'The Social and Electoral Influence
of the Trentham Interest 1800–60', *Midland History,*
II, 2 (1975–76), pp. 121–24.
S.R.O. 672/2/145.
Staffs. R.R. D593/N/3/2/16.
   9. Maurice Hunt, Ken Jones and Barrie Trinder, 'Holywell Lane: the rise and fall of an industrial
squatter community', *I.A.R.* (forthcoming).
   10. Ironbridge Gorge Museum, *Blists Hill Open
Air Museum* (1978), p. 16.
   11. William Ferriday-William Forester, 7 Mar.
1755, S.R.O. 1224.
   12. *A Description of Coalbrookdale . . . with two perspective views thereof,* copy in I.B.G.M.
   13. W. G. Muter, *op. cit.,* pp. 37–43.
   14. S.R.O. 245/14.
Unpublished analysis of census returns by Miss
Betsy Pope.
   15. CBD MS 3, 14 Aug. 1794.
CBD MS 2, ff. 4, 94.
See above p. 23.
   16. W. G. Muter, *op. cit.,* pp. 37–38.
CBD MS 3, 26 Mar. 1792.
   17. S.R.O. 1224/228.
N. J. Clarke, 'The Aqueduct: an East Shropshire
Industrial Settlement', *S.N.L.* 40, (1971).
S.R.O. 1150/898.
   18. D. R. Adams and J. Hazeley, *Survey of the
Church-Aston-Lilleshall Mining Area,* (1970), p. 38.

   19. J. W. Tonkin, 'Hinkshay Row, Dawley',
S.N.L. 33, (1967).
Susan Roberts, 'Hinkshay Rows', *S.N.L.* 44, (1973).
   20. C. R. T. Nankivell, 'Three Dwellings in the
Dark Lane Rows', *S.N.L.* 41 (1971).
   21. Mr. Wilkinson's Proposals to Messrs. Bishton and Rowley, 30 Nov. 1793, I.B.G.M., Lill. Co.
Colln.
Staffs. R.O. D593/H/14/2/24; D593/B/2/23.
   22. B.M. Add. MS. 21018.
   23. Commission on the Employment of Children,
Young Persons and Women in Agriculture, (1871),
extracts in *Salopian Journal* (4, 11, 25 Jan. 1871).
   24. The analysis of the Wrockwardine Wood census returns was carried out by Mr. E. Wood and
Mr. G. Herbert.
   25. Children's Emp. Comm. Rep. pp. 39, 81–82.
Staffs. R.O. D593/L/2/1.
   26. Parish Returns for the Archdeaconry of Salop, 1772, Lichfield Record Office, B/V/5.
Visitation of the Archdeaconry of Salop, 1799, copy
in S.R.O.
Arthur Young, *Tours in England and Wales* (1932), p.
153.
   27. Tithe Maps of Lilleshall, Wrockwardine
Wood and Wombridge, Lichfield Joint Record
Office.
   28. For the analysis of commercial facilities in
the coalfield based on directories I am indebted to
the work of Christopher Nankievell.
'A Short Account of Wellington, 1759', *Salopian
Shreds and Patches,* vol. 1, (1874–75), pp. 132–33.
Barrie Trinder and Jeff Cox, *op. cit.,* pp. 19–20.
   29. S. Bagshaw, *History, Gazetteer and Directory of
Shropshire* (1851), p. 441.
   30. *Universal British Directory* (1797), p. 867.
Trevor Rowley, *The Shropshire Landscape* (1972), pp.
179–233.
S. Bagshaw, *op. cit.,* p. 567.
Charles Hulbert, *History and Description of the County
of Salop* (1837), vol. 2, p. 348.
   31. S. Bagshaw, *op. cit.,* p. 557.
Probate records in Hereford Record Office.
   32. Edward Cassey, *Directory of Shropshire* (1871),
p. 136.
   33. *Primitive Methodist Magazine* (1846), pp. 418–
19.
   34. Samuel Hulme, *Memoir of the Revd. William*

Cooke, D.D. (1886), pp. 10–11.
'The Memoir of William Smith' ed. by Barrie Trinder, *T.S.A.S.*, vol. 58 (1965–68), p. 184.

35. *Salopian Journal* (16 Mar. 1853).
A. Raistrick, *Dynasty of Ironfounders* (1953), pp. 263–65.
(J. Fogerty), *Lauterdale* (1873), vol. 1, p. 145.

36. C. F. Peskin, 'Memories of Old Coalbrookdale' in *Trans. Caradoc and Severn Valley Feild Club*, vol. 11 (1941), pp. 217–18.

37. J. Randall, *History of Madeley* (1880), pp. 197–98.

38. W. H. Barclay, *The History of Wesleyan Methodism at Lawley Bank* (1858), p. 1.

39. *Ex inf.* the late Isaac Baugh.

40. Information from Shropshire Police Records, abstracted by John Golby, to whom I am grateful for permission to reproduce it here.

41. Ex. inf. Isaac Baugh and William Duce.

42. David Hey, *Packmen, Carriers and Packhorse Roads* (1980), p. 228.

43. Barrie Trinder and Jeff Cox, *op. cit.*, pp. 72, 180.

Notes to Chapter XVIII

1. W. Day, 'Report on Shropshire' in *Second Annual Report of the Poor Law Commissioners for England and Wales* (1836), p. 379.

2. S.B.L. MS. 328, f. 22, MS. 329, ff. 9, 202, MS. 333, ff. 33–34.

3. Arthur Young, *Tours in England and Wales* (1932), pp. 148–51.

4. B.M. Add. MS. 21018.

5. A. Birch, 'The Midlands Iron Industry during the Napoleonic Wars' in *Edgar Allen News* (Aug./Sep. 1952).
A. Birch, *An Economic History of the British Iron and Steel Industry 1784–1879* (1967), p. 266.
[J. Fogerty], *Lauterdale*, (1873), vol. 1, p. 36.

6. G. Gilpin-J. J. Guest, 12 Oct. 1817, in M. Elsas, ed., *Iron in the Making* (1960), pp. 3–4.

7. S.R.O. 245/145, 30 July 1796–27 Aug. 1796.

8. J. Randall, *The History of Madeley* (1880), p. 107.

9. C. R. Cameron, *Considerations suggested by the Murder of William Bailey* (1812), p. 12.
Mrs. [Lucy] Cameron, *The Oakengates Wake* (n.d.), p. 8.

10. B.M. Add. MS. 21018.

11. W. Day, *op. cit.*, p. 383.

12. Mrs. [Lucy] Cameron, *op. cit.*, pp. 8–11.

13. W. Day, *op. cit.*, p. 389.

14. B.M. Add. MS. 21018.
S.R.O. 2280/6/95.

15. For details of the charter master system see:
A. J. Taylor, 'The Sub-Contract System in the British Coal Industry' in *Studies in the Industrial Revolution* ed. by L. S. Pressnell, (1960), pp. 217 *et seq.*
John Holland, *The History and Description of Fossil Fuel, the Collieries, and the Coal Trade of Great Britain* (1968), p. 295.
H. Scott, 'Colliers' Wages in Shropshire 1830–50' in *T.S.A.S.* vol. 53, (1949–50), pp. 1–22.
T. S. Ashton and J. Sykes, *The Coal Industry in the 18th century* (1964), pp. 26–32, 100–14.

16. W. Day, *op. cit.*, pp. 383–85.
Salopian Journal (14 Dec. 1831).

17. J. Randall, *Broseley and its Surroundings* (1879),

pp. 180–82.

18. Children's Emp. Comm. Rep. p. 79.
Report of Meeting of Magistrates, 26 Aug. 1842, in National Library of Wales (appreviated hereafter to N.L.W.).
Calendar of Letters and Documents relating to Chartism in Shropshire (abbreviated hereafter to *Cal. Chartism Shropshire*) vol. 1, No. 48.

19. Children's Emp. Comm. Rep. p. 87.

20. J. M. Golby, 'Public Order and Private Unrest: a study of the 1842 Riots in Shropshire' in *University of Birmingham Historical Review*, vol. 11, (1968), pp. 157–169.
William Botfield-Earl of Powis, 25 Aug. 1842; Earl of Powis-Duke of Sutherland, 31 Aug. 1842; Earl of Powis-Sir J.-Graham, 30 Aug. 1842; Duke of Sutherland-Earl of Powis, 30 Aug. 1842; Minutes of Meeting of Ironmasters, 3 Sep. 1842, in N.L.W.
Cal. Chartism Shropshire, vol. 1, nos. 44, 55; vol. 2, nos. 14, 16, 22.

21. W. Day, *op. cit.*, p. 385.

22. Children's Emp. Comm. Rep., pp. 77–78.

23. J. W. Fletcher, *An Appeal to Matter of Fact and Common Sense* (1772), pp. 35–39.
Salop County Council, *An Abstract of the Quarter Sessions Rolls 1820–30* (1974).

24. L. J. Lee, ed. *A Full List and Partial Abstract of the Quarter Sessions Rolls* (for Shropshire), 1696–1800 (n.d.) and 1800–1820 (n.d.).

25. H. Moore, The Life of Mrs. Mary Fletcher (1817), p. 339.

26. S.B.L. Typescript of Madeley Parish Registers.

27. *Salopian Journal* (11 Jan. 1843).

28. H. Moore, *op. cit.*, p. 335.
S.B.L. Typescript of Madeley Parish Registers.

29. Children's Emp. Comm. Rep. pp. 83, 85.

30. *Salopian Journal* (22 June 1842).

31. Children's Emp. Comm. Rep. pp. 33, 34, 36, 54, 79–80.
Salopian Journal (22 June 1842).
Emanual Lovekin, "Mining Butty", in John Burnett, *Useful Toil* (1974), p. 291.

32. L. J. Lee, *op. cit.*, 1696–1800, pp. 56, 112; 1800–1820, pp. 160, 165, 190, 192, 197, 211, 227–28.

Ex. inf. Mrs. Pain of Madeley, tape recording collected by Mr. Ken Jones, Ironbridge Gorge Museum.

33. Staffs. R.O. D593/N/3/10/17.

34. Mrs. (Lucy) Cameron, *op. cit.*, pp. 5–6.

S.R.O. 673/2/145, *sub* Hayward, Benjamin.

S.B.L. Watton Colln., vol. 1, p. 360.

Derek Hudson, ed., *Munby: Man of Two Worlds* (ed. 1974), pp. 287–89.

Illustrated London News, (1846), vol. 1, p. 421.

Thomas Faulkner, *The History and Antiquities of the Parish of Hammersmith* (1839), p. 38.

Sir Richard Phillips, *A Morning's Walk from London to Kew* (1820), pp. 226–29.

I am grateful to Mrs. Barbara Jarvis of Shrewsbury and Miss Margaret Roake of Westminster for bringing the two latter sources to my attention.

Children's Emp. Comm. Rep. p. 41.

35. W. Day, *op. cit.*, p. 385.

Children's Emp. Comm. Rep., pp. 80–81.

36. Children's Emp. Comm. Rep., pp. 42–43.

37. *Ibid.*, pp. 49–50, 54–55.

38. For an excellent description of the work of a puddler, see W. K. V. Gale, *The British Iron and Steel Industry* (1967), p. 74.

39. Children's Emp. Comm. Rep., p. 80.

40. (J. Fogerty), *Lauterdale* (1873), vol. 1, p. 145. Children's Employment Commission (1862), 5th Report, 1866, XXIV, pp. 157–58.

Ex. inf., William Duce.

41. J. Randall, *The History of Madeley* (1880), p. 197; *The Clay Industries on the Banks of the Severn* (1877), p. 43.

Notes to Chapter XIX

1. H. M. Rathbone, *Letters of Richard Reynolds with a Memoir of his Life* (1852), p. 40.

2. Staffs. R.O. D593/L/2/20.

H. M. Rathbone, *op. cit.*, p. 293.

Visitation of the Archdeaconry of Salop, 1799, Copy in S.R.O.

3. C. S. Burne, *Shropshire Folk Lore* (1883), pp. 362–63.

Salopian Shreds and Patches 1885, p. 116.

T. J. Badger-Secretary of State, Home Department, 20 Aug. 1842. N.L.W.

Cal. Chartism Shropshire, vol. 1, no. 15.

4. Rules quoted in A. Raistrick, *Dynasty of Ironfounders* (1953), pp. 298–99.

S. Pollard, *The Genesis of Modern Management* (1965), p. 220.

5. S.R.O. 245/140.

6. W. Day, Report on Shropshire in, *Second Annual Report of the Poor Law Commissioners for England and Wales* (1836), p. 389.

S.R.O. 2280/6/95.

7. Luke Tyerman, *Wesley's Designated Successor* (1882), p. 524.

8. *Ibid.*, p. 528.

Visitation Returns, Box 69, Hereford Diocesan Record Office.

9. Joseph Benson, *The Life of the Rev. John William de La Flechère* (1835), p. 67.

10. B.M. Add MS. 21018.

H. M. Rathbone, *op. cit.*, p. 43.

Children's Emp. Comm. Rep. p. 87.

11. S.R.O. 245/14.

12. C. S. Burne, *op. cit.*, pp. 362–63.

S.B.L., Watton Collection, vol. 1, p. 360.

Mrs. [Lucy] Cameron, *The Oakengates Wake* (n.d.) p. 5.

13. *Methodist Magazine*, (1835), p. 378.

14. 'The Memoir of William Smith' ed. by B. S. Trinder in *T.S.A.S.* vol. 58, (1965–68), p. 181.

Shrewsbury Chronicle, (31 Jan. 1778).

15. C. S. Burne, *op. cit.*, p. 446.

Salopian Shreds and Patches (1885), p. 116.

J. Randall, *Broseley and its Surroundings* (1879), p. 180.

16. G. F. Carter and H. Walcot, *Historical Notes on the parish of Rodington* (n.d.), p. 15.

'The Memoir of William Smith' ed. by B. S. Trinder in *T.S.A.S.*, vol. 58, (1965–68), (p. 181).

17. Luke Tyerman, *op. cit.*, pp. 83, 87, 261.

18. For prize fighting see *Salopian Journal* (30 Jan. 1861, 28 Oct. 1863).

For cockfighting and bull-baiting:

Shrewsbury Chronicle (4 Oct. 1811).

S.R.O. 2280/6/95.

Methodist Magazine (1822), p. 732.

C. S. Burne, *op. cit.*, p. 446.

H. M. Rathbone, *op. cit.*, pp. 273–74.

Eric Richards, 'The Social and Electoral Influence of the Trentham Estate 1800–60', *Midland History*, vol. 3 (1975–6), pp. 121–24.

19. C. S. Burne, *op. cit.*, pp. 362–63.

J. T. Wilkinson, *Hugh Bourne* (1952), p. 58.

Salopian Shreds and Patches, 25 Feb. 1880.

Shrewsbury Chronicle (19 Sep. 1851).

20. *Salopian Journal* (13 Aug. 1836).

Ibid., (7 April 1841).

21. Anon, *A village dialogue on Bull-baiting and Cruelty of Animals* (n.d.), Houlstons' Tracts Nos. 27, 28.

22. L.S.F., Journal of Abiah Darby, f. 138.

23. S.R.O. 359/9.

24. *Primitive Methodist Magazine* (1846), pp. 418–19.

25. W. H. Barclay, *The History of Wesleyan Meth-*

odism at Lawley Bank (1858), pp. 5–6.

26. Arthur Lester, *Fifty Years* (1896), p. 16.
I.B.G.M. Lill. Co. Coll., Chartermasters' Book.
S.B.L. MS. 329, f. 146.

27. William Bosanquet-Mary Fletcher, 29 Sep. 1809, M.A.R.C., F.T.C.
Shrewsbury Chronicle (3 Nov. 1809).
Salopian Journal (11 June 1823, 12 Mar. 1828).

28. Lucy Jenkins-Mary Tooth, 18 Mar. 1837, 8 April 1837, M.A.R.C., F.T.C.
Salopian Journal (27 Sep. 1843).
For a full discussion of the Temperance movement, see B. H. Harrison, *Drink and the Victorians*, (1971).

29. W. H. Barclay, *op. cit.*, pp. 16–17.
Shrewsbury Chronicle (31 Jan. 1851, 3 June 1859).
Salopian Journal (2 April 1862).
Salopian Journal (26 Jan. 1853, 27 June 1860, 6 June 1862).
Arthur Lester, *op. cit.*, p. 16.

30. Parish Returns for the Archdeaconry of Salop, 1832, Lichfield Diocesan Record Office, B/V/5.
Luke Tyerman, *op. cit.*, p. 527.

31. Abiah Darby-John Fletcher, 22 June 1784, M.A.R.C., F.T.C.

32. Luke Tyerman, *op. cit.*, pp. 526–27.

33. H. M. Rathbone, *op. cit.*, pp. 264, 293.
Visitation of the Archdeaconry of Salop, 1799. Copy in S.R.O.

34. Luke Tyerman, *op. cit.*, p. 528.
Joseph Benson, *op. cit.*, p. 302.

35. William Jenkins-Mary Tooth, n.d. M.A.R.C., F.T.C.
H. Moore, *The Life of Mary Fletcher* (1817), p. 347.
See also E. P. Thompson, 'Time, Work Discipline and Industrial Capitalism' in *Past and Present* no. 38, (1967), pp. 57–97.

36. Robert Southey, *Life of John Wesley* (Hutchinson ed. n.d.), p. 326.
Luke Tyerman, *op. cit.*, p. 260.

37. Mrs. [Lucy] Cameron, *The Seeds of Greediness* (n.d.) Houlstons' Tract No. 22.
Mrs. [Lucy] Cameron, *Crooked Paths* (n.d.), Houlstons' Tract No. 25.

38. Mrs. [Lucy] Cameron, *An Honest Penny is worth a silver shilling* (n.d.).

39. Children's Emp. Comm. Rep. pp. 83, 86.

Notes to Chapter XX

1. E. P. Thompson, *The Making of the English Working Class* (1963), pp. 62–69.
E. P. Thompson, 'The Moral Economy of the English Crowd in the 18th Century' in, *Past and Present No.* 50, (1971), pp. 76–136.

2. The account which follows is drawn from contemporary letters reproduced in J. Randall, *Broseley and its Surroundings* (1879), pp. 232–34, and A. Raistrick, *Dynasty of Ironfounders* (1953), pp. 78–79, and from P.R.O. SP. Dom. Geo. II 1756, 136/25, 137/19.

3. A. Raistrick, *op. cit.*, pp. 79–80.

4. *Shrewsbury Chronicle* (14 Oct) 1782).

5. H. R. Rathbone, *Letters of Richard Reynolds with a Memoir of His Life* (1852), p. 46.
Shrewsbury Chronicle (9 Nov. 1782).

6. Joseph Benson, *The Life of the Rev. John William de La Flechère* (1835), p. 299.

7. William Reynolds-James Watt, 23 11 mo. 1782, B.R.L., B. & W. Colln., Box 2 'R'.
J. Randall, *History of Madeley* (1880), p. 364.
E. P. Thompson, *The Making of the English Working Class* (1963), p. 67.

8. *Shrewsbury Chronicle* (12, 19, 26 August 1791).

9. H. M. Rathbone, *op. cit.*, pp. 270–73.
Salopian Journal, (12 Aug. 1795).
C. Wingfield, *An Historical Record of the Shropshire Yeomanry Cavalry 1795–1887* (1888), pp. 87–89.
J. Tranter-Boulton and Watt, 27 July 1795, B.R.L., B. & W. Colln., Box 6 'C'.
Shrewsbury Chronicle (2, 23, 30 Jan., 24, 31 July 1795).

10. H. M. Rathbone, *op. cit.*, pp. 270–73.

11. H. M. Rathbone, *op. cit.*, pp. 47–48.

12. CBD MS. 2, f. 81.
S.R.O. 665/5967–68.
S.R.O. 1224/2214.
Salopian Journal, (5 Mar., 24 Sep. and 1 Oct. 1800).
H. M. Rathbone, *op. cit.*, p. 209.
Mrs. [Lucy] Cameron, *The Oakengates Wake* (n.d.), p. 11.

13. J. Randall, *Broseley and its Surroundings* (1879), pp. 230–31.

14. A. Birch, *An Economic History of the British Iron and Steel Industry 1784–1879* (1967), p. 270.
C. Wingfield, *op. cit.*, p. 106.
Salop County Council, *An Abstract of the Quarter Sessions Rolls, 1820–30* (1974), July 1820, f. 123, Oct. 1820, f. 119.

15. *Salopian Journal* (22 Mar. 1820).
Ibid., (22 Nov. 1820).
Ibid., (29 Nov. 1820).

16. *Ibid.*, (10 Jan. 1821).
Ibid., (17 Jan. 1821).

17. The account which follows is drawn from S.B.L. Watton Collection, vol. 2, f. 27, *Salopian Journal* (28 Mar. 1821); C. Wingfield, *op. cit.*, pp. 107–09, and P.R.O. HO 40/16/9, 15 & 33; J. Pidcock-B. Dickinson, 2 Feb. 1821 in S.R.O. 245/103.
Salop County Council, *op. cit.*, April 1821, f. 187.

18. W. Day, Report on Shropshire in, *Second Annual Report of the Poor Law Commissioners for England and Wales* (1836), p. 379.
W. Botfield-B. Dickinson, 21 Jan. 1830, S.R.O. 245/124.

19. The account which follows is drawn from *Salopian Journal* (7, 14 & 21 Dec. 1831); C. Wingfield, *op. cit.*, p. 142, S.R.O. 1649/1.

20. J. Randall, *The Clay Industries on the banks of the Severn* (1877), p. 44.

21. *Salopian Journal* (23 Feb. 1831).

22. *Ibid.*, (23 Mar. 1831).

Ibid., (11 & 25 May 1831).

23. J. P. Nichol, 'Wynnstay, Willey and Wenlock, 1780–1832, a study in local political history' in *T.S.A.S.* vol. 58, (1965–68), pp. 220–234.

24. S.R.O. 1649/1.

J. Randall, *Broseley and its Surroundings* (1879), pp. 239, 243.

25. *Salopian Journal* (4, 11 and 25 May 1831).

26. J. P. Nichol, *op. cit.*, p. 232.

27. H. Scott, 'Colliers' Wages in Shropshire 1830–50' in *T.S.A.S.* vol. 53, (1949–50), p. 4.

28. *Salopian Journal* (11 May 1842).

S.B.L. Watton Collection, vol. 4, f. 291.

29. *Salopian Journal* (11 & 18 May 1842).

Ibid., (1 & 8 August 1842).

Northern Star (28 May 1842).

'Emanuel Lovekin: mining butty', in John Burnett, *Useful Toil* (1974), p. 291.

30. S.B.L. Watton Collection, vol. 4, f. 179.

31. *Salopian Journal* (31 Aug. 1842).

Report on the Population in the Mining Districts, B.P.P., 1847–48, xxvi, p. 10.

32. *Ibid.*, (27 July 1842).

S.B.L. Watton Collection, vol. 4, f. 291.

Affidavits of G. Hughes and J. Jones, 21 July 1842,

in N.L.W., *Cal. Chartism Shropshire*, vol. 2, no. 10. Thos. Eyton-Earl of Powis 15 Aug. 1842 in *Ibid.*, vol. 1, no. 1; T. J. Badger to Secretary of State, Home Department, 20 Aug. 1842 in *Ibid.*, vol. 1, no. 15; Thos. Eyton-Earl of Powis, 21 Aug. 1842 in *Ibid.*, vol. 1, no. 20.

33. For a fuller account of this crisis see J. M. Golby, 'Public Order and Private Unrest: A Study of the 1842 riots in Shropshire' in *University of Birmingham Historical Journal* vol. 11. (1968), pp. 157–69.

34. For Llanidloes' riots see N.L.W. *Calendar of Letters and Documents relating to the Chartist riots in Montgomeryshire in the possession of the Rt. Hon. Earl of Powis* (1935).

35. C. Wingfield, *op. cit.*, p. 15.

Earl of Powis to J. C. Whitmore 21 July 1842, in N.L.W. *Cal. Chartism Shropshire* vol. 2, no. 7; T. J. Badger to Secretary of State Home Department, 20 Aug. 1842, in *ibid.*, vol. 1, no. 15.

J. M. Golby, *op. cit.*, p. 161.

36. *Salopian Journal* (22 June 1842).

37. Earl of Powis-Sir James Graham, 24 Aug. 1842 in, N.L.W. *Cal. Chartism Shropshire*, vol. 1, No. 38; W. Botfield-Earl of Powis 25 Aug. 1842 in *Ibid.*, vol. 1, no. 44; Earl of Powis-T. C. Eyton, 1 Sep. 1842 in, *Ibid.*, vol. 2, no. 20; Minutes of Meeting 3 Sep. 1842 in *Ibid.*, vol. 2, no. 22.

38. Sir James Graham-Earl of Powis, 31 Aug. 1842 in N.L.W. *Cal. Chartism Shropshire*, vol. 2, no. 17.

Notes to Chapter XXI

1. Sir John Clapham, *An Economic History of Modern Britain: Free Trade and Steel 1850–1886*, (1932), p. 49.

2. W. H. Williams, 'The Botfield Empire: Decline and Fall in *Shropshire Magazine* Jan. 1966, p. 24.

S.R.O. 245/140.

3. W. H. Williams, *op. cit.*, pp. 24–26.

A. Raistrick, *Coalbrookdale 1709–1966* (1966), pp. 20–21, 28.

W. G. Norris-Mrs. Darby, 25 Jan. 1887, S.R.O. 1987/20.

Arthur Lester, *Fifty Years* (1896), p. 15.

4. Sir John Clapham, *op. cit.*, p. 49.

G. R. Morton and M. Le Guillou, 'The South Staffordshire Pig Iron Industry' in, *The British Foundryman* (July 1967), pp. 282–83.

5. [J. Fogerty], *Lauterdale* (1873), vol. 1, pp. 36, 107.

W. G. Norris-A. Darby, 20 Sep. 1873, S.R.O. 1987/20.

6. R. F. Wearmouth, *Methodism and the Trades Unions* (1959), pp. 46, 52.

7. Dawley and Madeley Methodist Circuit Plan, October 1933, S.R.O. 1936.

B. S. Trinder, *The Methodist New Connexion in Dawley and Madeley* (1967), pp. 15–20.

8. J. H. D. Madin and Partners, *Dawley: Wellington: Oakengates* (1966), p. 79.

9. L. T. C. Rolt, *Landscape with Canals* (1977), pp. 54–57.

10. I. J. Brown, 'The End of an Era', *Newsletter of the Friends of the Ironbridge Gorge Museum* (No. 36, 1979), pp. 1–2.

APPENDIX ONE

PARTNERS IN SHROPSHIRE IRONWORKS SET UP 1755–58

Horsehay
Abraham Darby II, Ironmaster, Coalbrookdale.
Thomas Goldney II, Gentleman, Clifton.

Ketley
Abraham Darby II, Ironmaster, Coalbrookdale.
Thomas Goldney II, Gentleman, Clifton.
Richard Reynolds, Ironmaster, Ketley.

Lightmoor
Richard Syer, Gentleman, Norton, Culmington.
William Ferriday, Esq., Buildwas.
Joseph Biddle, Esq., Evesham.
Arthur Davies, Gentleman, Park House, Great Dawley.
George Goodwin, Gentleman, Coalbrookdale.
Thomas Turner, Gentleman, Madeley Wood.
Thomas Botfield, Little Dawley.
William and James Gibbons, Gentlemen, Little Dawley.
William Hallen, Gentleman, Coalbrookdale.
George Perry, Gentleman.

Madeley Wood
John Smitheman, Esq., West Coppice.
William Ferriday, Ironmaster, Buildwas.
William Hinton, Grocer, Madeley Wood.
William Hinton Jun., Clerk, Madeley Wood.
George Goodwin, Master Collier, Madeley.
Henry Rainsford, Gentleman, Much Wenlock.
Edmund Ford, Ironmaster, Madeley Wood.
Thomas Brooke, Master Collier, Madeley Wood.
John Jones, Master Collier, Madeley Wood.
Jane Phillips executrix &c. of Andrew Phillips, late of Bridgnorth, dec.
Edward Bickerton, Mercer, Bridgnorth.
John Yate, Mercer, Bridgnorth.
Joseph Biddle, Esq., Evesham [entered partnership 1760].

New Willey
Brooke Forester, Esq., Underdale.
Henry Marsh, Merchant, Bristol.
John Roberts, Merchant, Bristol.

William Reeve, Merchant, Bristol.
Corsley Rogers, Merchant, Bristol.
Austin Goodwyn, Merchant, Bristol.
Samuel Brice, Merchant, Bristol.
John Skrymster, Esq., Shrewsbury.
Edward Blakeway, Draper, Shrewsbury.
John Wilkinson, Ironmaster, Bersham.
William Ferriday, Esq., Buildwas.

Sources
(N.B. not all are the original agreements).
Horsehay, S.R.O. 1987/20. Ketley, Staffs. R.O. D593/B/2/5/11/2,
Lightmoor, S.R.O. 1681/10, Madeley Wood, S.R.O. 1681/14, New Willey, S.R.O. 1224/143.

APPENDIX TWO

STEAM ENGINES AT SHROPSHIRE IRONWORKS, c.1802

Willey
1. Blowing blast furnace. Boulton and Watt, 38 in. × 8 ft., 30.7 h.p. engine, supplied 1776.
2. Pumping back water over wheel driving boring-mill. Boulton and Watt engine of 1777. Inverted cylinder or 'Topsy Turvey' engine. Dimensions unknown. Still working 1796.
3. Driving boring-mill direct. 'Pirate' engine, 30 in. cylinder. Built at Bersham. Began work Jan. 1788.

Broseley (Coneybury)
4. Blowing blast furnace. 36 in., 36¹/₂ h.p. engine.
5. Working grinding and blacking-mills and other foundry equipment. 18 in. double acting 10 h.p. engine.
6. Operating boring-mill, 15 in., double acting 8 h.p. engine.

Calcutts
7. Blowing blast furnace. Brodie and Glazebrook 80 h.p. engine of 1798. 'Pirate' engine, probably built by Brodie, McNiven and Ormrod of Manchester.
8. Blowing blast furnaces. 60 h.p. engine of 1803 built by Murray and Wood.
9. Driving boring-mill. 'Pirate' engine of 1796.

Benthall
10. Blowing blast furnaces. 30 h.p. atmospheric engine, capable of blowing only one furnace at a time.

Barnetts Leasow
11. Blowing blast furnaces. Boulton and Watt, 48 in. × 5 ft., 20 h.p. engine, supplied 1797.
12. Blowing blast furnaces. Boulton and Watt, 36 in. × 8 ft., 55.2 h.p. engine, supplied 1801.

Wren's Nest
13. Operating forge hammers. Boulton and Watt, 36 in. × 8 ft., 27.6 h.p. engine, originally supplied 1779 to pump back water over wheel, altered to rotative motion and set to work hammers 1791.

Madeley Wood
14. Blowing blast furnaces. Boulton and Watt, 48 in. × 8 ft., 50 h.p. single acting engine, replacing earlier pair of engines which had pumped water from Severn on to a waterwheel.

Coalbrookdale
15. Pumping water from lower pool to upper furnace pool in order to supply waterwheels powering two blast furnaces and engineering shops. Boulton and Watt, 66 in. × 9 ft., 102.6 h.p. engine, supplied 1781.
16. Blowing bellows at Upper Forge. Boulton and Watt, 26 in × 6 ft. engine. Supplied 1787. Stopped 1793 but operating 1801.
17. Operating hammers at Upper Forge. Boulton and Watt engine supplied 1785.

Horsehay
18. Blowing blast furnaces. Boulton and Watt engine, probably installed when third furnace was built after 1803.

19. Blowing blast furnaces, returning water over waterwheels which powered various workshops, an atmospheric engine probably with a separate condenser added in 1800.

20. Working hammers in forge. Boulton and Watt 26 in. × 6 ft. engine supplied in 1784.

21. Working machinery in forge. Boulton and Watt engine, supplied in 1785.

22. Operating rolling-mill. Atmospheric engine converted to rotative motion. Probably one of those supplied to the works in 1770–71. Replaced 1809.

Ketley

23. Blowing blast furnaces. Boulton and Watt 58 in. × 7 ft. 6 in. 71.7 h.p. engine, supplied 1778–79. Originally used for pumping back water over a wheel.

24. Operating slitting-mill, Boulton and Watt 58 in. × 8 ft. 71.7 h.p. engine, supplied 1780 for pumping back water over wheel. Replaced by 1817.

25. Working hammers in forge. Boulton and Watt 26 in. × 6 ft. engine supplied 1784.

26. Working hammers in forge. Similar engine to above.

27. Working hammers in forge. Similar engine to above.

28. Operating boring-mill and other machinery in shops for fitting up steam engines. Atmospheric engine, 24 in. × 6 ft. converted to rotative motion.

Lightmoor

29. Blowing blast furnaces. Boulton and Watt 84 in. × 8 ft., 82.4 h.p. engine, supplied in 1800.

30. Purpose not known. Small side level independent type engine by Boulton and Watt. Sold 1802.

Old Park

31. Blowing blast furnaces. Common (i.e. atmospheric) 52 in. × 8 ft. engine supplied by Homfray of Lightmoor, 1789–90.

32. Operating forge hammers. Common engine. $35^{1}/_{2}$ in. cylinder. Supplied by Homfray of Lightmoor, 1789–90.

33. Operating forge hammers. Common engine. 36 in. cylinder. Supplied by Homfray of Lightmoor, 1789–90.

34. Blowing blast furnaces. Boulton and Watt, 54 in. × 7 ft., 54.3 h.p. engine, supplied 1801.

35. Operating rolling mill. Boulton and Watt 3 ft. 6 in × 8 ft., 56 h.p. engine, supplied 1801.

Snedshill

36. Blowing blast furnaces. Boulton and Watt 40 in. × 8 ft. 34.1 h.p. engine, supplied 1780. Dimensions given in 1799 as 42 in. × 7 ft.

37. Blowing blast furnaces. Atmospheric. 50 in. × 4 ft.

38. Operating forge hammers. Well-constructed common atmospheric engine.

39. Operating forge hammers. Similar to previous engine but with air pump and condenser.

Hollinswood

40. Blowing blast furnace. Atmospheric engine, open top cylinder with separate condenser. Date and dimensions unknown.

New Hadley

41. Blowing blast furnaces. Boulton and Watt type, 52 in. cylinder. Date unknown. Furnace came into blast 1804.

Donnington Wood

42. Blowing blast furnaces. Boulton and Watt 48 in. × 8 ft. 49.1 h.p. engine, supplied 1783–85.

Ironworks of which source of power is not known
Queenswood
Blowing blast furnaces. Engine of c. 1802.

Wrockwardine Wood
Blowing two blast furnaces. Engine(s) of c. 1801.

APPENDIX THREE

CHURCH ATTENDANCES IN EAST SHROPSHIRE
30 MARCH 1851

Attendances recorded by the 1851 Ecclesiastical Census at places of worship in the parishes of Benthall, Broseley, Madeley, Dawley, Little Wenlock, Stirchley, Priorslee, Wellington, Wombridge, Wrockwardine Wood and Lilleshall.

Church of England		9,393
Wesleyans	7,548	
Methodist New Connexion	1,538	
Primitive Methodist	3,445	
Total Methodists		12,531
Baptists	1,371	
Congregationalists	1,150	
Society of Friends	41	
Total old Dissenting denominations		2,562
Roman Catholic		1,000
Total		25,486

BIBLIOGRAPHY

i) *Manuscript sources; public collections*

BIRMINGHAM REFERENCE LIBRARY
Boulton and Watt Collection. Incoming and outgoing correspondence, lists of ironworks, maps, engine book.

BIRMINGHAM UNIVERSITY LIBRARY
Microfilms of the Journals and Notebooks of Joshua Gilpin, 1790–1801, copied from originals in the Division of Public Records, Pennsylvania Historical and Museum Commission, Harrisburg, Pennsylvania, USA.

BRITISH MUSEUM
Egerton MS. 1941 (Annotated drawings of John Wilkinson's Willey blowing engine of 1776), Add MS. 21018 (Joseph Plymley's survey of the portion of Shropshire in the diocese of Hereford, 1793, with later additions), Map Kxxxvi.16.1 (Madeley Wood Ironworks).

HEREFORD RECORD OFFICE
Bishops' Registers, visitation returns, returns of papists, probate records.

IRONBRIDGE GORGE MUSEUM TRUST LTD
a) Coalbrookdale Museum.
CBD MS. 1 – Coalbrookdale Stock Book, 1728–1738 (continuing S.B.L. MS. 330).
CBD MS. 2 – Coalbrookdale Settling Journal 1798–1808.
CBD MS. 3 – Minute Book of the Coalbrookdale Company 1789–1796.
CBD MS. 4 – Valuation and Profit and Loss Accounts, 1805–52.
Sundry letters, broadsheets, handbills &c.

b) Lilleshall Company Collection
Schedule of Deeds.
Chartermasters' Book 1764–1803.
Surveys, leases, agreements, accounts, maps and sundry papers.

c) General
Sundry papers, photostats &c.

KIDDERMINSTER PUBLIC LIBRARY
Stour Works Accounts, Stour General Accounts.

LIBRARY OF THE SOCIETY OF FRIENDS, FRIENDS HOUSE, EUSTON ROAD, LONDON
Journal of Abiah Darby.
Norris MSS. 14 volumes of transcripts of deeds, Quaker records, &c. made in the late 19th century by W. G. Norris.

LICHFIELD JOINT RECORD OFFICE
Visitation returns, Bishops' Registers, tithe maps, probate records.

METHODIST ARCHIVES AND RESEARCH CENTRE, JOHN RYLANDS UNIVERSITY LIBRARY, MANCHESTER
Fletcher-Tooth Correspondence. Several thousand letters, some written to John Fletcher, but the majority after his death in 1785 to Mary Fletcher and Mary Tooth.
Wesleyan Reform Collection, pamphlets &c.
Sundry circuit plans &c.

NORTHAMPTONSHIRE RECORD OFFICE
Journal of John Thornton.

PUBLIC RECORD OFFICE
Census Returns
Minutes of the Shropshire Canal Company

SCIENCE MUSEUM, SOUTH KENSINGTON
William Reynolds's Sketch Book.
Letters from Simon Goodrich to General Bentham, giving an account of a tour of engineering works in 1799. Goodrich Collection.

SCOTTISH RECORD OFFICE, H.M. GENERAL REGISTER OFFICE, EDINBURGH
Dundonald Collection, GD 233. Correspondence, chiefly between the 9th Earl of Dundonald and William Reynolds, plans, &c.

SHREWSBURY BOROUGH LIBRARY
(In 1974 the Borough Library was absorbed by the Shropshire County Library, but the manuscripts acquired by the Library remain a distinct collection, and are referred to throughout this book by the abbreviation S.B.L. and the appropriate number. At the time of writing (1980), the Shrewsbury Borough Library Collection is lodged in the Shropshire Record Office, Shirehall, Shrewsbury.)
MS. 328 Coalbrookdale Account Book, 1709–10.
MS. 329 Coalbrookdale Cash Book (1718–1732) (continued in MS. 331).
MS. 330 Coalbrookdale Stock Book 1718–1727 (continued in CBD MS. 1).
MS. 331 Coalbrookdale Cash Book 1732–1749 (continued from MS. 329).
MS. 332 Horsehay Account Book 1754–1762.
MS. 333 Horsehay Wages and Waste Book 1767–1774 (continued in S.R.O. 245/144).
MS. 334 Horsehay Day Book 1794–1798.
MS. 335 Horsehay Blast Furnace Weekly Accounts 1798–1807.
MS. 336 Horsehay Journal 1802–1805.
MS. 337 Horsehay Journal 1805–1808.
MSS. 2365–66 Broseley Estate Books.
MS. 2481 Survey of the Shropshire Estates of the Earl of Craven.
MS. 3190 Copy of Letter Book of Richard Ford, 1732–36.
MS. 3689 Minutes of the Proprietors of the Ironbridge.
Watton Collection of Newspaper cuttings, broadsheets, &c.
Typescripts of unpublished parish register.
Sundry papers, broadsheets, copies of deeds &c.

SHROPSHIRE RECORD OFFICE, SHIREHALL, SHREWSBURY
Charlton Collection, S.R.O. 625 and 676. Rentals, accounts, leases, &c. of the estates of the Charlton family of Apley Castle near Wellington.
Coalbrookdale Collection, S.R.O. 245. Accounts, correspondence &c. relating to the Coalbrookdale Company, including 245/144 Horsehay Wages and Waste Book 1774–1781 (continuing S.B.L. MS. 333), 245/145 Horsehay Wages Book 1796–1798 and Brierly Hill Tunnel Accounts 1793–94 (at opposite ends of the same volume), and 245/140, MS. account of the Horsehay ironworks in the 19th century by W. G. Norris.
Cooper Collection, S.R.O. 1681. Leases &c. relating to numerous concerns in east Shropshire.

Dawley U.D.C. Collection, S.R.O. 615. Poor law records for Dawley parish.

Dyas Collection, S.R.O. 796. Leases &c. relating chiefly to the estates of the Slaney family.

Forester Collection, S.R.O. 1224. Leases, rentals, accounts, surveys, correspondence, &c. relating to the lands of the Forester and Weld families, principally in Broseley, Willey and Little Wenlock.

Alderman Jones's Collection, S.R.O. 1649. Commonplace books of a member of a Jackfield barge-owning family.

Labouchere Collection, S.R.O. 1987 and 2448. Leases, accounts, correspondence, &c. relating to the Coalbrookdale ironworks and the Darby family, including the personal account books of Abraham Darby III.

Madeley Field coalworks and Madeley Wood furnaces, account books 1790–1797. S.R.O. 271.

Madeley Parish Records, S.R.O. 2280. Vestry accounts, glebe coalworks accounts and correspondence, MS. History of Wesleyan Methodism in Coalbrookdale by 'BB', printed and MS. material relating to John Fletcher, tithe map and award.

Dr. Mason (Pitt and Cooksey) Collection, S.R.O. 1190. Documents relating to the iron and clay works of the Onions family in Broseley and Madeley.

Shackerley Collection, S.R.O. 1781. Letters of Gilbert Gilpin.

Sutherland Collection, S.R.O. 38, 673 and 972. Leases, surveys, accounts, &c. relating to the estates of the Leveson Gower family, principally in Lilleshall and Ketley.

Thynne Collection, S.R.O. 1150. Agreements concerning the Botfield family and the Old Park Ironworks.

Wellington Poor Law Examinations Book. Draft for 1821 Census, Wellington Parish, S.R.O. 3129/4–5.

Wrockwardine Wood Primitive Methodist Circuit Records, S.R.O. 1861.

Typescript: Visitation Returns for the Archdeaconry of Salop, 1799.

Collections from which single items, not of major importance, have been taken are not listed.

STAFFORDSHIRE RECORD OFFICE

Sutherland Collection, D593. Leases, accounts, correspondence, surveys, rentals, &c. chiefly relating to the estates of the Leveson Gower family in Lilleshall and Ketley.

Jerningham Collection, D641. Correspondence &c. relating to the estates of the Jerningham family, Earls of Stafford, in the parish of Shifnal.

National Coal Board Collection, D876. William Reynolds's Executors' Accounts, 1803–10, and Madeley Wood Company Annual Statements, 1826–50.

WARRINGTON PUBLIC LIBRARY

Priestley Correspondence. Letters, chiefly written to John Wilkinson by Joseph Priestley.

ii) *Manuscript sources: private collections*
LADY LABOUCHERE, DUDMASTON, BRIDGNORTH

Correspondence &c. relating to the Coalbrookdale ironworks and the Darby family, including Hannah Rose's, 'Some account of the Family of the Darby's being what Hannah Rose has heard her Parents John and Grace Thomas say concerning them'.

MR. W. LAWRENCE, WELLINGTON, TELFORD
Despatch book of Thomas Dykes, 1801–02.

MADELEY WOOD METHODIST CHURCH
Property deeds of chapels in the Madeley Methodist Circuit.

iii) *Newspapers, periodicals &c.*
Aris's Birmingham Gazette.
Baptist Handbook.
Baptist Magazine.
Express and Star.
Methodist Magazine.
Methodist New Connexion Magazine.
Minutes of the Primitive Methodist Conference.
Minutes of the Methodist New Connexion Conference.
Minutes of the United Methodist Free Church Conference.

Minutes of the Wesleyan Methodist Conference.
Primitive Methodist Magazine.
Salopian Journal.
Salopian Shreds and Patches.
Shrewsbury Chronicle.
Shropshire Circular Letter.
Transactions of the Society of Arts.
Staffordshire Mercury.
Wesleyan Methodist Penny Magazine.

iv) *Older Printed Sources; books published before 1914*
(Works quoted in the text for purely comparative purposes are omitted from this list. Where reprinted editions have been used, the date of the reprint is quoted.)
Arthur Aikin, *Journal of a Tour through North Wales* (1797).
Annals of Church Pastoral Aid Work No. 5, (n.d. c. 1885).
Annual Register (1816).
Anon. *A Village Dialogue on Bull-baiting and Cruelty to Animals* (n.d.).
Art Journal, *Illustrated Catalogue of the International Exhibition of 1862.*
Joseph von Baader, *Neues System der fortschaffenden Mechanik* (1822).
Samuel Bagshaw, *History, Gazetteer and Directory of Shropshire* (1851).
William Bailey, *The Bristol and Bath Directory* (1787).
W. H. Barclay, *The History of Wesleyan Methodism at Lawley Bank* (1858).
Joseph Benson, *The Life of the Ref. John W. de la Flechère* (1835).
British Parliamentary Papers, 1842, VII, *Children's Employment Commission, Appendix to the first Report of the Commissioners.*
British Parliamentary Papers, *Reports of Commissioners on the Holyhead Road,* 1810 et seq.
British Parliamentary Papers, 1847–48, XXVI, *Report of the Commission . . . into . . . the Population of the Mining Districts.*
British Parliamentary Papers, 1866, XXIV, *Children's Employment Commission (1862) fifth report.*
C. S. Burne, *Shropshire Folk Lore* (1883).
William Camden, ed. and trans. by Richard Gough, *Britannia* (1789).
C. R. Cameron, *Considerations suggested by the Murder of William Bailey* (1812).
Mrs. (Lucy) Cameron, *The Novice* (n.d.).
Mrs. (Lucy) Cameron, *The Oakengates Wakes* (n.d.).
Mrs. (Lucy) Cameron, *The Seeds of Greediness* (n.d.).
Mrs. (Lucy) Cameron, *Crooked Paths* (n.d.).
Mrs. (Lucy) Cameron, *An Honest Penny is worth a Silver Shilling* (n.d.).
E. Cassey, *Directory of Shropshire* (1870).
Erasmus Darwin, *The Botanic Garden* (1791).
William Day, 'Report on Shropshire', in, *Second Annual Report of the Poor Law Commissioners for England and Wales* (1835).
Henry de Salis, *Bradshaws Canals and Navigable Rivers of England and Wales* (1964).
Charles Dibdin, *Observations on a tour through almost the whole of England . . . in a series of letters* (1801–02).
H. W. Dickinson, *John Wilkinson: Ironmaster* (1914).
Jean Dutens, *Memoirs sur les Travaux Publiques d'Angleterre* (1819).
E. Evans, *A History of Congregationalism in Shropshire* (1898).
J. W. Fletcher, *American Patriotism: Further confronted with Reason, Scripture and the Constitution: Being Observations on the Dangerous Politics taught by the Rev. Mr. Evans and the Rev. Dr. Price* (1776).
J. W. Fletcher, *An Appeal to Matter of Fact and Common Sense* (1772).
Posthumous Pieces of the late Rev. J. W. de la Flechère, ed. by M. Horne (1791).
[J. Fogerty], *Lauterdale* (1873).
H. E. Forrest, *Old Houses of Wenlock* (1914).
R. Galloway, *A History of Coalmining in Great Britain* (1882).
Eustace Greg, ed., *Reynolds Rathbone Letters and Diaries* (1905).
T. Gregory, *The Shropshire Directory* (1824).
Griffiths's Guide to the Iron Trade of Great Britain, ed. by W. K. V. Gale, (1967).
Thomas Harral, *Picturesque Views of the Severn* (1824).

John Holland, *The History and Description of Fossil Fuel, the Collieries and the Coal Trade of Great Britain* (1968).
James Houghton, *Periodic Letters on Husbandry and Trade*, No. 198, (1696).
Thomas Howell, *The Stranger in Shrewsbury* (1825).
Charles Hulbert, *Manual of Shropshire Biography, Chronology and Antiquities* (1839).
Charles Hulbert, *The History and Description of the County of Shropshire* (1837).
Charles Hulbert, *Memoirs of Seventy Years* (1852).
S. Hulme, *Memoir of the Revd. William Cooke, D.D.* (1856).
H. B. Kendall, *The Origins and History of the Primitive Methodist Church* (n.d.).
The Itinerary of John Leland, ed. by Thomas Hearne (1744).
Arthur Lester, *Fifty Years* (1896).
James Loch, *An Account of the Improvements on the estates of the Marquis of Stafford* (1820).
F. T. MacDermot, *The History of the Great Western Railway*, ed. by C. R. Clinker, (1964).
F. W. MacDonald, *Fletcher of Madeley* (1885).
John M'Owan, *A Man of God: a memoir of the Revd. Peter M'Owan*, ed. by G. Osborn, (1873).
J. Minshill, *The Shrewsbury Visitor's Pocket Companion or Salopian Guide and Directory* (1803).
H. Moore, *The Life of Mary Fletcher* (1817).
C. von Oeynhausen and H. von Dechen, *Railways in England 1826 and 1827*, ed. by Charles E. Lee, (1971).
Official Catalogue of the 1862 International Exhibition (1862).
Hugh Owen, *Some Account of the Ancient and Present State of Shrewsbury* (1808).
A. N. Palmer, *John Wilkinson and the Old Bersham Ironworks* (1899).
George Perry, *A Description of Coalbrookdale . . . with perspective views thereof* (n.d.).
George Perry, 'The Severn Navigation', in *Gentleman's Magazine* vol. 28 (1758).
John Petty, *The History of the Primitive Methodist Connexion* (1864).
John Phillips, *Phillips's Inland Navigation* (1805).
Thomas Phillips, *The History and Antiquities of Shrewsbury*, 2nd ed. by Charles Hulbert (1837).
Robert Plummer, *The Successful Class-Leader: a Memorial of Mr. Benjamin Pollard* (1861).
Joseph Plymley, *A General View of the Agriculture of Shropshire* (1803).
Joseph Prestwich, 'The Geology of the Coalfield of Coalbrookdale' in *Transactions of the Geological Society*, vol. 5, (1840).
John Randall, *The Severn Valley*, 1st ed. (1862), 2nd ed. (1882).
John Randall, *The Clay Industries on the Banks of the Severn* (1877).
John Randall, *Broseley and its Surroundings* (1879).
John Randall, *The History of Madeley* (1880).
John Randall, *The Wilkinsons* (n.d.).
John Randall, *A short Sketch of the Lives and Usefulness of the Rev. John and Mary Fletcher* (n.d.).
H. R. Rathbone, *Letters of Richard Reynolds with a Memoir of his Life* (1852).
Harry Scrivenor, *The History of the Iron Trade* (1967).
Samuel Smiles, *Industrial Biography: Ironworkers and Toolmakers* (1863).
Thomas Telford, *The Life of Thomas Telford*, ed. by John Rickman (1838).
Viaggio in Einhilterra di Carlo Castrone della Torre di Renzionico Comasco (1824).
Robert Townson, 'A Sketch of the Mineralogy of Shropshire' in *Tracts and Observations in Natural History and Physiology* (1799).
Luke Tyerman, *Wesley's Designated Successor* (1882).
Universal British Directory (1797).
Victoria History of Shropshire, vol. 1, (1908).
Journals of the Rev. John Wesley, ed. by Nehemiah Curnock, (1938).
C. Wingfield, *An Historical Record of the Shropshire Yeomanry Cavalry, 1795–1887* (1888).

v) *Modern Works*
D. R. Adams and J. Hazeley, *Survey of the Church Aston-Lilleshall Mining Area* (1970)
J. P. Addis, *The Crawshay Dynasty* (1951).
T. S. Ashton, *Iron and Steel in the Industrial Revolution* (1951).
T. S. Ashton and J. Sykes, *The Coal Industry in the 18th century* (1964).
David Atkinson, *The Tobacco Pipes of Broseley, Shropshire* (1975).
Franklin Barrett, *Caughley and Coalport Porcelain* (1951).
Alan Birch, *An Economic History of the British Iron and Steel Industry 1784–1879* (1967).
R. L. Brett, ed., *Barclay Fox's Journal* (1979).

F. Brook and M. Allbutt, *The Shropshire Lead Mines* (1973).
I. J. Brown, *The Mines of Shropshire* (1976)
I. J. Brown and D. R. Adams, *A History of Limestone Mining in Shropshire* (1967).
I. J. Brown and Barrie Trinder, *The Coalport Tar Tunnel* (1971).
The Diary of John Byng, ed. by C. B. Andrews (1934).
G. F. Carter and H. Walcot, *Historical Notes on the Parish of Rodington* (n.d.)
Rex Christiansen, *A Regional History of the Railways of Great Britain, Vol. VII, The West Midlands* (1973).
Sir John Clapham, *An Economic History of Modern Britain, vol. 2: Free Trade and Steel, 1850–1866* (1932).
A. and N. Clow, *The Chemical Revolution* (1952).
Evan Corlett, *The Iron Ship* (1975).
Neil Cossons, *The B.P. Book of Industrial Archaeology* (1974).
Neil Cossons and Harry Sowden, *Ironbridge: Landscape of Industry* (1977).
Neil Cossons and Barrie Trinder, *The Iron Bridge* (1979).
W. H. B. Court, *The Rise of the Midland Industries* (1953).
A. S. Davies, *The Charcoal Iron Industry of Powysland* (1939).
J. H. Denton, *A Tour of the Railways and Canals between Oakengates and Coalbrookdale* (1961).
H. W. Dickinson and Rhys Jenkins, *James Watt and the Steam Engine* (1927).
M. Elsas, *Iron in the Making* (1960).
Peter Forsaith, *The Eagle and the Dove, John Fletcher, Vicar of Madeley, towards a new assessment* (privately published 1979).
W. K. V. Gale, *The British Iron and Steel Industry* (1967).
W. K. V. Gale, *Iron and Steel* (1969).
W. K. V. Gale and Cyril Nicholls, *The Lilleshall Company Ltd.: a history 1764–1964* (1979).
Sir Alexander Gibb, *The Story of Telford* (1935).
G. A. Godden, *Caughley and Worcester Porcelains* (1969).
G. A. Godden, *Coalport and Coalbrookdale Porcelains* (1970).
Charles Hadfield, *The Canals of the West Midlands* (1966).
Charles Hadfield and John Norris, *Waterways to Stratford* (1962).
Charles Hadfield and A. W. Skempton, *William Jessop: Engineer* (1979).
The Hatchett Diary, ed. by Arthur Raistrick (1967).
Roger Hill, *A Telford Church: St. Leonard's, Malinslee* (1980).
Humphrey Household, *The Thames and Severn Canal* (1969).
Derek Hudson, *Munby: Man of Two Worlds* (1972).
Ironbridge Gorge Museum, *The Hay Inclined Plane* (1973).
Ironbridge Gorge Museum, *The Jackfield Tile Industry* (1978).
Ironbridge Gorge Museum, *The Tar Tunnel* (1980).
Ironbridge Gorge Museum, *The Quaker Burial Grounds* (1979).
Ironbridge Gorge Museum, *The Coalbrookdale Company and the S.S. Great Britain* (1979).
Ironbridge Gorge Museum, *Coalport: New Town of the 1790s* (1979).
Ironbridge Gorge Museum, *Shropshire Tragedies* (1980).
F. D. Klingender, *Art and the Industrial Revolution* (ed. by Sir. Arthur Elton, 1968).
L. J. Lee, ed. *A full list and partial abstract of the Quarter Sessions Rolls* (for Shropshire), *1696–1800* (n.d.).
L. J. Lee and R. G. Venables, eds., *A full list and partial abstraction of the Quarter Sessions Rolls* (for Shropshire) *1800–20* (n.d.).
M. J. T. Lewis, *Early Wooden Railways* (1970).
W. J. Lewis, *Lead Mining in Wales* (1967).
L. C. Lloyd, ed., *Wenlock 1468–1968* (1968).
J. Lord, *Capital and Steam Power* (1966).
J. H. D. Madin and Partners, *Dawley: Wellington: Oakengates* (1966).
H. Malet, *The Canal Duke* (1961).
Peter Mathias, *English Trade Tokens* (1962).
A. E. Musson and E. Robinson, *Science and Technology in the Industrial Revolution* (1969).
W. Grant Muter, *The Buildings of an Industrial Community: Ironbridge and Coalbrookdale* (1979).
National Library of Wales, *Calendars of Letters and Documents relating to Chartism in Shropshire*, vol. 1, (1941), vol. 2, (1949).
J. U. Nef, *The Rise of the British Coal Industry* (1932).
C. von Oeynhausen and H. von Dechen, *Railways in England 1826 and 1827*, ed. Charles E. Lee (1974).

Alistair Penfold, ed., *Thomas Telford: Engineer* (1980).
Sidney Pollard, *The Genesis of Modern Management* (1965).
Arthur Raistrick, *Dynasty of Ironfounders* (1953).
Ursula Rayska, *Victorian and Edwardian Shropshire from Old Photographs* (1977).
Arthur Redford, *Labour Migration in England, 1800–1850* (1964).
William Rees, *Industry before the Industrial Revolution* (1968).
Eric Richards, *The Leviathan of Wealth: the Sutherland Fortune in the Industrial Revolution* (1973).
L. T. C. Rolt, *Thomas Telford* (1958).
L. T. C. Rolt, *Tools for the Job* (1968).
L. T. C. Rolt, *Landscape with Canals* (1977).
L. T. C. Rolt and J. S. Allen, *The Steam Engine of Thomas Newcomen* (1977).
Trevor Rowley, *The Shropshire Landscape* (1972).
Salop County Council, *Canals and Railways: a list of Plans &c.* (1969).
Salop County Council, *An Abstract of the Quarter Sessions Rolls 1820–30* (1974).
R. S. Sayers, *Lloyds Bank in the History of English Banking* (1957).
H. R. Schubert, *The History of the British Iron Industry to 1775* (1957).
Shrewsbury Borough Library, *The Age of Steam* (1967).
Shropshire Parish Register Society, *The Register of Dawley Magna* (1923).
C. Singer and others, *A History of Technology* (1957).
R. F. Skinner, *Nonconformity in Shropshire 1662–1816* (1964).
D. J. Smith, *The Severn Valley Railway* (1968).
Stuart Smith, *A View from the Iron Bridge* (1979).
Svedenstierna's Tour in Great Britain 1802–03: the Travel Diary of an Industrial Spy, ed. by M. W. Flinn (1973).
Jennifer Tann, *The Rise of the Factory* (1968).
E. P. Thompson, *The Making of the English Working Class* (1963).
Barrie Trinder, *The Methodist New Connexion in Dawley and Madeley* (1967).
Barrie Trinder, ed., *A Description of Coalbrookdale in 1801* (1970).
Barrie Trinder, *The Darbys of Coalbrookdale* (1974).
Barrie Trinder, *The Most Extraordinary District in the World* (1977).
Barrie Trinder and Jeff Cox, *Yeomen and Colliers in Telford* (1980).
Victoria County History, Shropshire, vol. 2 (1973), vol. 3 (1979), vol. 8 (1968).
R. F. Wearmouth, *Methodism and the Trade Unions* (1959).
G. F. Westcott, *The British Railway Locomotive 1803–53* (1953).
P. J. Wexler, *La Formation de la Vocabulaire des Chemins de Fer en France*, 1778–1842 (1955).
T. H. Whitehead and others, *Memoirs of the Geological Survey of England and Wales: The Country between Wolverhampton and Oakengates* (1928).
J. T. Wilkinson, *Hugh Bourne 1772–1852* (1952).
Arthur Young, *Tours in England and Wales* (L.S.E. reprint, 1932).

vi) *Articles in Learned Journals or Symposia*
Sir Edward Benthall, 'Some 18th century Shropshire Potteries' in *T.S.A.S.* vol. 55, (1955).
Alan Birch, 'The Midlands Iron Industry during the Napoleonic Wars' in *Edgar Allen News* (Aug./Sept. 1952).
F. Bland, 'John Curr: Originator of Iron Tram Roads' in *T.N.S.* vol. 11, (1930–31).
S. R. Broadbridge, 'Joseph Banks and the West Midlands Industry, 1767' in *Staffordshire Industrial Archaeology Society Journal* vol. 2, (1971).
I. J. Brown, 'The Mines of the Madeley Court Company' in *S.N.L.* No. 38, (1970).
W. H. Chaloner, 'John Wilkinson: Ironmaster' in *History Today* (1951).
W. H. Chaloner, 'Isaac Wilkinson: Potfounder' in L. S. Pressnell, ed., *Studies in the Industrial Revolution* (1960).
Robin Chaplin, 'A Forgotten Industrial Valley' in *S.N.L.* No. 36, (1969).
Robin Chaplin, 'New Light on Thomas Farnolls Pritchard' in *S.N.L.* No. 34, (1968).
N. C. Clarke, 'The Aqueduct: an east Shropshire Industrial Settlement' in *S.N.L.* Nos. 39 and 40, (1970–71).
A. R. K. Clayton, 'The Shrewsbury and Newport Canals: Construction and Remains', in Alistair Penfold, ed., *Thomas Telford: Engineer* (1980).

Richard Cornes, 'A short topographical account of Bridgnorth by Richard Cornes 1739' in *T.S.A.S.* vol. 9, (1886).

Neil Cossons, 'Ironbridge – the First Ten Years', in *I.A.R.* vol. 3, (1979).

Richard Davey, 'The Newcomen Engine' in *Proceedings of the Institution of Mechanical Engineers* (1903).

A. S. Davies, 'The River Trade of Montgomeryshire' in *Montgomeryshire Collections*, vol. 43, (1934).

J. H. Denton and M. J. T. Lewis, 'The River Tern Navigation', in *Journal of the Railway and Canal Historical Society*, vol. 23, (1977).

M. W. Doughty, 'Samborne Palmer's Diary', in *I.A.R.*, vol. 3, (1979).

R. S. Edmundson, 'Coalport China Works, Shropshire; a comparative study of the premises and the background to their development', in *I.A.R.* vol. 3, (1979).

Graham Farr, 'The Severn Navigation and the Severn Trow', in *The Mariner's Mirror*, vol. 43, (1934).

A. H. Faulkner, 'The Wolverton Aqueduct' in *Transport History*, vol. 2, (1969).

M. W. Flinn, 'Abraham Darby and the Coke Smelting Process' in *Economica*, vol. 26, (1959).

M. W. Flinn, 'The Travel Diaries of Swedish Engineers as sources of Technological History', in *T.N.S.*, vol. 31, (1957–58).

E. A. Forward, 'Links in the History of the Locomotive: Trevithick's first locomotive, Coalbrookdale, 1803–03', in *The Engineer*, (22 Feb. 1952).

J. M. Golby, 'Public Order and Private Unrest: a study of the 1842 Riots in Shropshire' in *University of Birmingham Historical Review*, vol. 11, (1968).

Charles Hadfield, Telford, Jessop and Pontcysyllte', in *Journal of the Railway and Canal Historical Society*, vol. 15, (1969).

J. W. Hall, 'Joshua Field's Diary of a tour in 1821 through the Midlands' in *T.N.S.* vol. 6, (1925–26).

J. R. Harris, 'The Employment of Steam Power in the 18th century' in *History*, vol. 52, (1967).

A. T. Herbert, 'Jackfield Decorative Tiles in Use', in *I.A.R.*, vol. 3, (1979).

A. T. Herbert, 'Jackfield Decorative Tiles – A Victorian Art Industry', in The Design Council, *Design and Industry*, (1980).

M. C. Hill, 'Iron and Steel Bridges in Shropshire 1788–1901' in *T.S.A.S.*, vol. 56, (1956–57).

Marchant de la Houlière, 'Report to the French Government on British Methods of smelting iron ore with coke and casting naval canon' (1775), trans. and ed. by W. H. Chaloner, in *Edgar Allen News* (Dec. 1948/Jan. 1949).

E. Wyndham Hulme, 'The Statistical History of the Iron Trade 1717–50' in *T.N.S.*, vol. 9, (1928–29).

Maurice Hunt, Ken Jones and Barrie Trinder, 'Holywell Lane: the rise and fall of an industrial squatter community', *I.A.R.* (forthcoming).

B. L. C. Johnson, 'The Foley Partnerships' in *Economic History* Review, vol. 4, (1952).

B. L. C. Johnson, 'The Charcoal Iron Industry in the early 18th century' in *Geographical Journal*, vol. 117, (1951).

Ian Lawley, 'Art and Ornament in Iron: Design and the Coalbrookdale Company', in The Design Council, *Design and Industry*, (1980).

J. B. Lawson, 'Thomas Telford in Shrewsbury: the metamorphosis of an architect into a civil engineer', in Alistair Penfold, ed., *Thomas Telford: Engineer* (1980).

L. C. Lloyd, 'A beam engine at the Rats Pits' in *T.S.A.S.*, vol. 53, (1949–50).

L. C. Lloyd, 'The Records of a Borough Court in the 18th century' in *Archives*, vol. 7, (1965).

Emanuel Lovekin, 'Emanuel Lovekin: mining butty', in John Burnett, *Useful Toil*, (1974).

H. C. Maxwell Lyte, 'The Manuscripts of E. Lloyd Gatacre Esq.' in *T.S.A.S.* vol. 11, (1888).

R. Maguire and P. Matthews, 'The Iron Bridge at Coalbrookdale' in *Architectural Association Journal* vol. 74, No. 824, (1958).

G. R. Morton and M. Le Guillou, 'The South Staffordshire Pig Iron Industry' in *The British Foundryman* (July 1967).

G. R. Morton and N. Mutton, 'The Transition to Cort's Puddling Process' in *Journal of the Iron and Steel Institute* vol. 205, (1967).

R. A. Mott, 'English Waggonways of the 18th century' in *T.N.S.* vol. 37, (1964).

R. A. Mott, 'The Shropshire Iron Industry' in *T.S.A.S.* vol. 56, (1957–60).

R. A. Mott, 'Coalbrookdale – The Early Years' in *T.S.A.S.* vol. 56, (1957–60).

R. A. Mott, 'The Newcomen Engine in the 18th century' in *T.S.A.S.* vol. 58, (1965–68).

R. A. Mott, 'Abraham Darby I and II and the coke-iron industry' in *T.N.S.* vol. 31, (1957–58).

R. A. Mott, 'The Newcomen Engine in the 18th century' in *T.N.S.* vol. 35, (1962–63).

R. A. Mott, 'The Coalbrookdale Group Horsehay Works' in *T.N.S.* vol. 31, (1957–58).

R. A. Mott, 'The Coalbrookdale Group Horsehay Works Part II' in *T.N.S.* vol. 32, (1959–60).
Norman Mutton, 'An Engineer at work in the West Midlands' in *West Midlands Studies, Special Publication No. 1* (1969).
Norman Mutton, 'Charlcotte Furnace' in *T.S.A.S.* vol. 58, (1965–68).
Norman Mutton, 'The forges at Eardington and Hampton Loade' in *T.S.A.S.* vol. 58, (1965–68).
C. R. T. Nankivell, 'Three dwellings in the Dark Lane Rows' in *S.N.L.* No. 41, (1971).
J. P. Nichol, 'Wynnstay, Willey and Wenlock, 1780–1832, a study in local political history' in *T.S.A.S. vol. 58, (1965–68)*.
David Pannett, 'Fish Weirs on the River Severn' in S.N.L. No. 41, (1971) and No. 44, (1973).
C. F. Peskin, 'Memories of Old Coalbrookdale' in *Transactions of the Caradoc and Severn Valley Field Club*, vol. 11, (1941).
John Rhodes, 'Lead Smelting in the Severn Gorge' in *S.N.L.* No. 41, (1971).
Eric Richards, 'The Social and Electoral Influence of the Trentham Estate 1800–60', in *Midland History*, vol. 3, (1975–76).
Eric Richards, 'The Industrial Face of a great Estate: Trentham and Lilleshall 1780–1860' in *Economic History Review*, 2nd ser., vol. 27, (1975).
Clifton Roberts, 'Salopian China' in *The Connoisseur*, vol. 58, (1919–20).
Susan Roberts, 'Hinkshay Rows' in *S.N.L.* No. 44, (1973).
R. T. Rowley, 'Bouldon Mill', in *Shropshire Magazine* (Feb. 1966).
H. Scott, 'Colliers' Wages in Shropshire, 1830–50', in *T.S.A.S.*, vol. 53, (1949–50).
'A Short Account of Wellington, 1759' in *Salopian Shreds and Patches*, vol. 1, (1874–75).
Silvi Sogner, 'Aspects of the Demographic Situation in 17 parishes in Shropshire, 1711–60' in *Population Studies* (Feb. 1964).
W. A. Smith, 'A Swedish View of the West Midlands in 1802–03', in *West Midlands Studies*, vol. 3, (1969).
'The Memoir of William Smith', ed. by Barrie Trinder, in *T.S.A.S.*, vol. 58, (1965–68).
A. J. Taylor, 'The sub-contract system in the British Coal Industry' in *Studies in the Industrial Revolution*, ed. by L. S. Pressnell, (1960).
J. M. Tonkin, 'Hinkshay Row, Dawley', in *S.N.L.* No. 33, (1967).
S. M. Tonkin, 'Trevithick, Rastrick and the Hazledine Foundry at Bridgnorth' in *T.N.S.*, vol. 26, (1947–49).
Barrie Trinder, 'Early Railways in East Shropshire', in *S.N.L.* No. 39, (1970).
Barrie Trinder, 'Industrial Conservation and Industrial History' in *History Workshop Journal*, vol. 2, (1976).
Barrie Trinder, 'The First Iron Bridges', in *I.A.R.*, vol. 3, (1979).
Barrie Trinder, 'Coalport Bridge: a Study in Historical Interpretation' in *I.A.R.*, vol. 3, (1979).
Barrie Trinder, 'Two Probate Inventories from Industrial Shropshire', in *I.A.R.*, vol. 3, (1979).
Barrie Trinder, 'The Holyhead Road: an engineering project in its social context' in Alistair Penfold, ed., *Thomas Telford: Engineer*, (1980).
Barrie Trinder, 'Industrial Archaeology', in Alan Rogers and Trevor Rowley, eds., *Landscapes and Documents*, (1975).
Barrie Trinder, 'The Use of Iron as a Building Material' in Derek Linstrum *et al*, *Timber: Iron: Clay* (1975).
Barrie Trinder, 'Museum Projects as a Means of Community Education' in *Actes des 2ième Congrés International des Amis des Musées 1975*, (Brussels 1976).
Barrie Trinder, 'The Ironbridge Gorge Museum', in *The Local Historian*, vol. 9, (1971).
Barrie Trinder, 'The Ironbridge Gorge Museum: three years of progress', in *West Midlands Studies*, vol. 5, (1972).
Barrie Trinder, 'Religious Tracts as sources of Local History: Some West Midlands examples', in *The Local Historian*, vol. 10, (1972).
Barrie Trinder, 'Lead Smelters of the Ironbridge Gorge' in *Shropshire Caving and Mining Club Journal*, (1979).
Barrie Trinder, 'The Open Industrial Village in Industrial Britain' in Marie Nisser, ed., *The Industrial Heritage: Transactions of the Third International Conference on the Conservation of Industrial Monuments*, vol. 3 (Stockholm. Forthcoming).
M. D. G. Wanklyn, 'John Weld of Willey' in *West Midlands Studies*, vol. 3, (1969).
M. D. G. Wanklyn, 'Iron and Steelworks in Coalbrookdale in 1645', in *S.N.L.* No. 44, (1973).
W. H. Williams, 'The Botfields', in *Shropshire Magazine* (Dec. 1965/Jan. 1966).
W. H. Williams, 'The Wrockwardine Wood Glass House' in *The Around and About* (2 Dec. 1961).

vii) *Maps*

Anon., *Plan of the Donnington Wood Colliery, 1788, with later additions*. Whereabouts of original unknown.
Robert Baugh, *Map of Shropshire* (n.d., c. 1808).
Ordnance Survey, *First edition of the one-inch survey of England and Wales*, Sheet No. 41.
J. Rocque, *Carte Topographique de la Comté de Salop ou Shropshire* (1752).
G. Young, *Plan of the River Severn from the Meadow Wharf near Coalbrookdale to the City of Gloucester* (1786).
G. Young, *Plan of a Navigable Canal . . . from the Marquis of Stafford's Canal . . . to the River Severn* (1788).

INDEX

Darby family: 21, 42, 53, 61, 141, 155, 179–80, 198, 228, 239

Darby: Abiah, 14, 19, 23, 72, 116, 222

Abraham I, (d. 1717):
early life, 13; settles at Coalbrookdale and smelts iron with coke, 13–15, 55, 122, 179, 186; links with Tern ironworks, 15; death, 17; limits of knowledge of, 114; relics, 156

Abraham II, (d. 1763):
at Coalbrookdale works, 16–17, 19–20, 95, 182; at Horsehay works, 21–26, 28, 271; at Ketley works, 21, 23–28, 271; death and achievements, 24, 40; plans for Severn Bridge, 100; attitudes to money, 114–16; purchases farms, 36–37, 90; role in 1756 riots, 228; executors, 27

Abraham III, (d. 1789):
purchases Madeley Wood ironworks, 25, 41, 55; sells land for canal wharves to Richard Reynolds, 82; trustee of turnpike roads, 87; builder of the Iron Brige, 107–10, 116; interest in science, 116; purchases Hay Farm, 37, 127; purchases Lordship of Madeley, 23; mortgages shares to Rathbone family, 40–41

Abraham IV, (d. 1878): 140–41, 151, 155, 176, 179, 218

Alfred, 140, 155, 218, 223; Francis, 140, 155; Hannah, 116, 228; John, 13; Mary, 17; Samuel, 87, 220

Dark Lane, Shropshire: 77, 142, 194–95, 198, 200, 240

Darlaston, Staffs.: 184

Darlington: Earl of, 142

Darrall: Edward, 13, 201; Richard, 13

Dartmouth, Devon: 17, 93

Darwin: Erasmus, 116

Davies: Arthur, gent., 271; Edward, character in tract, 226; Owen, tailor, 187; Samuel, bargeman, 75; William, weaver, 188

Dawes: Samuel, ironmaster, 40

Dawley, Shropshire: 2, 23, 24, 26, 31, 46, 77, 86, 122, 136, 141–142, 168, 170, 172–74, 179, 183, 216, 223, 241
See also Mines

Dawley Bank: See Lawley Bank

Deal Flats: See Severn Navigation

Dean: See Forest of Dean

Dearman and Co., iron dealers: 49

Deists: 198

Denbigh: 183

Denbighshire: 24, 37, 97, 124, 182

Derby: 110

Derbyshire: 17, 52, 126, 182

Devon: 8, 126

Dibdon: Charles, actor, 105

Diet:
definition of luxuries, 164; use of tea, 205; four meals a day instead of three, 205; extravagant working class spending on food, 205–07; traditional working class Sunday dinners, 205–06; geese eaten on special occasions, 206; diet of potatoes and bacon, 226; children's treats, 226; rice and Indian corn imported at times of shortage, 229–31

Diglis, Worcs.: 69

Diligence, stage coach: 90

Dillion: —, 90

Discipline:
John Fletcher's concern, 158; class meetings, 163–64; necessary in highly capitalised undertakings, 217; forces imposing new forms of discipline, 217;

Discipline: *Cont'd.*
employers' need to control workers' leisure, 217–18; in ironworks, 217–19; suppression of bull-baiting &c., 220–23; changes by 1840, 223; attitude of employers to Methodist workers, 223; purpose of Sunday schools, 224–26; concepts of time, 225

Dissent: 136, 166–67, 176–68, 275
See also Baptists, Congregationalists, Methodists, Presbyterians, Quakers

Dog-fighting: 221

Doggies: 207–08

Dolgelley, Merioneth: 17

Donnington, Donnington Wood, Shropshire: 3, 75–77, 79–80, 85, 136, 150–51, 214, 217, 224, 236
See also: Ironworks, Mines, Glassworks

Dore: Matthew, 10

Dorsett: Francis, agent, 24, 30, 32, 121–22; Thomas, agent, 13, 30–32, 121–22

Doseley, Shropshire: 82

Dotti: Dominic, 185

Double turns: 215–16

Double way: See Railways

Doughty: family, 64; Thomas, bargeman, 65

Douzon or Dozen: measure of ore: 33

Dragoons, 168, 233

Dublin: 48, 148

Dudley: Earls of, 59

Dudley, Worcs.: 13–14, 17, 93, 179, 183

Dudley: Dud, ironmaster, 14

Dugard: Thomas, physician, 117

Dukes: William, surveyor, 87

Dumaresque: Captain, 55

Dundonald: 9th Earl of, See Cochrane, Archibald

Dundrum, Northern Ireland: 141

Dunham, Ches.: 157

Dunrobin, Co. Sutherland: 237

Durham, County: 16, 72, 182
See also Coal Mines

Durham Cattle: 37

Dutens: Jean, engineer, 105–06

Dyes: 133–34

Earl Gower and Company: 44–45, 58, 75, 77, 102

Earthenware: 8, 68, 125–28, 135
See also Potteries

East Anglia: 159

Easthope, Shropshire: 183

Easthope family: 64

Eaton under Haywood, Shropshire: 3

Eave's Mount: 65

Ecclesiastical Commissioners: 175–76

Edge: Benjamin, chainmaker, 129–30, 132

Edgmond, Shropshire: 31, 184

Education:
Lack of technical education in Shropshire, 155, 207; Coalbrookdale Institute and School of Art, 199; role of night schools in 1862 revival, 173; limited by employment of children, 224; growth of schools and Sunday schools, 224–25; opinions of Fletcher and John Wesley, 226

Eele; Martin, tar manufacturer, 8, 55

Egerton: Francis, 3rd Duke of Bridgewater, 27, 75, 122; Lady Louisa, 27

Ellesmere, Shropshire: 90

Ellesmere Port, Ches.: 151

Ellis: William, engraver, 111

Ellwell: William, 24

Spout Lane

Eaton Constantine

Little Wenlock

Coal Moor

Garmaston

Moor

Hall

Leighton

Buildwas

Sunnyside

10

11

12

Shineton

Bridge

Abbey

10

West Coppice

Belswardine

11

BENTHALL EDGE

10

Shinewood

EDGE

Benthall

Wyke

Harley

F. 12

11

WENLOCK

Downes

Pose Gate

Arlescott

Wille

Abbey

8

Mardh

B

12

Walton

19

11

Westwood Common

Atterley

Lea Farm

7

Callonghton

18

O

Beggarly Brook

Hawthorn

WENLOCK